Classification Made Relevant

Classification Made Relevant
How Scientists Build and Use Classifications and Ontologies

Jules J. Berman

ACADEMIC PRESS
An imprint of Elsevier

Academic Press is an imprint of Elsevier
125 London Wall, London EC2Y 5AS, United Kingdom
525 B Street, Suite 1650, San Diego, CA 92101, United States
50 Hampshire Street, 5th Floor, Cambridge, MA 02139, United States
The Boulevard, Langford Lane, Kidlington, Oxford OX5 1GB, United Kingdom

Notices
Knowledge and best practice in this field are constantly changing. As new research and experience broaden our
understanding, changes in research methods, professional practices, or medical treatment may become
necessary.

Practitioners and researchers must always rely on their own experience and knowledge in evaluating and using
any information, methods, compounds, or experiments described herein. In using such information or methods
they should be mindful of their own safety and the safety of others, including parties for whom they have a
professional responsibility.

To the fullest extent of the law, neither the Publisher nor the authors, contributors, or editors, assume any liability
for any injury and/or damage to persons or property as a matter of products liability, negligence or otherwise, or
from any use or operation of any methods, products, instructions, or ideas contained in the material herein.

Library of Congress Cataloging-in-Publication Data
A catalog record for this book is available from the Library of Congress

British Library Cataloguing-in-Publication Data
A catalogue record for this book is available from the British Library

ISBN 978-0-323-91786-5

For information on all Academic Press publications
visit our website at https://www.elsevier.com/books-and-journals

Publisher: Mara Conner
Editorial Project Manager: Jai Marie Jose
Production Project Manager: Punithavathy Govindaradjane
Cover Designer: Mark Rogers

Typeset by STRAIVE, India

Working together
to grow libraries in
developing countries

www.elsevier.com • www.bookaid.org

Other books by Jules J. Berman

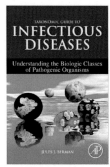

Taxonomic Guide to Infectious Diseases
Understanding the Biologic Classes of Pathogenic Organisms (2012)
9780124158955

Principles of Big Data
Preparing, Sharing, and Analyzing Complex Information (2013)
9780124045767

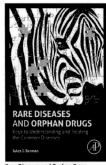

Rare Diseases and Orphan Drugs
Keys to Understanding and Treating the Common Diseases (2014)
9780124199880

Repurposing Legacy Data
Innovative Case Studies (2015)
9780128028827

Data Simplification
Taming Information With Open Source Tools (2016)
9780128037812

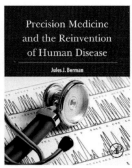

Precision Medicine and the Reinvention of Human Disease (2018)
9780128143933

Principles and Practice of Big Data
Preparing, Sharing, and Analyzing Complex Information, Second Edition (2018)
9780128156094

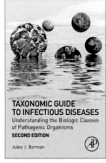

Taxonomic Guide to Infectious Diseases
Understanding the Biologic Classes of Pathogenic Organisms, Second Edition (2019)
9780128175767

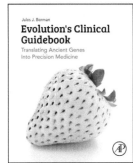

Evolution's Clinical Guidebook
Translating Ancient Genes into Precision Medicine (2019)
9780128171264

Logic and Critical Thinking in the Biomedical Sciences
Volume I: Deductions Based Upon Simple Observations (2020)
9780128213643

Logic and Critical Thinking in the Biomedical Sciences
Volume 2: Deductions Based Upon Quantitative Data (2020)
9780128213698

For Kenzie

Contents

About the author

Jules J. Berman has received two baccalaureate degrees from MIT: one in mathematics and the other in earth and planetary sciences. He holds a PhD from Temple University and an MD from the University of Miami. He completed his postdoctoral studies at the US National Institutes of Health, and his residency at the George Washington University Medical Center in Washington, DC. Dr. Berman served as Chief of Anatomic Pathology, Surgical Pathology, and Cytopathology at the Veterans Administration Medical Center in Baltimore, Maryland, where he held joint appointments at the University of Maryland Medical Center and at the Johns Hopkins Medical Institutions. In 1998, he moved to the US National Institutes of Health as Medical Officer and as the Program Director for Pathology Informatics in the Cancer Diagnosis Program at the National Cancer Institute. Dr. Berman is a past president of the Association for Pathology Informatics and the 2011 recipient of the Association's Lifetime Achievement Award. He has first-authored more than 100 journal articles and has written 20 science books. Books written by Dr. Berman, that may interest readers of *Classification Made Relevant,* include

Perl Programming for Medicine and Biology, Jones and Bartlett, 2007

Ruby Programming for Medicine and Biology, Jones and Bartlett, 2008

Methods in Medical Informatics: Fundamentals of Healthcare Programming in Perl, Python, and Ruby, CRC Press, 2010

Taxonomic Guide to Infectious Diseases: Understanding the Biologic Classes of Pathogenic Organisms, Elsevier, 2012

Principles of Big Data: Preparing, Sharing, and Analyzing Complex Information, Elsevier, 2013

Data Simplification: Taming Information with Open Source Tools, Elsevier, 2016

Principles and Practice of Big Data: Preparing, Sharing, and Analyzing Complex Information, Second Edition, Elsevier, 2018

Evolution's Clinical Guidebook: Translating Ancient Genes into Precision Medicine, Elsevier, 2019

Taxonomic Guide to Infectious Diseases: Understanding the Biologic Classes of Pathogenic Organisms, Second Edition, Elsevier, 2019

Logic and Critical Thinking in the Biomedical Sciences, Volume I: Deductions Based Upon Simple Observations, Elsevier, 2020

Logic and Critical Thinking in the Biomedical Sciences, Volume II: Deductions Based upon Quantitative Data, Elsevier, 2020

Preface

Doesn't everyone want the universe to make sense? Wouldn't it be great if we humans had a rational way of relating everything with everything else so that our world may become a bit less confusing? As it happens, we have a nifty little device to do just that. It is called a classification. While catalogs and indexes help us organize items, classifications organize relationships among classes. It is through our understanding of class relationships that we begin to understand our world. In *Classification Made Relevant*, we will explore three major themes:

1. That building classifications is one of the most intellectually rewarding pursuits available to serious scientists. We will see that the history of science is punctuated by moments of intense clarity when relationships among classes are suddenly revealed.
2. That the science of classification must be learned, just as we learn any other scientific discipline. Many of the disastrous classifications forced upon scientists have been produced by clueless individuals who neglected the fundamental rules of classification construction. We will take some pleasure in reviewing some of the most ill-conceived classifications, along with the common errors committed during their construction.
3. That classifications are devices by which we organize relationships among things and are not just a means by which we tidy up collections of items by inventing categories. Much of the book's narrative is driven by the notion that classifications embody the natural order of the universe. The relationships revealed by scientific classifications lead us to discover how the world operates. When we visit the great classifications of the natural world, we can begin to appreciate the unity of all the sciences.

For most of us, the subject of classification has never grabbed our full attention. We are not prepared to believe that the science of classification is a subject that requires a disciplined and rigorous course of study or that there exist classifications that play an important role in our everyday lives. In point of fact, classifications are vital to our existence. This book begins with a discussion of how the human mind is constantly sorting objects into classes, as we try to organize and simplify our environment. While we humans are busy sorting oranges and apples, the universe is preoccupied with enforcing a set of natural laws that all material things and all forces must obey. These natural laws determine the kinds of particles, atoms, molecules, and organisms we see around us and how they relate to one another. When we see how things can be sorted into defined classes that have explicit relationships with other classes, we begin the process of understanding our universe. The manner in which we define classes, their properties, and their relationships is best codified with the judicious use of a semantic language. Doing so permits computers, and humans, to analyze classifications and to draw new inferences about how our world works. Not everything in our world can fit into a traditional classification, and in such cases, we use ontologies to tie information and objects to one or to another of the natural classifications. We can model classifications and ontologies in object-oriented programming languages. By doing so, we can draw new inferences from the vast collections of data tied to classifications.

The first five chapters of this book are devoted to the theory and design of classifications. Chapter 5, "The Class-Oriented Programming Paradigm," explains how computer scientists model and analyze classifications and ontologies. Although the chapter is intended to be accessible to nonprogrammers, it is simply impossible to treat the topic fairly without including a few lines of code. For this chapter, most of the code is provided as one-liners consisting of one command whose resulting output can be examined. In those cases, no programming knowledge is required. A few short programs are provided, but these are not computer-ready applications and should not be used as such. These short programs are written in Perl, Python, or Ruby. Computer scientists can adapt snippets of this code to include in their own software programs in their preferred programming languages. Nonprogrammers can peruse the code and see just how easy it is to translate an algorithm into software written in any preferred computer language.

In the final three chapters, we will examine the three great classifications of the natural world: "The Classification of Life," "The Periodic Table of the Elements," and the symmetries exemplified in the "Classification Theorem of Finite Simple Groups." These chapters are not intended to be primers for biologists, chemists, or physicists. We study the great classifications so that we can see how they were developed and how they have been utilized. In the final chapter, we shall see how these classifications, taken together, encompass all of the sciences.

While composing the book, I settled on a set of concepts and questions that can be enjoyed by anyone with a college-level introduction to any of the natural sciences. To render the text accessible to the widest range of readers, I have tried to eliminate discipline-specific jargon. When the text bumps up against an unavoidable technical point that requires explanation, a link to an appropriate glossary item is included. The glossary provides term definitions and often includes an expanded discussion of the term's relevance to the chapter's topics. There are more than 300 glossary links included in the book, and you will find them listed at the bottom of paragraphs. If you prefer not to interrupt your reading with excursions to the glossary, you may find it rewarding to peruse the chapter glossaries, after you have read the narrative text.

1

Sitting in class

In the particular is contained the universal.

James Joyce

Section 1.1. Sorting things out

Let's begin this book with some provocative assertions in dire need of proof.

1. Classifications are the best way to encapsulate the relationships among objects.
2. The universe, and most things in it, can be reduced to a relatively small number of classes of things.
3. The inheritance of properties through ancestral classes is one of the strongest intellectual tools available to scientists.
4. "Triples" are the quantum of meaning in the information world.
5. Some items cannot be sensibly classified, but all such objects can be represented in alternate data structures, including ontologies; and ultimately linked to valid classifications.
6. Modern object-oriented programming techniques can fully model classifications and ontologies and permit us to apply algorithms that draw inferences from classifications and ontologies.
7. The assemblage of natural classifications is one of mankind's greatest intellectual achievements.
8. The natural sciences (i.e., biology, chemistry, and physics) obey scientific laws that govern our universe, and these laws are reflected in classifications.
9. Taken together, three great classifications (The Classification of Life, The Periodic Table of the Elements, and the symmetries exemplified by The Classification Theorem

of Finite Simple Groups) unify the natural sciences and clarify the relationships among all matter and forces in our universe.

10. Future advances in all of the sciences will depend on our ability to enhance existing classifications.

[Glossary Meaning, Modeling, Natural sciences, Ontology, Relationship, Triple]

When we reach the end of this book, we will have reviewed abundant evidence supporting every one of these claims. To arrive at that point, we will need to discuss what it means to be an object belonging to a class that belongs to a classification.

Our Classy Universe

Despite our sense that anything is possible in the vastness of space, we see an awful lot of sameness throughout the universe. Wherever we aim our telescopes, we see galaxies, most of which are flat and spiral, many having about the same size, and composed of the same objects: stars, planets, gas, dust, black holes, and abundant nothing in between. A small set of physical laws impose stability everywhere at once, and the result is the somewhat repetitious cosmos that we glimpse at night (Fig. 1.1).

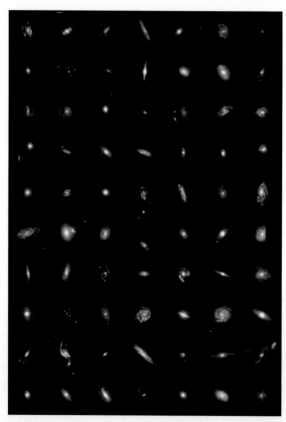

FIG. 1.1 The various classes of galaxies. Would it be an over-simplification to suggest that they all look much the same? *Source: U.S. National Aeronautics and Space Administration.*

As it happens, the universe is trending toward an even more bland and stable existence. The end-stage of stellar evolution seems to be mainly limited to just brown dwarfs, white dwarfs, neutron stars, and black holes [1]. White dwarfs are the end-stage objects for most main-sequence stars and can persist for about 10^{35} years. Black holes, another end-stage celestial object, have a predicted lifespan of 10^{64} years. As relatively short-lived main-series stars, like our sun, attain their various destinies, they leave behind a universe full of dead-end objects, predominantly white dwarf stars. The Milky Way is thought to have already accumulated 10 billion white dwarfs, and the number will only increase. At some point in the future, illuminated galaxies such as ours will be gone, and the universe will be filled with nearly perpetual end-of-life stars.

What is true on the cosmological scale is also true on the atomic scale. There are just 94 elements that occur in nature. A few dozen more can be created artificially, but these are short-lived atoms that do not account for much of what we find in our universe. Of the matter that we can observe, we note that Hydrogen, the smallest and simplest of elements, accounts for 92% of atoms in our universe. Helium, the second smallest atom, accounts for nearly everything else. The remaining 92 elements make do with about 1%–2% of matter. There is much less atomic variety than we might imagine.

Likewise, despite a large number of living species on our planet, they are all variations of a few common themes that can be encapsulated under a simple classification, wherein the root organism, and all of its descendants, are carbon-based and have a nucleic acid genome. This brings to mind what I refer to as the First Law of Classification, namely, "In a world where anything can happen, relatively little does." [Glossary Organism, Species]

There is a reason that the universe is stable and filled with objects having limited life-style options. Put simply, systems that are unstable cease to exist; that is what it means to be unstable. If there were no set of physical laws that apply everywhere in the universe, throughout time, then the universe would be chaotic. We would have matter suddenly dropping out of existence, or popping up again in strange and distant locations. We would not have repeatable chemical reactions. An experiment on Tuesday would yield a different outcome than the same experiment performed on Wednesday; and that is assuming that we would have a Tuesday, and a Wednesday, and an experiment. Or we might have nothing that we recognize as matter and energy. The entire universe might simply vanish, in a bang or a whimper.

[Glossary System]

We do not know the conditions of existence at the moment of the Big Bang. We can claim that the Big Bang was a gross violation of the conservation laws for matter and energy, an assertion that would suggest that our beginnings were not nearly as stable and non-chaotic as what we see today. Ilya Prigogine described mathematically how a stable system might arise from a chaotic system in his theory of dissipative structures, for which he was awarded the 1977 Nobel Prize in chemistry [2].

Steven Wolfram, a mathematician and a pioneer in computer science, conducted a fascinating set of computer simulations employing simple automata that generated graphic outputs consisting of collections of blocks emanating from a point. The automata made "decisions" such as put a block on top, put a block on the left side, make block black, make block white. An element of randomness was introduced at various points in the algorithms that controlled the automata [3]. Without going into a detailed description of their implementations, we can simply acknowledge that we would expect the graphic outputs of the automata to be random and unpredictable and that we would certainly not expect to see a rather fixed set of recurring patterns in the output. Regardless of preconceptions, Wolfram found that the outputs indeed had recurring patterns and that he could assign these patterns to classes [3]. After he chose classes for the patterns, he found additional properties of the output that characterized the classes. Regarding those classes, and their properties, he wrote, "But when I studied more detailed properties of cellular automata, what I found was that most of these properties were closely correlated with the classes that I had already identified. Indeed, in trying to predict detailed properties of a particular cellular automaton, it was often enough just to know what class the cellular automaton was in." He likened the process of finding classes and properties to building a natural classification of chemical substances or living organisms. This was a remarkable outcome for a set of computer simulations that should have been random, formless, and chaotic.

The topic of the spontaneous generation of order from chaos is best left to the mathematicians and the metaphysicians. Let's simplify the situation by agreeing that stable systems, by definition, persist longer than unstable systems, we can expect that stable systems will eventually replace unstable, chaotic systems. Indeed, we find ourselves governed by stable universal laws, applied to a small assortment of elementary particles. All the forces that control the behavior of matter act in a homogeneous space-time continuum. We can thank our simple, and non-chaotic universe for the birth of a world where the night sky is everywhere filled with twinkling stars, and we humans can sleep knowing that the sun also rises.

Section 1.2. Things and their parts

Thingyness

It has always struck me as amusing that in fictional encounters with alien life forms, authors typically create a classification of alien beings having a 1:1 correspondence with analogous human beings: here's the alien city, here's an alien house, here's a small alien baby, here's an alien military general preparing for war. Most science fiction movies depict aliens as being much more similar to humans than humans are to the other terrestrial life forms with whom we cohabit. Sadly, our most inventive authors seem incapable of imagining an unfamiliar form of existence, even when it's all make-believe. Of course, there are exceptions.

Here is a short excerpt from C.S. Lewis' classic novel *Perelandra*, wherein his fictional character, Elwin Ransom, arrives on Venus.

His first impression was of nothing more definite than of something slanted - as though he was looking at a photograph which had been taken when the camera was not held level. And even this lasted only for an instant. The slant was replaced by a different slant.

In *Perelandra*, the world is at first perceived to be formless. The traveler cannot distinguish one thing from another. Eventually, the world comes into focus, and all the "things" on Perelandra are sorted out. C.S. Lewis reminds us that the universe is a meaningless vision until the mind finds a way to sort reality into recognizable groups of things.

In *Perelandra*, the traveler experiences a brief period of disorientation upon his arrival in an alien land. In the science fiction novel *Solaris*, written by Stanislaw Lem, astronauts visit a strange planet that defies human understanding. An enigmatic planet comes to the attention of earth scientists who find that its erratic path through space seems to defy the laws of gravity. When the surface of the planet is observed from an orbiting science station, large artifacts mimicking human forms, are seen to assemble and disassemble. Soon, the residents of the science station are visited by apparitions that have the appearance of familiar humans. *Solaris* explores the reaction of the scientists to the inscrutable emanations of the planet, but the developing mysteries are never solved. As the book ends, the scientists slowly lapse into various forms of highly personalized insanity.

Science fiction often seems far-fetched, but it always aims to reveal basic truths about the human condition. The fact of the matter is that we often fail to perceive the things that share our reality. A favorite example, from the realm of archeology, involves the mystery of the Mayan glyphs. We have all seen images of these beautiful and ornate stone carvings. Forgotten by history for nearly 700 years, early twentieth-century archeologists uncovered these Mayan artifacts and attempted to fathom their meaning. Eric Thompson (1898–1975) stood as the premier Mayanist authority from the 1930s through the 1960s. After trying, and failing, to decipher the glyphs, he concluded that they represented mystic, ornate symbols; not language. The glyphs, according to Thompson, were unworthy of further study. Thompson was venerated to such an extent that, throughout his long tenure of influence, work in the area of glyph translation was suspended. When Thompson's influence finally waned, a new group of Mayanists came forward, hoping to mind meaning in the enigmatic glyphs. These new Mayanists, undeterred by naysayers, learned that the glyphs were more or less straightforward representations of the Mayan language, much as it is spoken today by Mayans who were taught their native speech. Breaking the code involved learning some symbology and mastering the proper way of moving from one symbol to the next, through the text [4] (Fig. 1.2).

FIG. 1.2 Mayan glyphs, displayed in Palenque Museum, Chiapas, Mexico. Early in the 20th century, prevailing wisdom held that these glyphs were purely decorative, with no semblance to language. *Source: Wikipedia, and entered into the public domain by its author, Kwamikagami.*

The early archeologists failed to perceive the glyphs as the "things" that they were. The issue of properly perceiving the things in our environment is a serious issue among philosophers. Let's look at a few "thingy" problems so that we can appreciate their relevance to the general topic of classification.

When we look at a boy on his bicycle, we tend to think of two specific items: the boy, and the bike. We don't usually think of a composite item (i.e., a boy-bike chimera), probably because we know what it means to be a boy, and we know that when a boy sits atop a bike, he does not suddenly transform into a composite structure. My dog Bailey, on the other hand, has an entirely different way of assessing the situation. When he sees a boy riding a bike, he is convinced that he is seeing a creature that is neither boy nor bike, but a horrible chimera that must be attacked and destroyed. Mind you, Bailey loves children and is indifferent to bicycles, but he bears a deep hatred of the creature that emerges when it engulfs boy and bike.

If you believe that my dog Bailey lacks common sense, you might want to reconsider after reading the next example. Humans never consider themselves composite items. We are so accustomed to thinking of ourselves as singular entities that we have invented the word "I" as a short and convenient way of referring to ourselves, without bothering to state our full names. I refer to myself as "I", and you refer to yourself as "I" and we both seem satisfied with that. What happens when an individual becomes pregnant? Does such an individual become two individuals, or does it become a composite creature?

Let's step around the special case of pregnancy, and just focus on the work-a-day human being. Most of the cells in a human are diploid cells, and these cells constitute our so-called "soma"; the brains, organs, muscle, bone, and connective tissue that walk and talk and watch television. The soma lives for some period before succumbing to inevitable but unscheduled death. Aside from the soma, each of us contains a specialized population of cells having its specialized genome, its own set of biological attributes, and the capacity for immortality. These are the haploid cells (i.e., gametes) that mature as oocytes (eggs) in the female and as sperm cells in males. The sperm cells are capable of living outside the body and fusing with oocytes obtained from another individual. The resulting zygote can multiply and develop into another organism also composed of a mixture of diploid somatic cells (doomed to death) and haploid cells (potentially immortalized through the process of conception). Are we humans two creatures in one: the diploid somatic organism and the haploid germinative organism? This is a tough question, but perhaps we can shed some light on the answer by referring to the plant kingdom. Some plants undergo alternating generations in which a haploid organism (gametophyte) produces a diploid organism (sporophyte), which produces a haploid organism, which produces a diploid organism, and so on. The haploid organism contains gametes that differentiate to form the structural cell types of the gametophytic plant. The sporophyte contains diploid cells that differentiate to form the soma of the sporophytic plant. The gametophyte and the sporophyte are two separate plants, distinguishable from each other. Knowing this to be true, would it be far-fetched to imagine that the gametes and the soma of the human species are, in fact, two very different organisms that happen to share the same physical space, most of the time? (Fig. 1.3).

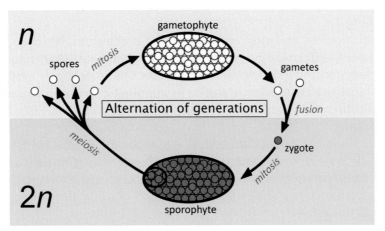

FIG. 1.3 The life cycle of plants alternates between a haploid organism (one complete set of chromosomes in each cell) and a diploid organism (two complete sets of chromosomes in each cell). *Source: Wikipedia, and entered into the public domain by its author, Peter Coxhead.*

Let's look at another example where we might misinterpret "thingyness." Two patients are seen by an oncologist (i.e., a physician specializing in cancer). Both of them happen to have a mass in their colon, and both of them have been given the same diagnosis: "adenocarcinoma of the colon". Each patient has their individual and unique genome, which, for each patient, is the same genome contained in the cell population that gives rise to their respective adenocarcinomas. In both cases, the tumor genome continuously mutates, producing a growth that is different from the genome of the patient in which it arises and that is different from the genome of the adenocarcinoma found in the other patient. The biology of each of the two tumors is unique, and the clinical outcome of the two patients are unlikely to be equivalent. This being the case, why would we give the same name, "adenocarcinoma", to the two biologically and genetically different tumors? As it happens, we assign the two tumors the same name because both tumors arose from the same type of cell in the same anatomic tissue. Physicians built a classification of neoplasms based on the tumor's cell type of origin; a cell that does not persist in the developed tumor. For a variety of reasons, this kind of indirect approach to "thingyness" seems to work for us; at least for the moment.

Let's examine one more perplexing aspect of "thingyness"; the issue of the "new thing". What do we mean when we refer to a new thing? Is a new thing something that comes into existence at once, without pre-existence in form or substance; or is a new thing just an old thing that has been modified in some way? A new day is just an old day that has completed one more revolution. A new snowstorm is just the convergence of pre-existing weather fronts. A new sandwich is just the assemblage of old ingredients that were laying around the kitchen. Today's squirrel is just the result of some combination of cellular death, cell renewal, and cell maintenance occurring in a population of billions of cells that constituted yesterday's squirrel. A new baby is just the result of the fusion of two old germ cells. How do we create a classification of discrete items, when we seem to live in a universe wherein everything develops over time, from pre-existing matter and energy?

Thingyness is the first, and most crucial, step-in classification. When we assign things to classes, we need to distinguish one thing from another, a task that is not as easy as it sounds. Our choice of "things" to be included in classification is largely a reflection of our perceptions of reality. Hence, every "thing" is just another hypothetical in our struggle to build a classification. [Glossary Gamete, Germ cell, Germ cell line, Germline, Haploid, Haploid organisms]

After we've chosen our things, our next task is to tackle the dilemma of "parthood". Specifically, if a thing is a composite of parts, and the parts are "things" in their own right, then how shall the classification deal with the relationships that exist between things and their parts? What happens when a thing's part is also a part of some other thing, belonging to another class of things?

Occasionally, I am asked to deliver a lecture on the topic of classification. Early in my talk, I always ask the group the following question. "Is a leg a subclass of humans?". With very few exceptions, the answer they tell me is, "Of course. All humans are born with legs, so a leg is an integral part of a human, and therefore a leg is a subclass of humans." I always respond that subclasses have the defining properties of their super-classes. A subclass of a human would need to be a type of human; just as the class containing the human species (i.e., Class Homo) would need to be a type of primate (i.e., a subclass of Class Primate). A leg is not a type of human, and therefore a leg is not a subclass of humans.

Parts have a special relationship to their "wholes". The word to describe this relationship is often referred to as "parthood." Mereology, from the Greek root translated as the study of parts, is the field devoted to parthood [5]. For anyone who might think that the concept of parthood is trivial and obvious, consider the following questions:

- Is an embryo a part of the woman who carries it in her womb?
- Is an embryo a part of the developed human who does not yet exist at the time that the embryo exists?
- Is an acorn a part of an oak tree into which it will develop?
- Is an acorn attached to a branch of an oak tree part of that tree?
- Is an acorn that has fallen to the ground a part of the oak tree from which it dropped?
- Is a caterpillar a part of the butterfly into which it will develop?
- Is collected garbage a part of the garbage truck in which it has been collected?
- Is Uranium a part of the Lead into which it will eventually transmute?
- Is a stairwell part of a man falling down a stairwell?
- Is a live person a part of the dead person he or she will become?
- Is a precancer a part of cancer into which it may eventually develop?
- Is a titanium hip a part of a human who has had a hip replacement?
- Is a cell from a human liver part of a human?
- Is a tissue culture prepared from human liver cells part of a human?
- Is midnight a part of yesterday or today?
- Is a pair of shoes part of any one specific item of apparel?
- Are the words you are currently reading a part of the author who wrote the words?

[Glossary Precancer]

The list goes on and on. We all have our perceptions of the relationships between acorns and oak trees and live persons and dead persons, but these perceptions will vary from person to person, and it is likely that none of our perceptions quite do justice to the mereologists' philosophy of "parthood." In "Chapter 3. Ontologies and Semantics" we will discuss some of the formal ways in which we can describe the relations between things, parts, and classes.

Section 1.3. Relationships, classes, and properties

Objects are related to one another when there is some fundamental or defining principle that applies to them mutually and which, ideally, helps us to better understand their nature. For example, when we say that force is mass times acceleration, we are describing a relationship between force and an accelerating mass. The equivalence, does not tell us what force is, and it does not tell us what mass is, but it describes how mass, force, and acceleration relate to one another, and it brings us a little closer to an understanding of their fundamental natures.

Possibly the most elegant relationship known is expressed by the Euler identity (Fig. 1.4).

$$\text{Euler Identity}\qquad e^{i\pi}+1=0$$

FIG. 1.4 The Euler Identity, which relates 7 fundamental mathematical concepts in a single assertion.

In the equation for the Euler Identity, 5 universal constants and 2 fundamental symbols of mathematics are related to one another, in a single mathematical assertion, as listed:

The number 0, the additive identity.
The number 1, the multiplicative identity.
The number pi (pi=3.141...), the fundamental circle constant.
The number e (e=2.718...), a.k.a. Euler's number, occurs widely in mathematical analysis.
The number i, the imaginary unit of the complex numbers.
The identity symbol "=" and the additive symbol, "+".

It is through relationships that we understand our world, but those relationships cannot be fully appreciated without some intellectual effort. The story is told of the statistician who was using the Gaussian distribution to describe a population trend. A friend with no knowledge of maths looked over the shoulder of the statistician and inquired the meaning of the odd-looking symbol for pi. The statistician said, "That's pi, the ratio of a circle's circumference to its diameter." His friend said, "Surely you jest. You can't expect me to believe that a population trend can have any relationship to the circumference of a circle!" [6].

The concepts of "relationship" and "similarity" are often mistaken for one another. To better understand the difference, consider the following. When you look up at the clouds, you may see the shape of a lion. The cloud has a tail, like a lion's tale, and a fluffy head, like a lion's mane. With a little imagination, the mouth of the lion seems to roar down from the sky. You have succeeded in finding similarities between the cloud and a lion. When you look at a cloud and you imagine a tea kettle producing a head of steam, and you recognize that the physical forces that create a cloud from the ocean's water vapor and the physical forces that produce steam from the water in a heated kettle are the same, then you have found a relationship.

Scientific laws are classifying rules because they state the relationships among classes of things. Because they apply everywhere and at any time, they are the strictest of all relationships. When different types of things obey the same scientific laws, we can infer that those things must be related to one another. In the next chapter, we will see that classifications are the embodiment of the natural laws that relate classes of things. [Glossary Universal laws versus class laws]

Now that we have repeatedly referred to the concept of a class, we should stop a moment and give "class" a proper definition.

A class is defined by the following properties:

1. Classes contain unique and identifiable objects (zero or more of them)

Uniqueness and identifiability are closely related concepts. When a factory's production line produces the same part, thousands of times in a day, it may stamp a unique number on each part. It is the assignment of a permanent and immutable identifying number that makes each part unique. When we have identifiable items, we can observe and record data (e.g., measurements) for the item. At any later time, we can use the unique identifier of the item to retrieve its data. Computer scientists work with so-called data objects. These are uniquely identified constructions that can be assigned to a class. Each data object has access to all of the methods of their assigned class. Data objects, as the name suggests, often contain data that can be accessed and modified. They may have a variety of methods that are specific for themselves (i.e., instance methods). A data object should contain self-descriptive data (i.e., data about itself, including its unique identifier). [Glossary Data object, Instance, Mutability, Unique identifier]

The objects belonging to a class are often referred to as instances or as members. In the Classification of Life, objects held within a class are the names of species, and the names of species are unique. Every species is assigned to a direct parent class, which biologists refer to as the genus (Latin for type or race) of the species. In the binomial system of biological classification, there are two parts to every species name. The first part of the species name is its genus, equivalent to a person's surname (family name). The name of the genus is always capitalized. The second part of the binomial is the species-specific name, equivalent to a person's given name, and is never capitalized. For example, *Homo sapiens* is our binomial species name, with "Homo" being the name of our genus or family, and "sapiens" being our species-specific name.

A class may contain as few as zero objects. As long as all the requisite class properties are satisfied, we have a class. There may be some advantage to having class methods without objects if those methods can be inherited by other classes or utilized by objects that may not belong to any class. A singleton class is a class that contains exactly one named object. A good example of a singleton class is the genus Class Homo. There is only one extant object belonging to Class Homo, and *H. sapiens* is our name. Computer scientists use singleton classes to permit one specific object to execute all of the methods available to a class. We shall learn more about these concepts in "Chapter 5. The Class-Oriented Programming Paradigm." [Glossary Singleton class, Singleton method]

2. Classes have a definition (i.e., the class definition) telling us what objects belong to the class and what objects do not belong to the class.

Class definitions are provided in plain written language and are typically collected in documents known as schemas.

3. The class may have class methods associated with it that can be used by every member of the class

Class methods can take the form of descriptors or algorithms that apply exclusively to members of the class, including descendant subclasses of the class. Methods available to all the members of a class that are not exclusive to the class and its descendant subclasses may also be provided, but such methods are not referred to as class methods. This is another topic that we will save for Chapter 5.

4. An object that is a member of a class cannot belong to any other class

As a logical corollary, a class definition cannot be written to include objects that logically belong to other classes. This corollary is true because otherwise, class definitions would conflict with one another. As a simple example, suppose I define a class of objects whose height, in feet, is exactly divisible by 2. We'll call this Class Even_height. This class would include objects of height 2 ft, 4 ft, 6 ft, and so on. At first glance, this would seem to be a proper class. It has a definition that includes members and that excludes non-members (e.g., objects whose height in feet is an odd number). Class Even_height may have its class methods. For example, an inclusion method might consist of something like, "Add the height of any two class objects to yield an allowable height of another class object." Class Even_height seems to be shaping up as a legitimate class. Now suppose I invent a class called Class Spheres. Spheres can come in any height, including heights that are exactly divisible by 2, and this would imply that members of Class Sphere are also members of Class Even_height. This situation is strictly forbidden insofar as a class definition must be written to exclude objects belonging to other classes. Hence, the existence of Class Sphere conflicts with Class Even_height. One of these classes, and possibly both of them, must not be permitted to exist. If we give the matter a little thought, we may realize that lots of completely unrelated objects can have all manner of height, even or odd and that creating a Class Even_height is a silly idea. As we begin to see that we have created an illegitimate class, we get our first inkling that creating a classification can be difficult.

5. A class is itself an identifiable object and may belong to a class (i.e., maybe a subclass of another class).

At first blush, we might think that classes, being nothing more than abstractions that hold real objects, cannot be considered a real object in need of identification. Therefore, we might infer that classes and their subclasses are all abstractions, and the only real items are the objects inserted in classes and subclasses. This is a bad way of thinking, on several counts. First, a class is composed of real objects, and something composed of real objects is, logically, a real object. Secondly, classes are unique and can be sensibly provided with a unique identifier. When we reach "Chapter 5. The Class-Oriented Programming Paradigm," we will see how useful it is to know that every class is itself a data object belonging to Class (the class of classes and consequently the classiest of classes). [Glossary Child class, Parent class, Subclass, Superclass]

Now that we have a definition of "class," can we begin to invent classes, and can we assign objects to our invented classes? Yes, but we need to proceed carefully, so as not to repeat common mistakes. For example, when I was a child, I learned that there were flowers, and trees, and bushes; leading me to believe that these were the three major classes of plants. All plants, I imagined, fell into one of these three classes. Of course, this pseudo-classification was nothing more than a categorization of plants into three morphologically distinctive groups that could be appreciated by school-age children without really delving very deeply into botanical science.

Sophisticated students, who may have taken a course in botany or agriculture, know that plants cannot be sensibly divided into flowers, trees, and bushes. Trees and bushes are simply features of species belonging to various classes of plants. Among botanists, there is no Class Tree, and there is no Class Bush. As for the flowers, there is a class for the flowering seed plants (Class Angiospermae) and another class of seed plants that do not flower (Class Gymnospermae). Both the Angiosperms and Gymnosperms contain species that grow like trees and bushes. Had botanists created a class just for trees, we would have been in a lot of trouble since we would have found tree species among classes of plants that differed from one another in almost every regard and having no class properties in common. We would also find trees and their close relatives that can grow as bushes or as demure lily pads. In point of fact, all of the trees in Class Angiospermae are types of flowering plants. We say that a plant is a tree if it happens to look tall and wistful and if it has a trunk from which branches or leafy clusters emanate; but these are just traits, not class-defining properties (Fig. 1.5). [Glossary Non-quantitative trait, Quantitative trait]

A class is a collection of things that share one or more properties that distinguish the members of the class from members of other classes. When creating classifications, the most common mistake is to assign class status to a property. When a property is inappropriately assigned as a class, then the entire classification is ruined. Hence, it is important to be very clear on the difference between these two concepts and to understand why it is human nature to confuse one with the other. A class is a holder of related objects (e.g., items, records, categorized things). A property is a feature or trait that can be assigned to an item (Fig. 1.6).

Much of our confusion comes from the way that we are raised to think and speak about the relationships between objects and properties. We say "He is hungry," using a term of equality, "is", to describe the relationship between "He" and "hungry". Technically, the sentence, "He is hungry" asserts that "He" and "hungry" are equivalent objects. We never bother to say "He has hunger," but other languages are more fastidious. A German might

FIG. 1.5 The lotus *Nelumbo nucifera*. This species of the lotus is only distantly related to water lilies, the flowers they superficially resemble. Instead, a close relative of *N. nucifera* is the common sycamore tree, also known as the plane tree. This would indicate that flowers and trees cannot be separate classes of organisms since some flowers may be more closely related to trees than to other flowers. *Source: U.S. National Gallery of Art public domain image.*

say "Ich habe Hunger" (I have hunger), indicating that hunger is a property of the individual, and avoiding any inference that "I" and "hunger" are equivalent terms (i.e., never "Ich bin Hunger"). The promiscuous use of equivalency relationships (i.e., "is", "are", and "am") produces all manner of mayhem. For example, imagine a situation wherein a scientist notes that a group of items happen to be hotter than other items. The scientist thinks "Those items are hot." Reflexively, the scientist creates a new class named "Hot Things," to accommodate all the items that are hot, such as a hot potato. Strictly speaking, a potato can have heat, but a potato can never be a type of heat. Heat is a property of an item, not the item itself. It can be difficult to break away from equating an item with a property of

FIG. 1.6 Photograph of copper-rich foods. These foods derive from unrelated classes of organisms (e.g., plant, crustacean, mammal) but they happen to share one property; copper-richness. We would not want to create a class of organisms named "Copper Rich", as such a class would contain unrelated organisms. *Source: Agricultural Research Service of the U.S. Department of Agriculture.*

the item. It may seem like a trivial point, but it is impossible to relate classes of things to one another if our classification does not distinguish classes from properties.

When inclusion in a class requires items to have a specific property that is characteristic of the class and absent from all other classes, we often name the class by its defining property. This is the source of much of our confusion. In the Classification of Life, we often choose names for classes that happen to reflect a class property. For example, Class Mammalia consists of animals having mammae (basically a ductal system leading to a nipple). Likewise, plants of Class Embryophyta consist of all plants that develop from an embryo. In these cases, biologists are not confused by the terminology insofar as it is commonly understood that the class name simply refers to a class property and is never equated to the property (e.g., a mammal is not a nipple). At other times, our choices are less discriminating and more problematic. For example, Class Rodentia, the rodents, includes rats, mice, squirrels, and gophers, which are other gnawing mammals. The word rodent derives from the Latin roots rodentem, rodens, from rodere, "to gnaw." Although all rodents gnaw, we know that gnawing is not unique to rodents. Rabbits (Class Lagormorpha) also gnaw. In retrospect, we probably could have chosen a better name than "Rodentia," if we had tried a bit harder.

Properties can be confused with classes for another reason, relating to the tendency of programmers to invent so-called compositional subclasses (i.e., subclasses composed of parts of the parent class). In "Chapter 5. The Class-Oriented Programming Paradigm," we will be explaining why the compositional programming style is not recommended for modeling classifications. For now, let's just say that in compositional programming, it is allowable to create a subclass of Class Human named Class Leg. In this case, Class Leg contains instances of a particular component of humans (i.e., their legs). In non-compositional programming, such as we will recommend for modeling classifications, there would never be a class named "Leg". "Leg", as noted previously, would simply be something that humans have, as a general feature or property, and we would give the property a descriptor, such as "has_a", when we want to assert the property for instances of the class. For example.

```
Fred has_a leg
```

How do we deal with properties other than class properties? Specifically, how do we deal with properties that are present in some of the members of the class, and not in others? Furthermore, how do we deal with properties that are present in members of several different classes? These important questions are sometimes ignored by classification builders, who are preoccupied with finding a set of properties that are class-specific and class-defining. When we are ready to discuss semantic languages ("Section 3.4. Semantic languages"), we will learn about instance properties (i.e., properties belonging to one or more members of a class), and properties with multi-class domains (i.e., properties that can be applied to a domain encompassing multiple classes). For now, let's just remember that a class is a collection of things, and a class property is a feature of all the things contained in the class. [**Glossary** Class Property versus class property, Classification builder, Domain, Property]

Section 1.4. Things that defy simple classification

We like to think that anything can be classified. This is not the case. Many things simply cannot be sensibly fitted into any classification, no matter how hard we try. Do not despair. We will learn, in "Section 3.2. Ontologies to the rescue," that everything in the universe can be placed in an organized data structure and linked to items and classes that are included in proper classifications. For now, let's just look at the kinds of things that cannot be classified, or that can only be classified after special treatment.

Composite items

The story is told of the Oxford scholar who remarked when the word "television" was coined that "no good would ever come of an invention the name of which was half in Latin and half in Greek" [7]. The pundit was asserting that a thing ought to be one thing or another thing and to describe television as a chimera of Latin and Greek was simply wrong. Pedantics notwithstanding, we must admit that much of what we observe in nature are composites. For example, humans are composites of trillions of individual living cells. Scientists can take a biopsy or a scraping of human tissue and grow a population of the extracted cells in a tissue culture flask. The cultured cells are free-living organisms that happen to contain a human genome. In addition to the trillions of human cells that form our composite bodies, we host a large assortment of resident organisms, including viruses, bacteria, fungi, single-cell eukaryotes, and even multicellular animals (e.g., Demodex folliculorum) [8,9]. The poet John Donne (1572–1631) was not far from the mark when he suggested that we are just "a volume of diseases bound together." [Glossary Eukaryote]

You might say that humans are non-obligate composite organisms, in that we can extract all of the viruses and bacteria and fungi, and microscopic animals from a human and we would still be left with an identifiable human being (albeit an unhealthy specimen). Such cannot be said for lichens, which are symbiotic colonies of fungi plus so-called algae or cyanobacteria. A lichen is not a lichen if it lacks one of its two composite organisms. There are at least 20,000 known species of lichens on earth, and no scientist would dispute that lichens are bona fide organisms. By convention, lichens are named for their fungal component and are classified as fungi (Fig. 1.7)

FIG. 1.7 A yellow lichen (*Caloplaca marina*) growing on a rock. Lichens are composites of at least two organisms (fungi plus algae) and cannot be accurately classified as a species. *Source: Wikipedia, and entered into the public domain by its author, Roger Griffith.*

There are numerous examples in nature in which an organism we see is an obligatory composite of two or more organisms. For physicians, one particular dual organism has been the object of a multi-layered medical puzzle. Onchocerca volvulus is a nematode that infects blackflies. When the blackflies bite humans, the injected organism migrates through the skin and other tissues. In the skin, it produces an itchy rash or nodules, a condition known as onchocerciasis. Onchocerciasis is a tropical disease that occurs mostly in

Africa and in tropical areas of South and Central America. Up to this point, we have been describing a simple parasitic infection, where the infectious organism causes tissue damage more or less confined to its migratory path in the skin.

In some instances, the nematode migrates to the eye of the infected patient, producing an inflammatory reaction that can lead to blindness. This condition is known as river blindness and is the second most common infectious cause of blindness worldwide [10]. It turns out that river blindness is not caused directly by Onchocherca volvulus. *Wolbachia pipientis* is a bacterium that is an endosymbiont of the Onchocerca [11]. It is the Wolbachia organism that is responsible for the local inflammatory reaction that leads to blindness [9].

The mysteries of Onchocerca volvulus, and its constant companion, *W. pipientis*, do not cease with our elucidation of the pathogenesis of river blindness. Nodding disease is a serious condition, first documented in the 1960s, that occurs almost exclusively in young children and adolescents living in certain regions of South Sudan, Tanzania, and Uganda. The disease stunts normal growth of the brain and produces seizures. During the seizures, the neck muscles do not support the weight of the head, resulting in a characteristic nod, emphasizing the name of the disease. It was noticed that nodding disease occurs in areas where river blindness is endemic. A recent paper found that patients with nodding disease have antibodies to Onchocerca volvulus proteins that cross-react with leiomodin-1, a protein expressed in areas of the brain affected by the disease [12]. If this early research is confirmed, then nodding disease will be seen as an infectious disease that elicits an antibody response, that subsequently elicits a neurologic disorder. If this hypothesis is correct, then elimination of the endosymbiont (*W. pipientis*) will lead to the elimination of its partner (Onchocherca volvulus), which will lead to the elimination of river blindness and nodding disease. A clinical trial is currently underway to determine whether doxycycline, an antibiotic active against *W. pipientis*, will successfully treat nodding disease [13]. The somewhat convoluted story of onchocerciasis reminds us that a composite organism cannot be usefully classified under any single class; its properties derive from multiple classes. [Glossary Pathogenesis]

All chemical species other than elements are composites of two or more elements. Such chemicals cannot be sensibly characterized by simply adding together the physical attributes of each of their constituent elements (Fig. 1.8).

Even energy has composite forms. For example, light is an electromagnetic wave. With each wave cycle, the charge component of light wanes as the magnetic component waxes, at a ninety-degree angle from one another. We cannot understand light without taking into account the composite (i.e., electrical and magnetic) nature of the wave [14].

In point of fact, everything in our universe either falls into a natural classification, or it can be related to things included in a natural classification. Hence, composite objects will always have relationships with classifiable objects, and these relationships can be expressed in meaningful statements. As it happens, there are excellent strategies in which such meaningful statements can be written, and these strategies will be discussed in "Section 4.2. Paradoxes." [Glossary Nonatomicity]

FIG. 1.8 Cerussite, also known as lead carbonate, is a transparent orthorhombic crystal that is a composite of lead, carbon, and oxygen atoms. Its features are not a simple aggregate of the features of its parts. Cerussite does not look anything like lead or carbon; and it is certainly not a gas, like oxygen. *Source: U.S. Geological Survey.*

Poorly labeled items

William Stanley Jevons (1835–1882), an English economist and logician, wrote "A word with two distinct meanings is two words." So true. Many of the words that we use in science have so many alternate meanings that they cannot be sensibly added to any legitimate classification.

We often encounter completely unrelated objects that are given the same name within a classification. For example, "parapsoriasis" is a specific-sounding diagnosis rendered by dermatologists. Actually, the name "parapsoriasis" is applied to a group of skin diseases that happen to be characterized by scaly or raised plaques that happen to look a bit like another clinical entity, "psoriasis"; hence the name "parapsoriasis" roughly meaning "like psoriasis". The conditions diagnosed as parapsoriasis may account for a host of distinct disorders, each having different causes, different histologic appearances, and different responses to treatment. It is a taxonomic sin to call different diseases under one common term, but bad habits die hard. [Glossary Histologic examination, Histology]

In the animal kingdom, the "worm" lost its scientific meaning a long time ago. Among the organisms that we call worms are the platyhelminths (flatworms), the nematodes (roundworms), and the annelids (the ringed worms). Each of these classes occupies its branch of the Classification of Life, and the organisms belonging to any one of these classes are not closely related to organisms belonging to the other branches. For example, a small squirming organism referred to as a "worm" may be an insect larva (i.e., not a helminth), or it may be one of several unrelated classes of organisms. Class Acanthocephala includes the thorny-headed worms. Class Annelida (which includes earthworms) descends from Class Lophotrochozoa, which includes mollusks. Acorn worms (Class Enteropneusta) are hemichordates whose closest phylogenetic relatives are the echinoderms, which include sand dollars and starfish. Class Chaetognatha contains the predatory marine arrow worms. Class Lophotrochozoa contains the Nemertea, or ribbon worms. Class Nematoda (roundworms) and Class Annelida (ringed worms, including earthworms) are more closely related to spiders and clams, respectively, than either one is related to Class Platyhelminthes (flatworms). The term "worm" has come to have no taxonomic meaning since soft, squiggly organisms are scattered throughout animal taxonomy, many having no close relationship to one another (Fig. 1.9). [Glossary Taxonomy versus classification]

A similar objection can be applied to the word "fly". The term "fly" should refer exclusively to members of Class Diptera (flies). As it happens, the term "fly" has been assigned, at one time or another, to just about any small flying insect, a few of which are dipterans: butterflies (Class Lepidoptera), dragonflies (Class Palaeoptera), mayflies (Class Palaeoptera). When a word is applied to morphologically similar, but phylogenetically unrelated organisms, it defies sensible classification.

Does it make a difference if we apply a technically inaccurate word to organisms having no close taxonomic relationship to one another? What is all the fuss about, anyway? The problem created by sloppy nomenclature is the havoc resulting from class noise. Whenever we combine items belonging to different classes under the same name, we cannot sensibly study the inherited properties of the items. The results of experiments conducted on collections of mixed-class items are seldom valid (for the class), and we produce science that is misleading and unhelpful. In the case of parasitic "worms", we produce drugs that we call antihelminthic (i.e., drugs that kill worms), knowing full well that such drugs cannot possibly be effective against all types of worms, insofar as the different classes of worms have no close evolutionary relationship and have sensitivities to toxins that are specific to their classes. [Glossary Class noise, Nomenclature]

Let's stop a moment to consider another example of class noise and its negative consequences. *Naegleria fowleri* is an example of a eukaryotic organism that is capable of

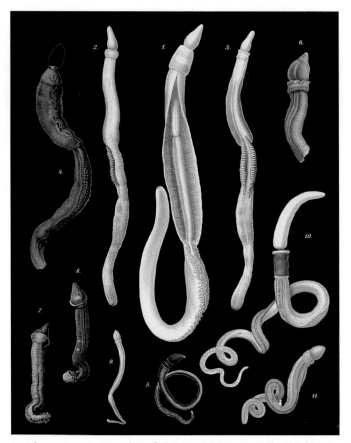

FIG. 1.9 Various species of acorn worm, a member of Class Deuterostomia, and a close relative of starfish and sand dollars. *Source: Johann Wilhelm Spengel, in Die Enteropneusten des Golfes von Neapel und der angrenzenden Meeres-Abschnitte Berlin: Verlag von R. Friedlander and Sohn, published 1893.*

producing lethal encephalitis in susceptible humans. *N. fowleri* grows in warm waters such as lakes and creeks. Swimmers in contaminated waters may develop an infection that spreads from the nasal sinuses to the central nervous system, to produce encephalitis that is fatal in 97% of cases [15]. Despite the hazard posed by Naegleria, health authorities do not generally test fresh-water sources to determine the presence of the organism. Do not expect to find warning signs posted at swimming holes announcing that the water is contaminated by an organism that produces a disease that has a nearly 100% fatality rate. It is simply assumed that anyone who spends any time around fresh water will eventually be exposed to Naegleria. As it happens, although many thousands of individuals are exposed each year to Naegleria in the U.S., only a few cases of Naegleria encephalitis occur in this country. In fact, since Naegleria was first recognized as a cause of encephalitis, in 1965, less than 150 cases have been reported [16]. Most of the reported cases have occurred in children and adolescents and are associated with recreational water activities [17,18]. As far as we can tell, individuals who develop Naeglerian encephalitis are generally immune competent. At present, we have no way of determining who is likely to be susceptible to Naeglerian encephalitis [19].

Historically, brain infections due to *N. fowleri* were lumped with the amoebic encephalitides. To this day, Nagleria fowleri, is commonly referred to as the "brain-eating amoeba." As it happens, Naeglerians are not amoebozoans. Naeglerians belong to Class Percolozoa, an entirely different class of single-celled eukaryotic organisms than Class Amoebozoa. The proper term for instances of encephalitis produced by *N. fowleri* is percolozoan encephalitis; not amoebic encephalitis. Let's take a look at the phylogenetic lineage of Naeglaria fowleri and compare it with *Acanthamoeba polyphaga*, a pathogen of Class Amoebozoa [19]. [Glossary Acanthamoeba]

Here is the lineage of *N. fowleri*:

Eukaryota
Bikonta
Heterolobosea
Schizopyrenida
Vahlkampfiidae
Percolozoa
Naegleria
N. fowleri

Here is the lineage of Acanthamoeba polyphagia

Eukaryota
Unikonta
Opisthokonta
Amoebozoa
Discosea
Longamoebia
Centramoebida
Acanthamoebidae
Acanthamoeba
Acanthamoeba polyphaga

Notice that at the very first phylogenetic split following Class Eukaryota, we see the two large classes of eukaryotic organisms: Class Unikonta (organisms with one undulipodium) and Class Bikonta (classes with two undulipodia). The Unikonts contain Class Fungi, Class Eumetazoa (animals), and Class Amoebozoa. Hence, all of the members of Class Amoebozoa, including all of the true amoeba known to cause amoebic encephalitis, are much more closely related to humans than they are to any of the members of Class Bikonta.

Class Bikonta contains all of Class Plantae (plants) plus several large classes of single-celled eukaryotes, including Class Percolozoa (to which *Naegleria fowleri* belongs). Hence, Naegleria, a member of Class Bikonta, is not at all closely related to any of the amoeba [19].

So what? What difference does it make if we lump *N. fowleri* with the pathogenic amoebas. They are all single-celled parasites; shouldn't we expect them all to respond similarly to the same treatments? It is exactly this type of fuzzy thinking that continues to block the advancement of modern medicine. Simply because two infectious organisms look similar to one another, grow in the same habitat, and produce clinically similar diseases does not indicate that the organisms will respond similarly to treatment. Unrelated classes of organisms, even if they look similar to one another, are driven by different sets of metabolic pathways. There is simply no rational reason to expect that a treatment regimen that is effective against members of Class Amoebozoa will be effective against members of Class Percolozoa [19]. [Glossary Metabolic pathway]

At present, Naegleria encephalitis is treated as though it were one of the amoebic encephalitides, with amphotericin B. With or without amphotericin B treatment, nearly all cases of percolozoan encephalitis are fatal [20]. We have much to learn about the biology of Class Percolozoa, before we find rational treatments for encephalitis produced by *N. fowleri* [9].

It should be noted that the clinical problem faced with infection with *N. fowleri* (i.e., pretending the organism is an amoeba when it is not), is not unique. As we learn more about the proper classification of living organisms, we continue to find diseases that have fallen through the cracks of our knowledge base (e.g., blastocystosis and pythiosis). In such cases, we tend to persist in treating them with the same drugs used to treat organisms that they superficially resemble. There is no logical justification for such behavior. The best course of action is what you might expect: more research, executed as quickly as possible. [Glossary Blastocystosis, Pythiosis]

In the aforementioned cases of worms and flies, one word has multiple meanings, rendering the word taxonomically uninformative. The fungi have the opposite problem. One fungal species may have two formally assigned taxonomic names, a feature that has confused biologists for many decades. The reason for doubly named fungal species relates to their two options for reproduction: sexual and asexual.

Both these forms of reproduction have their own morphologic appearances, in the same species of organism. Factors that determine the mode of reproduction for a cultured fungus are a mystery. A mycologist can observe a fungus that reproduces exclusively asexually, in a clinical setting, while another mycologist, observing the same species in a culture dish or growing in the wild, may observe sexual reproduction (i.e., exhibiting so-called fruiting bodies). Ignorant of the existence of an alternate morphologic form, taxonomists have assigned different names to the same organism, depending upon the mode of reproduction they happen to observe (i.e., sexual or asexual). Rather than harmonizing a dichotomous nomenclature under one preferred name, the ICBN (International Code of

Botanical Nomenclature) had ruled, in the past, that it is acceptable to assign two different binomials to an organism: a sexual (also called teleomorphic, perfect, or meiotic form), and an asexual (also called anamorphic, imperfect, or mitotic form). For instance, two binomials legitimately apply to the same organism: Filobasidiella neoformans (the teleomorphic form) and *Cryptococcus neoformans* (the anamorphic form). Clinical mycologists typically use the asexual name, because it is the asexual form that grows in human tissues. [Glossary Binomials]

The unchecked craziness of one species having several different names could not continue forever. The 18th International Botanical Congress assembled in 2011, in Melbourne, Australia, and at last formally recognized that a fungus was not a plant, and renamed themselves "The International Code of Nomenclature for Algae, Fungi, and Plants". More importantly, the Congress abolished longstanding provisions permitting the separate names for the different morphologic forms of a pleomorphic fungal species (i.e., names for the sexual and asexual morphologic forms) [21].

Artifacts

Artifacts (things made by humans through the use of artifice) pose another obstacle for classification enthusiasts. Human-made items such as stamps, automobiles, and teapots simply do not classify well. Artifacts tend to be composed of multiple parts and substances, all having different properties, making it difficult to assemble a collection of artifacts into a sensible classification.

What humans create, humans can modify. Classifications of artifactual items are often made complex due to modifications of the items, with subsequent modifications of their assigned classes, occurring over time. Malcolm Duncan has posted an insightful and funny essay entitled "The Chocolate Teapot (Version 2.3)" [22]. In this essay, he shows how modifications and additions to a product line (teapots in his example) make it impossible to sensibly classify items in a changing class structure. [4,23]. We will be discussing this issue further in "Section 3.5. Why ontologies sometimes disappoint us."

In most cases, catalogs, indexes, and blueprints are the best ways to organize collections of artifacts, and composite items. For stalwarts who insist on holding their artifacts in classes, there are several options discussed in "Section 3.6. Best practices for ontologies." [Glossary Blueprint, Catalog, Classification versus index, Index, Indexes]

Transitive items

Our definition of the idealized classification (discussed in "Section 2.1. Classifications defined") forbids the inclusion of transitives; things that change into other things, from moment to moment. The condition of intransitivity can be problematic.

In nature, there are many examples of objects that transit through different stages of their existence. For example, in human development, we pass through the following stages: conceptus, embryo, fetus, infant, adult. Each stage of existence is biologically different from all the others, but they all represent forms of existence of the same objects.

In the case of holometabolous insects, that undergo four life stages (i.e., egg, larva, pupa, adult), the different stages may exist as free-living animals with no obvious relation to one another. This is the case of the caterpillar and the butterfly. Early taxonomists, unaware of all the stages of the organisms they observed in their field-work, were prone to assigning different species names to each life stage, a practice that slowed progress in their fields of study. Likewise, an acorn is a phase (embryonic) in the development of an oak tree. We must not forget that the small acorn and the mighty oak are the same species.

In human medicine, some cancers change their morphology and behavior over time. For example, some slow-growing lymphomas may transform into aggressive tumors characterized by large tumor cells unlike the smaller cells observed in early cancer. It is important to recognize that these are different stages of the same class of tumor, despite their biological differences.

In the 1980s and 1990s, knowledge of cancer-causing genes and driver pathways was rudimentary, and clinical trial designers settled on a somewhat blunt classifier for cancers: stage. Some background is needed regarding the meaning of the cancer stage. When a cancer is diagnosed, a determination is made regarding its size, extent of local invasion, whether tumor deposits can be found in regional or distant lymph nodes, and whether cancer has metastasized to distant organs. This information is used to assign a clinical-stage to cancer. As an example, stage III lung cancer has spread to lymph nodes. The process of staging cancers required a lot of work, but the end product was the best available method for dividing cancer patients into clinically distinct subsets, at the time. Through the latter decades of the 20th century, cancer researchers designed clinical trials to test the response of candidate chemotherapeutic agents on populations divided by cancer stage. [Glossary Invasion, Oncologist, Staging, Tumor grading]

In retrospect, a very strong argument can be made that stage-stratified clinical trials were failures, generally. One of the prominent reasons for these failures was class blending. With the benefit of hindsight, it is easy to see that a clinical-stage is not a valid biological class. If we look at Stage III tumors, we know that some of the patients assigned to this class may have had tumors that progressed quickly through Stages I and II, exhibiting rapid growth and early invasiveness. Other patients may have had tumors with indolent growth history, requiring years or even decades to qualify as a Stage III tumor. The observation that biologically diverse tumors had attained the same clinical stage (i.e., similar size and similar status regarding metastases) at a certain point in time, does not put the tumors into a biologically homogeneous class.

Surprisingly, clinical trialists, as a group, had difficulty grasping the error of their ways. I remember having discussions in which the trialists refused to accept that there was any substantive difference between tumor stage and tumor class. Sometimes it helps to illustrate the problem from a different frame of reference. Imagine an automotive engineer who wants to test a new fuel additive on the performance of different classes of cars, driving at different speeds. To do so, she stands on the roadside of Interstate 95 and clocks the speed of cars passing on the road, simultaneously recording their license plate numbers.

With data in hand, she divides the cars into those that are driving slow, moderate, and fast; and she uses the license plate data to track the drivers in the three respective speed groups. After making the proper arrangements with all of the drivers, she engages in a carefully designed experiment, to determine whether there is a difference in the performance of cars receiving the fuel additive, comparing the three-speed groups (slow, moderate, and fast). No differences are found, and she concludes that the fuel additive works similarly regardless of driving speed. The problem here is that cars cannot be sensibly classified based on their highway speed. Basically, every car on the road can drive slowly or moderately, or speedily, depending on many factors (e.g., road conditions, traffic conditions, temperament of driver). Although at any moment on any highway we will find subpopulations of cars moving slow, or moderately, or fast, we cannot usefully classify automobiles as slow speed cars or moderate speed cars, or high-speed cars. Likewise, we can find populations of cancer patients in Stage I or Stage II, or Stage III of their disease, but we cannot classify patients into those stages.

The typical progression of a tumor from Stage I to Stage II to Stage III to Stage IV violates the intransitivity rule of classification. This alone should have told the trial designers, from the very start, that a clinical-stage cannot serve as the basis of a biological class. Hence, trials conducted by stage of tumor progression will contain groups of blended classes (i.e., the tumors collected by stage will belong to diverse biological classes), and such trials will seldom yield useful results. The importance of avoiding transitive classes cannot be over-emphasized. It is one of the most common errors committed by most of us, at one time or another, and has particularly unfortunate consequences when we begin to use our classifications to guide us in the design of experimental protocols. [Glossary Stage treatment bias]

Having made the previous remarks, we must confess that transitive objects have their way of sneaking into the most venerable of classifications. To give the problem a bit of perspective, consider that everything in the universe changes a tiny bit from moment to moment. Tomorrow, you will be a different organism that you are today, with many different cells, different experiences, and memories, different chemical content. You pretend to be the same person, but you are not. In the course of a day, you have transitioned to another version of yourself. The sense of being different, from one moment to another, is a favorite meme of science fiction writers. We see this displayed in every story that features a stolen identity, or a lost identity (i.e., amnesia), or a duplicate identity (i.e., a clone), or an unfamiliar identity (i.e., a man in the wrong body). The inconstancy of things that should never change is a concept that absorbs the human psyche. Let's tuck this problem away for the moment. We'll look at potential solutions in "Section 4.3. Linking classifications, ontologies, and triplestores."

Items that change their function from moment to moment

When an engineer designs a radio, she knows that she can assign names to components, and these components can be relied upon to behave in a manner characteristic to its type. A capacitor will behave like a capacitor, and a resistor will behave like a resistor.

The engineer need not worry that the capacitor will behave like a semiconductor or an integrated circuit. The engineer knows that the function of a machine's component will never change; but the biologist operates in a world wherein components change their functions, from organism to organism, cell to cell, and moment to moment.

Proteus is a Greek god who, according to legend, could morph into any animal shape he wished. Proteus is now the namesake for Proteobacteria, a large class of bacteria with widely diverse shapes, sizes, and biochemical attributes. Proteus is also the namesake for anything capable of changing itself radically, according to its needs. The term "protean" has been attached to many types of proteins. As an example, cancer researchers have devoted decades to determine the role of p53 in the development of cancer. Mutations in the gene coding for p53 may result in the disruption of normal cellular regulation, leading to the eventual emergence of malignant cells. In the past few decades, as more experimental data has been obtained, cancer researchers learned that p53 is just one of many proteins that play some role in carcinogenesis and that the role played by p53 changes depending on the species, tissue type, cellular microenvironment, and genetic background of cells. Under one set of circumstances, p53 may modify DNA repair; under another set of circumstances, p53 may cause cells to arrest the growth cycle [24,25]. It is impossible to construct a classification of proteins based on their functionality if their functionality is constantly changing. The classification builder must find some constant features upon which to build a classification. [Glossary Carcinogen, Carcinogenesis]

Collections of unrelated things having similar functionality

I may have thought, as a child, that when I grew up to be a scientist, I would never be fooled into mistaking a crude similarity for a formal biological class. Years later I was introduced to the endocrine system of animals. I was taught that animals have a class of organs that, for the most part, grow as bilateral matched glands (e.g., left and right adrenal glands, left and right gonad), or nearly symmetric glands attached at the midline (e.g., left-lobe and right lobe of the thyroid gland, left lobe and right lobe of the pituitary gland). These glands all participated in a chemical signaling system in which individual glands release hormones into the blood to produce various responses in receptor tissues. Those same glands respond in turn to circulating hormones released from other endocrine glands. Together, the endocrine glands, I was told, form a biological class of organs, and the tumors arising from the endocrine glands could all be unified under one general class of tumors.

There is much reason to believe that this is not the case. Beyond the defining feature of endocrine activity (i.e., the ability to secrete chemical signals into the blood), the endocrine glands are biologically quite different from one another. Some are large, like the thyroid, and some are small, like the islets of the pancreas that fit snugly between the parenchymal acini of the exocrine pancreas. Some endocrine glands, like the gastrointestinal tract, are single-cell structures sprinkled throughout the gut mucosa.

The hormones secreted by endocrine glands have no consistent chemical theme. Some endocrine hormones are polypeptides, some are steroids, some are catecholamines, some are iodinated conjugates. It is hard to imagine a common genetic or biochemical pathway that could account for this chemical diversity. Furthermore, the mode of action of the different hormones varies greatly, some acting on cell surface receptors, some acting on cytoplasmic receptors, some acting within the nucleus. With all these different activities, it would be highly unlikely that the endocrine glands share a common evolution or a common set of biochemical pathways. [Glossary Nucleus]

It turns out that there are many types of cells, derived from all of the embryonic layers in our bodies, that secrete chemical signals. Some secrete into the blood while others secrete short-acting molecules that act directly on neighboring cells (paracrine cells), and some cells produce signals that act on themselves (i.e., autocrine cells). Basically, the key feature separating endocrine cells from autocrine and paracrine cells is the distance between the secreting cell and its receptor cell. Otherwise, the signaling processes, and the general types of chemicals involved, are much the same.

Not only are endocrine factors produced by a wide variety of cells throughout our bodies, but we see chemical signaling in very simple species of multicellular organisms [26–30]. Endocrine activity is not limited to animals; plants too use chemical signals to moderate growth and development.

It has been suggested that the most direct and the fastest way to modify the phenotype of a species is to modify the endocrine system [27]. The endocrine system in animals is a major regulator of traits (e.g., size, metabolic rate, bone density). Mutations to the endocrine system are known to produce heritable modifications in the physiology of affected individuals. [Glossary Phenotype]

To summarize, endocrine activity is not limited to the identifiable endocrine glands in an animal. Many different types of cells of the body produce their chemical signals. How do these observations relate to the topic of classification? Because many diverse cell types have endocrine activity, we can infer that when we create an endocrine class (e.g., Class Endocrine), we will include cells and tissues that cut across other unrelated classes of tissues. When we refer to endocrine tumors (i.e., tumors derived from cells of Class Endocrine), we will be including biologically unrelated tumors. As it happens, endocrine glands develop from all of the germ layers of the embryo. For example, the cortices (outer layers) of the adrenal glands develop from the mesoderm. The medulla (inner core) of the adrenal glands develops from the neural crest. The adrenal cortical cells produce steroid molecules (e.g., cortisol), typical of other secretory cells of mesodermal origin. The adrenal medullary cells are specialized cells of the peripheral nervous system, of neural crest origin, and in concert with other cells of the peripheral nervous system. When we say that the adrenal glands belong to Class Endocrine, we put ourselves in conflict with our certain knowledge that the adrenal cortex is a member of Class Mesoderm (i.e., tissues arising from mesoderm) and that the adrenal medulla arises from Class Neural Crest. [Glossary Cell type, Germ layers]

At this point, you may be wondering why a class cannot include members of another class? The reason is that the behavior of a class member is determined by its ancestral lineage. If a class contains members of unrelated classes, those members will display an assortment of behaviors and inherited properties that will not extend to every member of the class. For example, in the case of the endocrine glands, it has been shown that the properties of the various tumors of endocrine glands are primarily determined by their embryonic class of origin, not by their endocrine behavior [31–34]. Specifically, inherited tumor syndromes that may involve tumors of endocrine glands will arise in tissues having the same embryologic lineage and will not occur in endocrine glands from other embryologic lineages. This observation suggests that we must classify endocrine glands based on their embryologic lineage; not based on one property that happens to be found in members of many different cell types (e.g., endocrine activity, in this case). Put simply, we cannot classify the tumors that arise in members of Class Endocrine, if Class Endocrine is not a valid class, whose members share a common feature that distinguishes them from members of other classes. The embryonic classes (e.g., Class Mesoderm, Class Neural Crest, Class Endoderm, Class Trophectoderm, Class Ectoderm) have their class properties, and every tissue in the developed human body develops from one, and only one, embryonic class. Therefore, a reasonable argument can be made to discard Class Endocrine and to assign the endocrine tumors to their respective classes of embryologic origin. [Glossary Ancestral lineage, Endoderm, Syndrome versus disease, Trophectoderm]

Things having multiple origins whose behavior is determined by their histories

> *Mille viae ducunt homines per saecula Romam (A thousand roads lead men forever to Rome)*
>
> *Alain de Lille in "Liber Parabolarum", circa 1175*

Lithium and boron are made in stars in great quantity but are also consumed in stars, with little net product released into space. The lithium and boron we find on earth are created not within stars but by cosmic ray collisions taking place on our planet. Suppose, just for the sake of argument, that the lithium that is produced in stars behaved entirely differently than the lithium produced by cosmic ray collisions? In that case, we would need a classification that somehow accommodated two behavioral forms of lithium. Fortunately, an atom of lithium is an atom of lithium, whether it was produced in a star or earth's stratosphere. This constancy of the elements, regardless of their mechanism of origin, is not shared by all types of classified items. In the case of human diseases, we have many examples of diseases whose behavior is determined by the biological mechanism leading to their development.

Let's take a few moments to learn a little bit about the so-called phenocopies of genetic diseases. A phenocopy is a non-inherited acquired disease that has the same or nearly the same, clinical features as an inherited genetic disease. Phenocopies may arise as the result of exposure to a toxic agent that happens to reduce the activity of some protein that is the same protein whose activity is reduced as the consequence of inherited genetic disease. Because both diseases are characterized by the same protein deficiency, we give both these conditions (i.e., genetic and phenocopy) the same name. [Glossary Inheritance]

In addition to toxins that produce disease by altering the same gene product that is affected by its genetic counterpart, we see many different biological mechanisms wherein a phenocopy may arise. For example, a toxin may alter a protein involved in the same metabolic pathway that corresponds to the metabolic pathway altered by some other protein involved by a genetic disease. In this case, both forms of the disease may share the same clinical features, but neither disease involves the same protein. Phenocopy diseases may be caused by epigenomic effects wherein some change to the genome other than genetic mutations may produce a disease with the same symptoms as the genetic counterpart. In theory, any genetic deficiency can be phenocopied by an epigenomic downregulation of the protein affected in the genetic disease, and we occasionally see examples of epigenomic alterations masquerading as genetic diseases [35]. Lastly mentioned, there is a large collection of autoantibody diseases that target specific proteins to produce a clinical picture that mimics that produced by a genetic disease affecting the same protein. Autoantibody disorders are a frequently occurring type of phenocopy disease. [Glossary Autoantibody disease versus autoimmune disease, Autoantibody diseases that are phenocopies of genetic diseases, Epigenome, Phenocopy disease]

At this point, you may be wondering why the existence of phenocopy diseases would present a dilemma for classification builders. You might be thinking that if two pathways (e.g., genetic and toxic) lead to the same set of clinical symptoms, then there is no harm done by giving the genetic and acquired forms of the disease the same name. The difficulty lies in the many ways, other than clinical symptomatology, that phenocopies differ from inherited diseases.

Here are just a few properties that characterize phenocopy diseases.

- Not rare (i.e., phenocopies are nearly always more common than their genetic equivalents)
- Association with an identified causal agent
- Disease cohorts confined to particular occupations or activities (e.g., smokers)
- Absence of disease in family members
- Often produces symptoms in organs known to metabolize or process ingested chemicals (e.g., liver, kidney, lungs)
- Often reversible
- Rapid onset of symptoms
- May develop in a wide range of ages of individuals exposed to the same agent
- May develop in a cluster of unrelated individuals (e.g., as an endemic or an epidemic)
- Lack characteristics of genetic mutation (by definition)

Because environmental agents often contribute to the cause of phenocopy diseases, and because many environmental agents have a direct action on cellular constituents, we would expect to see the rapid onset of symptoms and clusters of reported cases in high-risk locations. We also note that phenocopy diseases do not generally arise in infants, and tend to occur most often in older populations, as the cumulative toxic effects of environmental agents take their tolls. Generally, genes account for diseases in the young; environment accounts for their phenocopies in the older population. We can often observe the switch-over from genetic diseases to their phenocopies, with aging. In the case of all of the inherited cancer syndromes, genes account for the cancers that occur in childhood and early adulthood. As age increases, genes account for fewer and fewer cancers. By late adulthood, phenocopies dominate [36,37].

In a sense, the aging process itself is one of the great phenocopies of genetic diseases. Many of the cellular abnormalities that are considered pathognomonic of one or an other genetic diseases are found in occasional cells of otherwise unaffected individuals, increasing in number as the body ages. These might include Lewy bodies, amyloid plaques, neurofibrillary tangles, psammoma bodies [38], ragged red fibers [39], corpora amylacea [40], tubular aggregates [41], and other morphologic abnormalities familiar to anatomic pathologists. Although no one has made a complete survey of all the cellular abnormalities that arise in rare genetic diseases, it wouldn't be much of a stretch to suggest that most of them are phenocopied in increased numbers in the aging cells of normal individuals. [Glossary Anatomic pathologist, Rare disease]

Phenocopy diseases can be rare or common, depending on exposure conditions; while genetic diseases are almost always rare. It is noteworthy that in nearly every situation where we look at the differences in occurrence rates between a specific genetic disease and its phenocopy, the phenocopy is much more common. For example, in cases of colorectal cancer, 20% of cases have an identifiable predisposing inherited gene, while the remaining 80% are presumably phenocopies [42]. For breast cancer, about 5% of cases have a germline BRCA gene mutation. The vast majority of breast cancer cases are non-inherited phenocopies. About 15% of prion diseases occurring in humans are thought to be inherited, the remainder being phenocopies [43,44]. Pulmonary alveolar proteinosis occurs in inherited and sporadic forms. The acquired form of pulmonary alveolar proteinosis is the most common form, accounting for approximately 90% of cases [45]. Myasthenia gravis may rarely occur as a congenital genetic condition, but the common form of this disease is found in adults, as a phenocopy [46]. Likewise, the autoantibody phenocopy of thrombotic thrombocytopenic purpura is more common than the genetic form of the disease. The alcohol-related phenocopy of cirrhosis is much more common than the genetic form, due to a mutation in Keratin 18 [47,48]. [Glossary BRCA, Cirrhosis]

There may be a few exceptions to the rule. In 36 unrelated patients with hereditary angioedema, mutations were found in the gene coding for the serpin C1 inhibitor in 34 patients. The remaining two patients had antibodies against the C1 inhibitor [49], indicating that the genetic form of the disease seems to be more prevalent than its phenocopy [48].

Phenocopies, more so than genetic diseases, are often reversible by the elimination of a causative factor, or the introduction of a vitamin, or the reduction of a dietary constituent [50]. Genetic diseases are characterized by genes that persist in every cell of the organisms, through the life of the organisms; hence, genetic diseases cannot be easily reversed. There are exceptions, of course. Cumulative environmental exposures that produce chronic damage, particularly to non-dividing cell populations with limited repair capacity (e.g., neurons) are not generally reversible. Examples might include radiation damage, heavy metal poisoning to nerves and brain, and asbestos-induced lung disease [48].

Inherited diseases follow a common pattern that helps distinguish them from their non-genetic phenocopies [51].

Here are some of the biological features we might expect to find in inherited genetic diseases [48]:

- Usually progressive and irreversible unless there is medical intervention.
- Early age of onset.
- Types of organ dysfunctions that are otherwise rare in the general population (tremors, nystagmus, wasting).
- Usually rare (fatal genetic diseases are seldom common; common genetic diseases are seldom fatal).
- Neurocognitive impairments are sometimes present [51].
- Multiple dysmorphisms and multiple abnormalities are often encountered.

The phenocopy diseases help us to focus on the specific metabolic pathways that drive the disease phenotype. Knowing the operational pathway of a disease provides us with an opportunity to develop new strategies to repair, control, or bypass the metabolic damage caused by a flawed gene [48]. Unfortunately, our understanding of phenocopies and their genetic equivalents is incomplete, and we cannot distinguish one from the other, in every instance of their occurrence.

Because a named disease may have any of several distinctly different pathogeneses (i.e., steps leading to the development of the clinical entity), and because the biological features of the disease can be strikingly different in each form of the diseases, it becomes problematic to simply classify diseases by their name. At the same time, classification by name is one of the cornerstones of every classification. If we do not have named objects assigned to classes, how can we make sense of the classification? This ambiguity of identity is one of the chief reasons why disease classifications are notoriously inadequate.

Now that we understand the problems that arise when we try to classify diseases according to their names, what can we possibly do to remedy the situation? We will provide one possible solution when we reach "Section 4.3. Linking classifications, ontologies, and triplestores."

Things whose class assignment cannot yet be determined

A good classification is never complete until every member of the classification has a place in a class, and every member within a class has a defined relationship to every other member within the same class. When a classification is being constructed, it is common to have some objects whose properties are a mystery or objects that simply cannot be easily related to other objects. When classification builders encounter an object that they know belongs somewhere within the classification, but they don't know where to put it, they may reach for a Latin panacea, the venerable "incertae sedis". "Incertae sedis" is Latin for "uncertain placement." Using a Latin term puts a veneer of classical authority on the practice of classifying things that we do not understand. Other euphemisms for an indeterminate class of objects might include "miscellaneous" and "not otherwise specified." The idea here is that an unclassifiable object can be placed in a class with all the other unidentifiable objects until their true nature can be sorted out. By doing so, the classification builder satisfies the "completeness" dictum, insofar as every known object is assigned one specific class. It would be unkind to complain that the "incertae sedis" class is undefined, has no meaningful relationship to any other class, and contains objects that are unrelated to one another.

Let's look at a few famous examples wherein a miscellaneous class has been created as a stopgap measure.

The small "d" fungi

There are estimated to be several million fungal species, many fewer of which have been fully characterized. Many fungi cannot be grown in culture, thus amplifying the difficulties involved in studying their behaviors and morphologies. Before the advent of gene sequencing, it was common for one laboratory to observe a fungus under one set of conditions while another laboratory observes the same fungus under another set of conditions; leading each laboratory to announce its description and name for the same fungal species.

The proliferation of insufficiently characterized fungi, many of which being known by more than one name, has led mycologists to invent a pseudo-class of fungi, named the deuteromycetes (spelled with a lowercase "d", signifying its questionable validity as a true biologic class). Fungi of indeterminate class wait in a fungal purgatory until mycologists catch up with the millions of fungal species that are waiting for genetic sequencing and definitive classification [52]. [Glossary Problematica]

Protists

In the Classification of Life, nineteenth-century taxonomists did not know quite what to do with the many different one-celled eukaryotes they were collecting. As a stop-gap measure, they invented the Kingdom Protozoa, the class of all one-celled animals, the parent class of all multicellular organisms. Kingdom protozoa was a pseudo-class, consisting of all manner of organisms that were not closely related to one another, and which contained organisms that should have been assigned to separately named classes of single-celled eukaryotic organisms [53]. As a consequence, generations of students were taught that the protozoans were a biologically unified class of organisms having similar biological and biochemical properties. Medical students were introduced to "anti-protozoal" drugs, as though there could be a chemical agent that could target unrelated species (i.e., the so-called protozoans) while sparing every other type of organism. Is it any wonder that the world has been slow in finding drugs that are effective against particular species of single-celled infectious organisms?

Many decades passed before taxonomists caught up with the blunder and re-assigned individuals in class protozoa to proper classes of their own. Nonetheless, biologists are unwilling to abandon long-cherished terminology. Taxonomists who should know better have pleaded to retain obsolete and misleading plesionyms, such as "protist", "proto-ctista", and "protozoa" because doing so will enhance communication and facilitate teaching [54]. They raise a fair point, but surely the chief objective of science is to correct misconceptions, not perpetuate them. We have seen some evidence of progress. For example, the Society of Protozoologists, founded in 1947, has seen fit to update their name to Society of Protistologists, in 2005. Might it be asking too much for them to change their name, once again? An awkward but accurate title would be, "Society of Scientists Who Study Single-Celled Eukaryotic Organisms". [Glossary Plesionym]

Items on a spectrum

It can be impossible to classify things that have no sharp boundaries or that sit on a smooth spectrum of items. In many cases, the so-called spectrum is illusory and consists of many distinctly different things that seem blended when crowded together. The continuous color spectrum is a good example. There are no clearly defined colors. Red, orange, yellow, blue, indigo, and violet are somewhat arbitrary divisions of the color spectrum, with no defined wavelengths separating one color from another. The distinctive colors we perceive are an illusion produced by our brains. Using inputs from specialized retinal receptors that register some bands of wavelength more than others, the brain codifies colors to produce the simulacrum of a discrete reality. Despite our best perceptions, the electromagnetic spectrum is continuous and colors cannot be sensibly demarcated and classified.

Contrariwise, the emission "spectra" of elements are characterized by discrete wavelengths appearing as lines. In general, heavy elements have more emission lines than lighter elements, the reason being that as the atomic number increases, so too does the number of electrons and orbitals, providing more opportunities for orbital transitions, releasing energy at discrete wavelengths (Fig. 1.10).

FIG. 1.10 The characteristic emission lines of hydrogen. Discrete emission lines indicate that hydrogen does not radiate a continuous spectrum of electromagnetic energy. *Source: Wikipedia, and dedicated to the public domain by Merikanto, Adrignola.*

We commonly see the word "spectrum" used as a somewhat lame excuse to cover our ignorance of a subject. When we are told that a child is "on the autism spectrum," we are expected to believe that there is a smooth transition wherein one disease exhibits progressively worsening behaviors in an affected patient population. Maybe, but maybe not. We may be looking at a collection of distinct diseases, with some behavioral features in common, that blur our ability to distinguish one condition from another. And so, we co-opt the term "spectrum" to cover our ignorance.

In the 1980s, pathologists occasionally came upon a tumor arising in the gastrointestinal tract that seemed to have some of the morphologic features of a smooth muscle tumor (leiomyoma) and some of the features of a nerve sheath tumor (schwannoma), along with some features of benign tumors and other features of malignant tumors. Pathologists did not quite know what to do with this tumor, so they invented the so-called gastrointestinal stromal tumor spectrum, in which tumors at one end of the spectrum had purely smooth muscle features; while tumors at the other end of the spectrum had purely nerve sell features; and all mixtures of smooth muscle cells and nerve composed the gastrointestinal stromal tumor spectrum [55]. Today, we recognize that the spectrum was pure nonsense. The so-called spectrum has been replaced by three classifiable and biologically distinct tumors that can be diagnosed with certainty and without the need of pretending that they blend on a "spectrum" [56–59]. [Glossary Benign tumor]

Perhaps the most risible spectrum in the sciences is the "species spectrum". An astonishing number of scientists believe that "species" are arbitrary names that we apply to animals sitting on a genetic spectrum. At one end of the spectrum are the genes of primitive, one-celled organisms, and at the other end of the spectrum is the most complex organism on earth, the human being. We determine one organism from its neighbor on the spectrum by some arbitrary DNA cut-off. In this system, chimpanzees are distinguished humans by some indeterminate set of genes that the human has, and the chimpanzee lacks. We cannot devote the space in this book to explain why this conceptualization of species is incorrect, but we should be clear that every single assertion upon which the "species spectrum" hypothesis is based happens to be completely fallacious. The point to be made here is that if species sat on a spectrum of arbitrary cut-off points separating one species from another, then we could not create a classification of species. We would have no hierarchy of classes, no root class, no biological relationships among classes, and no classes at all.

The concept of a spectrum of items should be considered an example of an uncountable collection. In this sense, we are using the mathematical definition of "uncountable" to mean that the collection cannot be mapped to the numbers we use for counting (i.e., the integers). For example, the set of all real numbers is uncountable. When building a classification, we wouldn't want an animal that is 1.382726 monkeys. We want one monkey, or two monkeys, or, ideally, a barrel full of monkeys. As a general rule, items that obey integer laws are what we see in our useful classifications. As it happens, much of the physical realm is quantized (i.e., occur as specific constants or as integer multiples of a constant). For example, there is no such thing as a third of an electron or a half of a proton. Quantities of particles are exact integer numbers (e.g., Avogadro's number), and all particles of a kind are exactly identical to one another (i.e., every electron has exactly the same amount of "electron stuff" and weighs exactly as much as every other electron in the same reference frame). The dimensions of the universe are quantized (i.e., the four dimensions of space and time), and geometric symmetry transformations such as rotation and reflection are also quantized (e.g., 1 flip, 2 rotations, etc.). Quantum numbers of atomic particles are quantized and transitions of electrons between atomic shells are constrained to discrete jumps absorbing or emitting quantized amounts of energy. We'll be examining the quantum nature of the physical world in "Section 4.4. Saving hopeless classifications," and in "Section 8.6. Life, the universe, and everything." For now, all we need to remember is that classifiable items arrive in integer packages. [Glossary Quantum and quantized, Symmetry, Transformations]

Things having class, but no classification

It is possible for an object to be assigned to a class that cannot fit into a sensible classification. For example, a pen or a pencil might be legitimately assigned to Class Writing_Instrument, even if Class Writing_Instrument is not included in any natural classification. What do we do with items and classes that do not belong to a classification?

As it happens, there are logically useful and widely accepted ways in which we can identify items and assign them to classes that are not included in a classification. These will be discussed in "Section 3.4. Semantic languages."

Section 1.5. Classifying by time

Time is a curious entity because it establishes immutable relationships among events without carrying all the definitional encumbrances of a classification. That is to say that we can assign events to particular moments in time without fully understanding the events that are being recorded. All such events are related to one another by the time at which they occurred.

Why would we want to do such a thing? There are three very good reasons.

1. Timed events constitute a valid classification.
2. Timed events help scientists establish causal relationships, one of the most important goals of science.
3. We can accurately provide timed events with an immutable and unique identifier (i.e., the time at which the event occurred).
4. The classification of timed events can be organized as a blockchain, rendering the sequence of recorded events immutable and undeniable.

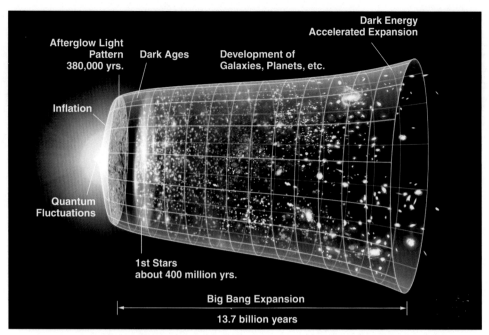

FIG. 1.11 The universe can be classified as a sequence of time intervals beginning with the Big Bang. The members of each class are related to one another by the time at which they exist, following the Big Bang (i.e., time 0). *Source: Public domain image produced by the U.S. National Aeronautics and Space Administration.*

Let's go back and look at each of these asserted reasons, to see why they are true.

First, can a sequence of timed events constitute a valid classification? A classification is a hierarchical collection of classes, in which the relationships among the classes are known, each class has one and only one parent class, class objects belong to one, and only one class and are intransitive (i.e., cannot shift from one class to another). When we collect events that occur over time, we can divide the events into classes defined by time intervals. The root class would represent the beginning of time (i.e., the moment of the Big Bang). Every class that followed would be a successive interval thereafter. Objects (i.e., events) that belong to one class are unique and intransitive. Within a class, objects are related by their individual times of occurrence (Fig. 1.11).

Scientists have made good use of timing historical epochs and filling them with events. The last 4.5 billion years, which corresponds roughly to the history of the sun and of the solar system, can be divided into about a dozen broad classes, holding all the events of earth history.

```
Pre-Cambrian Era, 4560-540 MYA
Cambrian Period, 540-500 MYA
Ordovician Period, 500-425 MYA
Silurian Period, 425-408 MYA
Devonian Period, 408-362 MYA
```

```
Carboniferous Period, 362-290 MYA
Permian Period, 290-245 MYA
Triassic Period, 245-208 MYA
Jurassic Period, 208-145 MYA
Cretaceous Period, 145-65 MYA
Tertiary Period, 65-1.64 MYA
Quaternary Period, 1.64 MYA - present
```

We can associate the emergence of classes of animals, and their branching's down to the species level, using a classification that is tied to sequentially occurring historical epochs (Fig. 1.12).

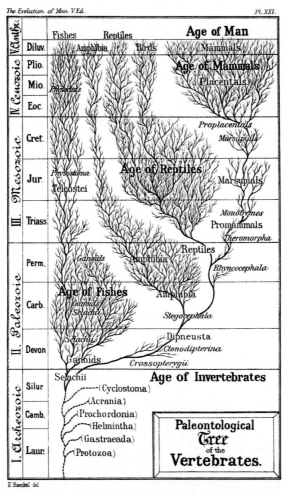

FIG. 1.12 A somewhat outdated illustration, by Ernst Haeckel, tying the evolution of animals to the sequentially occurring epochs of earth history. *Source: Haeckel's Paleontological Tree of Vertebrates, circa 1879).*

Regarding the second point, that timed events help scientists establish causal relationships, we can provide a few examples. Let's imagine that we have two events, A and B, and we know the time that these events occurred. If A causes B, then we would expect A to precede B. If we find that B precedes A, then we know our hypothesis is incorrect. Of course, A may precede B without actually being the cause of B. If we see a consistent pattern wherein A always precedes B, then it's likely that one of two hypotheses is correct: either A causes B, or A is a non-causal antecedent association for B. The distinction between a causal event and a non-causal antecedent association is often of critical importance to scientists. If A precedes and causes B, then we can prevent the occurrence of B if we prevent the occurrence of A. If A consistently precedes B but does not cause B, then A may provide a clue that leads us to the cause of B [19].

Historic debates over the causal link between smoking and lung cancer now serve as object lessons in the finer points of causality. In 1957, there was intense public debate over the role of smoking in the causation of lung cancer. Some of the arguments from the defenders of the tobacco industry played upon causality paradoxes, and they are worth reviewing here.

At the time, R.A. Fisher, a highly prominent statistician, raised an interesting point [60]. If we can associate A with B, then we need to be aware that A might be the cause of B, or B might be the cause of A, or some other factor, such as C, may be the cause of A or B, or neither A nor B may be causally related. In particular, this imaginative statistician suggested that lung cancer may be the cause of smoking and not vice versa. He suggested that as lung cancer develops, it irritates the lungs, hence motivating people to seek a remedy, such as the smooth taste of cigarette smoke, known to calm the bronchi and the tumor therein. As the tumor grew, and the lung irritation worsened, you might expect affected individuals to increase the number of cigarettes they smoke each day, thus explaining the dose/effect relationship between cigarettes and cancer. The same statistician suggested that a genetic condition may predispose individuals to an inclination to smoke and, independently, to a predisposition to cancer. Hence, smoking may not cause cancer, and cancer may not cause smoking, but both may be caused by an accident of genetics. The statistician forcefully testified that the causal link between smoking and lung cancer was mere speculation [19].

We now know a great deal about the temporal sequence of events that occur after individuals begin to smoke cigarettes. Specifically, the bronchial mucosa becomes inflamed and the normal mucosal epithelium is slowly replaced by squamous cells, a type of cell that is absent in normal lungs. As smoking continues, and time passes, the squamous cells lining the inflamed mucosa begin to display the morphologic features of nuclear atypia, the hallmark of precancerous change. Nuclear atypia worsens over time. These changes are, as a rule, not observed in non-smokers. Eventually, cancer may arise from this background of atypical squamous cells. In this particular case, a series of morphologic changes occur, in a temporal sequence that culminates in the appearance of lung cancer. Observations of the progressive changes occurring in the lung biopsies of smokers provide very strong evidence that smoking has a role in the development of lung cancer. Many factors may contribute to the development of lung cancer after smoking has started, and many factors may help sustain the growth of lung cancer. These issues notwithstanding, simple observations of the timing of events in disease development inform us that smoking leads to the development of lung cancer [19]. [Glossary Malignancy, Mucosa, Premalignancy]

If a scientist intends to build a classification but can find no sensible relationship among putative classes of objects, then constructing a timeline may be a convenient fall-back. Timelines can organize collections of things that arise sequentially, relating each thing to those that preceded it and to those that followed it. Timelines may support chains of inference and provide a way to frame credible relationships among objects, leading to a true classification.

One of the most important natural timelines was the Burgess Shale, discovered in 1909 by Charles Walcott. The Burgess Shale is a rock formation that embeds a timeline for the evolution of life forms through its ascending rock strata. By studying the ascending strata, scientists could say, with absolute confidence, when lifeforms lived. If there had been a single instance where lifeforms appeared out of order, then all of the evolutionary theory would have been discredited. For example, if the rabbit skeleton were found in the same layer as a fossilized trilobite; or a fossilized Tyrannosaurus rex was found in the same strata as the skeleton of a neanderthal, then we would have needed to rewrite all of our biology books. Fortunately for textbook authors, no such chronologic violations have been found (e.g., no bottles of Dr. Pepper grasped in the hand of a Neanderthal skeleton).

When we examine the ancestry of humans, we find that each ancestor appeared in a time following the appearance of its direct ancestor, and first appeared at a time preceding the appearance of its direct descendant(s). The evolution of humans fits into a handy timeline, as shown here:

First organisms 4100 mya (million years ago)
Prokaryota (3900 mya)
Eukaryota (2100 mya)
Holozoa (1300 mya
Apoikozoa (950 mya)
Metazoa (760 mya)
Eumetazoa (635 mya)
Bilateria (Triploblasts) (555 mya)
Nephrozoa (555 mya)
Deuterostomia (Enterocoelomata) (540 mya)
Chordata (530 mya)
Craniata/Vertebrata (500 mya)
Gnathostomata (419 mya)
Sarcopterygii (419 mya)
Tetrapodomorpha (390 mya)
Tetrapoda (367 mya)
Amniota (340 mya)

Synapsida (308 mya)
Mammalia (220 mya)
Theria (160 mya)
Eutheria (160–125 mya)
Boreoeutheria (124–101 mya)
Euarchontoglires (100 mya)
Euarchonta (99–80 mya)
Primatomorpha (79.6 mya)
Primates (75 mya)
Haplorrhini (63 mya)
Simiiformes (40 mya)
Catarrhini (30 mya)
Hominoidea (28 mya)
Hominidae (15 mya)
Homininae (8 mya)
Hominini (5.8 mya)
Hominina (4 mya)
Homo (2.5 mya)
Homo sapiens (0.3 mya)
H. sapiens (modern) (0.07 mya)

There are rocks on earth that date back to the origin of our planet, about 4.5 billion years ago. In a sense, the entire history of our planet is engraved in stone. Whereas observations of rock strata provide a coarse time-based classification, scientists have alternate methods for associating events with their times of occurrence. Observations of annual tree rings in living or dead trees have aided scientists to develop an accurate timeline of many types of natural events that have occurred in the past thousand years (Fig. 1.13).

Historians have used timelines to understand the relationships among events occurring throughout human history. Several studies focus on global events occurring immediately after Columbus' trip to the Americas in 1492 [61–63]. The authors of these works credit 1492 as the first year wherein the world became globalized, in terms of trade, culture, science, and ecology. Scientists have tacitly acknowledged the significance of 1492. We speak in terms of "new world" and "old world" monkeys, although Europe and Africa (the old world) is no older than the Americas (the new world). The Americas are "new" because they were unknown to Europeans before 1492. In botany, there is a modern term whose meaning is linked to the year 1492. The term is "neophyte" (from Greek "new" "plant"). A neophyte is a species of plant that is not native to a geographical region, being introduced at some point in the recent past. Long-established plants are called archaeophytes (old plants). Can we agree on the meaning of "recent"? In Great Britain, recently introduced plants are defined as plant species that were introduced after 1492, the year that every part of the world became accessible to trade and every species of life became vulnerable to transplantation.

FIG. 1.13 Cross-sections of trees are locked-in timelines, with each tree ring representing a sequential chronologic entry. The study of sequential tree rings to study events occurring through time is called dendrochronology. *Source: Wikipedia, and entered into the public domain by its author Adrian Pingstone.*

Likewise, we are all influenced by the Christian practice of dividing the human timeline into two eras: BC (before Christ) and AD (Anno Domini and beyond). It comes naturally to see history in terms of what preceded the event and what followed the event.

As an example of the use of time as an organizing principle, let's consider the dilemma of the philatelist. She has a large collection of stamps issued by different countries, at different times. There are no natural laws or principles that could be used to classify stamps. In point of fact, there is no compelling reason to produce a classification when a simple stamp catalog would satisfy most enthusiasts. The die-hard classification builder may want to consider organizing the stamps by the date of original issuance. There is only one first issuance of a stamp, and everyone understands the concept of time. The date can be correlated with local and world events, tying the stamp collection with other historically ordered classifications. Time is often the default organizing principle for almost any event-based classification (because the time or origin of an object or class is often fixed to a particular time).

Among biologists, embryologists are probably the scientists most likely to classify their knowledge domain using a timeline. Each embryologic structure develops from some embryonic structure that had developed earlier. Hence, the study of embryology consists largely of documenting interim structures, in their proper chronologic sequences. Specifically, the embryologist must learn, for each known embryologic structure, the name of the structure from which it arose, and the name of the structure to which it develops. The full description of human development, on the level of anatomy, are chronologically ordered classes of tissues. [Glossary Knowledge domain]

Trapping time in blockchain ledgers

Ledgers and blockchains are man-made devices by which we can permanently lock events relating to everything preceding and everything following.

We often think of events as properties of objects. For example, a patient named John Doe may have had blood drawn for glucose determination on 2021-2-07 13:11:29 (i.e., Sunday, February 7, 2021, at 1:11 and 29 s PM, Greenwich Mean Time). We think of the blood drawing and the associated glucose measurement as an event occurring to the patient. The event and its description become the permanent property of the object named John Doe.

We can re-examine the aforementioned scenario, this time thinking of the event itself as the primary data object, and John Doe as just a property of the event. Restated, at a certain time (i.e., 2021-2-07 13:11:29), an action occurs (i.e., a blood draw), and a measurement is made (i.e., blood glucose level), and the object associated with the glucose level is John Doe. In this case, John Doe belongs to the event, and the subject of the event is the unique time identified as "2021-2-07 13:11:29".

Nowadays, it is very easy for scientists to annotate all types of events, including all measurements, with the time at which the event occurred, and this can be done with a high degree of precision. Without going into the programming details, let's look at how the Python programming language allows us to determine time:

```
>>> import time
>>> time.time()

Output:
1593976054.161482
```

The output in this example ("1593976054.161482) is provided in epoch time. Epoch time, also known as Posix time or as Unix epoch time, is measured as the number of seconds elapsed since the first second of the year 1970, GMT (Greenwich Mean Time). Equivalent instructions for producing the high-resolution time, in Perl and Ruby are provided in this chapter's glossary, along with methods for converting the epoch time into standard time (date, hour, seconds, and fractions of a second).

The procedure for appending an exact time to a described event is known as time-stamping. If there is any doubt of the accuracy or authenticity of a time-stamp, a trusted time-stamp authority may be employed. [Glossary Authentication, Perl, Python, Ruby, Time-stamp, Trusted time-stamp]

A ledger is a permanent record of timed events (often referred to as transactions in the world of business), that are entered sequentially. A traditional ledger is a lined notebook, with pages stitch bound together. The order of occurrence of each event cannot be deleted or modified without producing a visible alteration to the ledger. One of the greatest advantages of the event-based classification is our ability to collect and lock object instances into an immutable digital ledger, at the moment when they are created. By doing so, each event is permanently sandwiched between the event that immediately preceded its entry and the event that follows. No out-of-sequence entry can be added to the ledger unnoticed.

In the world of computers, ledgers are created using blockchain technology. At its simplest, a blockchain is a collection of short data records received over time, with each record consisting of some variation on the following:

```
<head>--<message>--<tail>
```

Here are the conditions that the blockchain must accommodate [19]:

1. The head (i.e., first field) in each blockchain record consists of the tail of the preceding data record. By tying each record to its preceding record, the blockchain preserves the sequence of records, as they are received over time.
2. The tail of each data record consists of a one-way hash of the head of the record concatenated with the recorded message. We won't go into the details of a one-way hash here, but suffice it to say that the one-way hash is a seemingly random and unique character string that is generated for a particular text (in this case the head of the record concatenated with the recorded message). Every particular text has its unique one-way hash that can be recomputed from the text. [Glossary One-way hash, String]
3. Live copies of the blockchain (i.e., a copy that grows as additional blocks are added) are maintained on multiple servers.
4. A mechanism is put in place to ensure that every copy of the blockchain is equivalent to one another and that when a blockchain record is added, it is added to every copy of the blockchain, in the same sequential order, and with the same record contents.

Blockchain records are real-time transactions, acquired sequentially so that the nth record was created at a moment in time after the creation of the n-1th record and before the creation of the n+1th record. What do we achieve when with our blockchain [19]?

- Every blockchain header contains a buried contribution from the values in the entire succession of its preceding blockchain links.
- The blockchain is immutable. Changing any of the messages contained in any of the blockchain links would produce a different blockchain. Dropping any of the links of the blockchain or inserting any new links (anywhere other than as an attachment to the last validated link) will produce an invalid blockchain that can be immediately detected.

- The blockchain is undeniable. Every record in the blockchain must have existed, in its preserved sequential order.

The blockchain serves as a record of sequential events and can be used to re-generate all of the descriptions of events, as needed. The minimalist blockchain does not tell us the exact time that a record of the event was created, but it gives its relative time of creation compared with the preceding and succeeding records. When the exact time of an event is provided within the description of the event, the ledger can be used as an immutable record of sequences of events, along with the exact time at which the events occurred. Blockchains can be distributed as records are added, rendering each copy of the distributed blockchain current. Any tampering of the blockchain would produce incompatibilities among sequential versions (i.e., the distributed copies) and sequential records within any single version [19]. Fundamentally, blockchain records are equivalent to records contained in fossilized rock strata; but a lot easier to carry around. [Glossary Blockchain, Digital signature, Message digest, New data]

Glossary

Acanthamoeba The genus Acanthamoeba is a subclass of Class Amoebozoa. Most extant Amoebozoa species have no flagella, but a few species of Amoebozoans retain their ancestral single flagellum, characteristic of the unikonts. Because the Amoebozoans are unikonts, they are related to Class Opisthokonta, which includes Class Choanozoa, Class Animalia, and Class Fungi.

Amoebozoa move by flowing their cytoplasm from one area of the cell to another. The movement begins when a part of the cell wall, the lobopodium, is protruded. As cytoplasm flows into the lobopodium, the rest of the cell cannot help but follow. The amoebozoan genera vary greatly in size. Species producing disease in humans are about the size of human cells (10 to 40 μm), while at least one non-pathogenic species, Amoebozoa proteus, attains a size of 800 μm (on the verge of visibility with the unaided eye). A member of Class Amoebozoa, *Polychaos dubium*, has the largest known genome, at 670 billion base pairs. Compare this to the 3 billion base pairs of the human genome.

The members of Class Amoebozoa engulf and eat smaller organisms. Most members of Class Amoebozoa live in the soil or aquatic environments, where they are beneficial bacterial predators (Entamoeba is an exception, vide infra) [64]. The pathogenic members of Class Amoebozoa occur in tissues as trophozoites (the amoeboid feeding cells) or as cysts (round, infective cells resistant to desiccation).

Acanthamoeba species cause three distinctive clinical diseases: granulomatous amoebic encephalitis, amoebic keratitis, and cutaneous acanthamoebiasis [65,66]. Other free-living genera of Class Amoebozoa that are associated with human central nervous system infections are Balamuthia and Sappinia.

Anatomic pathologist Anatomic pathologists are physicians who have been trained to examine and evaluate lesions based on gross and microscopic findings. Anatomic pathologists perform autopsies and render diagnoses on tissue biopsies. They provide intraoperative consultations to surgeons by performing rapid analyses of quick-frozen sections of sampled tissues removed during surgery. All cytopathologists have received training in anatomic pathology. All forensic pathologists (physicians who perform autopsies for the Medical Examiner's Office) have received training as anatomic pathologists.

Ancestral lineage Every organism on earth, living or extinct, has a particular ancestral lineage. For example, here is the ancestral lineage of the common apple:

Malus domestica (malus domestica, cultivated apple)

Malus

Maleae (maleae, pyreae)

Amygdaloideae (amygdaloideae, maloideae)

Rosaceae (rosaceae, malaceae, rose family)

Rosales

fabids (fabids, eurosids i)

rosids

Pentapetalae

Gunneridae (gunneridae, core eudicotyledons)

eudicotyledons (eudicotyledons, eudicots)

Mesangiospermae

Magnoliophyta

Spermatophyta (spermatophyta, seed plants, seed plants)

Euphyllophyta (euphyllophyta, euphyllophytes)

Tracheophyta (tracheophyta, vascular plants, vascular plants)

Embryophyta (embryophyta, higher plants, land plants)

Streptophytina (charophyta/embryophyta group)

Streptophyta

Viridiplantae (viridiplantae, chloroplastida, green plants)

Eukaryota (eukaryota, eukaryotae, eukaryotes)

cellular organisms (cellular organisms, biota)

If you want to know your roots, then study the following listing of the ancestry of the common human.

Ancestry of the common human:

Homo sapiens (*homo sapiens*, man, human)

Homo (homo, humans)

Homininae (homininae, homo/pan/gorilla group)

Hominidae (hominidae, pongidae, great apes)

Hominoidea (hominoidea, ape, apes)

Catarrhini

Simiiformes (simiiformes, anthropoidea)

Haplorrhini

Primates (primates, primata, primate, primates)

Euarchontoglires

Boreoeutheria (boreoeutheria, boreotheria)

Eutheria (eutheria, placentalia, placentals)

Theria

Mammalia (mammalia, mammals)

Amniota (amniotes)

Tetrapoda (tetrapods)

Dipnotetrapodomorpha

Sarcopterygii

Euteleostomi (bony vertebrates)

Teleostomi

Gnathostomata (gnathostomata, jawed vertebrates)

Vertebrata (vertebrata, vertebrates)

Craniata

Chordata (chordates)

Deuterostomia (deuterostomes)

Bilateria

Eumetazoa

Metazoa (metazoa, animalia, animals, metazoans)

Opisthokonta (opisthokonts, fungi/metazoa group)

Eukaryota (eukaryotae, eukaryotes, eukaryotes)

Authentication In modern times, the term "authentication" is used to describe a process that determines if the data object that is received (e.g., document, file, image) is the data object that was intended to be received. The simplest authentication protocol involves one-way hash operations on the data that needs to be authenticated. Suppose you happen to know that a certain file, named temp.txt will be arriving via email and that this file has an MD5 hash of "a0869a42609af6c712caeba454f47429". You receive the temp.txt file, and you perform an MD5 one-way hash operation on the file.

In this example, we'll use the md5 hash utility bundled into the Cygwin distribution (i.e., the Linux emulator for Windows systems). Any md5 implementation would have sufficed.

```
c:\cygwin64\bin>openssl md5 temp.txt
MD5(temp.txt)= a0869a42609af6c712caeba454f47429
```

We see that the md5 hash value generated for the received file is identical to the md5 hash value produced on the file, by the file's creator, before the file was emailed. This tells us that the received, temp.txt, is authentic (i.e., it is the file that you were intended to receive). No other file will have the same MD5 hash. Any modifications to the temp.txt file, perpetrated by a malicious agent that intercepts the temp.txt file will change the MD5 hash of the file.

The authentication process, in this example, does not establish who sent the file (i.e., does not validate the signature of the sender), the time that the file was created, or anything about the veracity of the contents of the file. These would require a protocol that included signature, time-stamp, and data validation. In common usage, authentication protocols often include entity authentication (i.e., some method by which the entity sending the file is verified). Consequently, authentication protocols are often confused with signature verification protocols. An ancient historical example serves to distinguish the concepts of authentication protocols and signature protocols. Since early in recorded history, fingerprints were used as a method of authentication. When a scholar or artisan produced a product, he would press his thumb into the urn, or clay tablet, or the wax seal closing a document. Anyone doubting the authenticity of the urn could ask the artisan for a thumbprint. If the artisan's thumbprint matched the thumbprint on the urn, then the thumbprint would be considered authentic (i.e., produced by the artisan). Of course, this was not proof that the object was the creation of the person with the matching thumbprint. For all anyone knew, there may have been a hundred different urn makers, with just one artisan pressing his thumb into every urn produced. You might argue that the thumbprint served as the signature of the artisan. This would be only partly true. The ancients needed to compare the urn's thumbprint against the thumbprint of the living person who made the print. When the person died, civilization was left with a bunch of urns having the same thumbprint, but without any certain way of knowing whose thumb produced them. In essence, because there was no ancient database that permanently associated thumbprints with individuals, the process of establishing the authenticity of the urn or the signature of the artisan became very difficult once the artisan died. A good signature protocol permanently binds a unique authentication code to a unique entity (e.g., a person). Today, we can find a fingerprint at the scene of a crime; we can find a matching signature in a database; and we can link the fingerprint to one individual. Hence, in modern times, fingerprints are true "digital" signatures, no pun intended. Over the past decade, flaws in the vaunted process of fingerprint identification have been documented, and the science of identification is an active area of research [67].

Autoantibody disease versus autoimmune disease   The two terms are often used interchangeably, but they represent pathogenetically distinct conditions. Autoantibody diseases occur when the adaptive immune system synthesizes antibodies against some normal body constituent. This may occur when an antigen is an infectious organism elicits antibodies that happen to cross-react with a normal cellular protein; occasionally producing some adverse clinical consequence. In most cases, as far as anyone can tell, individuals with the common autoantibody diseases have normal functioning immune systems.

In autoimmune diseases, there is a primary dysfunction of the immune system, often producing an array of clinical sequelae, including the synthesis of one or more antibodies that react against self-antigens [68].

Autoantibody diseases that are phenocopies of genetic diseases   Many genetic diseases result from a gene mutation that reduces the activity of the protein encoded by the gene. Just as protein activity can be reduced by a gene mutation, protein activity can also be reduced by autoantibodies directed against the protein. In general, these autoantibody phenocopies occur more frequently than the genetic versions of the disease and occur in a much older population (i.e., adults, not infants).

Here are a few examples of autoantibody diseases that are phenocopies of rare genetic diseases: Auto-antibody forms of dystrophic epidermolysis bullosa [69], junctional epidermolysis bullosa [70], hemophilia A (factor VIII deficiency) [71], hemophilia due to antibodies to factor XI [72], hemophilia due to antibodies to factor XIII [73], psychosis [74], familial hypocalciuric hypercalcemia type i (antibodies reacting with the extracellular domain of the calcium-sensing receptor [75,76]), inherited thrombophilia (i.e., increased risk of thrombosis) due to protein C deficiency [77,78], inherited cutis laxa [79], hereditary angioedema (due to autoantibodies to C1 inhibitor [80]), congenital adrenal insufficiency [81], atransferrinemia [82], Bernard-Soulier syndrome [83], and Von Willebrand disease. The list of acquired forms of genetic diseases goes on and on [70,84–91].

Scanning the list of acquired autoantibody forms of otherwise inherited or de novo genetic diseases, it is obvious that most such conditions are deficiencies of circulating blood components (e.g., clotting factors and hormones). We should not be surprised. We can expect that autoantibodies will be raised against circulating proteins, having direct exposure to immunocytes. Proteins confined within cells, having no direct exposure to immunocytes under normal circumstances, might be less likely to excite an antibody response.

BRCA   BRCA1 and BRCA2 are Breast Cancer tumor suppressor genes that code for proteins involved in DNA repair. Women who inherit certain types of mutations in either BRCA1 or BRCA2 have about a 50% chance of developing breast cancer by age 70. About 1 in 400 women carry such mutations. Inherited BRCA1 and BRCA2 mutations are also associated with other tumors, particularly ovarian and prostate cancer [92].

Individuals born with a germline inactivating BRCA2 mutation have a variant type of Fanconi Anemia. Individuals born with a germline mutation characterized by a large intragenic deletion of BRCA1 may also have a variant type of Li-Fraumeni syndrome [93–95].

Benign tumor With a few exceptions, benign tumors are tumors that grow slowly but continuously, without invading or metastasizing. Many benign tumors are diploid. Some benign tumors are stable-aneuploid (i.e., varying from the normal chromosome number, without becoming increasingly aneuploid over time). There are rare examples of benign tumors that are progressively aneuploid [96].

As a general rule, benign tumors that grow slowly and have limited growth potential and benign tumors that are diploid, or near-diploid and that do not accumulate genetic alterations over time will seldom progress to become cancers. Benign tumors that grow relatively fast and have no apparent limit to their size, or benign tumors that are aneuploid and demonstrate genetic instability (i.e., become more genetically diverse over time) are likely to become cancerous over time.

Binomials Single words in any language seldom have any one meaning. Most words can mean one of several things depending on the context (i.e., depending upon flanking words). For example, the word rose can refer to the flower or to the past tense of "to rise". We can speak of golden retrievers and golden locks and golden parachutes, but the word "golden" is just a modifier until it is attached to a second word that establishes the meaning of a word phrase.

Two-word phrases tell us much more than single words. Some very interesting computer algorithms designed for indexing, searching, and understanding text involve abandoning single-word lists in favor of 2-word (also known as a doublet, binomial, 2-g) phrase lists and data structures [97–100].

Binomials are the preferred way of naming people in many cultures (e.g., Sally Smith, Li Wen) [101]. Not surprisingly, binomials have been used for both the common names of organisms (e.g., pin oak, white maple, box turtle), and for the formal latinized names of organisms (e.g., *Escherichia coli, H. sapiens*).

In the binomial nomenclature of organisms, the first word of the binomial is the genus or family name of the organism, corresponding to the full name of the direct parent class of the species. The second name is the species-specific name, corresponding to the given name of the species. By convention, the genus name has an uppercase first letter, and the given name is in all lowercase letters.

All classes above the species level are mono-nomials. Because there are millions of organisms, we might encounter instances where class names overlap (e.g., Pholidota the pangolins and Philodota the orchids).

Blastocystosis Blastocystis species are members of Class Stramenopile (also known as Class Heterokonta). Bastocystis organisms cause a human infection that clinically mimics irritable bowel syndrome [102]. It seems that most infections with Blastocystis species are subclinical and that it is common to find healthy carriers of the organisms. At present, our knowledge of how best to treat infections by members of Class Heterokonta is quite limited [103,104].

'Blastocystosis is yet another example of a medical term that seems to have been chosen with the intent to confuse health care workers, insofar as it can be easily mistaken for any of three similar-appearing but unrelated terms: blastomycosis, blastocyst, and blastomycetica. Blastomycoses is a fungal disease (Ascomycota). The blastocyst is the fluid-filled embryonic body characteristic of animals. Blastomycetica appears in the name of a fungal infection "erosio interdigitalis blastomycetica". This infection, despite what its name would imply, is a candidal infection of the web space between the third and fourth fingers of either hand. The infection was given its deceptive name in 1917, five years before the genus Candida was recognized [105]. As is often the case, the mistake stuck. All four terms come from the root word blastos (Greek for bud or embryo). Cystos (as in Blastocystis and blastocyst) is the Greek root meaning sac.

Blockchain As discussed in this chapter, a blockchain is a collection of short data records, with each record consisting of some variation on the following:

```
<head>--<message>--<tail>
```

Here are the conditions that the blockchain must accommodate:

1. The head (i.e., first field) in each blockchain record consists of the tail of the preceding data record.
2. The tail of each data record consists of a one-way hash of the head of the record concatenated with the recorded message.
3. Live copies of the blockchain (i.e., a copy that grows as additional blocks are added) are maintained on multiple servers.
4. A mechanism is put in place to ensure that every copy of the blockchain is equivalent to one another and that when a blockchain record is added, it is added to every copy of the blockchain, in the same sequential order, and with the same record contents.

We will soon see that conditions 1 through 3 is easy to achieve. Condition 4 can be problematic, and numerous protocols have been devised, with varying degrees of success, to ensure that the blockchain is updated identically, at every site. Most malicious attacks on blockchains are targeted against condition 4, which is considered to be the most vulnerable point in every blockchain enterprise.

By convention, records are real-time transactions, acquired sequentially, so that we can usually assume that the nth record was created at a moment in time before the creation of the n+1th record.

Let's assume that the string that lies between the head and the tail of each record is a triple. This assumption is justified because all meaningful information can be represented as a triple or as a collection of triples.

Here's our list of triples that we will be block-chaining.

```
a0ce8ec6^^object_name^^Homo
a0ce8ec6^^subclass_of^^Hominidae
a0ce8ec6^^property^^glucose_at_time
a1648579^^object_name^^Homo sapiens
a1648579^^subclass_of^^Homo
98495efc^^object_name^^Andy Muzeack
98495efc^^instance_of^^Homo sapiens
98495efc^^dob^^1 January, 2001
98495efc^^glucose_at_time^^87, 02-12-2014 17:33:09
```

Let's create our blockchain using these 9 triples as our messages.
Each blockchain record will be of the form:

```
<tail of prior blockchain link----the current record's triple----md5 hash of
the current triple concatenated with the header>
```

For example, to compute the tail of the second link, we would perform an md5 hash on:

```
ufxOaEaKfw7QBrgsmDYtIw----a0ce8ec6^^subclass_of^^Hominidae
```

Which yields:

```
=> PhjBvwGf6dk9oUK/+yxrCA
```

The resulting blockchain is shown here.

```
                          a0ce8ec6^^object_name^^Homo----ufxOaEaKfw7QBrgsmDYtIw
ufxOaEaKfw7QBrgsmDYtIw----a0ce8ec6^^subclass_of^^Hominidae----
PhjBvwGf6dk9oUK/+yxrCA
```

```
PhjBvwGf6dk9oUK/+yxrCA----a0ce8ec6^^property^^glucose_at_time----
P40p5GHp4hElgsstKbrFPQ

P40p5GHp4hElgsstKbrFPQ----a1648579^^object_name^^Homo sapiens----
2wAF1kWPFi35f6jnGOecYw

2wAF1kWPFi35f6jnGOecYw----a1648579^^subclass_of^^Homo----
N2y3fZgiOgRcqfx86rcpwg

N2y3fZgiOgRcqfx86rcpwg----98495efc^^object_name^^Andy Muzeack----
UXSrchXFR457g4JreErKiA

UXSrchXFR457g4JreErKiA----98495efc^^instance_of^^Homo sapiens----
5wDuJUTLWBJjQIu0Av1guw

5wDuJUTLWBJjQIu0Av1guw----98495efc^^glucose_at_time^^87, 02-12-2014 17:33:09----
Y1jCYB7YyRBVIhm4PUUbaA
```

Whether you begin with a list of triples that you would like to convert into a blockchain data structure, or whether you are creating a blockchain one record at a time, through transactions that occur over time, it is easy to write a short script that will generate the one-way hashes and attach them to the end of the nth triple and the beginning of the n+1th triple, as needed.

Looking back at our blockchain, we can instantly spot an anomaly, in the header of the very first record. The header to the record is missing. Whenever we begin to construct a new blockchain, the first record will have no antecedent record from which a header can be extracted. This poses another computational bootstrap paradox. In this instance, we cannot begin until there is a beginning. The bootstrap paradox is typically resolved with the construction of a root record (record 0). The root record is permitted to break the rules.

Now that we have a small blockchain, what have we achieved? Here are the properties of a blockchain

Every blockchain header is built from the values in the entire succession of preceding blockchain links.

The blockchain is immutable. Changing any of the messages contained in any of the blockchain links would produce a different blockchain. Dropping any of the links of the blockchain or inserting any new links (anywhere other than as an attachment to the last validated link) will produce an invalid blockchain.

The blockchain is recomputable. Given the same message content, the entire blockchain, with all its headers and tails, can be rebuilt. If it cannot recompute, then the blockchain is invalid.

The blockchain, in its simplest form, is a trusted "relative time" stamp. Our blockchain does not tell us the exact time that a record was created, but it gives its relative time of creation compared with the preceding and succeeding records.

With a little imagination, we can see that a blockchain can be used as a true time-stamp authority if the exact time were appended to each of the records in the container at the moment when the record was added to the blockchain. The messages contained in blockchain records could be authenticated by including data encrypted with a private key. Tampering of the blockchain data records could be prevented by having multiple copies of the blockchain at multiple sites, and routinely checking for discrepancies among the different copies of the data.

We might also see that the blockchain could be used as a trusted record of documents, legal transactions (e.g., property deals), monetary exchanges (e.g., Bitcoin). Blockchains may also be used for conducting elections (e.g., authenticating cast votes, validating voters, verifying the count, and providing undeniability to the results). The potential value of blockchains is enormous, but the devil hides in the details. Every implementation of a blockchain comes with its vulnerabilities, and much has been written on this subject [106,107].

Blueprint A blueprint is a schematic, containing detailed descriptions of the pieces of construction, with a diagram showing how the pieces fit together to form the final product.

The human genome is often referred to, incorrectly, as the blueprint for the development of the human body. When we look at human development, from the earliest stages of the embryo to the eventual appearance of a mature adult, we see nothing remotely resembling what we would expect to see if the genome were a blueprint. There are no identifiable "pieces" and no indication that anything is being fastened together to form a whole organism. Instead, we see clearly that human development follows successive transformations of living stages. This process in no way resembles the construction of a blueprint.

A much better analogy is that the genome operates like a recipe book, in which each successive recipe depends on the successful creation of the preceding recipe. In this case, there is a recipe for making a morula from a zygote, and a recipe for making a blastocyst from a morula, and a recipe for making an inner cell mass from a blastocyst, and a recipe for making a gastrula from an inner cell mass, and so on.

Carcinogen The term "carcinogen" refers to an agent that causes cancer, but there is considerable controversy over how to apply the term. Some people use the term "carcinogen" to mean a chemical, biological, or physical agent that produces cancer in animals, without the addition of any other agents or processes. Sometimes, the term "complete carcinogen" is used to emphasize the self-sufficiency of the agent as the primary underlying cause of cancer. Others in the field use the term "carcinogen" to include any agent that will increase the likelihood of tumor development. This definition would apply to agents that must be followed or preceded with another agent for tumors to occur or agents that simply increase the number of cancers occurring in a population known to be at risk of cancer.

Carcinogenesis The cellular events leading to cancer. Equivalent to the pathogenesis of cancer. Carcinogenesis in adults is a long process that involves the accumulation of genetic and epigenetic alterations that eventually produce a growing clone of malignant cells. The conjectured sequence of events that comprise carcinogenesis begins with initiation, wherein a carcinogen damages the DNA of a cell, producing a mutant clonal founder cell that eventually yields a group of cells that have one or more subtle (i.e., morphologically invisible) differences from the surrounding cells (e.g., less likely to senesce and die, more likely divide, less genetically stable, better able to survive in a hypoxic environment). After a time, which could easily extend into years, subclones of the original clone emerge that have additional properties that confer growth or survival advantages (e.g., superior growth in hypoxic conditions). The process of continual sub-clonal selection continues, usually for a period of years, until a morphologically distinguishable group of cells appear: the precancer cells. Sub-clonal cells from the precancer eventually emerge, having the full malignant phenotype (i.e., the ability to invade surrounding tissues and metastasize to distant sites). The entire process may take decades.

Catalog A complete listing of items that are available for retrieval. The items in a catalog are often stored as replicates, and the group of replicates is traditionally provided with an identifying catalog number, to facilitate retrieval and inventory tracking. Cataloging is fundamentally different from classifying. When we catalog, we are putting similar things together under a shared header. The category headers are intended to provide a distinction between one category and another, without providing any insight into the relationships among the different categories, and without providing any clue to the essential character of the included items. In contrast, when we classify, we are looking for fundamental relationships among classes.

Cell type The different cell types of the body are defined by morphologic, functional, and anatomic traits that, together, distinguish cells of one type from all other types of cells.

The number of different kinds of cells in an organism varies based on how you choose to categorize and count the different cells of the body, but most would agree that there are at least 200 different cell types in the body. Because we can classify thousands of different cancers in humans, we can safely say that one cell type may correspond to many different types of cancer. For example, both follicular carcinoma of the thyroid and papillary carcinoma of the thyroid seem to derive from the epithelial cells that give rise to normal thyroid glands. Follicular carcinoma of the thyroid and papillary carcinoma of the thyroid behaves differently from each other and each has its distinct genetic defects.

Child class The direct or first-generation subclass of a class. Sometimes referred to as the daughter class, or as the immediate subclass.

Cirrhosis A liver condition in which fibrous tissue proliferates in liver acini (the glandular portion of the liver) and around ducts and vessels. This results in the death of liver cells, and a marked reactive overgrowth of hepatocytes with distorted and enlarged liver acini. These changes result in a marked decrease in liver function and a subsequently high mortality rate.

Liver cirrhosis predisposes to liver cancer. In the U.S. about 80%–90% of hepatocellular carcinoma cases arise in cirrhotic livers.

Class Property versus class property It seems like a trivial distinction, but in object-oriented programming languages, there is an important and not very subtle difference between the concepts of Class Property (uppercase P) and class property (lowercase p). Class Property refers to the class of objects known as "Property" to which all properties belong (i.e., every property is an instance of Class Property). In a well-designed object-oriented programming environment, everything belongs to a class, and nothing may exist as unclassified abstractions. In other words, a well-designed object-oriented programming environment is itself a bona fide classification. Absent the condition that every element of classification must be assigned a class, our classification models would be incomplete, a violation of the fundamental rules of classification construction. Because all properties are members of Class Property, and because Class Property is a legitimate and necessary class, it must have an assigned parent class (often Class, the class of all classes, but sometimes Class Object, the class of all objects), and it must be included in a schema, such as RDF Schema, that provides definitions of all the classes and properties of the classification.

The term class property, appearing in lowercase letters, simply refers to a property of the class that is available to every member of the class, and that is inherited by the members of the subclasses of the class.

Class noise Refers to inaccuracies (e.g., misleading results) introduced in the analysis of classified data due to errors in class assignments (e.g., assigning a data object to class A when the object should have been assigned to class B). For example, if you are testing the effectiveness of an antibiotic on a class of people with bacterial pneumonia, the validity of your results will be jeopardized if your study population includes subjects with viral pneumonia or smoking-related lung damage.

There are two sources of class noise, the first being faulty assignment of class members. In the medical realm, this is equivalent to misdiagnosis. The second source, which is almost always much more difficult to detect, is a faulty class definition. For example, if you define Class Fish to mean all swimming animals, then you'll be including dolphins and scuba divers in the same class as guppies. You haven't made a mistake in the class assignment; the class was defined to include non-related members.

Classification builder The term "classification builder" is used nearly interchangeably with terms such as "sytematicists," "taxonomists," "ontologists," and "curators". These terms are applied somewhat differently in various disciplines. For example, systematics is essentially synonymous with the science of classification. In common usage, though, systematicists are biologists who study the diversity of animals and plants occurring through evolution. In the various life sciences, taxonomists are primarily concerned with the instances (i.e., class members) that fill the ranks of classes.

Because, strictly speaking, classifications are types of ontologies, the general term of ontologist is sometimes applied to anyone who works with ontologies or classifications. The term ontologist seems to be the preferred term in the field of bioinformatics and related computer scientists.

It is interesting that chemists, physicists, and mathematicians seldom associate themselves with any of the terms related to classification building. Traditionally, the "hard" sciences (e.g., chemistry, physics, and mathematics) have ignored the philosophy and the science of classification. Ironically, these fields are devoted to finding and organizing relationships among classes (e.g., particles, atoms, compounds, forces, shapes, spaces), and these activities are what the science of classification is all about. The hard sciences have benefited greatly from their classifications (e.g., The Periodic Table of the Elements and the Classification Theorem of Finite Simple Groups). A change of attitude is long overdue.

Classification versus index In practice, an index is an alphabetized listing of the important terms in a work (e.g., book), accompanied by the locations of each term within the work. Ideally, though, an index should be much more than that. The best indexes are novel conceptualizations of a corpus of work that enable users to locate the concepts that are discussed and created within the work. How does an idealized index differ from a classification? Classification is a way of organizing the relationships among concepts. An index is a way of locating concepts.

Data object A data object, as the name suggests, is a data structure that encapsulates some amount of data. Data objects in object-oriented programming languages typically encapsulate several items of data, including an object name, an object unique identifier, some described data expressed as data/metadata pairs. If the object is a member of a class, then the data object should encapsulate the name of the object's class and the name of the parent class of the object's class.

Digital signature As it is used in the field of data privacy, a digital signature is an alphanumeric sequence that could only have been produced by a private key owned by one particular person.

Operationally, a message digest (e.g., a one-way hash value) is produced from the document that is to be signed. The person "signing" the document encrypts the message digest using her private key and submits the document and the encrypted message digest to the person who intends to verify that the document has been signed. This person decrypts the encrypted message digest with her public key (i.e., the public key complement to the private key) to produce the original one-way hash value. Next, a one-way hash is performed on the received document. If the resulting one-way hash is the same as the decrypted one-way hash, then several statements hold true:

1. The document received is the same as the document that had been "signed".
2. The signer of the document had access to the private key that complemented the public key that was used to decrypt the encrypted one-way hash. The assumption here is that the signer was the only individual with access to the private key.

Digital signature protocols, in general, have a private method for encrypting a hash, and a public method for verifying the signature. Such protocols operate under the assumption that only one person can encrypt the hash for the message, and that the name of that person is known; hence, the protocol establishes a verified signature. It should be emphasized that a digital signature is quite different from a written signature; the latter usually indicates that the signer wrote the document or somehow attests to an agreement with the contents of the document. The digital signature merely indicates that the document was received from a particular person, contingent on the assumption that the private key was available only to that person [23].

To understand how a digital signature protocol may be maliciously deployed, imagine the following scenario: Lord Voldemort contacts you and tells you that he is Elvis Presley and would like you to have a copy of his public key plus a file and signature that he has encrypted using his private key. You receive the file and the public key; and you use the public key to successfully decrypt the file and signature, leading you to conclude that the file was indeed sent by Elvis Presley. You read the decrypted file and learn that Elvis advises you to invest all your money in a company that manufactures concrete guitars; which, of course, you do. Elvis knows guitars. The problem here is that the signature was validated, but the valid signature was not authentic [23].

Domain In the context of classification, the domain of a property is the list of classes to which the property may apply. If the domain of a property is confined to the members of a single class (e.g., hair growth is confined to Class Mammalia), then the property is a class property (i.e., a defining property of the class). In this case, the domain name tells us that if an animal has hair, then we can infer that the animal is a member of Class Mammalia. When a class is listed as the domain of a property, we can always infer that the property applies to the descendant classes of the class, since every descendant class inherits all of the properties of the ancestor.

Endoderm three embryonic layers eventually develop into the fully developed animal: endoderm, mesoderm, and ectoderm. The endoderm forms a tube extending from the embryonic mouth to the embryonic anus. The mucosa of the gastrointestinal tract, and the epithelial cells of the liver, pancreas, and lungs, all derive from the endoderm.

Epigenome The epigenome, at its simplest, consists of cell-type-specific chemical modifications to DNA that do not affect the sequence of nucleotides that comprise the genome. Such modifications may control the expression of genes. There are many kinds of non-sequence modifications that fall under the rubric of "epigenome." One of the best-studied epigenomic modifications is DNA methylation. The most common form of methylation in DNA occurs on Cytosine nucleotides, most often at locations wherein Cytosine is followed by Guanine. These methylations are called CpG sites. CpG islands are concentrations of CpG sites. There are about 29,000 to 50,000 CpG islands [108]. The patterns of methylation are inherited among cells of the same type (e.g., goblet cell to goblet cell, liver cell to liver cell). Alterations in methylation patterns are referred to as epimutations. Epimutations may persist in those specialized cells that are descendants from an epimutated cell [109].

Epigenome modifiers, other than methylation, include: histones, and non-histone nuclear proteins; conformational changes in DNA that influence gene expression (e.g., heterochromatin); protein interactions; RNA interactions; and any other physicochemical interactions that influence gene expression.

In general, the epigenome controls differentiation and the phenotype (i.e., observed biological characteristics) of the different somatic cell types of the body [110,111].

A simple way to think about the respective roles of genome and epigenome is as follows: The genome establishes the identity of an organism; the epigenome establishes the identity of the individual cell-types within the organism.

Eukaryote A member of Class Eukaryota, the large class of organisms whose cells contain a nucleus. There are three classes of living organisms: Class Viridae (the viruses); Class Prokaryota (organisms with no nucleus, comprising Class Bacteria and Class Archaea), and Class Eukaryota (organisms whose cells have at least one nucleus). In addition to having a nucleus, members of Class Eukaryota all seem to have evolved from organisms that contained mitochondria. Humans, and all animals, are descendants of Class Eukaryota. As descendants of Class Eukaryota, we humans are also full-fledged members of Class Eukaryota. Skeptics are urged to consider their geneology back through evolution. The gametes in humans are the result of a process that can be followed iteratively up through the chain of ancestors within a species, and up through the gametes of the parent species, and on and on, until reaching the single-cell eukaryotes; organisms that are, for all practical purposes, "all gamete." Hence, we humans are dues-paying members of Class Eukaryota. This also explains why all animals have hundreds of the same core genes, give or take some acquired mutations, that are found in single-celled eukaryotic organisms.

Gamete A differentiated germ cell (e.g., an egg in the female or a sperm cell in the male).

Germ cell A cell in the lineage that produces gametes (i.e., oocytes in females and sperm cells in males). Equivalent to a cell belonging to the germ cell line."

Germ cell line The germ cell line is one very specialized lineage of cells that produces fully differentiated gametes (ova in females and sperm in males). The primitive cells of the germ cell line can erase the epigenome, thus producing cells that may become totipotent (i.e., able to differentiate into any cell type).

The term "germ cell line" needs to be distinguished from "germline", the latter being the first cells to arise from the zygote, from which all of the cells of the embryo, including the cells of the germ cell line, will develop.

Germ layers Metazoans (i.e., members of Class Animalia) are triploblastic, meaning that the early embryo contains three layers, from which all of the tissues of the developed organism will arise. These three layers are ectoderm, endoderm, and mesoderm.

During embryogenesis, several additional germ layers arise (e.g., neuroectoderm and neural crest), but these layers are derivative of the three primary germ layers and not traditionally included when we use the term "germ layer".

The three primary germ layers traditionally exclude trophectoderm, the layer of cells that give rise to the extra-embryonic tissues that arise early in embryogenesis but which are not incorporated into the developed organism (e.g., extraembryonic placenta and amnion).

Also, the term "germ layer" must never be confused with "a layer of germ cells" (i.e., a layer of gametes and their precursors).

Germline The germline consists of the cells that derive from the fertilized egg of an organism. All of the somatic cells (i.e., the cells composing the body), as well as the germ cells of the body (i.e., oocytes and spermatocytes), arise from the same germline. The extra-embryonic cells (e.g., placental cells) have the same germline as the somatic cells. An inherited condition can be described as being in the germline; meaning that the mutation is in every cell that derives from the fertilized egg.

The word "germline" has confused many students, who use the term "germline cell" interchangeably with "germ cell" or with "germ cell line". In fact, if you search for a definition of germline on the web, you're apt to find the somewhat recursive definition that the germline constitutes all of the cells in the offspring that are produced by the germ cell lines of the parents. True, but apt to mislead.

It is best to think of a germline mutation by its functional definition, a mutation found in every cell in an organism.

Haploid From Greek haplous, "onefold, single, simple". Equivalent to the chromosome set of a gamete. In humans, this would be 23 chromosomes; one set of un-paired autosomes (chromosomes 1 to 22) plus one sex chromosome (X or Y chromosome). The somatic cells of the body (i.e., all cells that are not gametes) are diploid (i.e., having twice the haploid set of chromosomes)

Haploid organisms All multicellular organisms (i.e., all members of Class Plantae, Class Metazoa, and Class Fungi) may have both haploid and diploid stages of existence. That is to say that every animal, plant, and fungus can be envisioned as two different organisms each containing its distinctive type of cells (haploid or diploid). In humans, the haploid "organisms" are the gametes (oocytes or sperm).

Many fungi, algae, and bryophyte plants can grow either as haploid or as diploid organisms, depending on their life cycle stage. The soma of most animals (i.e., the body of the animal, excluding its component of gametes) are diploid, but some male bees, wasps, and ants are haploid organisms because they develop from unfertilized, haploid eggs [112].

Histologic examination All anatomic pathologists and many biologists spend countless hours examining tissues under a microscope. They study the different cells in the tissue and the relationship among the cells, and the morphologic changes that occur in cells after a biological event. In the case of pathologists, the biological event is the occurrence of a disease. Most human diseases can be diagnosed through careful histological examination of samples of involved tissues.

Histology Histology is the study of cells in tissues. The primary tools of the histologist are the microscope and glass slides. Thin slices of tissues are stained and mounted on glass slides, and the glass slides are examined under a microscope.

Index An index is an ordered collection of words, phrases, concepts, or subsets of classes of information (e.g., geographic names, names of persons, dates of events), linked to the locations where they occur. Great indexes provide a way of seeing the world created by the book, often in a manner that was unanticipated by the book's author. Ultimately, an index allows us to grow beyond the text, discovering relationships among concepts that were missed by the author. By all rights, indexers should be given published credit for their creative products, much like authors are given credit for their works [113].

Here are a few of the specific strengths of an index that cannot be duplicated by standard search operations conducted by word-processing software [114]:

1. An index can be read, as a stand-alone document, to acquire a quick view of the book's contents [115].

2. When you do a "find" search in a query box, your search may come up empty if there is nothing in the text that matches your query. This can be very frustrating if you know that the text covers the topic entered into the query box. Indexes avoid the problem of fruitless searches. By browsing the index, you can find the term you need, without foreknowledge of its exact wording within the text. When you find a term in the index, you may also find closely related terms, sub-indexed under your search term, or alphabetically indexed above or below your search term.

3. Searches on computerized indexes are nearly instantaneous because the index is precompiled. Even when the text is massive (e.g., Gigabytes, Terabytes), information retrieval via an index will be nearly instantaneous.

4. Indexes can be tied to a classification or other specialized nomenclature. Doing so permits the analyst to know the relationships among different topics within the index, and within the text [116].

5. Many indexes are cross-indexed, providing a set of relationships among different terms, that a clever data analyst might find useful.

6. Indexes can be merged. If the location entries for index terms are annotated with some identifier for the source text, then searches on a merged index will yield locators that point to specific locations from all of the sources.

7. Indexes can be embedded directly in the text [117]. Whereas conventional indexes contain locators to the text, embedded indexes are built into the locations where the index term is found in the text, with each location listing other locations where the term can be found. These in situ connections among terms can be hidden from the viewer using specialized formatting instructions (e.g., pop-up links). Programmers can reconstitute conventional indexes from embedded tags, as required.

8. Indexes can be created to satisfy a particular goal; and the process of creating a made-to-order index can be repeated again and again. For example, if you have a massive or complex data resource devoted to ornithology, and you have an interest in the geographic location of species, you might want to create an index specifically keyed to localities, or you might want to add a locality sub-entry for every indexed bird name in your original index. Such indexes can be constructed as add-ons when needed.

9. Indexes can be updated. If terminology or classifications change, nothing is stopping you from re-building the index with an updated specification, without modifying your source data.

10. Indexes can be created long after the corpus of text has been written. Such add-on indexes can be designed to encourage novel uses for the data resource.

11. Indexes can occasionally substitute for a text. For example, a telephone book, or its electronic equivalent, is an index that serves its purpose without being attached to any particular corpus of information.

Numerous computer algorithms for automatic indexing are widely available [23]. Many failed classifications could be replaced by indexes.

Indexes Every writer must search deeply into his or her soul to find the correct plural form of "index". Is it "indexes" or is it "indices"? Latinists insist that "indices" is the proper and exclusive plural form. Grammarians agree, reserving "indexes" for the third person singular verb form; "The student indexes his thesis." Nonetheless, popular usage of the plural of "index," referring to the section at the end of a book, is almost always "indexes," the form used herein.

Inheritance Inheritance, to the layman, indicates that a trait or disease occurring in an offspring can be attributed to some genetic condition or predisposition that is present in one or both of the parents. To the geneticist, the term "inheritance" has a much narrower meaning, and the difference in these two interpretations can lead to a great deal of confusion. It's best to take the time to explain the medical meaning of inheritance, and how the precise meaning of the term influences our understanding of the pathogenesis of genetic diseases.

For the geneticist, inheritance always indicates the passage of affected genes from the germline of a parent to the germline of the offspring. This means that the inherited genes are present in every cell of the parent. When a genetic abnormality is present only in the fertilized oocyte or the fertilizing sperm, then we do not speak of inheritance as the cause of the abnormality in the offspring; the mutation that is new to a parent's gamete is said to be de novo (i.e., new, and not inherited). Hence, Down syndrome (trisomy 21) is a condition that often comes from the mother (i.e., when there is a genetic defect in the oocyte) but which is seldom inherited from the mother.

The medical definition of inheritance is an anachronism that has persisted from the early days of genetics when there was no means to examine the cellular pathogenesis of the disease. In the case of Down syndrome, if both the mother and the father did not have Down syndrome, and if there was no history of Down syndrome in the family, then the infant with Down syndrome must not have inherited the condition. It is worth pointing out that this last statement is not always true. Cases of so-called translocation Down syndrome are inherited from a parent who does not have Down Syndrome. In these cases, one parent carries a balanced translocation between chromosome 21 and another chromosome, producing no gain or loss of chromosomal material in the affected parent. If this translocation is passed to the next generation, it can become unbalanced, producing extra genetic material from chromosome 21 in the offspring, with the consequent development of Down Syndrome.

Instance An instance is a specific example of an object that is not itself a class or group of objects. For example, "John Doe" might be an instance of a Class Person. The terms instance, instance object, class member is sometimes used interchangeably. The special value of the "instance" concept, in a system wherein everything is an object, is that it distinguishes members of classes (i.e., the instances) from the classes to which they belong.

Invasion In the field of cancer, the invasion occurs when tumor cells move into and through normal tissues.

All tumors that can metastasize can also invade, and, for this reason, it is inferred that invasion is involved in the process of metastasis. For metastasis to occur, tumor cells invade through the walls of lymphatic and blood vessels, thus gaining access to the general circulation, where they seed other organs.

Although all metastasizing tumors indeed can invade, it is not always true that an invading tumor can metastasize. Examples of non-metastasizing invasive tumors include basal cell carcinoma of the skin, and most tumors arising within the brain.

Knowledge domain A knowledge domain is a general subject or an academic discipline. We think in terms of the knowledge domain of classification or an ontology because we assume that their purpose is to cover exactly one domain of knowledge and no others. Of course, the term itself produces the false sense that knowledge can be neatly divided into distinct and separate domains. When we think about it, all knowledge is interrelated and it is impossible to assign any piece of information to one particular domain, to the exclusion of all others. Still, we need some convenient way to refer to the ways that we traditionally think of traditional subjects, so the term "knowledge domains" will need to suffice, for the moment.

Malignancy Synonymous with cancer. A tumor that progressively grows, invades, and if left untreated, kills.

Meaning In the computer sciences, "meaning" is achieved when described data is bound to a unique identifier of a data object. For example, "Claude Funston's height is five feet eleven inches," comes pretty close to being a meaningful statement. The statement contains data (five feet eleven inches), and the data is described (height). The described data belongs to a unique object (Claude Funston). Ideally, the name "Claude Funston" should be provided with a unique identifier, to distinguish one instance of Claude Funston from all the other persons who are named Claude Funston. The statement would also benefit from a formal system that ensures that the metadata makes sense (e.g., What exactly is height, and does Claude Funston fall into a class of objects for which height is a property?) and that the data is appropriate (e.g., Is 5 ft 11 in. an allowable measure of a person's height?). A statement with meaning does not need to be a true statement (e.g., The height of Claude Funston was not 5 ft 11 in. when Claude Funston was an infant).

Message digest Within the context of this book, "message digest", "digest", "HMAC", and "one-way hash" are equivalent terms.

Metabolic pathway According to traditional thinking, a metabolic pathway was a sequence of biochemical reactions involving a specific set of enzymes and substrates that produced a chemical product. The classic pathway has been the Krebs cycle. It was common for students to calculate the output of the cycle (in moles of ATP), based on stoichiometric equations employing known amounts of substrate.

As we have learned more about complex cellular systems, the concept of metabolic pathways has broadened to include linked actions among receptors, activators, enzymes, and structural macromolecules. The products of metabolic pathways are often cellular actions, rather than chemical products. Pathways may not always occur in a specific organelle. The pathways may interact with other pathways, and their direction and biological consequences may be complex and variable among different cell types or in different physiological states within one cell type. Still, the term "metabolic pathway" is a convenient conceptual device, permitting us to organize classes of molecules that interact with a generally defined set of partner molecules, to produce a consistent range of biological actions.

Modeling Modeling involves explaining the behavior of a system, often with a formula, sometimes with descriptive language. The formula for the data describes the distribution of the data and often predicts how the different variables will change with one another. Consequently, modeling often provides reasonable hypotheses to explain how objects within a system will influence one another.

Many of the great milestones in the physical sciences have arisen from a bit of data modeling supplemented by scientific genius (e.g., Newton's laws of mechanics and optics, Kepler's laws of planetary orbits, Quantum mechanics). The occasional ability to relate observations with causality endows modeling with great scientific impact.

Mucosa Refers to a surface layer of epithelial cells, the basement membrane upon which the epithelial cells sit, and the thin layer of connective tissue between the basement membrane and an underlying thin muscle layer (the muscularis mucosa).

Mutability Mutability refers to the ability to alter the data held in a data object, or to change the identity of a data object. The most useful data resources are immutable: data can be added, but data cannot be erased or altered. Data resources that are mutable cannot establish a sensible data identification system, and cannot support verification and validation activities.

For programmers, it is important to distinguish data mutability from object mutability, as it applies in Python and other object-oriented programming languages. Python has two so-called immutable objects: strings and tuples. Intuitively, we would probably guess that the contents of an immutable string object cannot be changed, and the contents of an immutable tuple object cannot be changed. This is not the case. Immutability, for programmers, means that there are no methods available to the object by which the contents of the object can be altered. Specifically, a Python tuple object would have no methods it could call to change its contents. However, a tuple may contain a list, and lists are mutable. For example, a list may have an append method that will add an item to the list object. We can change the contents of a list contained in a tuple object, without violating the tuple's immutability.

Natural sciences The natural sciences are those areas that explore things that are here in our universe, just waiting for us to observe and study. Hence, biology, chemistry, and physics and all their subdisciplines, are considered the natural sciences.

Mathematics has traditionally not been counted among the natural sciences, since humans have always taken credit for its creation. Aside from that, the conjectures of mathematics do not lend themselves to testability, one of the hallmarks of the natural sciences. For serious scientists, assertions that cannot be tested by experimentation are relegated to the level of pseudoscience and are not to be taken seriously. I suppose that a mathematician would argue that mathematicians think in terms of provability, not testability. Once a conjecture is formally proven, then it is known to be true, and testing becomes irrelevant.

In the past century, much of physics has become indistinguishable from mathematics. We have seen pure mathematicians receiving Nobel Prizes in physics, and we have seen physicists receiving Fields Medals in mathematics. Much of physics can be approached purely as a mathematical construct, that sometimes defies our intuitive notions. Perhaps mathematics is another "given" in our universe, whose fundamental constants and operations are just as much part of the fabric of the universe as is general relativity, hydrogen atoms, or mosquitoes. Hence, we should feel free to include mathematics in the natural sciences, if we wish it.

New data It is natural to think of certain objects as being "new", meaning, with no prior existence; and other objects being "old", having persisted from an earlier time, and into the present. In truth, there are very few "new" objects in our universe. Most objects arise in a continuum, through a transformation or a modification of old objects. When we study Brownian motion, wherein a particle's direction of motion, at a time "t", is chosen randomly, we are aware that the location of the particle, at a time "t" is predetermined by all of its prior locations, at times "t-1", "t-2", and so on. The new data is influenced by every occurrence of old data. For another example, the air temperature one minute from now is largely determined by weather events that are occurring now, but the weather occurring now is largely determined by all of the weather events that have occurred in the history of our planet.

Whenever we speak of "new" data, we must think in terms that relate the new data to the "old" data that preceded it. The dependence of new data on old data can be approached computationally. The autocorrelation function is a method for producing a measurement indicating the dependence of data elements on prior data elements. Long-range dependence occurs when a value is dependent on many prior values. Long-range dependence is determined when the serial correlation (i.e., the autocorrelation over multiple data elements) is high when the number of sequential elements is large [118].

Incidentally, in the same vein, a new idea is nearly always an old idea that you are hearing for the first time.

Nomenclature A nomenclature is an authoritative listing of terms intended to cover all of the concepts in a knowledge domain. A nomenclature is different from a dictionary for three reasons: (1) the nomenclature terms are not annotated with definitions, (2) nomenclature terms may be multi-word, and (3) the terms in the nomenclature are limited to the scope of a chosen knowledge domain.

Many nomenclatures group synonyms under a group code. For example, a food nomenclature might collect submarine, hoagie, po' boy, grinder, hero, and torpedo under one alphanumeric code such as "F63958". Optimally, the canonical concepts listed in the nomenclature are organized into a hierarchical classification [32,31].

Non-quantitative trait Non-quantitative traits can be described as being present or absent, without quantitative measures, that occur in individuals of a species, but which are not defining properties of the species. An example would be the trait of having blue eyes.

Unlike the quantitative traits, which always seem to be polygenic, with a non-Mendelian inheritance pattern, the non-quantitative traits can have a monogenic origin. An example is the horse's tolt. Some horses have a natural ability to use a specialized gait known as the tolt. This gait is common in a certain breed of the Icelandic horse and rare among all other horse breeds. Most horses, no matter how hard they try, cannot tolt. Recently, the tolt was found to come from a single gene mutation [119].

It should be noted that the term "trait" is used exceptionally by geneticists to indicate that an individual carries a recessive disease mutation on a single allele. For example, sickle cell disease occurs when an individual carries two recessive alleles of the characteristic hemoglobin mutation. Individuals with only one allele affected, who may develop some tendency toward red cell sickling, but who do not develop the complete sickle cell disease phenotype, are said to carry the sickle cell trait.

Nonatomicity   Nonatomicity is the condition that results in the assignment of a collection of objects to a single, composite object, that cannot be further simplified or sensibly deconstructed. For example, the human body is composed of trillions of individual cells, each of which lives for some length of time, and then dies. Many of the cells in the body are capable of dividing to produce more cells. In many cases, the cells of the body that are capable of dividing can be cultured and grown in plastic containers, much like bacteria can be cultured and grown in Petri dishes. If the human body is composed of individual living organisms, why do we resort to nonatomicity, insisting that each human is an irreducible living entity? Why don't we think of humans as an aggregate of individual organisms? Perhaps the reason stems from the coordinated responses of cells. When someone steps on the cells of your toe, the cells in your brain sense pain, the cells in your mouth and vocal cords say ouch, and an army of inflammatory cells rush to the scene of the crime. The cells in your toe are not capable of registering an actionable complaint, without a great deal of assistance.

Nucleus   The membrane-bound organelle that contains the genome and the apparatus necessary for transcribing DNA into RNA, for preparing RNA for its role in protein translation, and for replicating the DNA in preparation for cell division.

Eukaryotes consist of all the organisms whose cells contain nuclei. The prokaryotes, (eubacteria and archaeans), are organisms that do not contain a nucleus. Every organism on earth is either a eukaryote or a prokaryote, or a virus. The nucleus, though necessary for cell division, is not necessary for moment-to-moment cell survival. Mature red blood cells have no nucleus, but they manage to live for about 120 days.

Oncologist   Physician who specializes in treating patients who have cancer.

One-way hash   A one-way hash is an algorithm that transforms one string into a hashed string (a fixed-length sequence of seemingly random characters) in such a way that the original string cannot be calculated by operations on the one-way hash value (i.e., the calculation is one-way only). One-way hash values can be calculated for any string, including a person's name, a document, or an image. For any given input string, the resultant one-way hash will always be the same. If a single byte of the input string is modified, the resulting one-way hash will be changed and will have a totally different sequence than the one-way hash sequence calculated for the unmodified string.

Most modern programming languages have several methods for generating one-way hash values.

Here is a short Ruby script that generates a one-way hash value for a file, using the popular md5 algorithm:

```
require 'digest/md5'
file_contents = File.new("simplify.txt").binmode
hash_string = Digest::MD5.base64digest(file_contents.read)
puts hash_string
exit
```

Here is the output of the script, a one-way hash value for the chosen file (simplify.txt in this case):

```
OCfZez7L1A6WFcT+oxMh+g==
```

If we copy our example file to another file, with an alternate filename, the md5 algorithm will generate the same hash value. Likewise, if we generate a one-way hash value, using the md5 algorithm implemented in some other language, such as Python or Perl, the outputs will be identical.

One-way hash values can be designed to produce long fixed-length output strings (e.g., 256 bits in length). When the output of a one-way hash algorithm is very long, the chance of a hash string collision (i.e., the occurrence of two different input strings generating the same one-way hash output value) is negligible. One-way hash algorithms have been implemented in identification and deidentification systems, authentication systems, distributed ledgers, digital signatures, and cryptographic protocols [120–126].

Ontology   In the field of philosophy, ontology is the study of relationships and properties of things. In the sciences, when we speak of "an ontology" we are usually referring to a collection of classes and their relationships to one another. Ontologies are often rule-based systems (i.e., membership in a class is determined by one or more class rules). Ideally, we can use the rules of classes, applied to the members of classes, to draw inferences. For example, if we know that Sam is a member of Class "Friends_of_Fred" and we know that all members of Class "Friends_of_Fred" snore, then we can infer that Sam snores.

In practice, two features distinguish ontologies from classifications. Ontologies permit classes to have more than one parent class. For example, the class of automobiles may be a direct subclass of "motorized devices" and a direct subclass of "mechanized transporters". In addition, an instance of a class can be an instance of any number of additional classes. For example, a Lamborghini may be a member of class "automobiles" and also a member of class "luxury items". Likewise, the species class, "Horse", might be a child class of Equu, a zoologic term; as well as a subclass of "racing animals" and "farm animals", and "four-legged animals". Naturalists working in the pre-computer age simply could not keep track of the class relationships allowed by ontologies [114].

By convention, ontologies are typically prepared using a semantic language and are intended to be computer-ready (i.e., able to be easily analyzed with computer software).

A classification is a highly restrained ontology wherein instances can belong to only one class, and each class may have only one direct parent class. Hence, every classification is an ontology, while not every ontology qualifies as a classification.

We note that the definition of ontology and classification vary from source to source, but the definitions provided herein will apply in many real-world encounters.

Organism   A living entity that is composed of identifiable parts that act in concert to perform some measurable action(s). This definition permits us to think of organisms as biological systems confined to a defined structure.

Parent class   The immediate ancestor, or the next-higher class (i.e., the direct superclass) of a class. For example, in the classification of living organisms, Class Vertebrata is the parent class of Class Gnathostomata. Class Gnathostomata is the parent class of Class Teleostomi.

In a classification, which imposes single class inheritance, each child class has exactly one parent class; whereas one parent class may have several different child classes. Furthermore, some classes, in particular the bottom class in the lineage, have no child classes (i.e., a class need not always be a superclass of other classes). A class can be defined by its properties, its membership (i.e., the instances that belong to the class), and by the name of its parent class. When we list all of the classes in classification, in any order, we can always reconstruct the complete class lineage, in their correct lineage and branchings, if we know the name of each class's parent class.

Pathogenesis   The biologic events that lead to the expression of disease. The term "carcinogenesis" is synonymous with "pathogenesis of cancer". Full understanding of a disease process involves learning the disease's pathogenesis and learning the metabolic pathways operative in the disease. These pathways are the cellular consequences of the events that occur as pathogenesis proceeds. Understanding the pathogenesis of disease helps us find ways to prevent, diagnose, and treat the disease.

Perl   Perl is a free, readily available, and open-source programming language that can be used on any operating system. Perl is an example of a scripting language, for which the programmer writes scripts that need to be interpreted before they can be executed. C is an example of an executable langue, in that C programs do not need a stand-alone interpreter program to execute. Perl scripts can be run from any computer upon which the Perl interpreter file has been loaded, but this is accomplished seamlessly when the user has installed the bundled Perl distribution files that contain the interpreter and hundreds of specialized modules that can be called upon to perform specialized Perl language functions.

Perl is a favorite among part-time programmers because scripts are easy to write and because there is a large base of users that have added functionality to the language over the years and who provide support to new programmers through a variety of internet-based resources [127].

Phenocopy disease   A disease that shares the same phenotype as a genetic disease, but without the genotypic root cause. Most phenocopy diseases are caused by a toxin or drug. We typically think of a phenocopy disease as the non-genetic equivalent of a genetic disease.

Here are examples of phenocopy diseases followed by their genetic counterparts:

- Acquired porphyria cutanea tarda—inherited porphyria cutanea tarda [84,85]
- Acquired von Willebrand disease—inherited von Willebrand disease
- Aminoglycoside-induced hearing loss—inherited mitochondriopathic deafness
- Drug-induced methemoglobinemia—inherited methemoglobinemia
- Fetal exposure to methotrexate—Miller syndrome [128]
- Methylmalonic acidemia caused by severe deficiency of vitamin B12—inherited methylmalonic acidemia
- Scurvy—inherited collagenopathies
- Alcohol-induced sideroblastic anemia—inherited sideroblastic anemia
- Cardiomyopathy due to alcohol abuse—inherited dilated cardiomyopathy [129]
- Lead-induced encephalopathy—inherited tau encephalopathy [130]
- Myopathy produced by nucleoside analog reverse transcriptase inhibitors (i.e., HIV drugs)—inherited mitochondrial myopathy
- Pseudo-Pelger-Huet Anomaly—inherited Pelger-Huet Anomaly [90,131]
- Thalidomide-induced phocomelia—Roberts syndrome and SC pseudothalidomide syndrome [132]
- Warfarin embryopathy—brachytelephalangic chondrodysplasia punctata [133]
- Drug-induced cerebellar ataxia [134]—hereditary spinocerebellar ataxia [135]
- Chronic copper poisoning—Wilson disease
- Chronic iron overload hemochromatosis—inherited hemochromatosis
- Quinacrine-induced ochronosis—inherited ochronosis (i.e., mutation in the HGD gene for the enzyme homogentisate 1,2-dioxygenase) [136]
- Drug-induced Parkinsonism [137,138]—autosomal-dominant inherited Parkinsonism [139]
- Acquired pulmonary hypertension due to hypoxia, thromboembolism, left-sided heart failure, or drugs—inherited pulmonary hypertension [140]
- Acquired cirrhosis—genetic cirrhosis (due to mutation in keratin 18) [47]
- Anticoagulant drugs that inhibit thrombus formation—inherited Factor X deficiency (a form of hemophilia)

Phenocopy diseases provide important clues to the pathogenesis of rare and common diseases. The drug that produces a phenocopy disease is likely to share the same disease pathways observed in the genetic disease. Pharmacologic treatments for the phenocopy disease may be effective against the genetic form of the disease.

Phenotype   The set of observable traits and features of a biological object. For example, we can describe a dog as best as we can, and that description would be our assessment of its phenotype. If we describe a lot of dogs of a certain breed, we might come up with some consensus on the phenotype for the breed. A "disease phenotype" is the medical community's consensus on the observed features that characterize a disease. For example, the term "cancer phenotype" refers to the properties of growth, persistence, invasion, and metastasis that characterize virtually every cancer.

The concept of a phenotype exists in contrast to the concept of a genotype (the DNA sequence of the genome). The phenotype is the expression of environmental, genetic, and developmental influences and represents a totality of traits.

Plesionym Plesionyms are nearly synonymous words, or pairs of words that are sometimes synonymous; other times not. For example, the noun forms of "smell" and "odor" are synonymous. As a verb, "smell" does the job, but "odor" comes up short. You can small a fish, but you cannot odor a fish. Smell and odor are plesionyms to one another.

Precancer Precancers are the lesions from which cancers derive. Precancers have some of the properties of cancers, but not all of those properties. Most precancers are non-invasive and non-metastatic, so eliminating precancers cures the patient of cancer that might have eventually developed. Precancers also have some properties that cancers lack. Two of the most interesting properties of precancers (lacking in cancers) are their propensity for spontaneous regression and the ease with which they can be prevented or treated. Because all cancers seem to be preceded by an identifiable precancer stage, a successful strategy to eliminate all precancers would prevent the occurrence of all cancers [34,141].

Premalignancy Equivalent to precancer.

Problematica The term "problematica" is used by taxonomists to indicate a class of organism that defies robust classification [142]. The very existence of this term tells us that taxonomy is a delicate and tentative science. We must always be prepared to examine and test our current classification, and to make corrections whenever warranted.

Property Property, in the context of semantics, is a quantitative or qualitative feature of an object. In the case of spreadsheets, the column headers are all properties. In a classification, every class contains a set of properties that might apply to every member of the class (e.g., male cardinals have the "red feathers" property). Furthermore, instances may have their own set of properties, separate from the class. For example, the cardinal that I watch in my backyard seems to enjoy eating safflower seeds and cavorting in our birdbath, but I'm not sure that all cardinals share the same pleasures. From the standpoint of classifications, it is crucial to understand that a property may apply to multiple classes that are not directly related to one another. For example, insects, birds, and bats are not closely related classes of animals, but they all share the amazing property of flight.

Although a class can have no more than one parent class, a class can share properties with other classes. For example, Class File may be unrelated to Class Integer, but both classes may share a "print" method or the same "store" method.

In object-oriented programming languages, properties are often implemented as methods (short programs) that apply to instances of classes or classes.

Pythiosis A rare tropical disease caused by the oomycete (alternately called oomycotes) Pythium insidiosum. Until 1987, the disease was mistakenly believed to be caused by a fungus. The disease can disseminate through the body if the diagnosis is delayed or due to the lack of effective drugs against species of Class Oomycetes. The Oomycotes also include the organisms that produce late blight of potato (*Phytophthora infestans*), and sudden oak death (Phytophthora ramorum).

The oomycotes are a subclass of Class Heterokonta.

The only other member of Class Heterokonta is known to cause human infection is Blastocystis species, which can produce a disease that closely mimics irritable bowel syndrome. The heterokonts are a class of eukaryotic organisms that we barely understand, adding urgency to our research into this area. Both pythiosis and blastocystis are examples of infections that we would have had no chance of understanding without the benefit of a robust classification of organisms.

Python Python, like Perl and Ruby, is a free, readily available, and open-source programming language that can be used on any operating system. Python is a scripting language that has a large number of add-on libraries (e.g., numpy and scipy) that facilitate many of the analytic tasks that scientists commonly employ.

Python's chief advantage over Perl lies in the ease with which object-oriented programming can be implemented in the Python environment. Possibly, for this reason, Python is attracting more followers than Perl, in terms of the size of its growing user community [125].

Quantitative trait Quantitative traits are features that can be measured, and for which there is variation within the species population. Blood pressure is an example of a quantitative trait in humans insofar as we all have measurable blood pressure values, but the values vary greatly among individuals.

Quantitative traits can evolve very quickly within a species. For example, it may take only a few dozen generations for breeders to produce a large dog, such as a mastiff, or a small dog, such as a chihuahua. Between species of the same class of organism, traits can have truly enormous variations. For example, *Wolffia globosa* (duckweed) has been described as the world's smallest flowering plant, at 0.1–0.2 mm in diameter. Compare this with the weight or size of another angiosperm species, the giant redwood. The difference can be upwards of a trillion-fold.

Quantitative traits are polygenic and are inherited in a non-Mendelian fashion [143–145]. For example, at least 180 gene variants have been associated with variations of normal height. These 180 variants may represent only a fraction of the total number of gene variants that influence the height of individuals, as they account for only about 10% of the predicted spread [146].

Because blood pressure is an example of a quantitative trait, we would expect that commonly occurring hypertension (elevated blood pressure) would not have a monogenic origin (i.e., does not result from an abnormality in a single gene), Research scientists searching for the "hypertension gene" could have saved themselves a great deal of effort, if they had they simply recognized that hypertension is a quantitative trait and that a single gene defect could not account for the commonly observed wide variations in blood pressure found in the human population.

Quantum and quantized Quantum, from the Latin, meaning "amount" usually refers to the smallest amount of a discrete unit of a physical property. Quantum physics refers to the various values of properties that take on discrete numeric multiples, such as the multiples of n, where n is an integer or a half-integer. It is a surprising aspect of many laws of particle physics/field physics that relationships follow "quantized" rules, wherein properties are described by relationships containing gapless series of integers. Just to provide some perspective, a quantized automobile might drive at 0, 10, 20, 30, 40, 50, or 60 miles per hour (e.g., 10n, where $n=0,1,2...$), but at no speeds between these discrete multiples. Why is particle physics/field physics quantized? This question cannot be answered easily, but it is helpful to keep in mind that many of the properties of the universe that are familiar to everyone are quantized. For example, there is no such thing as a third of an electron or a half of a proton. Quantities of particles are exact integer numbers (e.g., Avogadro's number), and all particles of a kind are identical to one another (i.e., every electron has the same amount of "electron stuff" and weighs exactly as much as every other electron in the same reference frame). The dimensions of the universe are quantized (i.e., the four dimensions of space and time), and geometric symmetry transformations such as rotation and reflection are also quantized (e.g., 1 flip, 2 rotations, etc.). Quantum numbers of atomic particles are quantized and transitions of electrons between atomic shells are constrained to discrete jumps absorbing or emitting quantized amounts of energy. Insofar as the components of physical processes are quantized, it should not come as a complete surprise to anyone that many physical laws are quantized.

Rare disease As written in Public Law 107–280, the Rare Diseases Act of 2002, "Rare diseases and disorders are those which affect small patient populations, typically populations smaller than 200,000 individuals in the United States." [147]. Since the population of the U.S. is about 314 million, in 2013, this comes to a prevalence of about 1 case for every 1570 persons. This is not too far from the definition recommended by the European Commission on Public Health; a prevalence of less than 1 in 2000 people, or less than 50 in 200,000.

Relationship Two objects are related to one another when there is some fundamental or defining principle that applies to both objects and which, ideally, helps us to better understand the nature of both objects. For example, when we say that force is mass times acceleration, we are describing a relationship between force and an accelerating mass. The equivalence, does not tell us exactly what force is, and it does not tell us exactly what an accelerating mass is, but it describes how mass and force relate to one another, and it brings us a little closer to an understanding of their fundamental natures.

The concepts of "relationship" and "similarity" are often mistaken for one another. To better understand the difference, consider the following. When you look up at the clouds, you may see the shape of a lion. The cloud has a tail, like a lion's tale, and a fluffy head, like a lion's mane. With a little imagination, the mouth of the lion seems to roar down from the sky. You have succeeded in finding similarities between the cloud and a lion. When you look at a cloud and you imagine a tea kettle producing a head of steam, and you recognize that the physical forces that create a cloud from the ocean's water vapor and the physical forces that produce steam from the water in a heated kettle are the same, then you have found a relationship.

Ruby Ruby, like Perl and Python, is a free, readily available, and open-source programming language that can be used on any operating system. Ruby is a scripting language that has a large number of free Class Packages that can be easily installed, adding to the functionality of the Ruby environment.

Ruby, unlike either Python or Perl, is a purely object-oriented language. Everything in Ruby is an object. Ruby knows the type of every object (e.g., Array, Numeric, String, Class). Ruby Classes contain data and methods and can create unique instances of themselves (i.e., new class instances or class objects). Programmers have access to all the Ruby Classes in Ruby's built-in Class Library. In addition, programmers can create their classes to represent the natural world (e.g., living organisms, chemical processes, scientific laws), and to conform to the logical construction of modern data models (e.g., semantic languages including Resource Description Language). Unlike Python, the Ruby language imposes a "one class one parent" rule on its objects, hence simplifying its data object model. In terms of the elegance of its object-oriented environment and the understated simplicity of its programming style, Ruby surpasses both Python and Perl [100].

Singleton class In object-oriented programming languages, a Singleton class is a class that can have only one instance object.

Singleton method In object-oriented programming languages, a singleton method is a method that only operates for a single instance object.

Species The modern definition of species can be expressed in three words: "evolving gene pool" [148]. This elegant definition is easy to comprehend and serves to explain how new species come into existence [149,150]. Each member of a species (i.e., each organism) has a genome constructed from the species-specific gene pool. Hence, membership within a species is immutable (e.g., a fish cannot become a cat and a cat cannot become a goat) since the genome of any individual organism came from their species-specific gene pools. Species have a set of biological properties associated with any living entity: uniqueness, life, death, the issuance of progeny (i.e., new species), and the benefit of evolution through natural selection. Hence, we should think of a species as a biological entity; not as an artifactual abstraction created for the convenience of taxonomists.

It is estimated that 5 to 50 billion species have lived on earth, with more than 99% of them now extinct, leaving about 10 to 100 million living species [151]. Hence, we can conclude that there is an ongoing, global process of speciation (producing new species) and extinction (disappearance of species). Because there are tens of millions of animal species living today, we can infer that the process of speciation yields diversification.

Stage treatment bias If you carefully select a stage of the disease that is successfully treated by a particular treatment protocol, you can exaggerate the benefits of your treatment by ignoring disease stages for which your treatment is ineffective. One example is the use of prostatectomy for prostate cancer, a procedure that is credited with a high cure rate. Prostatectomy is only performed on patients with tumors confined to the prostate. If the prostate cancer has metastasized to lymph nodes in the region of the prostate or distant organs, then prostatectomy is contraindicated. Why is this? If cancer has spread beyond the prostate, then removing the prostate will not benefit the patient. An apt analogy is closing the barn door after the horses have left the barn. Prostate cancer confined to the prostate is often indolent. By age 80 to 90 years, 70% to 90% of men have prostate cancer confirmed at autopsy [152,153]. This indicates that prostate cancer is a very common disease that kills only a small proportion of affected individuals. Because prostatectomy is only performed on men whose prostate cancer is believed to be confined to the prostate, the cure rate is high. Restricting treatment to patients who have a stage of the disease that is known to be indolent in most cases virtually guarantees high survival rates.

Staging   The formal clinical process of determining the extent of disease, at the time of diagnosis. The term "staging" is commonly reserved for cancers.

String   A string is a sequence of characters. Words, phrases, numbers, alphanumeric sequences (e.g., identifiers, one-way hash values, passwords) are strings. A book is a long string. The complete sequence of the human genome (3 billion characters, with each character an A, T, G, or C, designating the four nucleotides of DNA) is a very long string. Every subsequence of a string is another string.

Subclass   A subclass is a descendant class of its direct line of ancestral classes. The members of a subclass inherit the properties and methods of the ancestral classes in their direct lineage. For example, all subclasses of mammals have mammary glands because mammary glands are a defining property of the mammal class. In addition, all subclasses of mammals have vertebrae because the class of mammals is a subclass of the class of vertebrates. The subclass that is the immediate descendant of a class is called the child class. In common parlance, when we speak of the subclass of a class, we are referring specifically to its child class.

Superclass   A superclass is an ancestral class of its direct line of descendants. For example, in the classification of living organisms, the class of craniates is a superclass of the class of mammals. The immediate superclass of a class is its parent class. In common parlance, when we speak of the superclass of a class, we are most often referring to its parent class.

Symmetry   Symmetry is invariance under a transformation [154]. For example, a physical system is symmetric under rotation (a type of transformation) if it stays the same after the rotation. The universe itself is symmetric under shifts in space or time because the same scientific laws apply everywhere and forever.

Syndrome versus disease   A disease is a clinical condition having particular pathogenesis. A syndrome is a constellation of physical findings that can occur together. The symptoms of a syndrome may or may not all have the same pathogenesis; and, hence, may or may not constitute a disease.

A true disease has one pathogenesis, despite its multi-organ manifestations and can be potentially prevented, diagnosed, or treated by targeting events and pathways involved in the development of the disease. A syndrome is a confluence of clinical findings that may or may not be pathogenetically related; hence, may or may not be amenable to any single therapeutic or diagnostic approach.

System   A set of objects whose interactions produce all of the observable properties, behaviors, and events that we choose to observe. Basically, then, a system is whatever we decide to look at (e.g., the brain, a cell, a habitat, the cosmos). The assumption is that the objects that we are not looking at (i.e., the objects excluded from the system), have little or no effect on the objects within the system. Of course, this assumption will not always be true, but we do our best.

Taxonomy versus classification   When we write of "taxonomy" as an area of study, we refer to the methods and concepts related to the science of classification, derived from the ancient Greek taxis, "arrangement", and nomia, "method." When we write of "a taxonomy", as a construction within a classification, we are referring to the collection of named instances (class members) in the classification. To appreciate the difference between a taxonomy and a classification, it helps to think of taxonomy as the scientific field that determines how the different items within the classification are named. Classification is the scientific field that determines how classes of items are defined and related to one another. A taxonomy is similar to a nomenclature; the difference is that in a taxonomy, every named instance must have an assigned class.

Here is an easy way to think of the difference between a classification and a taxonomy. The classification is equivalent to the schema, indicating all the names of the various classes, and their relationship to one another. When we fill up the classes with named items (i.e., the class instances), we have a taxonomy.

There is a tendency among modern scientists to dismiss the topic of taxonomy as being old-fashioned, and without much relevance in a world dominated by experimental studies and computational analyses. It is important to note that taxonomy is crucial to the advancement of science [155] and that it would be regrettable if modern scientists proceeded to create classifications and ontologies without having any training in taxonomic theory. George Gaylord Simpson, one of the giants of mid-20th century animal classification, wrote the following words, which apply today:

The former disrepute of taxonomy in general and classification, in particular, had as one result that these subjects were not, and in many cases still are not, taught to biologists and zoologists in training. Many of them have gone on to do taxonomic work of various kinds without ever having learned how. Some have remained virtually illiterate in this field, and their work has been a serious trial to their colleagues. Others have learned by experience but may still have occasional gaps in knowledge. A contribution, however small, to training in classification may not, then, be unwelcome.

George Gaylord Simpson [156]

Time-stamp A large portion of data analysis is concerned, in one way or another, with the times that events occur or the times that observations are made, or the times that signals are sampled. Here are three examples that demonstrate why this is so: (1) most scientific and predictive assertions relate how variables change with respect to one another, over time; and (2) a single data object may have many different data values, over time, and only timing data will tell us how to distinguish one observation from another; (3) computer transactions are tracked in logs, and logs are composed of time-annotated descriptions of the transactions.

Data objects often lose their significance if they are not associated with accurate time measurement. Because accurate time data is easily captured by modern computers, every collected data point should be annotated with the moment in time when they were measured.

It is remarkably easy to capture the time of occurrence of events (e.g., the time that a data point is measured). In the Windows operating system, the date and time are both available at the command line interface simply by entering the word "date" or "time" at the prompt.

Time can be saved in high resolution (i.e., seconds and decimal fractions of seconds). The standard time, also known as Posix time or as Unix epoch time, is measured as the number of seconds elapsed since the first second of the year 1970, GMT. The duration of any event can be easily calculated by subtracting the beginning time from the ending time. All modern computers and programming languages permit users to access the current Posix time.

In Python:

```
>>> import time
>>> time.time()
1593976054.161482
```

In Perl:

```
use Time::HiRes qw(gettimeofday);
($s,$ns) = gettimeofday();
print $s . "\." . $ns;
```

```
exit;
output: 1593977668.128996
```

In Ruby:

```
t = Process.clock_gettime(Process::CLOCK_REALTIME)
puts t
exit
output: 1593979747.730387
```

Unix epoch time can easily be converted to a recognizable format feature the data and the time in seconds. It is very important to understand, though, that country-specific styles for representing the date are a nightmare for data scientists. As an example, consider: "2/4/97". This date signifies February 4, 1997, in America; and April 2, 1997, in Great Britain and much of the world. There is no way of distinguishing with certainty 2/4/97 and 4/2/97.

It is not surprising that an international standard, the ISO-8601, has been created for representing date and time [157].

The international format for date and time is: YYYY-MM-DD hh:mm:ss.

The value "hh" is the number of complete hours that have passed since midnight. The upper value of hh is 24 (midnight). If hh = 24, then the minute and second values must be zero (think about it).

An example of and ISO-8601-compliant data and time is:
1995-02-04 22:45:00.
An alternate form, likewise ISO-8601-compliant, is:
1995–02-04 T22:45:00Z.

In the alternate form, a "T" replaces the space left between the date and the time, indicating that time follows the date. A "Z" is appended to the string indicating that the time and date are computed for UTC (Coordinated Universal Time, formerly known as Greenwich Mean Time, and popularly known as Zulu time, hence the "Z").

Here is a short Perl script, format_time.pl, that produces the date and time, in the American style, and ISO-8601-compliant forms:

```
($sec,$min,$hour,$mday,$mon,$year,$wday,$yday,$isdst) = gmtime();
$year = $year + 1900;
$mon = substr(("000" . ($mon+1)), -2, 2);
$mday = substr(("000" . $mday), -2, 2);
$hour = substr(("000" . $hour), -2, 2);
$min = substr(("000" . $min), -2, 2);
$sec = substr(("000" . $sec), -2, 2);
print "Americanized time is: $mday\/$wday\/$year\n";
print "ISO8601 time is:$year\-$mon\-$mday $hour\:$min\:$sec\n";
print "ISO8601 time is:$year\-$mon\-${mday}T$hour\:$min\:${sec}Z (alternate
form)";
exit;
```

Here is the output of the format_time.pl script.
output

```
c:\ftp>format_time.pl
```

```
Americanized time is: 16/3/2015
ISO8601 time is:2015-09-16 12:31:41
ISO8601 time is:2015-09-16T12:31:41Z (alternate form)
```

Here is a Python script, format_time.py, that generates the date and time, compliant with ISO-8601.

```
import time, datetime
timenow = time.time()
print(datetime.datetime.fromtimestamp(timenow).strftime('%Y-%m-%d %H:%M:%S'))
exit
```

Here is the output of the format_time.py script:

```
c:\ftp>format_time.py
2015-09-16 07:44:09
```

All serious scientists should annotate their data with the high-resolution time at which the measurement was obtained.

Transformations A transform is a mathematical operation that takes a function or a time series (e.g., values obtained at intervals of time) and transforms it into something else. An inverse transform takes the transform function and produces the original function. Transforms are useful when there are operations that can be more easily performed on the transformed function than on the original function.

Some examples might be helpful. In 1614, John Napier (1550–1617), a Scottish mathematician, published tables of logarithms and antilogarithms. The primary purpose of these tables was to facilitate multiplication, division and exponentiation. Napier had transformed multiplication with numbers into addition with the logarithms of those numbers, as shown:

```
if a = b x c
then log(a) = log(b x c) = log(b) + log(c)
and antilog(log(a)) = antilog(log(b) + log(c))
or a = antilog((log(b)) + (log(c)))
```

Simply put, we can multiply together any collection of numbers by transforming them to their logs, and replacing multiplication with summation; then determining the antilog (the inverse transform) of the summed logs. Hence, logarithms transform multiplication into summation. The division works much the same way, with the logarithms of the divisors subtracted, not added.

The most useful transform in mathematical analysis is the Fourier transform, which represents signals from the time domain as a sum of frequency components (i.e., converts from the time domain to the frequency domain). The Fourier transform is easily computed with great speed on modern computers, using a modified form known as the Fast Fourier Transform. Periodic functions (i.e., functions with repeating trends in the data, including waveforms and periodic time series data) can be represented as the sum of oscillating functions (i.e., functions involving sines, cosines, or complex exponentials). The summation function is the Fourier series. Often, just the first few components of the Fourier series serve as a suitable approximation of the original signal. Operations on the transformed function can sometimes eliminate repeating artifacts or frequencies that occur below a selected threshold (e.g., noise). The transform can be used to find similarities between two signals. When the operations on the transform function are complete, the inverse of the transform can be calculated and substituted for the original set of data (Fig. 1.14).

Let's look at an example wherein a function is approximated by just a few components of a Fourier series (Fig. 1.15).

$$\hat{f}(\xi) = \int_{-\infty}^{\infty} f(x) \; e^{-2\pi i x \xi} \, dx$$

$$f(x) = \int_{-\infty}^{\infty} \hat{f}(\xi) \; e^{2\pi i x \xi} \, d\xi$$

FIG. 1.14 The Fourier transform and its inverse. In this representation of the transform, x represents time in seconds and the transform variable zeta represents frequency in hertz.

Triple In computer semantics, a triple is an identified data object associated with a data element and the description of the data element. In the computer science literature, the syntax for the triple is commonly described as: subject, predicate, object", wherein the subject is an identifier, the predicate is the description of the object, and the object is the data. The definition of triple, using grammatic terms, can be off-putting to the data scientist, who may think in terms of spreadsheet entries: a key that identifies the line record, a column header containing the metadata description of the data, and a cell that contains the data.

The three components of a triple are:

1. the identifier for the data object.
2. the metadata that describes the data.
3. the data itself.

   In theory, all data sets, databases, and spreadsheets can be constructed or deconstructed as collections of triples.

Trophectoderm The trophectoderm is formed in the blastocyst stage and consists of cells derived from the concepts that are not part of the inner cell mass. The trophectoderm gives rise to the placenta and the amniotic membranes. Because these tissues are not incorporated into the developed animal, they are referred to as extra-embryonic tissue. Gestational trophoblastic neoplasia (e.g., tumors that arise in the pregnant mother's uterus, such as gestational choriocarcinoma), all come from the trophectoderm.

Trusted time-stamp It is sometimes necessary to establish, beyond doubt, that a timestamp is accurate and has not been modified. Through the centuries, a great many protocols have been devised to prove that a timestamp is trustworthy. One of the simplest methods, first employed in the late twentieth century, involved sending a digest (in the form of a one-way hash string) of a document to a trusted time-stamp authority. The timestamp authority saves the one-way hash of the message, adds a date-time to the digest, and returns a message, with the authority's digital signature. It may seem as though the modern trusted timestamp protocol is a lot of work, but those who routinely use these services can quickly and automatically timestamp huge batches of documents.

Tumor grading The process of assigning a tumor specimen to a biological category, based on morphologic features that seem to correspond to the biological aggressiveness of the tumor. Often, a tumor's grade is largely determined by the degree of nuclear atypia. A tumor with minimal nuclear atypia might be assigned a "low grade" suggestive of indolent behavior. A tumor of the same type, but with marked nuclear atypia might be labeled a "high grade" tumor with an expected aggressive clinical course. Sometimes grading is not based on nuclear atypia. In the case of prostate cancer, grading is based on glandular size, shape, and distribution.

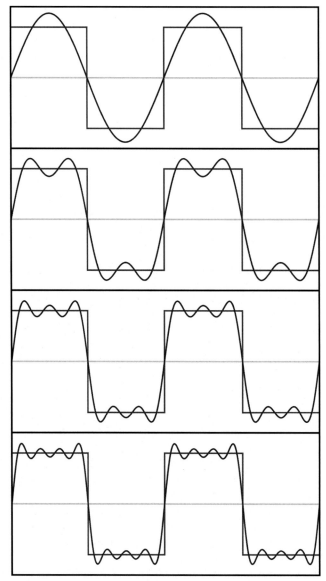

FIG. 1.15 A square wave is approximated by a single sine wave, the sum of two sine waves, three sine waves, and so on. As more components are added, the representation of the original signal or periodic set of data is more closely approximated.

The grade of a tumor should not be confused with the classification of a tumor. The tumor grade is a trait measured as an aggregate of features on a particular patient's tumor, at a particular moment in time. A tumor's classification is the name of the class of tumors into which a type of tumor is placed.
Unique identifier A unique identifier serves to identify an object in a manner that distinguishes the object from all other objects. Sometimes, the unique identifier is a measured feature of the object that

will not occur in any other object (e.g., iris pattern, retinal pattern, genome, fingerprints). More often, the unique identifier is a long, seemingly random character string generated by a software utility designed to generate such strings. The unique identifier for an object can serve as the name of the object to which it is permanently assigned.

Universal laws versus class laws A universal law applies to everything in the universe. In classification, a universal law would be equivalent to a class property of Class Root (the topmost object of the classification). Because everything in the classification is a descendant of Class Root, we can infer that everything in the classification inherits all of the class properties (e.g., laws and relationships) found in Class Root.

A class law applies to all of the members of a class and all of the subclasses of the class, and they apply wherever those items may exist, anywhere in the universe. Thus, class laws are universe-wide laws, but they are not universal laws.

References

[1] Adams FC, Laughlin G. A dying universe: the long-term fate and evolution of astrophysical objects. Rev Mod Phys 1997;69:337–72.

[2] Prigogine I, Stengers I. Order out of chaos: man's new dialogue with nature. Bantam New Age Books; 1984.

[3] Wolfram S. A new kind of science. Wolfram Media; 2002.

[4] Berman JJ. Repurposing legacy data: innovative case studies. Waltham, MA: Morgan Kaufmann; 2015.

[5] Varza A. Mereology. In: The Stanford encyclopedia of philosophy. Center for the Study of Language and Information (CSLI), Stanford University; 2016.

[6] Wigner E. The unreasonable effectiveness of mathematics in the natural sciences. Communications in pure and applied mathematics volume 13. New York: John Wiley and Sons; 1960.

[7] Gratzer W. Eurekas and euphorias: the Oxford book of scientific anecdotes. Oxford University Press; 2002.

[8] Berman JJ. Taxonomic guide to infectious diseases: understanding the biologic classes of pathogenic organisms. 1st ed. Cambridge, MA: Academic Press; 2012.

[9] Berman JJ. Taxonomic guide to infectious diseases: understanding the biologic classes of pathogenic organisms. 2nd ed. Cambridge, MA: Academic Press; 2019.

[10] Resnikoff S, Pascolini D, Etyaale D, Kocur I, Pararajasegaram R, Pokharel GP, et al. Global data on visual impairment in the year 2002. Bull World Health Organ 2004;82:844–51.

[11] Slatko BE, Taylor MJ, Foster JM. The Wolbachia endosymbiont as an anti-filarial nematode target. Symbiosis 2010;51:55–65.

[12] Johnson TP, Tyagi R, Lee PR, Lee MH, Johnson KR, Kowalak J, et al. Nodding syndrome may be an autoimmune reaction to the parasitic worm Onchocerca volvulus. Sci Transl Med 2017;9:377.

[13] Idro R, Anguzu R, Ogwang R, Akun P, Abbo C, Mwaka AD, et al. Doxycycline for the treatment of nodding syndrome (DONS): the study protocol of a phase II randomized controlled trial. BMC Neurol 2019;19:35.

[14] Burresi M, Kampfrath T, van Oosten D, Prangsma JC, Song BS, Noda S, et al. Magnetic light-matter interactions in a photonic crystal nanocavity. Phys Rev Lett 2010;105:123901.

[15] Centers for Disease Control and Prevention. *Naegleria fowleri* – primary amebic meningoencephalitis – amebic encephalitis, http://www.cdc.gov/parasites/naegleria/general.html; 2016. [Accessed 18 April 2017].

[16] Budge PJ, Lazensky B, Van Zile KW, Elliott KE, Dooyema CA, Visvesvara GS, et al. Primary amebic meningoencephalitis in Florida: a case report and epidemiological review of Florida cases. J Environ Health 2013;75:26–31.

[17] Grace E, Asbill S, Virga K. Naegleria fowleri: pathogenesis, diagnosis, and treatment options. Antimicrob Agents Chemother 2015;59:6677–81.

[18] Hebbar S, Bairy I, Bhaskaranand N, Upadhyaya S, Sarma MS, Shetty AK. Fatal case of *Naegleria fowleri* meningo-encephalitis in an infant: case report. Ann Trop Paediatr 2005;25:223–6.

[19] Berman JJ. Logic and critical thinking in the biomedical sciences, volume I: deductions based upon simple observations. Cambridge, MA: Academic Press; 2020.

[20] Garrison FH. History of medicine. Philadelphia: WB Saunders; 1921.

[21] Braun U. The impacts of the discontinuation of dual nomenclature of pleomorphic fungi: the trivial facts, problems, and strategies. IMA Fungus 2012;3:81–6.

[22] Duncan M. Terminology version control discussion paper: the chocolate teapot. Medical Object Oriented Software Ltd.; 2009. Available from: http://www.mrtablet.demon.co.uk/chocolate_teapot_lite.htm. [Accessed 30 August 2012].

[23] Berman JJ. Data simplification: taming information with open source tools. Waltham, MA: Morgan Kaufmann; 2016.

[24] Madar S, Goldstein I, Rotter V. Did experimental biology die? Lessons from 30 years of p53 research. Cancer Res 2009;69:6378–80.

[25] Zilfou JT, Lowe SW. Tumor suppressive functions of p53. Cold Spring Harb Perspect Biol 2009;00: a001883.

[26] Pang K, Ryan JF, Baxevanis AD, Martindale MQ. Evolution of the TGF-b signaling pathway and its potential role in the ctenophore, *Mnemiopsis leidyi*. PLoS ONE 2011;6(9), e24152.

[27] Cox RM, McGlothlin JW, Bonier F. Evolution endocrinology: hormones as mediators of evolutionary phenomena. Integr Comp Biol 2016;56:121–5.

[28] Grillo M, Casanova J, Averof M. Development: a deep breath for endocrine organ evolution. Curr Biol 2013;24:38–40.

[29] Bonett RM. Analyzing endocrine system conservation and evolution. Gen Comp Endocrinol 2016;234:3–9.

[30] Okabe M, Graham A. The origin of the parathyroid gland. PNAS 2004;101:17716–17,719.

[31] Berman JJ. Tumor taxonomy for the developmental lineage classification of neoplasms. BMC Cancer 2004;4:88.

[32] Berman JJ. Tumor classification: molecular analysis meets Aristotle. BMC Cancer 2004;4:10.

[33] Berman JJ. Modern classification of neoplasms: reconciling differences between morphologic and molecular approaches. BMC Cancer 2005;5:100.

[34] Berman JJ. Neoplasms: principles of development and diversity. Sudbury: Jones & Bartlett; 2009.

[35] Suter CM, Martin DI, Ward RL. Germline epimutation of MLH1 in individuals with multiple cancers. Nat Genet 2004;36:497–501.

[36] Houlston RS, Collins A, Slack J, Morton NE. Dominant genes for colorectal cancer are not rare. Hum Genet 1992;56:99–103.

[37] Whiffin N, Houlston RS. Architecture of inherited susceptibility to colorectal cancer: a voyage of discovery. Genes (Basel) 2014;5:270–84.

[38] Jovanovic I, Stefanovic N, Antic S, Ugrenovic S, Djindjic B, Vidovic N. Morphological and morphometric characteristics of choroid plexus psammoma bodies during the human aging. Ital J Anat Embryol 2004;109:19–33.

[39] Rifai Z, Welle S, Kamp C, Thornton CA. Ragged red fibers in normal aging and inflammatory myopathy. Ann Neurol 1995;37:24–9.

[40] Loiseau H, Marchal C, Vital A, Vital C, Rougier A, Loiseau P. Polysaccharide bodies: an unusual finding in a case of temporal epilepsy. Review of the literature. Rev Neurol (Paris) 1993;149:192–7.

[41] Chevessier F, Marty I, Paturneau-Jouas M, Hantai D, Verdiere-Sahuque M. Tubular aggregates are from whole sarcoplasmic reticulum origin: alterations in calcium binding protein expression in mouse skeletal muscle during aging. Neuromuscul Disord 2004;14:208–16.

[42] Boland CR. Clinical uses of microsatellite instability testing in colorectal cancer: an ongoing challenge. J Clin Oncol 2007;25:754–6.

[43] Gambetti P, Cali I, Notari S, Kong Q, Zou WQ, Surewicz WK. Molecular biology and pathology of prion strains in sporadic human prion diseases. Acta Neuropathol 2011;121:79–90.

[44] Hill AF, Joiner S, Wadsworth JD, Sidle KC, Bell JE, Budka H, et al. Molecular classification of sporadic Creutzfeldt-Jakob disease. Brain 2003;126:1333–46.

[45] Doerschuk CM. Pulmonary alveolar proteinosis—is host defense awry? N Engl J Med 2007;356: 547–9.

[46] Croxen R, Vincent A, Newsom-Davis J, Beeson D. Myasthenia gravis in a woman with congenital AChR deficiency due to epsilon-subunit mutations. Neurology 2002;58:1563–5.

[47] Ku NO, Wright TL, Terrault NA, Gish R, Omary MB. Mutation of human keratin 18 in association with cryptogenic cirrhosis. J Clin Invest 1997;99:19–23.

[48] Berman J. Precision medicine, and the reinvention of human disease. Cambridge, MA: Academic Press; 2018.

[49] Verpy E, Biasotto M, Brai M, Misiano G, Meo T, Tosi M. Exhaustive mutation scanning by fluorescence-assisted mismatch analysis discloses new genotype–phenotype correlations in angiodema. Am J Hum Genet 1996;59:308–19.

[50] Dobzhansky T. Genetics of the evolutionary process. New York: Columbia University Press; 1970.

[51] Solomon BD, Muenke M. When to suspect a genetic syndrome. Am Fam Physician 2012;86:826–33.

[52] Guarro J, Gene J, Stchigel AM. Developments in fungal taxonomy. Clin Microbiol Rev 1999;12:454–500.

[53] Scamardella JM. Not plants or animals: a brief history of the origin of Kingdoms Protozoa, Protista and Protoctista. Int Microbiol 1999;2:207–16.

[54] Schlegel M, Hulsmann N. Protists: a textbook example for a paraphyletic taxon. Org Divers Evol 2007;7:166–72.

[55] Antonioli DA. Gastrointestinal autonomic nerve tumors. Expanding the spectrum of gastrointestinal stromal tumors. Arch Pathol Lab Med 1989;113:831–8333.

[56] Berman J, O'Leary TJ. Gastrointestinal stromal tumor workshop. Hum Pathol 2001;32(6):578–82.

[57] Burger H, den Bakker MA, Kros JM, van Tol H, de Bruin AM, Oosterhuis W, et al. Activating mutations in c-KIT and PDGFRalpha are exclusively found in gastrointestinal stromal tumors and not in other tumors overexpressing these imatinib mesylate target genes. Cancer Biol Ther 2005;4:1270–4.

[58] Fletcher CD, Berman JJ, Corless C, Gorstein F, Lasota J, Longley BJ, et al. Diagnosis of gastrointestinal stromal tumors: a consensus approach. Int J Surg Pathol 2002;10:81–9.

[59] O'leary T, Berman JJ. Gastrointestinal stromal tumors: answers and questions. Hum Pathol 2002;33:456–8.

[60] Stolley PD. When genius errs: RA Fisher and the lung cancer controversy. Am J Epidemiol 1991;133:416–25.

[61] Fernandez-Armesto F. 1492: the year our world began. New York, NY: Bloomsbury Publishing; 2009.

[62] Mann CC. 1493: uncovering the new world Columbus created. New York: Knopf; 2011.

[63] Mann CC. 1491: new revelations of the Americas before Columbus. New York, NY: Vintage; 2006.

[64] Baldauf SL. An overview of the phylogeny and diversity of eukaryotes. J Syst Evol 2008;46:263–73.

[65] da Rocha-Azevedo B, Tanowitz HB, Marciano-Cabral F. Diagnosis of infections caused by pathogenic free-living amoebae. Interdiscip Perspect Infect Dis 2009;2009:251406.

[66] Marciano-Cabral F, Cabral G. Acanthamoeba spp. as agents of disease in humans. Clin Microbiol Rev 2003;2003:273–307.

[67] Anon. A review of the FBI's handling of the Brandon Mayfield case. U. S. Department of Justice, Office of the Inspector General, Oversight and Review Division; March 2006.

[68] Lleo A, Invernizzi P, Gao B, Podda M, Gershwin ME. Definition of human autoimmunity—autoantibodies versus autoimmune disease. Autoimmun Rev 2010;9:A259–66.

[69] Lapiere JC, Woodley DT, Parente MG, Iwasaki T, Wynn KC, Christiano AM, et al. Epitope mapping of type VII collagen. Identification of discrete peptide sequences recognized by sera from patients with acquired epidermolysis bullosa. J Clin Invest 1993;92:1831–9.

[70] Domloge-Hultsch N, Gammon WR, Briggaman RA, Gil SG, Carter WG, Yancey KB. Epiligrin, the major human keratinocyte integrin ligand, is a target in both an acquired autoimmune and an inherited subepidermal blistering skin disease. J Clin Invest 1992;90:1628–33.

[71] Sakurai Y, Takeda T. Acquired hemophilia A: a frequently overlooked autoimmune hemorrhagic disorder. J Immunol Res 2014;2014:320674.

[72] Salomon O, Zivelin A, Livnat T, Dardik R, Loewenthal R, Avishai O, et al. Prevalence, causes, and characterization of factor XI inhibitors in patients with inherited factor XI deficiency. Blood 2003;101:4783–8.

[73] Lorand L, Velasco PT, Rinne JR, Amare M, Miller LK, Zucker ML. Autoimmune antibody (IgG Kansas) against the fibrin stabilizing factor (factor XIII) system. Proc Natl Acad Sci U S A 1988;85:232–6.

[74] Velasquez-Manoff M. When the body attacks the mind. Atlantic 2016. July/August.

[75] Li Y, Song YH, Rais N, Connor E, Schatz D, et al. Autoantibodies to the extracellular domain of the calcium sensing receptor in patients with acquired hypoparathyroidism. J Clin Invest 1996;97:910–4.

[76] Pallais JC, Kifor O, Chen YB, Slovik D, Brown EM. Acquired hypocalciuric hypercalcemia due to autoantibodies against the calcium-sensing receptor. N Engl J Med 2004;351:362–9.

[77] Dahlback B. Advances in understanding pathogenic mechanisms of thrombophilic disorders. Blood 2008;112:19–27.

[78] Mitchell CA, Rowell JA, Hau L, Young JP, Salem HH. A fatal thrombotic disorder associated with an acquired inhibitor of protein C. N Engl J Med 1987;317:1638–42.

[79] Tsuji T, Imajo Y, Sawabe M, Kuniyuki S, Ishii M, Hamada T, et al. Acquired cutis laxa concomitant with nephrotic syndrome. Arch Dermatol 1987;123:1211–6.

[80] Frigas E. Angioedema with acquired deficiency of the C1 inhibitor: a constellation of syndromes. Mayo Clin Proc 1989;64:1269–75.

[81] Winqvist O, Karlsson FA, Kampe O. 21-Hydroxylase, a major autoantigen in idiopathic Addison's disease. Lancet 1992;339:1559–62.

[82] Larrick JW, Hyman ES. Acquired iron-deficiency anemia caused by an antibody against the transferrin receptor. N Engl J Med 1984;311:214–8.

[83] Stricker RB, Wong D, Saks SR, Corash L, Shuman MA. Acquired Bernard-Soulier syndrome. Evidence for the role of a 210,000-molecular weight protein in the interaction of platelets with von Willebrand factor. J Clin Invest 1985;76:1274–8.

[84] Bleiberg J, Wallen M, Brodkin R, Applebaum I. Industrially acquired porphyria. Arch Dermatol 1964;89:793–7.

[85] Cam C, Nigogosyan G. Acquired toxic porphyria cutanea tarda due to hexachlorobenzene. JAMA 1963;183:88–91.

[86] Clarkson K, Rosenfeld B, Fair J, Klein A, Bell W. Factor XI deficiency acquired by liver transplantation. Ann Intern Med 1991;115:877–9.

[87] Fishbein WN. Myoadenylate deaminase deficiency: inherited and acquired forms. Biochem Med 1985;33:158–69.

[88] Furie B, Greene E, Furie BC. Syndrome of acquired factor X deficiency and systemic amyloidosis in vivo studies of the metabolic fate of factor X. N Engl J Med 1977;297:81–5.

[89] Janka G, zur Stadt U. Familial and acquired hemophagocytic lymphohistiocytosis. Hematology Am Soc Hematol Educ Program 2005;2005:82–8.

[90] Juneja SK, Matthews JP, Luzinat R, Fan Y, Michael M, Rischin D, et al. Association of acquired Pelger-Huet anomaly with taxoid therapy. Br J Haematol 1996;93:139–41.

[91] Maran J, Guan Y, Ou CN, Prchal JT. Heterogeneity of the molecular biology of methemoglobinemia: a study of eight consecutive patients. Haematologica 2005;90:687–9.

[92] Walsh T, Casadei S, Coats KH, Swisher E, Stray SM, Higgins J, et al. Spectrum of mutations in BRCA1, BRCA2, CHEK2, and TP53 in families at high risk of breast cancer. JAMA 2006;295:1379–88.

[93] D'Andrea AD. Susceptibility pathways in Fanconi's anemia and breast cancer. N Engl J Med 2010;362 (20):1909–19.

[94] Stecklein SR, Jensen RA. Identifying and exploiting defects in the Fanconi anemia/BRCA pathway in oncology. Transl Res 2012;160:178–97.

[95] Silva AG, Ewald IP, Sapienza M, Pinheiro M, Peixoto A, de Nóbrega AF, et al. Li-Fraumeni-like syndrome associated with a large BRCA1 intragenic deletion. BMC Cancer 2012;12:237.

[96] Joensuu H, Klemi PJ. DNA aneuploidy in adenomas of endocrine organs. Am J Pathol 1988;132:145–51.

[97] Berman JJ. Automatic extraction of candidate nomenclature terms using the doublet method. BMC Med Inform Decis Mak 2005;5:35.

[98] Berman JJ. Doublet method for very fast autocoding. BMC Med Inform Decis Mak 2004;4:16.

[99] Berman JJ. Nomenclature-based data retrieval without prior annotation: facilitating biomedical data integration with fast doublet matching. In Silico Biol 2005;5:0029.

[100] Berman JJ. Ruby programming for medicine and biology. Sudbury, MA: Jones and Bartlett; 2008.

[101] Yoon CK. Reviving the lost art of naming the world. N Y Times 2016. August 2.

[102] Amin OM. Seasonal prevalence of intestinal parasites in the United States during 2000. Am J Trop Med Hyg 2002;66:799–803.

[103] Boorom KF, Smith H, Nimri L, Viscogliosi E, Spanakos G, Parkar U, et al. Oh my aching gut: irritable bowel syndrome, blastocystis, and asymptomatic infection. Parasit Vectors 2008;1:40.

[104] Stensvold CR, Suresh GK, Tan KS, Thompson RC, Traub RJ, Viscogliosi E, et al. Terminology for blastocystis subtypes: a consensus. Trends Parasitol 2007;23:93–6.

[105] Schlager E, Ashack K, Khachemoune A. Erosio interdigitalis blastomycetica: a review of interdigital candidiasis. Dermatol Online J 2018;24:1.

[106] Ugarte H. A more pragmatic Web 3.0: linked blockchain data; 2017. https://doi.org/10.13140/RG.2.2.10304.12807/1. Available from: https://www.researchgate.net/publication/315619465_A_more_pragmatic_Web_30_Linked_Blockchain_Data. [Accessed 27 October 2017].

[107] Anon. Blockchains: the great chain of being sure about things. The Economist; 2015. Available from: https://www.economist.com/news/briefing/21677228-technology-behind-bitcoin-lets-people-who-do-not-know-or-trust-each-other-build-dependable. [Accessed 27 October 2017].

[108] Bogler O, Cavenee WK. Methylation and genomic damage in gliomas. In: Zhang W, Fuller GN, editors. Genomic and molecular neuro-oncology. Sudbury, MA: Jones and Bartlett; 2004. p. 3–16.

[109] Lancaster AK, Masel J. The evolution of reversible switches in the presence of irreversible mimics. Evolution 2009;63:2350–62.

[110] Berman JJ. Armchair science: no experiments, just deduction. Kindle ed. Amazon Digital Services, Inc.; 2014.

[111] Berman JJ. Rare diseases and orphan drugs: keys to understanding and treating common diseases. Cambridge, MD: Academic Press; 2014.

[112] Mable BK, Otto SP. The evolution of life cycles with haploid and diploid phases. BioEssays 1998;20:453–62.

[113] Wallis E, Lavell C. Naming the indexer: where credit is due. Indexer 1995;19:266–8.

[114] Berman JJ. Principles of big data: preparing, sharing, and analyzing complex information. Waltham, MA: Morgan Kaufmann; 2013.

[115] Mallon T. The best part of every book comes last. N Y Times 1991. March 10.

[116] Shah NH, Jonquet C, Chiang AP, Butte AJ, Chen R, Musen MA. Ontology-driven indexing of public datasets for translational bioinformatics. BMC Bioinform 2009;10:S1.

[117] Lamb J. Embedded indexing. Indexer 2005;24:206–9.

[118] Downey AB. Think DSP: digital signal processing in Python, version 0.9.8. Needham, MA: Green Tea Press; 2014.

[119] Goldberg R. Horses' ability to pace is written in DNA. N Y Times 2012. September 11.

[120] Faldum A, Pommerening K. An optimal code for patient identifiers. Comput Methods Prog Biomed 2005;79:81–8.

[121] Rivest R. Request for comments: 1321. The MD5 message-digest algorithm. Network Working Group; 2015. https://www.ietf.org/rfc/rfc1321.txt. [Accessed 1 January 2015].

[122] Bouzelat H, Quantin C, Dusserre L. Extraction and anonymity protocol of medical file. Proc AMIA Annu Fall Symp 1996;1996:323–7.

[123] Quantin CH, Bouzelat FA, Allaert AM, Benhamiche J, Faivre J, Dusserre L. Automatic record hash coding and linkage for epidemiological followup data confidentiality. Methods Inf Med 1998;37:271–7.

[124] Berman JJ. Threshold protocol for the exchange of confidential medical data. BMC Med Res Methodol 2002;2:12.

[125] Berman JJ. Methods in medical informatics: fundamentals of healthcare programming in Perl, Python, and Ruby. Boca Raton: Chapman and Hall; 2010.

[126] Berman JJ. Principles and practice of big data: preparing, sharing, and analyzing complex information. 2nd ed. Waltham, MA: Morgan Kaufmann; 2018.

[127] Berman JJ. Perl programming for medicine and biology. Sudbury, MA: Jones and Bartlett; 2007.

[128] Ng SB, Buckingham KJ, Lee C, Bigham AW, Tabor HK, Dent KM, et al. Exome sequencing identifies the cause of a mendelian disorder. Nat Genet 2010;42:30–5.

[129] Piano MR. Alcoholic cardiomyopathy: incidence, clinical characteristics, and pathophysiology. Chest 2002;121:1638–50.

[130] Zhu H-L, Meng S-R, Fan J-B, Chen J, Liang Y. Fibrillization of human tau is accelerated by exposure to lead via interaction with His-330 and His-362. PLoS ONE 2011;6, e25020.

[131] Wang E, Boswell E, Siddiqi I, Lu CM, Sebastian S, Rehder C, et al. Pseudo-Pelger-Huet anomaly induced by medications: a clinicopathologic study in comparison with myelodysplastic syndrome-related pseudo-Pelger-Hu t anomaly. Am J Clin Pathol 2011;135:291–303.

[132] Schule B, Oviedo A, Johnston K, Pai S, Francke U. Inactivating mutations in ESCO2 cause SC phocomelia and Roberts syndrome: no phenotype–genotype correlation. Am J Hum Genet 2005;77:1117–28.

[133] Franco B, Meroni G, Parenti G, Levilliers J, Bernard L, Gebbia M, et al. A cluster of sulfatase genes on Xp22.3: mutations in chondrodysplasia punctata (CDPX) and implications for warfarin embryopathy. Cell 1995;81:1–20.

[134] Van Gaalen J, Kerstens FG, Maas RP, Harmark L, van de Warrenburg BP. Drug-induced cerebellar ataxia: a systematic review. CNS Drugs 2014;28:1139–53.

[135] Rossi M, Perez-Lloret S, Doldan L, Cerquetti D, Balej J, Millar Vernetti P, et al. Autosomal dominant cerebellar ataxias: a systematic review of clinical features. Eur J Neurol 2014;21:607–15.

[136] Penneys NS. Ochronosislike pigmentation from hydroquinone bleaching creams. Arch Dermatol 1985;121:1239–40.

[137] Langston JW, Ballard P, Tetrud JW, Irwin I. Chronic parkinsonism in humans due to a product of meperidine-analog synthesis. Science 1983;219:979–80.

[138] Priyadarshi A, Khuder SA, Schaub EA, Shrivastava S. A meta-analysis of Parkinson's disease and exposure to pesticides. Neurotoxicology 2000;21:435–40.

[139] Zimprich A, Biskup S, Leitner P, Lichtner P, Farrer M, Lincoln S, et al. Mutations in LRRK2 cause autosomal-dominant parkinsonism with pleomorphic pathology. Neuron 2004;44:601–7.

[140] Du L, Sullivan CC, Chu D, Cho AJ, Kido M, Wolf PL, et al. Signaling molecules in nonfamilial pulmonary hypertension. N Engl J Med 2003;348:500–9.

[141] Berman JJ. Precancer: the beginning and the end of cancer. Sudbury: Jones and Bartlett; 2010.

[142] Jenner RA, Littlewood TJ. Problematica old and new. Philos Trans R Soc B 2008;363:1503–12.

[143] Fisher RA. The correlation between relatives on the supposition of Mendelian inheritance. Trans R Soc Edinb 1918;52:399–433.

[144] Ward LD, Kellis M. Interpreting noncoding genetic variation in complex traits and human disease. Nat Biotechnol 2012;30:1095–106.

[145] Visscher PM, McEvoy B, Yang J. From Galton to GWAS: quantitative genetics of human height. Genet Res 2010;92:371–9.

[146] Zhang G, Karns R, Sun G, Indugula SR, Cheng H, Havas-Augustin D, et al. Finding missing heritability in less significant Loci and allelic heterogeneity: genetic variation in human height. PLoS One 2012;7, e51211.

[147] Rare diseases act of 2002. Public Law 107-280. 107th U.S. Congress. 6 November; 2002.

[148] DeQueiroz K. Species concepts and species delimitation. Syst Biol 2007;56:879–86.

[149] DeQueiroz K. Ernst Mayr and the modern concept of species. PNAS 2005;102(Suppl 1):6600–7.

[150] Mayden RL. Consilience and a hierarchy of species concepts: advances toward closure on the species puzzle. J Nematol 1999;31:95–116.

[151] Raup DM. A kill curve for Phanerozoic marine species. Paleobiology 1991;17:37–48.

[152] Sakr WA, Haas GP, Cassin BF, Pontes JE, Crissman JD. The frequency of carcinoma and intraepithelial neoplasia of the prostate in young males. J Urol 1993;150:379–85.

[153] Guileyardo JM, Johnson WD, Welsh RA, Akazaki K, Correa P. Prevalence of latent prostate carcinoma in two U.S. populations. J Natl Cancer Inst 1980;65:311–6.

[154] Schwichtenberg J. Physics from symmetry. 2nd ed. Switzerland: Springer International Publishing; 2018.

[155] Bennett BC, Balick MJ. Does the name really matter? The importance of botanical nomenclature and plant taxonomy in biomedical research. J Ethnopharmacol 2014;152:387–92.

[156] Simpson GG. The principles of classification and a classification of mammals. Bull Am Mus Nat Hist 1945;85:1–350.

[157] Klyne G, Newman C. Date and time on the internet: timestamps. Network Working Group; 2002. Request for Comments RFC:3339, available from: http://tools.ietf.org/html/rfc3339. [Accessed 15 September 2015].

2

Classification logic

Chapter outline

> *But, once I bent to taste an upland spring.*
> *And, bending, heard it whisper of its Sea.*
> **Ecclesiastes**

Section 2.1. Classifications defined

Classification is a hierarchical collection of classes that are related to one another. The hierarchy of classes is established by subclassing. Any class may have a subclass. Inversely, any class, except for the class at the very top of the hierarchy, must have a superclass (i.e., a class to which it is a subclass).

1. Each class of the hierarchy has a set of properties or rules that extend to every member of the class and all of the subclasses of the class, to the exclusion of unrelated classes. A subclass is itself a type of class wherein the members have the defining class properties of the parent class plus some additional property(ies) specific for the subclass.
2. In a hierarchical classification, each subclass may have no more than one parent class, whereas a class may have any number of subclasses. The root (top) class has no parent class.
3. A class instance is a member of a class. For example, your copy of this book is an instance of the class of objects known as "books."
4. Every instance belongs to exactly one class.
5. Instances and classes do not change their positions in the classification (e.g., a horse cannot become a sheep and a subclass of mammals cannot become a subclass of insects).

6. The members of classes may be highly similar to one another, but their similarities result from their membership in the same class (i.e., conforming to class properties), and not the other way around (i.e., similarity alone cannot define class inclusion).

It may come as a surprise, but the word "classification" has many different definitions. We will show that if we adhere closely to our provided definition, we can easily build robust computer models of our classifications, that will link to external data structures. We should admit, from the start, that ideal classifications are seldom encountered. There are examples of highly regarded classifications wherein the curators cannot assign a particular instance to a particular class with absolute certainty. There are also examples wherein an instance of a class can change its assignment from one class to another under a restrictive set of circumstances (e.g., transmutation of elements). There are also exceptions wherein subclasses may seem to have more than one legitimate parent class (e.g., hybrid species) and in which instances may be included in more than one class (e.g., Lie groups within Sporadic groups). We will see in "Chapter 8. Classifying the Universe," that even the most fundamental properties of classes, such as the law of conservation of energy, may have been violated during the "big bang" when our universe was seemingly created from nothing. These exceptions, all of which detract from the concept of an idealized classification, are generally tolerated, even in the most trusted classifications [1]. Curators understand that perfection in classification is something that is always pursued but seldom attained. [Glossary Curator]

Purposes of classifications

Classifications fulfill a variety of purposes, some of which are unique to classifications and not provided by any other data structures. A good classification does the following:

1. Defines objects and clarifies the relationships among classes of objects

Classification builders are constantly searching for the essence of a class; the key feature that is found in every member of the class, and that is absent from any object that is not a member of the class. For the classifications of the natural world, these class relationships mold our vision of reality.

2. Generalizes the properties of classes through inheritance

Every member of a class is also a member of its parent class and inherits the defining feature(s) of the parent class. Inheritance passes through all of the generations of a class so that the great-grandchild of a class has the defining features of its great-grandparent class and its grandparent class, its parent class, and its own class. Hence the properties of a class are generalized to all its descendant classes.

The importance of generalization cannot be overstated. The overriding purpose of science is to develop observations made on instances into generalizations that apply to classes. When, as legend has it, an apple fell on Newton's head, inspiring his work in gravitation, he was certainly not trying to find a mathematical expression that would apply exclusively to apples. The great scientist that he was, he immediately moved from the particular to the general. Likewise, when Darwin devoted 8 years of his life to the study of barnacles, he was considering how his observations on barnacles might extend to all classes of organisms. The process of finding general class relationships marks the difference between collecting facts and pursuing science. [Glossary Nongeneralizable predictor]

3. As a device for developing questions and hypotheses

In the natural sciences, the most important questions are always the most fundamental questions (e.g., "What is matter?," "What is energy?," "What is time?," "What am I?"). Because classifications embody the fundamental nature of reality, we can imagine why classifications might help us understand our world. We shall see, in later chapters of this book, that many of the most important advances in science have involved finding the relationships among seemingly unrelated classes of objects (e.g., forces, particles, atoms, compounds, organisms).

4. Determines what cannot exist within the classification

Classifications are complete, meaning that every legitimate member of the classification must have a place in one of its classes. Accordingly, if an object cannot fit into an assigned class, then it cannot belong to the domain of the classification. The condition of completeness seems somewhat trite, but we shall soon see (in "Section 2.3. The gift of completeness" of this chapter) that the property of completeness is one of the most powerful features of classifications.

5. Simplifies the knowledge domain

Order and simplification are the first steps toward the mastery of a subject.
Thomas Mann

Classifications drive down the complexity of their data domain, because every instance in the domain is assigned to a single class, and every class is related to the other classes through a simple hierarchy. By creating the classification of organisms, we eliminate the burden of specifying the relationships among instances (i.e., individual organisms). If oak belongs to Class Angiosperm, and birch belongs to class Angiosperm, then oak and birch are related by class. Likewise, if Class Angiosperm descends from class Plantae, then oak and birch both descend from Class Plantae. This tells us that oak and birch both enjoy all of the class properties of Class Angiosperm and Class Plantae. No matter how many objects are included in a classification, the hierarchical structure of classes can be absorbed and understood by the human mind. Life is great!

Let's consider the biomedical student who is struggling with the field of medical microbiology. There are well over 1400 well-studied species of infectious organisms, each being described in huge collections of literature. How can any single scholar manage to master the field of clinical microbiology? A survey of the Classification of Life informs us that all 1400 infectious organisms fall into a tractable set of 40 general classes.

When you learn the defining features of the 40 classes in which the clinically relevant organisms reside, you attain a general knowledge of the biological features of the included organisms and their relationships to other organisms. External sources of information, such as current textbooks and treatment guidelines, can be applied to specific infections, as needed.

What applies to the Classification of Life will apply to chemists using the Periodic Table of the Elements. The properties of elements; how they will bond to other elements to form chemical compounds; and how those resulting compounds may behave are all predictable, to some degree, by those who take a serious look at the Periodic Table.

6. Helps us understand the nature of the domain encompassed by the classification.

A completed classification permits us to see the totality of relationships among all the classes in its domain. Because science is fundamentally an examination of the relationships among class objects, a classification provides the structure in which everything within a domain can be understood. [Glossary Science]

7. Last and least, classifications help us to find objects included in classes

With the help of modern computers, we can write software programs that can quickly navigate through any classification to find a class and any or all of its members. By classifying every object as a member of a class, within a classification, we create an efficient data structure whereby we can find related objects instantly, regardless of the size of the classification. Because we have become adept at using classifications for search and retrieval, we sometimes lose sight of the other purposes of classification (i.e., points 1–6), devoting our attention to what we seem to do best. We will be mentioning some of the basic search and retrieval algorithms in later chapters and will include short software scripts as glossary entries. [Glossary Classification, Script]

Predetermination in natural classifications

The story is told of the military General who consulted his priest on the morning of the battle. The General asked, "Father, could you please pray that God will choose to be on my side in this battle?" The priest sighed and answered, "Sorry, no. But I will certainly pray that you choose to be on God's side."

The difference between the points of view of the military General and the priest is subtle but important. The General believed that God needed to be persuaded, by the priest, to side with the General's forces. The priest believed that the world has a particular nature and that it is the job of humans to discern God's design.

Some classification builders believe, quite wrongly, that it is their job to design a classification to suit their own needs or the needs of some particular community. In the case of the so-called natural classifications (i.e., the classifications that describe the order of the existing world), this approach is nonsensical. **Because the relationships among natural entities are predetermined, we can infer that a classification of natural entities is also predetermined. Hence, the job of the classification builder is to discover the natural order of things, not to invent them.**

When we look at the natural classifications, we see that the efforts of scientists have always led to a form that converges to our best understanding of how the natural world operates. In the case of the Classification of Life, the most recent analyses of genetic data have, for the most part, confirmed long-held perceptions of the evolution of new species, from previously existing ancestral species. Modern biologists are constantly adjusting the Classification of Life, following new information. When doing so, classes of organisms are never created to achieve any particular purpose, other than correctly reflecting nature (Fig. 2.1).

The Periodic Table of the Elements has been modified in many different ways, but the fundamental periodicity is a constant feature of our atomic universe, and it is unlikely that the representation of this reality, in the Periodic Table, will ever change.

The Classification of Finite Simple Groups has been proven, mathematically, to be complete (to be discussed in "Section 8.4. The Classification Theorem"). This means that the listed members of the finite simple groups are well-defined and that the classification will never expand. Being an abstract product of the human mind, can we assert that the Classification of Finite Simple Groups constitutes a representation of a predetermined natural world? Let's say yes. The Classification of Finite Simple Groups is unalterable and would hold equally well in any universe.

The situation is somewhat different for man-made objects, but our so-called man-made objects are composed of natural objects that obey the physical laws of nature. We will be discussing the ways of dealing with a variety of objects that do not easily fit into the classification paradigm, when we reach Chapter 4, "Section 4.3 Linking classifications, ontologies, and triplestores."

Features of great classifications

There are many classifications available to scientists, but three of these classifications seem to stand out from all the others: The Classification of Life, The Periodic Table of the Elements, and the Classification Theorem of the Finite Simple Groups. The reason that these classifications are important is that they cover the territory of the natural world: particles, chemicals, living organisms, and the physical laws that form the basis of the universe's operating system. Most other classifications (such as the classification of stars, classification of crystals, classification of diseases) depend in whole or in part on the afore-mentioned canons.

Here are some of the features that characterize the great classifications of nature:

1. The great classifications are typically brief

Unadorned classifications are simple schematics, listing their classes, in their hierarchy. They typically exclude the names of the members of classes. Taxonomies, which often accompany classifications, consist of the names of all of the known class members. A taxonomy is sometimes "poured" into a classification, producing a hierarchical class scaffold in which the names of members are attached to their appropriate class.

The classification of living organisms is a collection of classes that can accommodate every one of the billions of organisms that have ever lived on planet earth. Nonetheless, we

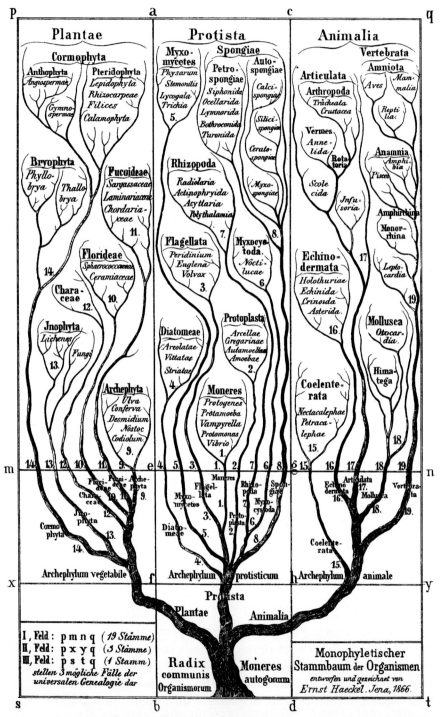

FIG. 2.1 Haeckel's 1866 rendering of the Classification of Living Organisms. *Source: Ernst Haeckel, Generelle Morphologie der Organismen: allgemeine Grundzuge der organischen Formen Wissenschaft, mechanisch begrundet durch die von C. Darwin reformirte Decendenz Theorie. Berlin, 1866.*

can view the major branches of the major classes of organisms in simple graphics. For example, here are all of the subclasses of Bacteria (Fig. 2.2).

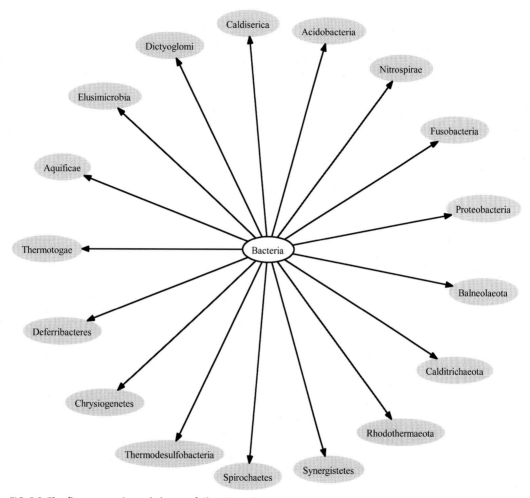

FIG. 2.2 The first-generation subclasses of Class Bacteria.

For any given living organism, its complete ancestral lineage, harking back to the first primordial life form appearing on earth, seldom exceeds more than 20 class levels. For example, the lineage of the octopus, as shown, is traversed up to the level of root cellular organisms, in just 16 ancestral classes.

Octopus
Octopodidae
Incirrata
Octopoda
Octopodiformes
Neocoleoidea
Coleoidea (coleoidea, dibranchiata)

Cephalopoda (cephalopoda, cephalopods, cephalopods)
Mollusca (mollusca, mollusks, mollusks, mollusks)
Lophotrochozoa
Protostomia
Bilateria
Eumetazoa
Metazoa (metazoa, animalia, multicellular animals, metazoans, animals)
Opisthokonta (opisthokonta, fungi/metazoa group)
Eukaryota (eukaryota, eukaryotae, eukaryotes, eucaryotes, eukaryotes)
cellular organisms (cellular organisms, biota)

The Periodic Table of the Elements can fit comfortably on a large index card. Many of us can remember our days as high school students when we kept a copy of the Periodic Table as the top page of our looseleaf notebooks, as a quick and easy reference (Fig. 2.3).

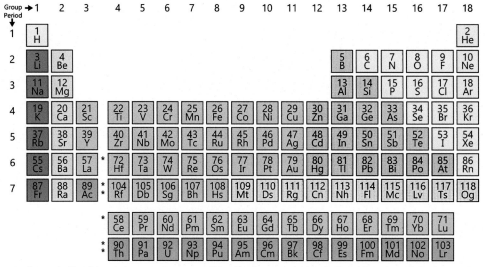

FIG. 2.3 The periodic table of elements. *Source: Wikipedia, from a graphic dedicated to the public domain by its author, Offnfopt.*

The whole of the Classification Theorem of Finite Simple Groups, one of the greatest intellectual achievements of modern mathematics, can be succinctly stated in just a few lines of simple text [2]. The proof of the Classification Theorem of Finite Simple Groups is a dense tract that plods on for well over 5000 pages (Fig. 2.4).

We will be revisiting the Classification Theorem, in "Section 8.3. Fearful symmetry." [Glossary Classification theorems]

2. The great classifications can be utilized in many different ways

A recurring theme that you will encounter throughout this book is that classifications do not have any particular objective, other than correctly expressing the preexisting

Classification Theorem

"Every finite simple group is either cyclic, or alternating, or it belongs to a broad infinite class called the groups of Lie type, or else it is one of twenty-six or twenty-seven exceptions, called sporadic."

FIG. 2.4 The Classification Theorem, representing the works of hundreds of scientists over dozens of years, and required thousands of pages of formal proof.

relationships among objects. Each user of a classification must invent his or her way of utilizing the classification. For example, the Periodic Table of the Elements can be examined row-by-row, to understand the periodicity of the elements. Or, the Table can be examined column-by-column, to understand the properties associated with a particular valence. Or, the Table can be examined block-by-block to study elements collected by their orbitals. Whichever way we choose to view the Table, we can draw important inferences concerning the nature of particles, atoms, and matter.

Likewise, the Classification of Life can be examined as the story of evolution, or as a chronology of planet earth, or as a study of species migrations, or as the foundation for comparative embryology and anatomy. Finally, the Classification Theorem of Finite Simple Groups can be studied as a map to the symmetry groups that determine the laws of energy, gravity, light, electricity, magnetism, relativity, and much more.

3. The great classifications are predictive

A great classification will teach us something we do not already know. When Mendeleev was developing his version of the Periodic Table of the Elements, in the 1860s, he was working in a crowded field. Lots of others had the same general idea and were developing Tables that looked much like Mendeleev's. The historical difference between Mendeleev and his contemporaries was that Mendeleev envisioned his Table as a tool for prediction. Mendeleev predicted the existence of numerous elements that were not known to exist. Before his death, in 1907, most of those predicted elements were discovered, thus vindicating Mendeleev's approach to classification.

The relationships established through the process of classification may lead us to infer the existence of objects that we cannot observe. Positrons, quarks, electrons, pions, neutrinos, Higgs bosons, fullerenes, genes, the epigenome, and even living organisms (e.g., Xanthopan morganii praedicta) are just some of the things that were predicted to exist (and eventually proven to exist) based on insights gained from the great classifications (Fig. 2.5). [Glossary Xanthopan morganii praedicta]

4. Great classifications are self-correcting

In "Section 2.4. A classification is an evolving hypothesis," we will see that our carefully crafted classes and class relationships are often just intelligent guesses. Hence, all scientific classifications must be tested and retested to determine whether our best

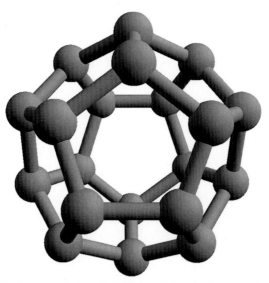

FIG. 2.5 Model of a Carbon-20 fullerene. Carbon, the third most abundant element in the universe, is a molecular acrobat, capable of creating complex bonds with other elements and with itself. Fullerenes, composed of arrangements of carbon atoms, are now known to occur naturally throughout the universe [3]. The bonding properties of carbon, as predicted by carbon's placement in the Periodic Table, led to the prediction of the existence of fullerenes, more than a decade before such molecules were detected. *Source: Wikipedia, and dedicated to the public domain by its author, Perditax.*

guesses hit the mark. It is not at all uncommon to detect small errors in classifications, necessitating re-assignments of class members. Sometimes a discovered error is so profound as to invalidate the classification, compelling scientists to come up with a new classification. In such cases, the fundamental errors of the original classification will likely dictate the structure of its replacement. The improved classification that emerges may not have been created without the assistance of the original, discredited classification. In the field of classification, even wrong guesses have great value.

5. Great classifications dissolve the artificial barriers between branches of science

Fundamental objects are interconnected. A living organism is composed of nonliving chemicals, and nonliving chemicals are composed of elemental atoms, and elemental atoms are composed of particles that operate under a few universal laws. Classifications built for different knowledge domains must ultimately connect, and the properties of connecting classes provide us with insight into the workings of complex systems.

When we combine all of the classifications of the natural sciences, we have a structure in place that will help us understand nothing less than the totality of the universe. In the final three chapters of this book, we will discuss the well-established significance of the three great classifications of the natural sciences (i.e., the Classification of Life, the Periodic Table of the Elements, and the classification of symmetry groups as exemplified by the Classification Theorem of Finite Simple Groups).

Section 2.2. The gift of inheritance

Inheritance is received from the ancestors of a class and inheritance extends through the descendants of a class. This means that if we humans are placental mammals (and we are), then we inherit all of the defining features of the Class Eutheria (the placental mammals). We humans all have hair, and we are all nourished during our gestations by a well-formed placenta. Going back further, Class Eutheria descended from Class Eukaryota, the cells that have a nucleus. Because Class Eutheria descended from Class Eukaryota, and because we humans have descended from Class Eutheria, then we can be certain that we, as humans, are composed of cells that have nuclei. At this point, you may feel obliged to notice that not all cells of the human body have nuclei. For example, red blood cells are anucleate (i.e., lack a nucleus), and they represent a large percentage of all the cells in our bodies [4]. No bother. We know that every enucleated red blood cell developed from a fully nucleated red cell precursor. [Glossary Anucleate cells]

A point of some confusion that crops up whenever inheritance is discussed is the notion that every child class is fundamentally different from its parent class. Therefore, we might think, the subclass inherits some of the features of the parent class; but not all of them. If this were not so, then there would be no difference between the child class and the parent class. This line of reasoning is incorrect. **In a classification, subclasses are not simply derivatives of their ancestral classes; subclasses are bona fide members of every ancestral class in their lineage**.

Let's think a bit about the Classification of Life. We, as humans, are members of every class of organisms in our ancestral lineage. For example, we are true eukaryotes; the reason being that the gametes in every organism represent the progeny of the gametes in the animal's ancestry. For a start, the gametes in our bodies are the cells produced by the fusion of two parental gametes. This process can be followed iteratively up through the chain of ancestors within a species, and up through the gametes of the parent species, and on and on, until reaching the single-cell eukaryotes, organisms that are, for all practical purposes, "all gamete." This explains why we have hundreds of the same core genes found in eukaryotic organisms, and why we are dues-paying members of Class Eukaryota, and Class Deuterostomia, and Class Craniata, and Class Eutheria, and every class in-between. Hence, we are eukaryotes, and we are deuterostomes, and we are craniates, and so on. The assertion that humans are eukaryotes must not be interpreted as dramatic hyperbole. We humans, are members of all our ancestral classes and we inherit all of the class methods and properties of every ancestral class in our lineage.

Here is a simple schematic indicating a few class relationships for numbers (Fig. 2.6).

We see that Class Numeric is a subclass of the Class Object, a root class. This tells us that Class Numeric is an object and inherits all of Class methods of Class Object. Likewise, Class Integer and Class Float are both subclasses of Class Numeric. This tells us that both Class Integer and Class Float inherit all of the class methods and class properties of Class Numeric and Class Object. At the bottom of the schematic, we see that Class Fixnum would inherit all of the class properties of Class Integer, Class Numeric, and Class Object; but would not inherit the class methods and properties of Class Float.

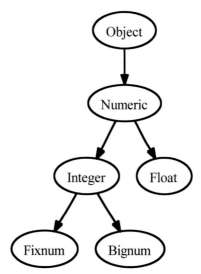

FIG. 2.6 Inheritance revealed in a schematic of classification for numeric objects.

Throughout this discussion, we have been referring to class methods and class properties. Are there methods and properties other than class methods and class properties? Yes! Within a class, there may be methods that are available to all the members of a class that are not in any way defining for the class. Such nonclass methods and properties may be present in classes outside the ancestral lineage of the class, and they may be absent within the ancestral lineage of the class. In addition, there may be methods and properties that are available to particular instances of a class, but which are not available to every instance of the class. That being the case, how do we learn which methods are available to the individual items in the classification? [Glossary Class method, Class property]

Nowadays, class properties and methods are recorded and organized in a schema, a topic that we will explore in "Section 3.4. Semantic languages." We will also see, in "Section 5.5. Listening to what objects tell us," that object-oriented programming languages allow us to instantly determine all of the inheritances of any object in any class. In that same section, we will see how computer scientists use this information to draw inferences about the classifications and their contained objects.

Section 2.3. The gift of completeness

> *It is difficult to find a black cat in a dark room, especially if there is no cat.*
>
> *Chinese proverb*

All classifications are complete. This means that there exists a class for any and every object member of the classification. When a zoologist encounters a newly discovered species of animal, she can be certain that this novel species can be assigned to a preexisting class of animals. If no such class exists, then the classification is incomplete; hence, invalid. Taxonomists must then revise the classification if they hope to validate its structure.

Completeness seems, at first blush, like a rather modest feature of a classification. It is easy to assume that any classification can be modified to accept new member objects; but no. The condition of completeness locks in the realms of our reality and dictates the allowable states of existence of class members. Violations of completeness are violations of the operating principles of our universe.

Let's take a look at some of the scientific advances that have been made, based on our understanding of the completeness of the classifications used by biologists, chemists, and physicists.

Completeness of crystal symmetries and the atomic nature of matter

It may seem difficult to believe, but the atomic theory of matter was unproven until just after the first decade of the 20th century. Until then, some of the greatest advances in the field of physics and chemistry were performed speculatively, on the expectation that atoms were real.

In the 19th century, one of the best arguments, short of proof, for the existence of atoms came when the classification of crystal symmetries was made complete. By empiric observation of crystals, it seemed that regardless of the shape of the gross crystal structure, the interfacial angles were restricted to a relatively small group of observable configurations. Scientists at the time suggested that all crystals were built from repetitions of certain types of fundamental shapes (the so-called unit cells). Applying their knowledge of group theory, mathematicians predicted that exactly 32-point groups represented all of the crystal classes. We won't be discussing groups until the very last chapter of this book (Chapter 8, "Section 8.5. Symmetry groups rule the universe"). For now, let's just focus on the mathematical assertion that all possible crystal symmetries are represented by 32-point groups [5]. Because this collection of 32 groups is complete, and because each group is a class representing symmetry transformations upon observable geometric shapes in crystals, we can say that the 32 mathematical groups comprise a classification. [Glossary Group, Point group, Symmetry group]

When we create a mathematical classification with 32-point groups, then we can expect to find not more than 32-point groups somewhere in nature, if our classification is correct. As it happens, back in 1830, a crystallographer named Johann Friedrich Christian Hessel painstakingly collected all the naturally occurring forms of crystals. At the end of his labors, he reported exactly 32 types of morphological symmetries. Had Johann found 33 crystal symmetries, then our mathematical representation of reality would have been in a great deal of trouble insofar as our classification would have provided an incomplete model of nature. Had Johann found only 31 crystal symmetries, then crystallographers would have been saddled with the job of finding, somewhere in nature, a crystal having the 32nd point group. As it happened, the mathematical classification of crystallographic point groups agreed with empirical observations of known crystals. Hence, the complete mathematical classification of crystals, based on point groups, accounts for the complete assortment of naturally occurring crystals.

Finally, because all naturally occurring crystals must be included in one of the 32-point groups, it was concluded that all crystals must be composed of discrete atoms occupying specific positions with respect to one another, and obeying strict geometric rules; without exception. Knowing that crystals are composed of the same elements found in gases and liquids and noncrystalizing solids, it seems reasonable to infer that all matter is composed of atoms. The contrary hypothesis, promoted by an imposing number of chemists and physicists at the time, was that matter was a sort of amorphous continuum, possibly consisting of nothing other than nonparticulate energy fields. The completeness of the classification of crystals bolstered the atomic theory of matter.

In the early 20th century, two important scientific achievements finally settled the argument in favor of the atomic theory of matter. X-ray crystallographic analysis (1912) demonstrated the atomic nature of crystals. At about the same time, Perrin provided experimental proof of the existence of atoms based on the observed effects of Brownian movements [6].

Mathematical completeness

In mathematics, there are several classification theorems, but the Classification Theorem of the Finite Simple Groups, and its proven completeness, is one of the most important intellectual achievements of mankind. As it happens, the physics of the universe is represented by groups (explained in detail in "Section 8.5. Symmetry groups rule the universe"). As it happens, the completeness of the Classification Theorem would suggest that all of the operational principles of the universe can be represented by one or another of the symmetry groups, finite or continuous, that can be logically mapped to the finite groups listed in the Classification Theorem.

One of the most complex of the symmetry groups listed in the Classification Theorem of Finite Simple Groups is the vividly named Monster Group. Freeman Dyson, a physicist, and a science visionary, predicted that even the Monster group would eventually be found to represent the behavior of some physical laws in the real world. His prediction seems to have been validated. Today, the study of the Monster group had led to a deeper understanding of string theory and black holes [7].

Completeness provides mathematicians with an opportunity to prove new theories that apply to every member of a complete class of abstract objects. For example, a proof may rely on finding some amenable class object (i.e., the special case) for which a valid proof can be successfully built. If the proof for the special case employs only general properties of the class of objects, then the proof will apply to all the members of the class of the objects.

Alternately, there may be situations in which a mathematician cannot, despite all her best efforts, find proof that applies to a class of objects. If the class is complete, and if she can devise tailored proofs for each member of the class, then she can infer that the proof must apply to the general class.

The gapless Periodic Table of the Elements

The Periodic Table of the Elements, as every student knows, has no gaps. As a historical sidelight, Mendeleev, who is credited with the idea that the completeness of the Periodic Table required that every vacancy be filled in with elements, was never awarded the Nobel Prize in Chemistry; these prizes went to some of the scientists who discovered the vacant elements. In 1906, the Nobel committee voted to give Mendeleev his long-overdue Nobel Prize, but the committee was overruled by the president of the Royal Swedish Academy of Sciences, who favored Henri Moissan, the man who filled the gap for element 9, Fluorine. Moissan got the prize, and, as fate would have it, both Mendeleev and Moisson died within weeks afterward. Because the Nobel prize is only awarded to living scientists, Mendeleev missed his last chance to be a Nobelist. Somewhat ironically, every student is taught the name of Mendeleev, while very few of us are familiar with the name of Moissan, the prize winner.

The gapless nature of the Periodic Table permits us to make a very bold assertion about our universe: that there are no elements present in distant worlds that are not also present here on earth. If there were nonearthly elements, then they would need to have an atomic number not found in the Periodic Table. But we know that the naturally occurring elements on earth fill the table. An "unearthly" element would have no place to fit. Therefore, such elements cannot exist. As it happens, there are just 94 naturally occurring elements. Above that number, the elements are produced under extreme conditions in laboratories and persist for only a fraction of a second. In "Section 7.4. Great deductions from anomalies in the Periodic Table," we will see how the elements fill the Table, and why, in theory, no element may have an atomic number exceeding 136.

Completeness of the Classification of Life and the singular origin of organisms

The biochemist knows his molecules have ancestors, while the paleontologist can only hope that his fossils left descendants.

Vincent Sarich [8]

When you can look around and see that everything shares the same improbable feature, you will often find that a single event was responsible for everything you see. Here's an example of the kind of thinking that applies generally, excerpted from a Robert Chambers' *Vestiges of the Natural History of Creation*, published in 1884 [9]:

"It is, in the first place, remarkable that all the planets move nearly in one plane, corresponding with the center of the sun's body. Next, it is no less worthy of attention, that the motion of the sun on its axis, those of the planets around the sun, and the satellites around their primaries, and the motions of all on their axes, are in one direction—namely, from west to east. Had all these matters been left to accident, the chances against the uniformity would have been, though calculable, inconceivably great. Of the motions of the twenty-three bodies known in the early part of this century, it was found by Laplace, that the adverse chances were as upwards of four million of millions to one. It is thus powerfully impressed on us that the uniformity of the motions, as well as their general adjustment to one plane, must have been a consequence of a single cause acting throughout the whole system"

We can look back at Chambers' words and agree with his conclusion, but we must acknowledge that his logic depended upon having a complete list of the heavenly bodies in our solar system, their paths, and the direction of their axial motions. It was the completeness of his knowledge that permitted him to find a general relationship that tied all the planets to a common origin, in time.

Biologists have used the completeness of the Classification of Life to draw a profound conclusion concerning the origin of life forms on earth. We should qualify our next remarks by noting that when we assert that the Classification of Life is complete, we are not claiming that we have studied every single species of life on planet earth. Common estimates of the number of living species on earth range from 10 million to 100 million. When we include all forms of microorganisms, including viruses, the estimates increase to the billions or more [10–17]. At present, only a few million species have been cataloged, and it seems likely that new species are forming at a rate that far outpaces our ability to detecting and characterizing them. The "completeness" of the Classification of Life reflects our somewhat shaky confidence that all of the major classes of organisms have been identified, and that some representative species from every known class of organism have been characterized.

When we survey representative organisms of the complete Classification of Life, we find that all living organisms, including all known classes of prokaryotes, eukaryotes, and viruses, have genomes coded in a nucleic acid (DNA or RNA). All living organisms produce and transfer energy in nucleotide molecules (e.g., ATP, NADPH). All live organisms have carbon-based structural molecules (e.g., amino acids, carbohydrates, lipids, nucleotides). All living organisms require water. Basically, all life on earth is about the same, on a molecular level. This universal sameness of molecular design and content suggests that all life on earth has a common ancient origin, an inference based upon a complete survey of the observable classes contained in natural classifications. **Among the various types of data structures, only the classification, with its completeness property, permits us to draw inferences that apply universally.**

Section 2.4. A classification is an evolving hypothesis

Every classification is a triumph over a paradox that smolders within the classification, for eternity. Poetic but true. Let's take a hard look at this paradox as we try to understand its full significance. Every classification creates a perception of reality, filled with objects, their relationships to one another, and the operational rules by which those relationships are achieved. To build the classification, we must first be aware of objects, and their relationships to one another, so that we can create the class hierarchy. But if we are aware of objects and relationships and classes, then we have a perception of the classification before we begin to create the classification. Hence, we must have a classification before we can begin to build the classification; this is the paradox.

The paradox of classification has its consequences:

1. Detractors

Those who would abandon the traditional methods of classification building have argued that such classifications only serve to perpetuate the biases of the classification builder. Every classification starts its existence with an "original sin"; this being the classification builder's imperfect interpretation of a knowledge domain. Everything that follows, as the classification is constructed, is tainted by sin, and cannot be accepted as scientific fact.

Within the biomedical community, a decades-long battle has raged over the methods by which biological classifications can be built. The two opposing camps consist of computational bioinformaticians and classical taxonomists. In the field of biology, computational bioinformaticians believe that the members of a biological class will all have similar genes and that these similarities can be graded by computational algorithms that compare many genes and their ancestral homologies, in many species, eventually yielding a complete and objective classification. A classification that is built by an algorithm is unbiased, and is thus superior to traditional classifications, generated with human biases and preconceptions. The traditional taxonomists scoff at the idea of a computer-generated classification, believing that computer algorithms simply look at superficial features among organisms. Only humans, they would say, have the skill, dedication, and inspiration required to find the essence of a class. [Glossary Algorithm, Bioinformatics, Class, Homolog]

2. Unreliability

From the paradox of classification emerges the following statement, that pops up repeatedly in the relevant literature: "A classification is an evolving hypothesis." This means that classifications are never built from certainty. Every classification begins with an inspirational guess about the basic structure of a knowledge domain. The guess may be nothing more than a hint about a possible class of things, or the root of a hierarchy of objects, or a fundamental law that dictates the behavior of some objects. In any case, from a first guess, the classification builder begins to collect objects into likely classes, and the effort of building a complex classification begins. These are the first steps in the growth of the evolving hypothesis that we call a classification.

As an evolving hypothesis, the classification must be continuously tested, to determine whether the original hypothesis and all consequent hypotheses are correct and consistent with one another. The process of testing hypotheses, as the classification is being built, is the only protection we have against the original sin of the classification builder. When errors are found, they must be corrected, even if the process of correction requires major revisions to the class hierarchy. The credibility of the classification grows as more and more of its foundational assertions are tested and validated. The structure of the classification hardens as we determine that class relationships and properties are self-consistent. [Glossary Validation]

Section 2.5. Widely held misconceptions

George Orwell wrote, in 1946, "When I sit down to write a book, I do not say to myself, 'I am going to produce a work of art.' I write it because there is some lie that I want to expose, some fact to which I want to draw attention, and my initial concern is to get a hearing [18]." If Orwell's opinion accurately describes the motive that drives creative writers, then it seems to me that it would apply even more so to science writers, for whom the notion of art for art's sake is never much of a consideration. In the particular case of classifications, most modern scientists ignore the subject entirely. It comes as no surprise that the scientific community holds a variety of ill-conceived beliefs that have served to diminish the legitimacy of classification as a subject worthy of inclusion in college curricula. Let's perish such foolish thoughts, beginning with these five widely held misconceptions.

Misconception 1. All humans are naturally adept at building classifications

Humans are constantly classifying their world. When we look at a blade of glass, we see it as one example of grasses that we have previously seen and categorized. Although we have never before observed this particular blade of grass, we presume that it is much like other blades of grass. Likewise, when we walk down the street and pass multiple buildings, we do not stop to examine every detail of every building. We are content in knowing that these unique buildings are much like other buildings that we have seen and passed throughout our lives. If we could not simplify our world, through classification, we would be overwhelmed by the complexity of our surroundings.

If humans are constantly sorting pieces of their world into neat and tidy classes, then we should all be fairly adept at the process. The truth is that we put objects from our environment into neat classes, but we are pretty bad at relating one class to another class, and we are terrible at building lineages of classes that ascend to the same root class. We only do half the job that we need to do.

Sorting objects into classes is an early and simple step in the process of classification. The next step involves thinking about the essential properties of the class that apply to every object of the class, and which exclude every object, not of the class. The step after that involves finding the relationships that connect one class to another. And the step after that involves building the scaffold that contains all of the classes. The subconscious mind doesn't do these hard tasks. We must stop and think and come up with some grand design for all those classes we made. Then, we need to test our guesses against reality. Finally, we must show that the finished classification allows us to predict how our world operates. None of this is done naturally. To create a classification, we need to whip our brains into shape and force it, by the strength of will, to think rationally.

The ancient Greek philosophers made some of the most important contributions to our modern understanding of classification. They divided everything into one of four visible classes (earth, air, fire, and water), and provided a fifth class that serves as the root of the classification. We refer to the fifth class as the fifth essence, or by its Latin equivalent, quintessence. When we succumb to the urge to wax poetic, we may refer to a favorite object as being "quintessential," meaning that it exemplifies the perfect and defining properties of its type. In retrospect, the ancients' upper-level classification of all things, in heaven and earth, was simplistic and wrong. Let's not allow their error to distract us from admiring their genius, for the ancient Greek philosophers understood that everything in our world must have an assigned place, in subclasses, embedded in a structure dominated by a root, quintessential, class.

Misconception 2. The purpose of classification is to facilitate search and retrieval

Search and retrieval algorithms are highly overrated. On a certain level, the process is absolutely trivial (i.e., when there is an exact search term, and the goal is to retrieve all of the sections of a document that contain the exact search term). Search and retrieval become a bit more difficult when you are looking for all the terms that match the meaning of a search term and covering all of the synonyms and near-synonyms that apply. The most advanced search and retrieval algorithms will dredge through data to provide answers to questions posed as sentences. In any case, regardless of what the search algorithm retrieves, you can never be certain that you will be delivered all of the relevant information you need or that you have the best possible answer to your question.

If search and retrieval is your sole interest, you should examine alternate data structures that might serve your purpose without demanding the time, energy, and thought lavished upon classifications. The strength of classifications comes from finding relationships among different classes of items and using those relationships to draw logical inferences about classes and their members. Fetching information is a chore that is best left to other forms of data organization. The practical value of indexes and concordances, which can be generated automatically and quickly, is often overlooked by data scientists. In point of fact, when indexes are tied to standard nomenclatures, they can be far more effective at search and retrieval than classifications. In my earlier book, *Data Simplification* I discuss the simplest ways in which indexes and concordances can be created and implemented [19]. [Glossary Concordance]

Misconception 3. We build classifications by grouping items according to their similarities

Assigning similar things to classes has nothing to do with the process of classification. As previously emphasized, all proper classifications of items are based on finding relationships, not similarities.

The first crude classifications of living organisms were similarity-based, producing classes such as flying animals (e.g., birds, bats, bumblebees) or swimming animals (e.g., fish, cephalopods, lampreys), or walking animals (e.g., man, bears, penguins) (Fig. 2.7).

Among various and sundry shortcomings, similarity-based approaches to classification cannot take into account the dissimilarities within a single entity during various stages of its life. For example, butterflies fly, but caterpillars do not; yet they are the same organism and hence both forms would be contained within the class of flying animals. Similarity-based approaches do not take into account the disparate ways by which species of animals achieve a similar property (Fig. 2.8).

FIG. 2.7 Animals of no close relationships who happen to share a similarity; flight. From top to bottom: gull, fox-bat, flying squirrel, flying fish. *Source: "The Outline of Science: A Plain Story Simply Told," by J. Arthur Thomson, 1922.*

Flying squirrels, birds, and "helicopter seeds" of maple trees all fly through the air, but they all achieve flight through different methods. The earliest animals' classifications did not add to our understanding of organisms and had value only as aids in animal identification.

Aristotle (384–322 BCE) was one of the first experts in classification to fully grasp the meaning of classification based on relationships. Perhaps his deepest insight came when he correctly identified a dolphin as a mammal. Through observation, he knew that a large group of animals was distinguished by a gestational period in which a developing embryo is nourished by a placenta, and the offspring are delivered into the world as formed, but small versions of the adult animals (i.e., not as eggs or larvae), and the newborn animals feed on milk excreted from nipples, overlying specialized glandular organs (mammae). Aristotle knew that these features, characteristic of mammals, were absent in all other types of animals. He also knew that dolphins had all these features; fish did not. He correctly reasoned that dolphin were a type of mammal, not a type of fish.

Aristotle was ridiculed by his contemporaries for whom it was obvious that dolphins were a type of fish. Unlike Aristotle, they based their classification on similarities, not on relationships. They say that dolphins looked like fish and dolphins swam in the ocean

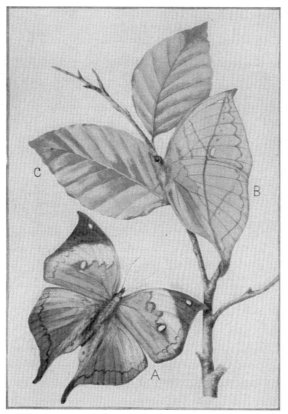

FIG. 2.8 The dead-leaf butterfly (Kallima inachis) is similar to a withered leaf when viewed from below, but nobody would assign these to organisms to the same class. *Source: "The Outline of Science: A Plain Story Simply Told," by J. Arthur Thomson, 1922.*

like fish, and this was all the proof they needed to conclude that dolphins were indeed fish. For about 2000 years following the death of Aristotle, biologists persisted in their belief that dolphins were a type of fish. For the past several hundred years, biologists have acknowledged that Aristotle was correct after all; dolphins are mammals. Aristotle discovered and taught the most important principle of classification; those classes are built on relationships among class members; not by counting similarities [20]. In fact, the act of searching for and finding relationships, not similarities, lies at the heart of science; it's how we make sense of reality (Fig. 2.9).

How is it then, that various species that belong to the same class often seem very similar to one another? George Gaylord Simpson, the eminent zoologist, provided a simple answer: "Individuals do not belong in the same taxon because they are similar, but they are similar because they belong to the same taxon." [Glossary Taxa, Taxon]

It is easy to succumb to the urge to classify organisms based on similarities. Classifications based on quantitating similarities among organisms are variously referred to as phenetic or phenotypic (from the Greek "pheno" meaning showing). When we attempt

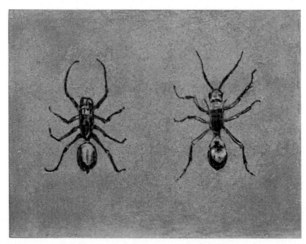

FIG. 2.9 Look closely at these two similar-appearing organisms. On the left is a small spider. On the right is an ant. *Source: "The Outline of Science: A Plain Story Simply Told," by J. Arthur Thomson, 1922.*

to classify by phenotypic similarities among objects, the result is sure to disappoint, for the following reasons:

1. Similarities among objects don't tell us much about the essential, defining properties of their contained objects. Often, similarity-based features are misleading, prompting major revisions in class structures [21]. At best, similarities serve as clues that might lead us to discover the definitive and heritable properties of classes.
2. Classes will contain unrelated items, a detractor known to biologists as polyphyly.
3. Classes will omit items that belong in the class, a detractor known to biologists as paraphyly.

These last two conditions (polyphyly and paraphyly) lead to class blending, wherein classes contain unrelated objects. When classes are blended with other classes, it becomes impossible to conduct valid experiments comparing different classes since the classes being compared are mixtures of one another. [Glossary Blended class, Paraphyly and polyphyly]

Misconception 4. Classifications are designed to fulfill a specific purpose

If it were true, that classifications are designed to fulfill a specific purpose, then we would have to deal with multiple classifications, all covering the same knowledge domain, based on the different intents of classification designers. As mentioned earlier, classifications are not created at all. We must recognize that there is a natural order to naturally occurring items. Hence, in the natural sciences, the job of the classification builder is to capture nature's classification; not to create her needs-based product. It is gratifying to see that when we successfully model classes that embody the natural relationships of the universe, we can fit one natural classification into another and build relationships unforeseen by the creators of the individual classifications. This point will be discussed in more detail when we reach "Section 8.6. Life, the universe, and everything."

Misconception 5. Catalogs, indexes, and identification systems are types of classifications

Indexes are terrific data organizing tools and should be the very first thing to come to mind when required to organize the data held in a corpus of text, regardless of size. I have devoted a full description of computational indexing methods in one of my earlier books, *Data Simplification* [19].

An index relates the individual items of a textual domain (e.g., a book or a document or collections thereof) according to some particular organizing principle. Most commonly, indexes relate all of the terms of a book to their page location in the book. Indexed terms are typically single words or noun phrases.

The single words included in an index are selected based on their high information content. In practical terms, this means that indexed words do not appear with high frequency, on every page (as we would see if words such as "a," "the," "for," and "when" were indexed), and indexed words must convey some special import related to the subject of the book.

The noun phrases included in an index of the book might include names of people or multiword geographic locations, technical terms (e.g., "parapsoriasis en plaque"), events (e.g., "War of the Roses").

Some very clever algorithms can automatically select index-worthy single words and phrases from any corpus of text, but the final selection of indexable items is typically made by a highly trained indexer. The human indexer selects, groups, and orders items based on her conceptualization of the text, and her assessment of the utility of the item for the intended readers. Furthermore, the index is seldom, if ever, created by the author or authors of the text. Hence, the index is a reconceptualization of the original text, in tabular form, comprising a new, creative, work [22].

Modern readers are deprived of the inventive approaches to indexing employed by book publishers of prior ages. It was not unheard of for a single book to be provided with multiple indexes, with any given index being devoted to names of persons, geographic locations, historical events, and so on. Because it is expensive to create and print multiple indexes, these practices have been abandoned. However, with modern algorithms and software implementations, it is quite possible to create multiple indexes for a single work or to combine indexes for collections of documents, in just a few seconds [19].

To summarize, indexes organize the individual items of a domain, according to their location in a text, permitting users to rapidly determine all of the locations of a particular item. In contrast, a classification is a method of relating classes of items.

The informatics literature seldom draws a clear distinction‘ between a classification and a catalog or between a classification system and an identification system. A catalog is a listing of physical things or parts of things that may be retrieved by the user. Often, catalogs contain inventoried items. Catalogs typically annotate each item with some sort of identifier and some descriptive information. The purpose of a catalog is to provide a means by which users can familiarize themselves with a collection and locate desired items.

An identification system helps us match an individual object with its assigned name. All identification systems use a set of features to determine the object that fits the features. For example, if we have a list of characteristic features: large, hairy, strong, African, jungle-dwelling, knuckle-walking; we might identify the organisms as a gorilla. The identifier system does not use class relationships to arrive at the name of an object. In the same example, we can identify an animal like a gorilla without knowing that a gorilla is a type of mammal or a member of Class Gorillini. Conversely, you can classify a gorilla as a member of Class Gorillini without knowing that gorillas are large and live in Africa. One of the most common mistakes in the biological sciences is to confuse an identification system with a classification system. The former simply provides a handy way to associate an object with a name; the latter is a system of relationships among objects.

Summarizing, indexes and catalogs help us find things. The Identifications system helps us name things. Classifications help us find relationships among classes of things.

As an aside, the lack of standard definitions for the terms commonly used in the data sciences has been an intractable problem. Some of the most general terms, such as "ontology," "data object," "schema," and even "classification," are either imprecisely defined, or they are precisely defined in different ways by different disciplines. Consequently, at conferences and workshops, participants keep missing the points raised by their peers, because all those present are babbling in an insular language. For this reason, we devote quite a bit of verbiage to definitional matters, in the hope of establishing a shared understanding of the fundamentals of classification. [Glossary Classification versus ontology, Diagnosis versus classification, Thesaurus]

Glossary

Algorithm An algorithm is a logical sequence of steps that lead to a desired computational result. Algorithms serve the same function in the computer world as production processes serve in the manufacturing world. Fundamental algorithms can be linked to one another, to create new algorithms. Algorithms are the most important intellectual capital in computer science [23,24].

Anucleate cells Cells that have no nuclei. Examples are red blood cells and keratotic squamous cells. Anucleate cells are postmitotic or end-stage forms that perform a function using the cellular machinery in their cytoplasm (keratin formation in the squamous cell and hemoglobin in red blood cells) until the cell eventually dies. It is possible to have proliferative conditions and even malignancies composed largely of anucleate cells, but the anucleate cells do not contribute to the growth of the tumor. Epidermoid cysts are nodules composed of the debris of anucleate squamous cells surrounded by a thin rim of proliferating nucleated squamous cells. Epidermoid cysts can grow to be large, approaching the size of an egg, and demonstrate how a small population of proliferating cells can give rise to a mass composed almost entirely of anucleate cells.

As another example, polycythemia vera is a blood clonal proliferative disorder characterized by an increase in the number of circulating mature red blood cells. Mature red blood cells are anucleate; so how can red blood cells proliferate? The population of anucleate cells is created by a nucleated erythroid stem cell population in the marrow. So, if you're looking for the origin of an increase in red blood cells, you should not devote your time to studying the mature red blood cells. Hunt for the nucleated precursor cells, which will contain the genetic defect leading to the overproduction of anucleate red blood cells.

Bioinformatics The science of the curation and analysis of biological data. The field of bioinformatics had focused on genomic data for several decades. Recently, the field has expanded its purview into epigenomics, proteomics, metabolomics, and so on.

The term "bioinformatics" should not be confused with "biomedical informatics"; the latter referring to applications of information systems (e.g., computers, hospital databases) to the practice and the science of medicine, and related fields of biology.

Blended class Blended classes (also known as class noise), refers to a mistake in proper classification, in which members are assigned to the wrong classes, or in which a class is created whose members are unrelated. These kinds of mistakes often arise when scientists use a single trait to establish class membership, or when taxonomists have created an untenable class. For example, if you were to make a Mouse class, and you included Mickey Mouse as one of the instances of the class, you would be blending a cartoon with an animal, and this would be a mistake. You should have been more discriminating when you created the "mouse" class. If you were to use the trait "ability to fly" to blend birds and houseflies and flying squirrels, then you made the error of building a class around a trait that could not sensibly serve as a class property.

After reading the preceding paragraph, you might be thinking that class blending is the kind of careless mistake that you will be smart enough to avoid. Don't be too confident. Class blending is a pervasive and costly sin that is committed by virtually every scientist at some point in his or her career. One error can easily set your research back a decade if you're not mentally focused on this often-subtle issue.

When you read old texts, written before scientists of the time knew anything about micro-organisms, it's clear that the cause of epidemics in those days was unknown. We recognize today that one of the plague bacteria is *Yersinia pestis*. But we do not know with certainty the specific causes of any of the major plagues in ancient Greece and medieval Europe. Typhus may have been involved. Measles and smallpox are likely causes of past plagues. Malarial outbreaks should not be overlooked. Now suppose you are a statistician, and you are magically whisked to Southern Italy, in the year 1640 CE, where people are dying in great number, of the plague, and you are a doctor trying to cope with the situation. You're not a microbiologist, but you know something about designing clinical trials, and one of the local cognoscenti has just given you an herb that he insists is a cure for the plague. "Give the sick this herb today, and their fevers will be gone by the next morning," he tells you. As it happens, the herb is an extract of bark from the Cinchona tree, recently imported from Brazil. It is a sure-fire cure for malaria, a disease endemic to the region; but you know none of this. Before you start treating your patients, you'll want to conduct a clinical trial.

In 1640, physicians knew nothing about the pathogenesis of malaria. Current thinking was that it was a disease caused by breathing insalubrious swamp vapors; hence the word roots "mal" meaning bad, and "aria" meaning air. You have just been handed a substance derived from the Cinchona tree, but you do not trust the herbalist. Insisting on a rational approach to the practice of medicine, you design a clinical trial, using 100 patients, all of whom have the same symptoms (delirium and fever) and all of whom carry the diagnosis of malaria. You administer the cinchona powder, also known as quinine, to all the trial subjects. A few improve, but most don't. You recall that the symptoms of malaria wax and wane, with the fever subsiding on its own every few days. It is not uncommon for malaria victims to recover, without any treatment. Everything considered you call the trial a wash-out. You decide not to administer quinine to your patients.

What happened? We know that quinine arrived as a miracle cure for malaria. It should have been effective in a population of 100 patients. Why did the clinical trial fail? The patients under study were assembled based on their mutual symptoms: fever and delirium. These same symptoms could have been accounted for by hundreds of other diseases that were prevalent in Italy at the time. The criteria employed to render a diagnosis of malaria was imprecise, and the trial population was diluted with nonmalarial patients who were guaranteed to be nonresponders. Consequently, the trial failed, and you missed a golden opportunity to treat your malaria patients with quinine, a new, highly effective, miracle drug. Basically, the trial was ruined by class noise.

It isn't hard to imagine present-day dilemmas, not unlike our fictitious quinine trial. If you are testing the effectiveness of an antibiotic on a class of people with bacterial pneumonia, the accuracy of your results will be jeopardized if your study population includes subjects with viral pneumonia or smoking-related lung damage. It is impossible to conduct rational trials for appropriate targeted therapies when the trial groups are composed of blended classes of individuals [25]. The medical literature is rife with the research of dubious quality, based on poorly designed classifications and blended classes.

One caveat, efforts to reduce class blending can be counterproductive if undertaken with excess zeal. For example, in an effort to reduce class blending, a researcher may choose groups of subjects who are uniform with respect to every known observable property. For example, suppose you want to actually compare apples with oranges. To avoid class blending, you might want to make very sure that your apples do not include any kumquats or persimmons. You should be certain that your oranges do not include any limes or grapefruits. Imagine that you go even further, choosing only apples and oranges of one variety (e.g., Macintosh apples and Navel oranges), size (e.g., 10 cm), and origin (e.g., California). How will your comparisons apply to the varieties of apples and oranges that you have excluded from your study? You may reach conclusions that are invalid and irreproducible for more generalized populations within each class. In this case, you have succeeded in eliminated class blending, at the expense of losing representative populations of the classes [19].

Class A class is a collection of members that share a property that is absent from members not in the class or its descendant classes.

The word "class," lowercase, is used as a general term. The word "Class," uppercase, followed by an uppercase noun (e.g., Class Animalia), represents a specific class within a formal classification.

Class method In object-oriented programming, A class method is an operation that is available to all of the members of the class, and all of the members of subclasses of the class (through inheritance).

In Ruby, class methods are sent directly to the class object, and the class object performs the method, as shown:

```
File.open
Array.new
```

Here, the class methods "open" and "new" are sent directly to the classes to which they belong (Class File and Class Array). If we were using an instance method, it would be sent to the instance of the class, not to the class itself.

To define a class method, the name of the class followed by a dot followed by the name of the method may appear in the definition line.

An example of a class method, name, for Class Person is shown.

```
class Person
   def Person.name
     "Jules"
   end
end
```

To define an instance method, simply list the method name. The method can be received by any object instance of the class.

Class property The term class property ("property" appearing in lowercase letters), simply refers to a property of the class that is available to every member of the class, and that is inherited by the members of the subclasses of the class. In object-oriented programming languages, properties are usually expressed as methods. For example, a property of all items in the Class File may be that they can be printed out to the computer monitor. The property might also be expressed as a method available to all of the items in the Class File, wherein the method automatically prints the item, when called. We might name the method "Print" or "Print_file", and the name of the method could also serve as the name of the property. For programmers, there is very little difference between a class property and a class method.

Classification A system in which every object in a knowledge domain is assigned to a class within a hierarchy of classes. The properties of the parent class are inherited by the child classes. Every class has one immediate parent class, although a parent class may have more than one immediate subclasses (i.e., child classes). Objects do not change their class assignment in a classification unless there has been a mistake in the assignment. For example, a rabbit is always a rabbit and does not change into a tiger.

Classifications can be easily modeled with computational algorithms and are nonchaotic (i.e., calculations performed on the members and classes of a classification should yield the same output, each time the calculation is performed).

Classification theorems In mathematics, classification theorems list all of the classes of objects of a given type (e.g., simple finite groups) and typically provide proof that the classification is complete, and that every object of a type belongs to exactly one of the classes. When examining two objects of a given type, there should be a way of determining whether the two objects belong to the same class.

Examples of classification theorems in mathematics include:

- Artin-Wedderburn theorem for semisimple rings
- Classification of Euclidean plane isometries
- Classification of Fatou components
- Classification of finite simple groups
- Classification of two-dimensional closed manifolds
- Classification theorem for finite-dimensional vector spaces
- Classification theorem of surfaces
- Enriques-Kodaira classification of algebraic surfaces (complex dimension two, real dimension four)
- Jordan normal form
- Nielsen-Thurston classification which characterizes homeomorphisms of a compact surface
- Rank-Nullity theorem (by rank and nullity)
- Structure theorem for finitely generated modules over a principal ideal domain
- Sylvester's law of inertia
- Thurston's eight model geometries, and the geometrization conjecture

Classification versus ontology A classification should be distinguished from an ontology. In an ontology, a class may have more than one parent class and an object may be a member of more than one class. A classification can be considered a restrictive and simplified form of ontology wherein each class is limited to a single parent class and each object has membership in one and only one class [26].

In general, ontologies are specified using a computer-readable descriptive language, such as RDF or OWL. Traditional classifications are seldom provided in any formal semantic language, and cannot be sensibly parsed and interpreted by computer applications. Consequently, computer scientists tend to apply the term ontology to any computer-ready listing of objects and classes.

Concordance A concordance is an index consisting of every word in the text, along with every location wherein each word can be found. It is computationally trivial to reconstruct the original text from the concordance. Before the advent of computers, concordances fell under the provenance of religious scholars, who painstakingly recorded the locations of all words appearing in the Bible, ancient scrolls, and any texts whose words were considered to be divinely inspired. Today, a concordance for a Bible-length book can be constructed in less than a second. Furthermore, the original text can be reconstructed from the concordance, in about the same time.

Curator   The word "curator" derives from the latin, "curatus," the same root for "curative," indicating that curators "take care of" things. A data curator collects, annotates, indexes, updates, archives, searches, retrieves, and distributes data. Curator is another of those somewhat arcane terms (e.g., indexer, data archivist, lexicographer) that are being rejuvenated in the new millennium. It seems that if we want to enjoy the benefits of a data-centric world, we will need the assistance of curators, trained in data organization.

Diagnosis versus classification   Diagnosis is the process by which a disease is assigned a name (i.e., a taxonomic term) belonging to a class of diseases. When a pathologist examines a tumor specimen and declares that the tumor is a squamous cell carcinoma of the skin, she is rendering a diagnosis (i.e., finding a specimen's location in a preexisting classification). Classification is different from diagnosis, the former referring to the process of inventing the class structure into which the taxonomy (e.g., the list of names of diagnosed diseases) must fit.

You'll occasionally hear someone saying something such as "The pathologist classified this lesion as a squamous cell carcinoma of the skin." This is an inaccurate use of terminology. Strictly speaking, pathologists diagnose lesions; they do not classify them. That is to say, the pathologist simply assigns the lesion the name of a disease that has a place in an existing classification.

Group   A group is a set having the properties of closure and associativity under an operation; having an identity element; and having an inverse element for every member of the set.

Specifically, for some operation (which we'll call "x" in this example, "closure" tells us that for all a, b in group G, the result of the operation, a x b, is also in G.

Associativity tells us that for all a, b, and c in G, (a x b) x c = a x (b x c).

To have an identity element, there must exist an element e in G such that, for every element a in G, the equation e x a = a x e = a hold. The identity element is unique within a group, and we speak of "the" identity element.

To have an inverse element, there must exist for each a in G, an element b in G, such that a x b = b x a = e, where e is the identity element.

Homolog   In the field of bioinformatics, "homolog" always refers to homologous genes. Genes from different organisms are considered homologous to one another if both descended from a gene in a common ancestral organism. If the homology was attained through speciation (i.e., the original gene persisted in the descendant species, with alterations), then the homologous genes are also orthologous. If the homology was attained through gene duplication (i.e., genetic alterations occurred in a duplicated inherited gene), then the homologous genes are also paralogous. Homologous genes of different species tend to have similar gene sequences, with sequence differences among the descendant species, and between the descendant species and the first parental species, accumulating over time.

Nongeneralizable predictor   Sometimes data analysis can yield results that are true, but nongeneralizable (i.e., irrelevant to everything outside the set of data objects under study). The most useful scientific findings are generalizable (e.g., the laws of physics operate on the planet Jupiter or the star Alpha Centauri much as they do on earth). Many of the most popular analytic methods are not generalizable because they produce predictions that only apply to highly restricted sets of data; or the predictions are not explainable by any underlying theory that relates input data with the calculated predictions. Data analysis is incomplete until a comprehensible, generalizable, and testable theory for the predictive method is developed.

Paraphyly and polyphyly   If the subclasses of a parent class omit any of the descendants of the parent class, then the parent class is said to be paraphyletic.

If a subclass of a parent class includes organisms that did not descend from the parent, then the parent class is polyphyletic.

A class can be paraphyletic and polyphyletic, if its subclasses exclude organisms that are its true descendants and if the subclasses include organisms that are not its descendants (Fig. 2.10).

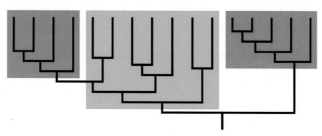

FIG. 2.10 Schematic (cladogram) of all the descendant branches of a common ancestor (stem at bottom of image). The left and the right groups represent clades insofar as they contain all their descendants and exclude classes that are not descendants of the group root. The middle group is not a valid clade because it does not contain all of the descendants of its group root (i.e., it is paraphyletic). Specifically, it excludes the left-most group in the diagram.

Point group The point group is formed from all of the symmetry transformations that can be performed on a geometric shape, about a fixed point.

Point groups play a role in the symmetry groups of crystals. There are 32 different point groups in crystals and 14 Bravais lattices [27]. Together they account for all 230 theoretical (and empirically observed) space groups of crystals.

Science Of course, there are many different definitions of science, and inquisitive students should be encouraged to find a conceptualization of science that suits their intellectual development. For me, science is all about finding general relationships among objects. In the so-called physical sciences, the most important relationships are expressed as mathematical equations (e.g., the relationship between force, mass, and acceleration; the relationship between voltage, current, and resistance). Scientific advancement is the discovery of new relationships or the discovery of a generalization that applies to objects hitherto confined to disparate scientific realms (e.g., evolutionary theory arising from observations of organisms and geologic strata).

Engineering would be the area of science wherein scientific relationships are exploited to build new technology.

Script A script is a program that is written in plain-text, in a syntax appropriate for a particular programming language, that needs to be parsed through that language's interpreter before it can be compiled and executed. Scripts tend to run a bit slower than executable files, but they have the advantage that they can be read and understood by anyone familiar with the script's programming language.

Symmetry group The set of all the transformations that leave a given object invariant (i.e., does not change the value of the object), and that meets the definition of a group.

Taxa Plural form of the taxon.

Taxon A taxon is a class. The common usage of "taxon" is somewhat inconsistent, as it sometimes refers to the class name, and at other times refers to the instances (i.e., members) of the class. In this book, the term "taxon" is abandoned in favor of "class," the term preferred by computer scientists.

Thesaurus A vocabulary that groups together synonymous terms. A thesaurus is very similar to a nomenclature. There are two minor differences. Nomenclatures include multiword terms; whereas a thesaurus is typically composed of one-word terms. In addition, nomenclatures are typically restricted to a well-defined topic or knowledge domain (e.g., names of stars, infectious diseases, etc.). Thesauruses, like dictionaries, may contain all the words of a language.

Validation Validation is the process that checks whether the conclusions drawn from data analysis are correct [28]. Validation sometimes starts with repeating the same analysis of the same data, using the methods that were originally recommended. Obviously, if a different set of conclusions is drawn from the same data and methods, the original conclusions cannot be validated. Validation may involve applying a different set of analytic methods to the same data, to determine if the conclusions are consistent. It is always reassuring to know that conclusions are repeatable, with different analytic methods.

In prior eras, experiments were validated by repeating the entire experiment, thus producing a new set of observations for analysis. Many of today's scientific experiments are far too complex and costly to repeat. In such cases, validation requires access to the complete collection of the original data, and to the detailed protocols under which the data was generated.

One of the most useful methods of data validation involves testing new hypotheses, based on the assumed validity of the original conclusions. For example, if you were to accept Darwin's theory of evolution, then you would expect to find a chronologic history of fossils in ascending layers of shale. This was the case. Thus, paleontologists studying the Burgess shall reserve provided some validation to Darwin's conclusions.

Validation is not quite proof. Nonetheless, the repeatability of conclusions, over time, with the same or different sets of data, and the demonstration of consistency among related observations, is about all that we can hope for in the natural sciences.

Xanthopan morganii praedicta When Darwin encountered a rare flower (Angraecum sesquipedale) having a great length from the tip of the flower to its nectary at the base of the flower's stamen, he predicted that there must be a pollinator capable of reaching the nectary; otherwise, the flower could not have evolved. 130 years after Darwin's prediction, a previously unknown moth was found feeding on the flower. The moth's proboscis was just long enough to reach the deep nectary. The moth was aptly named Xanthopan morganii praedicta.

References

[1] Parrochia D. Mathematical theory of classification. Knowl Organ 2018;45:184–201.

[2] Gorenstein D. Classifying the finite simple groups. Bull Am Math Soc 1986;14:1–98.

[3] Cami J, Bernard-Salas J, Peeters E, Malek SE. Detection of C60 and C70 in a young planetary nebula. Science 2010;329:1180–2.

[4] Sender R, Fuchs S, Milo R. Revised estimates for the number of human and bacteria cells in the body. PLoS Biol 2016;14, e1002533.

[5] Bravais A. Memoire sur les systemes formes par les points distribues regulierement sur un plan ou dans l'espace. J Ecole Polytech 1850;19:1–128.

[6] Perrin JB. Les Atomes ("The atoms"). Paris: Librairie Felix Alcan; 1913.

[7] Boya LJ. Introduction to Sporadic groups. In: Proceedings of the workshop, supersymmetric quantum mechanics and spectral design. Benasque, Spain; 2010.

[8] Sarich VM. Just how old is the hominid line? Yearb Phys Anthropol 1973;17:98–112.

[9] Chan EF, Gat U, McNiff JM, Fuchs E. A common human skin tumor is caused by activating mutations in beta-catenin. Nat Genet 1999;21:410–3.

[10] Whitman WB, Coleman DC, Wiebe WJ. Prokaryotes: the unseen majority. Proc Natl Acad Sci 1998;95:6578–83.

[11] Mora C, Tittensor DP, Adl S, Simpson AGB, Worm B. How many species are there on earth and in the ocean? PLoS Biol 2011;9, e1001127.

[12] Suttle CA. Environmental microbiology: viral diversity on the global stage. Nat Microbiol 2016;1:16205.

[13] Suttle CA. Marine viruses: major players in the global ecosystem. Nat Rev Microbiol 2007;5:801–12.

[14] Mihara T, Koyano H, Hingamp P, Grimsley N, Goto S, Ogata H. Taxon richness of "Megaviridae" exceeds those of bacteria and archaea in the ocean. Microbes Environ 2018;33:162–71.

[15] Anthony SJ, Epstein JH, Murray KA, Navarrete-Macias I, Zambrana-Torrelio CM, Solovyov A, et al. A strategy to estimate unknown viral diversity in mammals. MBio 2013;4(5), e00598-13.

[16] Schloss PD, Handelsman J. Toward a census of bacteria in soil. PLoS Comput Biol 2006;2, e92.

[17] Locey KJ, Lennon JT. Scaling laws predict global microbial diversity. Proc Natl Acad Sci U S A 2016;113:5970–5.

[18] Orwell G. Why I Write. Gangrel Magazine, Summer; 1946.

[19] Berman JJ. Data simplification: taming information with open source tools. Waltham, MA: Morgan Kaufmann; 2016.

[20] Berman JJ. Racing to share pathology data. Am J Clin Pathol 2004;121:169–71.

[21] Tenter AM, Barta JR, Beveridge I, Duszynski DW, Mehlhorn H, Morrison DA, et al. The conceptual basis for a new classification of the coccidia. Int J Parasitol 2002;32:595–616.

[22] Mallon T. The best part of every book comes last. New York Times 1991.

[23] Cipra BA. The Best of the 20th century: editors name top 10 algorithms. SIAM News 2000;33(4).

[24] Wu X, Kumar V, Quinlan JR, Ghosh J, Yang Q, Motoda H, et al. Top 10 algorithms in data mining. Knowl Inf Syst 2008;14:1–37.

[25] Committee on A Framework for Developing a New Taxonomy of Disease, Board on Life Sciences, Division on Earth and Life Studies, National Research Council of the National Academies. Toward precision medicine: building a knowledge network for biomedical research and a new taxonomy of disease. Washington, DC: The National Academies Press; 2011.

[26] Patil N, Berno AJ, Hinds DA, Barrett WA, Doshi JM, Hacker CR, et al. Blocks of limited haplotype diversity revealed by high-resolution scanning of human chromosome 21. Science 2001;294:1719–23.

[27] Bonolis L. From the rise of the group concept to the stormy onset of group theory in the new quantum mechanics: a saga of the invariant characterization of physical objects, events and theories. Riv Nuovo Cimento 2004;27:1–110.

[28] Committee on Mathematical Foundations of Verification, Validation, and Uncertainty Quantification; Board on Mathematical Sciences and Their Applications, Division on Engineering and Physical Sciences, National Research Council. Assessing the reliability of complex models: mathematical and statistical foundations of verification, validation, and uncertainty quantification. National Academy Press; 2012. Available from: http://www.nap.edu/catalog.php?record_id=13395. [Accessed 1 January 2015].

3

Ontologies and semantics

Chapter outline

I always wanted to be somebody,
but now I realize I should have been more specific.
Lily Tomlin

Section 3.1. When classifications just won't do

Here are a few examples of the circumstances wherein a classification will not suit your needs:

A classification just won't do when we intend to create an organized archive of descriptive information

A classification is just a collection of classes arranged as a hierarchy. There is no textual information other than definitions of classes and their properties. The hierarchy is established by requiring each class to contain, in its definition, the name of its parent class. There is no list of individual class members; that would be the taxonomy. Occasionally, we will encounter a taxonomy that has been poured into its classification, with each named item distributed to its rightful class position. This feature is an "add-on" and not an intrinsic part of the classification. As a rule, classifications do not contain detailed data sets.

Before the computer age, scientists were grateful for classifications that could be laid out in a simple arborized graph (e.g., The Classification of Life) or in a small schematic (e.g., The Periodic Table of the Elements), or in a few sentences (e.g., The Classification Theorem of the Finite Simple Groups). As computers gained acceptance, scientists

113

demanded that their classifications include data and that the data could be added without limit. Because the goal of classification is to distill information into a simple and parsimonious representation of the natural world, it would be counterproductive to insert an unlimited amount of information into the class structure.

A classification just won't do when we would prefer a compositional data structure

Outside of the natural sciences, particularly in the field of engineering, the components of objects often carry greater importance than the classes of objects. If we are building a data structure to contain relevant information about cars, we might want to know the make, model, and production year of the car. Beyond that, we might want to have a list of every part used in the car assembly, and how those parts fit with other parts. A data scientist might build something called a classification, listing cars by their manufacturing class, but the subclasses may contain parts of cars, not types of cars.

In semantic languages, the relationship between a class and its subclasses is an 'is_a' relationship. The subclass of a class must be a type of parent class. Engineers may not be happy with 'is_a' relationships among classes. They might prefer to create 'part_of' relationships, in which a subclass is created from parts of the parent class. Such data structures are sometimes referred to as compositional classifications. When we create 'part_of' subclasses, we eliminate a defining feature of every classification: inheritance. A part of an object cannot inherit the class property of the parent class, because class properties apply to the whole objects in the class. In the natural sciences, so-called compositional classifications are not classifications at all and must be handled with some other form of data representation. The topic of compositional class-oriented programming will be discussed in "Section 5.3. Classes and class-oriented programming."

A classification just won't do when we cannot find a theory or model for the classification

Most good classifications can be described in a sentence or two that tells us the underlying organizational principle upon which the classes were built. For example, the Periodic Table is a consecutive ordering of the elements, in rows that preserve the periodic behaviors of the elements. The Classification of Life is a tree-shaped sequential hierarchy of defined classes of organisms descending from a root class, over the past 4 billion years. The Classification Theorem of Finite Simple Groups is a mathematical proof yielding a complete listing of all possible classes of finite simple groups.

If classes and their various connections to one another are created without a clear understanding of a conceptual model for the developing classification, then it is unlikely that the final product will provide an internally consistent and useful representation of reality.

A classification just won't do when our intended data objects are demonstrably unclassifiable

People don't often stop to think about whether their data objects are classifiable; they just assume that anything can be classified if you just try hard enough. Sadly, this is not the case. In "Section 1.4. Things that defy simple classification," we reviewed several reasons why certain types of items cannot be classified. In such cases, a straightforward effort to create a classification will ultimately fail. Later in this chapter, we will discuss methods of dealing with unclassifiable items, without abandoning altogether our urge to use classifications.

Section 3.2. Ontologies to the rescue

When a classification is not up to the job, an ontology might be your best alternative. But what exactly is ontology? It is one of the great ironies of science that ontologies (Greek "ontos," that which is and "logia," natural discourse) which are intended to embody the meaning of things, are themselves poorly defined. So much so that is difficult to find any two authors who have equivalent definitions [1–4]. As I write this, I take some consolation in knowing that however I choose to define ontology, no colleagues of mine can invalidate my definition, since there are numerous vague and conflicting definitions floating in the info-verse, and no one can claim any credible authority on the point.

Let's start with a minimalist definition that most of us can accept.

> An ontology is a set of categories or classes in a knowledge domain that indicates their properties and the relationships between those classes.

This definition seems to be nearly identical to the definition of a classification. There are, however, some differences that we must understand. First ontologies contain categories, as well as classes. A category is a group of things, and the group may be constituted by any criteria that is convenient to the ontologist (e.g., by similarity, by age, by alphabetical order). A class differs from a category in the sense that all the members of a class must share some feature in common that is exclusive to the class. Secondly, there is nothing in the definition of an ontology that would indicate that the categories or classes must be structured as a strict hierarchy, with classes having a single parent class. Ontologists can create classes that have multiple parent classes, and classes may have relationships with any number of other classes. Finally, ontologists are not constrained to assign objects of only one class. An object can be assigned membership to multiple classes.

Aside from the basic definition, ontologies have one additional feature that we often employ in practice. Ontologies, unlike classifications, contain data and the data contained in ontologies is delivered in a semantic language. Because the contents of ontologies are composed in a semantic language, ontologies can be parsed by computer algorithms. In theory, a sophisticated computer algorithm can parse through an ontology, of any size, determining the relationships and properties of classes and their contained objects, all the while drawing logical inferences of the knowledge domain. Who could ask for anything more? [Glossary Parsing]

Now that we have a working definition for ontologies, we can see instantly that ontologies provide us with a solution for situations when a classification just won't do the job.

Conditions when an ontology comes in handy:

1. **When we intend to create an organized archive of descriptive information**

   A classification contains no annotative data. Ontologies can contain an unlimited amount of descriptive information provided that the information is prepared with a semantic language and that the objects of the information are linked to their classes within the ontology. If we treat ontologies as simply information assigned to classes, then we are reducing the ontologies to glorified filing systems.

2. **When we would prefer a compositional data structure**

   Ontologies place no restrictions on classes. A class can consist of parts of objects belonging to the parent class, as is the case in compositional data structures. We can add here that compositional classes do not retain inheritance. For example, if we created a Class Beak as a compositional subclass of Class Aves (birds), we could not expect the beaks to fly like birds.

3. **When we cannot find a theory or model for the classification**

   An ontology does not require a theory for the natural order of its classes. An ontology can have one model, or many models, or no model. Emphasizing the point, Natalya Noy and Deborah McGuinness wrote, "There is no one correct way to model a domain; there are always viable alternatives [2]." The lack of any testable theory for an ontology is a dramatic departure from our study of classifications. The classification builder struggles to embody the natural order of things in her classification, believing that there is only one natural order and only one true representation of that order. In point of fact, much of the work of classification building involves constantly testing classes and relationships to validate that the classification represents reality. All of that constant testing and validation can be omitted when we use an ontology.

4. **When our intended data objects are demonstrably unclassifiable**

   The objects held in an ontology can be arranged by any criteria that is convenient. A heritable class structure is not required; nor is a defining class feature that extends to all the members of the class. Of course, if the objects included in the ontology are not limited to a standard class structure, we have no way to ascertain whether we have produced a complete representation of a knowledge domain. Therefore the feature of classifications known as completeness is not guaranteed by ontologies.

In summary, ontologies expand the role of the traditional classification, a feature that is particularly appealing to non-taxonomists who deal with information analysis (e.g., anyone working in data science, informatics, library science, and computer science, bioinformatics). Currently, the term "classification" is fading rapidly in popularity, sloppily subsumed by the computer-ready concept of "ontology". In fact, it is possible to convert a classification into an ontology, by describing every element of the classification in proper semantic language. It is also possible to convert an ontology into a classification by adhering closely to a classification's strict rules for classes and properties. In practice, however, it would be exceedingly rare to come across a classification that could pass as an ontology or vice versa. We should probably resist thinking of ontologies as "classifications for the computer age" or as "classifications without all the fussy rules" or as "classifications delivered in a semantic language". All of these simplistic slogans are misleading and unhelpful. In the final section of this chapter, we will discuss ways in which ontologies and classifications can co-exist to one another's mutual benefit.

Section 3.3. Quantum of meaning: The triple

Three conditions must be satisfied in a meaningful assertion.

1. There is a specified object about which the assertion is made.
2. There is data that pertains to the specified object.
3. There is metadata that describes the data; metadata being defined as data that pertains to the specified object.) [Glossary Metadata]

The triple can be described as a sequence of subject-metadata-data, or, equivalently, as subject-predicate-object.

Here is an example:

```
"John Doe" "Height measured in feet" "6"
```

"John Doe" is the object of the triple, and "Height measured in feet" is the metadata, and "6" is the data.

When pressed, we could express non-quantitative information in the form of a triple.

```
"John" "loves" "Mary"
```

Here "John," the subject, is associated with the predicate "loves" and the object of his affections is "Mary".

Every complete assertion in the data universe is composed of triples, whether we know it or not. In fact, all well-structured databases and spreadsheets, and semantic structures can be tokenized as triples, and all collections of triples can be ported into any familiar data structure. We devote this section to triples because triples are the fundamental units of meaning in the information realm, much as atoms are the fundamental units of matter in the physical realm. Triples provide a solid foundation for all assertions, all relationships, and all efforts of reasoning with data. [Glossary Database, Spreadsheet]

In the case of classifications, triples can easily express the relationships among classes and their objects. For example, in the Classification of Life, we might say:

Homo sapiens common_name Humans
H. sapiens subclass_of Homo
Homo subclass_of Homininae
Homininae subclass_of Hominidae
Hominidae subclass_of Hominoidea
Hominoidea subclass_of Catarrhini

Catarrhini subclass_of Simiiformes
Simiiformes subclass_of Haplorrhini
Haplorrhini subclass_of Primates

In this case, we expressed the ascending classes from humans to primates, using only two metadata terms: common_name and subclass_of.

Let's look at some of the basic operations that can be conducted with sets of triples. Here are some triples, that may have been extracted from a medical report:

```
"Jules Berman" "blood glucose level" "85"
"Mary Smith" "blood glucose level" "90"
"Samuel Rice" "blood glucose level" "200"
"Jules Berman" "eye color" "brown"
"Mary Smith" "eye color" "blue"
"Samuel Rice" "eye color" "green"
```

Here are a few triples, as they might occur in a haberdasher's dataset.

```
"Juan Valdez" "hat size" "8"
"Jules Berman" "hat size" "9"
"Homer Simpson" "hat size" "9"
"Homer Simpson" "hat_type" "bowler"
```

We can combine the triples from a medical dataset and a haberdasher's data set, that apply to a common subject:

```
"Jules Berman" "blood glucose level" "85"
"Jules Berman" "eye color" "brown"
"Jules Berman" "hat size" "9"
```

We should take note of a few things. Each triple is a complete informational object and does not need to accompany any other triples in any order or any place. The portability of triples permits us to achieve data integration of seemingly unrelated data sets. [Glossary Data integration, Software agent]

Using unique identifiers in triples

In the examples of triples that we have seen, our human subjects were identified by their names (e.g., John). Names make poor identifiers because they are not unique. Many persons are named "John". A good triple will employ unique identifiers for its object. When we know the unique identifier for a data object, we can collect all of the information associated with the object. If information about the same identifier (corresponding to our "John") is held in numerous databases, we can collect all of the triples associated with the identifier, regardless of their locations. Furthermore, if we know the class that holds the object carrying the unique identifier, then we can infer that the object has all of the properties of its class, along with all the properties of its ancestral classes. Consider the following example [5].

Triples in resource #1

```
75898039563441    name                G. Willikers
75898039563441    gender              male
```

Triples in resource #2

```
75898039563441    age                 35
75898039563441    is_a_class_member   cowboy
94590439540089    name                Hopalong Tagalong
94590439540089    is_a_class_member   cowboy
```

Merged triples from resources #1 and #2

```
75898039563441    name                G. Willikers
75898039563441    gender              male
75898039563441    is_a_class_member   cowboy
75898039563441    age                 35
94590439540089    name                Hopalong Tagalong
94590439540089    is_a_class_member   cowboy
```

A stored collection of triples is known as a triplestore. The merger of two triplestores combines the triples related to identifiers (e.g., 75898039563441) from both resources. In this case, their merger tells us that the data objects identified as 75898039563441 and 94590439540089 are both members of the class cowboy. We now have two instance members from the same class, and this gives us some additional information related to the types of instances contained in the class and their properties.

Identifiers allow us to collect all of the data associated with a unique object while ensuring that we exclude that data that should be associated with any other object. There are various methods for generating and assigning unique identifiers for data objects [5–8].

UUID (Universally Unique Identifier) is an example of one type of algorithm that creates collision-free identifiers that can be automatically generated whenever new objects are created (i.e., during the run-time of a software application). Linux systems have a built-in UUID utility, "uuidgen.exe", that can be called from the system prompt. Equivalent UUID generators are readily available for every popular computer operating system [8,9]. [Glossary Identification, Syntax, UUID, Unique object, Uniqueness, Universally unique identifier, Utility]

Here are a few examples of output values generated by the "uuidgen.exe" utility: (Fig. 3.1)

The UUID utility produces a fixed-length character string suitable as an object identifier. The UUID utility is trusted and widely used by computer scientists. Independent-minded readers can easily design their unique object identifiers, using pseudorandom number generators, or with one-way hash generators.

Before we leave our discussion of the remarkably handy UUID utility, let's look at a little trick that is provided by the utility, that allows us to create a unique identifier string,

```
c:\cygwin64\bin>uuidgen.exe
0ffb2f8a-0934-491c-a23f-648d845d8dc9

c:\cygwin64\bin>uuidgen.exe
7478f639-58d7-4866-bef6-2e98fe400a84

c:\cygwin64\bin>uuidgen.exe
31826f46-bfdb-4a53-9f90-708c079ef6e9

c:\cygwin64\bin>uuidgen.exe
d2758900-b350-4e88-aca8-efce16aa9925
```

FIG. 3.1 Multiple outputs from the UUID generator utility. Notice that each time the utility is called from the command line, a new and unique identifier is created. [Glossary Command-line, Command-line utility]

in the customary UUID format, that has the added feature of embedding, in encrypted form, the time at which the unique identifier was created. Let's call the uuidgen.exe utility once more, adding the "-t" parameter to our command line. The "-t" parameter tells the uuidgen.exe utility to use the current time as a generator for the newly created identifier.

```
c:\cygwin64\bin>uuidgen.exe -t
```

The output of the command is shown here:

```
07d10b5c-f38e-11eb-bbb0-2c27d72775bb
```

Believe it or not, the time at which the UUID identifier was created is embedded in the character string. We can decrypt the time from the identifier with a command-line call to another UUID utility (uuidparse.exe, also bundled in Linux and Cygwin distributions).

```
c:\cygwin64\bin>uuidparse.exe 07d10b5c-f38e-11eb-bbb0-
2c27d72775bb
```

From the command line output, we find the date/time corresponding to the moment when the UUID was generated:

```
07d10b5c-f38e-11eb-bbb0-2c27d72775bb    2021-08-02 08:34:50,
697814-04:00
```

It is a bit unintuitive, but utilities such as uuidgen.exe, and the many simple one-way hash algorithms (e.g., md5sum.exe, sha1sum.exe, sha512sum.exe) are among the most useful tools available to programmers and non-programmers. In theory, identifier systems are incredibly easy to implement, if you follow these three easy steps:

1. Generate a unique character sequence, such as UUID, or a long random number.
2. Assign the unique character sequence (i.e., identifier) to each new object, at the moment that the object is created. In the case of a hospital, a patient's unique identifier

is created at the moment he or she is registered into the hospital information system. In the case of a bank, a customer's identifier is created at the moment that he or she is provided with an account number. In the case of an object-oriented programming language, such as Ruby, an object identifier is created when the "new" method is sent to a class object, instructing the class object to create a new class instance. [Glossary Method]

3. Preserve the identifier number and bind it to the object. In practical terms, this means that whenever the data object accrues new data, the new data is attached to the unique identifier. [Glossary Accrue]

An identifier system is a set of data-related protocols that satisfy the following conditions:

- Completeness. Every unique object has an identifier.
- Uniqueness. Each identifier is a unique sequence.
- Exclusivity. Each identifier is assigned to only one unique object.
- Authenticity. Objects that receive identification can be verified as the objects that they are intended to be.
- Aggregation. All information associated with an identifier can be collected.
- Permanence. An identifier is never deleted.

For a unique identifier system to work, no two objects can have the same identifier (obviously). A long character string, consisting of randomly chosen numeric and alphabetic characters is an excellent identifier because the chances of two individuals being assigned the same string are essentially zero.

After the identifier has been assigned, the identifier can always be used as a substitute for the name of the item associated with the identifier. For example, if John Smith is assigned the identifier "acabe08f-113c-4a24-a245-bc531904f18e", then he can be referred to as "acabe08f-113c-4a24-a245-bc531904f18e", so as not to confuse him with any of the other thousands of John Smiths in the world.

Even the best classifications contain ambiguities. Let's look at one example taken from the Classification of Life. Pholidota is the class that contains all the pangolins. In the European Bioinformatics Taxonomy, Class Pangolin is assigned a unique ID number: Taxonomy ID:9971.

The Classification of Life is an aggregate classification assembled from subclassifications (e.g., plants, protists, animals, bacteria) assembled by thousands of scientists laboring over the centuries. The scientists working on isolated subsets are, as a rule, unaware of the class names assigned to organisms outside their specialty. As it happens, the term "Pholidota" derives from the Greek, "pholidotos" meaning scaly, an adjective that could apply to lots of different organisms. Plant taxonomists applied the name Philodota to a class of orchids. Fortunately, the orchid Class Philodota was assigned Taxonomy ID:79446, a different identifier than the pangolin Class Philodota (Taxonomy ID:9971).

When we write a software program that takes the name of a class and retrieves data, we cannot be certain what data we might receive when we enter the term "Philodota" as our query. We could receive a lot of information of pangolins, or we might receive information related to orchids. If we search by a unique identifier, we can be certain that our Philodota data will correspond to the organism that we intended to search.

Replicate assignments of one name to different organisms is commonplace. For example, Acanthamoeba, a genus of single-cell eukaryotes that can be found as free-living amoeba or as parasitic pathogens [10]. Acanthamoeba is also applied to the sole identified species of mimiviruses, *Acanthamoeba polyphaga* [11]. The two organisms with the same name are distinguished by their unique identifiers. [Glossary Mimiviridae]

Some of the consequences of taxonomic vagaries would be comical if they were not fraught with deleterious clinical consequences. For example, when the name of a fungus changes, so must the name of the associated disease. Consider "Allescheria boydii," People infected with this organism were said to suffer from the disease known as allescheriasis. When the organism's name was changed to Petriellidium boydii, the disease name was changed to petriellidosis. When the fungal name was changed, once more, to Pseudallescheria boydii, the disease name was changed to pseudallescheriasis [12]. All three names appear in the literature (past and present), confusing generations of physicians [13].

Other forms of redundancies have an even greater prevalence. For example, there are many instances in which a class or a species is provided with more than one name. For example, Euura is a genus of sawflies, which, in fact, are not true flies (i.e., not members of Class Diptera). More to the point, the genus Euura has 26 synonymous class names, but Euura does not set the record for taxonomic redundancy. The species *Gluconobacter oxydans* is a member of Class Alphaproteobacteria. *G. oxydans* has 53 synonymous names. There are undoubtedly thousands of instances, possibly millions, in which one organism or class is provided with more than one alternate name. We also see instances of different organisms, with different names, having identical abbreviations. For example, *Escherichia coli* (a bacterium) and *Entamoeba coli* (an amoebozoan intestinal parasite) are both commonly known as *E. coli*.

Is there anything we might do to rectify a system that assigns multiple identifiers to the same object? Yes, but the process is messy. When an object has been assigned more than one unique identifier, then the object itself must be annotated with all the unique identifiers that apply. This requirement needs some explanation. Suppose you are registered as a patient at five different hospitals, and each of those hospitals assigns you a unique identifier; and all of the unique identifiers are different from one another. If the patient data from all five hospitals are aggregated, you would be counted as five different patients, based on your five different unique identifiers. If you knew all of your identifiers, you could scan the aggregate data and identify five entries that belong to you, and you could arrange to have these separate entries combined under one record. This is an onerous project, but if all of the unique identifiers were conveyed as triples in a triplestore, then it could all be done automatically, with a few software instructions.

To see how this might work, let's imaging that one patient has been re-registered by various departments in the hospital, on four different occasions spaced out over 30 years.

Different records pertaining to the patient are stored under four different assigned "unique" identifiers. These identifiers maybe something like the following:

```
c72f330e-9c34
9054e81b-5b03
679ffc42-9fa6
bbe42c4b-8f5b
```

Then we would need to construct four triples, that might look something like the following:

```
c72f330e-9c34    same_as    9054e81b-5b03
c72f330e-9c34    same_as    679ffc42-9fa6
c72f330e-9c34    same_as    bbe42c4b-8f5b
```

Because our triplestore contains triples telling us that the four different identifiers belong to the same patient, we can reconstruct a complete medical record for the patient, from all of his or her identifiers listed in the hospital database.

Of course, the best approach is to forbid subsequent identifiers once the first identifier has been assigned. In practice, errors of redundant names and identifiers are rampant in just about every large data set. Without exaggeration, maintaining a good identifier system is the most important role of every data curator. A data set that contains tainted identifiers or unidentified data has no value.

To summarize, when unique identifiers are properly linked to an object, we can modify and annotate our classifications and ontologies, regardless of size and complexity. When we lack properly linked unique identifiers, we cannot use data sensibly. In "Section 5.6. A few software tools for traversing triplestores and classifications," we will be looking at some examples of software techniques whereby we can analyze classifications and triplestores.

Section 3.4. Semantic languages

Semantics is the study of meaning (Greek root, semantikos, significant meaning). In the context of data science, semantics is the technique of creating meaningful assertions about data objects. A meaningful assertion is also known as a triple and consists of an identified data object, a data value, and a descriptor for the data value. Semantics involves creating triples, combining assertions about data objects (i.e., merging triples), and assigning classes to the data objects contained in triples; hence relating triples to other triples. In practical terms, semantics is how we express triples. The purpose of semantic languages is to provide a standard way of describing triples that we can all understand. RDF (Resource Description Framework) is a simple semantic language that has been designed specifically for the description of information on the web (i.e., WorldWide Web). The "Resource" in "Resource Description Framework" is the data held at a specific

URL (i.e., web address) or a specific network location. A simple example of triples described in RDF follows here. [Glossary URL, URN]

```
<rdf:Description
    rdf:about="http://www.the_url_here.org/ldip/">
    <dc:title>Normal Lung</dc:title>
  </rdf:Description>
```

Here, the subject of the triple is expressed as the URL identifier. The data associated with the subject is the character string "Normal lung", and the metadata tells us that "Normal lung" is a title. The notation <dc:title> informs us that the definition of the metadata is held in a publicly available document that is abbreviated here as "dc". If we had the entire RDF document, we would find a declaration near the top of the document, telling us that "dc" refers to the web location for the "Dublin Core" document, which contains definitions for a few dozen general document descriptors. [Glossary Dublin Core Metadata]

We could have prepared three triples is proper RDF syntax like the following:

```
<rdf:Description
    rdf:about="http://www.the_url_here.org/ldip/">
    <dc:title>Normal Lung</dc:title>
  </rdf:Description>
<rdf:Description
    rdf:about="http://www.the_url_here.org/ldip/">
    <dc:creator>Bill Moore</dc:creator>
  </rdf:Description>
<rdf:Description
    rdf:about="http://www.the_url_here.org/ldip/">
    <dc:date>2006-06-28</dc:date>
  </rdf:Description>
```

RDF permits us to collapse multiple triples that apply to a single subject. The following RDF:Description statement is equivalent to the three triples, directly above:

```
<rdf:Description
    rdf:about="http://www.the_url_here.org/ldip/">
    <dc:title>Normal Lung</dc:title>
    <dc:creator>Bill Moore</dc:creator>
    <dc:date>2006-06-28</dc:date>
  </rdf:Description>
```

An example of a short but well-formed RDF image specification document is:

```
<?xml version="1.0"?>
<rdf:RDF
      xmlns:rdf="http://www.w3.org/1999/02/22-rdf-syntax-ns#";
      xmlns:dc="http://purl.org/dc/elements/1.1/">
```

```
<rdf:Description
  rdf:about="http://www.the_url_here.org/ldip/">
  <dc:title>Normal Lung</dc:title>
  <dc:creator>Bill Moore</dc:creator>
  <dc:date>2006-06-28</dc:date>
</rdf:Description>
</rdf:RDF>
```

The first line tells you that the document is XML. The second line tells you that the XML document is an RDF resource. The third and fourth lines are the namespace documents that are referenced within the document (more about this later). Following that is the RDF statement that we have already seen. [Glossary Namespace, XML]

Do not get overly excited by any particular semantic language because they are all constantly changing, and all of them are subject to obsolescence. Examples of semantic languages include: RDF (Resource Description Framework), DAML (DARPA Agent Markup Language, fully expanded as Defense Advanced Research Projects Agency Agent Markup Language), DAML+OIL (DAML + Ontology Interchange Language), OWL (Web Ontology Language). Two stripped-down syntaxes for expressing triples are n3 (Notation3) and Turtle. [Glossary Notation3, OWL, RDF, RDF Schema, Turtle]

Strict adherence to any of the semantic languages is rarely encountered in real life. Most data are held in traditional databases and are either non-accessible (e.g., privately held and publicly withheld), uninterpretable (e.g., having meaning only to a small set of users), or meaningless (e.g., having been designed without any real meaning or having lost its meaning over time). Hence, what we stress in this chapter is the fundamental unit of ontologic meaning; the triple. Triples are the basic informational units employed by all semantic languages and are the intended conveyors of content for the so-called semantic web [14,15]. A well-constructed collection of triples (i.e., a triplestore) can always be converted into any popular semantic language, with a bit of effort. [Glossary Semantic web]

Descriptors and descriptive logic

Semantic languages come with formal ways of describing things, and the things that populate the world of classifications consist of classes, instances (i.e., class members), and properties. Everything we think of as "data" is just a value of a property assigned to a class or an instance, conveyed as triples. In the previous section, we defined a triple as a metadata/data pair associated with an identifier. All metadata descriptors are properties, in the sense that each data value is the value of a property represented by the metadata.

Here are a few descriptors that we regularly encounter in semantic languages:

"is_a" - Tells us that if A is_a B, then A is a type of B.

When B is a class of things, the "is_a" descriptor becomes identical in meaning to the instance_of descriptor. When we say that A is_a member of class B, it is equivalent to saying that A is an instance of Class B.

"has_a" - Tells us that if A has_a B, then A has something called B.

The "has_a" relationship does not tell us much about what B is. A statement such as "I have a craving for pizza" could be written with a has_a descriptor, but "craving for pizza" is not a class and the statement isn't exactly bursting with semantic rigor. In contrast, the "part_of" descriptor, provides a clear indication of a compositional relationship.

"part_of" - Tells us that if A part_of B, then A is a component of B. (e.g., A carburetor is part of a car).

We are tempted to say that has_a and part_of are inverses of each other. If a car has a carburetor, then certainly the inverse can be inferred (i.e., a carburetor must be a part of a car). We must return to the semantic vagueness of the has_a descriptor. If I have a craving for pizza, we cannot infer that craving for pizza is a component of myself.

We describe classes with a definition written in a simple (i.e., not particularly semantic) language such as English. The same is true for class properties, which are also composed in simple language. In the case of properties, our definition must include two additional descriptors: domain and range. The property domain is the list of classes that can use the property. If the domain is a single class, then the property only applies to that one class, and thus the property would be a class property. Conversely, if the domain of the property lists several classes, then we know that the property is not the class property of any single class. For example, a "can_fly" property might apply to birds, bats, airline pilots, and Rocky the flying squirrel. The "can_fly" property would have multiple domains and would not serve as the class property for any of those domains.

Properties must also be provided with a range. The range describes the data values that can be applied to the property. For example, "between 5 and 30" or "either yes or no" or "either true, false, or nil", or "name of a member of Class Person" might be ranges for four different properties. [Glossary Descriptor, Range]

Schemas and schema languages

A schema is a document composed in a semantic language, that lists and defines classes and properties. Each class should be provided with the name of its parent class if a parent class exists; and each property should be provided with its domain (i.e., the names of classes to which the property applies) and its range (i.e., the allowable values of the property). When a schema is prepared in conformance with the RDF format, it is usually referred to as an RDFS (RDF Schema).

The job of writing a good schema document is quite challenging. The author of the schema must be thoroughly versed in a semantic language and in the formal rules for composing schemas. Let's just look at one example of a specified property within a schema.

An RDF Schema declaration for the dateTime property might be:

```
<rdf:Property rdf:about="http://www.the_url_here.org/ldip_sch#dateTime">
  <rdfs:label>dateTime</label>
  <rdfs:comment>
```

```
    The date and time at which an event occurs, in ISO8601 format
    </rdfs:comment>
    <rdfs:domain rdf:resource="http://www.the_url_here.org/ldip_
    sch#Event"/>;
    <rdfs:range rdf:resource="http://www.the_url_here.org/ldip_xsd.
    xsd#iso8601"/>;
  </rdf:Property>
```

Let's look at the dateTime property. The first line announces that we will be declaring a Property within the current RDF schema document. The second line tells us the name (label) of the Property (dateTime). This might come in handy if we had different names for the property in different languages. The comment includes a definition of the element.

The next line specifies the domain (class) for the property. The domain of a property is the class or classes for which the property may be used. In this case, the domain class for which the dateTime property applies is Event. This makes sense. If you need to describe an event, you would certainly want to include the time that the event occurred.

When a property has multiple classes in its domain, all the classes in the domain share the same property (obviously). This achieves some of the functionality of multi-class inheritance, without actually needing to instantiate multiple classes under a single object. This is a subtle concept and does not need to be mastered at this time. Suffice it to say that as you create your RDF Schemas, you should try to design your properties to apply to multiple classes, and you should try to instantiate objects under a single class.

The range of the property element tells us what kind of data is described. In RDF Schemas, the range of a property is often "Literal", an element defined in the RDF syntax document that refers to any character string. You can see immediately that describing the range of a property as a character string does little to constrain or structure the expected values for a data element.

In the example that we provided, the dateTime property specified a range consisting of an element conforming to the ISO8601 date/time format. [Glossary ISO]

```
    <rdfs:range rdf:resource="http://www.the_url_here.org/ldip_xsd.
    xsd#iso8601"/>
```

In this case, the full statement of the range consists of a fictitious resource (i.e., a web page), and to the particular section of the resource wherein, the "ISO8601" format is defined. To fully comply with the RDF Schema definition of the dateTime property, we would need to visit the resource, pull out the ISO8601 specification, and compose our data in the prescribed format for time. This seems like a lot of work, but it is the kind of thing that computers do for us, simply and quickly. [Glossary ISO8601]

Because RDF Schemas are posted on the Internet, like Web pages, with their unique Web address, they can be linked from any other web document. The purpose of the RDF schema is to provide a reference from internet documents, particularly ontologies, to the definitions of classes and properties included in those documents. Anyone can incorporate the classes and properties of a public RDF Schema into their RDF documents and ontologies, linking back to the schema for their definitions. RDF schemas are intended to promote interoperability between ontologies and data structures that use the same classes and properties. A single ontology or data structure can link to any number of RDF Schemas, permitting the ontology creator to choose a variety of well-defined classes and properties for inclusion.

Conceptually, schemas seem like a terrific way to ensure a high level of uniformity among diverse ontologies and web-based data structures. Here are just a few problems that we may encounter:

1. When a schema simply disappears from the web, an ontology's links will be dead-ended. As a consequence, classes and properties included in the ontology will be undefined.
2. A schema can be constructed in ways that are incompatible with the construction of the ontology to which it is linked. This might result in ontologic relationships that simply make no sense [1].
3. The formal rules of schema construction, as described for the most popular schema format (i.e., RDFS), permit stylistic options that can result in schemas that are computationally incompatible with one another [1]. [Glossary RDFS]

Self-description, the stealth super-power of semantic languages

One of the greatest innovations of modern consumerism is the product label, with the contents of the container plainly displayed. Nowadays, when we buy a jar of peanut butter, the name of the product is specified, the amount of the product contained in the jar is provided, a list of nutritional values is there for us to consider, a complete list of ingredients is provided, and a "best buy" date is stamped somewhere on the jar.

Semantic languages permit objects to describe themselves, a feature that can be used to great effect by capable computer scientists. For example, an ontology of an automobile may contain numerous properties and classes in its schema document. The individual objects included in the ontology or triplestore will have properties that are fully described in one or other formal schemas. These properties will include relationships, functions, and types of data, Regardless of the size of an ontology or triplestore, we can write relatively simple software programs that will collect all of the data that describes any and every identified object in our ontology or triplestore.

Self-description is one of the most useful features provided by object-oriented programming languages and is closely related to the programming techniques known as introspection and reflection. We will be discussing self-description in more detail when we reach "Section 5.5. Listening to what objects tell us". [Glossary Introspection]

Limitations of the semantic web and linked data

The semantic web is a particular vision of the World Wide Web in which all web content is found in semantically endowed documents [16]. This would mean that all data assertions would be in the form of triples described in one of the standard semantic languages. Web content would presumably be displayed much as we see it today, but the underlying data would be accessible to computers capable of parsing and understanding semantically annotated data. Because semantic languages permit data objects to be placed in classes defined in web-accessible schemas, the semantic web would certainly constitute the largest ontology ever created [1]. [Glossary Standard]

Though the concept of the semantic web, championed by Sir Tim Berners-Lee, has its enthusiastic supporters, relatively little has been done in terms of making it a reality [17]. Several of the impedimenta to progress are listed here:

1. Much of the data on the web is wrong, thus inferences drawn from internet data will be wrong.
2. There are numerous semantic languages and each of them has its own set of complexities. Because of the vagaries of semantically annotated forms of data, the algorithms that examine such data would tend to be quirky.
3. Data on the web is constantly changing. Inferences drawn on Tuesday may be the opposite of inferences drawn on Wednesday. This means that any conclusions drawn from the semantic web would be tentative, at best.
4. Data linkages are non-uniform. One of the working principles of the semantic web is that data can be linked between locations. In practice, web data is prepared with linking terms expressing the equivalent data, using different words. For example, a person's birth date may appear in various nonstandard formats and may have various metadata descriptors (e.g., date_of_birth, birth_date, birthday). As a result, it is virtually impossible to use the web to collect all of the data related to a particular query.
5. Only a small proportion of web data is usable. Most web data do not come annotated with basic information. We often do not know who created the data, who owns the data, whether the data can be used and copied freely, when the data was created, how the data was prepared, and how the data was verified and validated.
6. Semantic languages often have idiosyncratic implementations. One person may understand the rules of a semantic language differently from another person. Some of the semantic languages are quite complex, and we can have no expectations that everyone will uniformly implement a syntax.
7. Web addresses (also known as uniform resource locators or URLs) can change, disappear, or their content can be radically modified over time.

In addition to the technical limitations, we can expect to find limitations imposed by human fallibilities. The Internet is an enticing venue for cherry-picking. Users of large troves of data tend to pick out the data that happens to support their world-views, ignoring conflicting information. Even when we have unbiased analysts (if such persons exist), for any data set collected from the semantic web, there may exist a set of totally contradictory data, sitting out of sight and unavailable.

Mathematics remains the finest descriptive language for the natural sciences

We should spare a few words here to discuss a form of expression that has been around for a very long time, but which is seldom recognized for its role as a semantic language. We are referring here to mathematics and its symbolics. It is through the use of algebraic notation that we convey the meaning of abstract mathematical objects (e.g., constants, variables), and operations (e.g., addition, subtraction, multiplication, division), and their relationships (e.g., equals, greater than, belongs to). The symbols of mathematics have been adapted to describe physical reality, through scientific laws and formulas. Mathematical symbols are used to construct proofs of theorems and documentation of calculations. The language of mathematics is defined so carefully that the notations left by one mathematician can be understood by other mathematicians hundreds of years later, without ambiguity.[Glossary Variable]

Anyone in any country, regardless of their native language, can understand the symbols of mathematics. The so-called standardized semantic languages (e.g., RDF, OWL, DAML/OIL) rely upon words taken from some written language (e.g., English). The meaning of descriptions prepared in a semantic language may change when statements are translated from English. We could make the argument that assertions written in a semantic language are unambiguously interpreted by computers, but a language that your computer understands and you do not make for a very uncomfortable situation. Will we trust our computers to interpret semantic language correctly, when we lack the facility to validate the computer's judgment?

The semantic strength and endurance of mathematical notations can be compared with any of the current versions of the semantic language that are in use today. How many of the documents composed with popular semantic languages can be relied upon to convey the same meaning to everyone? How many of the semantic languages will be in common use ten years from now? We cannot say. We should leave ourselves open to the possibility that the next great semantic language may involve a standardized implementation of mathematical notation.

Section 3.5. Why ontologies sometimes disappoint us

If man had limited himself to the accumulation of facts, then science would be nothing but a sterile nomenclature and the great laws of nature would have remained unknown forever.

Pierre Simon de Laplace

A dirty laundry list of common deficiencies

Let's go back to basic definitions. A classification is a collection of defined classes and their relationships with one another. Ontologies are best thought of as systems for holding triples (composed in a semantic language) and assigning classes to the identified objects of triples. This means that ontologies, unlike classifications, can become very large, and that computer algorithms can search through ontologies to draw inferences about classes and class instances. In fact, if the classes in an ontology meet the defining criteria of classification, then an ontology can fulfill all of the functions of classification, and much more. For this reason, data scientists may consider ontologies to be computer-friendly versions of traditional classifications. There are many caveats, as follows:

Ontologies can be enormous but incomplete

It is not hard to find ontologies that are designed to hold a lot of information about objects. Creating large ontologies full of facts about objects is not, in itself, sinful. Nonetheless, an ontology is not likely to have any scientific value, regardless of its information content, if it has not been designed thoughtfully. In particular, there is no requirement for completeness in an ontology. That is to say that the classes and the triples need not cover the object domain. Consequently, if the ontology is incomplete, then it is impossible to draw any inferences that require knowledge of the full object domain. Any conclusions you might want to draw may be proven false when we begin to look at classes of data that were excluded from the ontology.

In point of fact, there are circumstances when, as a collection grows in size, it becomes increasingly difficult to find what you need. As a trivial example, consider the perennial task of finding a needle in a haystack. As you add more hay, you make matters worse. You would be much better off if the haystack were small, consisting of a single straw adjacent to a single needle [18].

We can add here that there are no limits of object attributes in an ontology. A single object included in an ontology may be described with any number of attributes. For example, we can attach thousands of metadata/data pairs to a single person (e.g., height, weight, eye color, hat size, and so on). Great difficulties arise when the dimensionality of the data (i.e., the number of measured attributes for each data object) increases. The problem is known to mathematicians by the harrowing name of "the curse of dimensionality"! Basically, as the number of attributes for a data object increases, the multidimensional space encompassing the attributes becomes sparsely populated, and the distances between any two objects, even the closest neighbors, becomes absurdly large. When you have thousands of dimensions, the space that holds the objects is so large that clustering becomes incomputable and meaningless. The curse applies to any algorithm that compares data objects on their distances from one another, as implemented in several so-called classifier techniques (e.g., recommender, predictor, and support vector machine algorithms) [19]. [Glossary Classifier, Curse of dimensionality, Recommender, Support vector machine]

Ontologies can be promiscuously inclusive

Ontologies are not always defined in a manner that clearly determines the objects that do not belong. Consequently, ontologies may become polluted with irrelevant terms that should have been included in other ontologies.

Ontologies can have conflicting rules

Whereas classifications are composed of classes and subclasses, built upon the relationships of the different classes, ontologies are often rule-based systems that place objects into any number of different classes, based upon the object's adherence to the rules of the classes to which they are assigned. The task of anticipating how all the different rules may interact with one another, for every allowable combination of instances is difficult under the best of circumstances. When new rules are continuously added to the ontology, we can expect serious problems to arise [20].

Data integration and interoperability issues

It is tempting to think that schemas permit us to link together different ontologies whose knowledge domains overlap. It should be a simple matter to review the classes in the respective schema's of multiple ontologies, finding matches between classes and properties in both schemas. Unfortunately, it seldom works out so nicely.

Different schemas may apply different terms to the same object. For example, dermatopathologists refer to a certain species of skin tumor as "dermatofibroma." Pathologists who specialize in tumors of the soft tissue will refer to the very same species of the tumor as a "fibrous histiocytoma". A curator may review a schema prepared by a dermatopathologist and a schema prepared by a soft tissue pathologist and fail to recognize that both classes of the tumor, known by different names, refer to the same object.

Different schemas may contain discordant definitions for the same terms appearing in both schemas. As an extreme example, the biological property known as "regression" will have opposite meanings to oncologists and neurologists. When a neurologist says that the patient's tumor has undergone regression, she is indicating that the tumor has shrunk and the patient's condition has improved. When a neurologist says that a child has a neurologic condition has regressed, she is indicating the patient's condition has worsened. A single term that may have two opposite meanings is known as a Janus term, after the Roman god of doors, who is always depicted as having two faces staring in opposite directions.

Semanticists have invented structures for the primary purpose of supporting semantic representations of data in a format that enforces the correct interpretation of terms. This is done using so-called "namespaces," which are schemas that list one particular meaning for each term listed in the schema. If the semanticist uses the word "date" to mean the fruit *Phoenix dactylifera*, then she will append to the word "date" the name of the namespace schema that contains a definition of the fruit. If the semanticist uses the word "date" to refer to a social engagement, then she will append the word date to the name of the namespace that defines "date" as a friendly encounter between two individuals. Yes, data specialists must work very hard to achieve a simple description of information that we are accustomed to reaching effortlessly, from the context of the message. We must remember that computers need us to be explicit. Of course, if a name-space document suddenly disappears from the Web, or is modified, our carefully built semantic relationships will collapse.

Much more common than any of the aforementioned issues is the finding that individuals with different backgrounds will perceive the same object differently. When I look at a television, I see an appliance that lets me watch my favorite programs. When a technician looks at a television, she may see a device that has a 55 inch screen and a high-definition display. When an electrical engineer sees a television, she may see a digital signal processing device. We all have different perceptions of common objects. We base our understanding of classes and properties on our perceptions. Every ontology reflects our understanding of reality, making it difficult to map ontologies that were created by different persons. Discordances are most irksome for ontologies that deal with creative aesthetics ("Writing! You call that writing! That is not writing! That is scribbling!"). Classifications, which almost always deal with naturally occurring, measurable, and testable assertions, are less open to debate ("a rose is a rose by any other name").

These considerations would suggest that ontologies are not particularly interoperable. We cannot expect to seamlessly pass queries from one ontology to another and extract the information that we hope to find. [Glossary Nomenclature mapping]

Wrong choice of data structure

Ontologies are a great choice of data structure for users of a particular bent. When you need to tie a great deal of information to stable objects that belong to classes contained in classifications or stable Schemas, an ontology may be an ideal solution. When your users are simply interested in fetching information on a topic, indexes are probably the best option [9]. Indexes can be constructed on Gigabyte-sized corpuses of text in just a few seconds. They can be reconstructed and updated as needed. They can even be integrated with alternate indexes prepared for the same corpus of text, or tied to other indexes from other text sources [9]. Users interested in up-to-date searches for the information contained in a large body of text might prefer indexes, thus avoiding the fussiness and eccentricities of complex ontologies.

Sometimes ontologies solve a problem that nobody wants to solve. For example, anatomic ontologies exist, but they do not seem to be particularly popular among the intended users. Instead, anatomists tend to rely upon drawings and detailed photographs (e.g., radiologic images) as their source of information. There is an active industry centered on anatomic illustration. There is no equivalent effort centered on anatomic ontology. The issue is not that anatomic ontologies are scientifically invalid; it is just that they are not particularly useful, at this moment.

Issues of the Profession

Reinvented wheel syndrome

There's an often-repeated saying among information scientists: "Standards are so popular that everyone wants to have one for their very own." Although most ontologies are intended to serve as the standard way of classifying and collecting data, within a specified knowledge domain, those good intentions are seldom realized. Because ontologies are complex, offering an infinite number of options regarding their design, it would be very unlikely that any one ontologic representation of a knowledge domain would suit every potential user. Ontologies may have a highly complex and inscrutable set of class rules and relationships, or they may make use of a difficult semantic language, or they may be deeply embedded in commercial software. In such cases, potential users may prefer not to invest the time, energy, or money needed to fully implement the ontology. They may feel that they would be better off creating their own ontology, fashioned to meet their needs. As a consequence, we may see a proliferation of ontologies all covering, to some extent, the same knowledge domain.

Lack of community support

Ontologies have very little value without a community of users who are committed to testing the classes, relationships, rules, properties, and objects that compose the ontology. In addition, because ontologies generally provide an expansive framework to accommodate newly arriving object annotations, the community must be committed to continuously verifying the incoming data. It's easy to see how ontologies may lose their data integrity over time, without community support.

Impermanence

"Vidi nihil permanere sub sole." (I have seen that nothing under the sun endures).

Latin saying

Ontologies come and ontologies go. The causes of death are many, ranging from lack of popularity, lack of community support, loss of sustained funding, and abandonment when something better comes along. Ontologies tend to be complex, loaded with data, and expensive to create and maintain. When a large ontology dies, the professional consequences may be dire and may extend to a large number of involved personnel.

When working with ontologies, it is a good idea to prepare for the worst. All of the data annotations can be kept in a triplestore, connected to but separate from the class-based schema that defines the classes and properties of the ontology. If the ontology is abandoned, the data can be resurrected from the triplestore. New classes and properties, to which subjects of the triplestore will be assigned, can sometimes be added by linking the original triples to a different schema. [Glossary Abandonware]

Over-reach

Because there are no rules that dictate the limits of an ontology, we sometimes see onto-logic products that are so large and complex that they cannot be sensibly curated. If your ontology suffers from any of the following symptoms, you may find it advantageous to simplify your work [5].

- Nobody, even the designers, fully understand the ontology model [21].
- For any given problem, no two data analysts seem able to formulate the query the same way, and no two query results are ever equivalent. [Glossary Query]
- Analyses predicated upon the ontology yield results that contradict validated observations.
- The ontology cannot be debugged when errors occur. Tinkering with the ontology only makes matters worse.
- Errors occur without anyone knowing that the error has occurred.
- The ontology lacks competence. Good ontologies are endowed with the ability to support inferencing (i.e., drawing logical conclusions about the properties of members of the ontology using descriptive logic). Ontologies that support logical analyses are said to be competent.
- The ontology lacks modularity. It is impossible to remove a set of classes within the ontology without collapsing its structure. When anything goes wrong, the entire ontology must be re-designed, from scratch.
- The ontology lacks general scientific relevance since it cannot be fitted under a higher-level ontology or over a lower-level ontology.

Section 3.6. Best practices for ontologies

Building a useful and logically consistent ontology is always difficult and can involve a considerable investment of time and resources. Before beginning an ontology project, it is best to ask yourself a few questions:

1. Is this ontology necessary? (Why bother?)

Good ontologies are not easy to build, and the wise ontologist will always ask whether some other option might be preferable. It is not possible to create excellent indexes for extremely large collections of information, in a very short amount of time. An index bypasses the tricky problem of creating classes and carefully assigning each data object to the proper class. If all that is needed is a way of finding information related to terms, then a detailed index, often tied to a nomenclature that groups synonymous terms under one canonical concept, is the best option.

In some cases, ontologists will find a ready-made ontology that can be appropriated as a whole. In other cases, an existing ontology can be modified to conform specifically to a particular user's needs. Some ontologies are available in the public domain, while others may be encumbered by licenses and fees. On occasion, it will be to the user's advantage to negotiate a license.

There will be mornings when, rather than jumping into a new ontology project, it is best to just stay in bed.

2. Does this ontology create logical ambiguities, inconsistencies, and paradoxes?

No matter how much thought is put into the creation of a new ontology, the designer can expect to encounter flaws. The more complex the design, the more inconsistencies will be uncovered. My own experience would suggest that ambiguities are far and away the most common flaw in any ontology. Because ontologies are products of language, and because language is a crude way of expressing anything conceptual, we can expect to find many situations in which one semantic statement can be interpreted several different ways. Because one of the goals of an ontology is to promote a uniform understanding of concepts, ambiguities greatly diminish the value of an ontology. [Glossary Ambiguity]

3. Is this ontology testable?

Everything in science must be testable. An untestable ontology falls into the dim realm of pseudoscience. [Glossary Pseudoscience]

4. Has this ontology been designed as simply as possible?

Ask yourself, "Is this ontology comprehensible to me?" Should you be using an ontology that you cannot understand?

5. Does the ontology drive down the complexity of its knowledge domain?

Good ontologies, much like good classifications, should reduce complexity.

6. Is this ontology functional?

Specifically, does the ontology support information search and retrieval, and can it be used to construct logical inferences? In short, can the classification be implemented?

7. Was it designed to accommodate completeness?

Ontologies, unlike classifications, need not contain a complete representation of a knowledge domain. Still, an ontology should be able to accommodate all classes, objects, and relevant information that is relevant to its intended purposes.

8. How does the ontology handle versioning?

When an ontology undergoes multiple revisions that are released to the general public on a more or less regular basis, we can guess that the following may apply:

Older versions of the ontology will almost certainly persist among its intended users. It is very common for the user community to prefer an older version of an ontology over the newer version. This is particularly true if the ontology's objects and relationships have been deeply embedded in a popular software application.

Implementations of all of the versions of the ontology will be idiosyncratic. As a general rule for all complex standards, including formal ontologies, the complexity of the product may exceed human comprehension. Every implementation of a complex data product tends to be non-uniform and "not up to code". Consequently, no two implementations of an ontology will be equivalent to one another. A corporation or a government agency may purposefully veer from the standard ontology to accommodate some local exigency. In some cases, a corporation may find it prudent to add non-standard embellishments or functionalities that cannot be easily reproduced by their competitors.

Older versions of the ontology will likely be semantically incompatible with newer versions.

Semantic incompatibilities among versions of a complex ontology are seldom given any serious thought. Malcolm Duncan has posted an insightful and funny essay entitled "The Chocolate Teapot (Version 2.3)" [22]. In this essay, he shows how new versions of ontologies may unintentionally alter the meanings of classes of terms contained in earlier versions, making it impossible to comprehend relationships [23].

Suppose you have a cooking-ware terminology with a "teapot" item. Version 1 of the nomenclature may list only one teapot material, porcelain, and only two permissible teapot colors, blue or white. Version 2 of the terminology might accommodate two teapot sub-types: blue teapot and white teapot (i.e., in version 2, blue and white are sub-types of the teapot, not colors of teapot). If a teapot were neither blue nor white, it would be coded under the parent term, "teapot." Suppose version 3 accommodates some new additions to the teapot pantheon: chocolate teapot, ornamental teapot, China teapot, and industrial teapot. Now the teapot world is shaken by a tempest of monumental proportions. The white and the blue teapots had been implicitly considered to be made of porcelain, like all China teapots. How does one deal with a white teapot that is not porcelain or a porcelain teapot that is a China teapot? If we had previously assumed that a teapot was an item in which tea is made, how do we adjust, conceptually, to the new term "ornamental teapot?" If the teapot is ornamental, then it has no tea-making functionality, and if it cannot be used to make tea, how can it be a teapot? Must we change our concept of the teapot to include anything that looks like a teapot? If so, how can we deal with the new term "industrial teapot," which is likely to be a big stainless steel vat that has more in common, structurally, with a microbrewery fermenter than with an ornamental teapot? What is the meaning of a chocolate teapot? Is it something made of chocolate, is it chocolate-colored, or does it brew chocolate-flavored tea? Suddenly we have lost the ability to map terms in version 3 to terms in versions 1 and 2. We no longer understand the classes of objects (i.e., teapots) in the various versions of our cookware nomenclature. We cannot unambiguously attach nomenclature to objects in our data collection (e.g., blue China teapot). We no longer have a precise definition of a teapot or the subtypes of the teapot [9]. [Glossary Semantics]

Wishful thinking

There are many kinds of ontologies inhabiting the infoverse. It seems reasonable to survey some of the existing forms of ontologies to choose the ones we most prefer. The following wish list simply reflects the author's personal preferences.

Bad situation: Ontologies as unrestrained classifications

Ontologies lack many of the restraints imposed by classifications. Most importantly, when a child class in an ontology is assigned more than one parent class, then the behavior of the child class cannot be unambiguously determined. In "Section 5.1. This Chapter in a nutshell," we will see that there are many situations wherein an absence of the traditional restraints imposed by classifications results in unpredictable and chaotic ontologic systems.

Fairly good situation: Ontologies as triplestores tied to schemas

Ontologies can be built as triplestores in which the subjects of triples are assigned to classes, and in which both the classes and the metadata found in the triples are defined in schemas.

Let's create a small triplestore to demonstrate how this might work.

```
acf54bac name "Tweety Bird"
acf54bac in_class 7f912fe4

7f912fe4 is "Class Aves (birds)"
7f912fe4 described_in "http://www.place_I_put_my_schema.myschema.htm"

a3a290e7 is "name"
a3a290e7 described_in "http://www.place_I_put_my_schema.myschema.htm"

9629c05f is "is"
9629c05f described_in "http://www.place_I_put_my_schema.myschema.htm"

95a0d3b1 is "described_in"
95a0d3b1 described_in "http://www.place_I_put_my_schema.myschema.htm"

8781c200 is "in_class"
8781c200 described_in "http://www.place_I_put_my_schema.myschema.htm"
```

This tiny triplestore qualifies as a semantically pure, though informationally barren, ontology. Everything that this triplestore tells us can be written in one short sentence. "Tweety-bird is a member of Class Aves (birds)." Why did it take so many triples to convey this simple assertion? We needed to assign unique identifiers to all of our classes and instances, and to all of our properties. The triplestore contained one class (i.e., Class

Aves) and one class instance (Tweety-bird). The properties contained in the triplestore consist of the metadata descriptors (i.e., "is" "name" "in_class" "described_in").

When we look at the triplestore, we notice that the order of triples is immaterial. For example, the following triplestore is functionally identical to the original collection.

```
7f912fe4 described_in "http://www.place_I_put_my_schema.myschema.htm"
7f912fe4 is "Class Aves (birds)"
8781c200 described_in "http://www.place_I_put_my_schema.myschema.htm"
8781c200 is "in_class"
95a0d3b1 described_in "http://www.place_I_put_my_schema.myschema.htm"
95a0d3b1 is "described_in"
9629c05f described_in "http://www.place_I_put_my_schema.myschema.htm"
9629c05f is "is"
a3a290e7 described_in "http://www.place_I_put_my_schema.myschema.htm"
a3a290e7 is "name"
acf54bac in_class 7f912fe4
acf54bac name "Tweety Bird"
```

Because each triple is fully identified, we can always reconstruct its relationships to other entries, regardless of how the collection is ordered. In fact, the content of triplestores can be divided into groups of any size and distributed throughout a network (i.e., the Internet), and we could write a program that reconstructs the relations among identified objects (i.e., the subjects of triples), provided that we have access to all of the different datasets in which the identified subject occurs.

We notice that the website "http://www.place_I_put_my_schema.myschema.htm," appears as the location of a schema document. By convention, web addresses are accepted as unique and permanent identifiers for a web resource (i.e., anything found on the Internet). If we were to visit the fictional web location "http://www.place_I_put_my_schema.myschema.htm," we would expect to find a schema with plain language descriptions of the classes, instances, and metadata properties that were asserted to have been "described_in" the schema. A triplestore may contain classes, instances, and properties whose definitions are scattered in many different schemas. The obvious drawback to our use of schemas residing in files distributed through the internet is that it assumes that we shall have permanently accessible schemas with sensible and useful definitions of classes and properties. In practice, schemas come and go, as do definitions within schemas, and a triplestore that begins life as a well-defined data collection embedding a useful ontology may easily devolve into a collection of often uninterpretable assertions. To avoid pointing triples to non-existent schemas, ontology builders sometimes include all of their triples and all of the definitions for classes, properties, and descriptors in one file. Of course, the downside to this solution is that it encourages different ontologists to create their personalized idiosyncratic definitions, resulting in a non-uniform and inharmonious interpretation of the meaning of the data residing in triplestores. These aforementioned difficulties are entrenched limitations of the field, awaiting a satisfactory solution.

Looking back at the 13 somewhat convoluted assertions needed to indicate that tweety-bird is a member of Class Aves, we must ask ourselves whether triplestores are an enormous waste of time [17]. The good news is that databases don't care how many triples we create. Billions, trillions, it's all the same to a database. In fact, triplestores are an incredibly efficient way of storing information. In a real-life situation, a triplestore may contain millions of short assertions. A small number of those triples would tackle the preliminaries: pointers to schemas, identifiers for classes, instances, and properties. The remainder of the triples would consist of data assertions, in no particular order, that could be efficiently stored in a computer database. A well-constructed triplestore database should return instantaneous responses, regardless of the size of the triplestore. The modest personal computer should have no trouble finding classes and instances and drawing inferences based on their properties.

Most of the ontologies that are in use today can be thought of as triplestores restricted to one particular knowledge domain. If you were to download an ontology file, you would almost certainly see that it has been prepared in a syntax that is unlike that shown here, for Tweety Bird. The difference is purely cosmetic. Triples can be converted to statements rendered in a semantic language, such as OWL or RDF, and semantic language statements can be converted to simple triples.

Better situation: Ontologies as classifications revealed in a semantic language

Earlier in this chapter, we made the point that ontologies are not classifications dressed in a semantic language. The natural classifications are manageable collections of classes and their relationships, containing no annotative information. These classifications could be improved if they included identified class instances with metadata descriptors. Taxonomy.xml, the European Bioinformatics Institute's metadata-enhanced version of the Classification of Life is a prime example of a classification rendered with the attributes of an ontology. In "Section 5.6. A few software tools for traversing triplestores and classifications," we will see just how easy it is to combine the traditional strengths of classifications with the semantic and computational benefits of an ontology.

Best situation: Ontology as triplestores tied to one classification

In the opinion of this author, the best and most practical application of ontologies occurs when we have a classification rendered in a semantic language and associated with a triplestore in which every triple's subject is linked to a class within the classification, and every metadata descriptor is linked to a property within the classification. Under these conditions, the ontology becomes equivalent to a triplestore with pointers to a classification. Assuming that the classification is well-curated, these circumstances ensure that every assertion in the triplestore (and a triplestore can quite literally contain trillions of assertions), can have all of the computable advantages of a traditional classification (e.g., inheritance) and can be held within a class-oriented programming environment (to be discussed in some detail in "Section 5.1. This Chapter in a nutshell"). [Glossary Valid classification]

Glossary

Abandonware Software that was once shown to serve some useful purpose but which is no longer maintained, distributed, or used. Nearly all of the software ever written is now abandonware. In many cases, software loses its value if it is not continually de-bugged, enhanced, and aggressively marketed.

The term "abandonware" is commonly reserved for software created by graduate students as part of a funded research effort. Once the funding period ends and the students have moved to new pursuits, and there is no residual support or enthusiasm for marketing and distributing the software [24]. In addition, funding is traditionally rewarded for innovative ideas, and it is sometimes impossible to attract new funding to maintain the previously funded projects.

Accrue (Noun, accrual) In the context of clinical trials, accrual is the recruitment of patients into the study. Accrual is one of the most difficult aspects of clinical trial management [25]. In an analysis of 500 planned cancer trials, 40% of trials failed to accrue the minimum necessary number of patients. Of cancer trials that have passed through the early phases of a clinical trial, three out of five drugs failed to achieve the necessary patient enrollment to move into the final (i.e., phase III) clinical trial [26].

Furthermore, trial populations often fail to include sufficient numbers of minorities (e.g., African-Americans, Hispanics, children), yielding results that may not apply to a diverse population of patients [27].

Ambiguity An ambiguity occurs when a word, a phrase, or an assertion can be interpreted in more than one way. Here is an example:

"I didn't say you lied to me." Stressing "I," the sentence means that somebody else said that you lied to me.

"I didn't say you lied to me." Stressing "didn't," the sentence means that I had nothing to do with it.

"I didn't say you lied to me." Stressing "say," the sentence means that I didn't speak the assertion but I may have made the assertion in a written or other non-verbal communication.

"I didn't say you lied to me." Stressing "you," the sentence means that someone else lied to me.

"I didn't say you lied to me." Stressing "lied," the sentence means that I say you did something to me (other than lying).

"I didn't say you lied to me." Stressing "to," the sentence means that you lied but not to my face.

"I didn't say you lied to me." Stressing "me," the sentence means that you lied to someone else.

As another example of an ambiguous sentence, consider the following: "Wouldn't you like me to erase your file?" Is the question an assertion that the responder would like to have the file erased? If so, a reply of "yes" would result in the erasure of the file. Or does the questioner want to know if the responder would not like to have the file erased? In that case, a reply of "yes" would result in the file not being erased.

Some of us believe that if we keep our sentences short and direct, we can eliminate ambiguity. Perhaps, but who among us has not driven by the street sign that reads "SLOW CHILDREN AT PLAY" without wondering why none of the kids have much pep?

Classifier Refers to computational algorithms that assign a class (from an existing classification) to an object whose class is unknown [28]. There are many available classifier algorithms, and analysts have the luxury of choosing algorithms that match their data set attributes (e.g., sample size, dimensionality) and purposes [5,29,30].

Classifier algorithms assign class membership by similarity to other members of the class; not by relationships. For example, a classifier algorithm might mistakenly assign a terrier to the same class as a housecat, because both animals have many phenotypic features in common (e.g., similar size and weight, presence of a furry tail, four legs, tendency to snuggle in a lap).

To assign membership to classes, relationships are of paramount importance. Similarities, when they occur, arise as a consequence of relationships; not the other way around. At best, classifier algorithms provide a clue to classification, by sorting objects into groups that may contain related individuals.

Classifier algorithms are computationally intensive when the dimension is high and can produce misleading results when the attributes are noisy (i.e., contain randomly distributed attribute values) or non-informative (i.e., measure properties and traits whose values do not reflect relationships) [9].

Command-line Instructions to the operating system, that can be directly entered as a line of text from a system prompt (e.g., the so-called C prompt, "c:\>", in Windows and DOS operating systems; the so-called shell prompt, "$", in Linux-like systems).

Command-line utility Programs lacking graphic user interfaces, that are executed via command line instructions. The instructions for a utility are typically couched as a series of arguments, on the command-line, following the name of the executable file that contains the utility.

Curse of dimensionality As the number of attributes for a data object increases, the multidimensional data space becomes sparsely populated, and the distances between any two objects, even the two closest neighbors, becomes absurdly large. When you have thousands of dimensions (e.g., data values in a data record, cells in the rows of a spreadsheet, attributes of a data object), the space that holds the objects is so large that distances between data objects become difficult or impossible to compute, and most computational algorithms become useless.

The curse of dimensionality is one of those scary truths that all data analysts must face, so we should take a few moments to fully explain its mathematical foundation. First, let's understand what we mean when we talk about n-dimensional data objects. Each attribute of an object is a dimension. The object might have three attributes: height, width, and depth; and these three attributes would correspond to the familiar three-dimensional measurements that we are taught in geometry. The object is a large and complex data collection might have attributes of age, length of left foot, the width of right foot, hearing acuity, the time required to sprint 50 yards, and yearly income. In this case, the object is described by 6 attributes and would occupy 6 dimensions of data space [30].

Let's imagine that we've normalized the values of every attribute so that each attribute value lies between zero and two (i.e., the age is between 0 and 2; the length of the left foot is between 0 and 2; the width of the right foot is between 0 and 2, and so on for every dimension in the object.

The cube that encloses the set of data objects with attributes measuring between 0 and 2 will have sides measuring 2 units in length. The general formula for the volume of an n-dimensional cube is the length of a side raised to the nth power. In the case of a 260-dimensional cube, this would give us a volume of 2^{260}. Just to give you some idea of the size of this number, 2^{260} is roughly the estimated number of atoms contained in our universe. So, the volume of the 260-dimensional cube, of side 2 units, is large enough to hold the total number of atoms in the universe, spaced at least one unit apart in every dimension. Because there are many more atoms in the universe than there are data objects in our data sets, we can infer that all high-dimensional volumes of data will be sparsely populated (i.e., lots of space separating data objects from one another). In our physical universe, there is much more empty space than there is matter; in the info-verse, it's much the same thing, only more so.

So what? What does it matter that an n-dimensional data space is mostly empty, so long as every data object has an n-coordinate location somewhere within the hypervolume?

Let's consider the problem of finding a data object that lies within one unit of a reference object located in the exact center of the data space. As an example, we will continue to use n-dimensional data objects composed of attributes with normalized values between 0 and 2. We'll begin by looking at a two-dimensional data space. If the data objects in the 2-dimensional data space are uniformly distributed in the space, then the chances of finding a data object within one unit of the center of the space (i.e., at coordinate 1,1) will be the ratio of the circle of radius one unit around the center divided by the area of the square that contains the data space (i.e., a square whose sides have a length of 2). This works out to pi/4, or 0.785. This tells us that in two dimensions, we'll have an excellent chance of finding an object within 1 unit of the center [30]. **Basically, this is the likelihood that a randomly situated object will lie within our 1 unit circle and will not lie in the 4 corners between our circle and its enclosing square.**

$$V_n(R) = \frac{\pi^{\frac{n}{2}}}{\Gamma\left(\frac{n}{2}+1\right)} R^n$$

FIG. 3.2 General formula for the volume of sphere of a radius R, in n dimensions.

We can easily imagine that as the number of the dimensions of our data space increases, with an exponentially increasing n-dimensional volume, so too will the volume of the hypersphere that accounts for all the objects lying within 1 radial unit from the center. Regardless of how fast the volume of the space is growing, our hypersphere will keep apace, and we will always be able to find data objects in a 1-radial unity vicinity. Actually, no. Here is where the Curse of Dimensionality truly kicks in.

The general formula for the volume of an n-dimensional sphere is shown here: (Fig. 3.2)

Let's not get distracted by the lambda function in the denominator. It suffices to know that the volume of a hypersphere in n dimensions is easily computable. Using the formula, here are the volumes of a 1 radial unit sphere in multiple dimensions [31].

Hypersphere volumes when radius$=1$, in higher dimensions:

```
n=1,  V = 2
n=2,  V = 3.1416
n=3,  V = 4.1888
n=4,  V = 4.9348
n=5,  V = 5.2638
n=6,  V = 5.1677
n=7,  V = 4.7248
n=8,  V = 4.0587
n=9,  V = 3.2985
n=10, V = 2.5502
```

As the dimensionality increases, the volume of the sphere increases until we reach the fifth dimension. After that, the volumes of the 1-unit radius sphere begin to shrink. At 10 dimensions, the volume is down to 2.5502. From there on, the volume decreases faster and faster. The 20-dimension 1-radial unit sphere has a volume of only 0.0285, while the volume of the sphere in 100 dimensions is on the order of 10^{-40} [31].

How is this possible? If the central hypersphere has a radius of one unit, and the coordinate space is a hypercube that is 2 units on each side, then we know that, for any dimension, the hypersphere touches each and every facet of the hypersphere at one point. In the two-dimensional examples shown above, the inside circle touches the enclosing square on all four sides: at points (1,0), (2,1), (1,2), and (0,1). If an n-dimensional sphere touches one point on every face of the enclosing hypercube, then how could the sphere be infinitesimally small while the hypercube is immensely large?

The secret of the curse is that as the dimensionality of the space increases, most of the volume of the hypercube comes to lie in the corners, outside the central hypersphere. The hypersphere misses the corners, just like the 2-dimensional circle misses the corners of the square. This means that as the dimensionality of data objects increases, the likelihood of finding similar objects (i.e., objects at close n-dimensional proximity from one another) drops to about zero. When you have thousands of dimensions, the space that holds the objects is so large that distances between objects become difficult or impossible to compute. **You can't find similar objects if the likelihood of finding two objects near one another is always zero.**

Data integration The process of drawing data from different sources and knowledge domains in a manner that preserves the identities of data objects and the relationships among the different data objects.

The term "integration" should not be confused with a closely related term, "interoperability". An easy way to remember the difference is to note that integration applies to data; interoperability applies to software [23].

Database A software application designed specifically to create and retrieve large numbers of data records (e.g., millions or billions). The data records of a database are persistent, meaning that the application can be turned off, then on, and all the collected data will be available to the user.

Descriptor In the context of descriptive logic, a descriptor is a metadata tag that provides a relationship between one thing and another thing. In practice, descriptors are used in triples to provide the relationship between the subject of the triple and the subject of another triple. For example,

```
"c3a40c20-ab6e-11eb-a4c9-a41e32d4a58a"   has_a   "91ed0c52-ab6e-11eb-9967-
edd7da0ef48d"

"91ed0c52-ab6e-11eb-9967-edd7da0ef48d"   is_a    pocketbook

"c3a40c20-ab6e-11eb-a4c9-a41e32d4a58a"   name    Sally
```

These three triples tell that Sally has a pocketbook, and provides unique identifiers for Sally and Sally's pocketbook. The triples also provide three descriptors that establish relationships: "has_a", "is_a", and "name".

Commonly used descriptors are defined in documents, such as those published by the W3C (World-Wide_Web Consortium) so that anyone working with semantic languages can be reasonably confident that such descriptors will be understood and used much the same way by any computer program that analyzes data expressed in a semantic language.

Dublin Core Metadata There is a fundamental difference between creating a document for oneself and creating a document for others. If you've created a document for yourself, you do not need to include the name of the person who made the document, or the date that the document was created, or the purpose of the document, or restrictions on the use of the document, etc. But if you've made a document that can be obtained and used by anyone, you've got to include all this information and more.

Librarians understand the importance of having a set of information attached to every document that can be used to index documents for retrieval and that establish the terms under which the document can be distributed and used. The Dublin Core is a set of metadata elements (XML tags) that were initially developed by a group of librarians who met in Dublin, Ohio, in 1995. Every XML document should contain the standard set of annotations for the Dublin Core Metadata Element set [32,33].

ISO Abbreviation for International Standards Organization. The ISO is a non-governmental organization that develops international standards (e.g., ISO-11179 for metadata and ISO-8601 for date and time).

ISO8601 A standard for expressing time. In ISO8601 format, the value of a date/time must contain a plus or minus sign occurring zero or one times followed by 8 digits followed by a period followed by 6 digits followed by a letter Z, T, or a space followed by a plus or minus sign occurring zero or one time, followed by 4 digits.

Expressed in XML format, the pattern for time must fit the following pattern:

```
<simpleType name='iso8601'>
  <xsd:restriction base='string'>
    <pattern value=''[\+\-]?[\d]{8}\.[\d]{6}[ZT ][\+\-]{1}[\d]{4}"/>
  </xsd:restriction>
</simpleType>
```

The essence of the enforced datatype is found in the pattern value line:

```
<pattern value=''[\+\-]?[\d]{8}\.[\d]{6}[ZT ][\+\-]{1}[\d]{4}"/>
```

This line uses a Regular Expression (RegEx), that provides a pattern to which a date/time element must conform. RegEx is beyond the scope of this manuscript but has been described at length in the computer literature [34]. Computer programmers can easily write code that checks whether date/time annotations in a text comply with the ISO8601 standard.

Identification The process of providing a data object with an identifier, or the process of distinguishing one data object from all other data objects based on its associated identifier.

Introspection A method by which data objects can be interrogated to yield information about themselves (e.g., properties, values, and class membership). Through introspection, the relationships among the data objects can be examined. Introspective methods are built into object-oriented languages. The data provided by introspection can be applied, at run-time, to modify a script's operation; a technique known as reflection. Specifically, any properties, methods, and encapsulated data of a data object can be used in the script to modify the script's run-time behavior [9].

Metadata The data that describes data. For example, a data element (also known as a data point) may consist of the number, "6". The metadata for the data may be the words "Height, in feet." A data element is useless without its metadata. In XML, the metadata/data annotation comes in the form <metadata tag>data<end of metadata tag> and might be look something like:

```
<weight_in_pounds>150</weight_in_pounds>
```

In spreadsheets, the data elements are the cells of the spreadsheet. The column headers are the metadata that describes the data values in the column's cells, and the row headers are the record numbers that uniquely identify each record (i.e., each row of cells).

Method In programming languages, the term "method" is roughly equivalent to functions, subroutines, or code blocks. In object-oriented languages, a method is a subroutine available to an object (class or instance). In Ruby and Python, instance methods are declared with a "def" declaration followed by the name of the method, in lowercase. Here is an example, in Ruby, for the "hello" method, written for the objects of the Salutations class.

```
class Salutations
  def hello
    puts "hello"
  end
end
```

Mimiviridae Class Mimiviridae, discovered in 1992, occupies a niche that seems to span the biological gulf separating viruses from other organisms. Members of Class Mimiviridae are complex, larger than some bacteria, with enormous genomes (by viral standards), exceeding a million base pairs and encoding upwards of 1000 proteins. The large size and complexity of Class Mimiviridae exemplify the advantage of a double-stranded DNA genome.

Class Megaviridae is a newly reported (October 2011) class of viruses, related to Class Mimiviridae, but even larger [35]. The discovery of classes of giant viruses inspires biologists to reconsider the "non-living" status relegated to viruses and compels taxonomists to examine the placement of viruses within the Classification of Life [13].

Namespace A namespace is the metadata realm in which a metadata tag applies. The purpose of a namespace is to distinguish metadata tags that have the same name, but a different meaning. For example, within a single XML file, the metadata term "date" may be used to signify a calendar date, or the fruit, or the social engagement. To avoid confusion, the metadata term is given a prefix that is associated with a Web document that defines the particular use of the term. The term plus its prefix establishes a namespace.

For example, an XML page might contain three "date" tags, each prefixed with a code that identifies the namespace that defines a different meaning for the date tag.

```
<calendar:date>June 16, 1904</caldendar:date>
<agriculture:date>Thoory</agriculture:date>
<social:date>Pyramus and Thisbe<social:date>
```

At the top of the XML document you would expect to find declarations for the namespaces used in the XML page. You might see something like the following:

```
<root
xmlns:calendar="http://www.calendercollectors.org/"
xmlns:agriculture="http://www.farmersplace.org/"
xmlns:social="http://hearts_throbbing.com/"
>
```

The namespace web addresses are the locations that define the meanings of the tags that reside within their namespace.

Using namespaces, data objects residing in a triplestore can ensure that their metadata descriptors convey their intended meanings. Here is an example wherein two resources are merged, with their data arranged as assertion triples.

```
From triplestore 1

29847575938125      calendar:date      February 4, 1986
83654560466294      calendar:date      June 16, 1904

From triplestore 2

57839109275632      social:date      Jack and Jill
83654560466294      social:date      Pyramus and Thisbe

Merged triplestore

29847575938125      calendar:date      February 4, 1986
57839109275632      social:date      Jack and Jill
```

```
83654560466294        social:date        Pyramus and Thisbe
83654560466294        calendar:date      June 16, 1904
```

There you have it. The object identified as 83,654,560,466,294 is associated with a "date" metadata tag in both resources. When the resources are merged, the unambiguous meaning of the metadata tag is conveyed through the appended namespaces (i.e., social: and calendar:)

Nomenclature mapping Specialized nomenclatures employ specific names for concepts that are included in other nomenclatures, under other names. For example, the names for the physiologic responses caused by a reversible cerebral vasoconstrictive event include: thunderclap headache, Call-Fleming syndrome, benign angiopathy of the central nervous system, postpartum angiopathy, migraineur vasospasm, and migraine angiitis. The choice of a term will vary depending on the medical specialty of the physician (e.g., neurologist, rheumatologist, obstetrician). To mitigate the discord among specialty nomenclatures, lexicographers may undertake a harmonization project, in which nomenclatures with overlapping concepts are mapped to one another.

Notation3 Also called n3. A syntax for expressing assertions as triples (unique subject + metadata + data). Notation3 expresses the same information as the more formal RDF syntax, but n3 is easier for humans to read [36]. RDF and N3 are interconvertible, and either one can be parsed and equivalently tokenized (i.e., broken into elements that can be re-organized in a different format, such as a database record).

OWL Abbreviation for Web Ontology Language. OWL is a popular semantic language that provides a variety of standardized relationship descriptors (sometimes referred to as modeling primitives) that ontologists find helpful.

Parsing Much of computer programming involves parsing; moving sequentially through a file or some sort of data structure and performing operations on every contained item, one item at a time. For files, this might mean going through a text file line by line, or sentence by sentence. For a data file, this might mean operating on each record in the file. For in-memory data structures, this may mean operating on each item in a data structure (e.g., list, tuple, associative array).

Pseudoscience A set of beliefs or theories that cannot be tested (i.e., cannot be proven wrong). Pseudo-scientific beliefs are not necessarily wrong; we just have no way of knowing. Intelligent design is an example of a pseudoscientific belief. If we assert that humans were designed by an intelligent being, such as a superior but permanently absent alien life form, or an all-powerful but invisible entity, then we are making a pseudoscientific statement. There is no way to determine whether the assertion is false.

Query The term "query" usually refers to a request, sent to a database, to find information related to a specific word or phrase (i.e., the query term). In more technical terms, a query is a parameter or set of parameters that are submitted as input to a computer program, which searches a data collection for items that match or bear some relationship to the query parameters.

RDF RDF (Resource Description Framework) is a special syntax within XML that constrains content to assertions that consist of a declaration of a specified object followed by a metadata/data pair of information on the object. A syntactical specification, such as RDF, is the foundation for the semantic web, in which logical inferences can be drawn from meaningful assertions (RDF triples) distributed throughout the internet.

RDF Schema Resource Description Framework Schema (RDFS). A document containing a list of classes, their definitions, and the names of the parent class(es) for each class (e.g., Class Marsupiala is a subclass of Class Metatheria). In an RDF Schema, the list of classes is typically followed by a list of properties that apply to one or more classes in the Schema. To be accessible, RDF Schemas are posted on the Internet, as a Web page, with a unique Web address. Anyone can incorporate the classes and properties of a public RDF Schema into their RDF documents (public or private) by linking named classes and properties, in their RDF document, to the web address of the RDF Schema where the classes and properties are defined [23].

Key features of RDF Schemas:

1. RDF Schemas are written in XML but are completely unlike XML Schemas.

2. RDF Schemas contain declarations of the classes and properties that are used in RDF documents.

3. RDF Schemas, like all RDF documents, have no pre-determined order or composition, and consist of statements expressed as triples. The subject of every triple in an RDF Schema will be either Class or Property.

4. Every RDF Schema can be thought of as a child of the W3C RDF Schema that defines the "super" classes Resource, Class, and Property. All RDF Schemas will refer to the document that defines RDF syntax and to the document that defines the top-level schema, and therefore will begin something like this:

```
<?xml version='1.0' encoding='ISO-8859-1'?>
  <rdf:RDF
      xmlns:rdf="http://www.w3.org/1999/02/22-rdf-syntax-ns#";
      xmlns:rdfs="http://www.w3.org/2000/01/rdf-schema#">
```

5. An RDF document consists of triples <subject, metadata, value> provided in RDF format. RDF documents usually reference one or more RDF Schemas to instantiate the subject of each triple (i.e., to tell us which class in an RDF schema the subject is an instance of) and to provide subjects with class-appropriate metadata.

6. Documents composed of triples whose components are defined by RDF Schemas can be used to completely specify data objects.

RDF schemas are intended to promote interoperability between ontologies and other data structures that use the same classes and properties. As indicated in point 5, a single ontology or data structure can link to any number of RDF Schemas, permitting the ontology creator to choose a variety of well-defined classes and properties for inclusion.

RDFS Abbreviation for RDF Schema (Resource Description Framework Schema).

Range In the context of classification, the range of a property refers to the values that the property may have. For example, if the value of a property is always some integer number, the range of the property might be "integer". If the value of a property is always True or False, then the range of the property might be "True, False". In practice, the range of a property is often noncommittally listed as "literal" indicating that the value of the property is a character string.

Recommender A collection of methods for predicting the preferences of individuals. Recommender methods often rely on one or two simple assumptions: (1) If an individual expresses a preference for a certain type of product, and the individual encounters a new product that is similar to a previously preferred product, then he or she is likely to prefer the new product; (2) If an individual expresses preferences that are similar to the preferences expressed by a cluster of individuals, and if the members of the cluster prefer a product that the individual has not yet encountered, then the individual will most likely prefer the product.

Semantic web A vision of the Internet in which distributed information is organized as meaningful data triples (as described for RDF) that can be used to merge, interrogate, and retrieve heterogeneous information, to classify the subjects of triples into ontologies, and to draw logical inferences about the subjects' triples through the use of software agents.

Semantics The study of meaning (Greek root, semantikos, significant meaning). In the context of data science, semantics is the technique of creating meaningful assertions about data objects. A meaningful assertion, as used here, is also known as a triple and consists of an identified data object, a data value, and a descriptor for the data value. In practical terms, semantics involves creating triples, combining assertions about data objects (i.e., merging triples), and assigning classes to the data objects contained in triples; hence relating triples to other triples. As a word of warning, few if any informaticians would define semantics in these terms, but most definitions for semantics are functionally equivalent to the definition offered here [9].

Software agent A computer program that can operate in a somewhat autonomous fashion: collecting data, making logical inferences, and proceeding based on automated decisions. Though the definition of a software agent varies, most definitions convey the idea that software agents can interact with other software agents. This requires each software agent to contain instructions to describe itself using a standard data format that is understood by other agents. A special breed of software agent, the autonomous agent, proceeds through multiple interactions without human supervision.

Spreadsheet Spreadsheets are data arrays consisting of records (the rows), with each record containing data attributes (the columns). Spreadsheet applications permit the user to search records, columns, and cells (i.e., the data points corresponding to a specific record and a specific column). Spreadsheets support statistical and mathematical functions operating on the elements of the spreadsheet (i.e., records, columns, cells). Perhaps most importantly, spreadsheets offer a wide range of easily implemented graphing features. Quite a few data scientists perform virtually all of their work using a favorite spreadsheet application. Spreadsheets have only limited utility when dealing with large data (e.g., gigabytes or terabytes of data), or complex data (e.g., images, waveforms, text), and they do not easily support classified data (e.g., data objects that belong to classes within a lineage of classes). Additionally, spreadsheets do not support the kinds of methods and data structures (e.g., while loops, if statements, access to external modules, system calls, network interactions, reflection, complex data structures) that are supported in modern programming languages.

Standard A standard is a set of rules for doing a particular task or expressing a particular kind of information. The purpose of standards is to ensure that all objects that meet the standard have certain physical or informational features in common, thus facilitating interchange, reproducibility, interoperability, and reducing costs of operation. In the case of standards for data and information, standards typically dictate what data is to be included, how that data should be expressed and arranged, and what data is to be excluded. Standards are developed by hundreds of standards-developing agencies, but there are only a few international agencies that bestow approval of standards.

Support vector machine A machine learning technique that groups objects, by similarity. The method starts with a training set consisting of two groups of objects as input. The support vector machine computes a hyperplane, in a multidimensional space, that separates objects of the two groups. The dimension of the hyperspace is determined by the number of dimensions or attributes associated with the objects. Additional objects (i.e., test set objects) are assigned membership in one group or the other, depending on which side of the hyperplane they reside.

Syntax Syntax is the standard form or structure of a statement. What we know as English grammar is equivalent to the syntax for the English language. If I write, "Jules hates pizza," the statement would be syntactically valid, but factually incorrect. If I write, "Jules drives to work in his pizza," the statement would be syntactically valid but nonsensical. For programming languages, syntax refers to the enforced structure of command lines. In the context of triplestores, syntax refers to the arrangement and notation requirements for the three elements of a statement (e.g., RDF format or N3 format). Charles Mead distinctly summarized the difference between syntax and semantics: "Syntax is structure; semantics is meaning" [37].

Turtle Another syntax for expressing triples. From RDF came a simplified syntax for triples, known as Notation3 or N3 [38]. From N3 came Turtle, thought to fit even more closely to RDF. From Turtle came a highly simplified syntax, known as N-Triples.

URL Unique Resource Locator. The Web is a collection of resources, each having a unique address, the URL. When you click on a link that specifies a URL, your browser fetches the page located at the unique location specified in the URL name. If the Web were designed otherwise (i.e., if several different web pages had the same web address, or if one web address were located at several different locations), then the web could not function with any reliability.

URN   Unique Resource Name. Whereas the URL identifies objects based on the object's unique location in the Web, the URN is a system of location-independent object identifiers. In the URN system, data objects are provided with identifiers, and the identifiers are registered with and subsumed by, the URN.
For example:

```
urn:isbn-13:9780128028827
```

Refers to the unique book, "Repurposing Legacy Data: Innovative Case Studies", by Jules Berman.

```
urn:uuid:e29d0078-f7f6-11e4-8ef1-e808e19e18e5
```

Refers to a data object tied to the UUID identifier e29d0078-f7f6-11e4-8ef1-e808e19e18e5.
In theory, if every data object were assigned a registered URN, and if the system were implemented as intended, the entire universe of information could be tracked and searched.

UUID   UUID (Universally Unique IDentifier) is a protocol for assigning unique identifiers to data objects, without using a central registry. UUIDs were originally used in the Apollo Network Computing System [6]. Most modern programming languages have modules for generating UUIDs.

Unique object   Any object that can be described in such a way that the object can be distinguished from other objects. Every living and deceased organism is a unique object. Every moment in time (past, present, and future) is a unique object. In computer science, a unique object has been defined or specified and has been assigned a unique and permanent identifier (i.e., alphanumeric sequence).
We typically think of individual items as being unique, while classes of items are general objects that lack the quality of uniqueness. In computer science, this is absolutely not true. Classes of objects, such as species, are unique and should be fitted with a specifier (i.e., class definition) and an immutable unique identifier.

Uniqueness   Uniqueness is the quality of being demonstrably different from every other thing in the universe. For data scientists, uniqueness is achieved when a data object is bound to a unique identifier (i.e., a string of alphanumeric characters) that has not, and will never be, assigned to any other object. Interestingly, uniqueness can apply to classes of objects that happen to contain non-unique members, and to two or more indistinguishable objects, if they are each assigned unique identifiers (e.g., unique product numbers stamped into identical auto parts).

Universally unique identifier   Abbreviation: UUID. A protocol for producing unique identifiers (i.e., a long sequence of seemingly random alphanumeric characters) that can be attached to data objects [6]. This protocol is very useful, and most modern programming languages, including Perl, Python, and Ruby have modules for generating UUIDs [9]. The odds of two independently generated UUIDs matching one another are virtually nil.

Utility   In the context of software, a utility is an application that is dedicated to performing one specific task, very well, and very fast. In most instances, utilities are short programs, often running from the command line, and lacking any graphic user interface. Many utilities are available at no cost. In general, simple utilities are preferable to multi-purpose software applications [39]. Remember, an application that claims to do everything for the user is, most often, an application that requires the user to do everything for the application.

Valid classification   A classification that conforms with the definitional properties of a classification. The validity of classification has nothing to do with whether its underlying hypotheses are true.

Variable   In algebra, a variable is a quantity, in an equation, that can change; as opposed to a constant quantity, that cannot change. In computer science, a variable can be perceived as a container that can be assigned a value. If you assign the integer 7 to a container named "x", then "x" equals 7, until you re-assign some other value to the container (i.e., variables are mutable). In most computer languages, when you issue a command assigning a value to a new (undeclared) variable, the variable automatically comes into existence to accept the assignment. The process whereby an object comes into existence because its existence was implied by an action (such as value assignment), is called reification.

XML Acronym for eXtensible Markup Language. Although its acronym indicates that XML is a language, it is not. Charles Simonyi is credited with saying that "XML is not a language in the sense of a programming language any more than sketches on a napkin are a language." XML is a syntax for marking data values with descriptors (i.e., metadata). The descriptors are commonly known as tags. In XML, every data value is enclosed by a start-tag, containing the descriptor, and indicating that a value will follow, and an end-tag, containing the same descriptor and indicating that a value preceded the tag.

The enclosing angle brackets, "<>", and the end-tag marker, "/", are hallmarks of HTML and XML markup. Here is an example:

```
<date>June 16, 1904</date>
```

The tag, <date> and its end-tag, </date> enclose a data element, which in this case is the unabbreviated month, beginning with an uppercase letter and followed by lowercase letters, followed by a space, followed by a two-digit numeric for the date of the month, followed by a comma and space, followed by the 4-digit year. The XML tag could have been defined in a separate document detailing the data format of the data element described by the XML tag. ISO-11179 is a standard that explains how to specify the properties of tags.

If we had chosen, we could have broken the <date> tag into its constituent parts.

```
<date>
<month>June</month>
<day>16</day>
<year>1904</year>
</date>
```

Five properties of XML explain its extraordinary utility [40,41]. These are:

1. Enforced and defined structure (XML rules and schema)—An XML file is well-formed if it conforms to the basic rules for XML file construction recommended by the W3C (Worldwide Web Consortium). This means that it must be a plain-text file, with a header indicating that it is an XML file, and must enclose data elements with metadata tags that declare the start and end of the data element. The tags must conform to certain rules (e.g., alphanumeric strings without intervening spaces) and must also obey the rules for nesting data elements [15,40]. A metadata/data pair may be contained within other metadata/data pair (so-called nesting), but a metadata/data pair cannot straggle over other metadata/data pair. Most browsers will parse XML files, rejecting files that are not well-formed. The ability to ensure that every XML file conforms to basic rules of metadata tagging and nesting makes it possible to extract XML files as sensible data structures [9].

2. Reserved namespaces—Namespaces preserve the intended meaning of tags whose meanings change from web page to web page. When you encounter the XML tag <date>, would you know whether the tag referred to a calendar date, or the fruit known as a date, or the social encounter known as a date? To avoid confusion, metadata terms are assigned a prefix that is associated with a Web document that defines the term. For example, an XML page might contain three "date" tags, each prefixed with a code that identifies the different meanings of the term that apply within the designated namespace [9].

```
<calendar:date>June 16, 1904</calendar:date>
<agriculture:date>Thoory</agriculture:date>
<social:date>Pyramus and Thisbe<social:date>
```

At the top of the XML document, you would expect to find links to the three URL locations (i.e., web addresses) where the namespace definitions for the prefixes (i.e., "calendar:", "agriculture:" and "social:") can be found.

3. Linking data via the internet—XML comes with specifications for linking XML documents with other XML documents, or with any external file that has a specific identifier or web location. This means that there is a logical and standard method for linking any XML document or any part of an XML document, including individual data elements, to any other uniquely identified resource (e.g., web page) [9].

4. Logic and meaning—Although the technical methodologies associated with XML can be daunting, the most difficult issues always relate to the meaning of things. A variety of formal approaches have been proposed to reach the level of meaning within the context of XML. The simplest of these is the Resource Description Framework (RDF). The importance of the RDF model is that it binds data and metadata to a unique object with a web location. Consistent use of the RDF model assures that data anywhere on the web can always be connected through unique objects using RDF descriptions. The association of described data with a unique object confers meaning and greatly advances our ability to integrate data over the internet [9].

5. Self-awareness—Because XML can be used to describe anything, it can certainly be used to describe a query related to an XML page. Furthermore, it can be used to describe protocols for transferring data, performing web services, or describing the programmer interface to databases. It can describe the rules for interoperability for any data process, including peer-to-peer data sharing. When an XML file is capable of displaying autonomous behavior, composing queries, merging replies, and transforming its content, it is usually referred to as a software agent [9].

References

[1] de Bruijn J. Using ontologies: enabling knowledge sharing and reuse on the Semantic Web. Digital Enterprise Research Institute technical report DERI-2003-10-29; 2003. October.

[2] Noy NF, DL MG. Ontology development 101: a guide to creating your first ontology. Stanford Knowledge Systems Laboratory technical report KSL-01-05 and Stanford Medical Informatics technical report SMI-2001-0880; 2001.

[3] Gruber T. Ontology. In: Liu L, Ozsu MT, editors. The encyclopedia of database systems. Springer-Verlag; 2009.

[4] Haendel MA, Chute CG, Robinson PN. Classification, ontology, and precision medicine. N Engl J Med 2018;379:1452–62.

[5] Berman JJ. Principles of big data: preparing, sharing, and analyzing complex information. Waltham, MA: Morgan Kaufmann; 2013.

[6] Leach P, Mealling M, Salz R. A Universally Unique IDentifier (UUID) URN namespace. Network Working Group, Request for Comment 4122, Standards Track; 2017. Available from: http://www.ietf.org/rfc/rfc4122.txt. [Accessed 7 November 2017].

[7] Mealling M. RFC 3061. A URN namespace of object identifiers. Network Working Group; 2001. Available from: https://www.ietf.org/rfc/rfc3061.txt. [Accessed 1 January 2015].

[8] Berman JJ. Methods in medical informatics: fundamentals of healthcare programming in Perl, Python, and Ruby. Boca Raton: Chapman and Hall; 2010.

[9] Berman JJ. Data simplification: taming information with open source tools. Waltham, MA: Morgan Kaufmann; 2016.

[10] Marciano-Cabral F, Cabral G. Acanthamoeba spp. as agents of disease in humans. Clin Microbiol Rev 2003;2003:273–307.

[11] Fischer MG, Kelly I, Foster LJ, Suttle CA. The virion of Cafeteria roenbergensis virus (CroV) contains a complex suite of proteins for transcription and DNA repair. Virology 2014;466:82–94.

[12] Guarro J, Gene J, Stchigel AM. Developments in fungal taxonomy. Clin Microbiol Rev 1999;12:454–500.

[13] Berman JJ. Taxonomic guide to infectious diseases: understanding the biologic classes of pathogenic organisms. 1st ed. Cambridge, MA: Academic Press; 2012.

[14] Anon. Resource description framework (RDF). Available from: http://www.w3.org/RDF/. Comment. This is an excellent source of information for the W3C RDF specification.

[15] Ahmed K, Ayers D, Birbeck M, Cousins J, Dodds D, Lubell J, et al. Professional XML meta data. Birmingham: Wrox; 2001.

[16] Frauenfelder M. Interview with Sir Tim Berners-Lee technology review. Available from: http://www.technologyreview.com/articles/04/10/frauenfelder1004.asp; October 2004.

[17] Hitzler P, van Harmelen F. A reasonable semantic web. Semantic Web 2010;1:39–44.

[18] Li W. The more-the-better and the less-the-better. Bioinformatics 2006;22:2187–8.

[19] Chavez E, Navarro G, Baeza-Yates R, Marroquin JL. Searching in metric spaces. ACM Comput Surv 2001;33:273–321.

[20] Heathfield H, Bose D, Kirkham N. Knowledge-based computer system to aid in the histopathological diagnosis of breast disease. J Clin Pathol 1991;44:502–8.

[21] Mitra P, Wiederhold G. Chapter 5: An ontology-composition algebra. In: Staab S, Studer R, editors. Handbook on ontologies. 2nd ed. New York: Springer; 2009.

[22] Duncan M. Terminology version control discussion paper: the chocolate teapot. Medical Object Oriented Software Ltd.; 2009. 15 September. Available from: http://www.mrtablet.demon.co.uk/chocolate_teapot_lite.htm. [Accessed 30 August 2012].

[23] Berman JJ. Repurposing legacy data: innovative case studies. Waltham, MA: Morgan Kaufmann; 2015.

[24] Jaffe S. Scientists Abandon their Software: Good biology programs abound in universities, but academia offers little incentive to keep them current. Scientist 2004;18:47.

[25] Kitterman DR, Cheng SK, Dilts DM, Orwoll ES. The prevalence and economic impact of low-enrolling clinical studies at an academic medical center. Acad Med 2011;86:1360–6.

[26] English R, Lebovitz Y, Griffin R. Forum on drug discovery, development, and translation. Institute of Medicine; 2010.

[27] Anon. The precision medicine initiative cohort program – building a research foundation for 21st century medicine. Precision Medicine Initiative Working Group report to the Advisory Committee to the Director, NIH; 2015. 17 September.

[28] Wu X, Kumar V, Quinlan JR, Ghosh J, Yang Q, Motoda H, et al. Top 10 algorithms in data mining. Knowl Inf Syst 2008;14:1–37.

[29] Zhang L, Lin X. Some considerations of classification for high dimension low-sample size data. Stat Methods Med Res 2011. Available from: http://smm.sagepub.com/content/early/2011/11/22/0962280211428387.long. [Accessed 26 January 2013].

[30] Berman JJ. Principles and practice of big data: preparing, sharing, and analyzing complex information. 2nd ed. Waltham, MA: Morgan Kaufmann; 2018.

[31] Hayes B. An adventure in the nth dimension. Am Sci 2011;99:442–6.

[32] Anon. Dublin core metadata initiative. Available from: http://dublincore.org/. Comment. The Dublin Core is a set of basic metadata that describe XML documents. The Dublin Core were developed by a forward-seeing group library scientists who understood that every XML document needs to include self-describing metadata that will allow the document to be indexed and appropriately retrieved.

[33] Anon. Dublin core metadata element set, version 1.1: reference description. Available from: http://dublincore.org/documents/1999/07/02/dces/; 2021. Comment. This is the actual reference URL (Uniform Resource Loactor, or web site) for the Dublin Core elements.

[34] Berman JJ. Perl programming for medicine and biology. Sudbury, MA: Jones and Bartlett; 2007.

[35] Arslan D, Legendre M, Seltzer V, Abergel C, Claverie J. Distant mimivirus relative with a larger genome highlights the fundamental features of megaviridae. PNAS 2011;108:17486–91.

[36] Berman JJ, Moore GW. Implementing an RDF schema for pathology images. Available from: http://www.o/spec2img.htm; 2007. [Accessed 1 January 2015].

[37] Mead CN. Data interchange standards in healthcare IT–computable semantic interoperability: now possible but still difficult, do we really need a better mousetrap? J Healthc Inf Manag 2006;20:71–8.

[38] Anon. Primer: getting into RDF & semantic web using N3. Available from: http://www.w3.org/2000/10/swap/Primer.html. [Accessed 17 September 2015].

[39] Brooks FP. No silver bullet: essence and accidents of software engineering. Computer 1987;20:10–9.

[40] Berman JJ, Bhatia K. Biomedical data integration: using XML to link clinical and research datasets. Expert Rev Mol Diagn 2005;5:329–36.

[41] Berman JJ. Pathology data integration with eXtensible markup language. Hum Pathol 2005;36:139–45.

4

Coping with paradoxical or flawed classifications and ontologies

Chapter outline

> *Man of genius makes no mistakes. His errors are volitional and are the portals of discovery.*
>
> **James Joyce, Ulysses**

Section 4.1. Problematica

Some of the largest, best curated, and most respected classifications in use today are riddled with flaws [1–5]. The possible reasons for their shortcomings are many. It is a good idea to know how to assess deficiencies, early in the game.

Watch for these common flaws:

1. When the classes in the classification have no class properties that can be applied to the members of the class

Let's imagine that a classification builder finds that she has too many bird species within Class Aves, causing the overall classification to appear lopsided when displayed as a graphic. To even things out, she creates two subclasses of Class Aves, named Class Birds_ Weighing_Less_Than_One_Pound and Class Birds_Weighing_One_Pound_Or_More. Because every bird must weigh either less than a pound, or equal to a pound, or more than a pound, she feels that she has created a complete and sensible subclassification of the entire class of birds, while producing two classes of manageable size.

The problems caused by this kind of thinking are too numerous to count. Limiting ourselves to the issue of heritable properties, we can say that "weight" is not a class property;

155

it is a trait that varies greatly among individuals of a species and from moment to moment. Every bird is conceived as a single cell and thus most species of the bird goes through a period when its members weigh less than one pound. Furthermore, a species of birds of Class Birds_Weighing_One_Pound_Or_More may be the parent class of a species of birds that weigh, on average, much less than one pound. Hence, weight is not heritable through descendant classes.

We can also add that there is never a need to "even out" classes containing numerous members. In the Classification of Life, we have examples of classes with uncountable members (e.g., Class Hexapoda) and classes with just a few members (e.g., Class Prototheria). In the Periodic Table of the Elements, we have classes with many instances, such as Class Hydrogen, which comprises over 90% of the atoms of the universe, and classes of heavy elements that are seldom encountered, being laboratory creations that exist for a mere fraction of a second.

2. When the classes are named for properties that they lack

When we find a defining feature for a class, we sometimes take the easy way out and assign the class name's negation to its sister class. This is always a mistake. It is an intellectual failing to define a class by what it is not. Doing so deprives the sister class of a defining heritable feature. For example, a subclass of Class Tetrapoda developed a class-defining amniote egg (i.e., an egg adaptable for development on the land, by virtue of its amnion). This class was named Class Amniota. Its sister class was formerly named Class Anamniota (tetrapods lacking an amniote egg). Doing so was most unhelpful insofar as all animals preceding the evolution of Class Amniota lacked amniote eggs. Hence, all animals preceding Class Amniota have a defining feature in common with Class Anamniota. Likewise, using the term "agnathans" (jawless animals) to describe the sister class of Class Gnathostoma (animals having a jawed mouth), is not at all helpful.

Classes are best designated by a new property that belongs to every member of the class and which is inherited by all of its descendant classes. Hence, Class Anamniota was not a sensibly named class of animals. Our current Classification of Life does not contain a Class Anamniota, and the sister class of Class Amniota now has the familiar name "Class Amphibia," which is defined by several class-specific heritable features.

Classification by exclusion is not confined to organisms. Oncologists (i.e., physicians who specialize in cancer) refer to "Non-Hodgkin lymphomas" and "Non-small cell lung cancers." These terms add nothing to our understanding of the kinds of cancers they include. [Glossary Negative classifier, Non-Hodgkin lymphoma, Non-small cell lung cancer]

Even mathematicians can be sloppy with class names. Let's consider the so-called Sporadic groups (to be discussed in "Section 8.5. Symmetry groups rule the universe"). In the Classification Theorem, the finite simple groups are divided into classes: cyclic, alternating, Lie types, sporadic, or the Tits group (named for Jacques Tits).

The "sporadic" class, whose name indicates that its properties are unspecified, consists of groups that do not fall into the cyclic, alternating, or Lie type classes. This is yet another example of a class that is defined by what it is not (never a good sign). The Tits group has nearly all of the properties associated with a group of Lie type. Mathematicians do not quite know what to do with the Tits group, sometimes counting it as a singleton class (i.e., a class of only one member) and sometimes including it in the class of sporadic groups (defined by what it is not). As it stands today, if you ask mathematicians to tell you how many groups are included in the Sporadic class of finite simple groups, they will almost certainly answer, "26 or 27, depending on where you put the Tits group." This only goes to show that our finest mathematicians have difficulty finding an affirmative definitional property for their classes.

3. When the class members can just as easily be assigned to other classes in the same classification

For example, consider a classification of neoplasms (i.e., tumors) that has separate classes named "Tumors of the neck," "Radiation-induced tumors," and "Endocrine tumors." Thyroid cancers fit all three classes. This tells us that the classification has been constructed without any thought to eliminating the overlap among classes, or to finding one central theory of classes that provides a unique class assignment to every tumor. [Glossary Neoplasm]

4. When the classification does not help you predict the behavior of class members

For example, if we have a classification of minerals, we would hope that the class to which a particular mineral is assigned will tell us something about the properties of the mineral (e.g., conductivity, hardness, morphology). A class of minerals such as "Rocks of Brazil" will contain all manner of rocks and simply knowing that the rocks can all be found in Brazil doesn't give us any information that would help us to predict the properties of individual rocks.

5. When the classification does not indicate the relations of a class to other classes

For example, the classes "Big rocks" and "Small rocks" might help us sort a box of rocks by size, but the classes have no obvious relationships to one another, since any big rock can be pulverized into small rocks.

6. When the classification makes the domain more complicated than it had seemed, before being built

For example, many elements can exist in frozen, liquid, or gaseous states. We shouldn't create subclasses to accommodate the different states of the different elements. We would expect chemists to tell us why elements change their physical state based on class properties. We don't invent new subclasses to segregate each of the properties held by the superclass.

7. When the objects of the classification are simply unclassifiable

As discussed in "Section 1.4. Things that defy simple classification," not every object is classifiable. We cannot create classifications from unclassifiable items.

Some items are particularly difficult to classify, and we need to be very clever if we hope to find a classification that accommodates their particulars. As discussed previously, items composed of other items are always difficult to assign to any particular class. This would include artifactual objects that have various composite parts. Any modular creation, such as a software application with interchangeable parts (e.g., graphics module, user interface module) might be difficult to classify. A successful classification, in such cases, would hinge upon finding a class structure that bypasses the issue of modularity.

Humans and other animals can be considered modular structures. We, humans, have a set of organs that perform their particular jobs (e.g., liver, kidneys, brain); but we don't classify ourselves according to our modular components. The Classification of Life is built upon species ancestry. Each class descends from its immediate ancestral class, and classes inherit properties from their ancestors. The modularity of organisms is successfully bypassed.

Case studies of flawed classifications

Pseudoclassifications

Some decades ago, when I was fully engaged in medical research, I read an interview featuring a highly respected scientist working at Rockefeller University. Asked to comment on the quality of research training in medical schools, she responded that medical students are not trained to think like a scientist; they are trained to memorize lists. As a scientist trained at various medical schools, I was, at first, put off by her remarks. On further thought, I came to admit that physicians are indeed expected to memorize lots of lists; many involving differential diagnoses or steps in a procedure, or medications, or diseases of a certain category. For example, dermatologists are apt to encounter patients with rashes. Good dermatologists store in their minds a list of dermatologic conditions that cause rashes. Matching lists of the signs and symptoms and histories of various rashes to the patient's clinical presentation often leads the physician to a diagnosis. Sometimes a laboratory test, chosen from a list of tests relevant to dermatologic diseases, can definitively establish one particular diagnosis. Afterward, the dermatologist can look at a list of recommended treatments for the disease and prescribe something appropriate. Medical practice has much to do with lists and relatively little to do with understanding the biology of diseases.

It was not until I approached the World Health Organization's Classifications Tumor Classifications that the full horror of the list-centric approach of medicine became evident.

The World Health Organization (WHO) has published several tumor classifications, with separate classifications for various anatomic or physiologic divisions of the human body. Several of the classifications published by the World Health Organization are listed here:

Tumors of the Nervous System
Tumors of the Digestive System
Tumors of Hematopoietic and Lymphoid Tissues
Tumors of the Breast and Female Genital Organs

Tumors of Soft Tissues and Bone
Skin Tumors
Tumors of the Urinary System and Male Genital Organs
Tumors of Endocrine Organs
Head and Neck Tumors
Tumors of the Lung, Pleura, Thymus, and Heart

The advantage of listing tumors by their anatomic site is that pathologists have detailed information, collected over more than a century, of each of the tumors that are known to arise at any given location. These published tumor classifications are of great value to pathologists who want to familiarize themselves with the variety of tumors arising at any particular organ. The drawback with this sort of classification is that it groups together, tumors that have no common biology. For example, when we list tumors arising from the head and neck region, we might include tumors of the central nervous system, peripheral nervous system, muscle, salivary glands, oral and nasopharyngeal mucosa, thyroid, and parathyroid glands, and so on. These tumors are not biologically related. They do not form a coherent class, and they have no sensible parent class from which they can inherit class properties. In addition, when we classify by anatomic site, we lose the relationship among tumors that arise from very different locations but which share biological features. For example, an angiosarcoma (i.e., malignant tumor of vessels) of the head and neck region is likely to share properties with angiosarcomas that arise in the leg or the abdomen.

For the curators of a complete tumor taxonomy (i.e., the collection of all the named tumors), classifying tumors by topographic site adds enormous redundancy to the collection. For example, "Tumors of the Digestive System" would need to include lymphomas that occur in the digestive system, but we would expect these same lymphomas to be listed in "Tumors of the Haemopoietic and lymphoid tissues." Likewise, soft tissue tumors arising in the gastrointestinal tract would need to be included in "Tumors of the Digestive System," but must also appear in "Tumors of Soft Tissues and Bone." In fact, virtually every tumor included in any one WHO classification will be included in other WHO classifications. Having one instance object (i.e., name of a tumor) occurring in multiple classes within the classification is a violation of the uniqueness rule (i.e., a limit of one class per object).

The classification of tumors by anatomic site brings us right back to the criticism of medical science that started this topic: that medical education boils down to the memorization of lists of things. Science, to the contrary, is focused on discovering the order and relationships among classes of naturally occurring things. It is only when we move toward true classifications, and away from lists, that we can understand our world. Later in this chapter ("Section 4.4. Saving hopeless classifications"), we will see how we can create a classification of tumors that conforms to the fundamental rules of classification and that helps us relate our knowledge of other fields (e.g., genetics and embryology) to our understanding of tumor biology [6].

Erroneously named classes

To build a classification, each class must be well-defined and must contain members that we can confidently assign to the class. The problem here is that we commonly depend on the classification itself to give us a depth of understanding to its classes and their relationships to one another. As stated earlier, the classification must be completed before we truly understand its classes; and we cannot complete a classification without first providing its classes. We live with this paradox every day.

Consequently, it is not uncommon to miss the mark entirely, when defining classes of objects. A favorite example involves Charles Messier (1730–1817). Messier was intensely interested in comets, and he was annoyed by areas in space that were obscured by nebulous clouds of an undetermined nature. These nebulous areas blotted his view of comets, and he decided to warn his fellow astronomers not to waste their time gazing at cosmological eyesores. Messier found, mapped, and published 103 such regions, which came to be known as Messier objects. It turns out that the Messier objects, originally classified as comet-free zones, were the locations where nebulae were found. In these nebulae lie immense distributions of gases, where stars and galaxies are born. The Messier objects contain some of the most fascinating cosmologic curiosities in the known universe. Though Messier was completely mistaken in his understanding of his assigned classes, and their contained objects, he achieved scientific immortality just the same.

As Messier misunderstood what he saw, lying billions of light-years in the distance, generations of biologists misunderstood what they were observing, in their backyards, incorrectly. The language of biological science is peppered with taxonomically false terms. For example, the suffix "phyte" or "phyta" comes from the Greek "phyton" meaning plant. It is attached to all manner of nonplant organisms. As a case in point, heterokontophyta, the former name for the heterokonts, and still in common usage, is a single-celled eukaryote that is certainly not a plant. [Glossary Heterokonts]

Much of our terminological mischief harkens back to a time when it was common to divide all objects on earth into three classes: animal, vegetable, and mineral. Consequently, all of the nonmetazoan eukaryotes were thought of as vegetables or plants, and given names taken from the field of botany. So too the bacteria. Hence, the gut bacteria were called the human microflora (tiny flowers). Mycelial growth was described as vegetative. The sporocarp of fungi continues to be called a "fruiting body." The nearly meaningless term "fruiting body" is haphazardly applied to bacteria and slime molds, as well.

Just as we falsely apply strictly botanical nomenclature to nonbotanical terms, we also apply metazoan terms to nonmetazoan organisms. For example, the term "zoo" derives from the Greek "zoion," meaning an animal. We find "zoo" or "zo" appearing as a prefix, infix, or suffix for organisms that are single-celled eukaryotes, fungi, and almost anything but animals. [Glossary Pseudo-metazoans]

Biological nomenclature has changed a great deal in the past few decades. If you learned medical microbiology in the preceding millennium, you may be surprised to learn that kingdoms have fallen (the once mighty kingdom of the protozoans has been largely abandoned), phyla have moved from one kingdom to another (the microsporidians, formerly thought to be protozoans, are now fungi; myxozoans, formerly thought to be protists, are now cnidarians [7]; slime molds, formerly thought to be fungi, are now amoebozoans). [Glossary Phylum, Rank and taxonomic order].

Biological misclassifications have practical consequences. When we place an infectious organism in the wrong class, we assume that the organism will respond to the same general treatments known to be effective in the other members of the class. When the treatment fails, we can offer no rational alternative treatment; until we recognize that the organism has been misclassified.

Why do we make such mistakes? We define our classes knowing full well that our definitions cannot be validated until after the classification has been completed. Consequently, every version of a classification reveals errors in its structure.

Erroneously positioned classes

Early taxonomists mistakenly assigned Class Fungi as a subclass of Class Archaeplastida (plants), based on shared similarities (e.g., both live in soil and both grow as immobile, sessile multicolored structures). If we were to take a nature walk in the woods, we might find colorful mushrooms growing near flowers or upon trees. It is easy to see why a person uninitiated in the science of classification might mistakenly place fungi within the plant kingdom [8,9]. [Glossary Mushroom]

The early taxonomists who placed the fungi among the plants should have known better. Fungi synthesize chitin, unlike all plants; and fungi lack cellulose and chloroplasts, which are found in plants. The structural role of chitin in fungi and animals, as a molecule providing structural strength, should have been a clue to the close relationship between these two classes. Furthermore, fungi and animals are both heterotrophic, acquiring energy by metabolizing organic compounds obtained from the environment. Plants, unlike animals and fungi, are phototropic autotrophs, producing organic compounds from light, water, and carbon dioxide. [Glossary Chitin, Chloroplast evolution, Heterotrophic]

If we wished, we could look to the field of human medicine to find yet another fundamental difference between fungi and plants. It happens that all sorts of fungi inhabit humans; some as pathogens, and others as harmless colonists on skin or mucosal surfaces [8]. Moreover, many fungal species, previously believed to be nonpathogenic in humans, will readily invade human tissues in persons who are immunocompromised [9]. The facility with which fungi exist on or in humans would suggest that the internal environment of humans, including the composition of cellular and extracellular materials, provides the proper nutrients for fungal growth. Conversely, plant species never infect humans. Plants will grow in water, mud, clay, excrement. Epiphytes will grow on an iron railing. But plants draw the line when it comes to living in or on humans. The observation that fungi do well in humans, and plants do poorly, is yet another signal that fungi are not types of plants.

If fungi are not plants, then what are they? To answer this question, we need to look at the single class property of Class Opisthokonta, a class of eukaryotes, that distinguishes it from all other classes of living organisms. Members of Class Opisthokonta all descended from a single-celled organism having one undulipodium extending outwards from the posterior pole of cells. The undulipodium in eukaryotes is roughly analogous to the flagellum in bacteria, and the term "flagellum" is often used interchangeably with undulipodium [10]. Most modern fungi lost their tell-tale posterior undulipodium, somewhere along their evolutionary road [11]. When fungi changed their habitat, from water to soil, they could no longer use their tails to propel themselves. Hence, the fungal undulipodium, no longer serving a useful purpose, devolved. The undulipodium was retained by the chytrids, a group of fungi that never left their aquatic habitat. All members of Class Plantae are descendants of Class Bikonta, eukaryotes with two undulipodia. Hence, the retention of the single posterior flagellum among the chytrid fungi leaves no doubt that fungi are opisthokonts, not plants. Both Class Fungi and Class Metazoa (the animals) are subclasses of Class Opithokonta. We humans do not routinely depend upon our posterior undulipodia. Nonetheless, a characteristic undulipodium is attached to every human spermatocyte. We are very much opisthokonts, just like our cousins, the fungi [8,9] (Fig. 4.1).

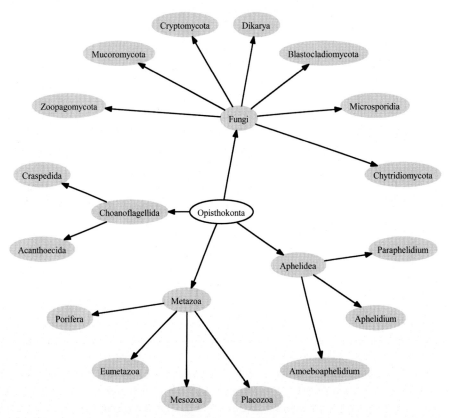

FIG. 4.1 Class Opisthokonta is the parent class of Class Fungi, Class Metazoa (all animals), Class Aphelidea (fungus-like organisms sometimes included within Class Fungi), and Class Choanoflagellida (single-celled organisms, some species of which may live in tight colonies).

The misconception that fungi are a class of plants has been hard to expunge. Universities, steeped in tradition, continue to assign their mycologists to the Department of Botany. Until about a decade ago, the taxonomy of fungi was decided by the International Committee for BOTANICAL Nomenclature. To this day, we find published taxonomies that identify fungi as types of flowers [12].

The take-away lesson here is that classifications serve as tentative hypotheses for a knowledge domain. Everything about a classification deserves skeptical analysis and reanalysis. We learn the most when we investigate anomalies and incongruities in the structure of the classification. We learn absolutely nothing when there is no classification waiting for our criticisms. [Glossary Reanalysis]

Instances confused with classes

Suppose we are cosmologists, and we create a class named Solar System, to contain the sun and the planets and the moons, and everything else that seems to fit. If we also have a class named Milky Way Galaxy, then the solar system would logically be one of the star systems contained in Class Milky Way Galaxy. But wait. We have already stipulated that the solar system is a class. Now we are asserting that the solar system is an instance within the Class Milky Way Galaxy. Can our solar system be both a class and an instance of some other class? Maybe we should have defined the solar system as a subclass of Class Milky Way Galaxy. In that case, the Class Solar System would be a subclass of Class Milky Way Galaxy and would contain, for instance, the sun and the moon, and the planets. Would that work?

No, it would not work. A moment's thought should tell us that we have hopelessly ruined our cosmological classification by confusing instances with classes. The solar system cannot be a subclass of Class Milky Way Galaxy because the solar system is not a type of galaxy! Furthermore, Class Milky Way Galaxy cannot be a valid class because it is just one particular instance of the general class of galaxies (i.e., Class Galaxy).

It is extremely easy to confuse instances with classes, and the confusion is vastly compounded by semantic languages that draw no clear distinction between classes and instances [13]. As an example of a semantic paradox, it is permissible to create an object that serves as the subclass of some class and as an instance of some other class. Under this condition, it is possible to design a semantically compliant ontology in which a class is an instance and a subclass of the same class [13].

Let's return to our classification of the cosmos. How should we have designed a classification in which instances are not confused with classes, and every instance has one assigned class? It is difficult to say. The fundamental design of any classification is never easy. We may have simply made classes of all the recognizable types of things we commonly observe in space:

Class Galaxy
Class Star
Class Black hole
Class Planet
Class Moon

Class Space rocks
Class Space gas

The root class might be Class Matter, and all the above-named heavenly bodies would be sister subclasses of Class Matter inheriting the properties of matter. Members of Class Star that appear in a particular galaxy might have a "belongs_to" property to which the name of the galaxy can be attached. Likewise, members of Class Moon might have a "belongs_to" property to which the name of a planet could be attached. Notice that none of the classes consist of any specifically named cosmologic body. Classes are always general terms and contain exclusively general subclasses of the general term. So Milky Way Galaxy could never be a subclass of Class Galaxy. The Milky Way Galaxy can never be anything more than an instance.

Ontology models that ignore the natural order

For the traditional classification builder, the mindset of modern ontologists is simply unfathomable. The classification builder is constantly trying to understand the basic nature of his knowledge domain so that she can create a classification that exactly matches reality. The ontologist, however, seems to believe that his ontology can be anything she wants it to be. Here is a quotation from a manuscript intended as an introduction to ontologies. "There is no one correct way to model a domain [14]." The manuscript continues in the same vein, concluding "there are always viable alternatives. The best solution almost always depends on the application that you have in mind and the extensions that you anticipate [14]."

If we maintain that our ontology is a model of the real world, it would seem that there should be only one true ontologic design (i.e., one possible set of classes and class relationships). If we say that the design of an ontology depends on the application that we have in mind, then we are saying that the ontology need only satisfy a particular set of goals. The modern ontologist has a very different way of thinking than the traditional classification builder, and this disparity in mindset is responsible for much of the miscommunication between traditionalists and modern computer-ready ontologists.

Here is an example of how a traditionalist may be disappointed by a modern ontology. Let's imagine that an ontology has been constructed as a knowledge domain for human anatomy. The ontology is built to be maximally useful for students and professionals from many different medical disciplines. Accordingly, the ontologists have created a class of objects of particular interest to ophthalmologists, and a class of objects of interest to podiatrists, and a class of objects of interest for endocrinologists. The ontology is built class-by-class, as additional disciplines of medicine are added to the mix. The goal is to eventually have an ontology that covers every field of medicine.

After the ontology has been completed and released to the scientific community, a researcher decides to use the ontology to understand the developmental biology of lymph nodes and plans to map out the location of every lymph node. After spending several unproductive hours working with the ontology, the traditionalist seeks help from one of the ontology designers. The conversation might go something like this.

> Scientist: "I just tried using your ontology to map out the anatomic location of lymph nodes in the human body, and all I can find are references to some particular nodes in a few particular locations, such as foot, eye, chest. I can't find all the lymph nodes that have been described anatomically."
>
> Modern ontologist: "Ok. First tell me, what discipline of medicine are you studying?"
>
> Scientist: "I'm not studying any particular discipline. I just have a general question about the locations of lymph nodes."
>
> Modern ontologist: "Our ontology is designed for specific medical disciplines. You're trying to use it in a way that was never intended."
>
> Scientist: But your ontology is named "Ontology of Human Anatomy."
>
> Modern ontologist: "Yes."
>
> Scientist: "There is only one model of human anatomy. It hasn't changed over thousands of years. Shouldn't your Ontology of Human Anatomy contain all the anatomic relationships of the human body?"
>
> Modern ontologist: "You haven't heard a word I've said, have you?"

When we admit that an ontology has no single correct model, then we are essentially saying that any ontology we create imposes the designer's concept of how the system works. In addition, we are operating under the assumption that objects and classes have no natural order, and we can define classes as we wish.

It is difficult to argue with success. The modern ontologist's approach has had enormous utility, providing application builders with a set of objects, classes, and properties that can be implemented in useful software programs. A traditionalist might complain that ontologies that fail to correctly model the natural order are of limited value. If the class relationships and rules are not designed to be universally true, and if the ontology is not fully representative of reality, then the ontology cannot have enduring scientific significance.

International Classification of Diseases

Diseases have always been difficult to classify because all of the noninfectious common diseases result from the action of various contributing causes, acting through a variable sequence of events, occurring over a variable length of time. As an example, let's consider cirrhosis of the liver. Cirrhosis is a condition wherein the liver becomes diffusely fibrotic, usually due to some chronic and progressive process that kills hepatocytes (i.e., liver cells). Cirrhosis can result from inherited mutations (e.g., hemochromatosis, alpha-1-antitrypsin deficiency), or through the ingestion of toxic chemicals (e.g., alcohol), or due to contamination of the liver by a source of chronic radiation (e.g., thorotrast), or by inhalation of a chemical in the environment (e.g., carbon tetrachloride, polyvinyl chloride), or by infectious agents (e.g., hepatitis virus).

The clinical course of individuals with cirrhosis can greatly vary, partly due to the variety of ways in which the disease can develop. Cirrhosis is just one example of a well-known disease that can have many different pathogeneses (steps in development) and clinical attributes. We could add ischemic heart disease (including the common term, "heart attack"), chronic obstructive pulmonary disease (including emphysema), hypertension, pneumonia, gastritis, encephalitis, and so on. It would be difficult to name a commonly occurring disease that does not represent a collection of biological causes and attributes spread through a population. Viewed this way, diseases cannot be readily classified.

The International Classification of Diseases (ICD) is a nomenclature of the diseases occurring in humans, with each listed disease assigned a unique identifying code. The ICD is owned by the World Health Organization but can be used freely by the public. The currently used version of ICD is version 10 (ICD-10).

Let's take a moment to inspect the higher order of classes in the International Classification of Disease. Here are 10 of the 28 major classes of disease that are in draft form, awaiting inclusion in the upcoming release of ICD version 11, which is scheduled for worldwide implementation in January 2022 [15].

```
Certain infectious or parasitic diseases
Neoplasms
Diseases of the blood or blood-forming organs
Diseases of the immune system
Endocrine, nutritional, or metabolic diseases
Mental, behavioral, or neurodevelopmental disorders
Sleep-wake disorders
Diseases of the nervous system
Diseases of the visual system
Diseases of the skin
Diseases of the circulatory system
Diseases of the musculoskeletal system or connective tissue
```

How do we fill these ICD-11 classes of disease? Does acute leukemia fall into class "Neoplasms," or should it go into "Diseases of the blood or blood-forming organs." Is Alzheimer's disease one of the "Mental, behavioral, or neurodevelopmental disorders" or is it one of the "Diseases of the nervous system"? Why would we want to include adrenal insufficiency, an endocrine disease, and scurvy, a nutritional deficiency, in the same class of "Endocrine, nutritional, or metabolic diseases"?

What do we do with a disease such as streptococcal sore throat that begins as an acute infection, but may progress to an immune process that subsequently affects the heart (i.e., rheumatic fever)? In this case, one disease transitions from "Certain infectious or parasitic diseases" to "Diseases of the immune system" and "Diseases of the musculoskeletal system or connective tissue."

There is no single way, by application of logic, to assign diseases to the high-level classes of ICD-11. No matter. The creators of ICD-11 have assigned every disease to some location in the classification, and those individuals who receive the proper training can successfully code diseases according to the prescribed, listings under each class.

The World Health Organization has provided the following definition of ICD-11 [15]:

"ICD is the foundation for the identification of health trends and statistics globally, and the international standard for reporting diseases and health conditions. It is the diagnostic classification standard for all clinical and research purposes. ICD defines the universe of diseases, disorders, injuries and other related health conditions, listed in a comprehensive, hierarchical fashion that allows for:

- Easy storage, retrieval, and analysis of health information for evidence-based decision-making.
- Sharing and comparing health information between hospitals, regions, settings, and countries.
- Data comparisons in the same location across different periods."

Nowhere in the definition does it state that the ICD has an internally logical construct. Here are some of the shortcomings of ICD-11, based on the minimal criteria for a logical classification, as stipulated earlier in this chapter:

1. Assigns biologically unrelated diseases to the same class, based solely on anatomic location.
2. Assigns diseases that are pathogenetically related into biologically unrelated classes.
3. Provides no set of class-defining features that adequately separates the members of a class, and its descendants, from the other classes. Instead, the ICD-11 employs exception lists added to each class that exclude diseases that meet class criteria but which must, nevertheless, be assigned to some other class.
4. Has no competence (i.e., cannot be used to draw inferences and create new hypotheses based on methods derived from the class properties).
5. Cannot be proven either right or wrong. Because no inferences can be drawn from a standardized listing of diseases, with no logical structure, then there is no way to test that the listing is either correct or incorrect. It is what it is.

We should not criticize ICD-11 harshly; it may well be the very best disease classification in existence. We must remember that creating a not-so-good classification is a necessary step toward creating a good classification.

It is always instructive to look through a classification to get a sense of what is included. When we review ICD-10 codes, we find that many of the entries are disturbingly specific, requiring multiple conditions to occur at one moment in time, and not involving anything that we would commonly interpret as a disease process.

Ponder the following entries:

```
Y92.146 Swimming-pool of prison as the place of occurrence of the
  external cause
Y92.241 Hurt at the library
V97.33 Sucked into a jet engine
X52 Prolonged stay in a weightless environment
W56.22 Struck by orca
V91.35 Hit or struck by falling object due to accident by canoe or
  kayak
V00.01 Pedestrian on foot injured in collision with roller-skater
V91.07 Burn due to water-skis on fire
```

Have we come very far from our 17th-century versions of the ICD, whose causes of death include "fainted in a bath," "frighted," and "itch" [16]?

The International Classification of Diseases serves a purpose. It provides standardized codes by which healthcare organizations can keep track of the medical conditions encountered in their catchment population. This data can be collected from multiple institutions, and statistically valid data related to the incidence of various diseases can be produced. Nonetheless, we should remark that the ICD does not provide the scientific foundation expected from a competent classification. We cannot use the classification to understand disease processes or to understand the biological relationships of one class of disease with another class of diseases, and we cannot test the classification to see if it is biologically valid.

The Diagnostic and Statistical Manual of Mental Disorders

In the past half-century, we have witnessed incredible advances in the field of brain imaging. Scientists can now determine the brain areas that are selectively activated during specific physiologic functions. New imaging techniques include: positron emission tomography, functional magnetic resonance imaging, multichannel electroencephalography, magnetoencephalography, near-infrared spectroscopic imaging, and single-photon emission computed tomography. With all of these available technologies, you would naturally expect that neuroscientists would be in a position to make remarkable progress in the field of psychiatric illnesses. Indeed, the brain research literature has seen hundreds, if not thousands of early studies purporting to find associations that link brain anatomy to psychiatric diseases. Alas, none of these early findings have been validated. Excluding degenerative and traumatic brain conditions (e.g., Alzheimer's disease, Parkinson's disease, chronic traumatic encephalopathy), there is, at present, no known psychiatric condition that can be consistently associated with a specific functional brain deficit or anatomic abnormality [17]. [Glossary Association]

What thwarted the ambitions of researchers in this promising young field? One problem seems to be that we have no biological classification for any of the psychiatric diseases. Historically, diagnoses are rendered based on grouping diseases that have similar symptoms, without any knowledge of the underlying biological mechanism that causes the symptoms to appear. When we do so, we create aggregate objects (in this case names of psychiatric disorders) that cannot be rationally classified. [Glossary Aggregate disease]

In 2013, a new version of the Diagnostic and Statistical Manual of Mental Disorders (DSM) was released. The DSM is the standard classification of psychiatric disorders and is used by psychiatrists and other healthcare professionals worldwide. The new version was long in coming, following its previous version by 20 years. Spoiling the fanfare for the much-anticipated update was a chorus of loud detractors, who included among their ranks a host of influential and respected neuroscientists. They complained that the DSM classifies diagnostic entities based on collections of symptoms; not on biological principles. For every diagnostic entity in the DSM, all persons who share the same collection of symptoms will, in most cases, be assigned the same diagnosis; without taking into account the biological events leading to those symptoms [18].

For example, Rett syndrome is a highly complex neurodevelopmental disorder often accompanied by a variety of neurologic and somatic dysfunctions [19]. Repetitive hand movements and the absence of verbal skills are commonly noted. In early versions of the DSM, Rett syndrome was classified as a pervasive developmental disorder, in the same class of disease that includes autism. Subsequently, we have learned a great deal about the pathogenesis of Rett syndrome. Most cases are associated with a mutation of the MECP2 gene located on the X chromosome, and virtually all cases occur in females. Medical researchers are carefully studying the developmental processes affected in Rett syndrome, but the early DSM, which misclassified Rett syndrome as a form of autism, only served to confuse researchers. The latest version of the DSM removes Rett syndrome entirely from the classification, conceding that Rett syndrome is not even a mental disorder [20].

When individuals with unrelated diseases, are studied together, simply because they have some symptoms in common, the results of the study are unlikely to have any validity [21]. Dr. Thomas Insel, a former Director of the National Institute of Mental Health, was quoted as saying, "As long as the research community takes the DSM to be a bible, we'll never make progress." When the very first version of the DSM was introduced to the world, in 1952, its creators were hailed as heroes [22]. Today, with little progress in the field, and with diseases still grouped by symptoms, the DSM is vilified by some of the most active and influential members of the field [22,20].

The much anticipated, but ultimately impossible, molecular classification of diseases

For well over 150 years, the diagnosis of disease has been based on microscopic examination [23]. The fundamental reasoning that justified the morphologic diagnosis of the disease is based on the concept that diseases of the body are caused by diseases of cells in the body; and those diseased cells provide us with morphologic clues to diagnosis. This system has worked fairly well, with some notable limitations. Most significantly, patients having the same diagnosis, based on pathological examination, may respond quite differently to the same treatment. One patient may recover fully. Another patient may die [20]. [Glossary Lesion]

As an increasing number of diseases have been examined by advanced molecular techniques, it has become apparent that patients grouped under a single morphological diagnosis may have genetically distinctive diseases. In some cases, response to treatment can be more accurately determined by their characteristic genetic sequences rather than by somewhat imprecise and subjective morphologic features. In many of those cases, the genetic findings seem to be both pathognomonic (i.e., seen in every case of the disease and not seen in any other diseases or the normal population) and causal [20].

A growing number of scientists and physicians have concluded that morphologic examination of tissue might have run its course, and that new genetic and molecular methods may be the best way to diagnose and classify diseases. This sentiment was expressed by the Director of the U.S. National Institutes of Health, who convened an ad-hoc committee of the National Research Council to develop a framework for the classification of human diseases, based on molecular biology [21].

The disappointing news is that despite the advances to medicine brought by molecular techniques, a classification of diseases, based on genetic analyses, is not feasible.

Here is a lengthy list of arguments against a gene-based classification of diseases.

1. Many diseases do not have a genetic basis

The nongenetic diseases would include the diseases caused by environmental toxins, and the so-called wear and tear degenerative diseases, such as osteoarthritis. It is difficult to create a classification of diseases around a concept that does not apply to all diseases.

2. There are many diseases whose causes and genetic characteristics are unknown

These would include the many developmental diseases that are observed at birth (i.e., congenital anomalies). Of the clinically significant congenital anomalies, an estimated 60% are so-called sporadic, meaning that they have no discernible genetic cause or environmental cause. Of the 12%–25% of clinical congenital anomalies that have a genetic cause, the majority of these are characterized by chromosomal anomalies. Because chromosomal anomalies involve many genes within a gene region, we can seldom associate the conditions associated with the chromosomal anomaly with any single gene. This means that the overwhelming majority of congenital anomalies that occur in humans are unclassifiable under a genetic classification of human diseases.

3. Genes are just one factor among many that contribute to the development of diseases

It is impossible to build a classification that is determined by one component of disease development while ignoring all the others.

4. The same gene mutations that play an important role in the clinical expression of one particular disease may have a negligible role when found in some other disease

For example, malignant melanomas having the BRAF V600E mutation respond well to treatment with vemurafenib, while colorectal carcinomas with the identical mutation do not respond to the same drug [24,25]. The rationale for developing a gene-based classification of diseases is that diseases classified by the same mutation will respond similarly to mutation-targeted therapies. How will we deal with conditions that do not comply with the fundamental rationale underlying a molecular classification of disease?

5. The genetic aberrations found in diseases may involve a large set of mutations that defy classification

In the case of cancer, the advanced stage cancers found in adults are nearly always highly unstable genetically, and a single tumor may have thousands of different mutations. Multiple samples, selected from different locations in the same tumor, may yield widely different genetic profiles. Classifying such tumors by a genetic marker can be an impossible task [26].

6. The genes that drive disease in one stage of development may be absent in later stages

For example, BRAF V600E mutations are found more often in dysplastic nevi, the presumed precursors of melanoma, than in melanomas that arise therefrom. Likewise, human epidermal growth factor receptor 2 is more often overexpressed in ductal carcinomas in situ (i.e., noninvasive breast cancers) than in the invasive breast cancers into which they develop. Similarly, fibroblast growth factor 3 mutations decrease as the bladder tumor grade increases, over time [27]. It is difficult to classify a disease based on gene mutations that may not be present in the cells of the disease in every stage of its development. [Glossary Carcinoma in situ]

7. A single disease, occurring in different individuals, may result from one of many distinct molecular defects

For example, breast cancer may result from inherited defects in p53 (as in the Li Fraumeni syndrome), or PTEN (as in Cowden syndrome), or from STK11 (as in Peutz-Jegher syndrome), or from none of the above. [Glossary Cowden syndrome]

8. A single gene may produce many different diseases

We now know of hundreds of instances wherein various mutations of a single gene are the root causes of multiple phenotypically diverse diseases [32]. Because a single mutated gene may produce many different diseases, it would be difficult to build a classification based solely on gene-based correlations [20]. [Glossary One-gene-to-many-diseases, Root cause]

9. Healthy individuals carry putative disease-causing genes

An ideal class property applies to every member of the class and its descendant classes and is absent in all other classes. For a while, there was hope that most of the inherited diseases and most cancers could be defined by a set of disease-specific mutations, one of which would be present in every individual with the disease; none of which would be present in individuals without the disease. Such hopes were dashed when rare healthy individuals, without any sign of disease, were shown to carry "disease-specific" gene mutations.

One of the earliest surprises came when the bcr/abl fusion gene, thought to be pathognomonic for chronic myelogenous leukemia, was present in healthy individuals, a finding that was confirmed by several different laboratories [28–30]. Disease genes involved in the pathogenesis of other hematologic disorders were also found in healthy individuals [31,33,34].

Genome testing on large populations confirms the presence of disease genes in the healthy population [35]. Many of the putative disease genes are now recognized as common polymorphisms, indicating the discordance between genotype and phenotype (i.e., between the genetic findings and the clinical findings) [36]. Classification of disease cannot be based on gene mutations if those mutations are commonly present in unaffected individuals. [Glossary Genotype]

10. There is no way to separate genetic diseases and diseases caused by the environment

It is difficult to classify diseases by a genetic mutation when we know that many so-called genetic diseases are biologically complex processes with multiple genetic and environmental components.

If you recall, this part of our discussion began with a request, from the Director of the U.S. National Institutes of Health to the National Research Council, for a new framework for the classification of human diseases, based on molecular biology [21]. How did the National Research Council respond? After due deliberation, the National Research Council advised that a framework for a new classification of disease based solely on molecular biology is not feasible [21]. Sometimes, creating a new classification is not the wisest course of action. [Glossary Unstable taxonomy]

Section 4.2. Paradoxes

Paradoxes are fun. Plus, whenever we encounter a paradox, we can expect to learn a lesson in logic that will improve our professional skills. Let's look at five examples of paradoxes that involve classifications or ontologies.

In 1975, while touring the Bethesda, Maryland campus of the National Institutes of Health, I was informed that their Building 10, was the largest all-brick building in the world, providing a home to over 7 million bricks. Soon thereafter, an ambitious construction project was undertaken to greatly expand the size of Building 10. When the work was finished, building 10 was no longer the largest all-brick building in the world. What happened? The builders used material other than brick, and Building 10 lost its classification as an all-brick building. This poses something of a paradox; objects in a classification are not permitted to move about from one class to another (i.e., the nontransitive property of classifications).

Apparent paradoxes that plague any formal conceptualization of classifications are not difficult to find. Before we return to the "all-brick Building 10 paradox" let's look at a few more puzzles.

Consider the "Bag" class of objects. A "Bag" is a collection of objects, and Class Bag is included in most object-oriented programming libraries. A "Set" is also a collection of objects, and is a subclass of Class Bag, with the special feature that duplicate instances are not permitted. For example, if Kansas is a member of the set of U.S. States, then you cannot add a second state named "Kansas" to the set; although you can add as many Kansas objects to a bag as you might wish. If Class Bag were to have an "increment" method, that added "1" to the total count of objects in the bag, whenever an object is added to Class Bag, then the "increment" method would be inherited by all of the subclasses of Class Bag, including Class Set. But Class Set cannot increase in size when duplicate items are added. Hence, inheritance creates a paradox in the Class Set.

Consider the geometric class of ellipses; planar objects in which the sum of the distances to two focal points is constant. Class Circle is a child of Class Ellipse, for which the two focal points of instance members occupy the same position, in the center, producing a radius of constant size. Imagine that Class Ellipse is provided with a class method called "stretch," in which the foci are moved further apart, hence producing flatter objects. When the parent class "stretch" method is applied to members of the Class Circle, the circle stops being a circle and becomes an ordinary ellipse. Hence the inherited "stretch" method forces members of Class Circle to transition out of their assigned class (in violation of the intransitivity condition of classifications).

The Suggested Upper Merged Ontology (SUMO) is an ontology designed to contain classes for general types of objects that might be included in other, more specific knowledge domains. Class HumanCorpse, in SUMO, is customized to contain "A dead thing which was formerly a Human." Class HumanCorpse is a subclass of Class OrganicObject; not of Class Human. Class Human is reserved for the living. This means that we humans, once we cease to breathe, transit from Class Human to Class OrganicObject, a class that excludes live humans but welcomes dead humans. A member of Class Human, in the SUMO ontology, will change its class and its ancestral lineage, when it least wants to.

One last dalliance before leaving SUMO. Consider these two classes from the SUMO ontology, both of which happen to be subclasses of Class Substance: Class NaturalSubstance and Class SyntheticSubstance. It would seem that these two subclasses are mutually exclusive. However, diamonds occur naturally, and diamonds can be synthesized. Hence, diamond belongs to Class NaturalSubstance and Class SyntheticSubstance.

The ontology creates two mutually exclusive classes that contain the same item, thus creating a paradox [18]. [Glossary SUMO]

How does a data scientist deal with class objects that disappear from their assigned class and reappear elsewhere? Let's revisit all of our listed paradoxes and see if we cannot rectify the problems.

1. Building 10 at NIH was defined as the largest all-brick building in the world. Strictly speaking, building 10 was a structure, and it had a certain weight and dimensions, and it was constructed of brick. "Brick" is just an attribute or property, and properties should not form the basis of a class, if they are not a constant feature shared by all members of the class (i.e., some buildings have bricks; others do not). Had we not conceptualized an "all-brick" class of building, we would have avoided any confusion.

2. Class Set was made a subset of Class Bag, but the increment method of class Bag could not apply to Class Set. We created Class Set without taking into account the basic properties of Class Bag, which must apply to all its subclasses. Perhaps it would have been better if Class Set and Class Bag were created as sister classes of Class Collection; each with its own nonparadoxical set of properties.

3. The circle paradox could have been avoided by refraining from creating Class Circle. Circles are simply ellipses with a distance of zero between their two focal points. They do not need their own designated class.

4. Class HumanCorpse was not created as a subclass of Class Human. This was a mistake, as all humans will eventually die. If we were to create two classes, one called Class Living Human and one called Class Deceased Human, we would certainly cover all possible human states of being, but we would be creating a situation where members of a class are forced to transition out of their class and into another (violating Rule 3). The solution, in this case, is simple. Life and death are properties of organisms, and all organisms can and will have both properties, but never at the same time. We can assign organisms the properties of life and death, without creating classes limited to either of these properties.

5. The concepts "NaturalSubstance" and "SyntheticSubstance" would appear to be subclasses of "Substance." Are they really? Would it not be better to think that being "natural" or being "synthetic" are just properties of substances; not types of substances. If we agree that diamonds are a member of class substance, we can say that any specific diamond may have occurred naturally or through synthesis. We can eliminate two subclasses (i.e., "NaturalSubstance" and "SyntheticSubstance") and replace them with two properties of class "Substance": synthetic and natural. By assigning properties to a class of objects, we simplify the ontology (by reducing the number of subclasses), and we eliminate the paradox created when a class member belongs to two mutually exclusive subclasses.

A classification of the mind

Science is, in reality, a classification and analysis of the contents of the mind.
Karl Pearson in The Grammar of Science, *1900*

I used to think that the brain was the most wonderful organ in my body. Then I realized who was telling me this.
Emo Philips

Nowhere are the paradoxes of classification more in evidence than when we try to classify our minds. No matter how hard we try, we cannot be objective because our minds impose upon our conscious thoughts a subconscious representation of reality that we cannot fully understand. Of course, scientists have never been discouraged by the impossible. In the case of a classification of the mind, the general approach has been that if we can make some tentative assertions, and if we can show, by experiment, that these assertions are valid, then we can construct some semblance of a credible classification that can be continuously tested and improved.

What can we begin to say about the classification of the human mind?

1. The individual objects of the classification of the mind are thoughts.
2. The two largest classes of thoughts are conscious thoughts and subconscious thoughts.
3. Our conscious minds have limited access to the subconscious minds, but dreams provide us with some clues since dreams are the products of the subconscious mind.
4. Ultimately, all of our thoughts, including all of our observations of the external world, are internal constructions that should not be held as accurate renditions of reality.
5. Our human brains develop just like other organs of the body, with anatomic form and functionality that is generally typical of the species.
6. The subconscious of one human is likely to hold many of the same thoughts as are found in most other humans, insofar as every brain draws from the same species gene pool, and these genes must code for all of the intrinsic thought processes provided at birth. These would almost certainly include instincts, drives (e.g., the drives for food, shelter, love, companionship, sex), and certain species-typical behaviors.
7. Our minds integrate our subconscious and conscious thoughts. It is reasonable to guess that all manner of mental dysfunction might result when subconscious and conscious thoughts are poorly integrated.

We can say with some certitude that all of our perceptions, even those that we consider direct observations of external events, are concoctions of the mind. If we look outside our window and we watch a robin flying from branch to branch in our front lawn tree, we must understand that what we see is a highly processed mental representation of stimuli received primarily through our eyes. In our minds, we watch a kind of homemade movie starring a simulated robin. We can shut our eyes and replay the movie in our minds, though the replayed movie may not have as much detail as our first movie, which, in turn, would certainly not have all the detail of the actual scene. Later that night, while we sleep, our subconscious may play the movie again, but this time, the robin may be replaced by a hawk or a snake. Basically, what we see is whatever our minds deliver.

Somewhat less certain, but worthy of our consideration, is the notion of the collective consciousness (i.e., thoughts inherited and shared by most or all members of the species). It is difficult for us to think in terms of "inherited thoughts," but we accept this concept without any skepticism when we examine nonhuman animal behavior (e.g., chicks imprinting on the mother hen, wolves baying at the moon, fixed action patterns in hunting dogs). There is no rational reason to think that humans are special in this regard. The human genome codes for a brain that functions from the moment of birth, and probably much earlier. How the genes code for instinctual behaviors is unknown, but all humans draw their genes from the species gene pool, and the notion of "species-wide thoughts" should not be considered particularly controversial.

Carl Jung examined the idea of collective intelligence, acting on both the conscious and subconscious levels. The inherited intelligence of our species is claimed to provide us with cross-cultural symbols, myths, personality archetypes, dreams, drives, and even memories; all of which act to shape the human psyche. Jung taught that these thoughts must be properly integrated into our conscious psyches; otherwise, all manner of psychiatric disorders may arise [37].

It is tempting to dismiss Jungian psychoanalysis as a pseudoscience, insofar as its theories are built on clinical and personal observations; not on controlled laboratory experiments. Jung's philosophy and his approach to psychoanalysis and dream interpretation cannot be proven or disproven. Perhaps, when we find many examples of universal myths and symbols that are present in diverse cultures, widely separated by time and geography, we may temper our skepticism. By asserting the existence of a collective subconscious and conscious intelligence, and populating that domain with defined objects (e.g., symbols, myths, archetypes), alchemies (seen as transformations toward a more perfect state of existence), and relationships (i.e., dreams and other forms of intrusion of the unconscious into the conscious mind), Jung was building a classification of the elements of the mind.

For modern scientists, the topic of collective intelligence may seem ridiculous. What purpose would be served by dwelling on how we humans think? *Homo sapiens*, the apes who know things, have made great progress using the scientific method. We design experiments intended to prove or disprove our hypotheses. We record our findings in the scientific literature so that generations of scientists can benefit from earlier works. On a certain level, we have proven that we humans can think pretty well, without devoting much energy to understanding how we think.

In response, we observe that humans are not, as a group, driven by logic. Whatever accounts for our intelligence seems to be something very different from Vulcan-like logic.

Furthermore, there is a great deal of mental illness in our society, and we don't have a very good handle on how to prevent, diagnose, or treat disorders of the mind.

Perhaps the field of study that is the best indicator of our inability to understand ourselves is found in AI (Artificial Intelligence). AI attempts to build computers that think as humans do. Over the years, as computers have become faster and more powerful, the field of AI has made some progress. Currently, computers can defeat humans in the game of chess, and computers excel at the television game show "Jeopardy." Still, AI experts will admit that these achievements in no way involve an understanding of human thought processes. They have merely programmed calculations performed on sets of data. We have made very little progress toward building machines that think like humans because we know almost nothing about how humans think. [Glossary Artificial intelligence]

An unclassified world is an incomprehensible world. Classifications assemble the relationships among objects that help us understand the essence of the objects, and allow us to predict how objects of different types interact. It is highly unlikely that much headway will be made in the field of AI until we begin to assemble and test a classification of the human mind. It may be that when we make real progress in AI, we will gain the ability to understand and treat mental disorders.

Section 4.3. Linking classifications, ontologies, and triplestores

Triplestores linked to classifications, ontologies, and schemas

Aside from the computational advantages of triplestores, which can accommodate billions or trillions of triples representing meaningful computer-parsable assertions, they offer three features lacking in classifications and ontologies.

1. Objects in triplestores that are also included in classifications or ontologies can be directly linked from their records in the triplestore to their class objects

For example, if object "07171502-6fd7-11eb-a5b4-989cb31ecde1" in a triplestore is asserted to be a cultured specimen of *Staphylococcus aureus*, then we can add assertions indicating that "07171502-6fd7-11eb-a5b4-989cb31ecde1" is a sample of *S. aureus*, a species included in the Classification of Life and for which there is a wealth of readily available information. We can infer that "07171502-6fd7-11eb-a5b4-989cb31ecde1" will have inherited the class attributes of Staphylococcus and all of the classes ancestral to Staphylococcus. In addition, we can use the triplestore to find any of the contained triples of "07171502-6fd7-11eb-a5b4-989cb31ecde1," from which we might move a bit closer to finding new class attributes of Staphylococcus. In the same manner, an object in a triplestore that is a member of a class included in an ontology can be asserted to be a type of object included in the ontologic class. When we can link objects in triplestores to objects in classifications or ontologies, we vastly increase our ability to test hypotheses and draw new inferences about instances and classes.

2. Objects in triplestores that are not included in classifications or ontologies may sometimes represent components of objects in classifications

In previous chapters, we discussed various types of objects that could not be sensibly classified. Foremost among the unclassifiable objects are the multicomponent structures (e.g., aggregate rocks, electronic equipment). When the components of an object are instances of classification, we can compose triples of the objects that describe each component and we can compose additional triples that link such components to their class within a classification or an ontology. Once again, the classified components of an object will inherit the properties of its class and its ancestral classes. Hence, unclassifiable objects, when included in triples, have the opportunity of benefiting from classifications, if their components are asserted in triples.

3. Metadata found in triplestores may represent properties defined in schemas

We must not forget that every triple consists of an identified object followed by some metadata and some data. The metadata tells us what we need to know to make sense of the data. In the following triple, "weight_in_ounces" is the metadata that helps us understand the significance of "16."

```
2d147188-6fdb-11eb-8d83-b70afc122f0f "weight_in_ounces" 16
```

All metadata are properties of the object. In the above case, the unique object "2d147188-6fdb-11eb-8d83-b70afc122f0f" has the property of "weight_in_ounces." We might guess that "2d147188-6fdb-11eb-8d83-b70afc122f0f" is a bag of potato chips, or maybe a book. We don't know exactly, but we do know that it is something with weight and that the weight can be measured in ounces, and that in this triple the number of ounces is 16.

Because "weight_in_ounces" is a property, it may be listed in a schema that provides definitions of properties. In turn, a triple can link "weight_in_ounces" to the schema in which it is defined. Proceeding in this manner, all of the metadata included in triplestores can be linked to the schemas that contain their definitions. Wherever the metadata is found in any triplestore, we can be certain that if that metadata (itself a unique object with a unique identifier) is properly linked to a schema, then everyone who uses the same unique metadata object will have access to the same schema definition for the metadata. Doing so may provide some added level of interoperability among triplestores, and between triplestores and classifications or ontologies.

Upper ontologies combined with lower ontologies

As we mentioned previously, ontologies have no completeness requirement. This means that an ontology need not contain all of the classes representative of a knowledge domain. An ontology need not be designed to fit within any single knowledge domain and may contain classes that belong to several different knowledge domains. The price paid for this kind of subject flexibility is the loss of class inheritance. Nonetheless, ontologies can be created with well-defined classes, properties, and instances that can be used by other ontologies, when we properly link their related classes.

An example of an ontology that serves as a source of objects for other ontologies is SUMO. SUMO is designed to contain many thousands of terms that might be used by focused ontologies (i.e., lower-level ontologies) from many different realms. Terms such as "chemical substance," "human," "person," "home address" are the kinds of instances that might be included in an upper-level ontology. When an ontology references a term found in an upper-level ontology (using a namespace or using with triples that specify how objects are linked), we can be fairly confident that the meaning of the term and its properties will be equivalent in any other ontology that references the same upper-level ontology.

Classifications extracted from classifications

The branches of well-constructed classifications are themselves valid classifications of the knowledge domain rooted at the branching point. In the case of the Classification of Life, we can choose any class (e.g., Class Metazoa, Class Aves, Class Mammalia) to serve as the root class for all the descendants of the class. This kind of deconstruction of the major classification into subclassifications is done all the time, permitting scholars to concentrate their attention on a particular subdiscipline. We can add that, among data structures, only classifications permit us to simply cut out a section of itself while preserving the hierarchy and relationships existing among the extracted classes.

Classifications combined with other classifications

Just as we can deconstruct a classification by removing branches, we can also construct large classifications by connecting branches together wherever they have a common junction.

For example, the Classification of Life was, of necessity, created by combining subclassifications. The bacteriologists worked on the two kingdoms of the prokaryotic organisms (i.e., bacteria and archaea); the zoologists worked on the metazoans, the botanists worked on plants, and so on. The task of building the Classification of Life is simply too big to tackle without breaking it down into parts. **One of the best features of classifications is that they can be assembled seamlessly from subclassifications, to produce a final product that is incredibly easy to understand, in its entirety.** [Glossary Archaea]

It is not until the subclassifications are tied together that we can easily understand the relationships among the major kingdoms of life. For example, we cannot determine the full ancestral lineage of any existing organism without access to a complete classification that extends from the species to the root of the total classification. As another example, we can study the classification of plants for the duration of our careers, but we will never understand the relationships between plants and insects until we have connected their respective subclassifications, and study their coevolution.

Ontologies combined with classifications

Ontologies can be easily subsumed by one or more classifications. For example, we might create an ontology of the minerals found in Arizona. Minerals are chemical compounds composed of elements and have a specific chemical formula and crystalline structure. It would be feasible to tie individual instances of the ontology of minerals to the Periodic Table of the Elements and a classification of crystal structures. Although an ontology of minerals may not qualify as a classification, the elements of the mineral are certainly classified, as are the crystal structures of the mineral. Hence, the elemental and structural components of minerals will inherit class properties of their respective classifications.

Let's look at one more example. There is a class of tumors that develops from the cells of the neural crest. This class of tumors includes hundreds of different types of tumors such as schwannomas, paragangliomas, and melanomas. The neural crest evolved exclusively in Class Craniata and is found only in subclasses of Class Craniata. From this, we can infer that tumors of the neural crest are found only in extant species that are subclasses of Class Craniata. Examples of subclasses of Class Craniata include fish, birds, and mammals. As it happens, pathologists who collect samples of tumors from many different types of animals confirm that neural crest tumors occur in craniates and do not occur in noncraniates. This is an example of how an ontology (e.g., an ontology of tumors classified by developmental tissue of origin) can be usefully linked to a classification (i.e., the Classification of Life). [Glossary Craniata]

Section 4.4. Saving hopeless classifications

Building a classification when detractors consider the effort unnecessary

Building a classification is never easy. History has taught us that for every great classification, there are vocal detractors, many of whom find the enterprise to be either futile or pointless. All three of the great classifications of the natural sciences have had their detractors. We remember Aristotle ("Section 2.5. Widely held misconceptions"), whose efforts to produce a classification of animals were ridiculed through two millennia. We also note the travails of Dioscoridis, a 1st-century botanist. Dioscorides wrote De Materia Medica in about 60 CE, providing one of the earliest and most influential taxonomies of botanical medicine [38]. This scholarly work also contained thoughtful discussion bemoaning the then-current state of botanical classification. Dioscorides asked why his contemporaries had organized their listings of herbs alphabetically. Doing so separated herbs that were closely related and made it difficult to understand the relationships and shared properties of related plants. Theophrastus, four centuries earlier, had wisely divided seed plants into angiosperms (flowering plants) and gymnosperms (non-flowering plants such as cycads and pines). The classification of Theophrastus did not seem to influence herbalists in the time of Dioscoridis. History would indicate that Dioscoridis' quite reasonable questions went largely unanswered over the subsequent 1700 years. Sometimes, noble efforts to create new classifications are abandoned simply for lack of enthusiasm. In the case of the classification of plants and living organisms, interest in the subject matter waned until the 18th century, when Carl Linnaeus momentously stepped into the fray.

Through most of the 19th century, as the elements were being discovered, there was some interest in organizing these new-found substances into a classification. As early as 1829, Johann Wolfgang Dobereiner noted repeated patterns of physical characteristics of elements, based on their molecular weights. By the mid-19th century, Lothar Myer, Joseph Needham, John Newlands, and Dmitri Mendeleev were all converging on a table for the elements that clarified the periodic nature of atomic properties and that established simple relationships among the elements (Fig. 4.2).

No.		No.		No.		No.		No.		No.		No.		No.	
H	1	F	8	Cl	15	Co & Ni	22	Br	29	Pd	36	I	42	Pt & Ir	50
Li	2	Na	9	K	16	Cu	23	Rb	30	Ag	37	Cs	44	Os	51
G	3	Mg	10	Ca	17	Zn	24	Sr	31	Cd	38	Ba & V	45	Hg	52
Bo	4	Al	11	Cr	19	Y	25	Ce & La	33	U	40	Ta	46	Tl	53
C	5	Si	12	Ti	18	In	26	Zr	32	Sn	39	W	47	Pb	54
N	6	P	13	Mn	20	As	27	Di & Mo	34	Sb	41	Nb	48	Bi	55
O	7	S	14	Fe	21	Se	28	Ro & Ru	35	Te	43	Au	49	Th	56

FIG. 4.2 The Newlands Periodic Table, circa 1866. Several contemporaries of Mendeleev, noticing some periodicity linking atomic weights with chemical properties, created other versions of the Periodic Table. *Source: Wikipedia, from a work by John Alexander Reina Newlands (1838–1898).*

Meanwhile, many of their peers in the community of chemists and physical scientists saw no need to find hidden relationships among the elements. Some of the most prominent chemists of the time held the opinion that atoms had no physical existence. As late as 1905, Ernst Mach and Wilhelm Ostwald, both eminent scientists of their time, insisted that the fundamental component of physical existence was energy and that atoms were fictions invented as a sort of intellectual crutch to help us cope with an inscrutable physical reality [39]. It was about that time that Albert Einstein published his theoretical work on Brownian motion, confirmed experimentally by Jean Perrin, and the atomic theory became the atomic fact [39].

In the 1860s, there was considerable resistance to classifying elements based on unexplained periodicities observed when elements were arranged by atomic weight. Voices within the Royal Chemical Society indicated their indifference to classification efforts when they suggested that a facile and useful solution to the whole problem would involve simply putting the elements in alphabetic order.

Luckily, Mendeleev and his contemporaries prevailed, and Mendeleev's 59 element table was eventually accepted by the scientific community. Mendeleev was a relative latecomer to the field of element classification. As mentioned previously, the important idea championed by Mendeleev was that the Periodic Table was predictive. Once the table was made, Mendeleev could predict the missing elements, and describe many of their chemical features. It was the concept of using classification to draw new and testable inferences about the knowledge domain that Mendeleev promoted better than most scientists of his era, earning him his preeminent place in history.

Building a classification when detractors consider the effort to be nonsensical

We shall be discussing the Classification Theorem of the Finite Simple Groups when we reach Chapter 8. For now, it suffices to note that symmetry groups represent the symmetry transformations that underlie the foundational scientific laws of physics and chemistry. Leading up to the effort to prove the Classification Theorem were choruses of lamentations coming from physicists whose training was rooted in mathematical analysis, a branch of mathematics disconnected, at the time, from group theory. Einstein, along with most of his contemporaries were astonished by the growing influence of group theory. At one point, Einstein wrote, half-seriously, "Since the mathematicians have now invaded the theory of relativity, I do not understand it myself anymore!" Yielding to the need of understanding group theory, Einstein simply found himself a mathematician to help out with the math. A contingent of German physicists referred to group theory as "Gruppenpest" (group pest), indicating their general disdain for the subject. [Glossary Mathematical analysis]

It is always a problem when a classification is built on a conceptual model that seems to defy one's concept of reality. Such is the case with the Classification Theorem of Finite Simple Groups, which includes abstract constructions that far exceed the number of spatial dimensions envisioned by classical physicists. For example, the Leech lattice, one of the sporadic groups listed in the Classification Theorem (to be discussed in "Section 8.5. Symmetry groups rule the universe"), has 24 dimensions [40]. Ernst Mach (1838–1913), a classical physicist, summarized the then-prevailing sentiment as follows [41]:

> *Seldom have thinkers become so absorbed in revery, or so far estranged from reality, as to imagine for our space several dimensions exceeding the three of the given space of sense.*
>
> *Ernst Mach*

As it happened, the traditional reliance upon a three-dimensional space was a sticking point that slowed the advance of physics throughout the 19th century. It was the work of Einstein, Minkowski, Lorentz, Klein, and Poincare that led to our current understanding that space must have at least four dimensions, referred to as spacetime, if observations within frames of reference are to make any sense.

We now know that observable phenomena in the "real" universe are represented by symmetry groups. We can now imagine a universe having, at a minimum, 10 dimensions [42]. Furthermore, physicists are finding that some of the most complex and unworldly symmetry groups have physical relevance [40,43].

Work on the Classification Theorem of Finite Simple Groups proceeded through much of the latter half of the 20th century, an effort involving hundreds of mathematicians. The Classification Theorem is now considered to be one of the greatest achievements in the field of mathematics.

Finding the valid hierarchy for our classification

Class hierarchies of the natural world are discovered, not created. The hierarchy of class relationships forms the scaffold of the classification. If the scaffold is poorly constructed, the classification will tumble. In the Classification of Life, classes create their subclasses, through the act of speciation. For many classes of organisms, there is not much question as to the name of the parental class. For some classes, determining the parental class is challenging.

There are numerous species whose genome is composed of pieces of DNA obtained from species other than the parental species. For example, bacterial species obtain genetic material from other bacterial species through horizontal transfer. Plants commonly interbreed to produce fertile hybrids of mixed species [44]. Various classes of viruses routinely swap whole segments of their genome with viruses belonging to other classes in a process known as reassortment. Even animals acquire genes from other species. For example, bdelloids, microscopic rotifers, obtain about 10% of their genetic material from other species including bacteria, plants, and fungi. We humans are not above doing a bit of gene swapping with other species. About 8% of human genes happen to be derived from viruses. Conversely, an unknown quantity of animal DNA has transferred into various species of virus. In summary, every major kingdom of living organisms engages in interspecies exchanges of genetic material, a situation that makes life difficult for classification builders. [Glossary Horizontal gene transfer, Multiparental inheritance, Reassortment]

The problem is as follows. Our definition of a classification stresses the importance of a mono-parental class hierarchy. Each class of organisms has one parent class, without exception. This being the case, how do we reconcile the existence of species whose genomes are derived from more than one parent class? Doesn't the widespread occurrence of gene transfer across species tell us that the Classification of Life produces a false representation of biological reality [45]?

Before giving up on our traditional Classification of life, let's take a look at how taxonomists have handled the dilemma of mixed-species heritage in living organisms. The aforementioned bdelloid rotifer, a tiny animal that is best observed under a microscope, famously declines the benefits of sex and meiosis, preferring to reproduce exclusively by mitotic parthenogenesis [46]. The all-female league of bdelloids has managed to diversify over 500 species, thus defying generations of evolutionary biologists who would insist that prolific speciation is impossible absent the gene shuffling that occurs with sexual reproduction. The bdelloids bypassed the messiness of sex, preferring to simply take the genes they need (about 10% of their genome) from other organisms [46]. Apparently, the accessory genetic material adds to the gene pool of the bdelloids, thus facilitating the emergence of new species. [Glossary Parthenogenesis]

Bdelloids are not the only animals that acquire genes through horizontal gene transfer. Tardigrades, also known as water bears, are tiny animals that have obtained about one-sixth of their genome from many types of living organisms, including bacteria, archaeans, plants, and fungi [47]. The acquisition of functional genes from other organisms seems to provide tardigrades with some survival advantage, as they are widely considered the hardiest animals on earth. Aside from enduring a wide range of environmental conditions here on earth, the tardigrades are held to be capable of surviving the extreme cold, and the blistering cosmic radiations of outer space. Bdelloids and tardigrades are mosaic animals, composed of genes taken from other animals. Yet, bdelloids and tardigrades seem to be distinct species of animals, with their own characteristic features that are common to all the members of each species. A good way to think about this is to forget about what happens with individuals of a species and to concentrate on the species as a whole. Every species stemmed from one parent species. If individuals of the species manage to collect some DNA from some other species, then that DNA enters into the gene pool of the species, where it has an opportunity to be utilized by other individuals of the species. Gene pools are constantly evolving, and a bit of extra DNA from an extraneous source simply expands the gene pool that is available to every member of the species. It does not change the hierarchical relationship between a child species and the parent species from which it evolved. We can say with confidence that if there had been no parent species, then the child species would never have come into existence. Despite repeated acquisitions of foreign DNA into the genomes of animal species at points along the metazoan lineage, there remains a persistent ancestral identity that marks a preserved mono-parental lineage. Even though bdelloid rotifers obtain much of their DNA from the horizontal transfer, the progeny of rotifers are typical rotifers; not some morphologic amalgam of different species.

The inherent frustrations of classifying species that engage in horizontal gene transfer climaxed in the middle of the 20th century when there was an effort to assign bacteria to classes on a strictly mono-parental basis. Before that time, bacteria were distinguished from one another based on a behavioral (e.g., class-based nutrient requirements), metabolic (e.g., classed as anaerobic versus aerobic), histologic (e.g., classed as Gram-positive and Gram-negative), or morphologic (e.g., classed as rods or cocci) basis that was not necessarily related to genetic ancestry. Hence, the known bacterial species could be named and diagnosed, but no true classification existed. When molecular biologists developed methods for sequencing the genomes of various organisms, there was hope that bacterial classification could be based on genomic sequencing. This hope was somewhat deflated when it was determined that horizontal gene transfer (i.e., the exchange of genetic material among different species) was rampant in the bacterial kingdom. At the time, it was feared that bacteria were just a mish-mash of genes popping in and out of organisms, with no stable genetic identity. The thinking went that if the gene pool is constantly being flooded with the genes of other species, then there is no stable gene pool; hence, no sensible way of assigning species and no credible classification of bacterial organisms. Bacterial taxonomy seemed hopeless.

In 1977, the field of bacterial taxonomy changed much for the better when Carl Woese and George E. Fox announced that there existed a class of bacteria that contained species that were genetically different from all other species of prokaryotes. They named these bacteria Archaebacteria, later known as Class Archaea (from the Greek meaning original or first in time); the name indicating that the Archaea predated all other classes of prokaryotes (i.e., organisms having no nucleus). When we compare species of Class Bacteria with species of Class Archaea, we are not likely to notice any striking visual differences. The bacteria have the same shapes and sizes as the archaea. All species of bacteria and all species of archaea are single-celled organisms, and they all have a typical prokaryotic cytologic structure. As it happens, Class Bacteria contains all of the prokaryotic organisms that are known to be pathogenic in humans. The archaeans, so far as we can currently tell, are nonpathogenic. Many archaeans are extremophiles, capable of living in hostile environments (e.g., hot springs, salt lakes), but some Archaean species occupy less demanding biological niches (e.g., marshland, soil, human colon). Class Archaea does not hold a monopoly on extremophiles; some bacterial species live in extreme environments (e.g., the alkaliphile *Bacillus halodurans*).

Woese and Fox showed that despite extensive horizontal gene transfer in ancient and modern prokaryotes, there are fundamental differences among prokaryotes that establish excellent criteria for assigning biological classes according to a traditional mono-parental lineage [48,49]. Furthermore, the differences between classes can be exploited to establish the different subclasses of prokaryotic organisms, and the chronology of their evolution. The key finding that allowed Woese and Fox to build a classification of bacteria lies in the fact that prokaryotes do not swap their ribosomal RNA. The archaeans have one form of ribosomal RNA; the bacteria have another. Over time, small changes in ribosomal RNA accumulate, and the ancestry of archaeans and bacterial subclasses can be determined by comparing ribosomal RNA sequences among classes of bacteria. Later studies indicate that additional genes other than ribosomal RNA may serve equally well as keys to the classification of prokaryotes [50]. Despite the acquisition of genes from other species, a core set of genes have allowed us to establish a hierarchical classification of the prokaryotes. [Glossary Prokaryotes]

Let's look at another situation in which one class may appear to have divergent origins (e.g., one class having two parent classes). When I worked at the U.S. National Cancer Institute, I participated in a project to develop a classification of cancers based on their embryologic development [6,51–53]. The central idea of the classification is that each cancer arises from cells that derive from one, and only one, of the original embryonic layers. We expected that tumors would exhibit the biological pathways and epigenetic controls typical of their embryologic development.

We assigned each of the human tumors (and there are thousands of them) to one of these 6 embryologic tissues:

Germ cell
Trophectoderm
Mesoderm
Endoderm/Ectoderm
Neuroectoderm
Neural Crest

We subclassed the major embryonic classes into subclasses, with subclasses, with subclasses being the derivative embryologic structures developing from top embryologic classes (Fig. 4.3).

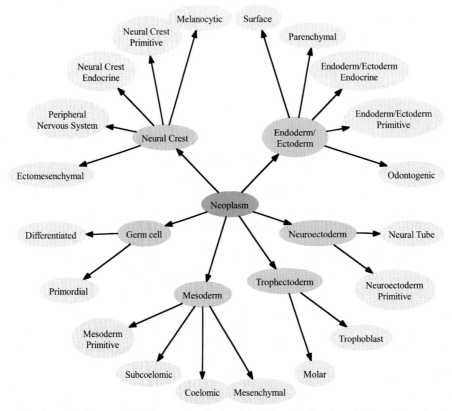

FIG. 4.3 A classification of Cancers, based on embryologic origins. The Classification of Cancers essentially shadows preexisting classifications of embryologic development.

We need to stop here and take note that when we base a classification upon an existing domain of knowledge (embryology, in this case), that has been previously classified, then the secondary classification (the classification of cancers, in this case) is born complete [54,55]. Because every anatomic structure has its roots in an embryonic structure, and because every cancer has an anatomic origin, we can infer that every cancer can be assigned to an embryologic class.

The neoplasms classification seemed to come together neatly until we ran up against an embryologic anomaly associated with tumors arising from the bone. Everyone who is taught anatomy is taught that there are two types of bones in the human body. The first type, which accounts for most of the bones in our torso and extremities, is called endochondral bone. Endochondral bone forms from osteogenesis occurring within a zone of cartilage at either end of the bone. As ossification proceeds, the cartilaginous growth zone moves distally, relative to the ossified bone, and the bone lengthens. The long bones of the leg and arms are examples of bones formed by endochondral ossification. The second type of bone is intramembranous bone, also known as dermal bone. Intramembranous bone arises through osteogenesis within a preshaped mesenchymal matrix. The bones of the skull, and most of the bones of the head, are dermal bones [56,57]. [Glossary Dermal bone, Endochondral bone]

Every student of anatomy is expected to know the difference between endochondral and intramembranous bone, but fewer students are aware that these two types of bone are derived from completely separate embryologic anlagen. Specifically, endochondral bones derive from the mesoderm; intramembranous bones derive from the neural crest. Regardless of embryologic origin, all bone cells (i.e., osteocytes) look alike histologically, have the same functionality, and are subject to the same acquired diseases; and that would include cancer. Specifically, we cannot distinguish a bone cancer arising from a neural crest bone from a cancer arising from a mesodermal bone. [Glossary Acquired disease, Anlagen, Mesoderm]

Here is the problem. How can we classify bone cancers by embryologic origin if identical bone cancers can derive from either neural crest or mesoderm? Remember, the uniqueness rule of classification forbids us from assigning two classes to a single class instance. To answer this question, let's take a step back, way back, to the origin of the neural crest, as revealed in The Classification of Life.

A developed neural crest first appeared in Class Craniata, and was, in fact, the defining evolutionary advancement responsible for the appearance of this major class of animals. The earliest known undisputed craniates are jawless fishes that lived 480 million years ago. All animals that preceded Class Craniata lacked a neural crest. All animals living today that are not members of Class Crainata lack a neural crest. How do we know when an animal qualifies as a member of class Craniata? As a rule of thumb, any animal that has a demarcated skull and face, with two eyes and a nose, is almost certainly a craniate. The reason this is so is that the neural crest accounts for the teeth, jaws, the bones of the face, and a cranial vault lined by meninges [56–58]. [Glossary Neural crest]

The neural crest serves as the embryologic origin of a wide variety of tissues, including all of the peripheral nervous system, several endocrine tumors, all melanocytes (pigment-forming cells found mostly in the skin), and all dermal bones. Tumors of cells that arise from the neural crest occur exclusively in members of Class Craniata, reaffirming our rationale for classifying tumors by their embryologic origin.

When we considered the acquired bone diseases occurring in adults (e.g., osteoarthritis, Paget disease of bone, osteomyelitis, toxin-induced bone necrosis, and cancer of the bones), we see very little difference in the manner in which these acquired conditions affect either the neural crest-derived bones or the mesoderm-derived bones. However, when we confine our attention to developmental disorders of bones, observed in infants, we see a great difference in disease development depending on their embryologic origins. The reason for this is fairly obvious. A neural crest-derived bone may be indistinguishable from a mesoderm-derived bone, but their developmental pathways (i.e., the mechanism by which embryologic tissues develop) will be different. Accordingly, we would expect that developmental disorders of neural crest-derived bones will be different from developmental disorders of mesoderm-derived bone. This turns out to be true. We see profound differences among genetic malformations affecting bones, based on their embryologic origin. There are hundreds of developmental anomalies that are confined to the bones and soft tissues of neural crest origin, including cleft palate and cleft lip, craniosynostosis (premature fusion of cranial sutures), macrocephaly, microcephaly (small skull), and jaw defects that include agnathia (missing jaw).

Knowing that there are developmental disorders, included genetic defects, that account for observed clinical differences in bones, depending on their embryologic tissue of origin, we may feel justified in dividing all bone cancers into two separate classes: bone cancers of neural crest origin and bone cancers of mesoderm origin (Fig. 4.4).

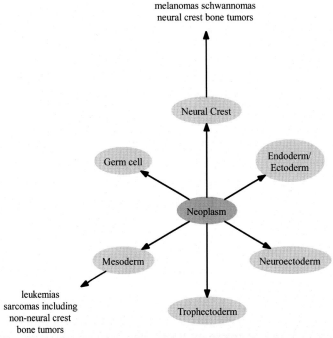

FIG. 4.4 This schematic of the embryologic classes of cancers provides for the subclassing of bone cancers into those that derive from the neural crest and those that derive from mesoderm.

If there are biological differences that distinguish osteosarcomas arising from bones of neural crest origin from osteosarcomas arising from bones of mesodermal origin, then we might expect that we will eventually run across chemotherapeutic agents that have very different effects in each of these two cancers. For example, a chemotherapeutic agent that is active against a key metabolic driver in neural crest-derived tumors may be more effective in treating an osteosarcoma of the skull than osteosarcoma arising in the femur. In addition, an agent that effectively treats several different types of neural crest tumor will be likely to have some beneficial effect on osteosarcomas of neural crest origin. If the developmental origin is a noncontributory factor in the biology of bone cancers, then we may be guilty of overreach when we decided to subdivide bone cancers by embryologic origin.

The take-away lesson here is that apparent anomalies in classification may sometimes prompt us to assign classes based on features that are not directly observable in the object being classified, but which are known to be present in the established ancestors of the object. In the particular example under discussion, we have no objective way to distinguish bone cancers of neural crest origin from bone cancers of mesoderm origin. Our decision to assign these tumors to separate classes is based on our knowledge of developmental biology; not on our knowledge of tumor biology.

Deciding whether a classification effort is likely to be worthwhile

In the case of the Classification of Life, the Periodic Table of the Elements, and the Classification Theorem of Finite Simple Groups, the benefits of classification have been obvious. All the same, many classifications have been total failures. Some of these failed classifications have persisted as enduring relics of dubious value, as discussed in "Section 4.1. Problematica." How can we decide when to proceed with a classification project and when to just concede that the task is impossible.

There is no certain way to judge a classification before it has been built, but the following general guidelines may sometimes help.

Indicators that a classification will be successful:

1. You have a theory or model of reality that can serve as the fundamental principle by which classes can be created and organized.
2. Your theory of the classification is complete and would predict the existence of classes and instances that are not yet known.
3. There is inheritance in the system from which instances of classes acquire properties.
4. The instances of the classification are all classifiable.

Indicators that a sensible classification cannot be created:

1. The proposed instances of the classification are unclassifiable (see "Section 1.4. Things that defy simple classification").
2. You are certain that there are no sensible relationships among the proposed classes.
3. You simply do not know enough to rationally assign instances to classes.
4. Your hypotheses and predictions inferred from your classification have been proven wrong.
5. You cannot enunciate a theory or model for the classification as a whole.

One additional caveat. Never base your decision on the concerted opinions of your colleagues. The prevailing consensus is often wrong.

Glossary

Acquired disease Everything is acquired, even inherited diseases are acquired. In common parlance, an "acquired disease" results from conditions occurring in the environment or as the result of events, processes, or behaviors that happened after birth. Some so-called acquired diseases are genetic conditions that were not clinically expressed at birth (i.e., not congenital). For example, the condition known as focal epilepsy with a speech disorder is referred to as an acquired disease because children reported to have this disease are typically born without clinical signs of the condition. Recent analysis indicates that the disease is caused by a germline mutation, and does not fit the definition of an acquired disease [59].

Contrariwise, diseases that are thought to be genetic may prove to be acquired (i.e., not accountable by genetic mutation or variation). A likely example is lactase deficiency. Lactase is an enzyme that is required for the digestion of lactose, a major ingredient of milk. Without lactase, ingested lactose is not absorbed from the gut and is instead metabolized by gut flora to yield gases; thus, producing flatulence. Infants normally ingest milk as the sole or primary component of their diets, and most healthy babies are born with the genetic wherewithal to generate intestinal lactase. After weaning, generally around year two, intestinal lactase levels diminish to the point where many older children and adults become lactase deficient and lactose intolerant. Hence, lactase deficiency can be considered an acquired disease.

As an additional example, consider infectious diseases. It seems obvious that all infectious diseases are acquired. Nonetheless, there is great variation in susceptibility to infectious diseases, and genetics plays a role in determining who acquires an infection and who does not. The term "acquired" is applied throughout medical literature in such an inconsistent manner that it scarcely retains any biological meaning.

Aggregate disease A condition that includes multiple disorders all having the same clinical phenotype. For example, COPD (Chronic Obstructive Pulmonary Disease) has been called an aggregate of many "small COPDs" representing individual diseases that happen to be difficult to distinguish from one another [60]. Aggregate diseases would include all of the so-called end-stage conditions (e.g., end-stage kidney, end-stage heart) produced by longstanding or chronic pathologic processes that irreversibly diminish the organ's function, often replacing most of the organ with fibrous tissue. The majority of common diseases (e.g., heart attacks, asthma, common cold, constipation) are aggregates of conditions that have many different pathogeneses.

Anlagen Embryologic precursors for fetal organs and tissues. It is important to know that the anlagen of an organ are not a miniature version of the organ, and does not contain any of the differentiated cells that will eventually appear in the developed organ. The anlagen contain stem cells growing within an architectural framework that does not have the appearance of the organ that will eventually emerge. As an example, imaginal discs are the insect equivalent of analagen and consist of small sacs of committed stem cells. For example, insect wings grow from imaginal discs that are biologically committed to developing into a wing. An insect wing does not grow from a tiny wing.

Archaea For decades, archaean species were considered just another class of bacteria. This changed in 1977. Woese and Fox had been studying ribosomal RNA. Because ribosomal RNA is a fundamental constituent of all cellular organisms, sequence comparisons in the genes coding for ribosomal RNA are considered a reliable way to estimate the degree of relatedness among organisms. In 1977, Woese and Fox surprised biologists when they demonstrated profound differences in the sequence of ribosomal RNA that distinguished archaean species from all other bacteria [49]. Much more shocking was their finding that the sequence of archaean ribosomal RNA was more closely related to eukaryotic cells than to other bacterial cells. Other sources have since shown that the archaeans share with the eukaryotes a variety of features that are lacking in the bacteria. These include the presence of histones in some archaeans, the manner in which DNA is replicated and organized, and the finding that archaeans and eukaryotes share several transcription factors (proteins that bind to DNA and control the transcription of DNA to RNA) [61]. Woese and Fox proposed that the archaeans (then called archaebacteria) comprised a kingdom, separate but equal to the bacteria. That paper, and the many contributions of Woese that followed, sharpened our understanding of terrestrial biology, and sparked a controversy that shook the foundations of taxonomic orthodoxy [62,63].

Artificial intelligence Artificial intelligence is the field of computer science that seeks to create machines and computer programs that emulate human intelligence. The field of artificial intelligence sometimes includes the related fields of machine learning and computational intelligence.

Association In the context of diseases, an association is anything that happens to occur more frequently in the presence of a disease than it occurs in the absence of the disease. Even when we know that one thing is associated with another thing, it can be very difficult to express the association in a mechanistically useful manner. For example, in 2000, a Concorde, a supersonic transport jet, crashed on take-off from Charles de Gaulle Airport, Paris. Debris left on the runway, possibly a wrench, flipped up and tore the underside of the hull. All passengers were killed in the subsequent few seconds as the plane exploded and crashed. What is the association here? Is it, "debris associated with a jet crash," or do we need to be more specific, "wrench associated with a jet crash"? Do jets need to be afraid of wrenches in general, or only with wrenches that are left out on the runway? If the association contains an implied mechanism that ties an object with a result, wouldn't we need to confine the association to wrenches that are run over by the jet, because if the jet tires miss the wrench, the wrench would not flip up and tear the underside of the plane. This would bring us to the assertion: "Wrenches that are run over by a jet's tire and that flip upwards are associated with jet crashes."

It can be difficult to develop a sensible way to determine whether a disease association is causal. In general, we look to see if the associated factor always segregates with the disease (i.e., is found in every instance of disease and is found in no instances of the control population) and if the association always precedes the development of disease and does not occur as a late finding in chronic or fully developed instances of the disease. Such findings do not establish proof of causality, but they can be considered supportive evidence.

For example, scientists have long wondered whether tau proteins, a hallmark of several neurodegenerative diseases, are causal factors, or just bystanders in such diseases. Frontotemporal dementia and parkinsonism linked to chromosome 17 (FTDP-17) is an inherited disease characterized by mutations in the gene coding for Tau. In this disease, a specific Tau inclusion is always found in the pathologic lesions, and never in control subjects. Most importantly, the appearance of the tau inclusion always precedes the development of neural degeneration; hence, the inclusion does not occur as a consequence of neural degeneration. These observations have led researchers to believe that altered Tau protein plays a causal role in the pathogenesis of FTDP-17 [64].

The problem of determining genetic causality is magnified many times when we are dealing with gene polymorphisms (i.e., gene variants found in a population) that are associated with diseases that have various causes, poorly understood pathogeneses and complex phenotypes. Like so many other types of scientific observations, associations serve as clues, not as answers [32].

Carcinoma in situ Noninvasive carcinoma. Because carcinoma in situ is not invasive, it is localized to its original place of origin (hence, in situ, or place). Carcinoma in situ is the last phase in the development of a precancer. After invasion begins, the lesion is no longer a carcinoma in situ, and no longer a precancer. If we knew how to stop the progression from carcinoma in situ to invasive carcinoma, we could eliminate most deaths from cancer.

Chitin Chitin is a long-chain polymer built from units of *N*-acetylglucosamine and found in the cell walls of every fungus. It is analogous to cellulose, in plants, which is built from units of glucose. Importantly, chitin is never found in plants, and cellulose is never found in fungi. Aside from its presence in fungi, chitin is found in some members of Class Protoctista and some members of Class Animalia (particularly arthropods). Chitin is the primary constituent of the exoskeleton of insects.

The structural role of chitin in Class Fungi and Class Metazoa (animals) serves as a clue to the close relationship between these two classes. It happens that chitin was not discovered until 1930 (by Albert Hoffmann); well before that time, Class Fungi had been incorrectly assigned to the plant kingdom.

Chloroplast evolution Chloroplasts are the organelles (little membrane-wrapped replicating structures within cells) that produce glucose and oxygen, via oxygenic photosynthesis, a process that can be loosely described as:

```
carbon dioxide + water + light energy -> carbohydrate + oxygen.
```

With very few exceptions, chloroplasts are found in all members of Class Plantae. Aside from photosynthesis occurring in plants, we can also observe photosynthesis in cyanobacteria. Photosynthesis produced by cyanobacteria is thought to account for the conversion of our atmosphere from an anoxic environment to an oxygen-rich environment. Did photosynthesis, a complex chemical pathway, evolve twice in terrestrial history; once in cyanobacteria and once again in primitive plants?

Present thinking on the subject holds that the evolution of photosynthesis occurred only once, in the distant past, and all photosynthesis ever since, in cyanobacteria and plants, arose from this one event. It is presumed that plants acquired photosynthesis when they engulfed photosynthesizing cyanobacteria that evolved into self-replicating chloroplasts. This conclusion is based on the observation that chloroplasts, unlike all other plant organelles, are wrapped by two membranous layers. One layer is believed to have been contributed by the captured cyanobacteria, and one layer presumably came from the capturing plant cell as it wrapped the cyanobacteria in its cell membrane.

Cowden syndrome An inherited disease syndrome characterized by hamartomas of the brain, face, breast, colon, and other organs and a predisposition to developing cancers of the breast, thyroid, and endometrium [65–67].

Cowden disease is caused by loss of function in the tumor suppressor gene PTEN, the phosphatase, and the tensin homolog gene. PTEN mutations are commonly found in the sporadically occurring brain, breast, and prostate cancers.

Craniata Craniata is the class of animals that have a skull encasing a brain. The most important embryological advance, responsible for the emergence of Class Crainata, was the neural crest. Before the appearance of organisms of class Craniata, there were no animals with an embryologic neural crest, the neural crest was primitive and incapable of producing all of the cell types and derivative tissues found in organisms of Class Craniata. With the appearance of the neural crest came all of the tumors that derive from the neural crest, including many of the tumors of the connective tissue of the head, tumors of the peripheral nervous system, several endocrine tumors, and tumors of melanocytic origin. Tumors of the neural crest can occur in all Craniates (including mammals and fish) and are absent in noncraniates (e.g., arthropods).

Dermal bone Bone that arises by calcification of a preshaped mesenchymal matrix. The bones of the skull, and most of the bones of the head, are dermal bones [56,57]. Dermal bone formation is synonymous with intramembranous bone formation. Dermal bones are embryologically derived from the neural crest, whereas endochondral bones (i.e., bones growing from epiphyseal growth zones and comprising virtually every bone other than bones of the head and neck) are all derived from mesenchyme.

Endochondral bone Bone that forms through ossification of growing zone cartilage at each end of the bone. Long bones (for example, the femur) are all endochondral bones. There are two major types of bone, based on their pattern of development, and on their embryologic origin: endochondral bone and dermal bone. Dermal bones develop by ossifying a preformed matrix. Endochondral bones are of mesenchymal origin. Dermal bones are of neural crest origin. Regardless of their distinctly different origins, endochondral bones and dermal bones are composed of the same types of cells, have equivalent functions, and are subject to the same set of degenerative conditions that occur commonly in aging mammals.

Genotype Characteristic genetic sequence for an organism. Every organism on earth has a unique genotype, with the possible exception of identical twins and some organisms that replicate asexually.

Heterokonts Also known as stramenopiles. A class of single-celled eukaryotes. There are over 25,000 species of heterokonts, including some types of algae, unicellular diatoms, and single-celled components of plankton. Also includes organisms that are pathogenic in plants (late blight of potato caused by *Phytophthora infestans*, and sudden oak death caused by Phytophthora ramorum. Heterokonts are also known to cause two diseases in humans: blastocystosis and pythiosis.

Heterotrophic An organism is heterotrophic if it must acquire organic compounds from the environment as its energy source. All animals and all fungi (both of Class Opisthokont) are heterotrophs. In contrast, members of Class Plantae, and chloroplast-containing members of Class Protoctista, are phototropic autotrophs; producing organic compounds from light, water, and carbon dioxide.

Horizontal gene transfer The direct transfer of genetic material between organisms, by mechanisms other than by reproduction (i.e., other than the transfer of DNA from parents to offspring). The very first eukaryotic ancestors derived their genetic material by horizontal gene transfer from prokaryotes (bacteria and archaean organisms), viruses, and possibly from other now-extinct organisms that might have preceded the eukaryotes. The early eukaryotes almost certainly exchanged DNA between one another, and we see evidence of such exchanges in modern single-celled eukaryotes and fungi [68,69].

To an unknown extent, horizontal gene transfer occurs throughout the animal kingdom. For example, tardigrades, a microscopic animal, has a genome of one-sixth of which was derived from bacteria, archaeans, plants, and fungi [47].

It should be noted that many of the most significant evolutionary advances came from interspecies gene acquisitions. The primordial mitochondrion that helped to create the first eukaryotic cell was an acquisition from a bacterium. The very first chloroplast in the most primitive precursor of the plant kingdom was a pilfered cyanobacterium.

Lesion All diseases result from pathologic abnormalities of specific populations of cells. The specific locations in which these diseased cells can be found are referred to as lesions. Clinicians can biopsy lesions (i.e., remove a tissue sample), and pathologists can study the morphology of the affected cells under a microscope, often establishing the name of the particular disease responsible for the lesion.

Mathematical analysis The area of mathematics that deals with infinite series and limits. Crudely, mathematical analysis is advanced calculus. Though mathematical analysis is an incredibly powerful tool, giving us the Fourier Transform, numerical analysis, signal processing, and much of the important breakthroughs in modern physics achieved in the early 20th century, it can be somewhat cumbersome to apply, and even more cumbersome to understand someone else's work. Vector algebra, matrix algebra, and Group theory have, to an extent, simplified some of the earlier works achieved with mathematical analysis [70].

Mesoderm The embryonic germ layer that lies between Ectoderm and Endoderm, giving rise to the mesenchyme, the latter consisting of most of the connective tissue, muscles, and bones of the body. The kidneys and the uterus are organs that are derived entirely from the mesoderm.

Multiparental inheritance In ontologies, multiparental inheritance occurs when a child class has more than one parent class. For example, in an ontology, a member of Class House might have two different parent classes: Class Shelter, and Class Real Estate. Multiparental inheritance is permitted in ontologies but is forbidden in classifications, which restrict inheritance to a single parent class (i.e., each class can have at most one parent class, though it may have multiple child classes).

Medical taxonomists should understand that when multiparental inheritance is permitted, along with multiclass assignments (in which an object may belong to more than one class), we can see all manner of strange relationships. For example, a class may be an ancestor of a child class that is itself an ancestor to its parent class (e.g., a single class might be a grandfather and a grandson to the same class). The combinatorics and the recursive options become computationally absurd.

Taxonomists who rely on simple, uniparental classifications do so on epistemological grounds. They hold that an object can have only one nature, and therefore can belong to only one defining class, and can be derived from exactly one parent class. Traditional taxonomists who insist upon uniparental class inheritance believe that assigning more than one parental class to an object indicates that you have failed to grasp the essential nature of the object [71,72,18].

Mushroom A mushroom is a fleshy fungal sporocarp (i.e., structure in which spores are produced) that we can observe with the naked eye as an outgrowth, usually from the ground or from a tree trunk. Most, but not all, mushrooms are ascocarps (i.e., the sporocarp of a fungus of Class Ascomycota).

Negative classifier One of the most common mistakes committed by ontologists involves classification by negative attribute. A negative classifier is a feature whose absence is used to define a class.

It is often a bad idea to use negative classifiers to class definitions. An example is found in the Collembola, popularly known as springtails, a ubiquitous member of Class Hexapoda, and readily found under just about any rock. These organisms look like fleas (same size, same shape) and were formerly misclassified among the class of true fleas (Class Siphonaptera). Like fleas, springtails are wingless. The true fleas lost their wings when they became parasitic. Springtails never had wings, an important phylogenetic distinction. If we were to classify insects by their lack of wings, we would produce a nonsensical classification. Today, springtails (Collembola) are assigned to Class Entognatha, a separate subclass of Class Hexapoda.

As another example of poor taxonomy, based on a negative classifier, let's look at Class Fungi. All species of Class Fungi were formerly believed to have a characteristic absence of a flagellum. Based on the absence of a flagellum, the fungi were excluded from Class Opisthokonta (a class defined by a posterior flagellum). The fungi were erroneously classified as a type of plant. However, the chytrids, members of an early class of fungi, were subsequently shown to have a posterior flagellum. We now know that all fungi descended from a species of opisthokonts having a posterior flagellum. Except for the chytrid fungi, all other species lost their posterior flagellum in the mists of evolutionary history. The erroneous confusion of fungi and plants set back modern taxonomy by decades; due, in part, to our reliance upon a negative classifier.

Neoplasm Neoplasm means "new growth," and is a near-synonym for "tumor." Neoplasms can be benign or malignant. Leukemias, which grow as a population of circulating blood cells, and which do not generally produce a visible mass (i.e., do not produce a tumor), are included under the general term "neoplasm." Hamartomas, benign overgrowths of tissue, are typically included among the neoplasms, as are the precancers (precursor lesions cancers), which are often small and scarcely visible.

As a former research scientist, who was always desperately searching for tumor specimens suitable for laboratory analysis, I was painfully aware that "neoplasm" is also an apt anagram, for "no sample."

Neural crest Phylogenetically, the developed neural crest first appeared in Class Craniata. All descendants of Class Craniata, which includes nearly all vertebrates, have a neural crest. In embryological development, the neural crest derives from a specialized compartment of cells lying between the ectoderm and the primitive neural tube. The neural crest gives rise to the peripheral nervous system, to the connective tissue of the cranium, to several endocrine glands, and to the connective tissue component of the teeth, and much more. Indeed, the cell-type versatility of the neural crest is so vast that it is difficult for us to confidently fathom its full biological role.

Non-Hodgkin lymphoma Lymphoid neoplasms are divided into two categories: Hodgkin lymphoma and non-Hodgkin lymphoma. Non-Hodgkin lymphoma comprises every lymphoid neoplasm other than Hodgkin lymphoma. The diagnosis of Non-Hodgkin lymphoma, communicated to a patient, is always uninformative and needlessly confusing. "Non-Hodgkin lymphoma" is one example of a diagnosis that informs patients what their diagnosis is not (i.e., it's not Hodgkin lymphoma), declining to specify what their diagnosis happens to be.

Non-small cell lung cancer Small cell lung cancer is a highly malignant cancer, most occurring in the lung, and composed, as the name implies, of small cells with scant cytoplasm. Small cell carcinomas of the lung tend to metastasize (i.e., spread to different organs) while the primary lung cancer is still small. Because the cancer is often widespread at the time of diagnosis, surgical treatment for the primary lung tumor is seldom of great benefit. For other types of lung cancer, surgical resection is more likely to be an option. In addition, the treatment options for lung cancers other than small cell carcinoma can be substantially different from the approaches reserved for small cell carcinoma. Due to the biological and clinical differences between small cell carcinoma and other cancers of the lung, oncologists have found it convenient to divide all lung cancers into two categories: small cell lung cancer and non-small cell lung cancer.

One-gene-to-many-diseases Various alterations in a single gene can result in any of several different diseases.

Here are just a few examples for which mutations in a single gene (listed in all uppercase characters) may result in more than one disease (listed directly below the name of the "root cause" gene)

```
LMNA gene
  Emery-Dreifuss muscular dystrophy
  Familial partial lipodystrophy
  Limb-girdle muscular dystrophy
  Dilated cardiomyopathy
  Charcot-Marie-Tooth disease
  Restrictive dermopathy
  Hutchinson-Gilford progeria syndrome.
CEP290 gene
  Bardet-Biedl syndrome 14
  Joubert syndrome 5
  Leber congenital amaurosis 10
  Meckel syndrome 4
  Senior-Loken syndrome 6
COL11A2 gene
  Stickler syndrome type III
  Fibrochondrogenesis-2
  Form of non-syndromic hearing loss
  COL2A1 gene
  Stickler syndrome type I
  Osteoarthritis with mild chondrodysplasia
  Achondrogenesis type II
  Czech dysplasia
PIGA gene
  Paroxysmal nocturnal hemoglobinuria
  Multiple congenital anomalies-hypotonia-seizures syndrome-2
  PRKAR1A gene
  Acrodysostosis with hormone resistance
  Carney complex, type 1
```

Parthenogenesis Reproduction from an ovum without fertilization by a sperm. Occurs in plants, invertebrates, and some vertebrates but does not occur in mammals, a class of animals that uses genomic imprinting. Mammalian imprinting may interfere with parthenogenesis. There are about 80–100 genes in mammals that are imprinted, and many of these genes are vital to normal embryogenesis and fetal development. In parthenogenesis, all genes have maternal derivation. A parthenogenic embryo would lack paternally imprinted genes. There is experimental evidence that the paternally imprinted genes are required for the normal development of a human embryo [73,74].

Phylum A major class of organism. With respect to classes of animals, a phylum is a class wherein all the members have the same basic body type.

Prokaryotes Every organism on earth is either a prokaryote (organisms with no nucleus), a eukaryote (organisms with a nucleus), or a virus (genetic material wrapped in a capsid). There are two major classes of prokaryotes: Class Bacteria and Class Archaea.

In 1977, Woese and Fox surprised biologists when they demonstrated profound differences in the sequence of ribosomal RNA that distinguished archaean species from all other bacteria [49]. Much more shocking was their finding that the sequence of archaean ribosomal RNA was more closely related to eukaryotic cells than to other bacterial cells. Other sources have since shown that the archaeans share with the eukaryotes a variety of features that are lacking in the bacteria. These include the presence of histones in some archaeans, how DNA is replicated and organized, and the finding that archaeans and eukaryotes share several transcription factors (proteins that bind to DNA and control the transcription of DNA to RNA) [61].

Pseudo-metazoans The syllable "zoo" or "zoa" is attached to organisms that fall into the animal kingdom (i.e., Class Metazoa). In many cases, the "zoo" or "zoa" have been formally attached to organisms that are not, in fact, animals. Here is a list of taxonomically misnamed pseudo-metazoans:

- Amoebozoa (a one-celled eukaryote and not an animal)
- Apoikozoa (synonymous with Choanozoa, a sister class to animals, an not an animal)
- Bradyzoites (an encysted form of sporozoan, such as Toxoplasma gondii, and not belonging to any member of Class Animalia)
- Choanozoa (same as aforementioned Apoikozoa)
- Encephalitozoon (a member of Class Microsporidia, a descendant of Class Fungi, and not an animal)
- Enterocytozoon (another member of Class Microsporidia, a descendant of Class Fungi, and not an animal)
- Euglenozoa (a class of single-cell eukaryotes, and not an animal)
- Filozoa (an ancestral class for the metazoans, and hence not an animal)
- Holozoa (another ancestral class for the metazoans and hence, not an animal)
- Mesomycetozoea (a nonmetazoan opisthokont; hence, not an animal)
- Percolozoa (a descendant of Class Excavata, and not an animal)
- Protozoa (single-celled eukaryotes and hence, not animals)
- Sporozoan (synonymous with apicomplexan, single-celled eukaryotes that are not animals)
- Sporozoites (an infective, motile form of some sporozoans, and hence not an animal)
- Sulcozoa (a class of single-celled eukaryotes, and hence not an animal)
- Trichozoa (a subclass of Class Excavata, and hence not an animal)
- Trophozoite (a growth stage of some sporozoans, and hence not an animal)
- Zoopagomycota (a type of fungus, and hence not an animal)
- Zoospores (a taxonomically nonspecific term referring to a swimming spore, and not an animal)

Rank and taxonomic order   In hierarchical biological nomenclatures, classes are given ranks. The order of the ranks, from highest to lowest in the hierarchical classification is the taxonomic order. In early versions of the classification of living organisms, it was sufficient to divide the classification into a neat handful of descending divisions: Kingdom, Phylum, Class, Order, Family, Genus, Species. Today, the list of divisions has nearly quadrupled. For example, Phylum has been split into the following divisions: Superphylum, Phylum, Subphylum, Infraphylum, and Microphylum. The other divisions are likewise split. The subdivisions often have a legitimate scientific purpose. Nonetheless, the current taxonomic order is simply too detailed for any but the most determined of readers to memorize.

Aside from the needless layers of complexity created by the classical rankings, there is the virtually unsolvable issue of versioning. Changes in the named rank of organisms produce a ripple effect throughout all of the descendant branches of the classification [75]. This entails changing ranks in textbooks, software programs, and reciprocating standards (i.e., classifications other than the classification of living organisms that include organismal rankings in their design).

Is this growing nomenclature for class rankings really necessary? Not at all [75]. Taxonomic complexity can be easily averted by dropping named ranks and simply referring to every class as "Class." Modern specifications for class hierarchies encapsulate each class with the name of its superclass. When every object yields its class and superclass, it is possible to trace an object's class lineage. For example, in the classification of living organisms, if you know the name of the parent for each class (i.e., its superclass), you can write a simple software program that generates the complete ancestral lineage for every class and species within the classification, without resorting to a specialized nomenclature [76]. Furthermore, the complex taxonomic ranking system for living organisms does not carry over to the ranking systems that might be used for other scientific domains (e.g., classification of diseases, classification of genes, etc.) and creates an impediment for software developers who wish to write programs that traverse the hierarchy of multiple classifications, in search of relationships among data objects. Hence, the venerable ranking nomenclature, which has served generations of biologists, may need to be drastically simplified for the current era, wherein computationally-driven research prevails.

Reanalysis   Subjecting a study to a new analysis, using a data set that had previously undergone analysis. First analyses should always be considered tentative until they undergo reanalysis and validation. One could argue that the most important purpose of the analysis is to serve as the prelude to reanalysis. Although there have been instances when reanalysis has discredited published conclusions, it should be remembered that the goal of reanalysis is to confirm, strengthen, and extend prior knowledge.

Reassortment   Often confused or used interchangeably with "recombination," but reassortment is generally reserved for a viral event wherein two similar segmented viruses exchange part of their genomes during the co-infection of a host cell. Reassortment seems to be the major mechanism accounting for new influenza virus strains.

Root cause   The earliest event or condition that is known to set in motion a chain of additional events that can result in some specified result. Of course, we can never be certain what the earliest event is in any process. For example, infections from *Naegleria fowleri* result from exposure to free-living organisms in their natural habitat (pond and river water). The organism travels from the nose to the brain, where it causes meningoencephalitis. It seems self-evident that *N. fowleri* is the root cause of Naeglerian meningoencephalitis. Maybe not. Because these organisms are widely found in water, it is presumed that millions of people are exposed to the organism, but only rare individuals develop meningoencephalitis. It is not known why most people are unaffected by the organism, while others develop rapidly progressive meningoencephalitis. Perhaps the root cause of the disease is a very specific deficiency in the host defense system rendering rare individuals susceptible to infection with a ubiquitous organism. If so, the root cause shifts one step back, from the organism to the host. Geneticists have a saying, "Genes load the gun; environment pulls the trigger."

Even in the simplest of cases, it is difficult to assign a root cause with any certainty. We never know if we've looked back far enough. Still, we do the best that we can, and we apply the term "root cause" in this book with the understanding that we may need to modify our thinking if evidence of an earlier event comes to light.

The term "root cause" is nearly synonymous with "underlying cause."

SUMO Knowing that ontologies reach into higher ontologies, ontologists have endeavored to create upper-level ontologies to accommodate general classes of objects, under which the lower ontologies may take their place. One such ontology is SUMO, the Suggested Upper Merged Ontology, created by a group of talented ontologists [77]. SUMO is owned by IEEE (Institute of Electrical and Electronics Engineers), and is freely available, subject to a usage license [12].

Unstable taxonomy A taxonomy that is prone to change over time. You might expect that a named species would keep its name forever, and would never change its assigned class. Not so; taxonomists are continually fussing with the classification of living organisms, as new information is received and analyzed. For example, in the Classification of Life, Class Fungi has recently undergone profound changes, with the exclusion of myxomycetes (slime molds, currently assigned to Class Amoebozoa) and oomycetes (water molds, currently assigned to Class Heterokonta), and the acquisition of Class Microsporidia (formerly classed as a protozoan).

References

[1] Kumar A, Smith B. The universal medical language system and the gene ontology: some critical reflections. In: Gunter A, Kruse R, Neumann B, editors. Advances in artificial intelligence, lecture notes in computer science, vol. 2821. Berlin, Heidelberg: Springer; 2003.

[2] Campbell JR, Carpenter P, Sneiderman C, Cohn S, Chute CG, Warren J. Phase II evaluation of clinical coding schemes completeness, taxonomy, mapping, definitions, and clarity. J Am Med Inform Assoc 1997;4:238–50.

[3] Ceusters W, Smith B, Goldberg L. A terminological and ontological analysis of the NCI thesaurus. Methods Inf Med 2005;44:498–507.

[4] Kohler J, Munn K, Ruegg A, Skusa A, Smith B. Quality control for terms and definitions in ontologies and taxonomies. BMC Bioinformatics 2006;7:212.

[5] Yu JB, Gross CP, Wilson LD, Smith BD. NCI SEER public-use data: applications and limitations in oncology research. Oncology 2009;23:288–95.

[6] Berman JJ. Neoplasms: principles of development and diversity. Sudbury: Jones & Bartlett; 2009.

[7] Chang ES, Neuhof M, Rubinstein ND, Diamant A, Philippe H, Huchon D, et al. Genomic insights into the evolutionary origin of Myxozoa within Cnidaria. PNAS 2015;48:14912–14,917.

[8] Berman JJ. Taxonomic guide to infectious diseases: understanding the biologic classes of pathogenic organisms. 1st ed. Cambridge, MA: Academic Press; 2012.

[9] Berman JJ. Taxonomic guide to infectious diseases: understanding the biologic classes of pathogenic organisms. 2nd ed. Cambridge, MA: Academic Press; 2019.

[10] Margulis L. Undulipodia, flagella and cilia. Biosystems 1980;12:105–8.

[11] Liu YJ, Hodson MC, Hall BD. Loss of the flagellum happened only once in the fungal lineage: phylogenetic structure of Kingdom fungi inferred from RNA polymerase II subunit genes. BMC Evol Biol 2006;6:74.

[12] Suggested Upper Merged Ontology (SUMO). The OntologyPortal Available from: http://www.ontologyportal.org [Accessed 14 August 2012].

[13] de Bruijn J. Using ontologies: enabling knowledge sharing and reuse on the Semantic Web. Digital Enterprise Research Institute technical report DERI-2003-10-29, October; 2003.

[14] Noy NF, DL MG. Ontology development 101: a guide to creating your first ontology. Stanford Knowledge Systems Laboratory technical report KSL-01-05 and Stanford Medical Informatics technical report SMI-2001-0880; 2001.

[15] Anon. Classifications. World Health Organization; 2017. http://www./classifications/icd/en/. viewed July 4.

[16] Bowker GC, Star SL. Sorting things out: classification and its consequences (inside technology). Cambridge, MA: MIT Press; 2000.

[17] Borgwardt S, Radua J, Mechelli A, Fusar-Poli P. Why are psychiatric imaging methods clinically unreliable? Conclusions and practical guidelines for authors, editors and reviewers. Behav Brain Funct 2012;8:46.

[18] Berman JJ. Data simplification: taming information with open source tools. Waltham, MA: Morgan Kaufmann; 2016.

[19] Chahrour M, Zoghbi HY. The story of Rett syndrome: from clinic to neurobiology. Neuron 2007;56:422–37.

[20] Berman J. Precision medicine, and the reinvention of human disease. Cambridge, MA: Academic Press; 2018.

[21] Committee on A Framework for Developing a New Taxonomy of Disease, Board on Life Sciences, Division on Earth and Life Studies, National Research Council of the National Academies. Toward precision medicine: building a knowledge network for biomedical research and a new taxonomy of disease. Washington, DC: The National Academies Press; 2011.

[22] Belluck P, Carey B. Psychiatry's guide is out of touch with science, experts say. The New York Times; May 2013.

[23] Virchow R. Die Cellularpathologie in ihrer Begrundung auf physiologische und pathologische Gewebelehre. Berlin: August Hirschwald; 1858.

[24] Yang H, Higgins B, Kolinsky K, Packman K, Go Z, Iyer R, et al. RG7204 (PLX4032), a selective BRAFV600E inhibitor, displays potent antitumor activity in preclinical melanoma models. Cancer Res 2010;70:5518–27.

[25] Carlson RH. Precision medicine is more than genomic sequencing. Available from: http://www.medscape.com/viewarticle/870723_print; 2016. [Accessed 11 March 2017].

[26] Gerlinger M, Rowan AJ, Horswell S, Larkin J, Endesfelder D, Gronroos E, et al. Intratumor heterogeneity and branched evolution revealed by multiregion sequencing. N Engl J Med 2012;366:883–92.

[27] Kato S, Lippman SM, Flaherty KT, Kurzrock R. The conundrum of genetic "drivers" in benign conditions. J Natl Cancer Inst 2016;108.

[28] Bayraktar S, Goodman M. Detection of BCR-ABL positive cells in an asymptomatic patient: a case report and literature review. Case Rep Med 2010;2010, 939706. Available from: https://www.hindawi.com/journals/crim/2010/939706/. [Accessed 22 September 2016].

[29] Bose S, Deininger M, Gora-Tybor J, Goldman JM, Melo JV. The presence of typical and atypical BCR-ABL fusion genes in leukocytes of normal individuals: biologic significance and implications for the assessment of minimal residual disease. Blood 1998;92:3362–7.

[30] Biernaux C, Loos M, Sels A, Huez G, Stryckmans P. Detection of major bcr-abl gene expression at a very low level in blood cells of some healthy individuals. Blood 1995;86:3118–22.

[31] Basecke J, Griesinger F, Trumper L, Brittinger G. Leukemia- and lymphoma-associated genetic aberrations in healthy individuals. Ann Hematol 2002;81:64–75.

[32] Berman JJ. Rare diseases and orphan drugs: keys to understanding and treating common diseases. Cambridge, MD: Academic Press; 2014.

[33] Sidon P, El Housni H, Dessars B, Heimann P. The JAK2V617F mutation is detectable at very low level in peripheral blood of healthy donors. Leukemia 2006;20:1622.

[34] Brassesco MS. Leukemia/lymphoma-associated gene fusions in normal individuals. Genet Mol Res 2008;7:782–90.

[35] Xue Y, Chen Y, Ayub Q, Huang N, Ball EV, Mort M, et al. Deleterious- and disease-allele prevalence in healthy individuals: insights from current predictions, mutation databases, and population-scale resequencing. Am J Hum Genet 2012;91:1022–32.

[36] Bell CJ, Dinwiddie DL, Miller NA, Hateley SL, Ganusova EE, Mudge J, et al. Carrier testing for severe childhood recessive diseases by next-generation sequencing. Sci Transl Med 2011;3. 65ra4.

[37] Jung CG. Memories, dreams, reflections. New York: Vintage Books; 1961.

[38] Dioscoridis P. De Materia Medica. Lyon: Apud Balthazarem Arnolletum; 1554.

[39] Newburgh R, Peidle J, Rueckner W. Einstein, Perrin, and the reality of atoms: 1905 revisited. Am J Phys 2006;74:478–81.

[40] Boya LJ. Introduction to sporadic groups. In: Proceedings of the workshop, supersymmetric quantum mechanics and spectral design. Benasque, Spain; 2010.

[41] Mach E. Erkenntniss und Irrtum: Skizzen zur Psychologie der Forschung (Knowledge and error: sketches on the psychology of enquiry). Leipzig: Kessinger; 1905.

[42] Williams M. A universe of 10 dimensions. Universe Today; 2014.

[43] Eguchi T, Ooguri H, Tachikawa Y. Notes on the K3 surface and the Mathieu group M_24. Exp Math 2011;20:91–6.

[44] Margulis L, Schwartz KV. Five kingdoms: an illustrated guide to the phyla of life on earth. 3rd ed. New York: W.H. Freeman; 1998.

[45] Koonin EV. Darwinian evolution in the light of genomics. Nucleic Acids Res 2009;37:1011–34.

[46] Nowell RW, Almeida P, Wilson CG, et al. Comparative genomics of bdelloid rotifers: insights from desiccating and nondesiccating species. PLoS Biol 2018;16, e2004830m. Tyler-Smith C, Ed.

[47] Boothby TC, Tenlen JR, Smith FW, Wang JR, Patanella KA, Nishimura EO, et al. Evidence for extensive horizontal gene transfer from the draft genome of a tardigrade. Proc Natl Acad Sci U S A 2015;112:15976–15,981.

[48] Woese CR. Bacterial evolution. Microbiol Rev 1987;51:221–71.

[49] Woese CR, Fox GE. Phylogenetic structure of the prokaryotic domain: the primary kingdoms. PNAS 1977;74:5088–90.

[50] Wu D, Hugenholtz P, Mavromatis K, Pukall R, Dalin E, Ivanova NN, et al. A phylogeny-driven genomic encyclopaedia of bacteria and archaea. Nature 2009;462:1056–60.

[51] Berman JJ. Tumor classification: molecular analysis meets aristotle. BMC Cancer 2004;4:10.

[52] Berman JJ. Tumor taxonomy for the developmental lineage classification of neoplasms. BMC Cancer 2004;4:88.

[53] Berman JJ. Developmental lineage classification and taxonomy of neoplasms. Available from: http://www.o/neoclxml.gz [Accessed 14 August 2017].

[54] Anon. Nomina embryologica veterinaria. Knoxville, Tennessee: International Committee on Embryological Veterinary Nomenclature; 2003.

[55] The International Anatomical Nomenclature Committee. Nomina anatomica. 5th ed. Baltimore: Williams and Wilkins; 1980.

[56] Jiang X, Iseki S, Maxson RE, Sucov HM, Morriss-Kay GM. Tissue origins and interactions in the mammalian skull vault. Dev Biol 2002;241:106–16.

[57] Kuratani S. Craniofacial development and the evolution of the vertebrates: the old problems on a new background. Zool Sci 2005;22:1–19.

[58] Trainor PA, Melton KR, Manzanares M. Origins and plasticity of neural crest cells and their roles in jaw and craniofacial evolution. Int J Dev Biol 2003;47:541–53.

[59] Lesca G, Rudolf G, Bruneau N, Lozovaya N, Labalme A, Boutry-Kryza N, et al. GRIN2A mutations in acquired epileptic aphasia and related childhood focal epilepsies and encephalopathies with speech and language dysfunction. Nat Genet 2013;45:1061–6.

[60] Rennard SI, Vestbo J. The many "small COPDs", COPD should be an orphan disease. Chest 2008;134:623–7.

[61] Koonin EV, Galperin MY. Sequence, evolution, function: computational approaches in comparative genomics. Boston: Kluwer Academic; 2003.

[62] Mayr E. Two empires or three? PNAS 1998;95:9720–3.

[63] Woese CR. Default taxonomy: Ernst Mayr's view of the microbial world. PNAS 1998;95(19):11043–6.

[64] Delacourte A. Tauopathies: recent insights into old diseases. Folia Neuropathol 2005;43:244–57.

[65] Brownstein MH, Mehregan AH, Bikowski JBB, Lupulescu A, Patterson JC. The dermatopathology of Cowden's syndrome. Br J Dermatol 1979;100:667–73.

[66] Haibach H, Burns TW, Carlson HE, Burman KD, Deftos LJ. Multiple hamartoma syndrome (Cowden's disease) associated with renal cell carcinoma and primary neuroendocrine carcinoma of the skin (Merkel cell carcinoma). Am J Clin Pathol 1992;97:705–12.

[67] Schrager CA, Schneider D, Gruener AC, Tsou HC, Peacocke M. Clinical and pathological features of breast disease in Cowden's syndrome: an underrecognized syndrome with an increased risk of breast cancer. Hum Pathol 1998;29:47–53.

[68] Fitzpatrick DA. Horizontal gene transfer in fungi. FEMS Microbiol Lett 2012;329:1–8.

[69] Keeling PJ, Palmer JD. Horizontal gene transfer in eukaryotic evolution. Nat Rev Genet 2008;9:605–18.

[70] Bonolis L. From the rise of the group concept to the stormy onset of group theory in the new quantum mechanics: a saga of the invariant characterization of physical objects, events and theories. Riv Nuovo Cimento 2004;27:1–110.

[71] Berman JJ. Principles of big data: preparing, sharing, and analyzing complex information. Waltham, MA: Morgan Kaufmann; 2013.

[72] Berman JJ. Repurposing legacy data: innovative case studies. Waltham, MA: Morgan Kaufmann; 2015.

[73] McGrath J, Solter D. Completion of mouse embryogenesis requires both the maternal and paternal genomes. Cell 1984;37:179–83.

[74] Barton SC, Surani MAH, Norris ML. Role of paternal and maternal genomes in mouse development. Nature 1984;311:374–6.

[75] Adl SM, Simpson AGB, Farmer MA, Anderson RA, Anderson OR, Barta JR, et al. The new higher level classification of eukaryotes with emphasis on the taxonomy of protists. J Eukaryot Microbiol 2005;52:399–451.

[76] Berman JJ. Methods in medical informatics: fundamentals of healthcare programming in Perl, Python, and Ruby. Boca Raton: Chapman and Hall; 2010.

[77] Niles I, Pease A. Towards a standard upper ontology. In: Welty C, Smith B, editors. Proceedings of the 2nd international conference on formal ontology in information systems (FOIS-2001), Ogunquit, Maine, October 17–19; 2001.

5

The class-oriented programming paradigm

Chapter outline

Object-oriented programming is more than just classes and objects; it's a whole programming paradigm based around objects (data structures) that contain data fields and methods. It is essential to understand this; using classes to organize a bunch of unrelated methods together is not object orientation.

Junade Ali [1]

Section 5.1. This chapter in a nutshell

For the edification of those readers who know nothing about computers, and who may feel intimidated by the title of this chapter, we begin with one of my favorite quotations:

Computer Science is no more about computers than astronomy is about telescopes.

Edsger W. Dijkstra

What Dijkstra said is absolutely true. We shall see that the basic paradigms of computer science have wide application in the natural sciences. Biologists, chemists, mathematicians, and physicists who have no interest in computers or programming would do well to avail themselves of the fundamental concepts that are fueling progress in computer science. In particular, we cannot fully realize the benefits of classifications and ontologies unless and until we understand the paradigm of class-oriented programming. The practical goals of classification include generating testable hypotheses, drawing profound inferences, determining the lineages of objects, finding the relationships among objects and classes of objects, and enlisting class properties. Class-oriented programming techniques are perfectly suited to achieving these goals rapidly, and with a minimum of effort.

Science, especially in the past half-century, has become a team activity. Scientific efforts are often described as projects or as initiatives that are conducted by a group of individuals, with each group member having their specialized field (e.g., statistics, programming, chemical analysis, etc.). The specialists are expected to confine their efforts to their own areas of expertise, without becoming directly involved in the activities of their colleagues. In the case of group projects involving classifications or ontologies, a "mind your own business" mentality is untenable. If you have any serious desire to fully understand and analyze a large classification or a complex ontology, non-programmers must be versed in the fundamentals of software objects, and object-oriented programming. Left to their own devices, your team's programmers may not create a program that models a classification or an ontology in a manner that preserves the fundamental relationships upon which these data structures were designed. In most cases, it will be up to the naturalist (i.e., biologist, chemist, or physicist) to steer the programmer to the correct class model. The purpose of this chapter is to prepare scientists to be active partners with programmers and computer scientists. We will provide naturalists with just enough insight into the programming process to work effectively on the data modeling process. To do so, we will be examining three programming paradigms:

1. Basic object-oriented programming (i.e., how programmers create and utilize simple programmable data objects).

An object-oriented programming language is one in which the components of a program are objects, and the objects are capable of executing methods (i.e., short little programs made specifically for particular objects). For many programmers, the attraction of the object-oriented paradigm is that programmable objects can be created that have immediate access to libraries of previously prepared methods. Having pre-built methods at their disposal saves programmers time and facilitates the construction of short, readable, and powerful programs.

2. Class-oriented programming that preserves inheritance (i.e., always the preferred paradigm for modeling classifications)

When every object is assigned to a particular class, and the methods available to an object are chosen from a library of methods created specifically for the object's class, then we have elevated our object-oriented programming language into a class-oriented programming language. When we create classes that exactly mirror the classes and the class relationships found in a well-designed classification, we can begin to write programs that analyze and draw inferences from the classification. When this occurs, the programming environment becomes a computer implementation of the classification. In this chapter, we shall explain, for non-programmers, how a traditional classification can be modeled by a modern object-oriented programming environment.

3. Class-oriented programming that captures parthood relationships, sometimes referred to as a compositional style of object-oriented programming

When we are primarily interested in what's inside objects, rather than the relationships among classes of objects, we can use class-oriented techniques to create subclasses of objects composed of the parts of the objects. For example, we might want to create a class of objects that are used in the construction of an automobile. In this case, the class is not a true subclass in the sense that each of the parts of an automobile is not a type of automobile. Nonetheless, object-oriented programmers have developed successful strategies for treating parthood relationships using class-oriented programming. When they do so, they forego the inheritance relationship that is definitionally important when we create faithful computer models of classifications.

When we confuse the two different types of class-oriented programming styles (inheritance classes for classifications, and compositional classes for some types of ontologies), we risk introducing catastrophic programming errors that are impossible to rectify. In this chapter, we will learn how to avoid these kinds of mixed-paradigm errors, without relying on any particular programming skills. For any programmers who may be reading this chapter, the lessons learned here can be applied to your projects implemented within your favorite object-oriented programming language.

Section 5.2. Objects and object-oriented programming languages

An object, in an object-oriented programming paradigm, is a container that is uniquely identified, that holds data, and responds to methods (i.e., tiny programs) sent to it by the programmer. The container that we refer to is just a specific place in a computer's memory where data can be stored. The identifier is just some unique number created by the object-oriented programming environment when the object is created, that stays assigned to the object for the duration of the object's existence.

How are objects utilized in object-oriented programming languages? Basically, all objects have a basic set of universal methods, regardless of their assigned class. Data objects can be created, they can accept data put into them, they can delete that data, and they can retrieve the data when requested.

Let's pretend that we can communicate with the object-oriented programming environment using plain English sentences, and we want to try out a few instructions, using the definition of an object described in the preceding paragraph. Our conversation with the computer might go something like this:

1. Object creation

```
Computer, please create a new object and name it 'Zorro'.
```

That was easy. The computer complies, and now we have a new data object named Zorro. Zorro is automatically assigned an identification number that is known to the computer and that is not displayed to us unless we do something extra (as we shall in see step 7).

2. Object data insertion

```
Computer, please put the number 5 into Zorro.
```

Ok, now Zorro is holding some data, but what does "5" mean? Let's do this over again and put something a bit more meaningful into Zorro. First, let's undo our previous step.

3. Object data deletion

```
Computer, please delete '5' from Zorro.
```

OK, now Zorro contains no data and is ready for us to add something new.

4. Object additional data and metadata insertion

```
Computer, please put '5 pesos' into Zorro."
```

We put "5 pesos" into our data object, Zorro. Without any forethought, we have just created a triplet, consisting of: (1) an identified object (Zorro, identified by a hidden identifier string supplied by the computer when Zorro was created); (2) Metadata (pesos being a descriptor for the data that follows); and (3) data (the number 5). We can add as many triples as we like, without limit, to our Zorro object.

5. Object data retrieval

```
Computer, please tell me what is inside Zorro."
```

The computer will tell us that Zorro contains 5 pesos.

Have we accomplished anything by showing the equivalence between data objects and triples? Yes, indeed. Now we know that our data objects, in addition to having a variety of computational methods at their disposal, can also be exported as a semantically meaningful collection of triples, and directly queried as a triple store.

Every object in an object-oriented programming language can execute all of the built-in methods that have been created for members of Class Object. Aside from the simple methods that we have just reviewed, most object-oriented languages will include other built-in methods for Class Object, and some of these methods might involve different ways of extracting information about the object (e.g., a method to learn the class of the object, or the parent class of the object).

Objects in Class Object can be subclassed to handle specialized contents and methods. For example, a subclass of Class Object may be Class String (i.e., objects composed of sequences of characters). An object of Class String will inherit the methods of Class Object and it will have all of the methods available to members of Class String. Class String methods may include methods such as "uppercase", transforming the string into all uppercase characters, or "reverse", putting the string object into reverse order of characters. Likewise, a subclass of Class Object may be Class Number, in which case the class methods that apply to instances of Class Number may be "add" or "multiply" or "divide". We can supplement class methods to the pre-built collection whenever we please.

One of the very best object-oriented programming languages, in terms of ease of use and clarity of language is Ruby. In Ruby, everything is an object. This would include integers, character strings, constants, and anything that can be included in a Ruby program. As full-fledged members of Class Object (the class of all objects), every Ruby object inherits, at a bare minimum, all of the methods bestowed by the Ruby environment upon Class Object. Just for fun, let's look at Ruby's listing of the methods inherited through Class Object (Fig. 5.1).

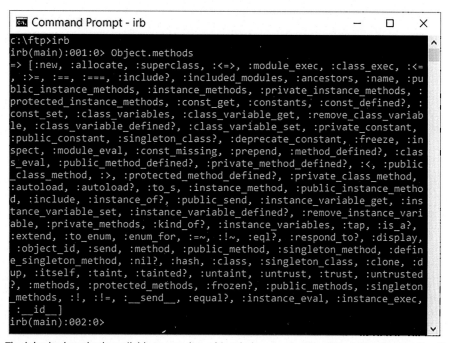

FIG. 5.1 The inherited methods available to any data object belonging to Class Object, listed by sending Ruby's Object Class the message "methods".

The aggregate of pre-built methods that come included with the programming environment is referred to as the "standard library". User-created methods can be collected as libraries, to supplement the "standard library". The community of Ruby users has created hundreds of methods (so-called *gems*) that can be freely retrieved from various web locations. Like Ruby, both Perl and Python have vast collections of methods prepared by their user communities, all available for general use. [Glossary Ruby gem, Ruby standard library]

We have already used several of the built-in methods that would be available to any object in any object-oriented programming environment (object creation in step 1, object data insertion in step 2, and object data deletion in step 3). Let's continue our computer conversation, in plain English, as we create a simple method specifically for our object.

6. Object methods creation

```
Computer, please create an object method called
 "print_my_identifier" that displays the identifier of an object
```

Once we have an object, we can create methods for the object or whole classes of objects (so-called class instance methods). Here we have told the computer to create a generic object method, that could apply to any object, called "print_my_identifier". We won't delve into the specifics of how to actually code a method; we'll just pretend that the computer does this sort of thing for us. If we were writing a real program, we would use some computer coding techniques to construct a new method, but let's not be unduly awed by the programmer's skill. Simple methods usually require just a few lines of computer code. Anyone can learn to code if they have a mind to.

7. Object method execution

```
Computer, please send the method "print_my_identifier" to the
 Zorro object
```

The computer returns to us a numeric string as Zorro's unique identifier. Let's just say that the computer has assigned 472056y199399375 to the Zorro object. This same identifier number will stay with Zorro for as long as our object persists, and the computer will not assign this identifier to any other data object that it creates for us.

Now we have a unique identified object, (i.e., Zorro, permanently associated with a unique identifier number "472056y199399375"), that contains data (i.e., "5"), that is associated with a data descriptor ("pesos"). Every data object is equivalent to the collection of triples whose identifier is the identifier of the data object. The data object, Zorro, that we have created, is now equivalent to two triples:

```
472056y199399375 "name" "Zorro"
472056y199399375 "pesos" "5"
```

As previously noted, data objects are semantically equivalent to aggregates of triples, and we always have the option to export our objects as triplestores. Likewise, we can use the object-oriented programming environment to convert triplestores into programmable objects. By doing so, we can apply the methods provided by object-oriented programming languages to our triples (i.e., our objects). In this manner, we can fully analyze all the data contained in our triplestores.

Simplistically, we have just seen everything that object-oriented programming languages provide (i.e., objects and methods), but we haven't yet seen anything that would suggest that object-oriented programming languages have any great advantage over traditional programming languages, all of which have been analyzing huge collections of data without the benefit of the object-oriented paradigm. **The real power of object-oriented programming does not come into play until we create classes that fit into a**

hierarchy that can pass methods to subclasses, through inheritance. Put another way, the power of the object-oriented paradigm reaches its climax when it achieves a classification-oriented paradigm. [Glossary Object-oriented programming language]

Section 5.3. Classes and class-oriented programming

When we employ a basic, object-oriented programming techniques, we create objects, but the objects we create need not belong to any specific class within a structured classification. In contrast, when we employ class-oriented programming, every object must belong to a class. Classes may have subclasses, and the properties of the class are inherited by the subclasses. All object-oriented programming languages allow users to create classes, and the classes that users create can model a classification or an ontology. Common parlance excludes the term "class-oriented" programming. The reason for this is that the style of class-oriented programming always involves using programming languages that are referred to by their most generic and agnostic descriptor (i.e., object-oriented programming language). **The difference between object-oriented programming and class-oriented programming depends upon whether the programmer has built a class-based hierarchical structure.**

Let's imagine that we are programmers who use our object-oriented skills to create classes to hold our objects. Let's add two restrictions to the way we write our programs: that every object belongs to exactly one class; and that every class has exactly one parent class. Does this sound familiar to us? Class-oriented programming environments are essentially computerized classifications.

From this point forward, we will be using the actual syntax used by programmers when they write code. Ruby is a popular object-oriented programming language. We'll be using Ruby syntax, but code written in virtually any other object-oriented language would look quite similar.

Class-oriented programming, being an extension of object-oriented programming, requires programmers to perform a few special tasks, as shown here:

1. Create new classes in the programming environment to accommodate each of the classes contained in a classification that is being modeled

Every object-oriented programming language should support the facile creation of user-defined classes. Classes are typically created just by invoking the class name. Here is how the class Rodentia (i.e., rodents) would be created in Ruby:

```
class Rodentia
end
```

It seems almost too simple to be true, but all that is required to create a class is to include a statement with the word "class" followed by the name of the class that you would like to create (i.e., Rodentia, in this case), followed by the word "end" indicating the command has ended.

2. When each class is being created, indicate the name of its parent class

In Ruby, the parent class of a class being created is indicated by a "<" character. In the following example, in which part of the Classification of Life is being modeled, we see how an ancestral class lineage can be created in a few simple lines of actual Ruby code.

```
class Bilateria < Eumetazoa
end

class Eumetazoa < Metazoa
end

class Metazoa < Opisthokonta
end

class Opisthokonta < Eukaryota
end

class Eukaryota < Cellular Organisms
end

class Cellular_Organisms < Class
end
```

In the example above, we have modeled the ascending lineage of Class Bilateria, with just a few command lines. When Class Bilateria is created, we inform Ruby that Class Bilateria is a subclass of Class Metazoa. Class Metazoa is a subclass of Class Opisthokonta, and so on until we come to the root of the Class of Life, Class Cellular_organisms. This class has no higher class of living organisms. Nonetheless, because Class Cellular_Organisms is a proper class in Ruby, it can inherit properties from the generic class known as Class Class. Class Class has its own set of properties, which can be inherited by Class Cellular_organisms, and all of its descendant subclasses. At this point, none of our created classes have any methods or any members.

3. Create class instances

When we program with objects, we nearly always want our objects to be of a certain type, and to behave in a manner that is determined by its type. Accordingly, object-oriented programming languages permit us to create objects that are instances, these being members of a particular class. In the Classification of Life, the names of species are our instances, and the genus of the species is the parent class of the species. Let's create the species commonly known as an apple.

```
class Malus < Maleae
end

apple = Malus.new
```

Here we created a new class called Malus, which is the genus name for fruits that would include the common apple. Class Malus is the child class of Class Maleae, so we created Class Malus to indicate its parent Class Maleae. After creating Class Malus, we created an instance of the class, using the "new" method, and we called this instance "apple". All object-oriented programming languages have a pre-built "new" method, or its functional equivalent, that allows us to create new class objects.

4. Provide the classes with any additional properties that would qualify as class properties

```
class Malus
  def falls_on_head
    puts "Kaboing!"
  end
end


apple = Malus.new
apple.falls_on_head
```

In the first 5 lines, we created Class Malus, and we included in the class an instance method named "falls_on_head" that prints the word "Kaboing" to the computer screen. Methods simply sit inside the programming environment, doing nothing until they are called for by an object belonging to the appropriate class. In line 6, we created a new instance of Class Malus, and named this instance object "apple." In line 7, we sent the "falls_on_head" instance method to "apple", and this prompted the method, located in Class Malus, to execute. When the "falls_on_head" method executes, it prints the word "Kaboing!" on our computer monitor.

Every instance of Class Malus has access to the "falls_on_head" method. Every instance of every descendant subclass of Class Malus has access to the "falls_on_head" method. You can see that inherited methods afford a great economy of code writing, because many different classes and instances can use a method that was written only one time, and included in a class library, along with a vast number of other available methods.

With minor modification, we can expand the power of the "falls_on_head" method.

```
class Malus
  def falls_on_head(x)
    puts "Kaboing. #{x}"
  end
end

apple = Malus.new
apple.falls_on_head("Sorry.")
```

The output of this short program would be the words "Kaboing. Sorry." printed on the computer monitor. The falls_on_head(x) method receives the text that we attached to the message received by the apple object. The method, revised here, prints out the word

"Kaboing" followed by the received text, "Sorry." In this example, an instance object of Class Malus (i.e., our apple) passed some information back to its class method, which was used by the method when it returned its output. This trivial exercise demonstrates how programmers send methods and data between instance objects and classes.

5. Create modules for properties that apply to unrelated classes, and insert these modules inside all such classes

Module creation is a powerful tool available to class-oriented programmers, allowing them to create methods that can be used by classes that are not directly related to one another. Modules can be thought of as programs that are available to one or more classes. Modules, unlike classes, do not have instances; but the instances of a class that contains a module have access to the module methods inserted into the class. In the next section of this chapter, we will be explaining why this technique is of paramount importance for class-oriented programmers who are modeling traditional classifications. For now, let's just look at a simple example that demonstrates how a module is created and employed.

When a class is provided with a module, the module method will be inherited by all the descendants of the class, much the same was as a class method would be inherited. In the following Ruby script, the class Container contains a module named HelloModule with one method named say_hello, whose function is to print out the word "hello" when called.

```
class Container                  #Here we create Class Container
    module HelloModule           #Here we create a module
        def say_hello            #Here we create a module method
                                    say_hello

            puts "hello"
        end
    end
include HelloModule
end

class SubContainer < Container   #A subclass of Class Container is
                                    created

end

my_object = SubContainer.new     #An instance of Class
                                    SubContainer is created
my_object.say_hello              #A module method (say_hello) is
                                    sent to the object
exit
```

The word "hello" is printed on the screen, representing the value returned by the module method "say_hello" that was sent to the instance object created for Class SubContainer. The striking aspect of this simple script is that an object of Class SubContainer was able to use a module method that had been placed in a parent class.

Programmers who are using an object-oriented programming language to model a classification will want to include modules within classes. A single module can be included in multiple classes, without altering the hierarchy of the classification. For any class, Ruby can tell us the included modules, using the "included_modules" method.

```
> String.included_modules
=> [Comparable, Kernel]
```

In the example above, Class String is shown to include two modules: Comparable and Kernel. The practical significance of modules will become obvious in the next section of this chapter when we discuss how programmers avoid ontologic dilemmas.

To summarize, the difference between object-oriented programming and class-oriented programming depends upon whether the programmer has provided every class with relationships to other classes, permitting instances to make heavy use of class inheritance. Otherwise, class-oriented programming is syntactically no different from object-oriented programming (i.e., it looks much the same when you look at written code). All of the general techniques of object-oriented programming will apply to class-oriented programming.

Compositional style class-oriented programming

It is important to understand that the most popular style of object-oriented programming today is described as "compositional" [2,3]. Compositional programming represents a radical departure from the type of programming that we have been describing, in which a traditional classification is faithfully modeled within the object-oriented programming environment. If we want to enjoy the benefits of compositional programming techniques while preserving the logical integrity of formal classifications, then we must pause a moment to bask in the allure of compositional style.

In compositional class-oriented programming, the items contained in a child class are related to the parent class through a "part_of" relationship; not through the "is_a" relationship prescribed for traditional classifications. For example, if we have a class "Automobile", then a compositional subclass of "Automobile" might be "Interior". The items in class Interior might be "glove compartment", "radio", "bucket seat", "cup holder", and so on. Another subclass of "Automobile" might be "Chassis" and might include such things as "axle", "drive train", "muffler". In other words, the subclasses of a class comprise all the parts of the parent class. In traditional classifications, every child must be a type of the parent class. If we have an "Automobile" class, then the subclasses might be "Gas-powered car", "Electric-powered car", or "Hybrid car".

Compositional subclasses forfeit the inheritance. For example, a "glove box" cannot inherit the properties of an automobile because a "glove box" is not an automobile; it is simply a small part of the automobile. This being so, why would anyone wish to create compositional subclasses? The answer is that most real-world programming applications are concerned primarily with things and their associated parts and properties. When we program compositionally, we can write software that quickly retrieves parts of an object, and applies object methods that were created for a particular object, regardless of the subclass in which it was found. Staying with the example of an "Automobile" class, we could write a program that lists all of the parts of an automobile, or a program that lists all of the items that have been marked as being "flammable" (i.e., have a "flammable" property). We can write a program that takes a specification document for a car and checks to determine whether the document contains all the required items. To do these kinds of things, we need to write lots of little methods for the classes, subclasses, and instances because our objects will not inherit through an ancestral lineage. Regardless, we can always use the inspection methods provided by object-oriented languages to find all the methods that apply to any particular object and to modify those methods, as needed. Furthermore, methods applicable to several classes can be shared, using modules (vida supra).

As a general rule, compositional programming works very well in situations where the class structure cannot be accommodated by a traditional classification. Despite everything we have read about the value of classifications, we must accept that most object-oriented software is designed to model objects that are unclassifiable. In such cases, a compositional approach to object-oriented programming makes a lot of sense. Because many ontologies permit a variety of features common to compositional programming (e.g., multi-class inheritance, multi-class membership, methods with object-specific functionality), it is easy to see why compositional programming might be the style of choice for modern ontologies.

Because compositional-style object-oriented programming is popular, and because it is well-suited to modeling ontologies, is there any advantage to applying object-oriented programming techniques to traditional classifications? The answer is yes, for the following reasons:

1. Class-oriented programming languages can fully represent traditional classifications.
2. Object-oriented classification models can import their structure directly from semantic language documents.
3. Compositional programming sacrifices inheritance.
4. Traditional classifications generate hypotheses.
5. Using modules, the power of compositional programming can be achieved with traditional classifications.

Let's elaborate on these points.

Class-oriented programming languages can fully represent traditional classifications. Using Ruby as an example, we have seen how classes and instances are created and how we assign classes to their parent classes. We have also seen how class methods, which are equivalent to class properties, are created and assigned. These are the only steps involved in porting a traditional classification into an object-oriented programming environment. A programmer should have no trouble taking a file in which all of the classes and instances of a classification are listed, along with the named parent class of each child class, and instantly assembling all of the classes and instances as programmable objects.

Object-oriented classification models can import their structure directly from semantic language documents. Schemas were discussed in "Section 3.4. Semantic languages." Briefly, a schema contains definitions of classes and properties and includes the name of the parent class for each listed class, and the domain and the range of properties (i.e., the classes in which the property applies, and the structure of the property's value (e.g., integer, string, Boolean). If a schema has been composed in a semantic language (e.g., RDF Schema), then a computer program could port the classes and properties directly into an object-oriented programming environment, providing the general scaffold of the classification, to which class instances (not included in the schema) can be separately added.

An important feature of object-oriented languages is the ability to load data into objects. This feature permits a programmer to parse through a triplestore, and whenever it encounters a triple whose subject (i.e., the identifier of the triple) corresponds to a created data object, it simply adds the triple to the existing object.

Compositional programming sacrifices inheritance. As mentioned, in compositional programming, subclasses are typically composed of the components of the parent class. Components of an object lack the composite properties of the object (e.g., we can drive an assembled car, but we cannot drive a rear-view mirror). Therefore, components of an object cannot inherit the methods of their parent classes.

Traditional classifications generate hypotheses. When a classification has been modeled within a class-oriented programming environment, all class relationships are retained, and all class objects are assigned their proper classes. Hence, the banal functions of classification, such as searching and retrieving items that have been organized into classes, are facilitated by an object-oriented model. It should be noted that the primary advantage of class-oriented programming has less to do with locating and retrieving objects via their class assignments; and much more to do with deepening our understanding of the classification itself. Using object-oriented programming techniques, we can draw inferences about classes, and we can generate new hypotheses about how classes relate to one another. We cannot do such things with compositional classes, which consist of items having no particular relationship to one another, other than their inclusion in a composite object.

Using modules, the power of compositional programming can be achieved with traditional classifications.

In modern programming languages, a module is a section of invoked code that contains methods and constants assigned to a namespace (the declared module name). In object-oriented programming languages, modules are typically used to provide objects with methods that are not available to them through simple inheritance.

Although modules are not classes, modules lie at the heart of class-oriented programming. Modules provide a way for classes to acquire methods that enhance the functionality of the class without changing the identity and the purpose of the class. Many of the built-in Ruby classes contain modules that are common to other Ruby classes.

Let's see how a single module can be used by unrelated classes.

```
#!/usr/local/bin/ruby

module HelloModule
    def say_hello
      puts "hello"
    end
end
```

```
class Container
  include HelloModule
end

class Pastry
  include HelloModule
end

class SubContainer < Container
end

class Cookie < Pastry
end

my_object = SubContainer.new
my_object.say_hello

my_dessert = Cookie.new
my_dessert.say_hello

exit
```

In the example shown above, the module HelloModule has a single method (say_hello). When the HelloModule's say_hello method is invoked, and the word "hello" is sent to the monitor. Various unrelated classes (e.g., Class Pastry and Class Container) could use the say_hello method in the HelloModule module.

A module differs from a class in several ways.

1. A module is created with the "module Modulename" statement, (not the "class ClassName" statement), and the statement is never followed by the name of an assigned parent module (i.e., modules are not classes and, accordingly, do not have parent classes).
2. Modules cannot create instance objects.
3. Modules can be included in built-in or added class libraries, or they can be coded into class definitions inside scripts, or they can exist as stand-alone routines within a script, that can be called with an "include" statement or a scope operator. If the module definition is part of an external file, the external file can be required into the script, with the "require" command. [Glossary Scope operator]
4. Module methods are added to a script using an "include" statement

By including modules within classes, the user has access to the module methods via the class's instance objects. The user does not need to put include statements in the script (because the module is included through the class) and the user does not need to know which class methods were created for the class and which methods were included in the class through a module. As far as the programmer is concerned, the Module methods included in a class are just like any other heritable class method.

Some programmers think of modules as a sneaky way to gain a multi-class inheritance. Though technically true, this thinking is counter-productive. You should think of modules as a way of enhancing a Class without changing the intrinsic identity of the class. Module methods provided to a class should be methods that are natural extensions of features that are characteristic of the class. If you have a Neoplasm class, it might be reasonable to include a Growth module with a doubling_time method. A Growth module may be appropriate to include in unrelated classes (i.e., not ancestors and not descendants) of the Neoplasm class. An Amoeba class might appropriately include a Growth module. A Bacteria class may include the Growth module as well. The point here is that modules can provide methods that are not specific to any class. Classes create objects of a specific type, but these objects may need methods that dissimilar objects also need. Through the careful and disciplined use of modules, we can vastly expand the utility of classes without changing the identity of the class and without violating the definitional properties of traditional classifications. [Glossary Class-oriented programming versus object-oriented programming, Inheritance polymorphism, Mixins, Module]

Section 5.4. In the natural sciences, classifications are mono-parental

Ontologies often exhibit multi-class parentage, meaning that a class may have more than one parent class (i.e., direct superclass). There are various reasons why ontologies allow multi-class parentage:

1. There is a commonly held view that the natural world is designed in such a way that objects inherit properties from multiple classes. For example, a dog is an animal (Class Canis), and it would be expected to be created with the functionalities typically assigned to canines. Dogs are also domesticated pets and would seem to qualify as objects belonging to Class Pets. To the modern ontologist, there may seem to be no reason not to assign your dog to Class Canis and Class Pets.
2. It is incredibly easy to create multiple parent classes for any class. Many object-oriented programming languages allow programmers to create classes with multiple parent classes, or to create classes that have no parent classes at all.
3. By assigning more than one parent class to a class, the instances within the class stand to inherit methods from every one of the parent classes, endowing such instances with a vast array of methods available for the programmer.
4. Assigning multiple parent classes to a class is commonplace in so-called "compositional" programming. In this technique, subclasses consist of parts that, together, compose the parent class [2,3]. For those programmers who prefer compositional programming, multiclass parentage is a routine practice. [Glossary Compositional classes]

The question confronting data scientists is, "Should I model my data as a classification, wherein every class has one direct parent class; or should I model the resource as an ontology, wherein classes may have multi-parental inheritance?" This question lies at the heart of several related fields: database management, computational informatics, object-oriented programming, semantics, and artificial intelligence. Computer scientists are choosing sides, often without acknowledging the problem or fully understanding the stakes involved. In many cases, the choice of a multi-parental ontology versus a mono-parental classification is made without forethought, at the moment when a programmer selects their preferred object-oriented language.

When a programmer builds object libraries in the Python or the Perl programming languages, she is working in a permissive environment that supports multiclass object inheritance, by default. In Python and Perl, any object can have as many parent classes as the programmer prefers. In contrast, when a programmer chooses to program in the Ruby programming language, she shuts the door on multiclass inheritance. A Ruby object can have only one direct parent class. Most programmers are unaware of the liberties and restrictions imposed by their choice of programming language, until they start to construct their class libraries, or until they begin to use class libraries prepared by other programmers [4]. By then, it may be too late to change the structural model of the knowledge domain.

Does the choice of class parentage (mono-parental versus multi-parental) make a difference? Yes, very much so.

Let's look at a simple example, wherein a class is provided with two parent classes (not just one, as is the case in proper classifications).

We pretend that we are writing a program that simulates the functionality of humans, based on their personalities. In our model class structure, we have created a class called "Class Knowledge_seeker." We fill Class Knowledge-seeker with inquisitive humans who serve as our data objects. Class Knowledge_seeker has two parent classes: Class Guru_enthusiast and Class Douglas_Adams_fan. It seems that, in our classification, all seekers of knowledge are very enthusiastic about Indian gurus, and they are also big fans of Douglas Adams, the brilliant creator of the "Hitchhiker's Guide to the Galaxy."

In our program, a knowledge seeker would like to learn the meaning of life. In object-oriented programming, methods are "sent" to objects, the method is executed, and the result is returned to the object. In this example, we'll use a handy method named "meaning_of_life" and we will send the request to execute the method to an instance of Class Knowledge_seeker called "self".

```
self.meaning_of_life
```

Do we have any reason to think that the "self" object contains the "meaning_of_life" method as part of its programmed repertoire? The beauty of object-oriented programming is that the "self" object does not need to have direct access to the methods being sent. In a class-oriented programming environment, methods are carried up the class lineage until a class is encountered that happens to contain, in its class library, the program that can execute the method that was sent to the original receiving object ("self" in this case). **The object that receives the method need not possess the method. The object receiving the method only needs to have some ancestor in possession of the method.** The method will be executed with the ancestor's method and the result will be returned to the original object that received the message. Every object knows its ancestral lineage and has no trouble sending a method request up through its hierarchy. When a class is encountered that can execute the method, the search stops, and the result is generated. If no class has access to the method, then an error is generated. This is how inheritance works in class-oriented environments.

In the case of multi-parental classification, when an object receives a request to execute a method, the programming environment must choose one of the parental lineages in which to search for the method. When the method name "meaning_of_life" is sent to "self", an instance of Class Knowledge_seeker, the method name first looks around within the Knowledge_seeker class for the method of the same name. In this case, the "meaning_of_life" method is not found within Class Knowledge_seeker, and the method must be sent to the next higher class. In this case, Class Knoledge_seeker has two parent classes. Should the message go to Class Guru_enthusiast or Class Douglas_Adams_fan? It just so happens that Class Guru_enthusiast contains a method named "meaning_of_life," and this method is programmed to return the character string, "Life is a river!" when executed. There also happens to be a method named "meaning_of_life" in Class Douglas_Adams_fan, and this method returns the integer "42" when executed.

Here is the dilemma. The meaning_of_life method, when sent from the Knowledge_seeker class, will return the character string "Life is a river" if sent to the Guru_enthusiast parent class, and the method of the same name will return the integer "42" if sent to the Douglas_Adams_fan class. It is unlikely that both possible responses are correct.

In class-oriented programming, every data object is assigned membership to a class of related objects. Once a data object has been assigned to a class, the object has access to all of the methods available to the class in which it holds membership, and to all of the methods in all the ancestral classes. If classes are constrained to single parental inheritance, then the methods available to the programmer are restricted to a tight lineage. When the object-oriented language permits multi-parental inheritance, a data object can have many different ancestral classes spread horizontally and vertically through the classification, and methods of the same name, but different functions, may appear throughout its ancestral classes. There is no way to determine how a search for a named method will traverse its ancestral class libraries; hence, the output of a software program written in an object-oriented language that permits multiclass inheritance is unpredictable [4].

Object-oriented programming is a bit like putting a message in a bottle and throwing it out to sea. If the bottle can go anywhere, you cannot know who will receive it and how they will reply. If the bottle is restricted to one particular sea lane, the result becomes predictable.

In ontologies, classes are typically connected by relational rules and are not typically constrained to mono-parental class lineages. Under such circumstances, a class may be an ancestor of a child class that is an ancestor of its parent class (e.g., a single class might be grandfather and grandchild to the same class). An instance of a class might be an instance of two classes, at once. The combinatorics and the recursive options can become difficult or impossible to compute.

Those who use ontologies that use multiclass inheritance will readily acknowledge the complexities of their models. The ontology expert justifies the model on the certainty that reality itself is complex and unpredictable. A faithful model of reality cannot be created with a simple-minded classification. A belief is held that with time and effort, modern approaches to complex systems will isolate and eliminate computational impediments, these being the kinds of problems that computer scientists are trained to solve. For example, recursion within an ontology can be avoided if the ontology is acyclic (i.e., class relationships are not permitted to cycle back onto themselves). For every problem created by an ontology, an adept computer scientist will find a solution. Basically, ontologists believe that the task of organizing and understanding information no longer resides within the ancient realm of classifications [4]. [Glossary Data modeling]

For traditionalists, who believe in the supremacy of classifications over ontologies, their faith has nothing to do with the computational dilemmas incurred with multiclass parental inheritance. They base their faith on epistemological grounds; on the nature of objects. They hold that an object can only be one thing. You cannot pretend that one thing is two or more things, simply because you insist that it is so. One thing can only belong to one class. One class can only have one parent class; otherwise, it would have a dual nature. Assigning more than one parental class to an object is a sign that you have failed to grasp the essential nature of the object. The classification expert believes that ontologies do not accurately represent reality [4].

Mono-parental class systems in classifications

As stated, many times previously, classifications are mono-parental systems; each class has one and only one parent class, while a class may have any number of child classes, including zero. The relationship of the derived class is commonly known as an "is_a" relationship, indicating that a class is a bona fide member of its ancestral classes and inherits all of the class properties of its ancestral classes.

There is a tendency to say that everyone can implement whatever type of model for their knowledge domain as may suit them (i.e., multiclass or single class, compositional classes or hierarchical classes). For classifications that model the natural world (e.g., The Classification of Life, The Periodic Table of the Elements, and the Classification Theorem of Finite Simple Groups), there is no freedom of choice in the class structure. In the natural world, the job of the classification builder is to faithfully model the existing classification created by nature; not to impose a new order under which the universe must strive to abide.

In point of fact, whenever we examine classification of the natural world, we observe a simple mono-parental hierarchy of classes. There are a few logical reasons that would seem to justify this current state of affairs:

1. If the universe were a multi-parental classification, then individual objects in the universe would have dual (or higher) identities and would operate under multiple sets of laws, producing a chaotic universe. The universe is not chaotic. As we shall see in "Section 8.2. Invariances are our laws," our universe operates under sets of laws that apply to specific classes of items (e.g., fields, particles, spacetime geometries).
2. Living organisms exhibit ancestral traits with characteristic heritable traits appearing in ancestral classes. The inheritance of the species genome, from parent to child organism, provides the biological rationale for the mono-parental class system of all life on earth.
3. No successful multi-parental class system has ever been created for a natural system.

In the above list, item 3 stands on shaky grounds. We all recognize that the absence of a positive can never serve as proof of a negative. In this particular case, the absence of any natural classifications having multi-parental class structure cannot serve as proof that such classifications cannot exist. The fact remains that some very intelligent scientists have tried to build multi-parental classifications and have failed in doing so. In "Section 4.1. Problematica," we listed some of the ontology models that dared to ignore the natural order of things. These included: The International Classification of Diseases, The Diagnostic and Statistical Manual of Mental Disorders, and The molecular classification of diseases. All of these classifications have major limitations that can be traced, in some ways, to their acceptance of multi-class inheritance.

In the biomedical sciences, the classification that comes closest to having a successful implementation of multi-class inheritance seems to be the Gene Ontology (better known as GO). GO provides items with three distinct class systems having three distinct ancestral lineages: Biological Process, Cellular Component, and Molecular Function. The thinking here is that a biological entity may have inherited biological processes (e.g., metabolic pathways), inherited cellular components (e.g., parts of cells and anatomic parts), and inherited molecular functions (e.g., regulatory pathways and signals in the genome). GO is built to segregate the three ways in which items are classified. In a sense, GO consists of three proper classifications connected in one database. Thus, the creators of the Gene Ontology have narrowly created 3-class inheritance, without strictly violating the fundamental rules of classification. Kudos to them.

It would seem fair to conclude that when we confine ourselves to the natural world, as described by mathematics, physics, chemistry, and biology, the "one class one parent" rule holds sway, without exception.

Section 5.5. Listening to what objects tell us

Back in "Section 3.4. Semantic languages," we discussed a feature that is provided by semantic languages that allow us to fully understand all of the objects and object relationships contained in classification or ontology. We called this feature self-description. Because semantic languages include descriptors such as "name", "subclass_of", "part_of", "is_a", "type_of" "identifier", "has_property", "domain", "range". a computer can parse through a document consisting of triples composed in a descriptive semantic language and find all of the included relationships (e.g., the unique identifier of an object, it's class membership, its available properties, and so on. Because both classifications and ontologies can be represented in a semantic language, we can use computers to fully analyze their structures, assuming that the semantic representation has been properly prepared.

When we have modeled a classification or an ontology using an object-oriented programming language, we have at our immediate disposal a host of built-in self-describing methods that will facilitate the construction of computer programs capable of quickly understanding all of the relationships among our objects and classes. The process of deploying such methods, in our computer programs, is known as introspection.

To get a rough idea of the value of introspection, when dealing with class structures, we can try out a few methods, from a command-line, without bothering to write a formal script. Non-programmers will have no trouble understanding what we see.

Ruby can always tell you the complete ancestry of any objects, including the classes and the modules available for its use, in proper order, ascending the class hierarchy.

In all the following examples, the "=>" symbol indicates Ruby's response to a command.

```
> Integer.ancestors
=> [Integer, Numeric, Comparable, Object, Kernel, BasicObject]

> String.ancestors
=> [String, Comparable, Object, Kernel, BasicObject]

> Array.ancestors
=> [Array, Enumerable, Object, Kernel, BasicObject]

> NilClass.ancestors
=> [NilClass, Object, Kernel, BasicObject]

> Method.ancestors
=> [Method, Object, Kernel, BasicObject]

> Class.ancestors
=> [Class, Module, Object, Kernel, BasicObject]

> Object.ancestors
=> [Object, Kernel, BasicObject]
```

In every case, when we sent the "ancestors" to an object, Ruby returned to us the object's ascending lineage. The top class, in every case, is Class BasicObject. This is the "root" of Ruby; and Class BasicObject has no parent class. Every object in Ruby is a descendant of Class BasicObject and inherits all of the properties of Basic Object.

Seeing these listed examples of object hierarchies, all of which converge upon Class BasicObject, we can appreciate that the built-in Ruby environment is itself a valid classification. Moreover, if we were to insert a classification into Ruby (e.g., if we were to model the Classification of Life within Ruby), we would need to put the top class in our classification as a subclass of some existing Ruby classes. Hence, any classification that we model in Ruby would be a subclassification of Ruby itself, and would automatically inherit all of the built-in Ruby methods for all of the classes that sit above our modeled classification.

For example, if our "root" class for the Classification of Life were named Class Organism, and we instructed Ruby to make Class Organism a child class of Class String, then every organism in our modeled Classification of Life would inherit the methods of Class String and the ancestral classes of Class String. Let's see how this would work, in Ruby:

```
class Organism < String
end
```

That was simple. We have created a new class, Class Organism, in Ruby, and we placed this class as a child class of Class String. Why did we choose to make Class Organism a child class of Class String when we know that an organism is not a string. Technically, all of our organisms and all of our class relationships will be described using strings (i.e., sequences of alphanumeric characters that we recognize as words). We will certainly want to search for and compare names of organisms, and for that reason, it makes sense to put our Classification of Life under Class String. If we were modeling some other classification in Ruby, we might choose an alternate parent class. For example, if we were to use ruby to model the symmetry groups to be discussed in "Section 8.5. Symmetry groups rule the universe," we might opt to model our classification under some other class from which we could install and draw upon a collection of available Ruby math modules.

Now that we have created a Class for our organisms, let's check to see if Ruby has included Class Organism in its revised hierarchy by sending the "ancestors" method to Class Organism:

```
Organism.ancestors
=> [Organism, String, Comparable, Object, Kernel, BasicObject]
```

Yes, our root class of the Classification of Life is now ensconced in Ruby, and we could add all of the classes of the Classification of Life as subclasses of Class Organism, preserving the current version of the classification. If we had a suitable computer-parsable file of the class hierarchy, we could do the job almost instantly.

Every newly created instance object must be assigned a class, in any purely class-oriented programming language (such as Ruby). In contrast, objects can be created that are not assigned to classes, in loosely structured object-oriented programming languages. Ruby keeps track of the class of every object, and we can always determine an object's class with the "class" method.

Let's begin by creating a new instance object of Class String, putting the string "hello world" into the object. Just to show how forgiving Ruby is, we won't bother giving the new object a name.

```
> String.new("hello world")
=> "hello world"
```

Ruby returned the contents of the newly created string, this being "hello world". Now let's find the name of the class and the class ancestry for our newly created object.

```
> "hello world".class
=> String
```

When we concatenate the "ancestors" method to the "class" method, we get the ordered names of the classes and modules of the instance object's ancestry.

```
> "hello world".class.ancestors
=> [String, Comparable, Object, Kernel, BasicObject]
```

When the "class" method is sent to "hello world", ruby tells us that "hello world" is a member of Class String. When the chained methods "class. Ancestors" is sent to Hello world, Ruby tells us that "hello world" is an instance of Class String, and the ancestral classes of Class String are "Comparable, Object, Kernal, and BasicObject."

If we are specifically interested in the parent class of a class, we can use the "superclass" method.

```
> Fixnum.superclass
=> Integer
```

When the "superclass" method is sent to Class Fixnum, ruby tells us that the parent class of Class Fixnum is Class Integer.

If we have an object that is not a class and would like to know the name of the superclass of the class in which it resides, we can just chain together the "class" and "superclass" methods.

```
>my_array = Array.new([1,2,3])
=> [1, 2, 3]

>my_array.class.superclass
=> Object
```

When we create a new instance of Class Array, we can determine the superclass of its class by chaining the class and superclass methods and sending the chain to the instance.

Once we have the name of a class, we can always determine the methods available to the class, using the "methods" method. Let's look at all of the methods available to Class String (Fig. 5.2).

```
irb(main):001:0> String.methods
=> [:try_convert, :new, :allocate, :superclass, :<=>, :module_exec, :class_exe
c, :<=, :>=, :==, :===, :include?, :included_modules, :ancestors, :name, :publ
ic_instance_methods, :instance_methods, :private_instance_methods, :protected_
instance_methods, :const_get, :constants, :const_defined?, :const_set, :class_
variables, :class_variable_get, :remove_class_variable, :class_variable_define
d?, :class_variable_set, :private_constant, :public_constant, :singleton_class
?, :deprecate_constant, :freeze, :inspect, :module_eval, :const_missing, :prep
end, :method_defined?, :class_eval, :public_method_defined?, :private_method_d
efined?, :<, :public_class_method, :>, :protected_method_defined?, :private_cl
ass_method, :autoload, :autoload?, :to_s, :instance_method, :public_instance_m
ethod, :include, :instance_of?, :public_send, :instance_variable_get, :instanc
e_variable_set, :instance_variable_defined?, :remove_instance_variable, :priva
te_methods, :kind_of?, :instance_variables, :tap, :is_a?, :extend, :to_enum, :
enum_for, :=~, :!~, :eql?, :respond_to?, :display, :object_id, :send, :method,
 :public_method, :singleton_method, :define_singleton_method, :nil?, :hash, :c
lass, :singleton_class, :clone, :dup, :itself, :taint, :tainted?, :untaint, :u
ntrust, :trust, :untrusted?, :methods, :protected_methods, :frozen?, :public_m
ethods, :singleton_methods, :!, :!=, :__send__, :equal?, :instance_eval, :inst
ance_exec, :__id__]
```

FIG. 5.2 By sending the "methods" message to Class String, in the Ruby command-line environment, we receive a list of all of the class methods of Class String.

Methods that act on a class are not strictly equivalent to methods that act on instances of a class (i.e., instance methods). When the "methods" message is sent to the newly created instance of Class Array, my_array, Ruby lists all of the methods available to the instance (Fig. 5.3).

When we are not certain whether an object belongs to a class, we can always check, using the "instance_of?" method. Let's create a new instance of Class Hash, and let's leave the new object empty. [Glossary Associative array]

```
>hash1 = Hash.new
=> {}
>hash1.instance_of?(Array)
=> false
>hash1.instance_of?(Hash)
=> true
```

When the "instance_of?" method was sent to the new object, with "Array" as its parameter, Ruby returned "false," indicating that the object is not an instance of Class Array. When the "instance_of?" method was sent to the new object, with "Hash" as its parameter, Ruby returned "true," indicating that the object is an instance of Class Hash.

```
irb(main):001:0> my_array = Array.new([1,2,3])
=> [1, 2, 3]
irb(main):002:0> my_array.methods
=> [:fill, :assoc, :rassoc, :uniq, :uniq!, :compact, :compact!, :flatten, :to_
h, :flatten!, :shuffle!, :shuffle, :include?, :combination, :repeated_permutat
ion, :permutation, :product, :sample, :repeated_combination, :bsearch_index, :
bsearch, :select!, :&, :*, :+, :-, :sort, :count, :find_index, :select, :rejec
t, :collect, :map, :pack, :first, :any?, :reverse_each, :zip, :take, :take_whi
le, :drop, :drop_while, :cycle, :insert, :|, :index, :rindex, :replace, :clear
, :<=>, :<<, :==, :[], :[]=, :reverse, :empty?, :eql?, :concat, :reverse!, :in
spect, :delete, :length, :size, :each, :slice, :slice!, :to_ary, :to_a, :to_s,
 :dig, :hash, :at, :fetch, :last, :push, :pop, :shift, :unshift, :frozen?, :ea
ch_index, :join, :rotate, :rotate!, :sort!, :collect!, :map!, :sort_by!, :keep
_if, :values_at, :delete_at, :delete_if, :reject!, :transpose, :find, :entries
, :sort_by, :grep, :grep_v, :detect, :find_all, :flat_map, :collect_concat, :i
nject, :reduce, :partition, :group_by, :all?, :one?, :none?, :min, :max, :minm
ax, :min_by, :max_by, :minmax_by, :member?, :each_with_index, :each_entry, :ea
ch_slice, :each_cons, :each_with_object, :chunk, :slice_before, :slice_after,
:slice_when, :chunk_while, :lazy, :instance_of?, :public_send, :instance_varia
ble_get, :instance_variable_set, :instance_variable_defined?, :remove_instance
_variable, :private_methods, :kind_of?, :instance_variables, :tap, :is_a?, :ex
tend, :to_enum, :enum_for, :===, :=~, :!~, :respond_to?, :freeze, :display, :o
bject_id, :send, :method, :public_method, :singleton_method, :define_singleton
_method, :nil?, :class, :singleton_class, :clone, :dup, :itself, :taint, :tain
ted?, :untaint, :untrust, :trust, :untrusted?, :methods, :protected_methods, :
public_methods, :singleton_methods, :!, :!=, :__send__, :equal?, :instance_eva
l, :instance_exec, :__id__]
```

FIG. 5.3 The "methods" method sent to the my_array instance object yields the built-in instance methods available to the instances of Class Array.

As we learned from our discussion of triples, objects have no real meaning unless they are assigned a unique identifier. Ruby automatically assigns every object a unique identifier, at the moment of its creation. We can discover the id of any object by sending the object the "object_id" method. Let's create the "my_array object", and immediately afterward ask Ruby to tell us the object's identifier number.

```
>my_array = Array.new([1,2,3])
=> [1, 2, 3]
>my_array.object_id
=> 20612470
```

In Ruby, everything is an object, including classes of things. Because every object is assigned an identifier, we can use the "object_id" method to find the identifier of any class. Here, we retrieve the object id of the Array class.

```
>Array.object_id
=> 19475900
```

In summary, just about anything we would want to know about a class or an instance is made available to us, through introspection methods. How can such information be used by scientists? In the case of non-programmers, a few introspection commands can be used to ascend the lineages of a classification, or determine all of the instance objects of a class, or find the properties of instances and classes. In Chapter 6, "The Classification of Life," we will show that many important inferences about the nature of living organisms can be drawn by simply examining the structure of their classification. When a classification is modeled by a class-oriented programming language, we can use introspection methods to reveal everything currently known about the relationships of classes, objects, and properties. In most cases, all the information we might need can be gathered with a single built-in command.

For skilled programmers, introspection tools support a technique known as "reflection," wherein information about objects is used, during the run-time of a program, to dynamically determine its behavior and its output. For example, we might want to write a program that collects objects having a particular property, and to send an appropriate method to each of those objects, collecting the results, and displaying a summary of findings. The programmer need not know what objects will be used in the script before the script's execution. The selection of objects will be accomplished using introspection methods that occur during run-time.

Remarks for non-programmers

For non-programmers who may be interested in pursuing a nascent interest in object-oriented programming, there is a large number of excellent programming languages at your disposal. Java seems to be the most popular choice for professional programmers. In many cases, a professional will use an objectified version of a traditional language in which they have expertise. For non-programmers, Python seems to be highly popular at this time. Python would be a very good choice for anyone who is working with colleagues who have committed themselves to this language.

If you are a lone wolf or a contrarian, you might want to consider Ruby. Here is a list of Ruby's features that you might find attractive [5]:

1. Available at no cost with a simple installation available for Windows users.
2. Comes with all of the conditional blocks (e.g., if statements, for statements, loop ranges) and many iterative methods that all programmers have come to expect from a modern programming language.
3. Specifically designed to be an object-oriented programming language (i.e., object-orientation is not a feature added to a procedural language, as an afterthought).
4. Well suited to model traditional classifications, enforcing a mono-parental class structure.
5. Comes with a large standard library, and has an active user group that has prepared a large library of easily installed add-on methods (cleverly named Ruby Gems).
6. Provides elegant and easy implementations of object orientation techniques (i.e., inheritance, reflection, polymorphism, encapsulation, abstraction). Learning Ruby has been compared to learning chess. It takes about an hour to learn the rudiments, but enthusiasts can spend a lifetime sharpening their skills.
7. Supports the open-world logic paradigm.

A note about point 7 in the list. There are two paradigms in which the truth of assertions is evaluated in programming languages: closed world and open world. In the closed world programming paradigm, operations that test truth (i.e., conditional statements in programs such as "if", "unless" "until", "equals") must return either "true" or "false". Nothing else will do. In the open world paradigm, there is a third option known as "nil" indicating that nothing can be said on the subject. Every conditional statement, in the open world, is "true, false, or nil".

Perl and Python have closed world languages, in which every statement is either true or false, with all non-zero values considered "true" and "0" considered "false". In an open world language, such as Ruby, conditional statements evaluate as "true, false or nil."

For example, consider this conditional statement:

"If Fred likes pizza, we'll go to an Italian restaurant for dinner."

If we don't know the first thing about Fred, then Perl and Python would return the if condition (i.e., whether or Fred likes pizza) as false, because any statement in Perl and Python that cannot evaluate to true, must evaluate to false.

In Ruby, the condition "If Fred likes pizza" would evaluate to "nil". Ruby doesn't know anything about Fred and cannot determine whether the condition is true or false.

Now, let's pretend we've moved on in our program, and have learned that Fred is a member of Class Pizza_enthusiasts and that the defining class property of Class Pizza_enthusiasts is that all members like pizza. At the moment that we assign Fred to Class Pizza_enthusiasts, we learn that the program in Perl and Python made an error. The conditional statement, "If Fred likes Pizza" was falsely evaluated as false, and our program suddenly has a bug that might be very difficult to detect and correct.

The equivalent program, in Ruby, makes no error when it evaluated the condition, "If Fred likes pizza" as "nil". Nil simply indicates that nothing can be said. Nil is never false and never true. Nil only indicates that nothing is known. In this circumstance, using the so-called nil-inferencing of the open-world programming paradigm saved us from an error [5].

The philosopher Ludwig Wittgenstein wrote, "Whereof one cannot speak, thereof one must be silent." Open-world programmers would agree. In the case of programmers who deal with classifications, nil inferencing is particularly important insofar as we are constantly creating classes for which our knowledge is limited. We do not want to assert that an inference is false, just because we did not have all the information needed to establish its truth. It's often better to say that a conclusion has a nil value and to wait for more data to clarify the situation. [Glossary Abstraction, Encapsulation, Polymorphism, Reflection]

Section 5.6. A few software tools for traversing triplestores and classifications

The taxonomy.xml file is available at no cost and contains a curated Classification of Life, in an annotated XML format. The file is currently more than 5 Gigabytes in length, but with a little effort, novice programmers can use this file determine the ascending lineage of any organism or construct a graphic representation of the branched descendants of any class of organisms. In this section, we will be providing short scripts and code snippets.

Non-programmers can skip this last section of the chapter, without losing any of the book's narrative message.

Taxonomy.xml can be downloaded from the EBI (European Bioinformatics Institute) web site. XML files are nice to have because they are readable by humans, and because they can be parsed, by computer, into categories of information. When you read a few hundred lines from an XML file, you can quickly learn how the records are organized, and how the data contained in one record might be related to the data contained in other records.

A typical line from the XML file is shown here, for the "Cellvibrio":

```
<taxon scientificName="Cellvibrio" taxId="10"
 parentTaxId="1706371"
rank="genus" hidden="false" taxonomicDivision="PRO"
 geneticCode="11">
```

The line of XML code tells us that Cellvibrio is a genus, meaning that it will contain species. Cellvibrio is assigned a taxonomy identification number, "10" and we are informed that the taxonomy id number of its parent class is "1706371". We can expect that every species and class of organism included in the taxonomy will be similarly annotated. Knowing the identification number of every organism included in the taxonomy, along with the identification number of its parent, we can climb up or down the ancestral lineage of any organism, and we can determine the phylogenetic relationship among any list of organisms included in the taxonomy. We can also relate taxonomy records with those of any other data set that utilizes the same identifiers, codes, class relationships, and descriptors. Hence, the taxonomy XML file has vast utility outside of its limited content.

The downside of XML files, particularly XML files that capture triples, is that semantic orthodoxy yields excessively large and verbose files that are unsuitable for rapid data retrieval and data analysis. The Romans expressed the situation well: "Obscurum per obscurius, ignotum per ignotius," roughly translated as "the explanation is more obscure than the thing it explains." When speed and memory are considerations, it is often wise to transform the data from the XML file into a very simple flat file, in which the data values in records are sequentially listed in rows, with each data value separated from one another by a delimiter. [Glossary Flat-file]

We will be using the Perl programming language in the examples below. Perl is a free, readily available, and open-source programming language that can be used on most operating systems. Perl is popular among part-time programmers because short programs known as scripts are easy to write and because there is a large base of users that have added functionality to the language over the years and who provide support to new programmers through a variety of internet-based resources [6].

The following Perl script reduces the enormous taxonomy.xml file (exceeding 5 Gigabytes in length) to a simple flat file that lists a triple for each included organism.

The triple consists of the name of the organisms, its id number, and the id number of its parent class. Believe it or not, this information is all that you will ever need to reconstruct a hierarchical classification and to construct all of the lineage lists and graphic representations of class hierarchies that appear throughout the book.

```perl
open(TAXO,"taxonomy.xml");
open(OUT,">taxonomy.out");
$line = " ";
print OUT "root\|1\|0\|\n";
print "root\|1\|0\|\n";
while ($line ne "")
   {
   $line = <TAXO>;
   if ($line =~ /^\<taxon scientificName\=\"([^\"]+)\"/)
      {
      $name = $1;
      if ($name =~ /[^ ]+ [^ ]+/)
         {
         $name = $&;
         next if (exists($ok{$name}));
         $ok{$name} = " ";
         }
      if ($line =~ / taxId\=\"([^\"]+)\"/)
         {
         $id = $1;
         if ($line =~ / parentTaxId\=\"([^\"]+)\"/)
            {
            $parentid = $1;
            print OUT "$name\|$id\|$parentid\n";
            }
         }
      }
   }
exit;
```

We won't go into details of how this script works. Programmers should have no trouble understanding the code, and may choose to rewrite this script in their preferred language. The output of the script is the taxonomy.out file, a very simple triplestore that exceeds 27 megabytes in length (Fig. 5.4).

Each record of the triplestore occupies one line of the output file and has the following general format:

```
organism name|taxonomy id of organism|taxonomy id of the parent
   organism
```

We can do an awful lot with this simple and short condensation of the taxonomy.xml file. Here follows a Perl script that parses through the taxonomy.out file to produce 4 SDBM files.

```
root|1|0|
Bacteria|2|131567
Azorhizobium|6|335928
Azorhizobium caulinodans|7|6
Buchnera aphidicola|9|32199
Cellvibrio|10|1706371
Cellulomonas gilvus|11|1707
Dictyoglomus|13|203488
Dictyoglomus thermophilum|14|13
Methylophilus|16|32011
Methylophilus methylotrophus|17|16
Pelobacter|18|213421
Syntrophotalea carbinolica|19|2812025
Phenylobacterium|20|76892
Phenylobacterium immobile|21|20
Shewanella|22|267890
Shewanella colwelliana|23|22
Shewanella putrefaciens|24|22
Shewanella hanedai|25|22
halophilic eubacterium|27|49928
Myxococcales|29|28221
Myxococcaceae|31|80811
Myxococcus|32|31
Myxococcus fulvus|33|32
Myxococcus xanthus|34|32
```

FIG. 5.4 The first output screen of the taxonomy.out file, consisting of a list of all of the organisms included in the large taxonomy.xml file, along with the id of the organism and the id of the parent class of the organism.

Each of these SDBM files is a persistent database, the entries of which are permanently available to any subsequently written Perl script, without necessitating a line-by-line parse through the 27+ Megabyte taxonomy.out the file from which they were extracted. We will use Perl commands to create SDBM files containing the relationships among parent classes, child classes, and identification (id) numbers. In this manner, if we know the name of a class, we can instantly determine its parent class. If we know the name of a parent class, we can instantly determine its child classes. If we have the name of a class, we can instantly determine its identification number. If we have an identification number, we can instantly determine the name of the class to which it applies. [Glossary SDBM]

```
use Fcntl; use SDBM_File;
open(TAXO, "taxonomy.out");
tie%parent_children, "SDBM_File", 'parent', O_RDWR|O_CREAT|O_EXCL,
  0644;
tie%child_parent, "SDBM_File", 'child', O_RDWR|O_CREAT|O_EXCL,
  0644;
```

```
tie%name_id, "SDBM_File", 'name', O_RDWR|O_CREAT|O_EXCL, 0644;
tie%id_name, "SDBM_File", 'id', O_RDWR|O_CREAT|O_EXCL, 0644;
$line = " ";
while ($line ne "")
   {
   $line = <TAXO>;
   $line =~ s/\n//o;
   @linearray = split(/\|/,$line);
   next if (exists($name_id{$linearray[0]}));
   if (exists($parent_children{$linearray[2]}))
      {
      $_ = $parent_children{$linearray[2]};
      next if (tr/|// > 20);
      $parent_children{$linearray[2]} = $parent_children{$linearray
[2]} . "\|" . $linearray[1];
      }
   else
      {
      $parent_children{$linearray[2]} = $linearray[1];
      }
   $child_parent{$linearray[1]} = $linearray[2];
   $name_id{$linearray[0]} = $linearray[1];
   $id_name{$linearray[1]} = $linearray[0];
   }
exit;
```

This file produces 4 persistent databases, in 8 external files:

parent.pag, parent.dir
child.pag, child.dir
id.dir, id.pag
name.pag, name.dir

Here is what these files contain:

The "parent" database file contains the identifiers of the child classes for each parent class identifier.
The "child" database file contains the identifier of the parent class of each child class identifier.
The "id" database file contains the name of a species or class corresponding to each species or class identifier.
The "name" database file contains the taxonomic identifier for each named species or class).

An equivalent program can be written for virtually any modern programming language. In one of my previous books, I listed similar scripts, that also produced persistent database files, with equivalent versions coded in Perl, Python, and Ruby [7].

When we have our database files prepared, a simple Perl script (taxmlback.pl) can compute the ascending lineage of any species or class of organism included in the European Bioinformatics Institute's Taxonomy file (taxonomy.xml). For this script, we use the SDBM persistent database files described in the Glossary entry "Taxonomy.xml file".

```
use Fcntl;
use SDBM_File;
print "What organism would you like to find?\n";
$lookup = <STDIN>;
$lookup =~ s/\n//;
tie%child_parent, "SDBM_File", 'child', O_RDWR, 0644;
tie%name_id, "SDBM_File", 'name', O_RDWR, 0644;
tie%id_name, "SDBM_File", 'id', O_RDWR, 0644;
for (0..40)
    {
    print $lookup . "\n";
    $organism_id = $name_id{$lookup};
    $parent_id = $child_parent{$organism_id};
    $lookup = $id_name{$parent_id};
    exit if ($lookup eq "root");
    }
exit;
```

Let's look at an example of the output, searching on the blue crab, *Callinectes sapidus*: (Fig. 5.5).

We can also write a simple Perl script (child_list.pl) that will provide us the names of the child classes (i.e., direct subclasses) of any class.

```
use Fcntl; use SDBM_File;
print "For What parent organism would you like a list of children?
 \n";
$lookup = <STDIN>; chomp($lookup); print "Subclasses are...\n";
tie%parent_children, "SDBM_File", 'parent', O_RDWR, 0644;
tie%id_name, "SDBM_File", 'id', O_RDWR, 0644;
tie%name_id, "SDBM_File", 'name', O_RDWR, 0644;
if (exists($name_id{$lookup}))
    {
    $organism_id = $name_id{$lookup};
    if (exists($parent_children{$organism_id}))
        {
```

```
Callinectes sapidus
Callinectes
Portunidae
Portunoidea
Heterotremata
Eubrachyura
Brachyura
Pleocyemata
Decapoda
Eucarida
Eumalacostraca
Malacostraca
Multicrustacea
Crustacea
Pancrustacea
Mandibulata
Arthropoda
Panarthropoda
Ecdysozoa
Protostomia
Bilateria
Eumetazoa
Metazoa
Opisthokonta
Eukaryota
cellular organisms
```

FIG. 5.5 Output of the taxmlback.pl script for *Callinectes sapidus* (the blue crab).

```
@child_id_array = split(/\|/, $parent_children
  {$organism_id});
foreach $id_number (@child_id_array)
    {
    print "$id_name{$id_number}\n";
    }
  }
}
exit;
```

When we input "Eukaryota", we get the following output:

```
c:\ftp\pl>children_list.pl
For What parent organism would you like a list of children?
Eukaryota
Subclasses are...
Rhodophyta
Cryptophyta
Heterolobosea
Viridiplantae
Opisthokonta
```

```
Alveolata
Stramenopiles
Euglenozoa
Glaucocystophyceae
unclassified eukaryotes
Malawimonadidae
Katablepharidophyta
Rhizaria
Apusozoa
Amoebozoa
Jakobida
Breviatea
Hemimastigophora
Rhodelphea
Haptista
CRuMs
Metamonada
```

The hierarchical graphs of the descendant branches of parent classes appearing as figures through much of Chapter 6 were produced by versions of the following script, modified to display multiple generations of subclasses.

```perl
open (TEXT, "parent_children.txt");
open (OUT, ">taxo_dot.dot");
print OUT "digraph G \{\n";
print OUT "size\=\"10\,10\"\n";
print OUT "ranksep\=\"4\.40\"\n";
print OUT "dpi \= \"1200\"\n";
$line = " ";
while ($line ne "")
   {
   $line = <TEXT>;
   $line =~ s/\n//o;
   if ($line =~ / /)
      {
      $parent = $`;
      next if ($parent =~ / /);
      $child{$parent} = $';
      }
   }
print "Enter a class whose descendants you would like to find\n";
$lookup = <STDIN>;
$lookup =~ s/\n//;
```

```
die "sorry no match" unless (exists($child{$lookup}));
print OUT "$lookup \[label\=\"$lookup\"\]\n";
print OUT "node \[style\=filled color\=lightgray\]\n";
@childarray = split(/\, /, $child{$lookup});
foreach $thing (@childarray)
   {
   print OUT "$lookup -> $thing\n" unless ($thing =~ / [a-z]*/);
   #this gets rid of any multi-word classes, which lack formal
    assignment
   }
print OUT "\}";
close OUT;
$lookup = $lookup . "\.png";
system("twopi -Tpng taxo_dot.dot -o $lookup");
system($lookup);
exit;
```

The script, when executed from the command line, prompts us to enter the name of a class of organisms. in this case, we have entered "Platyhelminthes", the formal name for flatworms, as shown.

```
c:\ftp\taxonomy>taxo_1dot.pl
Enter a class whose descendants you would like to find
Platyhelminthes
```

The final output of the Perl script is an ancestry graph, as shown here (Fig. 5.6):

How did the Perl script produce the graphic display? This Perl script prepares a specialized script prepared in the GraphViz scripting language (taxo_dot.dot). The GraphViz script contains information that can be used by a graphing utility known as twopi. Twopi is bundled into the GraphViz software package that is available at no cost. The Perl script calls the twopi utility (twopi.exe) that interprets and executes the taxo_dot.dot script. [Glossary GraphViz]

Here is the taxo_dot.dot script created at runtime by the Perl script taxo_1dot.pl

```
digraph G {
size="10,10"
ranksep="4.40"
dpi = "1200"
Platyhelminthes [label="Platyhelminthes"]
node [style=filled color=lightgray]
Platyhelminthes -> Trematoda
Platyhelminthes -> Cestoda
Platyhelminthes -> Monogenea
Platyhelminthes -> Catenulida
```

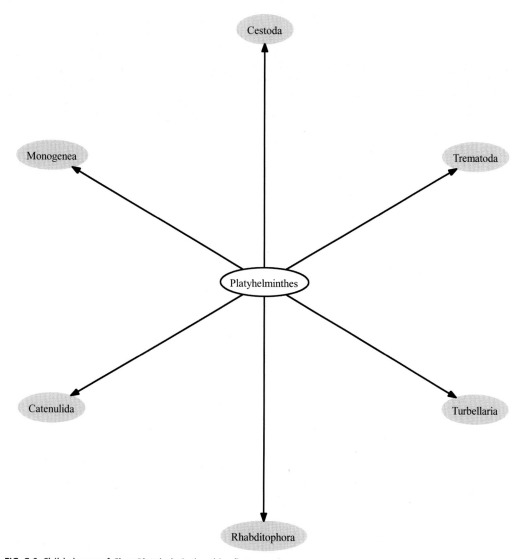

FIG. 5.6 Child classes of Class Platyhelminthes (the flatworms).

```
Platyhelminthes -> Rhabditophora
Platyhelminthes -> Turbellaria
}
```

This is an example of metaprogramming, in which one program creates another program. In this case, our taxo_1dot.pl program used the in which one program creates a program in another language and makes an external call to the interpreter (for the other language) to execute the newly created program.

This may seem like a complex algorithm, requiring multiple external files and the installation of two different programming languages. Nonetheless, the output is obtained with a relatively small number of lines of code. With a little tweaking, novice programmers can create multi-level hierarchies for any parent class.

Using Triplestores

A triplestore is simply a data file or a database composed entirely of triples (statements consisting of an item identifier plus the metadata describing the item plus an item of data. The triples in a triple store need not be saved in any particular order, and any triplestore can be merged with any other triplestore; the basic semantic meaning of the contained triples is unaffected.

Here is the triplestore, as the plain-text file, triple.txt:

```
9f0ebdf2^^object_name^^Class
9f0ebdf2^^property^^subclass_of
9f0ebdf2^^property^^property
9f0ebdf2^^property^^definition
9f0ebdf2^^property^^object_name
9f0ebdf2^^property^^instance_of
9f0ebdf2^^subclass_of^^Class
9f0ebdf2^^instance_of^^Class
701cb7ed^^object_name^^Property
701cb7ed^^subclass_of^^Class
701cb7ed^^definition^^^^the metadata class
77cb79d5^^object_name^^instance_of
77cb79d5^^instance_of^^Property
77cb79d5^^definition^^the name of the class to which the object is
 an instance
a03fbc3b^^object_name^^object_name
a03fbc3b^^instance_of^^Property
a03fbc3b^^definition^^word equivalent of its predicate identifying
 sequence
de0e5aa1^^object_name^^subclass_of
de0e5aa1^^instance_of^^Property
de0e5aa1^^definition^^the name of the parent class of the referred
 object
4b675067^^object_name^^property
4b675067^^instance_of^^Property
4b675067^^definition^^an identifier a for class property
c37529c5^^object_name^^definition
c37529c5^^instance_of^^Property
c37529c5^^definition^^the meaning of the referred object
```

```
a29c59c0^^object_name^^dob
a29c59c0^^instance_of^^Property
a29c59c0^^definition^^date of birth, as Day, Month, Year
a34a1e35^^object_name^^glucose_at_time
a34a1e35^^instance_of^^Property
a34a1e35^^definition^^glucose level in mg/Dl at time drawn (GMT)
03cc6948^^object_name^^Organism
03cc6948^^subclass_of^^Class
7d7ff42b^^object_name^^Hominidae
7d7ff42b^^subclass_of^^Organism
7d7ff42b^^property^^dob
a0ce8ec6^^object_name^^Homo
a0ce8ec6^^subclass_of^^Hominidae
a0ce8ec6^^property^^glucose_at_time
a1648579^^object_name^^Homo sapiens
a1648579^^subclass_of^^Homo
98495efc^^object_name^^Andy Muzeack
98495efc^^instance_of^^Homo sapiens
98495efc^^dob^^1 January, 2001
98495efc^^glucose_at_time^^87, 02-12-2014 17:33:09
```

[Glossary Plain-text]

A perusal of the triples provides the following observations:

1. Each triple consists of three-character sequences, separated by some convenient characters (a double-caret, in this case). The first character sequence is the object identifier. The second is the metadata and the third is the value. For example:

```
7d7ff42b^^subclass_of^^Organism
```

The individual parts of the triple are:

```
7d7ff42b is the identifier
subclass_of is the metadata
Organism is the data
```

Our triples are expressed in a format different from RDF, or Notation3, or Turtle. Do we care? No. We know that with a few lines of code, we could convert our triplestore into an alternate format we might prefer. Furthermore, our triplestore could be converted into a spreadsheet, in which the identifiers are record keys, the metadata are column headings, and the data occupy cells. We could also port our triples into a database if we so desired.

2. Using triples, we have defined various classes and properties. For example:

```
03cc6948^^object_name^^Organism
03cc6948^^subclass_of^^Class
```

With one triple, we create a new object, with the name Organism, and we associate it with a unique identifier (03 cc6948). With another triple, we establish that the Organism object is a class. Because Organism is a subclass of Class, it will inherit all of the properties of its parent class.

Let's skip down to the bottom of the file:

```
98495efc^^object_name^^Andy Muzeack
98495efc^^instance_of^^Homo sapiens
98495efc^^dob^^1 January, 2001
98495efc^^glucose_at_time^^87, 02-12-2014 17:33:09
```

Here we create a few triples that provide information about a person named Andy Muzeak. We learn, from the next triple that Andy Muzeack is an instance of Class *Homo sapiens*. As such, we infer that Andy Muzeack inherits all the properties contained in class Homo (the parent class of Class *Homo Sapiens*) and all the ancestors of Class Homo, leading to the top, or root ancestor, class Class. We learn that Andy Muzeack has a "dob" of January 1, 2001. By ascending the list of triples, we learn that "dob" is a property, with a unique identifier (a29c59c0), and a definition, "date of birth, as Day, Month, Year." Finally, we learn that Andy Muzeack has a glucose_at_time of "87, 02-12-2014 17:33:09." Elsewhere in the triplestore, we find that the "glucose_at_time" metadata is defined as the glucose level in mg/Dl at time drawn, in Greenwich Mean Time.

If we wished, we could simply concatenate our triplestore with other triplestores that contain triples relevant to Andy Muzeack. It would not make any difference how the triples are ordered. If Andy Muzeack's identifier is reconcilable, the metadata is defined, and each triple is assigned to a class, then we will be able to fully understand and analyze the data held in the triplestore.

Of course, when we have millions and billions of triples, we could not perform our analyses by reading through the file. We would need scripts and/or a database application.

At this time, there are many software implementations, both open source and commercial, for triplestore databases. Readers with facility with the MUMPS language may choose to investigate the value of using native MUMPS as a triplestore database. MUMPS, also known as the M programming language, is one of a small handful of ANSI-standard (American National Standard Institute) languages. It was developed in the 1960s and is still in use, primarily in hospital information systems and large production facilities. Versions of MUMPS are available as open-source, free distributions [8,9]. The MUMPS installation process can be challenging for those who are unfamiliar with the MUMPS environment.

Stalwarts may find that MUMPS has native features that render it suitable for storing triples and exploring their relationships [10].

If we don't want to deploy triplestore databases, we can use any standard programming language to retrieve information from triplestores that are prepared as simple lists of triples. Let's look at a very simple Ruby script that will look at any given list of triples and provide all of the information about all of the uniquely identified objects in the triples.

The Ruby script hashofhash.rb takes 6 triples and tells us everything we may want to know about the identified objects in our triplestore:

```ruby
class NestedHash < Hash
  def initialize
    blk = lambda {|h,k| h[k] = NestedHash.new(&blk)}
    super(&blk)
  end
end

class Hash
  def Hash.new_nested_hash
    Hash.new{|h,k| h[k]=Hash.new(&h.default_proc) }
  end
end

a = Hash.new_nested_hash

a["58302256"]["has_a"]["circle"]=""
a["92164588"]["has_a"]["square"]=""
a["58302256"]["has_a"]["triangle"]=""
a["92164588"]["has_a"]["circle"]=""
a["58302256"]["is_a"]["shape"]=""
a["92164588"]["is_a"]["shape"]=""

puts "unique identifiers are: ";
puts a.keys * ", ";puts;
puts "metadata for 58302256 are: ";
puts a["58302256"].keys * ", "; puts;
puts "has_a data for 58302256 are: ";
puts a["58302256"]["has_a"].keys * ", ";
puts;
a.keys.each do
  |x|
  print x.to_s; print "->"; puts a[x]["has_a"].keys * ","
end
puts;
a.keys.each do
```

```
   |x|
   a[x].keys.each do
     |y|
     print x.to_s ;print " "; print y.to_s; print "->"; puts a[x][y].
     keys * ","
   end
 end
 exit
```

Ruby creates nested hashes of the following triples:

```
["58302256"],["has_a"],["circle"]
["92164588"],["has_a"],["square"]
["58302256"],["has_a"],["triangle"]
["92164588"],["has_a"],["circle"]
["58302256"],["is_a"],["shape"]
["92164588"],["is_a"],["shape"]
```

In a nested hash, each consecutive element of the triple is a key to what precedes it in the triple. When we have a nested hash, we can collect all of the keys to the triple that relate to the triple's identifier number (i.e., the identified object of the assertion). The output of the hashof hash.rb script is provided as a screenshot (Fig. 5.7).

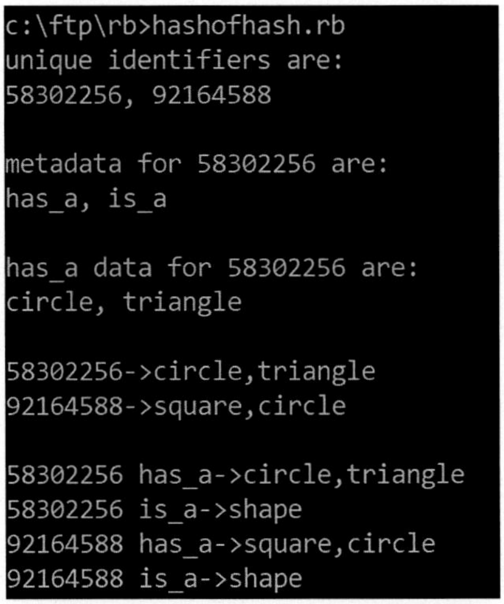

FIG. 5.7 The output of hashofhash.rb script.

Everything we need to know about the triples and the triplestore can be retrieved with a few lines of code. In the hashofhash.rb screen, we can produce the list of all the unique identifiers in the triplestore. For any and all identifiers, we can determine the scope of their metadata terms. For any and all unique identifiers, we can determine the scope of their data.

When the triplestore contains class relationships for identified objects, we can trace the lineage of those objects. Let's look at a few Perl scripts that explore triple.txt files, the short triplestore that we created earlier.

This simple Perl script, parent.pl, will tell us the parent class of any class entered on the command line.

```perl
open(TEXT, "triple.txt");
$line = " ";
$subclass = "subclass_of";
$object_name = "object_name";
$class_identifier = "";
$new_parent_identifier = $ARGV[0];
$class = $ARGV[0];
while ($line ne "")
   {
   $line = <TEXT>;
   $line =~ s/\n//o;
   @three = split(/\^\^/, $line) if ($line ne "");
   $triple{$three[0]}{$three[1]}{$three[2]} = "";
   }
for $identifier (keys %triple)
   {
   if (exists($triple{$identifier}{$object_name}{$class}))
      {
      $class_identifier = $identifier;
      last;
      }
   }
@parent_array = keys (%{$triple{$class_identifier}{$subclass}});
print "$class is a subclass of $parent_array[0]";
exit;
```

Here is the output of parent.pl, for three different input classes.

```
c:\ftp>parent.pl "Homo sapiens"
Homo sapiens is a subclass of Homo
c:\ftp>parent.pl "Homo"
Homo is a subclass of Hominidae
c:\ftp>parent.pl "Property"
Property is a subclass of Class
```

Here is a short Perl script, class_prop.pl, that traverses the triple.txt file, and lists the contained properties.

```perl
open(TEXT, "triple.txt");
$line = " ";
```

```
$object_name = "object_name";
$class_identifier = "";
$instance = "instance_of";
$property_class = "Property";
$property = "property";
while ($line ne "")
   {
   $line = <TEXT>;
   $line =~ s/\n//o;
   @three = split(/\^\^/, $line) if ($line ne "");
   $triple{$three[0]}{$three[1]}{$three[2]} = "";
   }
for $identifier (keys %triple)
   {
   if (exists($triple{$identifier}{$instance}{$property_class}))
      {
      @property_names = keys (%{$triple{$identifier}
      {$object_name}});
      print "$property_names[0] is an instance of Class Property\n";
      }
   }
exit;
```

Here is the output of the class_prop.pl script:

```
subclass_of is an instance of Class Property
instance_of is an instance of Class Property
the definition is an instance of Class Property
object_name is an instance of Class Property
glucose_at_time is an instance of Class Property
property is an instance of Class Property
dob is an instance of Class Property
```

We have shown just a few ways of tracing the relationships among classes. Any classification that provides unique identifiers for objects and that indicates the class and the parent class of every object can be analyzed using similar programming techniques.

Glossary

Abstraction Generally, an abstraction is something that has no physical existence, but which can be applied to physical objects. For example, the number "3" is a pure abstraction. Nonetheless, it can be applied to both abstract and physical objects. For example, "3 + 1 = 4" describes an abstract relationship among abstractions; while "3 monkeys" describes something real, establishing a physical relationship between "3" and "monkeys".

In the context of object-oriented programming, abstraction is a technique whereby a method is available to many different types of objects, but for which the specific characteristics of the object receiving the method may be used to return a result that is suited to the object. Abstraction, along with polymorphism, encapsulation, and inheritance, are fundamental and essential features of object-oriented programming languages.

Associative array An associative Array (also known as hash table, map, symbol table, dictionary, or dictionary array) is a data structure consisting of an unordered list of key/value data pairs. The proliferation of synonyms for "associative array" suggests that these data structures have great utility. Associative arrays are used in Perl, Python, Ruby, and most modern programming languages. Here is an example in which an associative array (i.e., a member of Class Hash) is created in Ruby.

```
my_hash = Hash.new
my_hash["C05"] = "Albumin"
my_hash["C39"] = "Choline"
my_hash.each {|key,value| STDOUT.print(key, " - ", value, "\n")}
exit
```

The first line of the script creates a new associative array, named my_hash. The next two lines create two key/value elements for the associative array (C05/Albumin and C39/Choline). The next line instructs ruby to print out the elements in the my_hash associative array. Here is the output of the short ruby script.

```
Output:
C05 --- Albumin
C39 --- Choline
```

Class-oriented programming versus object-oriented programming Class-oriented programming, also known as Class-based programming is a style of object-oriented programming in which there are methods assigned to classes, and these methods are inherited by every instance of the class, and by every instance of every descendant subclass of the class. It differs in style from traditional object-oriented programming, which relies heavily on methods written for particular object instances.

Class-oriented programming languages embody a specified representation of the real world in which all objects reside within defined classes having methods that apply to all of the members of the class. Powerful scripts can be written with just a few short lines of code, using class-oriented programming languages, by invoking the names of methods inherited by data objects assigned to classes.

Ruby and Python are examples of two object-oriented languages that could support a pure class-oriented approach to programming if the programmer deliberately assigns all objects and methods to a hierarchical class system. Of the two languages, Ruby seems to be better suited to a pure class-oriented approach, as it comes with a built-in class system that is intended to accommodate additional subclassing. Nonetheless, both languages give programmers the flexibility to either permit or circumvent a purely class-oriented approach. Perhaps Smalltalk is the language that comes closest to being a purely class-oriented language [11].

Compositional classes The objects in a compositional class are components of the objects of the parent class. This means that the objects of a class are related to the parent class by the "part_of" relationship. This kind of class hierarchy differs from the kind of class hierarchy described in this book for classifications, which are based on an "is_a" relationship between a child class and parent class.

Compositional classes are permissible in ontologies and have been employed very successfully by computer programmers when dealing with models of constructed systems that are controlled by the programmer (e.g., computer games, inventories, etc.) [3]. Such systems have no natural order, and the imperatives of the programmer are directed toward software interfaces, modularity, reusability, and other features that have no bearing on natural classifications. For classifications that capture the order of natural objects (e.g., living organisms, atoms, forces), compositional programming techniques are often inappropriate but may have utility when designing ontologies that interact with traditional classifications.

Data modeling Refers to the intellectual process of finding a mathematical expression (often, an equation) or a symbolic expression that describes or summarizes a system or a collection of data. In many cases, mathematical models describe how different variables will change with one another. Data models simplify the systems they describe, and many of the greatest milestones in the physical sciences have arisen from a bit of data modeling supplemented by scientific genius (e.g., Newton's laws of mechanics and optics, Kepler's laws of planetary orbits) [12].

Encapsulation The concept, used in object-oriented programming, that a data object contains its associated data. Encapsulation is tightly linked to the concept of introspection, the process of accessing the data encapsulated within a data object. Encapsulation, Inheritance, and Polymorphism are available features of all object-oriented languages.

Flat-file A file consisting of data records, usually with one record per file line. The individual fields of the record are typically separated by a marking character, such as "|" or " ". Flat files are usually plain-text (i.e., composed of the ASCII characters displayed by the keys of a standard keyboard).

GraphViz GraphViz is a free, open-source, an application that produces graphic representations of hierarchical structures that are described in the GraphViz scripting language. GraphViz is free software and is available at:

```
http://www.graphviz.org
```

GraphViz has sub-applications:dot, fdp, twopi, neato, and circo. The twopi application, which we use here, creates graphs that have a radial layout. Because the GraphViz language is designed with the same goal as RDF Schema (i.e., to describe the relationships among hierarchical classes of the object). Hence, it is always possible to directly translate an RDF Schema into the GraphViz language. This is a type of poor-man's metaprogramming (using a programming language to generate another program). When an RDF Schema has been translated into the GraphViz language, the GraphViz software can display the class structure as a graph.

Inheritance polymorphism In object-oriented programming, polymorphism is the condition in which the action of a named method is determined by an object's class hierarchy.

When you send a method to an object, the method may not always be included in the method definitions of the object's class. When this happens in an object-oriented programming environment, such as Ruby, the ancestral classes of the object are searched in ascending order, and Ruby dispatches the first method it finds in an ancestor class that has the same name as the sender method, assuming that the arguments for the method are consistent with the arguments required by the ancestor method. Higher classes may have a method of the same name, that has some different function. If that is the case, the method is polymorphic for the methods of the same name that happen to appear in the class definitions of the ancestors of the class.

Mixins Mixins are a technique for including modules within a class to extend the functionality of the class. The power of the mixin is that methods can be inserted into unrelated classes. In practice, mixin methods are generally useful functions that are not related to the fundamental and defining methods for a class. A good way to think about non-defining methods included in a class is that "mixins" are to object-oriented programming languages what "properties" are to classifications. A single property may apply to multiple, unrelated classes. The mixin technique is available in both Python and Ruby.

Module In programming languages, a module is a section of invoked code that contains methods and constants assigned to a namespace (the declared module name). Modules provide a convenient way for classes to acquire methods that add to the functionality of a class, without adding class methods that must be restricted to the class, and without providing functionality that changes the class definition.

Well-designed object-oriented programming languages can always tell us the name of any modules that have been included in a class. In the Ruby programming language, we can send the included_modules method to the name of any class, and Ruby will list the modules contained in the class. In the example shown here, we send Ruby's "included_modules" introspection method to Class String.

```
> String.included_modules => [Comparable, Kernel]
```

The output tells us that Comparable and Kernel are modules included with Class String

There are several differences between a class and a module, but the most relevant difference, for classification modelers, is that modules cannot create instance objects. Classes always include a method by which they can create new instance objects of their class.

Object-oriented programming language Although the purpose of this book is not to teach programming techniques, it is worth noting that all of the general features of an object-oriented programming language are found in classifications and ontologies. In particular, all objects are assigned a class; classes have parent classes, and the class-specific properties and behaviors of ancestral classes (i.e., the class methods) are inherited by all of the classes in its descendant lineage. Hence, data objects assigned to formal classifications or ontologies can be seamlessly adapted to an object-oriented framework [5,12].

Plain-text Plain-text refers to character strings or files that are composed of the characters accessible to a typewriter keyboard. These files typically have a ".txt" suffix to their names. Plain-text files are sometimes referred to as 7-bit ascii files because all of the familiar keyboard characters have ASCII values under 128 (i.e., can be designated in binary with, just seven 0 s and 1 s). Most plain-text files exclude 7-bit ascii symbols that do not code for familiar keyboard characters. Occasional plain-text files will contain ascii characters above 7 bits (i.e., characters from 128 to 255) that represent characters that are printable on computer monitors, such as accented letters.

Polymorphism In the realm of object-oriented programming, polymorphism is one of the constitutive properties of an object-oriented language (along with inheritance, encapsulation, and abstraction). Methods sent to object receivers have a response determined by the class of the receiving object. Hence, different objects, from different classes, receiving a call to a method of the same name, will respond differently. For example, suppose you have a method named "divide" and you send the method (i.e., issue a command to execute the method) to an object of Class Bacteria and an object of Class Numerics. The Bacteria, receiving the divide method, will try to execute by looking for the "divide" method somewhere in its class lineage. Being a bacteria, the "divide" method may involve making a copy of the bacteria (i.e., reproducing) and incrementing the number of bacteria in the population. The numeric object, receiving the "divide" method, will look for the "divide" method in its class lineage and will probably find some method that provides instructions for arithmetic division. Hence, the behavior of the class object, to a received method, will be appropriate for the class of the object.

In the realm of biology, polymorphism refers to genetic polymorphism, indicating that variants of a gene occurring in the general population. Polymorphism is usually restricted to variants that occur with an occurrence frequency of 1% or higher. If a variant occurs at a frequency of less than 1%, it is considered to be sufficiently uncommon that it is probably not steadily maintained within the general population. The commonly occurring polymorphisms are assumed to be benign or, at worst, of low pathogenicity; the reasoning being that natural selection would eliminate frequently occurring polymorphisms that reduced the fitness of individuals within the population. Nonetheless, different polymorphisms may code for proteins with at least some differences in functionality.

Reflection A programming technique wherein a computer program will modify itself, at run-time, based on the information it acquires through introspection. For example, a computer program may iterate over a collection of data objects, examining the self-descriptive information for each object in the collection (i.e., object introspection). If the information indicates that the data object belongs to a particular class of objects, then the program may call a method appropriate for the class. The program executes in a manner determined by descriptive information obtained during run-time; metaphorically reflecting upon the purpose of its computational task.

Ruby gem In Ruby, gems are external modules available for download from an internet server. The Ruby gem installation module comes bundled in Ruby distribution packages. Gem installations are simple, usually consisting of commands in the form, "gem install name_of_gem" invoked at the system prompt. Ruby will automatically fetch the gem from its recorded location somewhere on the Internet. After a gem has been installed, scripts access the gem with a "require" statement, equivalent to an "import" statement in Python or the "use" statement in Perl.

Ruby standard library In addition to the built-in Ruby class library, the Ruby interpreter is distributed with a standard library. The standard library consists of a suite of programs that can be "required" into your own Ruby scripts (i.e., called from your own Ruby script by invoking "require" followed by the name of the program).

For example, the Date standard library could be required into a script with the following line of code:

```
require 'date'
```

Anyone using a current version of Ruby is likely to have the same libraries included in their installation. Hence, scripts that use programs from the Standard Library are likely to be portable among users.

SDBM Abbreviation: Simple Database Module. Collections of key/value pairs are commonly used in computer programs to retrieve information about objects of interest. For example, I might have a set of millions of records, with each record containing the date of birth and the name of an individual, along with lots of other information. If I am particularly interested in knowing the date of birth of any particular individual, then I might want to create a data object containing all of the key/value pairs corresponding to the individuals (i.e., the keys) and their respective dates of birth (i.e., the values). I could then quickly retrieve any information I needed from the object containing the key/value pairs. The drawback is that I would need to reconstruct the object containing the key/value every time I ran the program. This might take a bit of time if the original data set is large. The SDBM module provides programmers with a way to create the data object containing key/value pairs that persist in computer memory, as a file, after the program has stopped executing. Whenever the programmer needs to access any of the key/value pairs, she simply opens the external SDBM file, bypassing the need to open and parse the original, large, data record file. From the SDBM file, she can quickly retrieve any or all of the key/value pairs that she needs to find.

Scope operator A class can create a new constant. Constants are never declared within methods because the scope of a class constant extends to all the methods of the class. Different classes can declare constants that have the same name. Ruby provides the scope operator (::) to reach into classes and pull out class constants. The scope operator is also be used to call module methods without including the module.

Examples:

```
irb>Math.constants => ["PI", "E"]
irb>Math::PI => 3.14159265358979
irb> Math::E => 2.71828182845905
irb>Math::sqrt(4) => 2.0
```

Ruby also lets us call Module methods and constants using the scope operator. This assures us that even if multiple modules are included in the script, and they all have a method of the same name, Ruby will use the method in the namespace of the scoped module.

```
module HelloModule
   def say_hello
      puts "hello"
   end
end
include HelloModule
HelloModule::say_hello
exit
```

In this case, the scope operator command consists of the name of the module (HelloModule representing the namespace of the module) followed by a double colon followed by the method name.

References

[1] Ali J. Mastering PHP design patterns. PACKT books. Birmingham, England: Packt Publishing Limited; 2016.

[2] Booch G. Object-oriented analysis and design with applications. 2nd ed. Boston, MA: Addison-Wesley; 1994.

[3] Gamma E, Helm R, Johnson R, Vlissides J. Design patterns: elements of reusable object-oriented software. Boston, MA: Addison-Wesley; 1995.

[4] Berman JJ. Principles of big data: preparing, sharing, and analyzing complex information. Waltham, MA: Morgan Kaufmann; 2013.

[5] Berman JJ. Ruby programming for medicine and biology. Sudbury, MA: Jones and Bartlett; 2008.

[6] Berman JJ. Perl programming for medicine and biology. Sudbury, MA: Jones and Bartlett; 2007.

[7] Berman JJ. Methods in medical informatics: fundamentals of healthcare programming in perl, python, and ruby. Boca Raton: Chapman and Hall; 2010.

[8] Anon. GT.M high end TP database engine: industrial strength NoSQL application development platform. Available from: http://sourceforge.net/projects/fis-gtm/; 2015. [Accessed 29 August 2015].

[9] Anon. MUMPS database and language. ANSI standard MUMPS. Available from: http://sourceforge.net/projects/mumps/files/; 2015. [Accessed 29 August 2015].

[10] Tweed R, James G. A universal NoSQL engine, using a tried and tested technology. Available from: http://www.mgateway.com/docs/; 2010. [Accessed 29 August 2015].

[11] Goldberg A, Robson D, Harrison MA. Smalltalk-80: the language and its implementation. Boston, MA: Addison-Wesley; 1983.

[12] Berman JJ. Data simplification: taming information with open source tools. Waltham, MA: Morgan Kaufmann; 2016.

6

The classification of life

Chapter outline

The biochemist knows his molecules have ancestors, while the paleontologist can only hope that his fossils left descendants.

Vincent Sarich [1]

Section 6.1. All creatures great and small

The Classification of Life, also known as the Classification of Living Organisms, and sometimes as the Tree of Life, is instantly recognizable, in any of its graphic forms. It was created through the labor of thousands of naturalists, working over the past two millennia. Throughout this long period, contributors have honed their skills through careful observations, debates, reviews, and, lately, through the introduction of new scientific methods (e.g., genome sequencing). It was all well worth the effort. It is only through classification that our living world makes any sense. It is through the Classification of Life that we have come to understand the history of life on earth, the movement of continents, the process of evolution, the embryologic and anatomic development of animals, the emergence and regulation of complex metabolic pathways, and the inherited molecular sequences that lead us to new drugs that are effective against the various classes of pathogenic organisms [2]. Scientists have collected an enormous amount of information about thousands of plants and animals, but without an understanding of how each organism fits into the Classification of Life, such information cannot lead to an understanding of our biological world that explains our past and predicts our future.

Classification Made Relevant. https://doi.org/10.1016/B978-0-323-91786-5.00008-2
Copyright © 2022 Elsevier Inc. All rights reserved.

How was the Classification of Life created? As discussed in "Section 2.4. A classification is an evolving hypothesis," all classifications arise from paradox. A natural classification, such as the Classification of Life, is intended to discover the existing classification that nature has created for us. However, to form the early rudiments of classification, the classification builder must begin with a settled worldview that presupposes knowledge of the major classes of organisms and their relationships to one another; knowledge that can only be attained after the classification has been completed. This is the central paradox of natural classifications. Because it is impossible to build a classification objectively without imposing upon it our own subjective biases and preconceptions, modern scientists have been encouraged to find a purely objective computational approach to classification.

Currently, molecular biologists are adept at determining the genome sequence of whole organisms. Imagine an experiment wherein you take DNA samples from every organism you encounter: bacterial colonies cultured from a river, unicellular non-bacterial organisms found in a pond, small multicellular organisms found in soil, crawling creatures dwelling under rocks, and so on. It would seem as though it would be a straight-forward project to group organisms based upon sequence similarity. An algorithm would compare the sequences of the different organisms and would assign organisms to species classes based on the similarities of their genome sequences. After genomically similar species classes have been established, the algorithm would begin to compare each of these classes against one another and group those classes based on their degree of genomic similarities; thus, finding the parent classes of the species classes. Once done, the computer would compare each parent class against all the other parent classes and group the most similar classes under one grandparent class. This approach would be repeated until there was only one root class sitting at the top of a pyramid of classes, with the species classes at the very bottom of the pyramid. In theory, one computer program, executing over a large dataset containing genome sequences for every earthly organism, could create a complete biological classification.

What would we learn from a classification produced by iterative comparisons of genome sequences among a dataset of organisms? We may think that we have created a useful classification, but we haven't really because we lack information about the organisms that are clustered together into classes. A cluster may be contaminated by organisms that share some of the same gene sequences, but are phylogenetically unrelated (i.e., the sequence similarities result from chance or convergence, but not by descent from a common ancestor). The sequences do not tell us much about the biological properties of specific organisms, and we cannot infer which biological properties characterize our newly created classes. We have no certain knowledge of whether the members of any given cluster of organisms can be characterized by any particular gene sequence (i.e., we do not know the characterizing gene sequences for classes of organisms). You do not know the genus or species names of the organisms included in the clusters, because we began our experiment without a presumptive taxonomy. Basically, we simply know what we knew before we started; that organisms have unique gene sequences that can be grouped by sequence similarity. We do not know whether the grouped organisms represent valid classes.

When we think a bit more deeply about the process of automatically computing a biological classification, we run up against a few points that should give us pause:

1. There are many possible sequence comparison algorithms available to computational biologists. Each will yield a different classification as its output. Those different classifications can't all be correct, can they?
2. We can be certain that our database will not contain sample DNA from every organism. We might expect our algorithm to produce a very different classification, depending on which organisms are included in our samples.
3. Algorithms designed to cluster items into classes and to put classes into a connected structure will always yield a classification. The certainty of a result informs us that fundamentally conflicting or anomalous data, that might inspire a savvy biologist to question the wisdom of proceeding with the computations, never stops the algorithm from completing its task. In other words, no matter what garbage is included in the original data, the algorithm will produce a classification, faulty though it may be.

A purely computational approach to classification is anathema to traditional taxonomists, who have long held that a species is a natural unit of biological life and that the nature of a species is revealed through the intellectual process of building a consistent taxonomy [3]. In practice, the taxonomist begins with a root object that embodies the fundamental features of every class and every species within the classification. In the case of the taxonomy of living organisms, this root object might be "the living cell". Once the root object is chosen, the taxonomists can begin to create broad subclasses containing properties that are inclusive for the class and exclusive of other classes (i.e., Class Prokaryota, which lack a nucleus, and Class Eukaryota, which have a nucleus). Then, based on observing the properties of the prokaryotes, she might define additional classes that include some organisms and exclude others. This goes on until every organism has a class, and every class is a subclass of the parent class, in a lineage that extends back to the root class. The root class, which contains every member of the classification, is the full embodiment of the classification (i.e., the top-class of the classification equals the classification). If this last assertion seems difficult to accept, let's think about the root class of the Classification of Life. In this case, the root is "cellular organisms." So far as we can tell, every living organism is a cellular organism, hence the root class contains the full collection of earthly organisms, extinct or extant.

When biologists build a classification in which each class is literally the parent class of its child classes (i.e., each subclass derives biologically from organisms in the parent class), the resulting classification is said to be phylogenetic. The word phylogenetic comes from the Greek word "phylon", meaning clan or race, plus "genetikos", meaning origin or birth. It is important to emphasize that the suffix "genetic" in "phylogenetic" does not indicate that the classification is built upon an analysis of genetic sequences. It just happens that words such as genetics, genes, and genesis all happen to share the same Greek root. The actual techniques by which a biologist builds a phylogenetic classification may or may not involve gene sequence comparisons.

The process of determining classes and subclasses is sometimes referred to as cladistics, in which the biologist searches for specific inherited characteristics present in closely related classes that appear at a certain point in the classification (i.e., absent from classes above that point; absent from non-descendant classes below that point). Finding inherited features that are shared by closely related classes allows the biologist to tentatively infer that the classes belong to the same clade (i.e., family of descendants). If all the members of a class have developed from a common ancestor, and if all of the descendants of the common ancestor are included in the class, and if these constraints extend to every class in the classification, the classification is said to be monophyletic. The goal of cladistics is to create a hierarchical, monophyletic classification. [Glossary LUCA]

When a monophyletic classification of organisms is built, the biologist can expect that all of the species within a class will have many of the same genes, metabolic pathways, and anatomy. Shared properties among closely related species allow scientists to generate new hypotheses that may apply to all the members of a class. Without an accurate classification of living organisms, medical scientists would need to approach every human infectious disease as a sui generis (i.e., one of a kind) disorder, requiring its own research effort. Using a biological classification, medical researchers can apply general approaches to diagnosis, prevention, and treatment to classes of infectious organisms. Without the classification of living organisms, the pace of medical research would slow to a standstill.

Up to this point, we have regarded the role of a sequence-based classification of organisms with some skepticism. Although a strictly molecular approach to classification has its limitations, we have seen that thoughtful biologists can use molecular data to draw profound conclusions about the classification of living organisms [4,2]. Let's look at one example where a phylogenetic classification built on sequence analysis has proven to be of value.

The molecular clock is a metaphor describing an analytic method by which the age of phylogenetic divergence of two species can be estimated by comparing the differences in sequence between two homologous genes or proteins. The name "molecular clock" and the basic theory underlying the method were described in the early years of the 1960s when the amino acid sequence of hemoglobin molecules was determined for humans and other hominids [5]. It seemed clear enough at the time that if the number of amino acid substitutions in the hemoglobin sequence, as compared among two species, was large, then a very great time must have elapsed since the divergence of the two species from a common ancestor. The reason being that sequence changes occur randomly over time, and as more time passes, more substitutions will occur. Conversely, if the differences in the amino acid sequence of hemoglobin between species are very small, then the time elapsed after the divergence of the two species from a common ancestor must have been small.

Back in "Section 4.3. Linking classifications, ontologies, and triplestores," we described the work of Woese and Fox who, in 1977 created a phylogenetic classification of bacteria, using a molecular clock. The molecular clock consisted of the gene coding for ribosomal RNA, a highly conserved gene retained in all organisms, which mutates very little over time [6]. The two major classes of prokaryotic organisms (i.e., Class Archaea and Class Bacteria) have distinctive and characteristic ribosomal RNA. By comparing the changes of this molecule over time, the authors computed a phylogenetic classification and timeline of the prokaryotes. As with all simple and elegant theories in the biological sciences, the devil lies in the details. Today, we know that analyses must take into account the presence or absence of conserved regions (whose sequences will not change very much over time). Various technical impediments confront every effort to create a phylogenetic classification using only sequence data (e.g., nonphylogenetic property, nonphylogenetic signal, long-branch attraction). Consequently, analysts must apply a host of adjustments before they can claim to have a fairly well-calibrated molecular clock [7,8]. We can only stress that every classification, regardless of how it is created, requires validation. [Glossary Apomorphy, Clade, Cladistics, Law of sequence conservation, Long branch attraction, Monophyletic, Monophyletic class, Nonphylogenetic property, Nonphylogenetic signal, Ortholog, Phylogeny, Synapomorphy]

Section 6.2. Solving the species riddle

It is once again the vexing problem of identity within variety; without a solution to this disturbing problem there can be no system, no classification.

Roman Jakobson

The concept of species did not come naturally; it had to be invented. After it was invented, it took centuries to reach anything approaching a consensus on its exact definition.

In the early days, every life stage of an organism was considered to be a separate thing. For example, the frog and its tadpole were considered separate organisms. Likewise for the butterfly and the caterpillar. Ditto for the oak tree and its acorn. Perhaps the early taxonomists reasoned that the acorn and the oak were different things, with different biological properties. They each deserved their own species name. The fact that the acorn was known to grow into the oak tree seemed an irrelevant detail at the time. Today, when we look at an acorn and an oak tree we assign them both the same species (e.g., *Quercus alba*), but we also must acknowledge that they are very different things. If an acorn is not an oak tree, then why do we insist that an acorn and an oak tree are the same species? (Fig. 6.1).

To this day, many scientists believe that the concept of "species" is a mere abstraction invented by taxonomists, having no physical meaning in the natural world. I have encountered medical scientists who believe that all living organisms can be assembled on a spectrum that ranges, in terms of complexity, from the simplest bacteria up to the most complex animal, a spot egotistically reserved for *Homo sapiens*. Along this spectrum, biomathematicians can collect feature data such as gene sequences, geographic habitat, diet, size, mating rituals, hair color, the shape of skull, and so on, for a variety of different animals. After a bit of computational analysis, these biomathematicians can cluster animals based on their similarities, and we could assign the clusters names, and the names of our

FIG. 6.1 *Schizura concinna*. Eggs, caterpillars, pupa, and moths all have the same species name. *Source: Public work produced by the United States Department of Agriculture.*

clusters would be our species. Recognizing that there is a multitude of ways by which we might select the features to be measured in our data sets, and by which we choose the weights assigned to the different features (e.g., should we give more weight to gene sequence than to the length of gestation?), and by which we pick our algorithms for assigning organisms to groups, species assignments would be fluid. Not to worry. Species are just abstractions that can be assigned and reassigned at will, and we should not be concerned that our results will vary from investigator to investigator. Of course, all of these ideas are complete nonsense [9]. [Glossary Cluster analysis]

Because speciation accounts for everything we see in the living world, we must have a firm understanding of the meaning of species and the process of speciation, if we are to presume that we know anything at all about biology. This being the case, it is somewhat embarrassing that it has taken centuries for taxonomists to come to any generally accepted definition of "species," that can be sensibly applied to the construction of species taxa [3].

What exactly is a species? The modern definition of species consists of just three words: "evolving gene pool." The original gene pool of a species begins as a breakaway subset of the gene pool of its parent species; hence every new species begins its existence as a collection of members of the parent species. In most cases that have been studied, some geographic barrier (e.g., a mountain range, or a body of water) isolates a subset of the parent species, more or less permanently. Over time, the evolving gene pool of the new species becomes sufficiently different from the gene pool of the parent species that the new species has observable heritable features that are not present in the parent species. Eventually, the new species can no longer mate successfully with the parent species.

The definition of species as an evolving gene pool provides us with an explanation for why we do not see new types of animals suddenly popping up in the landscape. Every member of a new species is also a member of the parent species. The difference between the old species and the new species is its gene pool (i.e., the aggregate of the genomes of the individuals belonging to the species). The distinction between a child species and its parent species is observed over time; not immediately [9].

Species have three properties that inform us that a species is a true biological entity.

1. A definition that clarifies identity. Despite its obviousness, the definition of a species as an evolving gene pool is one of the greatest advances in the field of biology. Without this definition, a species could be anything anyone claims it to be, and the classification of living organisms would be little more than a large list of somewhat arbitrary names and categories.
2. The class "species" has a biological function that is not available to individual members of the species; namely, speciation. Species are the only biological entities that can produce new species.
3. Species can die. When the species gene pool is gone, the species ceases to exist. This occurs when procreation ceases, and the gene pool shrinks to nothing. We tend to think of the "fitness" of a species in terms of the length of time the species exists. For example, the celebrated horseshoe crab, belonging to a subclass of arthropods (i.e., Class Limulidae), is often considered to be fit because it has survived for about 450 million years all the while looking much like it does today. **Another viewpoint would hold that the horseshoe crab is an evolutionary failure insofar as it has not speciated to produce a great diversity of descendant species.** In the time that the horseshoe crab

has lingered on our shores, another subclass of arthropods, the insects, have become the most numerous, most diverse, and most active living force on earth. Many insect species have died, but many more have successfully speciated to produce the enormous diversity of life that we see today. [Glossary Survival of the fittest]

4. Species evolve. Individuals, despite claims to the contrary, do not evolve. Evolution requires a pool of genes that accumulate gene variants over time. Hence, species evolve. Individuals merely propagate, occasionally adding to the species gene pool.

A species is not an abstraction. A species is a living entity determined by its ancestry; and the ancestry of a species can be traced through its gene pools. Taxonomists now understand that "species" is the fundamental building block of the living world, no less real than the concept of a galaxy to astronomers, or the number "e" to mathematicians, or the self-referencing identifier "me" to existentialists. Our current definition, equating species with an evolving gene pool, serves as a great unifying theory in the life sciences. As an aside, the concept of species as an evolving gene pool solves at once four taxonomic puzzles:

1. The uniqueness of individuals of a species

If every individual of a species is genetically unique, and different from every other individual of the same species, then how do they belong to the same species? The definition of species as an evolving gene pool indicates that the genetic composition of individuals of a species need not be identical just so long as all of the individuals derive their genes from the same collective gene pool.

2. How members of a species may have completely different properties

Returning to our dilemma at the beginning of a discussion, how can an acorn and an oak have the same species name when they are so different types of organisms? The acorn and the oak from which the acorn grows are genetically identical. Every acorn and every oak draw its genes from the same species gene pool (e.g., the gene pool for the common white oak tree of North America, *Quercus alba*).

3. The transitive nature of organisms within the same species

If the acorn and the oak were separate species, and the non-transitive rule of classification would be violated every time an acorn matures into a sapling. By identifying the transient developmental stages of organisms under the same species name, we avoid transitions in which one species transforms into another.

4. The exclusion of the individual from the classification of life

When we examine the Classification of Life, we see that the bottom class is the genus, and the members of the genus class are the various species designated with the genus name. In the case of humans, the bottom (genus) class of our lineage is Homo, and Class Homo happens to have one extant member; *H. sapiens*. The species *H. sapiens* has no listed members! If you're looking for your name somewhere in the Classification of Life, you will be sorely disappointed. The reason for this omission is that the individual is subsumed by the species. The species is the gene pool from which the individual is assembled. Individuals, such as you and me, are genetic permutations drawn from an evolving gene pool.

As mentioned earlier in this section, species are the only entity capable of speciating. What is the purpose of all this speciation? Don't we have a sufficient number of species on our planet, without adding to the confusion? As it happens, speciation is the driver of evolution. Basically, without speciation, natural selection would have precious little to select from. Let's spend a bit of time examining the relationship between speciation and evolution.

It is conservatively estimated that from 5 billion to 50 billion species have lived on earth [10], with somewhere between 10 and 100 million now inhabiting the planet. Perhaps the greatest number of species comes from the prokaryotes (bacteria plus archaea), which are estimated to have between 100 thousand and 10 million species. Viruses are also plentiful. It is estimated that there may be hundreds of thousands of marine species of viruses and phages [11]. The number of virus species that live in or infect mammals is estimated to be about 320,000 [12]. These are only estimates, but they indicate that viruses, despite their minimalist physicality, have accounted for themselves admirably [13].

The eukaryotes are estimated to have about 9 million species [14]. Adding up the estimates for prokaryotes, eukaryotes, and viruses, we get a rough and conservative 10–20 million living species. To get an idea of the wide range of estimates, we must not overlook a 2016 study that estimates at least a trillion species of organisms on earth [15]. From this staggeringly large number of terrestrial species, we can infer that speciation is an almost inevitable process.

We are taught in school that evolution brings us greater and greater fitness, producing organisms that are more complex and more functional over time. There is little evidence to support this assertion. Evolution enhances the fitness of a species for a particular environment, but there is no reason to believe that evolution produces improved organisms, in any absolute sense. Basically, every organism on earth struggles to survive, as best as it can, under prevailing conditions. If evolution drove species toward perfection, you might think it would have succeeded by now.

The natural process that accounts for the vitality and resilience of our biosphere, more so than improvements through natural selection, is diversification. Because successful species will speciate, we can expect the number of species on the planet to continually increase, until we face the next global extinction event. When that time comes, and it may be upon us now, the factor that will preserve life on earth will not be evolution. We cannot evolve our way out of the consequences of a nuclear catastrophe or a moon-sized meteoric collision, or a 6-degree rise in temperature occurring in the span of a human lifetime. The process that will preserve life on earth will be the diversification of species. Of the hundreds of millions of species on earth, the odds are that some of them will have the genetic wherewithal to survive when the other species die. [Glossary Results]

Section 6.3. Wherever shall we put our viruses?

The first task of any classification builder is to determine which kinds of things belong to the classification, and which do not. If we are building a classification of mental disorders, we would certainly want to include schizophrenia and depression, but we might feel justified excluding buyer's remorse or writer's block, neither of which rise to the level of a clinically serious disease. Where shall we classify such disorders as mescaline-induced hallucinations or thyrotoxic mania? These two disorders express themselves clinically by altered mental status, but they have a known origin that is external to the brain (i.e., drug ingestion in the case of mescaline hallucinations and increased thyroid activity in the case of thyrotoxic mania). Do the aforementioned conditions truly belong in a classification of mental disorders? If we decide to put all conditions that have a psychiatric component into our classification of mental disorders, then should they all belong to a special class of disorders caused by factors extrinsic to the brain, or should they be assigned to share a place among the classes of intrinsic mental disorders? Whatever we decide to do, our choice will influence our conceptual understanding of our classification.

At the end of the nineteenth century, the builders of the Classification of Life had a major decision to make, regarding a newly discovered class of infectious agents. In 1892, Dmitri Ivanovsky demonstrated that an agent capable of slipping through very tiny pores in a filter was the cause of a disease of the tobacco plant. This agent, which came to be known as the tobacco mosaic virus, was much smaller than any known bacteria. In fact, the tobacco mosaic virus was too small to be seen under conventional light microscopes. After this first demonstration of disease-causing viruses, biologists uncovered many more pathogenic and non-pathogenic viruses, infecting a wide range of living organisms. In the early days, scientists lacked the tools to characterize viruses, but they were forced to make a far-reaching decision concerning the biological nature of this new entity. Are viruses living organisms, or are they inanimate agents, like toxic chemicals? It would seem that viruses replicated and spread, like any organism, but there were many examples of chemical reactions that yielded increasing amounts of product that spread readily from place to place, as gases or as aerosolized fluids. Moreover, viruses were so small that it seemed inconceivable at the time that they could accommodate the anatomic complexity of a true organism.

In 1936, Bawden and coworkers demonstrated that viruses consisted of protein and nucleic acid. In 1956, Gierer and Schramm showed that the viral protein of the tobacco mosaic virus could be entirely removed and that the remaining nucleic acid could infect a plant and reproduce itself as a complete virus. At this point, it seemed certain that viruses were nonliving agents consisting of nothing more than nucleic acid wrapped in protein. Hence, viruses were excluded from the Classification of Life.

It is a quirk of human nature that when a decision has been reached, based on an incomplete set of information, then all information subsequently acquired is interpreted so as to confirm the original decision. Nobody likes to seem foolish, and highly respected scientists are loathe to admit that their professional opinions were incorrect. Hence, almost every new discovery concerning viruses was interpreted in such as way as to reinforce the prevailing notion that viruses are non-living agents. An argument was built that viruses lack key features that distinguish life from non-life. Specifically [16]:

- Viruses depend entirely on host cells for replication.
- Viruses do not partake in metabolism.
- Viruses do not yield energy.
- Viruses cannot adjust to changes in their environment (i.e., no homeostasis).
- Viruses do not respond to external stimuli.

When it was shown that all viruses contain DNA or RNA, the genomic ingredient of all living organisms, it was claimed that in the case of viruses, these sequences were basically inert molecules, wrapped in a capsid, capable of producing mayhem only when introduced to a host cell. [Glossary Capsid]

In the first edition of my book *Taxonomic Guide to Infectious Diseases* (2012), I fell in line with tradition and consigned viruses to the realm of the "unliving." At that time, I followed the Baltimore Classification which divides viruses into seven groups based on whether their genome is DNA, RNA, single-stranded or double-stranded, the sense of the single strand, and the presence or absence of reverse transcriptase. If I had been thinking clearly, I would have asked myself how the different genomic forms of viruses had come into being. Surely, the various forms of viruses had not sprung into existence independently of one another. It seems highly unlikely that classes of viruses having so many common features (e.g., size, presence of capsid, host-dependence, high rates of replication) could have each arisen without a common ancestor. If, as seems likely, the viruses descended from a common ancestor, then the viruses must have evolved into their current classes. Finally, if evolution is a property of living organisms, then can we not conclude that viruses are forms of life?

By the time the second edition of my book was written, in 2019, I had come to re-evaluate the status of viruses and expressed my opinion that viruses could be considered living organisms if we so chose. Today, it is hard for me to take seriously any suggestion that viruses are lifeless.

Consider the following activities of viruses, that would seem to indicate that viruses are living organisms:

1. Viruses, like us, have a nucleic acid genome

Every living organism has a nucleic acid genome. The presence of a nucleic acid genome in viruses, and the absence of a nucleic acid genome in non-living objects, would suggest that viruses are living organisms.

2. Viruses replicate

Replication is a property observed in all living species. It has been argued that viral replication is completely dependent on the host cells (i.e., viruses cannot replicate in isolation), and therefore not an achievement of the virus. To this criticism, we might reply that every organism depends on other organisms for various vital functions (e.g., symbiosis and other forms of mutualism; parasitism, carnivory, and other forms of heterotrophy). A virus's dependence on its host is not relevant to its status as a living organism.

3. Viruses hijack their host cells

After infection, host cells forego many of their normal functions and the newly synthesized viral products may cause cell death (so-called viral cytolytic effect) or may produce disturbances in cellular physiology (so-called cytopathic effects). In either case, the host cells, after infection by virions, become something more akin to viral factories than to eukaryotic organisms, and these new living entities are referred to as virocells, suggesting that the virus has created its form of cellular life. [Glossary Virion, Virocell]

4. Viral strains breed true

A virus of any particular strain will replicate to produce viruses of the same strain.

5. Viruses adapt to their external environment

It has long been assumed that extracellular viral existence is relegated to long-term storage: a lifeless viral genome double-wrapped in a protein capsid, and an envelope that is mostly purloined from the cell membranes of a former host. This is not always true. The Acidianus Tailed Virus can be cold-stored at room temperature for long periods, without changing its morphology. When the temperature rises, they undergo a structural transformation, forming bipolar tails [17]. This tells us that viruses can react to external stimuli and perform biological activities, much as free-living organisms do.

6. Viruses speciate and evolve

It has long been accepted that there are distinct species of viruses. The definition of a viral species, as suggested in 1985, is much the same definition as we see for the living organism: an evolving gene pool [18].

If viral replication were perfect, every replicated virus of a particular strain would be identical to every other virus of the same strain, and each virus would contain the full gene pool of its strain. Of course, perfection is elusive, and viruses cannot replicate without introducing new mutations or some captured genes snipped from a host cell. Hence, if we collect lots of viruses of the same strain, we will find a gene pool (i.e., the totality of genes found in the strain) that is much larger than the genome found in any single virus particle of the strain. Moreover, we would expect that some of those genes floating in the pool may confer certain survival advantages on viruses, leading to their gradual increased presence within the members of the strain. In point of fact, virus species exhibit chemical, structural, and physiological diversity. Through natural selection, viruses have adapted to a wide range of hosts, habitats, sizes, mechanisms of infection, and capsids.

7. Giant viruses, first discovered in 1992, occupy a niche that seems to span the biological gulf connecting living organisms with viruses

These viruses are functionally complex, larger than some bacteria, with enormous genomes (by viral standards), exceeding a million base pairs and encoding upwards of 1000 proteins. Some giant viruses are capable of repairing their DNA, a feature not found in previously known virus families. Biologically, the life of a mimivirus is not very different from that of obligate intracellular bacteria (e.g., Rickettsia). The discovery of giant viruses has compelled biologists to critically reconsider the "non-living" status relegated to viruses.

Let's suspend our disbelief for the moment, and pretend that we have proven, beyond any doubt, that viruses are indeed living organisms. In that case, we face the burden of assigning each species of the virus to a class within the Classification of Life. Just how many different viruses are there? We do not have an answer to this question, but we know enough to guess that the total number of virus species exceeds the number of all non-viral species of organisms [19,20]. Viruses are found everywhere in our environment, and every class of living organisms host viruses. In the oceans, which account for most of the forms of life on earth, viruses are the predominant life forms in terms of the numbers of organisms [11]. A single class of newly characterized aquatic viruses, the Megaviridae, appears to have more species and more classes than all of the bacterial and archaean species found in ocean water [21]. Hence, as we welcome viruses into the Classification of Life, we automatically enlarge the size of our classification by a factor of 2, at the very minimum. For particles that were formerly considered to be lifeless, viruses have done extremely well for themselves [13].

Impediments to viral classification

If we accept that viruses are living organisms, on equal footing with bacteria, archaeans, and eukaryotes, then we must accept the challenge of creating a classification of viruses based on phylogeny (descent from evolving ancestral species), and abandon viral groupings based solely on phenetics (i.e., based on physical similarities), such as the previously mentioned Baltimore classification. Having a robust phylogenetic classification of viruses, along the same lines as the classification of all other living organisms, is an ambitious goal; but its achievement may not be possible, at present. [Glossary Phenetics]

Let's take a look at a few of the impediments to establishing a viral phylogeny that is both comprehensive, testable, and credible.

1. There are many known and unknown viral species

Simply put, the greater the number of species, the more work there is to prepare a taxonomy. Every new species requires a certain irreducible amount of study, and if new species are being discovered at a rate that exceeds our ability to describe and classify known species, then the list of unassigned species will become infinitely long, over time.

2. There is no accepted concept of a "root" virus

The classification of cellular organisms is built on the premise that each of the major classes (i.e., bacteria, archaeans, and eukaryotes) have a root or founder class, with a hypothesized set of class-defined features, from which all subclasses descended. In the case of viruses, we really have no way of describing the ancestor of all extant viruses, and we do not have a strong reason to assume that all the viruses we see today came from any single class of viruses.

Furthermore, we define viruses as being obligatory parasites, requiring one of the major classes of cellular organisms for a host. If this were the case, then viruses, as we have come to define them, could not have existed before the existence of host organisms to parasitize. Hence, if viruses existed before the emergence of cellular life, then the root of the viruses was not a virus, insofar as they could not have parasitized cellular hosts. If the root of the viruses was not a virus, then it may have been almost anything, and we could not rule out the existence of multiple root organisms, accounting for the widely varying versions of viral genomes that we observe today.

Games of phylogenetic logic are harmless fun, but they illustrate how it is impossible to create a top-down classification of viruses if we know nothing about the biological features that would define the top class.

3. There is a high rate of mutation in viruses

For the most part, viruses do not repair their genomes. A notable exception is the megavirus Cafeteria roenbergensis [22]. Presumably, we will find that other megaviruses have DNA repair pathways, but the small, simple viruses have rates of mutation in DNA and RNA, with no mechanism to repair the damage. This means that genome-damaged viruses have two choices: to die or to live with, and replicate their mutations. Viral genomes tend to mutate quickly, producing lots of variants. Species mutability is particularly prevalent among the RNA viruses (e.g., influenza virus, Newcastle disease virus, foot, and mouth disease virus).

4. Multiparental lineage of viruses

Viral reassortment is a process wherein genome segments (roughly, the viral equivalent of eukaryotic chromosomes) are exchanged between two viruses infecting the same cell. Viral reassortment has been observed in four classes of segmental RNA viruses: Bunyaviridae, Orthomyxoviridae, Arenaviridae, and Reoviridae. Following reassortment, a new species of the virus may appear, and this new species will contain segments of two parental species. This poses a serious problem for traditional taxonomists, who labor under the assumption that each new species has one and only one parental species [23]. It is the uniparental ancestry of biological classifications that accounts for their simplicity, and for the concept of lineage, wherein the ancestry of any species can be computed from as an uninterrupted line of classes stretching from the species level to the root level. When a species has more than one parent, then its lineage is replaced by an inverted tree. The tree branches outwards with each class reaching to more than one parent class, iteratively, producing a highly complex ancestry wherein the individual classes have mixed heritage.

The genomic promiscuity of viruses is so troubling to taxonomists that it has been used to argue that viruses are not living organisms, through a chain of reasoning somewhat like the following [24]:

1. Viruses are constantly changing due to extensive horizontal gene transfer, endosymbiosis, hybridization, and re-assortments among themselves.
2. Hence, Viruses are transitive, frequently changing from one kind to another.
3. Transitivity is forbidden in classifications (i.e., a properly classified species cannot transform itself into another species).
4. Hence, viruses cannot be classified within the Classification of Life.
5. Hence, viruses cannot be included among living organisms.
6. Hence, viruses are not living organisms.

Can we think our way out of this dilemma?

Classifying viral classes despite their high mutation rates

How is it that you keep mutating and can still be the same virus?
Chuck Palahniuk, in his novel, "Invisible Monsters"

Despite the impediments to viral classification, we need not lose all hope. We can find some consolation in the history of bacterial classification. As recently as the mid-twentieth century, many taxonomists had abandoned the quest for a phylogenetic classification of bacteria. As discussed in "Section 4.4. Saving hopeless classifications," bioinformaticians largely solved the riddle of bacterial classification by tracking the evolution of "molecular clock" genes.

Just as the field of bacterial classification was saved by science, we may have already found a new approach that will enable us to create a satisfactory classification of viruses. It seems that viruses, like all other organisms on earth, contain conserved genes that permit us to trace the ancestral lineage of viral species [25–28]. Despite the high mutation rate of viral RNA, and DNA, the stability in genes that code for constitutive proteins may help us establish phylogenetic lineages for some classes of viruses. [Glossary Mutation rate]

Why do viruses contain conserved genes? Presumably, much of the stability of viral species is imposed by the host organisms [29]. How so? All viruses must replicate within a host, and the process by which a virus infects and transforms a cell is very much dependent upon its host. Viruses are forced to adopt to some level of host preference and must fine-tune all their functions to the available conditions within the host [29]. Thus, for viruses to successfully replicate, they must evolve into relatively stable host-compatible species. This is what we observe when we study viruses.

A demonstration of host-specific constraints on viruses is found by noting the specificity of viruses for the so-called kingdoms of organisms. Virus infections are found in Class Archaea, Class Bacteria, and Class Eukaryota, but there is no instance in which any single class of viruses is capable of infecting more than one of these classes of cellular organisms. Furthermore, within a class of cellular organisms, there are only rare instances of classes of viruses that can infect distantly related subclasses. For example, there are virtually no viruses that can infect both Class Animalia and Class Plantae (rare exceptions are claimed [30]). Furthermore, as the host evolves, so must the virus. Hence, we might expect to find ancestral lineages of viruses that shadow the lineage of their host organisms.

Sometimes we see genes that rapidly mutate while conserving particular gene motifs that we assume to code for protein segments that are essential for the activity of the protein. Conserved molecular gene motifs help us to classify viruses into biological groups that share phylogenetic origins [31,32]. For example, despite the sequence variations that occur in rapidly mutating viruses, scientists are finding that the three-dimensional folds of protein molecules are conserved and that viruses can be grouped into so-called fold-families, which can, in turn, be grouped into fold superfamilies, that preserve phylogenetic relationships among viral lineages [31].

At least for the DNA viruses, there seems to be a limited number of ways that virions can assemble, and the particular methods of virion assembly are associated with a limited number of families [33]. Among the retroviruses, it has been shown that viral ancestral lineages can be determined by looking at inherited variations in so-called "global" genomic properties (e.g., translational strategies, motifs in Gag and Pol genes, and their associated enzymes) [32]. [Glossary Retrovirus]

Highly innovative work in the field of viral phylogeny is proceeding, from a variety of approaches, including: inferring retroviral phylogeny by sequence divergences of nucleic acids and proteins in related viral species [32]; tracing the acquisition of genes in DNA viruses [34]; and dating viruses by the appearance of viral-specific antibodies in ancient host cells [35]. Because viruses evolve very rapidly, it is possible to trace the evolution of some viruses, with precision, over intervals as short as centuries or even decades [31,36–38].

In 2017, the ICTV (International Committee on Taxonomy of Viruses) recognized 9 orders, 131 families, 46 subfamilies, 803 genera, and 4853 different viral species [39]. The number of known viral species (4853) is thought to represent a tiny fraction of the total number.

Let's return to the question posed at the top of this subsection, taken from Chuck Palahniuk's novel: "How is it that you keep mutating and can still be the same virus?" It would seem that mutational variations of a virus do not generally produce a new viral species. Instead, variations produce diversity in the viral gene pool of the species. If new mutations do not produce an alteration in the specificity of its host organisms, essentially establishing a separate viral gene pool for the variant, then the mutational variants will usually preserve their membership in the same viral species. Still, all those viral genomic variants complicate the job of the viral taxonomist. Basically, the high rate of mutation in viruses yields lots of genomic variation among viral populations, making it easy for bioinformaticians to claim the discovery of new species that are just minor variants of existing species. We can easily imagine a situation wherein new species are discovered, and old species are declared extinct because we simply do not have the time and manpower to carefully examine every genomic variant for the structural and physiologic features that determine its correct taxonomic classification. Today, bioinformaticians off-handedly refer to the variant genomes, resulting from mutations and replication errors, as quasi-species [40]. For the traditional taxonomist, who are trying to create a simple phylogenetic classification of viruses, the vague concept of "quasi-species" must be particularly exasperating.

Where do we put the root class of the viruses?

We know that viruses have been on earth for a very long time [41,42]. We also know that viruses infect all classes of extant organisms (i.e., archaeans, bacteria, and eukaryotes). Is it possible that viruses preceded all other life forms on earth? Evidence that viruses were the first organisms on earth is based in part on the observation that some archaeans, bacteria, and eukaryotes have homologous genes that code for capsid proteins, such as would be derived from a class of viruses. The simplest explanation for homology for a viral-type gene, in all extant cellular forms of life, is that an ancient gene in the very first self-replicating organisms came from a viral species that lived at a time that preceded the emergence of other forms of life [43]. Today, genetic materials of viral origin are present in abundance in eukaryotic cells. At least 8% of the human genome is composed of fragments of RNA viruses [35,44,45].

Tentatively, we can place the root of the viruses as a stand-alone kingdom positioned alongside Class Archaea, Class Bacteria, and Class Eukaryota. Modern classifications draw lineages for viruses that lead up to the root (i.e., Class Viridae) without taking any detours through non-viral classes. For example, consider the simple ancestral lineage of the Variola virus (i.e., smallpox virus) provided by the European Bioinformatics Institute:

Variola virus (smallpox virus)
Orthopoxvirus
Chordopoxvirinae
Poxviridae
dsDNA viruses, no RNA stage
Viridae

Of course, this class lineage could be entirely wrong, at the top level. It is not beyond the possibility that Class Viridae was the legitimate parent class of the very first self-replicating cellular organisms. This would put Class Viridae as the root of all life on earth. We cannot eliminate the possibility that various classes of viruses began as spin-offs of early archaeans and bacteria genomes, much like transposable elements that escaped from their host cells. We cannot discount such a possibility because we encounter instances of naked nucleic acids acting as infectious agents. In particular, we recognize viroids as small molecules of infectious RNA. The first viroid was discovered in 1971 and was shown to be the cause of potato spindle tuber disease [46]. Today, several additional plant diseases are known to result from viroid infection. If the naked nucleic acid is all that is needed to establish a new viral species, then we can easily imagine that new viral species may have originated on numerous occasions, throughout earth's history. [Glossary Transposable element]

If new viral organisms arose through the "escape" of nucleic acids from cellular organisms, This would give us viral lineages that might look something like the following, with Class Bacteria making a cameo appearance just before we take the final step to Class Viridae, a putative parent class to all self-replicating organisms:

Variola virus (smallpox virus)
Orthopoxvirus
Chordopoxvirinae
Poxviridae
dsDNA viruses, no RNA stage
Bacteria
Viridae

The fact is, we do not know all that much about the beginnings of life on earth. Quoting John Galsworthy, "The beginnings and endings of all human undertakings are untidy."

Life is what we make of it

You must accept one of two basic premises: Either we are alone in the universe, or we are not alone in the universe. And either way, the implications are staggering.

Wernher von Braun

At this point, with all these arguments swimming in our heads, we might regroup and ask ourselves another pressing question: "Why bother? Does it really make any difference whether viruses are living or dead?" In point of fact, some scientists flatly refuse to take a position. In a manuscript published by Eugene Koonin and Petro Starokadomskyy, the authors wrote, "the question is effectively without substance because the answer depends entirely on the definition of life or the state of 'being alive' that is bound to be arbitrary" [47].

If the definition of life is arbitrary, then let's play with the idea that life has been defined from the view of humans, using *H. sapiens* as the prototypical example of a living organism. Let's turn the tables around, and imagine a definition of life from the view of viruses [41]. Doing so, we suddenly see numerous reasons why a virus might not believe that humans qualify as living organisms.

1. Humans cannot replicate (they merely procreate)

In an effort to strengthen their species' gene pool, humans undergo a strange mating process in which the chromosomes of both parents are hopelessly jumbled together to produce an unique offspring, unlike either the father or the mother. In doing so, humans miss out on the replicative process, performed with the greatest enthusiasm by every virus.

Self-replication is one of the fundamental features of life. Because humans cannot replicate themselves, they barely qualify as living organisms. At least, this is what the viruses think.

2. Humans do not behave in a manner that preserves the survival of their species

Humans have created a variety of weapons and have adopted a set of behaviors that may wipe out most of the multicellular organisms on earth. Viruses generally respect one another's right to live.

3. We can thank viruses for the existence of humans

Viruses are constantly donating DNA to humans, and humans have used this DNA to evolve [35]. In point of fact, if there were no viruses, there would be no DNA replication, no adaptive immune system, no placentas, and no humans [48].

4. Humans may have descended from viruses

Nobody knows much about the earliest forms of life, and there is plenty of room for conjecture. It's quite feasible that the earliest genetic material consisted of sequences of RNA, and that these RNA molecules moved between the earliest forms of cells. If this were the case, then the earliest genomes were essentially RNA viruses, and this would place humans as direct, but distant descendants of viruses.

There is a current theory, among many competing theories, that the first eukaryotic nucleus was a giant virus that was not successful in transforming its proto-eukaryotic host into a virocell totally [41,49,50]. A hybrid giant virus/virocell/proto-eukaryote may have stabilized and replicated to form an early, nucleated cell; the first eukaryote.

5. Humans serve viruses; not vice versa

We are taught to think of viruses as fragments of nucleic acids wrapped by a capsid (i.e., the virion). To a virus, extracellular existence must be akin to a state of suspended animation. Virions come back to life when they invade a eukaryotic cell and create a virocell; a living organism consisting of the hijacked eukaryotic cell whose nuclear machinery is redirected to synthesize viral progeny. If every eukaryotic cell is conceptualized as a potential virocell, then every eukaryotic species is a potential slave owned by the viral kingdom. The viruses probably think they're doing us a favor. Frankly, most of the cells in a metazoan body lead to a vegetative existence, doomed to a fully differentiated, post-mitotic, and short existence. Viruses re-animate post-mitotic cells, and create a thriving center for viral life from a lackluster population of eukaryotic cells, by re-animating them, as virocells. [Glossary Post-mitotic]

6. Humans ingest and metabolize all forms of organisms (i.e., bacteria, plants, animals, fungi, single-celled eukaryotes), non-selectively. This would indicate that humans are merely chemical factories that consume anything and produce excrement.

Viruses are selective about which organisms they infect. Viruses are found in every major class of organisms, but do not cross-infect other the top classes (e.g., viruses that infect bacteria never infect archaean or eukaryotic species). This would suggest that viruses are capable of choosing to infect one class of organism, over another.

7. Unlike living viruses, humans lack the basic capacity of going dormant. From the moment of birth, they must engage in an exhausting effort to acquire food to fuel their metabolic activities, until they eventually die.

All kidding aside, if we cannot distinguish life from non-life, how will we determine whether forms of life exist beyond our planet? It would be terrible to think that we may be too stupid to recognize life when we come upon it. Shortly, we will need to address the definition of life anew, when our artificial intelligence systems attain self-consciousness and our robots become self-replicating. Perhaps, one day, an autonomous android will ponder whether infectious software viruses are living organisms. As strangers in a strange land, it behooves us to think deeply about the meaning of life.

Section 6.4. Using the classification of life to determine when aging first evolved

Omnes vulnerant, ultima necat. (All hours wound; the last one kills.)

Latin motto

Whenever we contemplate the grim facts of life, the inevitability of aging and death intrudes upon our psyche and darkens our soul. It seems to us that we all must grow old and die. The inevitable consequence of life is death.

Actually, the process of aging, leading to death, is something that applies to only a fraction of living organisms. We shall see that aging is an evolved trait that only applies to animal classes descended from a few subclasses of bilaterians. The remainder of the classes of life, including single-celled eukaryotes, bacteria, archaeans, many species of plants, and various branches of metazoans (i.e., animals), simply do not age. They can live thousands of years. When they die, it is typically due to some misadventure (e.g., predation, starvation, suffocation, desiccation, etc.). Even among the animals for which aging and death come naturally, there are wide variations in lifespan, as though the trait of aging is something that is more fully expressed in some classes of animals than in others.

Before going any further, let's define aging. Aging is a sequence of events that occur in an organism, over time, that reduces the ability of the organism to survive, and which eventually results in the death of the organism. We infer that aging is genetically controlled because all of the members of a species will undergo that same aging process, more or less, and will reach the same end-point (i.e., death) at roughly the same age. In the case of humans, we can all expect to die from the aging process before the age of 120 years, unless we die earlier, from intervening events.

On a cellular level, the simplest definition of aging involves two biological steps:

1. The replacement of dividing cell populations with cell populations that can no longer divide and can no longer be replaced by younger cells. A cell that cannot divide has no physiologic option but to continue functioning until it eventually dies. The length of time that a cell may live, without dividing, varies greatly from days (e.g., epidermal cells and cells lining the gut) to several months (e.g., red blood cells), to many years (e.g., neurons, cartilage cells). In the case of epidermal cells, gut lining cells, and red blood cells, the defunct non-dividing cells are replaced by new cells generated by a reserve cell population. In the case of neurons and cartilage cells, there is no replacement after death. [Glossary Epidermis]

2. Organ and tissue dysfunction due to the gradual loss of the non-dividing cell populations that are not replaced. The gradual or rapid death of neurons may lead to defects of mentation. The loss of cartilage cells leads to joint dysfunction resulting in osteoarthritis. The loss of muscle cells that have lost the ability to divide leads to a reduction in muscle cells (i.e., sarcopenia) and generalized weakness. Most of the degenerative changes associated with the aging process in humans are a consequence of having no capacity to replace non-dividing cells with new cells.

Why are we discussing aging in a book devoted to classification? In this section, we shall reveal how aging evolved just one time in the history of our planet, as an acquired class trait, at one point in the evolution of a particular ancestral class of animals. All of the descendant classes of animals inherited the class property of aging, and no classes of animals that did not descend from that first-to-age class of animals have that same aging trait. Most importantly, the key information with which we will draw these inferences all come from our examination of the Classification of Life. Without the Classification of Life, our knowledge of aging, an evolved trait, would be non-existent.

Let's take a step back to the first forms of cellular life on earth. Cellular organisms fall into one of two broad classes: the prokaryotes (cells with no nucleus, comprising Class Bacteria and Class Archaea); and the eukaryotes (cellular organisms containing a nucleus). When we think of aging, we generally confine ourselves to processes that occur in multicellular organisms because single-celled organisms (i.e., all of the prokaryotes and most of the eukaryotes) continue to divide so long as they are well-nourished, uncrowded, and protected from environmental pathogens (Fig. 6.2).

Nearly all of the child classes of Class Eukaryota are single-celled organisms or simple colonies of single-celled organisms. None of the single-celled organisms undergo anything akin to aging. When one cell divides to become two daughter cells, nothing remains of the original cell other than its genome replicated in the daughters. The two daughter cells emerge as brand-new individuals, not as aged replicates of the parent cell. Hence, the continuously dividing single-cell eukaryotes and all of the prokaryotes have a lifestyle that evades our concept of aging.

Only two of the original Eukaryotic classes became ancestors of complex multicellular organisms: Class Viridiplantae, the ancestral class of all plants; and Class Opisthokonta, the ancestral class of all animals. Organisms from both of these major eukaryotic classes achieved the dubious ability to age and divide. However, most of the branches of Class Viridiplantae and Class Opisthokonta lack the ability to age.

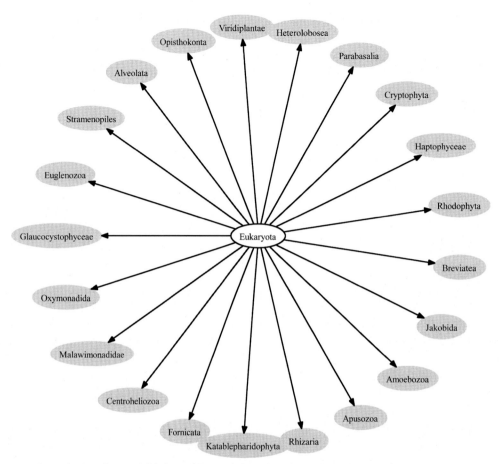

FIG. 6.2 Class Eukaryota has 21 child classes (direct subclasses). Only Class Opisthokonta (adjacent to Class Viridiplantae, near the top of the figure) contains subclasses that exhibit what we have come to think of as aging.

In the plant kingdom, aging, when it occurs, follows a different biological pathway than what we see in the animal kingdom. For example, many individual trees can live hundreds or even thousands of years. Methuselah, a Great Basin bristlecone pine residing in Inyo County, California, is reputed to be about 5000 years old, which seems to be about the observed limit for the lifespan of any individual standing tree [51].

Some species of trees self-clone. Self-cloning occurs within a copse, producing a group of trees all having the same genetic identity, with new clonal growths replacing dying trees. It is not unreasonable to consider the copse itself as a single biological organism, characterized by one genome and by a stable collection of growing and dying cells. Such clonal organisms are virtually immortal. A copse of Quaking Aspen (*Populus tremuloides*), living in Fishlake National Forest, Utah, is thought to be hundreds of thousands of years old [52]. Considered as a single organism, the Quaking Aspen colony occupies 106 acres and has an aggregate weight of about 6 million kilograms. Farmers in ancient and modern times have benefited from the self-cloning nature of plants by developing the agricultural technique known as coppicing. Young trees are cut to near-ground level, and new, clonal trees re-shoot from the stump. By repeated cuttings, the trees are maintained as juveniles. Regularly coppiced trees never seem to age or die; they just spread out from the center. Individual coppiced trees have been maintained for centuries [51] (Fig. 6.3).

FIG. 6.3 A grove of quaking aspen trees, all belonging to the same clonal growth, are referred to, collectively, as Pando. *Source: Wikipedia, produced for the U.S. Department of Agriculture.*

Unlike most animal species, individual plants contain totipotent cells that can divide indefinitely and from which portions of plants, or fully formed plants, can regenerate. Not so for most metazoans (animals) who, in the natural course of development, lose their totipotent cells as they differentiate to develop mature organs. Because all of Class Viridiplantae is characterized by species that maintain a totipotent cell population, we can infer that every member of the class (i.e., all plants) has a mechanism for achieving continuous clonal growth. Hence, death in the kingdom of plants is much more like a biological option than it is an inevitability.

Other than Class Viridiplantae, the only class of eukaryotes that experience anything akin to aging is found in Class Opisthokonta. Class Opisthokonta has child classes: Class Fungi, Class Choanoflagellida, Class Metazoa, and Class Aphelidia. Organisms of Class Fungi have no upper bound in terms of size or age. The Malheur National Forest in Oregon is host to a fungus (Armillaria ostoyae, the honey mushroom) that covers 2200 acres of land, to an average depth of about 3 ft. It is estimated, based on growth rates, to be about 2400 years old. Class Aphelidea are basically fungi and do not experience aging, as we recognize it. Likewise, members of Class Choanoflagellida are single-celled organisms that grow in close-packed social colonies, but have not attained status as a multicellular organism and do not exhibit aging in the usual sense. Consequently, among the child classes of opisthokonts, it is only Class Metazoa that contains aging organisms (Fig. 6.4).

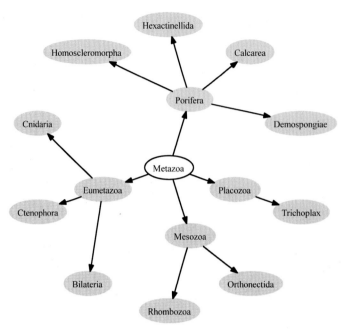

FIG. 6.4 Class Metazoa, a child class of Class Opisthokonta, contains all of the animals on earth.

The child classes of Class Metazoa are: Class Porifera (the sponges); Class Placozoa (with one extant species, Trichoplax); Class Mesozoa; and Class Eumetazoa (so so-called true animals, of which we humans belong).

Sponges, among which are some of the longest-living animals, belong to Class Porifera. Estimates based on the growth rates of Antarctic sponges suggest a very long lifespan in these animals. A two-meter-high sponge, discovered in the Ross Sea, is estimated to be 23,000 years old. Due to fluctuation in the levels of the Ross Sea, skeptical scientists doubt that the specimen could have lived for much more than 15,000 years. Still, a low-estimate 15,000-year lifespan is impressive enough.

Class Placozoa contains one extant species, Trichoplax, a flat organism, about 1 mm in diameter, that lacks internal organs. Trichoplax can regenerate their entire bodies from small groups of cells. As such, they are essentially immortal.

Class Mesozoa is an informal class containing simple, minuscule animals. There is currently some controversy over the legitimacy of Class Mesozoa, with some evidence suggesting that the monophyletic mesozoan species are subclasses of the lophotrochozoans. In any case, the accepted mesozoan species do not exhibit anything akin to the aging process observed in most eumetazoans.

It is only within Class Eumetazoa that the aging process is found, so let's look at the subclasses of Class Eumetazoa to see which subclasses exhibit aging. Class Eumatazoa has three subclasses: Class Cnidaria, Class Ctenophora, and Class Bilateria (Fig. 6.5).

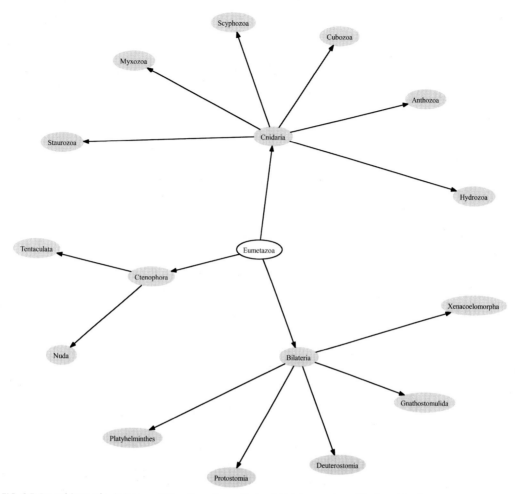

FIG. 6.5 Branchings of subclasses of Class Eumetazoa (animals) giving us the cnidarians (also known as the coelenterates), the ctenophores (the comb jellies), and the bilaterians (animals whose embryos have bilateral symmetry along a central axis).

Some members of Class Cnidaria seem to be immortal. The medusae (fully mature form) of the jellyfish *Turritopsis nutricula* has the rare ability to revert to its immature polyp stage, basically reversing its life cycle. The immature polyp can reproduce by budding. There seems to be no limit to the number of times in which a medusa may form from a budding polyp and revert to a polyp stage. Hence, the jellyfish *T. nutricula,* and several other species, including Turritopsis dohrnii and *Hydractinia carnea* may be immortal [53–56].

Class Ctenophora (the comb jellies) contains the bdelloid rotifers, tiny creatures whose females can clone themselves. Although the body of the short-lived female dies, its clone with the identical genome persists, basically sidestepping the entire issue of aging.

Within Class Bilateria, we have the following subclasses: Platyhelminthes, Deuterostomia, Protostomia, Gnathostomulida, and Xenacoelomorpha.

Class Platyhelminthes (the flatworms) contain species that regenerate their bodies
from small pieces. In particular, the planarian flatworms can be cut into pieces, and an
entire organism can be regenerated from each of the pieces. Hence, researchers quip that
planarian are "immortal under the edge of a knife." Observations of blastemal whole-body
regeneration indicate that planarian cells are totipotent and able to form blastemas. We do
not know how planaria manage to maintain a population of totipotent stem cells, but it
has been suggested that a key step involves the maintenance of normal telomere length in
planaria [57]. Telomeres are sequences of non-coding DNA attached to the termini of
chromosomes. Without telomeres, cells cannot divide. Telomeres are typically lost from
non-dividing somatic cells in animals that age. [Glossary Telomere]

Another subclass of Class Platyhelminthes, Class Turbellaria, contains species that
clone themselves by transverse or longitudinal division. Still, other turbellarians reproduce by budding. The term "aging" does not easily apply to species that can regenerate
whole organisms from single slices, or that divide themselves into two parts to produce
two clones of themselves or that self-reproduce by simple budding. Clearly, members
of Class Platyhelminthes did not get the memo instructing them to curl up and die
(Fig. 6.6).

FIG. 6.6 *Pseudobiceros bedfordi*, a species of the Turbellarian flatworm (Class Platyhelminthes). *Source: Wikipedia,
and contributed to the public domain by its author, Jan Derk.*

Class Gnathostomulida consists of tiny aquatic organisms that are self-reproducing
hermaphrodites. Much like the comb jellies, their reproductive lifestyle essentially
bypasses the issue of aging.

Class Xenacoelomorpha is closely related to both Class Deuterostomia and Class Protostomia and has been included within the deuterostomes by some taxonomists [58].

The xenacoelomorphs are tiny aquatic hermaphroditic animals that engage in sexual reproduction. Just to simplify things, we'll tentatively include Class Xenacoelomorpha alongside the deuterostomes and protostomes in our discussion of the aging classes of animals.

Without prolonging the suspense, we can say that with the evolution of Class Protosomia and Class Deuterostomia, the process of aging first evolved. As far as anyone can tell, all of the species, extant or extinct, that descended from either of these two classes exhibit some form of the aging process. All of the classes that are not descended from either Class Deuterostomia and Class Protostomia contain species that do not age; at least, they do not age in a manner that we would consider equivalent to aging as seen in deuterostomes or protostomes. [Glossary Totipotent stem cell]

Let's summarize. Single-celled eukaryotes are ageless. Although we haven't discussed them, the prokaryotes and the viruses are ageless in the same sense as the single-celled eukaryotes are ageless: they replicate to produce exact copies of themselves. Of the three major classes of multicellular organisms (i.e., plants, fungi, and animals), the plants and the fungi contain ageless species. Of the remaining class of multicellular organisms (i.e., Class Metazoa), the classes produced by the first several phylogenetic branching's are ageless. **All of these ageless organisms are characterized by continuous growth and or continuous cell renewal, both of which imply the existence of a non-declining population of stem cells. In no instance is long life based on the ability of cells to persist as a collection of long-lived non-dividing cells.**

The idea that aging is an evolutionary advancement seems a bit absurd to those of us who stare in the mirror to see our thinning hair and our turkey necks, as we contemplate our inevitable deaths. It's best to shirk these depressing thoughts and to think of aging as a trait that benefits the species (at the great expense of individual members of the species). The sad fact is that as we age, our gametes accumulate mutations and other forms of cellular degeneration, and the progeny of a mating between two middle-aged adults will, on average, be less fit than a mating between two young adults. From the point of view of a species, the purpose of procreation is to produce new, unique gametes, and to enlarge the gene pool with potentially beneficial genes. Remember, a species is simply an evolving gene pool, and species achieve immortality by speciating, not by simply persisting. For the species, there is no need to preserve individual organisms that carry damaged gametes. In the Classification of Life, aging is an evolved trait that arose when Class Bilateria branched and produced the protostomes and the deuterostomes, about 550 million years ago. Having this starting point (and divergence point) may provide us with a few clues to the nature of aging.

If aging is an evolutionary advancement, presumably achieved through a genetic acquisition, then can we find, isolate, and eliminate the "aging gene", and thus achieve immortality, like the planarium or the jellyfish, or the sponge? The answer to this question is "No!", there is no single gene that accounts for the aging process, and we can prove this logically. If aging were caused by a single gene, we would expect rare occurrences of mutations of the gene, leading to instances of human immortality. Outside of science fiction, immortal humans do not exist. Therefore, there is no "aging gene." Aging is a quantitative trait (i.e., some individuals age more slowly than others, some species age differently than others). Quantitative traits are almost always polygenic (i.e., involving multiple genes and gene-regulatory mechanisms). [Glossary Polygenic disease]

Where might we expect the genes that account for aging to be expressed? Later in this chapter, in "Section 6.6. How the classification of life unifies the biological sciences," we shall see that the defining properties of classes, and most major evolutionary innovations, are expressed in the embryo. We shall learn that adult organism plays a secondary role in evolution, and the processes we see as aging in fully developed animals are likely to be a by-product of some combination of genes that enhance the embryo, in some manner. If this is the case, medical scientists who study aging should devote some of their attention to the embryo; and maybe a little less time to observing superannuated adults. Most of the rare genetic diseases of aging (i.e., the progerias) are manifested in very young children, indicating that aging, as a biological process, begins at the earliest stages of life. [Glossary Progeria]

To what do we owe all of our inferences and hypotheses regarding aging? Such ideas come to us courtesy of the Classification of Life. It is by observing the behavior of classes of organisms and determining the lineages that carry particular class traits, that we learn something about the evolution and biology of aging. Without the Classification of Life, we would be in the situation of knowing that some species of organisms seem to age, and others do not, but we would have no concept of aging as an evolved trait inherited through an ancestral lineage.

Section 6.5. How inferences are drawn from the classification of life

Once we have created a classification, we can learn a great deal about its domain (i.e., the system being classified) just by taking a look at the class structure and by counting classes. As an example, let's consider how we measure the biological success of a species. When we consider the full Classification of Life, we tend to switch to a long view of success. Well over 99% of the species that have lived on earth are now extinct [10]. With very few exceptions, the destiny of a species is no different from the destiny of individuals of the species: death and extinction. Under the circumstances, the biological success of a class is determined by the success of its descendant subclasses.

When we look at descendants of Class Rodentia, we see, in just three branchings, a wide variety of species, many of which are extant. This indicates that Class Rodentia was successful. We can be fairly certain that none of the original species inside Class Rodentia are living today, because we do not see evidence of modern rodent species in fossils from the age when members of Class Rodentia first appeared, about 66 million years ago [59]. Ultimately, the destiny of a successful class is speciation, not perpetuation (Fig. 6.7).

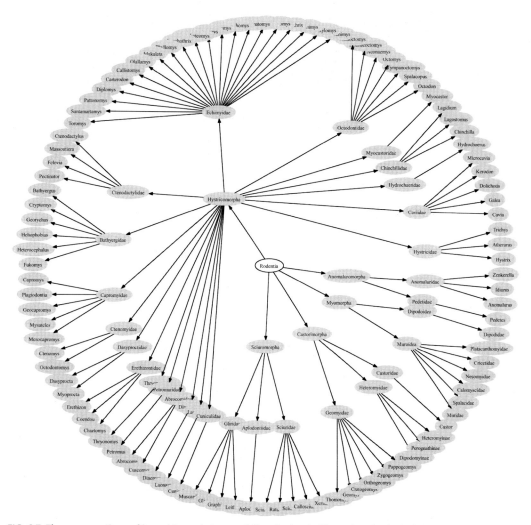

FIG. 6.7 Three generations of branching subclasses of Class Rodentia (the rodents). The individual third-generation subclasses are too numerous to be individually annotated in the graph.

When we see living species having a small population, we should not assume that the species is unsuccessful. The wolf (*Canis lupus*), whose numbers have greatly diminished in just the past few generations, has sub-speciated to produce the domesticated dog (*Canis lupus familiaris*). It would be tragic to lose a species such as a wolf, but if the wolf were to disappear, its success as a species would be validated by the modern dog.

When we have a complete classification, we can determine the success and the failures of classes just by counting. Ants, springtails, spiders, birds all seem to be speciating nicely. Other classes have not fared nearly so well. For example, Class Mammalia has two extant subclasses: Class Theria and Class Prototheria. Class Theria has done well, producing the extant marsupials (Class Metatheria), and the placental mammals (Class Eutheria). Class Prototheria (the monotremes), consists mostly of extinct species known only through their fossils. Currently, there are only five extant species of monotremes: the duck-billed platypus and four species of echidna (spiny anteaters). Fossils of monotreme species that died without speciating are found in England, China, Madagascar, and Argentina, and date back to the Mesozoic era (252–66 million years ago) (Fig. 6.8).

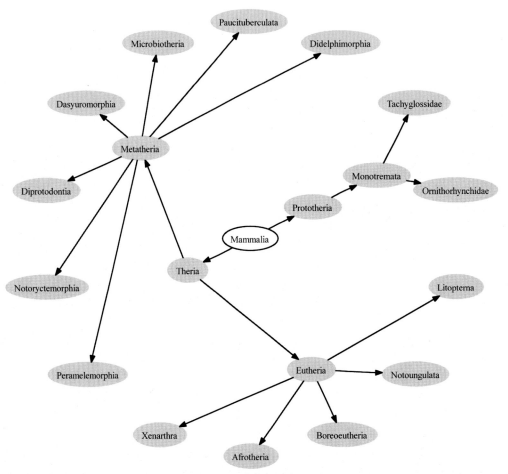

FIG. 6.8 Branching's of Class Mammalia. Two large subclasses of the mammals are Class Metatheria (the marsupials) and Class Eutheria (the placental mammals). A third subclass, Class Monotremata, consists of about half a dozen extant poorly populated species (e.g., duckbilled platypus) and a cluster of extinct species.

All placental mammals are alike, more, or less

Class Eutheria (the placental mammals) is reputed to contain widely diverse species. As an example of the great physical diversity of eutherians, we see tiny mice and large humans, ferocious tigers and timid rabbits, seafaring whales, and burrowing moles. At first blush, it is hard to imagine that all of these animals belong to the same general class.

One of the greatest values of any classification is its ability to make us look beyond the superficial as we concentrate our attention on the properties that apply to all the members of a class.

All eutherians develop from embryos that look remarkably similar among the eutherian species; all eutherian embryos and fetuses are nourished by a placenta for the length of their gestations; all eutherian have a nearly identical skeletal framework if we ignore quantitative differences in the size and shape of bones; all eutherians have brains and nervous systems that are anatomically similar; all eutherians have a nearly equivalent set of neural crest derivatives; all eutherians have a corpus callosum connecting the left and right hemispheres of the brain; all eutherians have the same complement of organs, for the most part; all eutherians have hair. When we compare genes, there is very little difference between one eutherian and another. The list of shared properties goes on and on.

For the comparative histologist, who studies the cells and tissue organization of different animals, under a microscope, the family resemblances among all eutherians are incredibly striking. There are, in the adult human, a bit more than 200 types of cells that are morphologically distinguishable by microscopic examination using a standard staining technique. With a few exceptions, every cell in the human has a close counterpart in every other eutherian species. That is to say that there really is hardly any observable difference between a hepatocyte in a mouse and a hepatocyte in a human. By the same token, human neurons are much like mouse neurons; human bone cells are much like mouse bone cells; and so one for nearly every one of the 200+ cell types found in mice and men and every other eutherian organism.

Basically, the differences among the eutherians are quantitative, not qualitative. When we talk about quantitative differences, we are discussing traits, where traits are defined as measurable differences in properties, such as the length and thickness of a bone, the weight of an individual, how high an individual can jump, and so on. Even in the case of the giraffe, whose neck may be 6-ft in length, there are just 6 cervical vertebrae, the same number as is found in all the eutherians. The vertebral bones in the giraffe's neck may be larger and thicker than ours, but those are quantitative differences, not qualitative differences.

Here are some of the mechanisms that account for the quantitative differences among the qualitatively equivalent eutherians:

1. Endocrine regulation

Endocrine stimulation or repression can produce startling differences in the size and shape of animals. As an example, consider the differences between a bull and a cow. Like anything else in life, endocrine activity is ultimately controlled by the genome, and genetic alterations influencing the endocrine system can be inherited.

2. Small polygenic changes

Often, small changes in many individual genes that code for proteins involved in a particular metabolic pathway may result in significant changes in metabolic activity.

3. Epigenetic modifiers

Back in "Section 1.4. Things that defy simple classification," we introduced the topic of the epigenome (i.e., the various chemical modifications that alter the expression of genes, without changing the sequence of nucleotides in genes). The epigenetic modifiers change the way that genes behave, and these changes are often reflected in heritable quantitative variations that we call traits. For example, when we observe variations among related species or between subgroups of one species, we often find differences in transcription factor binding, one of the many epigenetic mechanisms controlling the genome [60,61].

4. Selection from the existing species gene pool

Animal and plant breeders can produce large changes in species within a few generations, simply by breeding for specific traits.

All of our observations on eutherians, as a group of very closely related species, despite their superficial differences of appearance, could not have been made without the benefit of The Classification of Life.

Listening to our sister classes

Robert Frost, in his poem "The Road Not Taken," wrote: "Somewhere ages and ages hence: Two roads diverged in a wood, and I took the one less traveled by, And that has made all the difference."

How could Robert Frost be certain that choosing the road less traveled "made all the difference" in his life? Without putting too fine a point on it, wouldn't Frost need to have somehow duplicated himself at the divergence of roads, and watched how each of the duplicate Frosts proceeded down their separate paths? It is conceivable that both the Frosts may have ended at the same destination, with nothing to indicate that their lives followed divergent pathways. Frost, you see, was operating at a disadvantage that modern-day biologists have overcome. In essence, we can watch the evolutionary pathways followed by species that diverge at a point in time. We do this by studying sister classes and their descendant subclasses.

In many cases, we have lost the living representatives of ancestral sister classes through extinction. Currently, one living species represents the sister class to all other angiosperms (i.e., flowering plants). This species, Amborella trichopoda, is an unassuming shrub found only on the small Pacific Island of New Caledonia. It is feared that Amborella trichopoda is on the brink of extinction. A botanist wrote, in a 2008 Ph.D. thesis (translated from the French), "The disappearance of Amborella trichopoda would imply the disappearance of a genus, a family and an entire order, as well as the only witness to at least 140 million years of evolutionary history [62]". [Glossary Sister class and cousin class]

Having a verifiable member of a sister class has several uses. By studying sister species, we can sometimes:

1. Verify phylogenetic relationships and taxonomic trees

We can't go back and study the class from which sister lineages arose. That class has speciated out of existence. If we want to discover what that class must have been like, we must study the child classes of the parent class. If a class and its sister both share the same trait, then it is reasonable to infer that the trait was inherited from the parent class. Hence, by comparing sister classes and their descendant subclasses. we can follow the evolutionary pathways that diverged at a point in time.

2. Distinguish acquired properties from inherited ancestral properties

If a class and its sister do not share the same property, and if the property is present in a class that is not closely related to either of the sibling classes, then it is reasonable to infer that the property is most likely convergent (i.e., acquired independently, and not inherited by shared ancestry) in the classes that have the common property. [Glossary Convergence, Homoplasy, Mimicry versus convergence]

3. Improve our understanding of embryologic development

As an example, amphioxus, also known as lancelet, is a cephalochordate, the sister class to Class Craniata. Amphioxus lacks a neural crest. Therefore, structures present in amphioxus that are homologous to structures in craniates could not have arisen purely through the action of the neural crest. By comparing amphioxus development with the development of craniates, we can learn a great deal about the specific role of the neural crest in craniate development [63].

4. Serve as the comparison species for a molecular clock analysis determining the time at which the sister classes diverged [Glossary Molecular clock]

When two classes split, the molecular clock is essentially reset, with new mutations arising in either class at a rate that is presumed to be fairly constant for homologous genes. By comparing the sequences in homologous genes in sister classes, we can determine whether a gene has been tightly conserved.

5. Determine candidate genes responsible for diseases occurring in the sibling class

If a type of disease occurs in one class of animals, but not in the sister class, then we might look for genes or gene variants that are present in one class and not the other. Such genes may possibly hold the key to an important pathogenetic step in the development of the disease. For example, HIV infections are devastating for humans but less so for several closely related primates [35]. In some cases, it may be shown that an effective antiviral gene is present in a sister species that is currently free of virus infection. In such cases, it may be possible to identify the antiviral gene in the resistant species and to develop a treatment for members of the non-resistant sister class [35].

6. Find the first ancestral class of species in which an evolutionary change may have occurred

For example, it is common to find viruses that are present in the genome of a species or a class of animals, and absent from its sister class. To name a few, the PtERV retrovirus is not present in the human genome but is present in Class Pan (chimpanzees and bonobos) and Class Gorillini (gorillas). Similarly, a lineage of rhadinovirus as well as species of the foamy virus are absent from humans but are found in closely related primates [35].

Intelligence evolving independently in distantly related classes

Animal intelligence is impossible to quantify, but we humans like to believe that we know which animals are intelligent and which animals are not. Class Mammalia, which includes humans, whales, dolphins (basically, small whales), dogs, and cats is generally regarded to be a fairly smart class. Birds, we find, are also capable of a high level of intelligence. The closest ancestral class containing birds (Class Aves) and mammals (Class Mammalia) is Class Amniota (the amniotes being tetrapods characterized by the presence of a specialized membrane that covers and protects the embryos of class members).

Are there any intelligent animals outside of Class Amniota? Apparently so, and these intelligent animals emerge from a class that is commonly considered to be among the dumbest of animals, the mollusks. We are referring here to the members of Class Cephalopoda (i.e., octopi, cuttlefish, and squids), a descendant class of Class Mollusca, and a fairly close cousin to clams (Class Bivalvia) and snails (Class Gastropoda). The cephalopods, particularly octopi and cuttlefish, are credited with being highly intelligent animals (Fig. 6.9).

When we examine the ancestors of mollusks and mammals, in the Classification of Life, we find that they have no closely shared ancestry (Fig. 6.10).

Applying our anthropocentric concepts of intelligence, octopi are extraordinarily smart [64,65]. Functionally, the octopus brain supports both short and long-term memory, sleep, and the ability to explore objects and learn their shapes [66]. For example, octopi easily open jars of food shut with a screw-cap lid. Captive octopi are known to respond with different behaviors based upon their established relationships with individual human caretakers and visitors. They seem to resent captivity and have been known to contrive ingenious strategies to escape confinement and to seek a more hospitable environment. Octopi have a social life, and some female octopi exhibit some of the most protective brooding behavior observed in the animal kingdom [67]. The list of anecdotes reporting high intelligence in the three subclasses of cephalopods is long and wondrous. Considering that we humans have no seriously creditable way of measuring intelligence, it is unlikely that we will ever fathom the full scope of the octopus's mind.

On the anatomic and physiologic level, the octopus brain and nervous system have virtually no resemblance to that of humans [64]. Mollusks, like all invertebrates, have a distributed nervous system. Octopi, like other mollusks, have multiple brains, for each of the 8 arms, plus a central brain. How all of these anatomically isolated brains coordinate

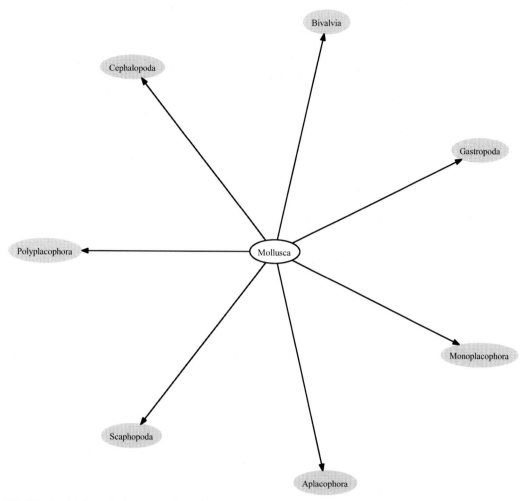

FIG. 6.9 Class Mollusca is the parent class of the cephalopods (containing octopi, squid, and cuttlefish), which are close cousins to the bivalves (containing clams) and the gastropods (containing snails and slugs).

thought and action is an area of active investigation, but we can readily see that the brains of the octopus are organized much differently than the centralized amniote brain. Aside from gross anatomy, we see fundamental differences between the brains of octopi and amniotes on the cellular level. The axons of amniotes are wrapped by cells that produce myelin (glial cells in the brain and Schwann cells in the peripheral nervous system). Myelin greatly increases the conduction velocity of neural impulses. The axons of neurons in octopi are unmyelinated, greatly reducing the speed with which impulses are conducted [65]. Hence, we can infer that quick nervous system responses in the octopus must be achieved through a mechanism that does not require fast conduction through long axons.

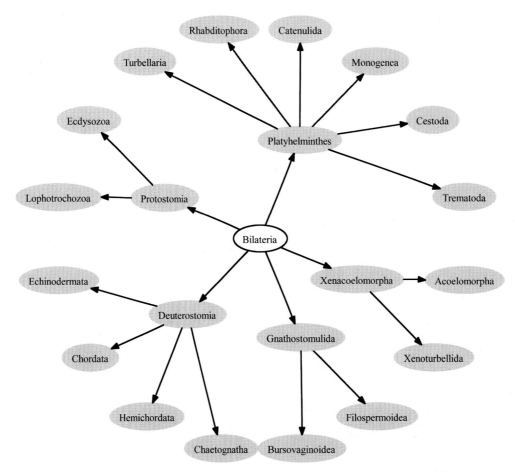

FIG. 6.10 Class Mollusca is the child class of Class Lophotrochozoa, a subclass of Class Protostomia. Class Amniota is a descendant class of Class Chordata. The graph indicates that members of Class Mollusca (including the cephalopods) are related to Class Chordata (including the amniotes) only by the most distant ancestral class (i.e., Class Bilateria).

The fact that cephalopods and humans are both highly intelligent, despite coming from distantly related classes, and (in the case of the cephalopods) from a class whose super-classes and sister classes are devoid of any discernible intelligence, merits a few inferences:

1. The intelligences that arose on earth arose entirely independently of one another, using entirely dissimilar anatomic and physiologic strategies

Because the two classes of animals that exhibit high intelligence have no close ancestors and are radically dissimilar in the anatomic and cellular organizations of their respective brains, we can conclude that their intelligence evolved independently.

One additional supportive observation is that the first cephalopods may have appeared as early as 522 million years ago [68]. The first amniotes seem to have appeared about 312 million years ago [69]. The asynchronous appearances of cephalopods and amniotes seem to indicate that the two classes evolved independently of one another.

2. High intelligence evolved at least twice in the history of the planet: Once in class Amniota and once in class Cephalopoda

Because the evolution of higher intelligence evolved independently in Class Amniota and Class Cephalopoda, we can infer that intelligence evolved more than once. Insofar as there may be additional intelligent classes of animals, extinct or extant, but unknown to us, we can infer that intelligence evolved at least twice in the history of the earth.

3. In the case of the octopus, intelligence may have arisen de novo, without preceding small steps achieved throughout its ancestral lineage

The parent and sister classes of Class Cephalopoda exhibit no signs of much intelligence. Hence we suspect that intelligence evolved de novo in the cephalopods.

4. Intelligence does not appear to confer any great evolutionary advantage, in terms of speciation

Neither Class Cephalopoda nor Class Amniota are particularly outstanding classes, in terms of the number of descendant species. There are about 800 living species of cephalopods, representing well under 1% of the species of mollusks. The gastropods (e.g., snails and slugs) account for about 80% of the approximately 100,000 known mollusk species. Among Class Amniota, the extant subclasses are reptiles, birds, and mammals, which represent a small portion of living animals. The putatively smartest subclass of the amniotes is Class Primata (the primates), most species of which are barely managing to survive. The self-appointed smartest of the smartest classes, Class Homo, contains merely one species, *Homo sapiens*. These facts would all suggest that intelligence barely registers as a factor in the diversification of species.

5. Intelligence may evolve again, in some unpromising class of animals. For that matter, the existence of two independent paths toward high intelligence may auger the development of intelligent life elsewhere in the universe.

The history of evolution is marked by occurrences that are so unlikely that they seem to have occurred once, and never again. The prototypical example of a non-repeating isolated evolutionary advancement is oxygenic photosynthesis. It would seem that the metabolic pathway for oxygenic photosynthesis required the independent development of two interacting pathways, both of which involved the evolutionary acquisition of a chain of complex enzymes. As far as we can tell, oxygenic photosynthesis evolved once, in ancient cyanobacteria, and all oxygenic photosynthesis occurring today involves the inheritance of ancient genes coding for the cyanobacterial pathway. Traits that evolve more than once in earth's long history are considered to be generally repeatable. That is to say that the traits are evolutionarily attainable and may arise in other organisms, at any time.

Regarding intelligence in the universe outside our planet, it is a rather chilling fact that many of the most intelligent animals on earth are predatory carnivores (e.g., humans, hawks, tigers, and octopi). We can only hope that intelligent life elsewhere in the universe does not evolve with the same predatory tendencies.

It is important to point out that none of the listed inferences could have been attained without the Classification of Life. By examining lineages and comparing features of one class against another we can begin to understand general biological relationships among living organisms.

Orthodiseases and the Classification of Life

Orthodiseases are conditions observed in non-human species that result from alterations in genes that are homologous to the genes known to cause diseases in humans. For example, if a loss of function mutation in a particular gene in humans were associated with an inherited blood cell disorder; and if a loss of function mutation in the homologous gene in a zebrafish resulted in lymphocytosis (proliferation of circulating lymphocytes), then we would consider the condition in zebrafish to be an orthodisease of the human genetic counterpart. To qualify as an orthodisease, the zebrafish need not be clinically identical to the human counterpart; it just needs to have, as its root cause, a defect in a homologous gene. Just as a reminder, two genes are homologous if they both are descended from the same ancestral gene. [Glossary Orthodisease]

Orthodiseases are important for two important reasons:

1. We are discovering the root mutations responsible for genetic diseases at a rate that far exceeds our ability to understand how the mutation produces its clinical phenotype. Orthodiseases often reveal the biological consequences of a mutation.
2. It is relatively cheap, fast, and easy to perform disease research in non-mammalian animals.

It's one thing to know the gene defect that is associated with human disease; it is quite another thing to understand how that gene defect contributes to the development of disease. Most experiments conducted on mammalian models of disease are very expensive to conduct and are often not helpful. Historically, the drug development process employs mouse models to identify candidate drugs for clinical trials in humans, but few such mouse-inspired trials have shown success [70–73]. The National Academy of Sciences recently convened a workshop entitled, "Therapeutic development in the absence of predictive animal models of nervous system disorders" [74]. Mouse models for common neurological disorders, such as Alzheimer's disease and Parkinson's disease have been largely unsuccessful [74,75]. In fact, multiple mouse models for Parkinson's disease have been developed, including the "parkin knockout mouse" and LRRK2 knockouts, but none have shown dopamine degeneration, motor dysfunction, or even the synuclein bodies that are characteristic of human Parkinson's disease [76]. Likewise, mouse models of Alzheimer's disease fail to develop the neurofibrillary tangles and neuronal losses that are hallmarks of the human disease. Even if refinements in the mouse model may produce mice with a disease marked by the same pathological changes that are observed in the human disease, the treatments developed for mice may not carry over to clinical trials in humans [72,77]. One of the repeated themes emerging from the National Academy of Sciences workshop is that animal models cannot predict how humans will respond to drugs that perturb the complex system of pathways involved in common human diseases [74]. The situation in the neurosciences is sufficiently discouraging that signs of a withdrawal from animal research by the pharmaceutical industry have been reported [78].

Where mammalian models of human genetic diseases have failed, we may find success studying the orthodisease equivalents of human diseases, in non-mammalian organisms. Organisms such as the nematode *Caenorhabditis elegans*, the fruit fly *Drosophila melanogaster*, the zebrafish *Danio rerio*, or the yeast *Saccharomyces cerevisiae*, can be propagated, manipulated genetically, and studied in the laboratory. Experiments on these non-mammalian species are conducted at much lower cost, and in much less time, than comparable experiments on rodents and other mammals [79].

At this point, we must ask the obvious question: "Why would an orthodisease in the yeast *S. cerevisiae* have any relevance to a disease occurring in humans?" Surely, the two diseases will have completely different clinical phenotypes. No yeast can develop heart disease or gout or an ovarian neoplasm!

The justification for orthodisease models of human pathologic processes follows the following line of reasoning:

1. The mutations that account for most genetic diseases in humans occur in conserved genes; the reason being that conserved genes are essential (otherwise, they would not be conserved). If a malfunction occurs in an essential gene, it is likely to produce some pathological consequences. Mutations in non-conserved genes, even when they result in an impairment of the gene product, tend not to produce disease.

2. A conserved gene is the one that is found throughout much of its phylogenetic lineage in roughly the same form and sequence. From this definition, we can infer that many conserved genes in humans will have close homologs throughout much of the eukaryotic lineages. As it happens, nearly 75% of human disease-causing genes are believed to have a functional homolog in the fly [80].

3. If a gene is essential for humans, it is probably essential for other organisms, and mutations of the gene will likely produce an orthodisease in some of these eukaryotic organisms.

4. Conserved genes tend to have a similar function (i.e., similar substrates and similar products) in every organism. The homologous conserved genes of humans that are found in non-mammalian animals are likely to participate in metabolic pathways that are at least similar to the pathways found in humans.

5. Drugs that are effective in modifying metabolic pathways in model organisms are likely to have similar biological effects in humans.

There is abundant observational and experimental evidence that seems to support our logic-based justification, and the study of human disease pathogenesis using non-mammalian orthodisease models is flourishing [79–84]. Where traditional animal models are failing, biologists are finding success with single-cell eukaryotes and insects. Though we can expect disease phenotypes to diverge among species affected by orthologous genes, we might be able to study specific pathways that have been conserved through most of the history of eukaryotic evolution. For example, the 2013 Nobel Prize in Physiology or Chemistry was awarded for work on vesicular transport disorders. Progress in this area came from studies of human inherited transport disorders [85]. However, the vesicular transport pathway was dissected by studying orthologous genes in yeast [83]. [Glossary Observational data]

Though yeast has many homologous genes with humans, there has been concern that the homologs may not participate in the same pathways in yeast as they do in humans. In a large study of pathway proteins involved in human spinocerebellar ataxias, it was found that the human genes coding those proteins have yeast homologs that code for proteins that participate in similar pathways [86]. This tells us that, for yeast models of the spinocerebellar ataxias, homologous pathways exist for homologous genes, supporting the relevance of the yeast model for human disease (Fig. 6.11).

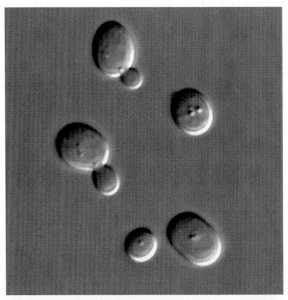

FIG. 6.11 The yeast *Saccharomyces cerevisiae*, a model organism for human disease research. *Source: Wikipedia, entered into the public domain by its copyright holder, Masur.*

The nematode *Caenorhabditis elegans* is a well-studied organism. Despite its different phylogenetic lineage (i.e., Class Protostomia, not Class Deuterostomia, containing humans) more than 65% of human disease-causing genes currently identified have a counterpart [87]. As a hermaphroditic organism, *C. elegans* has a particularly useful property that enhances its value in disease research. When organisms are exposed to mutagens, the first-generation progeny self-fertilize producing some second-generation offspring that are homozygous for the mutation. This has allowed researchers to study how specific mutations disrupt development and cause disease. [Glossary Mutagen]

When using nematodes (roundworms) to study human disease processes, we must be very careful to remember that biological systems are always complex and that the final phenotype resulting from a gene mutation is an emergent property of the total system, developing over time. For example, the root cause of human retinoblastoma (a cancer of retinal stem cells) is a mutation in the RB1 gene. Mutating the homologous gene in the nematode results in ectopic vulvae, a condition that is unmistakably different from retinoblastoma [84]. Nonetheless, pathways involved in causing retinoblastoma (in humans) and in causing ectopic vulvae (in *C. elegans*) may share many important commonalities, including sensitivity to potentially useful gene-targeted drugs (Fig. 6.12). [Glossary Trilateral retinoblastoma]

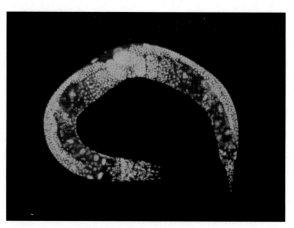

FIG. 6.12 *Caenorhabditis elegans*, a nematode (roundworm) about 1 mm in length. *C. elegans* serves as a model organism for human disease research. *Source: Wikipedia, from a public domain work from the U.S. National Institutes of Health.*

Another example of a useful orthologous organism is the fruit fly, *Drosophila melanogaster*. Drosophila contains homologs of the genes that cause tuberous sclerosis, a hamartoma-cancer syndrome in humans. The brain tubers (hamartomas of the neuroectoderm, also called phakomas), for which tuberous sclerosis takes its name, contain large, multinucleate neurons. Loss of function of the same genes in Drosophila produces enlarged cells with many times the normal amount of DNA [88]. The tuberous sclerosis orthodisease in Drosophila is being studied to help us understand cell growth control mechanisms in humans. [Glossary Hamartoma]

In addition, loss-of-function mutations in Drosophila genes, that are homologous to human tumor suppressor genes, have resulted in neoplasms growing from imaginal disc cells. These findings support the hypothesis that carcinogenesis involves conserved genes that have been evolving through the insect and the human evolutionary lineages [89]. [Glossary Loss-of-function mutation, Tumor suppressor gene]

The zebrafish (*Danio rerio*) is a species of small freshwater minnows. Their common name comes from the distinctive horizontal stripes on the sides of their bodies; a somewhat inaccurate appellation insofar as most of the stripes on zebras (*Equus quagga*) are nearly vertical. Zebrafish eggs are fertilized outside the mother's body, allowing scientists to inject DNA or RNA into one-cell-stage embryos, to produce transgenic or knock-out strains of zebrafish strains. Zebrafish are easy to grow, in large or small schools, and their development can be closely monitored, from egg onwards (Fig. 6.13).

FIG. 6.13 Zebrafish, a model organism for the study of human diseases. *Source: Wikipedia, and entered into the public domain by its author, Azul.*

Zebrafish share with humans the same class hierarchy, down to the level of Class Euteleostomi. At this point, the ancestors of the zebrafish branched to Class Actinopterygii (i.e., ray-finned fish accounting for at least 30,000 species of extant fish), while the ancestors of humans branched to Class Sarcopterygii (i.e., the lobe-finned fish). En route to Class Euteleostomi, the ancestors of humans and ray-finned fish descended through Class Metazoa, Class Bilateria, Class Craniata, Class Vertebrata and Gnathostomata. In doing so, zebrafish acquired nearly all the cell types that are present in humans today. Consequently, zebrafish and humans are not all that distant from one another, developmentally, and these two species have inherited the same class-determined immunologic systems, central nervous systems, and peripheral nervous systems. This being the case, it should not be surprising to learn that 70% of human genes are found in zebrafish [90].

In the past few decades, the zebrafish has become a very useful model for studying developmental and disease-related pathways in humans [91]. For example, zebrafish, as members of Class Chordata (like humans) develop chordomas (as do humans). As a fellow member of Class Craniata, the zebrafish has been an excellent model for neurocristopathies (i.e., diseases of the neural crest), including Waardenburg-Shah syndrome and Hirschsprung's disease [91–94]. [Glossary Neurocristopathy]

As was the case with *C. elegans*, it is important not to overinterpret experiments using zebrafish. In one large study, a gene in the zebrafish was shown to modulate its susceptibility to mycobacterial infection [95]. Naturally, there was hope that the orthologous gene in humans would be associated with human susceptibility to tuberculosis. Despite a large study involving 9115 subjects, no such association was found [96]. Again, we learned that the genetic root cause of a disease does not fully account for pathogenesis, which is an emergent property of the system in which the mutation is expressed. [Glossary Multi-step process]

Let's look at a few specific examples of orthodiseases. Because all animals of Class Craniata have a neural crest, all craniates are capable of developing tumors of the neural crest. Men and fish are cousins, and both belong to Class Craniata. Because man and fish both have neural crests, we both develop neural crest tumors [91,93,97]. It is easy to find schwannomas and melanomas in fish. It would be impossible to find such tumors in organisms that do not descend from Class Craniata. Do not expect to find schwannomas in a tarantula or a crab or a beetle or in any of the crowd of faceless species (i.e., non-craniates) that dwell among us. [Glossary Schwannoma]

Consider the carcinoid, a tumor arising primarily from the gut, that was formerly believed to be of neural crest origin. Carcinoid tumors are composed of cells containing small round cytoplasmic organelles known as either neurosecretory granules or dense-core granules. These granules contain hormone-like peptides that are similar to the hormones produced by endocrine cells of neural crest origin. It was presumed that neural crest cells had migrated to the gut during embryonic and fetal development and that neural crest cells dwelling in the gut were the source of the neuroendocrine cells composing carcinoid tumors [98].

For those of us who study the Classification of Life, the strongest argument against a neural crest origin for carcinoid tumors is based upon a simple observation made on crabs. Crabs, like humans, have a gut, and the crab gut is lined by endocrine cells that can secrete neuropeptides, just like carcinoid cells [99]. Crabs unlike humans, are not members of Class Craniata and therefore lack a neural crest. If the crab has no neural crest, it cannot have cells that derive from the neural crest. Therefore, neuroendocrine cells of the crab's gut do not derive from the neural crest. We can infer that gut neuroendocrine cells arose in animals before the evolution of the neural crest, in Class Craniata. Hence, there is no reason to think that the neuroendocrine cells that compose carcinoid tumors derive from the neural crest. It is currently believed that carcinoid tumor cells derive from specialized cells of endodermal origin, not of neural crest origin.

Here is one more example wherein our knowledge of the Classification of Life helps us reach a better understanding of tumor biology. The neural crest appeared as the defining class property of Class Craniata. The neural crest is the only embryonic tissue that can produce both muscle cells and neural cells, from the same stem cell population.

Pathologists occasionally encounter tumors composed of cells that contain muscle cells, mixed with neural cells. Tumors have a clonal origin, meaning that the cells that we observe in a tumor are all derived, at some point in cancer development, from single cells. Of all the embryonic anlagen, only the neural crest can produce muscle cells and neural cells. Hence, a tumor, of presumed clonal origin, that differentiates as a mixture of neoplastic muscle cells and neural cells, must have originated from a neural crest cell. As it happens, a mixed neural/muscle tumor has been shown to express the EWS/FLI1 fusion gene, a marker that seems to be specific for tumors of neural crest origin [100]. Thus, experimental evidence supports a neural crest origin of mixed muscle/nerve tumors, the same conclusion reached through our understanding that all members of Class Craniata (including humans) have a neural crest.

Section 6.6. How the classification of life unifies the biological sciences

Classification unifies evolution, embryology, and anatomy

If we want to understand the Classification of Life, then we must take some time to study human embryology. The reason for this is that class properties are tightly coupled to the milestones of embryonic development achieved through evolution. For example, when we look at classes of eukaryotic organisms, we can reconstruct the sequential recipes for embryonic development.

```
Class Eukaryota: Marked by the pre-embryonic zygote
Class Embryophyta: Marked by the evolution of the plant embryo
Class Sporophyta: Marked by the evolution of the plant seed
Class Metazoa: Marked by the formation of the blastulated embryo
Class Eumetazoa: Marked by the formation of a two-layered embryo
Class Bilateria: Marked by the formation of the three-layered
  embryo
Class Deuterostomia: Gastrulation and formation of an enterocoelom
Class Chordata: Marked by the formation of an embryonic backbone
Class Amniota: Marked by the evolution of egg-laying, on land
Class Eutheria: Marked by the evolution of the placenta
```

The list shown here demonstrates how each class's defining property represents an innovation in embryologic development. There is a simple reason why this is so. **You cannot modify a part until you have the part (and all parts of the developed organism develop from embryonic structures).** This condition imposes an order in the development of classes of organisms imposed by the development of the embryo, from which the organisms develop. To illustrate, you can't have angiosperms (flowering plants) until you have spermatophytes (seed plants, which will produce the seeds from which flowers grow). Such advances are always found in the embryo because you can't have a change in the adult without first having a change in the anlage of the involved adult part. It is exclusively through embryonic development that fully developed organisms acquire their distinguishing class properties. Hence, every evolutionary feature expressed in adult organisms (e.g., feathers on birds, placentas in mammals, fins on fish) must have arisen in the embryo. [Glossary Evo-devo]

Some readers must be thinking that our claim that the properties of classes of organisms are expressed in the evolving embryo seems much like a rephrasing of the discredited and often vilified maxim that "Ontogeny recapitulates phylogeny." We must digress a moment to explain the meaning and history of this catchy but misleading phrase, and why it does not strictly apply here.

Near the end of the nineteenth century, one of the greatest evolutionary biologists to have ever graced this world made a small blunder that ravaged his scientific reputation, and that provided creationists with enough ammunition to attack the theory of evolution through the following century. The biologist was Ernst Haeckel (1834–1919), and his blunder can be summarized in three memorable words: "Ontogeny recapitulates Phylogeny."

What is the meaning of "Ontogeny recapitulates phylogeny?" There are many interpretations of this three-word bombshell, but let's try to keep it simple. Ontogeny is embryonic development. During embryonic development, the anlagen of organs appear, and their anatomic arrangement is determined. Phylogeny is the evolutionary descent and diversification of species from common ancestors. The slogan "ontogeny recapitulates phylogeny" asserts that during the embryologic development of an organism, it will reproduce all of the embryologic forms of its ancestors. For example, as the human embryo develops, it will begin as a simple eukaryote (the zygote) and progress to a ball of cells (recapitulating the proposed ancient gallertoids that preceded animals) and then a blastula (recapitulating an embryonic early metazoans) and then a two-layered organism (recapitulating an embryonic eumatazoan), followed by a trophoblast (recapitulating an embryonic bilaterian), and so forth until a human fetus emerges. [Glossary Gallertoid]

If ontogeny truly recapitulated phylogeny, we could reconstruct the entire phylogenetic ancestry of any living species, simply by capturing every phase of its embryologic development. For example, somewhere in human development, we could expect to find an embryo that had the same form as the embryo of the ancestral organism for all living apes.

Haeckel's theory holds up moderately well, at least for the early embryo. In some species, observations seem to provide strong confirmation. For example, amphibians evolved from sarcopterygian fish. Every species of amphibia passes through a "fishy" stage of development before emerging as fully developed frogs, toads, salamanders, or caecilians. This being the case, why has Haeckel's theory been discredited? There are two large flaws in the proposition that "ontogeny recapitulates phylogeny."

1. Evolutionary innovations are ontogenetically non-sequential

No law limits evolutionary innovations to temporal order. For example, Class Eutheria (the placental mammals) is characterized by the evolution of the placenta. The placenta is not an add-on at the end of ontogeny. The placenta begins to form at the earliest stage of embryonic development. Hence, one of the defining embryologic features of eutherians, a class of organism positioned way down the ancestral lineage of animals, is found by examining the very earliest embryo (corresponding to a class very high in the class lineage of animals). If ontogeny were a sequential recapitulation of phylogeny, then we would expect the first appearance of the placenta to occur late in embryonic development, at the stage that recapitulates the entrance of Class Eutheria.

Today, it's easy for us to imagine new mutations arising in any gene, potentially affecting any stage of embryonic development. In Haeckel's hay-day, DNA and the genetic code were unknown, and genes were a vague abstraction.

2. Embryologic processes occur concurrently, and the pace of those processes will vary among species

We think of embryologic development as a stepwise affair: first the zygote, then the blastula, then the gastrula, and so on. We lose sight of the fact that sequential processes can branch, with each branch of the process developing simultaneously with other branches. Moreover, the pace at which different branches of embryonic development progress may vary among different organisms of the same ancestral lineage. This tells us that even if the order of events is the same in every species, variations in speed will cause some branches of development to fall "out of step" with other branches when we compare different species. Hence, there can be no expectation that any temporal stage of embryonic development will have a corresponding temporal stage of development in an ancestral embryo. Once again, nature violates "ontogeny recapitulates phylogeny."

Putting aside his professional difficulties arising from the assertion that ontogeny recapitulates phylogeny, Haeckel was one of the greatest naturalists in the history of science. Today, Haeckel is best remembered for his remarkable legacy of beautiful and detailed drawings of classes of organisms, some of which serve as illustrations in this book.

Evolutionary advances of the embryo determine many of the class properties upon which the Classification of Life is built, thus reminding us that the genomes of living organisms are primarily devoted to the task of producing the embryo. The cellular activities related to adult behavior (e.g., walking, gathering food, eating) are impressive, but not nearly so much as the activities of embryonic development. We see evidence of the overwhelming dominance of the embryonic life form in those organisms that spend the majority of their lives passing through stages of development, with the adult organism appearing for a brief time, primarily to procreate (e.g., butterflies, cicadas). It is in the embryo and the fetus that germ layers are created, cell types are programmed, metabolic pathways are established, and organs are formed. The embryo deals the cards, and the adult organism plays the hand that it is dealt. Lewis Wolpert emphasized the disproportionate significance of embryonic development when he wrote, "It is not birth, marriage, or death, but gastrulation which is truly the most important time in your life."

Because it is the embryo, not the adult organism, that is the primary recipient of evolution, we should not be surprised to find that retained evolutionary innovations of the embryo may easily work to the detriment of the adult organism. In 2021, the 17-year cicadas arose as adult organisms, throughout the Eastern United States. The larval form of the cicada lives underground on tree roots for 17 years, at which time the adult emerges to live for a few short weeks before dying. In their brief adult existence, they do their best to mate and the fertilized females deposit their eggs in trees. The eggs develop to the nymph stage, which burrows into the base of the tree, to begin another 17-year cycle. As anyone in the Eastern U.S. can tell you, the adult cicadas are ungainly flyers, have almost no ability to evade capture by predatory animals, and seem all too eager to drop dead on sidewalks and driveways. Evolution never favored the survival of the adult cicada. Evolution is mostly about the survival of the embryo. In this case, the embryo evolved to survive 17 years underground (Fig. 6.14).

FIG. 6.14 The short-lived adult form of the Eastern 17-year cicada, Snodgrass *Magicicada septendecim*.

Once we tie evolution to embryology, it becomes easy to see that human anatomy evolved before the time when humans came into existence. Here is an example demonstrating that the adult structure of an organism is little more than an evolutionary afterthought. In every mammal, the left and right vocal cords are innervated by the recurrent laryngeal nerves. This nerve, follows a circuitous route from the spinal cord (via the vagus nerve), down the length of the neck, into the thorax, and back up again to its final destination in the larynx. When we humans decide to speak, our larynx is on the job. There doesn't seem to be any lapse whatsoever between the thought and the action. The close temporal relationship between thought and speech results from the close spatial relation between brain, mouth, larynx, and upper thorax. Nerve impulses need not travel very far before they can be translated into action. Such is not the case for giraffes, whose right recurrent laryngeal nerve may attain a length of 15 ft. Giraffes, despite their gregarious nature, have almost no vocal power thanks, in no small part, to needlessly long recurrent laryngeal nerves [101].

Why does evolution put up with the absurdity of anatomy? At this point, it should be obvious that evolution is all about the embryo, not the adult organism. In the embryo, the recurrent laryngeal nerve is tiny, and its future length has nothing whatsoever to do with the success of the development of the embryo.

Inherited symmetry; it's all about the embryo

Class Bilateria, the trophoblasts, have three embryonic layers (endoderm, mesoderm, and ectoderm). Animals of Class Bilateria display bilateral symmetry (i.e., their bodies can be divided into two symmetrical halves by a plane that runs along a central axis) [102]. Hence, the bilaterians have laterality, with an anterior head, a posterior tail, a dorsal back, and a ventral belly.

Starfish are members of Class Bilateria, with axial symmetry and five arms. But wait. How is it possible for a 5-armed organism to have bilateral symmetry. Shouldn't a symmetrical starfish have four arms, or maybe six arms? (Fig. 6.15).

FIG. 6.15 A Red-knobbed starfish with five arms, openly violating axial symmetry. *Source: Wikipedia, released into the public domain by its author, Arpingstone.*

We must remember that class lineage has everything to do with sequential embryologic processes, and very little to do with what we observe in adult organisms. Adult organisms often display secondary changes due to developmental events that occur after a fundamental embryologic process has occurred. Yes, the adult starfish violates axial symmetry, but the embryonic starfish has lovely symmetry, and it is the embryo that expresses the phylogenetic innovations of its ancestors (Fig. 6.16).

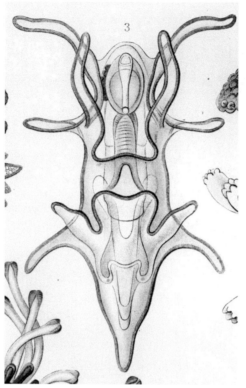

FIG. 6.16 Diagram of a starfish larva, illustrating a bilateral body plan. *Source: Wikipedia, from a drawing by Ernst Haeckel published in "Kunstformen der Natur", 1904.*

Likewise, we humans are descendants of Class Bilateria. When we look at adult humans, we see some indication that we arose from a bilateral embryo (e.g., two kidneys, two lungs, two lobes to our brains), but we also see asymmetrical organs (one spleen, one liver, and a wandering alimentary tract that crisscrosses the body's central axis). What happened to break our beautiful embryonic symmetry?

There are numerous examples in which embryonic symmetry is lost by twists and turns of embryonic tissues, during the fetal period: an axial twist of the early brain, producing the optic chiasm [103]; a twist of the intestines, shifting the liver to the right side of the chest; a fusion and twist of the embryonic aortic arches, producing the heart. Some bilaterians work hard to preserve their symmetry. For example, when an arm is amputated, in young jellyfish of species *Aurelia aurita*, the body rearranges the remaining arms so that they are evenly spaced around the body [104]. So far as we can tell, embryonic development in bilaterians begins with perfect symmetry. Asymmetry arises at various times during development (Fig. 6.17).

[Glossary Chiasm], [Glossary Ontogeny]

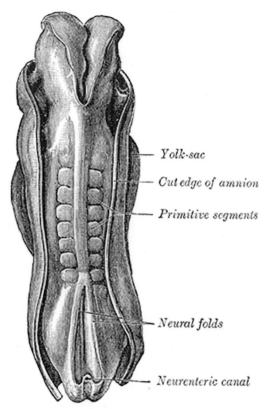

Yolk-sac

Cut edge of amnion

Primitive segments

Neural folds

Neurenteric canal

FIG. 6.17 Drawing of the dorsum of a human embryo, 2.11 mm. in length. In the early embryonic stages, the human anatomy has bilateral symmetry, as we would expect from any member of Class Bilateria. *Source: 20th U.S. edition of Gray's Anatomy of the Human Body, originally published in 1918.*

The Classification of Life meets chemistry

> *An animal is a chemical reaction so unstable that it is instantly reversed at death.*
>
> Steve Jones, from his book "In the Blood"

For many centuries, it was assumed that all living cells were imbued with a life force. This seemed sensible because, otherwise, we humans would be nothing more than chemistry sets. As it turns out, despite wishing it were otherwise, we are just chemistry sets. The chemical reactions that occur within our cells can be easily replicated in test tubes. If a life force is present in living organisms, it does not seem to be a necessary component of cellular metabolism.

If we assume that all organisms are just fancy chemistry sets, then we must ask: "Were all organisms built with the same manufacturer's chemistry set, or did our chemicals come from a wide range of suppliers?" It would seem that we were all built from the same source of chemicals. As it happens, molecules have geometric chiralities. A molecule is chiral if it cannot be superimposed upon its mirror image. The chiral forms are "D" (dexter or right) and L (levo or left) isomers, with the "D" and "L" referring to the respective directions in which light is reflected off the molecule. In a non-enzymatic molecular synthesis, such as might occur in a test tube, "D" and "L" forms are produced in near-equal quantities. To the surprise of chemists, the same molecules, when found in living organisms, occur almost exclusively with a particular chirality; and the same chirality extends throughout the classes of living organisms. For example:

> D-isomers of saccharides prevail over L-isomers in living organisms.
> L-isomers of phospholipids prevail over D-isomers in living organisms.
> All Amino acids of proteins have the S (left) configuration [105].
> All ribose units in nucleic acids have the R (right) configuration [105].

Let's stop to consider why an organism might evolve to prefer one isomeric form of the metabolic molecule. In the case of enzymatic metabolism of "D" and "L" forms of substrate molecules, chirality is an issue. The catalytic units of enzymes operate by fitting the substrate molecule (e.g., a saccharide) into a matching site. A D-isomer of a molecule will not fit into a site that matches the L-isomer of the same molecule. Hence, only one form of the isomer can be metabolized by a particular enzyme.

We see that monochirality is required for a variety of metabolic functions. Polypeptides synthesized by a random distribution of amino acids with right and left chirality would not function very well. Likewise, a nucleic acid built from a mixture of ribose molecules having randomly either left or right chirality could not achieve the regular helical structure observed in our genomes.

The prevalence of identical chemical monochiralities observed in virtually every living organism would suggest that chemical substrates of particular chirality were selected at some remote moments in time, and the genes enforcing those selections promulgated throughout all of the living organisms that subsequently evolved [105]. Chirality-specific sites in enzymes and synthetic machinery also tell us that gene evolution is highly constrained to code for just those particular forms of proteins that recognize a specific molecular chirality in substrate molecules [106]. The observations that all living organisms have the same chirality would suggest that all life on the planet arose from a common ancient ancestor. If the organisms of the earth arose independently, without a common ancestor, then we would not expect all organisms to have the same isomeric preferences.

We can draw one more valuable inference from the chiral specificity of molecules in all known living organisms. The absence of any organisms that defy the general features of chirality indicate that the Classification of Life is complete. Otherwise, we would have encountered exceptions to the classification that would necessitate reconstruction of the class hierarchy and the addition of new branches to accommodate the organisms with alternate chiralities.

Chemical diversity

When we think about what we were all taught about rocks and minerals, we get the impression that our planet is filled with an endless variety of naturally occurring chemicals. In point of fact, the number of minerals that formed before the emergence of terrestrial life is quite limited. There are under 100 naturally occurring elements, and there are about 6000 cataloged minerals. An earnest mineralogist could learn them all if she put her mind to it. When it comes to gathering a list of all the chemical compounds on earth, the really big numbers don't come into play until we begin counting the chemical species produced by living organisms.

Let's do just a simple review of the chemical diversity provided by living organisms. There are many millions of species of living organisms on the planet. There are so many species of organisms that we will probably never know their true extent. Estimates vary from tens of millions up to trillions [15]. Each species of organism has its species-specific genome template, and each individual of the species has its variant of the species genome. All of these many trillions of genomes represent unique molecules, so we can say, just as a first pass, that nearly all of the distinct chemical molecules found on planet earth are produced by organisms, and are not found as the residue of planet creation. When we consider that each of the individual genomes from all these organisms is busy coding for organic molecules (e.g., proteins, lipids, carbohydrates, and various types of nucleic acids in addition to those found in the genome's DNA), then we greatly expand the number of molecular species kindly provided by living organisms.

We can think of living organisms as small chemical factories, specializing in the synthesis of carbon-based molecules. Carbon, the third most abundant atom in the universe, has four electrons in its outer shell, rendering the atoms ripe for electron sharing via stable covalent bonds with hydrogen, oxygen, nitrogen, and with other carbon atoms. Because carbon is the main bonding ingredient in every organism, we can hypothesize that all organisms arose from a common, carbon-based ancestor. If we were to encounter even one species on planet earth that was not carbon-based, then we would almost certainly need to change our modern vision of the root origin of life on earth.

In a sense, it is quite evident that living organisms would be the major creators of chemicals since all organisms are fundamentally chemical reactions confined within tiny membranous bags that are themselves composed of chemicals. Among the extant organisms populating the earth, which species are credited as the greatest contributors to the diversity of chemical species?

We must begin by confessing that Class Metazoa (animals) is filled with metabolic underachievers in terms of the diversity of their synthesized chemicals [107]. The prokaryotes are far more productive [108]. Among the eukaryotes, only Class Archaeplastida (i.e., plants) and Class Fungi seem to be making any effort to impress [109,110]. The eukaryotes largely rely on endosymbiotic relationships with current or former prokaryotes to perform complex biosynthesis (e.g., mitochondria and chloroplasts captured from former bacteria). Otherwise, eukaryotes are saddled with the rather hum-drum tasks of synthesizing organelles and membranes and manipulating the basic ingredients that sustain cellular life (carbohydrates, structural and enzymatic proteins, lipids, nucleic acids). An awful lot of the metabolic effort in eukaryotes is devoted to the eternal activities of eating and digesting food. Hence, the fundamental chemical constituents of living organisms were established about 3 or 4 billion years ago, and haven't changed much since. DNA, RNA, proteins, and lipids, and the biological machinery for their manufacture and modification were all established about two billion years ago.

Some estimates suggest that the first fungi appeared as early as 1.3 billion years ago, while the first land plants may have evolved 700 million years ago. The first fossils of vascular land plants are dated to about 480 million years ago, just after the end of the Cambrian explosion (about 500 million years ago). Regardless of the timing, we can surmise that following the Cambrian explosion, plants, fungi, and metazoans were obliged to evolve their coping mechanisms for planetary cohabitation. [Glossary Cambrian explosion]

Whereas animals rely on their body structure for both aggressive and defensive activities (e.g., running toward prey and running away from predators), plants and fungi rely on their ability to synthesize bioactive chemicals that act as respiratory poisons (e.g., cyanide), neuromuscular agents (e.g., nicotine), irritants (e.g., capsaicin), and a host of other chemical warfare agents. When we eat plants and mushrooms, we can expect to ingest some of the chemicals that the plants created, to kill us. For example, cycasin is a toxin and carcinogen found in the seeds and the pollen of every class of cycad tree [111]. Among the fungi, Aspergillus flavus, a ubiquitous fungus found growing on peanuts and other crop plants, synthesizes aflatoxin, one the most powerful liver carcinogens known [112]. Peanut butter manufacturers take pains to harvest peanuts under conditions that minimize their contamination with aflatoxin; and they measure the amounts of aflatoxin in manufactured peanut butter to ensure that batches that exceed an allowed level will never reach the market.

Fungi produce alpha-amanitin, a strong, often fatal toxin, produced by the mushroom Amanita phalloides. Another fungal product is gyromitrin, a hydrazine compound present in most members of the common False Morel genus. Nobody is quite sure how small quantities of gyromitrin and other related hydrazine molecules may affect the health of mushroom eaters, but the hydrazines, as a group, seem to be toxic to humans.

Weaponized molecules play no role in the primary functions of plant and fungal cells (i.e., do not participate in cellular physiologic processes), and are referred to as secondary metabolites or as idiolites [109]. The terminology conveys the idea that if all the secondary metabolites in a plant cell or a fungal cell were to disappear, then the cells would survive happily, provided that no predatory organisms spoiled their fun.

Secondary metabolites account for a large portion of the chemical diversity in bacteria, plants, and fungi [110]. Plants devote 15%–25% of their genes to producing enzymes involved in the synthesis of secondary metabolites; of which several hundred thousand have been reported [113]. We presume that every secondary metabolite is bioactive under some set of circumstances; otherwise, the synthetic method for creating the chemical would not have evolved. In point of fact, the discipline of medicinal chemistry, as it was pursued in the 20th century, consisted of finding appropriate secondary metabolites from bacteria, fungi or plants, that would have some utility in the prevention or treatment of human diseases.

Of course, when it comes to unbridled chemical diversity, disconnected from any apparent survival benefit, nothing beats the arrogance of contemporary humans. Chemists create, in their laboratories, at least one million new chemical species yearly. There are over 100 million man-made chemicals, dwarfing anything we might expect to come from any other living organism, and prompting the somewhat sexist adage: "Whatever a chemist can imagine, he can make" [114].

In summary, virtually all chemical diversity arises as to the result of organismal diversity, which is, in turn, encapsulated within the Classification of Life.

Protein diversity

The earth's proteome consists of the translational products of the different protein-coding genes contained in the various organisms inhabiting our planet. The estimates of the planetary proteome vary widely. The lowest number seems to be 5 million [115]. Elsewhere, we read that the human intestine contains about 40,000 species of bacteria producing a whopping 9 million unique bacterial genes [116–118]. It seems plausible that before all the counts come in, we'll find that there are billions of protein species in the total collection. [Glossary Translation]

What organism is responsible for contributing the greatest number of protein species to earth's proteome? Currently, it is impossible to know, but one thing is certain: humans, for all our complexity, are slouches when it comes to creating protein species. The human genome contributes a meager 20–25 thousand protein-coding genes to the proteome. Other, seemingly less complex, animals have a larger genetic repertoire than humans. For example, the nearly microscopic crustacean *Daphnia pulex* (the water flea) has 31,000 genes. Plants tend to have way more genes than animals. For example, rice has an estimated 46–56 thousand protein-coding genes [119].

Certainly, the millions, or perhaps billions, of distinct proteins in Earth's proteome deserve a classification of their own. When we try to pin down a guiding principle by which to classify proteins, we seem to run into insurmountable problems, regardless of which principle we follow. Let's consider some of our options:

1. Protein classification by amino acid sequence

Conformationally similar proteins may be encoded by highly dissimilar sequences. In these cases, the conformation might be conserved between species, while the gene sequences may be largely irrelevant except for some small segments that confer similar conformational shapes to parts of the protein. Hence, if we try to classify proteins according to their amino acid sequences, we will produce a classification where the relationships among classes will not always correlate with protein function, which is partly determined by the shape. Hence, it becomes difficult to classify proteins by amino acid sequences.

Furthermore, a classification of proteins based on amino acid sequence would be incompatible with our classification of living organisms, in which organisms of the same class are expected to have similar metabolic pathways and protein functionalities. Because the sequence of amino acids in a protein does not always correlate with functionality, then the assembled classes of proteins will not correlate with the class properties of organisms.

2. Protein classification by function

One additional revelation has shaken our early notions of pathways, this being the observation that a single protein may have many different biological functions, and that a single function may be served by a multitude of different proteins. In "Section 1.4. Things that defy simple classification," we discussed the many cellular roles played by the p53 protein [120,121]. It is difficult to predict biological outcomes when pathways change their primary functionality based on cellular context. Various mutations in p53 have been linked to 11 clinically distinguishable cancer-related conditions, and there is little reason to assume that the same biological role is played in all of these 11 disorders [122]. [Glossary Ataxia telangiectasia, Cancer progression, DNA repair, Druggable driver, Initiation, Li-Fraumeni syndrome, Mutation]

Likewise, the Pelger-Huet anomaly and Hydrops-ectopic calcification-'moth-eaten' (HEM) are both caused by mutations of a gene, coding for the lamin B receptor. Pelger-Huet anomaly is a morphologic aberration of neutrophils wherein the normally multi-lobed nuclei become coffee bean-shaped, or bilobed, with abnormally clumped chromatin. The condition is called an anomaly, rather than a disease because despite the physical abnormality, affected white cells seem to function adequately. HEM is a congenital chondrodystrophy that is characterized by hydrops fetalis (i.e., accumulations of fluid in the fetus), and skeletal abnormalities. It would be difficult to imagine any two diseases as dissimilar to one another as Pelger-Huet anomaly and HEM. How could these disparate diseases be caused by a mutation involving the same gene? As it happens, the lamin B receptor has two separate functions: preserving the structure of chromatin and serving as a sterol reductase in cholesterol synthesis [123]. These two different and biologically unrelated functions, in one gene product, account for two different and biologically unrelated diseases. [Glossary Congenital disorder, Neutrophils]

An example wherein different proteins have evolved to serve one equivalent function is found in the evolution of lens crystallins [124,125]. In the following cases, the protein comprising the principal lens protein, serving to produce a clear, refractive lens, varies among animals, on a phylogenetic basis, as shown:

alphaA-Crystallin in vertebrates derives from the gene coding for a small heat shock protein homolog

delta1-Crystallin, found in birds and reptiles, derives from the gene coding for argininosuccinate lyase homolog

zeta-Crystallin, found in guinea pig, camel, and llama, derives from gene coding for quinine oxidoreductase

pi-Crystallin, found in gecko, derives from the gene coding for glyceraldehyde-3-phosphate dehydrogenase

nu-Crystallin, found in elephant shrew, derives from the gene coding for retinaldehyde dehydrogenase

omega/L-Crystallin, found in cephalopods and scallops, derives from the gene coding for a homolog of aldehyde dehydrogenase

J3-Crystallin, found in cubomedusan jellyfish, derives from the gene coding for a homolog of saposin

In all these cases, we see that the product of a gene may serve multiple unrelated functions (e.g., as zeta-Crystallin and as quinine oxidoreductase), and in which one function is served, in different species, by the products of alternate genes. Of course, the evolution of this phenomenon has sparked lively debate, but we can take it as one more example of the molecular flexibility of metabolic pathways [126,127]. Because we cannot assign one function to one protein, we cannot create a sensible classification of proteins, based on function.

3. Protein classification by conformation

In many cases, the function of a protein is determined by its shape. For example, the shape of a protein at its active site determines enzyme activity. The shape of an antibody protein determines its attachments to an antigen. The shape of a collagen molecule determines its structural function. It seems only logical that we can build a useful classification of proteins according to their conformational types.

In point of fact, proteins can be organized into broad classes depending on their shapes. Such classes include globular proteins, fibrous proteins, membranous proteins, and disordered proteins. The disordered protein lacks any fixed three-dimensional structure, but may include partially structured domains.

Classifying proteins based on conformation is made difficult for several reasons:

- A protein may transition from one conformation to another, and a single protein molecule may have several different conformations under various conditions. Proteins that can adopt different conformations under one amino acid sequence are known as metamorphic proteins [128]. Hence, it becomes difficult to classify such proteins according to their conformation.
- Establishing conformational similarities can be computationally intensive, and even impossible, when the number of structurally characterized proteins grows to be very

large. Hence, if we decide to classify proteins based on observed conformation, we could easily miss finding the conformations that determine class relationships.
- Intrinsically disordered proteins account for a sizeable portion of the total number of proteins. It is difficult to classify by conformation a protein that has no discernible conformation.

Nonetheless, we need not lose all hope. The conformational properties of proteins are achieved through evolutionary processes, including pre-translational alterations (e.g., subtle changes in the sequence of the genes that code for the protein) and post-translational changes (e.g., protein adduct attachments and protein folding pathways). It seems possible that a given conformation in a protein may arise through different sets of protein folding pathways, in different organisms, and these pathways (not the product) may be evolutionarily conserved in a species.

As it happens, particular conformations of proteins seem to be characteristic of specific classes of organisms. For example, one particular conformation (named DUF1285) is found in alpha, gamma, and delta proteobacteria. Another conformation (PB002487) is found in beta-proteobacteria. The UPF0598 conformation is found in metazoans [128].

It remains to be seen whether it would be possible to build a classification of proteins based on their shapes, but such a classification might be compatible with the Classification of Life if the protein conformation process is shown to be a property of the class of organism in which the protein is assembled and shaped.

4. Algorithmic protein classification

With all the aforementioned impediments to classification, maybe we should hand the job over to a computer. There are excellent algorithms available that can group proteins using a set of different properties (i.e., function, sequence, conformation, folding family) and produce a complete classification in which the proteins are grouped by their similarity measures.

This approach sounds good, but it violates the rule that classifications are classes of relationships; not similarities. Any similarities that may exist among proteins belonging to the same class are a consequence of their class assignment. We must always keep in mind Gaylord Simpson's admonition, "Individuals do not belong in the same taxon because they are similar, but they are similar because they belong to the same taxon."

Aside from that, computational taxonomy is highly limited by the information available. If there are millions of protein species, then it would be difficult to collect a rich set of data on every protein member. At this point, much of our most trusted information about proteins is faulty [129–131]. Scientists make mistakes, and it may be difficult to find the errors in a fast-growing database having many independent contributors. In addition, there are technical difficulties determining function and conformation for a protein whose conformation is disordered; and there are many such proteins.

In summary, it may be premature, at this time, to create a protein classification. Because every distinct, naturally occurring protein molecule is synthesized by a living organism, it is reasonable to simply store information about individual proteins as properties of its species-of-origin. In this manner, the classification of proteins can be temporarily subsumed by the Classification of Life. At some point in the future, when the general relationships among proteins become simplified and less mutable, a valid protein classification may emerge.

Structural diversity of organisms

Structural diversity is perhaps the only form of diversity in which Class Metazoa (animals) seems to take the lead over other forms of life (e.g., prokaryotes, single-cell eukaryotes, plants, fungi). One animal may look strikingly different from another animal, despite belonging to the same genus. Structural diversity took off in the Cambrian period (541–485 million years ago), when nearly all the extant metazoan body plans were established. Although there were simple multicellular animals who lived before the Cambrian (i.e., about 600 million years ago), it would seem that the dominant eukaryotes were standard issue unicellular organisms. The pre-Cambrian animals varied in terms of size and shape and external structures (e.g., wavy membranes, pseudopods, undulipodia, and cilia), but they couldn't compete with the diversity of structures that arose in the Cambrian explosion. We can think of the Cambrian as the era when metazoan diversity shifted from chemical to structural diversity, the latter being the preferred mechanism for moving organisms to capture prey. Interestingly, plants never evolved muscle cells. Chemical diversity is the preferred mechanism for immobile organisms, such as plants and fungi, to attack or defend themselves.

The key event that propelled the attainment of structural diversity in metazoans was almost certainly the evolution of specialized junctions, particularly the desmosome, that uniquely characterize animal cells. The desmosomes act like rivets, and soft animal cells serve as somewhat modular building blocks that can be assembled into almost any shape and size imaginable (e.g., ducts, glands, acini, cavities, membranes). The emergence of desmosome-lined cells allowed the evolution of the embryonic blastocyst, which happens to be the defining feature of all metazoan life.

In the Cambrian period, much of the structural diversity occurred when hardened tissues of different shapes, sizes, and purposes proliferated. These included cuticles, bones, teeth, and cartilage composed of collagen, keratin, chitin, and hydroxyapatite deposited into proteinaceous matrices (i.e., bone). These tough accessories permitted the animal kingdom to produce a multitude of species with variable-shaped outer and inner structures. The field of paleontology has, until recently, been devoted to understanding the characteristic design of the hard structures that distinguish one animal from another.

Among the animals, the holometabolous insects probably take the prize when it comes to structural diversity, insofar as a single organism may pass through multiple stages of life, each having a distinctive structural morphology. [Glossary Holometabolism]

Fungi and plants display a fair amount of structural diversity; usually simple variations on common themes (e.g., stalk, leaves, flowers). With few exceptions, the plant kingdom does a much better job with colors than does the animal kingdom. Plants rely on flavo-noids (particularly anthocyanins) and carotenoids to produce their wonderful and vivid colors. For the most part, animals have a single pigment molecule, melanin, as their primary source of coloration. An assortment of colors can be coaxed from the melanin molecule by controlling the concentration and spatial distribution of melanin within cells, and by making small modifications to the base molecule. Other colors, such as the red of hemoglobin, are produced with iron and other metal cofactors bound to proteins. [Glossary Cofactor]

   The value to humans of molecular diversity

For humans, the molecular diversity of living organisms allows us to find new antibiotics, new anti-cancer agents, and new methods to control and modify just about any metabolic pathway or regulatory mechanism we choose to study. In fact, scientists have been exploiting the chemical diversity of plants and fungi for thousands of years. To name just a few: white willow trees, whose bark gives us aspirin; cinchona trees, whose bark gives us quinine; weeping belled flowers of the foxglove plant, the source of digitalis; smooth black-berried belladonna plants, the source of atropine; red-petaled *Papaver somniferum*, the black-trimmed centers from which plump seed heads bulge with opium; roses whose fruits are a source of the anti-scorbutic, Vitamin C; yellow-blossomed sweet clover, whose moldy silage provided warfarin; the autumn crocus and the flame lily, both of which are natural sources of the gout medication, colchicine; and tobacco plants, the source of nicotine.

   In the late nineteenth century, there was a rush of discoveries of highly effective anti-biotics developed from common fungi (e.g., penicillin from *Penicillium chrysogenum*). More recently, we have been exploiting the genetic machinery of various gene-targeted treatments. Thanks to genetic diversity we have found the thermophilic Taq polymerase (from *Thermus aquaticus* bacteria) used in PCR (polymerase chain reactions) and the gene-editing enzymes used in CRISPR/Cas9 (prokaryotic species) and Cre-LoxP (bacteriophage P1), and CAR-T (lentiviral and gammaretroviral vectors) [132–135]. [Glossary CAR T-cell therapy, CRISPR]

   How did we know how to find the molecules that we would need to fight disease? Much of the early advances in the pharmacology of natural substances can be credited to a combination of luck and persistence. Ultimately, though, discoveries of the properties of individual species are directed by our knowledge of the Classification of Life. It is through an understanding of the classes of organisms that ancient healers understood which groups of plants were edible, which groups of plants were poisonous, and which groups of plants were medicinal. As mentioned in "Section 4.4. Saving hopeless classifications," one of the earliest, and most influential, classifications of herbal medicines were the *De Materia Medica*, written by the Greek physician and botanist Dioscorides in 60 CE [136]. This scholarly work contained a thoughtful discussion on the topic of taxonomic organization of groups of medicinal plants. Today, we have a fair idea of the various properties of classes of organisms, and we stand a good chance of finding an organism most likely to have a medically useful attribute, based on a deep understanding of the Classification of Life.

The Classification of Life meets geography

When we examine the full Classification of Life, one of the unexpected findings that we encounter, for plants and animals, is that whole classes of animals are often restricted to one particular location.

For example:

- Lemurs live on Madagascar and nowhere else.
- The platyrrhines, the New World monkeys, live only in Mexico and Central and South America.
- Most marsupials (Class Metatheria) live in Australia, and Australia hosts many types of marsupials that are not present on any other continent.
- Likewise, Australia hosts the highest number of eucalyptus trees, and many species are found nowhere else on earth.
- Reptiles are confined to a band flanking the equator and encircling the planet, with the highest concentration of reptiles living more or less on the equator.
- Mammals of Class Xenarthra are largely confined to South America.
- The Avocado plant is native to Central and South America and has only recently been exported, through human agency, to the other areas around the globe, all having a warm climate, hospitable to the fruit.

The list goes on and on. Sometimes the geographic location is best explained by climate. In the case of the reptiles, all of which are cold-blooded, they naturally prefer a hot climate, and we find most classes of reptiles living near the equator. Sometimes a geographic preference is determined by food sources. The giant panda has evolved to eat a specific species of bamboo and dwells only in South Central China, where its bamboo grows. Sometimes the geographic location is determined by geographic limitations to migration. For example, frogs are killed by seawater. Hence, frogs are seldom found on islands. Lemurs evolved on Madagascar from ancestral species that gave rise to all of the closely related species that are found uniquely on Madagascar, an island that affords no opportunity for lemurs to migrate to Africa, its closest continent. The avocado seed is encased in a large, hard stone. When dinosaurs and giant sloths roamed South America, the gullet was sufficiently large to eat avocados whole, including its indigestible stone. The avocado plant spread wherever these behemoths happened to defecate. When the dinosaurs and giant sloths died out, there were no animals capable of spreading the avocado's seed, and the plant remained in just those areas of South American where it had previously grown [137].

For the most part, zoologists and botanists have no problem explaining the geographic preference of any particular class of extant organism. **The observation that zoologists and botanists were not prepared to explain was the presence of fossils of animals and plants on continents where the extant descendants of those fossils are never found.** For example, why would we expect to find in Patagonia (at the Southern tip of South America) fossils of eucalyptus trees, whose extant species are only found in Australia?

The presence of fossils of organisms on continents where the descendant organisms do not live has helped geologists substantiate one of the most daring hypotheses ever conceived. We are, of course, referring to the slow separation and movement of continents on their tectonic plates, a process that proceeds over hundreds of millions of years. The hypothesis, known as continental drift, was first proposed by Alfred Wegener in 1912 and was soon expanded into a book [138]. When first proposed, it seemed ridiculous that anyone would imagine that continents could move, but Wegener's hypotheses, now known as continental drift, have since been validated many different ways.

An ancient supercontinent known as Pangea, itself formed from coalescing continents, began splitting apart about 175 million years ago. At that time, the continent of Australia was closely apposed to South America. Ancient Eucalyptus trees remain today as fossils on the previously connected South American/Australian land, thriving only in Australia. Hence, Eucalyptus fossils are found in South America [139]. The same type of argument holds for a wide number of animals and plants whose ancient ancestors, in fossil form, are found in incongruous locations (Fig. 6.18).

Here is one more example of fossils found where we would least expect them. The tip of Mount Everest is the highest point on earth, with an elevation of 29,029 ft. One might expect Mount Everest to have had a volcanic origin, wherein convulsions of earth heaped forth magma that solidified into the majestic Himalayan mountains. If that were the case, the Himalayan mountains, Everest included, would be composed of igneous rock such as basalt, granite, gabbro, and so on. This is definitely not the case. The Himalayans are largely composed of limestone, a sedimentary rock that is formed at the bottom of oceans, from ocean salts and dead marine life, compressed by the weight of miles of water. The limestone at the summit of Everest contains the skeletons of long-extinct classes of marine organisms (e.g., trilobites), and ancient species of currently extant classes of organisms (e.g., small crustaceans). The fossil-bearing limestone at the top of Mount Everest is quite similar to the fossil-bearing limestone found in flat ranges of sedimentary rock located in sites where oceans held sway, many millions of years ago. Why is Mount Everest built from ancient limestone? There can only be one answer. Everest formed when an enormous force pushed the ocean bottom up and up and up until limestone poked through the clouds. What force could have caused the ocean bottom to rise? Continental drift delivered the Indian subcontinent to Asia, about 40 or 50 million years ago. As the subcontinent closed in on Asia, a body of water, the Tethys Sea, got in its way, and the sea-bottom was squeezed backward and upwards as the collision proceeded. Thus, was born the Himalayan mountains. The collision of India and Asia has never stopped. To this day, the Himalayan mountains continue to rise, at about 1 cm per year. One centimeter seems like such a small and insignificant number, but a growth rate of 1 cm per year translates to about 10 km in a million years. For Everest, a million years is a trifle; about one-fiftieth of its current age.

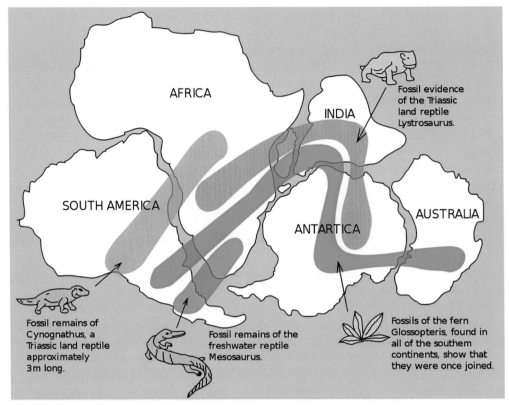

FIG. 6.18 As the continents have drifted from Pangea, the supercontinent, so have the fossil remains of species that lived on the once-connected landmasses. *Source: U.S. Geological Survey.*

The Classification of Life meets bioinformatics

When we think of bioinformatics, we naturally turn to the human genome and its sequence. But bioinformaticians will tell us that the human genome would have very little scientific significance if it could not be related to the genomes of other organisms included within the Classification of Life.

We understand the human genome through our exploration of organisms belonging to our ancestral classes. The field of bioinformatics grew to maturity at about the same time that biologists gained access to a fairly robust classification of all the branches of life, in a form that was suitable for annotation with genome sequences collected from a large number of species. Today, it's fairly easy to study genes and their homologs that may be present in many different organisms. By comparing sequences of homologous genes, bioinformaticians can determine where, in the Classification of Life, a gene first appeared, and which lines of descendant organisms may have retained the genes. Bioinformaticians now have some idea of which genes are relatively new, and the prevalence of new and ancient genes in any species' genome.

One of the most startling outcomes of cross-species sequence analyses was the finding that we humans have far fewer genes than anyone expected; and a large proportion of our genes are present in ancient ancestors.

Let's look at a few striking facts that genome sequencing has brought to light:

1. There are over 500 core genes that are present in all extant metazoan (i.e., animal) species [140].
2. Not only do we find homologs of human genes in single-celled eukaryotic organisms, but we also find homologies that extend up our ancestral lineage and into the bacterial kingdom (as in the case of an actin homolog in the proteobacteria *Haliangium ochraceum* [6]).
3. The human genome and the chimpanzee genome are between 97% and 92% alike, indicating that closely related species have nearly the same set of genes [141].
4. Approximately 60% of the annotated protein-coding genes in the mouse genome originate from prokaryotic and basal eukaryotic ancestors [142], and there is every reason to believe that the same can be said for all mammals, including humans.
5. Nearly 75% of human disease-causing genes are believed to have a functional homolog in the fly [80].
6. Pax6 is a regulatory gene that controls eye development. This gene, like so many other basic regulatory genes, has been strictly conserved throughout metazoan evolution. Remarkably, Pax6 in mice is so similar to its homolog in insects that the corresponding genes from either species can be interchanged and function properly [143].
7. Nearly identical gene families are found among metazoan classes. Gene families are ancient and have evolved through all the lineages descending from the first organisms to carry the gene family's founder gene. [Glossary Founder effect, Gene pool, Natural selection, Non-homologous, Paralog]

Comparisons among the genome sequences of organisms have led to some of the most important general laws of biology. Let's list here some of the insights that could not have been achieved without the Classification of Life.

1. The law of sequence conservation and its corollary. If a sequence is conserved through evolution (i.e., if we can find a closely similar sequence that is present in various animal species having a shared ancestral class), then that sequence must perform a useful function for the organism.

Furthermore, highly conserved sequences (i.e., with very little difference among class members), are likely to have a very important function. This law is so useful and so fundamental to bioinformatics and to gene-based computational algorithms that it may as well be known as the First Law of Bioinformatics.

The corollary to the law is that genomic sequences that degenerate over time, and for which there are large variations in closely related species, must not have a very important function in the organism.

2. All evolving organisms have genomes containing sequences of DNA that have no conserved function (so-called junk DNA). In fact, if we knew absolutely nothing at all regarding our genomes, we could infer that some junk DNA must be present [144,145]. The logic is as follows:

   a. Suppose our genomes were packed full of functional genes, with no non-functional DNA sequences.
   b. In that case, every gene would be conserved. The Law of Gene Conservation tells that that genes that have a useful purpose are conserved.
   c. If every gene in our genome is conserved, then the genome cannot evolve. Evolution can only occur in genes that are not fully conserved, insofar as evolution involves the acquisition of genetic variation in genes, and this would mean that some genes would not be conserved.
   d. But we know that evolution occurs all the time.
   e. Therefore, our original premise is incorrect, and our genome must contain non-functional DNA.

3. The set of genes in humans are inherited from ancient ancestors in the human lineage. This in itself is a compelling argument for evolution (among many equally compelling arguments)

If humans did not inherit their genes from ancient ancestors, then we would expect human genes and ancestral genes to be non-homologous. Because nearly every identified human gene seems to be homologous to genes found in ancestors, then we can infer that our genes were inherited from ancestral organisms.

4. The ancestors of humans are probably the same ancestors of all the eukaryotic classes (e.g., plants, single-cell organisms)

Essentially every extant organism, even those that seem to have no biological commonalities with humans, have about the same set of core genes. This would strongly suggest that all living organisms have a common root.

5. The differences among the eukaryotes are largely accounted for by differences in gene regulation, not by differences in the types of genes present in the genome

Because all eukaryotes contain many of the same genes, the differences in behavior between one organism and another cannot be easily accounted for by differences in genes. However, all of the structural and metabolic proteins are coded for by genes. Therefore, the differences among species must be accounted for by regulatory modifiers (e.g., regulators that determine which genes are transcribed and translated, and the relative levels of transcription and translation of genes).

A specific example wherein genes simply cannot account for the differences we see among species is found when we compare placental mammals (Class Eutheria) with a marsupial mammal (Class Metatheria). 20% of conserved noncoding elements found in placental mammals are missing in the opossum, a marsupial [146–148]. We conclude that the differences between eutherians and metatherians must be accounted for by regulatory processes, insofar as there seems to be very little difference in their genes, and large differences in their noncoding sequences, which are known to contain regulatory elements.

Relatively early in eukaryotic phylogeny, cells evolved diverse methods for regulating their genomes. These would include the evolution of the epigenome, wherein the DNA or genetic material is modified by base methylations, and these modifications are themselves modified at every step of cell-type development. Aside from the complexities of the epigenome, there are a host of genome modifiers that micromanage every aspect of gene expression, including [60,61]:

- Transcription: transcription factors, promoters, enhancers, silencers, pseudogenes, siRNA, miRNA, competitive endogenous RNAs
- Post-transcription: splicing, RNA silencing, RNA polyadenylation, mRNA stabilizers
- Translation: translation initiation factors, ribosomal processing
- Post-translational protein modifications: chaperones in mammals, protein trafficking

Chromatin, the structural backbone of the genome is modified by the attachment of proteins (histones and non-histone varieties), and by the wrapping of units of DNA into tight nucleosomes. There are numerous ways in which chromatin is modified, including remodeling factors, histone deacetylases, heterochromatin-binding proteins, and topoisomerases [149]. Disruptions of any of these regulatory processes may produce disease in humans and other metazoans [150–160]. Readers interested in the subject are encouraged to read the following glossary items, most of which list examples of human diseases caused by particular mutations in regulatory sequences [4]. [Glossary Alternative RNA splicing, Cis-acting regulatory element, Epistasis, Gene regulation, Homeobox, Promoter, Regulatory DNA element, Regulatory RNA element, Trans-acting regulatory element, Transcription, Transcription factor]

6. Animals can tolerate mutation in regulatory machinery more easily than they can tolerate mutations in genes

An inherited mutation in a protein-coding gene may result in the total inactivation of its protein product. If that protein plays a crucial role in the organism, the mutation may be fatal. In point of fact, virtually all fatal gene disorders involve mutations of protein-coding genes. Regulatory sequences act to modify the activity of protein-coding genes, either by coding for regulatory protein factors or by exerting some other form of direct or indirect effect on gene transcription. If a mutation involves a regulatory region of the genome, the result is, typically some mild reduction or increase in the amount of protein being produced in cells. Hence, germline mutations in regulatory sequences tend to produce non-fatal, often mild, diseases.

7. Gene families are never species-specific

How can we justify this rule? We know that all gene families are ancient. However, individual species are, for the most part, not ancient (remember, species continuously speciate). Hence, gene families arise within lineages of organisms. Hence, we would expect multiple species arising through the lineage to have the same gene family.

An example of an ancient gene family are the globins, whose function in the red blood cells of many animals is the distribution of oxygen from an external source (e.g., air or water) to tissues throughout the body [161,162]. The genes of the globin family are so ancient that they are present in bacteria. It is believed that the original globin molecule evolved in bacteria before the evolution of oxygenic photosynthesis (i.e., before 2.3 billion years ago) at a time when all organisms were anaerobic. Oxygen is toxic to anaerobic organisms. The purpose of the first globins in bacteria was to scavenge oxygen, thus protecting anaerobic cells from oxygen-induced toxicity. Following the advent of oxygenic photosynthesis, when the earliest aerobic organisms were evolving, the oxygen-scavenging properties of the early globins were modified to facilitate the extraction of oxygen from the air, and the delivery of oxygen to the intracellular enzymes participating in the pathways for oxidative phosphorylation. A variety of hemoglobinopathies affect humans, all involving the globin gene family [161].

In summary, clever scientists have been able to accumulate lots of facts about life on our planet, but they couldn't have made much sense of their findings without the Classification of Life.

Glossary

Alternative RNA splicing A normal mRNA editing mechanism whereby one gene may code for many different proteins [163]. In humans, about 95% of genes that have multiple exons can be spliced together in alternate ways, yielding different proteins.

Altered proteins may result from mutations occurring in splice sites or from defects of the splicing apparatus (i.e., spliceosome disorders). It has been estimated that 15% of disease-causing mutations involve splicing [164,165]. Normal cells eliminate most abnormal splicing variants through a post-transcriptional editing process. Cancer cells are known to contain numerous splicing variants that are not found in normal cells [166,167].

Apomorphy A new trait, appearing in a species, that is passed to all the descendant species of the class. The apomorph is called the synapomorphy when observed in the descendant species. There isn't much difference between the terms "apomorphy" and "synapomorphy", other than their positions in the class lineage. As a mnemonic, you may find it convenient to remember that the apomorph sits at the apex.

Ataxia telangiectasia Also known as Louis-Bar syndrome and as Boder-Sedgwick syndrome, and caused by a mutation of the ATM gene, resulting in a defect in DNA repair. Cells of individuals with ataxia-telangiectasia are highly vulnerable to radiation toxicity. The clinical phenotype of ataxia-telangiectasia is cerebellar ataxia (a body movement disorder secondary to cerebellar impairment), telangiectases (small focal vascular malformations), immune deficits predisposing to ear, sinus and lung infections, and a predisposition to malignancy (e.g., lung, gastric, lymphoid, and breast cancers).

The gene that is mutated in ataxia-telangiectasia is ATM. The normal ATM gene product phosphorylates DNA repair enzymes following DNA breakage.

CAR T-cell therapy In August 2017, gene therapy for the treatment of children and young adults with B-cell acute lymphoblastic leukemia was approved by the U.S. Food and Drug Administration [168]. The therapy is centered on several stunning refinements of an old and nearly defunct approach, using a patient's immune system to destroy cancer cells. The successful methodology that was developed is known as CAR-T (Chimeric Antigen Receptor for T cells) [135,169–171]. Here are the steps involved in deploying CAR-T [169]:

1. Choose some antigen in the disease-causing cells that are present in high concentration in those cells or that is unique to those cells. It is best if the antigen lies on the cell surface, where it can easily bind to T-cell receptors. In cancers, the target cells for this procedure will be the cancer cells themselves. In the case of CAR-T therapy for B-cell acute lymphoblastic leukemia, the target antigen is CD-19, a B-cell surface antigen. Researchers are hoping that this technique can be applied to diseases other than cancer [170]. Perhaps, in the future, the target cells may be the chief effector cells within many different types of lesions (e.g., parasitic infections).

2. Create the chimeric receptor to the antigen. This is the step that awaited several advances in genetic engineering [135]. Basically, the different units of a receptor designed to provide the greatest possible biological response, when bound to an antigen, are combined with a unique antigen-recognizing subunit. The final product is an artificial receptor molecule capable of arming T cells.

3. Determine the gene sequence that encodes the artificial receptor, and synthesize it in a vast number.

4. Enclose copies of the synthesized gene in an appropriate vector (e.g., lentivirus).

5. Extract a sample of T cells from the patient.

6. Transfect those T cells with the vector.

7. Grow the transfected T cells, now expressing the chimeric receptor, in culture.

8. Deplete the patient of his or her T cell population, to "make room" for the cultured T cells that it will soon receive.

9. Transfuse the cultured and transfected T cells into the patient.

10. Wait as the transfused T cell recognize and destroy the patient's cancer cells.

11. Watch to see if the patient develops any adverse events, and treat complications aggressively [171].

In the case of B-cell acute lymphoblastic leukemia, a rare form of cancer, the results have been nothing short of miraculous. In early trials, complete and lasting remissions have been achieved in more than two-thirds of treated patients [170]. As is so often the case, early successes come to rare diseases. The common diseases come later, if at all. At present, CAR-T therapy is not particularly effective against common solid tumors, possibly due to the enormous phenotypic heterogeneity of epithelial tumors, and the emergence of cells that lack the target antigen, following an initial response to treatment [170].

CRISPR CRISPR (Clustered Regularly Interspaced Short Palindromic Repeats) is a gene-editing tool. In the U.S. the direct clinical uses of CRISPR are focused on repairing somatic mutations (e.g., repairing the sickle cell mutation in young or adult patients). Applications might involve taking unhealthy cells from a patient, editing the DNA to repair or eliminate the disease gene, growing the repaired cells in culture, and infusing the cells back into the patient.

CRISPR has been heralded as a way to cure and eventually eliminate genetic diseases [132,172]. To do so, scientists would need to edit germline human cells. At the current time, editing of the human germline DNA (i.e., the DNA of human embryos) will not be funded by NIH and would most likely not meet approval by the FDA [173]. Efforts to use CRISPR to edit the germline of non-human animals are proceeding rapidly [133].

Cambrian explosion Studies of shale strata indicate that something very special happened, in the history of terrestrial animals, in a relatively short period, stretching from about 550 to 500 million years ago. In this 50-million-year span, nearly all of the major phyla of animals that we see today came into existence. We call this era the Cambrian explosion. The word "Cambrian" is a latinized form of the Welsh language word for Wales, where shale deposits of the Cambrian age were first studied. The word "explosion" tells us that paleontologists have come to think of a span of 50 million years as a blinding flash in earth's history.

Our understanding of the major classes of animals is based almost entirely on fossils found in rock. Animals certainly preceded the Cambrian period, but such animals were soft and uncalcified and would be under-represented in the fossil record [174,175]. Furthermore, our reliance on body plans, as the only measure of a phyla's emergence, is somewhat presumptuous. It may very well be that the defining expression of phyla may not have developed until well after the Cambrian explosion [176–178]. In particular, the bryozoans (tiny invertebrate aquatics that filter food particles from water), seem to have arisen sometime after the Cambrian.

Cancer progression The acquisition of additional properties of the malignant phenotype, in a tumor, over time. Progression is achieved through a variety of mechanisms (e.g., genetic instability [179], epigenetic instability, and aberrant cell death regulation [180]) and results in the eventual emergence of subclones that have growth advantages over other cells in the same tumor. The presence of subclones of distinctive phenotype and genotype, within a single tumor, accounts for tumor heterogeneity [181].

Capsid The protein shell of a virus that encloses the genetic material of the virus when the virus is outside its host cell. The capsid aids the virus with its attachment to the target host cell, and with the penetration of the viral genome into the host cell.

Chiasm Whereas the term "decussation" is rooted in the Latin word "deca," meaning ten, and refers to the geometric shape of the corresponding Roman numeral, "X", the synonymous term, "chiasm," comes from the Greek. The Greek number ten, "chi" is also represented by the familiar "X". In practice, the term "chiasm" refers specifically to the point of cross-over at the center of the "X" shape. The most notable anatomic chiasm is the optic chiasm, where a portion of the left and right optic nerves cross over to the contralateral sides of the brain.

Cis-acting regulatory element A gene regulation function that is exerted by some segment of genetic material on another segment of genetic material. In most instances, a short sequence of DNA regulates the transcriptional activity of a nearby gene that codes for a protein. The Cis-acting elements typically regulate gene transcription by functioning as binding sites for transcription factors (i.e., the proteins encoded by trans-acting regulatory elements). Polymorphisms (i.e., sequence variants) in these noncoding cis-elements have strong effects on the phenotype of cells, by modifying the levels of gene expression. The best understood types of cis-acting elements are enhancers and promoters. The cis-acting sequence of DNA is often activated or inactivated by some diffusible molecule that attaches to it. *cis*-Acting processes apply to RNA as well as to DNA.

Clade A class plus all of its descendant classes. A clade should be distinguished from a lineage, the latter being a class and its ascendant classes. Because a class can have more than one child class, a pictogram of a clade will often look like a branching tree. In a classification, where each class is restricted to one parent class, ascending lineages (from the Latin linea, "a line"), are represented as a non-branching line of ancestors, leading to the root (i.e., top-class) of the classification.

Cladistics The technique of creating a classification from hierarchical clades. Each branch of the classification includes a parent species and all its descendant species while excluding species that did not descend from the parent.

The goal of cladistics is to create a hierarchical classification that consists exclusively of monophyletic classes (i.e., no paraphyly, no polyphyly in any branch).

Cluster analysis Clustering algorithms provide a way of taking a large set of data objects that seem to have no relationship to one another, and to produce a visually simple collection of clusters wherein each cluster member is similar to every other member of the same cluster. The algorithmic methods for clustering are simple. One of the most popular clustering algorithms is the k-means algorithm, which assigns any number of data objects to one of the k clusters [182]. The number k of clusters is provided by the user. The algorithm is easy to describe and to understand, but the computational task of completing the algorithm can be difficult when the number of dimensions in the object (i.e., the number of attributes associated with the object), is large. Aside from computational difficulties, there are drawbacks to the algorithm, including:

1. The final set of clusters will sometimes depend on the initial, random choice of k data objects. This means that multiple runs of the algorithm may produce different outcomes.

2. The algorithms are not guaranteed to succeed. Sometimes, the algorithm does not converge to a final, stable set of clusters.

3. When the dimensionality is very high, the distances between data objects (i.e., the square root of the sum of squares of the measured differences between corresponding attributes of two objects) can be ridiculously large and of no practical meaning. Computations may bog down, cease altogether, or produce meaningless results. In this case, the only recourse may involve eliminating some of the attributes (i.e., reducing the dimensionality of the data objects).

4. The clustering algorithm may succeed, producing a set of clusters of similar objects, but the clusters may have no practical value. They may miss important relationships among the objects, or they might group objects whose similarities are non-informative.

5. The most important drawback is that grouping by similarity is not a valid basis for classification. Objects may share many properties and still be fundamentally different.

At best, cluster analysis produces groups that can be used to start piecing together a valid classification, based on relationships (not similarities).

Cofactor When biochemists use the term "cofactors," they are referring to chemicals that bind to enzymes, to activate the enzyme or to enhance the activity of the enzyme. Some enzymes or enzyme complexes need several cofactors (e.g., the pyruvate dehydrogenase complex which has five organic cofactors and one metal ion). Vitamins are often cofactors for enzymes.

Congenital disorder Includes all the congenital anomalies (i.e., structural or anatomic deformities) plus the genetic diseases, including metabolic disorders, and acquired diseases of the embryo or fetus, that are present at birth.

Convergence In evolution, convergence occurs when two species independently acquire an identical or similar trait through adaptation; not through inheritance from a shared ancestor. Examples are: the wing of a bat and the wing of a bird; the opposable thumb of opossums and primates; the beak of a platypus and the beak of a bird.

In disease biology, convergence occurs when diverse pathogenetic sequences all lead to the same clinical phenotype. Convergence accounts for all of the common diseases because a disease with many convergent pathways is apt to occur often. Disease convergence can also be observed in rare diseases that have genetic heterogeneity. In these instances, different mutated genes may lead to the same clinical phenotype. The biological basis for disease convergence is that there are a limited number of ways in which an organism can respond to a biological perturbation. By this reasoning, we would expect that there would be a limited number of clinical phenotypes. Furthermore, if the number of disease phenotypes is constant for any species, then this would imply that the human race cannot encounter any new diseases. No matter what metabolic pathways are involved in a disease process, the resulting disease would be limited to one of a finite number of feasible clinical phenotypes.

DNA repair Except for damaged DNA, damaged cellular molecules need not be repaired. They are simply replaced with newly synthesized molecules. Because DNA is the template for its replication, damaged DNA molecules cannot be replaced with newly synthesized DNA molecules; the damage must be repaired in situ if the organism is to continue replicating faithfully. Repairing DNA is of such great importance to cellular life that mammals have at least seven different DNA repair pathways, each specializing in a particular type of damage repair (e.g., direct reversal repair, mismatch repair, nucleotide excision repair, homologous recombination, base excision repair, single-strand break repair, non-homologous end joining, and Fanconi Anemia DNA crosslink repair). Some types of DNA lesions are substrates for more than one pathway, and how these pathways interact are complex [183].

Druggable driver A driver pathway that serves as a molecular target for a therapeutic drug. The ideal druggable driver would have the following properties:

1. The driven pathway is necessary for the expression of disease but is not necessary for the survival of normal cells (i.e., you can eliminate the pathway without killing normal cells).

2. There must be a pathway protein that is necessary for the activity of the pathway (i.e., if the protein is removed, the pathway cannot proceed). Such a pathway protein would be a logical drug target.

3. The potential target protein is biologically suitable as a drug target. For example, the targeted protein must be chemically stable and should have sites that can bind to a small drug molecule.

4. The protein target is itself not necessary for the survival of normal cells (i.e., targeting the protein must not kill the patient).

Epidermis The outermost anatomic layer of skin, composed of multi-layered squamous epithelial cells. The bottom (basal) layer of epithelial cells (cells closest to the underlying dermis) is the generative layer and contains a population of dividing cells, that give produce the non-dividing squamous cells that arise through the epidermis (for weeks), and eventually slough off. As non-dividing cells rise through the epidermis, they change their shape, structure, and chemical content. The top layer consists of flat, anucleate cells filled with keratin. These cells eventually slough into the air. House dust consists largely of sloughed, keratinized cells.

Epistasis A gene's role may be influenced by other genes; a phenomenon called epistasis. For example, a gene may be active only when a particular allele of one or more additional genes is also active. Because dependencies among genes can be expected in complex biological systems, the role of epistasis in the penetrance of disease genes and the pathogenesis of disease phenotypes is presumed to be profound. For example, there are at least 27 epistatic interactions claimed to be associated with the occurrence of Alzheimer's disease [184]. Epistatic interactions can be synergistic or antagonistic [185].

It should be kept in mind that genes do not directly interact with other genes; genes are just sequences of DNA in chromosomes. Interactions between genes must be mediated through other molecules, and there is a multitude of mechanisms whereby an epistatic effect may ensue. Examples might include coding for transcription factors that control the expression of other genes, modifying regulatory systems that control gene expression, modifying the synthesis of proteins encoded by a gene, changing metabolic pathways that use the proteins encoded by genes, and so on. Epistatic interactions are complex, and attempts to predict the functional effect of single or multiple gene variations are typically futile [186,187].

Evo-devo The study of the evolution of developmental processes.

Founder effect Occurs when a specific mutation enters and spreads through a population due to the successful procreational activities of a founder, the animal that carried and introduced the mutation to the gene pool. In the case of diseases, when members of a family having a specific disease that is marked by an identical mutation, the disease may have been propagated through the population by a founder effect. This is particularly true when the disease is confined to a separable sub-population, as appears to be the case for Navaho neurohepatopathy, in which the studied patients, all members of the Navaho community, have the same missense mutation.

Not all diseases characterized by a single gene mutation arise as the result of a single founder effect. In the case of cystic fibrosis, a founder effect can be observed in a subset of the affected population. In this case, one allele of the cystic fibrosis gene accounts for 67% of cystic fibrosis cases in Europe. Hundreds of other alleles of the same gene account for the remaining 33% of cystic fibrosis cases [188].

Perhaps the most famous "founder" is the so-called "mitochondrial eve." Mitochondria are inherited whole from the cytoplasm of maternal oocytes. Hence, all of us can, in theory, trace our mitochondria back up to the woman from whom all humans living today have descended.

Gallertoid Animals are thought to have evolved from simple, spherical organisms floating in the sea, called gallertoids. The living sphere was lined by a single layer of cells enclosing a soft center in which fibrous cells floated in the extracellular matrix. As the gallertoids evolved to extract food from the seabed floor, they flattened out. The modern animals most like the gallertoids are the placozoans, discovered in 1833, plastered against the wall of a seawater aquarium. These organisms are just under a millimeter in length and are composed of about 1000 epithelial cells. Except for being flat, rather than round, they closely resemble the gallertoids, with an outer lining of cuboidal cells, and an inner gelatinous matrix holding a suspension of fibrous cells.

Gene pool   The imagined aggregate collection of genetic material from all of the members of a species.

Gene regulation   Gene expression is influenced by many different regulatory systems, including the epigenome (e.g. chromatin packing, histone modification, base methylation), transcription, and post-transcription modifiers (e.g., transcription factors, DNA promoter sites, DNA enhancer sites, cis- and trans-acting factors, alternative RNA splicing, miRNA and competitive endogenous RNAs, additional forms of RNA silencing, RNA polyadenylation, mRNA stabilizers), translational modifiers (e.g., translation initiation factors, ribosomal processing) and post-translational protein modifications.

Disruptions of any of these regulatory processes produce disease in humans and other metazoans [150–159]. Moreover, anything that modifies any regulatory process (e.g., environmental toxins, substrate availability, epistatic genes) can influence gene regulation; potentially causing disease.

Hamartoma   Hamartomas are typically benign growths that occupy a particular biological niche, with some features of neoplasia (i.e., a clonal expansion of an abnormal cell) and some features of hyperplasia (i.e., the localized overgrowth of tissue). Hamartomas may be composed of tissues derived from several embryonic lineages (e.g., ectodermal tissues mixed with mesenchymal tissue). This is seldom the case in cancers, which are clonally-derived neoplasms wherein every cell is derived from a single cell type.

Hamartomas occasionally occur in abundance in inherited syndromes; as in tuberous sclerosis. The pathognomonic lesion in tuberous sclerosis is the brain tuber, the hamartoma from which the syndrome takes its name. Tubers of the brain consist of localized but poorly demarcated malformations of neuronal and glial cells [189]. Like other hamartoma syndromes, the germline mutation in tuberous sclerosis produces benign hamartomas as well as carcinomas; indicating that hamartomas and cancers are biologically related.

Another genetic condition associated with hamartomas is Cowden syndrome. Cowden syndrome is associated with a loss of function mutation in PTEN, a tumor suppressor gene [190].

Holometabolism   Complete metamorphosis, as observed in all insect species of Class Endopterygota, involving four developmental stages: egg, larva, pupa, and imago or adult. The term "holometabolism" is reserved for insects, but we see a complete multi-stage metamorphosis in other animals, such as the European eel, a type of fish.

Homeobox   Genes that code for transcription factors involved in anatomic development in animals, fungi, and plants. Hox genes are specialized homeobox genes found in metazoans that determine the axial relationship of organs. Mutations of homeobox genes are associated with remarkably specific, often isolated, anatomic alterations. Examples are:

MSX2 homeobox gene mutation, which produces enlarged parietal foramina.

PITX1 homeobox gene mutation, which produces Rieger syndrome (hypodontia and malformation of the anterior chamber of the eye including microcornea and muscular dystrophy).

PITX3 homeobox gene mutation, which produces anterior segment dysgenesis of the eye, moderate cataracts, and anterior segment mesenchymal dysgenesis.

NKX2.5 homeobox gene, which produces atrial septal defect and atrioventricular conduction defects.

SHOX homeobox (short stature homeobox) gene mutation is the root cause of Leri-Weill dyschondrosteosis (deformity of the distal radius, ulna, and proximal carpal bones as well as mesomelic dwarfism).

The reason why homeobox mutations tend to produce diseases in isolated anatomic locations or involve some specific function probably results from the coordinated regulatory activity of the individual homeobox genes. For example, one gene might regulate the synthesis of a group of proteins exclusively involved in the growth of particular skull bones; another homeobox gene might regulate proteins involved in insulin production.

Homoplasy A trait found in a species that was not present in its ancestor. It is generally believed that species develop homoplasies when none of the traits inherited from ancestors happens to fulfill their needs [191]. A homoplastic trait may appear in a skip wise manner in different subclasses of species belonging to the same class of animals, depending on their survival requirements. An example of a common homoplastic trait in various insect species is the loss of wings. Species of some subclasses of insects have lost their wings, while most other classes of insects have retained their ancestral wings.

In object-oriented programming languages, a homoplasy would be modeled as an instance method, in contrast to a class method, which would model an apomorphy.

Initiation In the field of cancer, the term "initiation" refers to the inferred changes in cells following exposure to a carcinogen, that may eventually lead to the emergence of cancer in the cell's descendants. Though we know much about the changes that occur in cells exposed to carcinogens, the essential and defining changes that begin the process of carcinogenesis are still unknown. The process that begins with initiation and extends to the emergence of cancer is called carcinogenesis.

In the field of molecular biology, the term "initiation" has a distinctly different meaning, preferring instead to the necessary molecular events that allow a process (e.g., replication, transcription, or translation) to begin [51].

LUCA Abbreviation for Last Universal Common Ancestor, also known as the cenancestor. Assuming that all organisms on earth descend from a common ancestor, then LUCA is the most recent population of organisms from which all organisms now living on Earth have a common descent. LUCA is thought to have lived 3.5 to 3.8 billion years ago [192].

Law of sequence conservation If a sequence is conserved through evolution (i.e., if we can find a closely similar sequence that is present in various animal species having a shared ancestral class), then that sequence must perform a useful function for the organism. Furthermore, highly conserved sequences (i.e., with very little difference among class members, over time), are likely to have a very important function. This law is so useful and so fundamental to genomics and to gene-related computational algorithms that it may as well be known as the First Law of Bioinformatics.

The corollary to the law is that genomic sequences that degenerate over time, and for which there are large variations in closely related species, must not have a very important function in the organism.

Li-Fraumeni syndrome A rare inherited cancer syndrome, associated with a mutation of the p53 tumor suppressor gene. Affected individuals are at risk of developing rhabdomyosarcoma, soft tissue sarcomas, breast cancer, brain tumors, osteosarcoma, leukemia, adrenocortical carcinoma, lymphoma, lung adenocarcinoma, melanoma, gonadal germ cell tumors, prostate carcinoma, and pancreatic carcinoma.

Long branch attraction When gene sequence data is analyzed, and two organisms share a similar sequence in a stretch of DNA, it can be very tempting to infer that the two organisms have a relatively close common ancestor. This inference is not necessarily correct. Because DNA mutations arise stochastically over time, two species with distant ancestors may achieve the same sequence in a chosen stretch of DNA, by chance alone (i.e., not through inheritance). When mathematical phylogeneticists began modeling inferences for gene data sets, they assumed that most such errors would occur when the branches between compared classes were long (i.e., when a long time elapsed between evolutionary divergences). Long-branch attraction occurred when non-sister classes were mistakenly assigned the same ancient parent class, based on sequence similarities. In practice, errors of this type can occur whether the branches are long, or short, or in-between. Over the years, the accepted usage of the term "long-branch attraction" has been extended to just about any error in phylogenetic grouping due to gene similarities acquired through any mechanism other than inheritance from a shared ancestor. This would include random mutational and adaptive convergences [193].

Loss-of-function mutation Any mutation that produces a reduction in the normal activity of a gene product (i.e., protein). Mutations that produce an abnormality in the function of a gene product, without a reduction in the amount of gene product produced, are known by the somewhat misleading term, "gain-of-function" mutations.

For example, sickle cell disease is caused by a very specific gene mutation that alters one amino acid in the sequence of hemoglobin, resulting in an abnormality in the hemoglobin molecule that renders red blood cells prone to sickling (a specific type of red cell deformation). Sickle cell disease is a disease caused by a gain-of-function mutation.

For any given gene, many potential gene sequence mutations might result in a loss of function of the gene product. There are only a few possible gene mutations that will result in a specific alteration of a gene product characteristic of a disease. Hence, the vast majority of diseases caused by a single mutation in a single gene (i.e., monogenic diseases) are caused by loss-of-function mutations.

Mimicry versus convergence In nature, there are many instances when two different organisms may look alike. Often, the species that mimics another species gains a survival advantage. For example, a predator may ignore a butterfly if the butterfly is mistaken for a leaf, and a small insect may ignore a predatory larger insect that appears to be a twig.

Evolutionary convergence is different from mimicry. In convergence, organisms of different classes evolve the same morphologic or biochemical traits independently, to achieve a certain functionality that suits their similar environments. One example is found in new world vultures and old-world vultures, which look similar to one another and which both feed on carrion, but the old-world vultures are related to eagles and hawks, while the new world vultures are related to storks. An example of chemical convergence is found in syntheses by elephants and butterflies of a compound ((Z)-7-dodecen-1-yl acetate) which serves as a pheromone for both species.

Molecular clock The molecular clock is a metaphor describing an analytic method by which the age of phylogenetic divergence of two species can be estimated by comparing the differences in sequence between two homologous genes or proteins. The name "molecular clock" and the basic theory underlying the method were described in the early years of the 1960s when the amino acid sequence of hemoglobin molecules was determined for humans and other hominids [5]. It seemed clear enough at the time that if the number of amino acid substitutions in the hemoglobin sequence, compared among two species, was large, then a very great time must have elapsed since the phylogenetic divergence of the two species. The reason being that sequence changes occur randomly over time, and as more time passes, more substitutions will occur. Conversely, if the differences in amino acid sequence between species are very small, then the time elapsed between the species divergence must have been small.

As with all simple and elegant theories in the biological sciences, the devil lies in the details. Today, we know that analyses must take into account the presence or absence of conserved regions (whose sequences will not change very much over time). Indeed, analysts must apply a host of adjustments before they can claim to have a fairly calibrated molecular clock [7,8].

Molecular clocks provide biologists with information related to the timing of species divergences, possibly corroborating the prior chronology, or tentatively establishing new timelines.

Monophyletic If all the members of a class have developed from a common ancestor, and if all of the descendants of the common ancestor are included in the class, and if these constraints extend to every class in the classification, then the classification is monophyletic. The goal of cladistics is to create a hierarchical classification that consists exclusively of monophyletic classes. The Classification of Life seeks to attain monophyly, but there are many instances of classes that are non-monophyletic, containing species that do not belong in the class or excluding species that should be included.

Monophyletic class A class of organisms that includes a parent organism and all its descendants, while excluding any organisms that did not descend from the parent. If a subclass of a parent class omits any of the descendants of the parent class, then the parent class is said to be paraphyletic; hence, not monophyletic. If a subclass of a parent class includes organisms that did not descend from the parent, then the parent class is polyphyletic; hence not monophyletic [194].

The Classification of Life seeks to attain monophyly. As the requirement for monophyly is imposed on classes, it becomes necessary to get rid of the classification of long-cherished polyphyletic or paraphyletic class names (ratites, protozoa, reptiles). Some of the names of classes that were shown to violate monophyly have been expunged from the Classification of Life, but retained in textbooks as "informal" classes; for no reason other than habit.

Multi-step process All of life can be described as a multi-step process, wherein each cellular event is directly preceded by some other event. Because every biological event has a preceding event, it can be inferred that every cellular event that occurs in any organism can be iteratively traced backward through history, to the first cellular event that occurred on the planet, some 4 billion years ago.

Diseases are multi-step processes, but it is impractical to trace diseases back to their origin, 4 billion years in the past. For practical reasons, determining the root cause of a disease requires us to choose an arbitrary cut-point where we say that pathogenesis begins, and we call this cut-point the root cause [9].

Mutagen A chemical that produces alterations in the genetic sequence of DNA molecules. Most mutagens are carcinogens, and most carcinogens are mutagens. Contrariwise, there are examples of carcinogens that are not mutagens and examples of mutagens that are not carcinogens. These somewhat inconsistent findings reflect the fact that carcinogenesis is a multistep process occurring over time. This being the case, we would expect carcinogenic agents with different properties (i.e., mutagenic, non-mutagenic) to have effects on different steps of carcinogenesis.

Mutation Alternations in the nucleotide sequences of genomic DNA. These would include point mutations (changes in a single nucleotide) and segment mutations (e.g., losses of a string of nucleotides) and structural variations that delete, amplify, or move segments of DNA.

Some of the mutations that account for genetic diseases are: deletions (e.g., Duchenne muscular dystrophy), Frame-shift mutations (e.g., factor VIII and IX deficiencies), fusions (e.g., chronic myelogenous leukemia, hemoglobin variants), initiation and termination codon mutations (e.g. a type of thalassemia), inversions (a type of thalassemia), nonsense mutations (familial hypercholesterolemia), point mutations (e.g., sickle cell disease, glucose-6-phosphate dehydrogenase deficiency), promoter mutations (e.g., a type of thalassemia), RNA processing mutations, including splice mutations (e.g. Phenylketonuria) [195].

Mutation rate Over the years, many estimates for the spontaneous mutation rates have appeared in the literature. In humans, point mutations (i.e., mutations that occur in a single nucleotide base within the genome) seem to occur with a frequency of about 1 to 3×10^{-8} per base [196–198]. Cancer cells, which are generally characterized by genetic instability and multiple genetic abnormalities, seem to have high rates of spontaneous mutation, with estimates about a hundred-fold higher than mutation rates in normal cells (e.g., 210×10^{-8} mutations per base) [199]. When we extrapolate the mutation rate for the many cells that compose a human body, we might expect that trillions of mutations occur every few seconds [200]. Past estimates were somewhat speculative and provided little information about the rate of repair of mutations. Furthermore, estimates were generally restricted to one specific type of genetic error (i.e., point mutations). With the advent of next-generation sequencing, it became possible to look for mutations of all types, in the entire genome of cells, comparing the number of mutations found in different tissues of the same person, or persons of different ages. These kinds of studies will tell us a great deal about the mutational burden on humans. In a recent study wherein samples of chronically sun-exposed eyelid skin were examined for oncogene mutations, the researchers found that about a quarter of the skin cells contained activating mutations in oncogenes [201]. We shouldn't be surprised by these findings. It has been estimated that by the time we reach the age of 60 years, every nucleotide in our genome has been mutated in at least one cell of the body [202].

Natural selection The tendency for favorable heritable traits to become more common over successive generations. The traits are selected from expressed genetic variations among individuals in the population.

Neurocristopathy A disease of cells that derive from the neural crest. Examples include MEN2 (multiple endocrine neoplasm syndrome type 2), aganglionic diseases of the GI tract, and neurofibromatosis.

Neutrophils Circulating blood cells are either red (red blood cells) or white (white blood cells). More accurately, blood cells are either red or they are unpigmented. The red cells greatly outnumber the white cells, but there is a large variety of circulating white cells, dominated by lymphocytes, platelets, monocytes, and granulocytes (neutrophils, eosinophils, basophils). The granulocytes can be distinguished from one another by the dyes that can be absorbed by the different types of their contained granules. Eosinophils retain a pink dye. Basophils retain a blue dye. Neutrophils do not retain dyes of either color. The most numerous types of white cell are the neutrophil, and, among the granulocytes, the neutrophil is the most important defender against infections.

Non-homologous Two very similar proteins, genes, and organs can be non-homologous because homology requires that both objects derive from a common ancestral object. Because similar objects can be non-homologous, it is a bad idea to build a biological classification based entirely on similarities among objects.

Nonphylogenetic property Properties that do not hold true for a class; hence, cannot be used by ontologists to create a classification. For example, we do not classify animals by height, or weight because animals of greatly different heights and weights may occupy the same biological class. Similarly, animals within a class may have widely ranging geographic habitats; hence, we cannot classify animals by locality. Case in point: penguins can be found virtually anywhere in the southern hemisphere, including hot and cold climates. Hence, we cannot classify penguins as animals that live in Antarctica or that prefer a cold climate.

Scientists commonly encounter properties, once thought to be class-specific, that prove to be uninformative, for classification purposes. For many decades, all bacteria were assumed to be small; much smaller than animal cells. However, the bacterium Epulopiscium fishelsoni grows to about 600 μm by 80 μm, much larger than the typical animal epithelial cell (about 35 μm in diameter) [203]. *Thiomargarita namibiensis.* an ocean-dwelling bacterium can reach a size of 0.75 mm, visible to the unaided eye. What do these admittedly obscure facts teach us about the art of classification? Superficial properties, such as size, seldom inform us how to classify objects. The ontologist much thinks very deeply to find the essential defining features of classes.

Nonphylogenetic signal DNA sequences that cannot yield any useful conclusions related to the evolutionary pathways. Because DNA mutations arise stochastically over time (i.e., at random locations in the gene, and at random times), two organisms having different ancestors may, by chance alone, achieve the same sequence in a chosen stretch of DNA. When gene sequence data is analyzed, and two organisms share the same sequence in a stretch of DNA, it can be tempting to infer that the two organisms belong to the same class (i.e., that they inherited the identical sequence from a common ancestor). This inference is not necessarily correct. When mathematical phylogeneticists began modeling inferences for gene data sets, they assumed that most of class assignment errors based on DNA sequence similarity would occur where the branches between sister taxa were long (i.e., when a long time elapsed between evolutionary divergences, allowing for many random substitutions in base pairs). They called this phenomenon, wherein non-sister taxa were assigned the same ancient ancestor class, "long-branch attraction". In practice, errors of this type can occur whether the branches are long, or short, or in-between. The term "nonphylogenetic signal" refers to just about any pitfall in phylogenetic grouping due to gene similarities acquired through any mechanism other than inheritance from a shared ancestor. This would include random mutational and adaptive convergence [16,193,194].

Observational data Data obtained by measuring existing things, and not the result of an experiment designed to obtain a particular type of result. The data collected in hospitals, as part of their ordinary work, is considered observational data because it is based on observations on patients, even though those observations may be obtained through the use of highly technical equipment. The data obtained by prospective randomized clinical trials are considered non-observational, even though the data is obtained by observing patients because the data would not exist without the implementation of a designed trial.

Ontogeny The development of the adult organism from embryonic structures.

Orthodisease Orthodiseases are conditions observed in non-human species that result from alterations in genes that are homologous to the genes known to cause diseases in humans.

Ortholog Refers to a gene found in different organisms that evolved from a common ancestor's gene through speciation. As an empiric observation, orthologs in different species often have the same or similar functionality [143,204–208]. It is assumed that a gene and its encoded protein have greater similarity to their orthologs in another species than to any of the other genes/proteins in its genome. This basic assumption drives the algorithms designed to determine the evolutionary lineage of orthologs in different species [209,210]. Orthology is a type of homology.

Paralog A paralogous gene. Refers to genes found in different species of organisms that evolved from a common ancestor's gene after gene duplication. Paralogs permit the organism to get new functionality from a gene, through natural selection, without losing the functionality of the gene that has been duplicated. A paralog is a type of homolog. All homologs are either orthologs or paralogs.

Phenetics The classification of organisms by feature similarity, rather than through relationships. Taxonomists are generally opposed to the idea of phenetics-based classifications, preferring to build classifications by finding the relationships that connect one class to another. Taxonomists have long held that a species is a natural unit of biological life and that the nature of a species is revealed through the intellectual process of building a consistent taxonomy; an intellectual process that is not based on phenetics [3].

Phylogeny A method of classifications based on ancestral lineage. The Classification of Life is a phylogenetic classification.

Polygenic disease A disease whose underlying cause involves alterations in multiple genes. In general, the development of polygenic diseases is highly dependent upon environmental modifiers that trigger bouts of disease, that enhance or reduce susceptibility to disease, or that seem to serve as the apparent root cause of the disease.

As an example, consider a patient with no known underlying medical condition who is stung by a bee and immediately succumbs to anaphylactic shock. It is tempting to say that the root cause is the bee sting, but we know that most individuals who are stung by a bee do not develop an anaphylactic response. Clearly, some underlying condition must have predisposed the patient to develop shock. You want to blame a gene passed to the child from a parent, but if there was no parental or familial history of anaphylaxis, then it would be hard to blame on an inherited gene. A de novo mutation (a mutation originating in the patient's zygote), but such mutations may be rare, while anaphylactic responses are not particularly uncommon. In such instances, we look toward a polygenic explanation, wherein multiple gene variants together produce a physiological condition that predisposes the individual to anaphylactic shock. Of course, we cannot be certain that we are correct until we identify all of the modified genes and demonstrate the biological mechanism by which they exert their effect. That's a very tall order. In the meantime, we work under the tentative assumption that we are correct. That's science.

There are many common conditions in which the majority of cases are presumed to be polygenic (e.g., diabetes, obesity, hypertension).

Post-mitotic Refers to fully differentiated cells that have lost the ability to divide. For example, the epidermis of the skin has a basal layer of cells, each of which is capable of dividing to produce one post-mitotic cell plus another (replacement) basal layer cell. The post-mitotic cells sit atop the basal cells, where they gradually flatten out (i.e., become squamous shaped) and lose their nucleus as the cells rise through the epidermal layers, pushed up by the next generation of cells produced by the dividing basal cells.

The top layer of the epidermis sloughs off into the air and is replaced by post-mitotic epidermal cells in the next lower layer. Much of the small flakes of house dust that we see dancing in the beams of sunlight passing through our windows are composed of post-mitotic squamous cells, sloughed from our skin. This cycle of cell renewal from the bottom and cell sloughing from the top is typical of most epithelial surfaces of the body (e.g., the epidermis of the skin, gastrointestinal tract, and glandular organs). Aside from epithelial surfaces, post-mitotic cells arise from populations of mitotic cells that have exhausted their regenerative potential. One theory of aging holds that certain cell types of the body (e.g., fibroblasts) have a limited number of mitotic cell cycles. When a biologically determined number of cell cycles have elapsed, such cells cannot divide further and become post-mitotic cells that eventually wear out and die.

Progeria   Any of several rare genetic conditions of premature aging, typically characterized by early-onset atherosclerosis and diabetes. All of the progerias, despite differences in their root genetic causes, seem to involve defects in normal cellular renewal processes (e.g., stem cell regeneration, maintenance of stem cells, DNA repair in dividing cell populations).

Promoter   The DNA site that binds RNA polymerase plus transcription factors, to initiate RNA transcription. Promoters are cis-acting regulatory elements.

Examples of promoter mutations causing disease are found in subsets of patients affected by beta-thalassemia, Bernard-Soulier syndrome, pyruvate kinase deficiency, familial hypercholesterolemia, and hemophilia [211].

As a general rule, promotor mutations, as well as all mutations that affect genomic regulatory systems, cause disease by reducing the quantity of a normal protein; not by producing altered protein, and not by eliminating gene products. Because the drop in protein production may be small, promoter diseases may produce milder diseases than those resulting from gene defects that eliminate a protein entirely.

Regulatory DNA element   Sites in DNA that bind to other molecules (e.g., transcription factors and RNA polymerase) to regulate transcription. Promoters and enhancers are types of regulatory DNA elements.

Regulatory RNA element   Transcribed RNA can influence the subsequent transcription and/or translation of other RNA species. The various RNA regulatory elements include: antisense RNA (including cis-natural antisense transcript and trans-acting siRNA), long non-coding RNA, microRNA, piwi-interacting RNA, repeat-associated siRNA, RNAi, small interfering RNA, and small temporal RNA.

Mutations of regulatory RNA elements may cause disease. For example, miR-96 is expressed exclusively in the inner ear and the eye. Mutations in the miR-96 precursor molecule may cause a rare form of autosomal dominant hearing loss [212].

Results   The term "results" is often confused with the term "conclusions." The "results" consist of the full set of experimental data collected by measurements.

In practice, the "results" that scientists provide to the public, to justify their conclusions, are a small subset of data that has been distilled from the full set of raw results. It is wrong to think, as many do, that the "Results" section of a journal article represents all of the relevant data obtained from an experiment or project. In many cases, the data provided in the text of a journal article is specifically chosen to support the narrative preferred by the authors. Serious scientists who are interested in the results of an experiment should insist upon obtaining all of the experimental data generated by the experiment.

Results should be distinguished from conclusions. Conclusions are the inferences drawn from the results. As a general rule, results need to be verified, usually by demonstrating that they are repeatable. Conclusions need to be validated, usually by showing that the conclusions hold true for a variety of conditions.

Retrovirus   An RNA virus that replicates through a DNA intermediate. The DNA intermediate may become integrated into the host DNA, from which viral RNA is transcribed. When the integration of the virus occurs in germ cells, the viral DNA can be inherited by the offspring. Through this mechanism, the human genome carries a legacy of retroviral DNA. Ancient retroviruses account for about 8% of the human genome [35].

Schwannoma A tumor composed of neoplastic Schwann cells, that are normally found wrapped around the axonal extensions of peripheral nervous system neurons. Schwann cells and the cells they ensheath derive from the neural crest. Animals that have no neural crest will lack Schwann cells and cannot develop Schwannomas (tumors of Schwann cells).

Schwannomas of the acoustic spinal nerves occur in neurofibromatosis type 2, a neurocristopathy.

Sister class and cousin class Two classes of organisms are sisters of one another if they both have the same direct superclass (i.e., parent class). This practice of referring to "sister" classes is just one example of the inappropriate application of gender assignment to biological entities that have no gender. A better, though still inaccurate, term for classes having the same direct superclass would be the gender-neutral term "sibling classes," but the term "sister class" seems to be solidly entrenched in modern nomenclature. All species descended from either of two sister classes will have the same closest common ancestor, this being the parent class of the sister classes.

Two classes are cousin classes if they have a common grandparent class. Because taxonomists don't generally distinguish levels of "cousinality", the term cousin class is informally extended to any two classes that share any ancestral class above the parent class. Of course, this means that, technically, every class is a sister or a cousin to every other class. By convention, we reserve the "cousin class" term for non-siblings who share a relatively close ancestor (e.g., a grandparent or great-grandparent in common).

Survival of the fittest This phrase was first used by Herbert Spencer, a contemporary of Darwin's, in his Principles of Biology (1864) and referred to natural selection as a process that favored the survival of the fittest "races" (Spencer's terminology). The term was not intended to refer to the survival of the fittest individuals of a species. Moreover, fitness, as it applies to species, refers to the ability of the species to speciate, to produce a diverse class of descendant species over time. There is nothing in the theory of evolution through natural selection that specifically addresses the issue of the survival of individuals in the species.

Synapomorphy A trait found in all the members of a clade (i.e., shared by the species descending from the ancestral species in which the trait first appeared). Neural crest cells may be considered a synapomorphic trait shared by all subclasses of Craniata.

Other examples of synapomorphic traits include the following [213]:

- The single posterior undulipodium of Class Opisthokonta
- Collagen synthesis and formation of polar bodies during spermatogenesis in Class Metazoa
- Hox and ParaHox genes of Class Parahoxozoa
- Serotonin synthesis in Class Planulozoa
- Enterocoely in Class Deuterostomia
- Notochord in Class Chordata
- Larvae with prototroch in Class Trochozoa
- Molted cuticle of Class Ecdysozoa
- Discrete excretory organs of Class Nephrozoa, such as nephridia

Telomere Chromosomes have a long padding sequence of repetitive DNA, at their tips, and this sequence is called the telomere. Animal cells lose a fragment of DNA from the tip of the chromosome with each cell division. This happens because one strand of DNA is replicated as sequential fragments, with each fragment requiring a template sequence beyond its end to initiate replication. Absent the telomere, the last fragment in the DNA strand has no extension template and is not replicated. By furnishing padding at the tips of chromosomes, the telomere sequence sacrifices fragments of itself for the sake of pre-serving the coding sequences of the chromosome. As all good things come to an end, the telomere padding exhausts itself, after about 50 rounds of mitosis. At this time, the cell ceases further replication and will eventually die.

Cells that continually renew throughout life, such as bone marrow stem cells, skin and hair follicle basal layer cells, and intestinal basal crypt cells, retain an enzyme, telomerase, that restores telomere length. If such cells contain a loss of function mutation in any of the genes encoding the components of the telomerase complex, then the ability of those cells to continuously divide will be impaired.

A mutation in the telomerase gene is the root cause of dyskeratosis congenita, a rare inherited con-dition in which bone marrow failure frequently occurs [214]. Telomerase gene mutations have also been found in some cases of adults having bone marrow failure, and these late-occurring conditions are presumed to be variant forms of dyskeratosis congenita [215]. We see the clinical consequences of a telomerase deficiency in the blood-forming cells of the bone marrow because these cells are the most highly replicative in the body [216]. A defect in the replicative capacity of dividing cells would be expected to reveal itself clinically as bone marrow failure.

Cancer cells, like bone marrow cells, continuously divide and have high concentrations of telome-rase. The ability of some cancer cells to restore their telomeres contributes to their continuous capacity to divide without limit, a phenomenon sometimes called cancer cell immortality. Telomerase insuffi-ciency has been suggested as a possible cause of spontaneous regression in tumors, a rarely observed phenomenon [217].

Totipotent stem cell A stem cell that can produce, after cell division, differentiated cells of any type. This would include cells of any of the three embryonic layers (ectoderm, endoderm, and mesoderm), germ cells, and cells of the extra-embryonic tissue (e.g., trophoblasts). A totipotent stem cell is different from a pluripotent stem cell, the latter of which cannot produce cells of trophoblast lineage [218].

As pertains to development in members of Class Eutheria (placental mammals), there is a short period when all of the cells are totipotent. During the so-called pre-embryonic period, corresponding to the first two weeks following fertilization, the zygote (i.e., fertilized ovum) travels to the uterus, implants, and begins to build the extra-embryonic tissues, and the blastocyst. The cells of the pre-embryo are, to the best of anyone's knowledge, totipotent. In the third week following fertilization (fifth week since the last menstrual period), the three layers of the embryo form, and the embryonic cells differentiate to the extent that they are no longer totipotent.

In the past few decades, we have come to learn that the primary difference between an embryonic stem cell and a fully differentiated cell of the body (i.e., a somatic cell) is the erasure of the epigenome. Epigenomic erasure is a process by which virtually all of the epigenomic modifications present in the mature cell are erased, and the cell is returned to its uncommitted state, much like that of a totipotent stem cell [219–222].

Trans-acting regulatory element In molecular biology, a trans-acting agent is usually a regulatory sequence of DNA, that acts through an intermediary molecule (e.g., transcription factor or RNA mol-ecule), on some other location of the chromosome or some other chromosome. In contrast, cis-acting elements do not operate through intermediary molecules and exert their effects in close proximity to themselves. Cis- and trans- elements work in concert to regulate gene expression.

Transcription The process in which genomic DNA serves as a template for the synthesis of RNA. After a considerable amount of processing, particular types of RNA (messenger RNA transcribed from genes that code for proteins) are translated into protein molecules. Newly synthesized protein molecules are modified further before being "set free" into the cell.

Transcription factor A protein that binds to specific DNA sequences to control the transcription of DNA to RNA. The human genome codes for several thousand different transcription factors [223].

One transcription factor can regulate gene expression in multiple tissues. Consequently, transcrip-tion factor diseases may involve several organs [224]. For example, Waardenburg syndrome types 1 and

2 whose root causes are mutations in the PAX3 and MITF transcription factor genes, are associated with lateral displacement of the inner canthus of each eye, pigmentary disturbance including a frontal white blaze of hair, heterochromia iridis, white eyelashes, leukoderma, and cochlear deafness. Transcription factor diseases tend to have a dominant inheritance pattern, as insufficiency of one transcription factor allele is sufficient to produce a syndromic phenotype [225].

Translation Translation is the process by which mRNA (messenger RNA) is used as a template to produce a sequence of amino acids that constitute nascent protein molecules. The mRNA involved in translation was produced from a DNA template in a process known as transcription. Transcription is a cellular process that involves a variety of complex steps including editing and splicing.

Chains of amino acids freshly translated from an mRNA template typically undergo a variety of modifications before they are finally folded into their fully functional three-dimensional structure. In many cases, protein molecules are combined with other protein molecules and non-protein cofactors (e.g., metals such as heme and zinc) to produce large protein complexes. Errors in the post-translational process can have negative consequences. An example of a rare disease caused by a defect in a post-translational process is a congenital disorder of glycosylation type IIe, caused by homozygous mutation in a gene that encodes a component of a Golgi body protein that is involved in post-translational protein glycosylation; the COG7 gene [226]. This rare disease produces a complex disease phenotype in infants, with multiple disturbances in organs and systems plus various anatomic abnormalities.

All living organisms on earth follow the same processes of transcription and translation, more or less, and this is another indicator that all classes of life on earth descended from a common ancestor.

Transposable element Also called a transposon, and informally known as jumping gene. The name "transposable element" would seem to imply that a fragment of the genome (i.e., the transposable element) physically moves from one point in the genome to another. This is not the case. What actually happens (in the case of Class II transposons) is that a copy of the DNA sequence of the transposon is inserted elsewhere in the genome, resulting in the sequence now occupying two different locations in the genome. In the case of Class II transposons, the DNA sequence of the transposon is translated into RNA, then reverse-transcribed as DNA, and reinserted at another location; likewise resulting in two of the same sequence in two locations in the genome [227]. You can see how transposable elements might bloat the genome with repeated elements.

Transposons are the ancient remnants of retroviruses and other horizontally transferred genes that insinuated their way into the eukaryotic genome. Because transposon DNA is not necessary to cell survival, the sequences of transposons are generally not conserved, and mutations occurring over time yield degenerate sequences that no longer function as retroviruses. As luck would have it, not all mutations to transposable elements are without benefit to the host cell. A transposon is credited with the acquisition of adaptive immunity in animals. The RAG1 gene was acquired as a transposon. This gene enabled the DNA that encodes a segment of the immunoglobulin molecule to rearrange, thus producing a vast array of protein variants [228]. A role for transposons in the altered expression of genes in cancer cells has been suggested [229].

Trilateral retinoblastoma The occurrence of bilateral retinoblastomas is sometimes followed by the occurrence of a pineoblastoma, and this is referred to as trilateral retinoblastoma. The pineal gland has an evolutionary anlage identical to that of the eye. The difference is that neuroectoderm-derived photoreceptors of the pineal gland took up residence deep within a midline recess in the brain, while the photoreceptors of the eyes developed as paired external structures. The evolved pineal gland, like the evolved eyes, reacts to filtered sunlight, though any light reaching the pineal has had a lot more filtering than the light reaching the retinas. In response to light cessation, the pineal gland releases melatonin, a hormone that influences circadian rhythms (e.g., sleep). The same germline mutation that leads to bilateral retinoblastomas may occasionally cause a pineoblastoma. Pineoblastomas share a common morphology (i.e., histologic appearance) and homology (i.e., development from equivalent embryonic anlagen) with retinoblastomas [230].

Tumor suppressor gene A gene that serves to arrest, delay, or makes less likely, one or more of the cellular events involved in the pathogenesis of cancer. Loss of function of a tumor suppressor gene is associated with an increased risk of developing cancer; sometimes an increased risk for many different types of cancer. As you might guess, our genome has not evolved to produce genes whose only purpose is to wait for an opportunity to intervene around to intervene whenever some tumor begins to develop. Tumor suppressor genes have roles in normal cell function, such as participating in DNA repair, or regulating cell division or cell death.

Virion The infective form of a virus outside the host cell. Viruses can be thought of as having two alternating forms: the virion and the virocell.

Virocell The name given to a host cell that has been commandeered by a virus to devote its cellular machinery to the mass production of virus particles. When we think of viruses as living organisms, it is best to envisage the virocell, which consists of a viral factory built from the wreckage of the host cells; and not the virion, which is simply a vehicle for transporting a virus safely from host to host.

References

[1] Sarich VM. Just how old is the hominid line? Yearb Phys Anthropol 1973;17:98–112.

[2] Berman JJ. Evolution's clinical guidebook: translating ancient genes into precision medicine. Cambridge, MA: Academic Press; 2019.

[3] DeQueiroz K. Ernst Mayr and the modern concept of species. PNAS 2005;102(Suppl 1):6600–7.

[4] Berman J. Precision medicine, and the reinvention of human disease. Cambridge, MA: Academic Press; 2018.

[5] Zuk O, Hechter E, Sunyaev SR, Lander ES. The mystery of missing heritability: genetic interactions create phantom heritability. Proc Natl Acad Sci U S A 2012;109:1193–8.

[6] Wu D, Hugenholtz P, Mavromatis K, Pukall R, Dalin E, Ivanova NN, et al. A phylogeny-driven genomic encyclopedia of bacteria and archaea. Nature 2009;462:1056–60.

[7] Schwartz JH, Maresca B. Do molecular clocks run at all? A critique of molecular systematics. Biol Theory 2006;1:357–71.

[8] Drummond AJ, Ho SYW, Phillips MJ, Rambaut A. Relaxed phylogenetics and dating with confidence. PLoS Biol 2006;4, e88.

[9] Berman JJ. Logic and critical thinking in the biomedical sciences, volume I: deductions based upon simple observations. Cambridge, MA: Academic Press; 2020.

[10] Raup DM. A kill curve for Phanerozoic marine species. Paleobiology 1991;17:37–48.

[11] Angly FE, Felts B, Breitbart M, Salamon P, Edwards RA, Carlson C, et al. The marine viromes of four oceanic regions. PLoS Biol 2006;4, e368.

[12] Anthony SJ, Epstein JH, Murray KA, Navarrete-Macias I, Zambrana-Torrelio CM, Solovyov A, et al. A strategy to estimate unknown viral diversity in mammals. MBio 2013;4(5), e00598-13.

[13] Koonin EV, Wolf YI. Evolution of microbes and viruses: a paradigm shift in evolutionary biology? Front Cell Infect Microbiol 2012;2:119.

[14] Mora C, Tittensor DP, Adl S, Simpson AGB, Worm B. How many species are there on earth and in the ocean? PLoS Biol 2011;9, e1001127.

[15] Locey KJ, Lennon JT. Scaling laws predict global microbial diversity. Proc Natl Acad Sci U S A 2016;113:5970–5.

[16] Berman JJ. Taxonomic guide to infectious diseases: understanding the biologic classes of pathogenic organisms. 1st ed. Cambridge, MA: Academic Press; 2012.

[17] Haring M, Vestergaard G, Rachel R, Chen L, Garrett RA, Prangishvili D. Virology: independent virus development outside a host. Nature 2005;436:1101–2.

[18] Kingsbury DW. Species classification problems in virus taxonomy. Intervirology 1985;24:62–70.

[19] Suttle CA. Environmental microbiology: viral diversity on the global stage. Nat Microbiol 2016; 1:16205.

[20] Suttle CA. Marine viruses: major players in the global ecosystem. Nat Rev Microbiol 2007;5: 801–12.

[21] Mihara T, Koyano H, Hingamp P, Grimsley N, Goto S, Ogata H. Taxon richness of "Megaviridae" exceeds those of bacteria and archaea in the ocean. Microbes Environ 2018;33:162–71.

[22] Fischer MG, Kelly I, Foster LJ, Suttle CA. The virion of Cafeteria roenbergensis virus (CroV) contains a complex suite of proteins for transcription and DNA repair. Virology 2014;466:82–94.

[23] Morgan GJ. What is a virus species? Radical pluralism in viral taxonomy? Stud Hist Phil Biol Biomed Sci 2016;59:64–70.

[24] Van Regenmortel MHV. The metaphor that viruses are living is alive and well, but it is no more than a metaphor. Stud Hist Phil Biol Biomed Sci 2016;59:117–24.

[25] Argos P, Kamer G, Nicklin MJ, Wimmer E. Similarity in gene organization and homology between proteins of animal picornaviruses and a plant comovirus suggest common ancestry of these virus families. Nucleic Acids Res 1984;12:7251–67.

[26] Kamer G, Argos P. Primary structural comparison of RNA-dependent polymerases from plant, animal and bacterial viruses. Nucleic Acids Res 1984;12:7269–82.

[27] Goldbach R. Genome similarities between plant and animal RNA viruses. Microbiol Sci 1987;4: 197–202.

[28] Koonin EV, Dolja VV. Evolution and taxonomy of positive-strand RNA viruses: implications of comparative analysis of amino acid sequences. Crit Rev Biochem Mol Biol 1993;28:375–430.

[29] Bandin I, Dopazo CP. Host range, host specificity and hypothesized host shift events among viruses of lower vertebrates. Vet Res 2011;42:67.

[30] Balique F, Lecoq H, Raoult D, Colson P. Can plant viruses cross the kingdom border and be pathogenic to humans? Viruses 2015;7:2074–98.

[31] Nasir A, Caetano-Anolles G. A phylogenomic data-driven exploration of viral origins and evolution. Sci Adv 2015;1, e1500527.

[32] Jern P, Sperber GO, Blomberg J. Use of Endogenous Retroviral Sequences (ERVs) and structural markers for retroviral phylogenetic inference and taxonomy. Retrovirology 2005;2:50.

[33] Krupovic M, Bamford DH. Double-stranded DNA viruses: 20 families and only five different architectural principles for virion assembly. Curr Opin Virol 2011;1:118–24.

[34] Hughes AL, Friedman R. Poxvirus genome evolution by gene gain and loss. Mol Phylogenet Evol 2005;35:186–95.

[35] Emerman M, Malik HS. Paleovirology: modern consequences of ancient viruses. PLoS Biol 2010;8, e1000301.

[36] Mohammed MA, Galbraith SE, Radford AD, Dove W, Takasaki T, Kurane I, et al. Molecular phylogenetic and evolutionary analyses of Muar strain of Japanese encephalitis virus reveal it is the missing fifth genotype. Infect Genet Evol 2011;11:855–62.

[37] Bannert N, Kurth R. The evolutionary dynamics of human endogenous retroviral families. Annu Rev Genomics Hum Genet 2006;7:149–73.

[38] Rasmussen MD, Kellis M. A Bayesian approach for fast and accurate gene tree reconstruction. Mol Biol Evol 2011;28:273–90.

[39] Anon. Taxonomy. International Committee on Taxonomy of Viruses; 2018. https://talk.ictvonline.org. [Accessed 18 October 2018].

[40] Andino R, Domingo E. Viral quasispecies. Virology 2015;479–480:46–51.

[41] Forterre P. Defining life: the virus viewpoint. Orig Life Evol Biosph 2010;40:151–60.

[42] Forterre P. Three RNA cells for ribosomal lineages and three DNA viruses to replicate their genomes: a hypothesis for the origin of cellular domain. PNAS 2006;106:3669–74.

[43] Bamford DH. Do viruses form lineages across different domains of life? Res Microbiol 2003;154:231–6.

[44] Horie M, Honda T, Suzuki Y, Kobayashi Y, Daito T, Oshida T, et al. Endogenous non-retroviral RNA virus elements in mammalian genomes. Nature 2010;463:84–7.

[45] Griffiths DJ. Endogenous retroviruses in the human genome sequence. Genome Biol 2001;2. reviews1017.1–reviews1017.5.

[46] Diener TO. Potato spindle tuber "virus": IV. A replicating low molecular weight RNA. Virology 1971;45:411–28.

[47] Koonin EV, Starokadomskyy P. Are viruses alive? The replicator paradigm sheds decisive light on an old but misguided question. Stud Hist Phil Biol Biomed Sci 2016;59:125–34.

[48] Valas RE, Bourne PE. The origin of a derived superkingdom: how a gram-positive bacterium crossed the desert to become an archaeon. Biol Direct 2011;6:16.

[49] Filee J. Multiple occurrences of giant virus core genes acquired by eukaryotic genomes: the visible part of the iceberg? Virology 2014;466–467:53–9.

[50] Forterre P, Gaia M. Giant viruses and the origin of modern eukaryotes. Curr Opin Microbiol 2016;31:44–9.

[51] Berman JJ. Rare diseases and orphan drugs: keys to understanding and treating common diseases. Cambridge, MD: Academic Press; 2014.

[52] Mitton JB, Grant MC. Genetic variation and the natural history of Quaking aspen. Bioscience 1996;46:25–31.

[53] Schmich J, Kraus Y, De Vito D, Graziussi D, Boero F, Piraino S. Induction of reverse development in two marine hydrozoans. Int J Dev Biol 2007;51:45–56.

[54] Martinez DE. Mortality patterns suggest lack of senescence in hydras. Exp Gerontol 1998;33:217–25.

[55] Rich N. Can a jellyfish unlock the secret of immortality? N Y Times 2012. November 28.

[56] Martinez DE, Bridge D. Hydra, the everlasting embryo, confronts aging. Int J Dev Biol 2012;56:479–87.

[57] Tan T, Rahman R, Jaber-Hijazi F, Felix DA, Chen C, Louis EJ, et al. Telomere maintenance and telomerase activity are differentially regulated in asexual and sexual worms. Proc Natl Acad Sci U S A 2012;109:4209–14.

[58] Philippe H, Brinkmann H, Copley RR, Moroz LL, Nakano H, Poustka AJ, et al. Acoelomorph flatworms are deuterostomes related to Xenoturbella. Nature 2011;470:255–8.

[59] Kay EH, Hoekstra HE. Rodents. Curr Biol 2008;18:R406–10.

[60] Kasowski M, Grubert F, Heffelfinger C, Hariharan M, Asabere A, Waszak SM, et al. Variation in transcription factor binding among humans. Science 2010;328(5975):232–5.

[61] Zheng W, Zhao H, Mancera E, Steinmetz LM, Snyder M. Genetic analysis of variation in transcription factor binding in yeast. Nature 2010;464:1187–91.

[62] Pillon Y. Biodiversite, origine et evolution des Cunoniaceae: implications pour la conservation de la flore de Nouvelle-Caledonie [Ph.D. thesis]. University of New Caledonia; 2008.

[63] Holland LZ. Laudet the chordate amphioxus: an emerging model organism for developmental biology. Cell Mol Life Sci 2004;61:2290–308.

[64] Hochner B. An embodied view of octopus neurobiology. Curr Biol 2012;22:R887–92.

[65] Adamo SA. Octopus: multiple minds or just a slow thinker? Anim Sentience 2019;2019:278.

[66] Godfrey-Smith P. The mind of an octopus. Sci Am Mind 2017;28:62–9.

[67] Webb J. Broody octopus keeps record-breaking four-year vigil. BBC News Sci Environ 2014. 30 July.

[68] Hildenbrand A, Austermann G, Fuchs D, Bengtson P, Stinnesbeck W. A potential cephalopod from the early Cambrian of eastern Newfoundland, Canada. Commun Biol 2021;4:388.

[69] Benton MJ, Donoghue PCJ. Palaeontological evidence to date the tree of life. Mol Biol Evol 2006;24:26–53.

[70] Pound P, Ebrahim S, Sandercock P, Bracken MB, Roberts I. Reviewing animal trials systematically (rats) group. Where is the evidence that animal research benefits humans? BMJ 2004; 328:514–7.

[71] Hackam DG, Redelmeier DA. Translation of research evidence from animals to humans. JAMA 2006;296:1731–2.

[72] Van der Worp HB, Howells DW, Sena ES, Porritt MJ, Rewell S, O'Collins V, et al. Can animal models of disease reliably inform human studies? PLoS Med 2010;7, e1000245.

[73] Rice J. Animal models: not close enough. Nature 2012;484:S9.

[74] National Academies of Sciences, Engineering, and Medicine. Therapeutic development in the absence of predictive animal models of nervous system disorders: proceedings of a workshop. Washington, DC: The National Academies Press; 2017.

[75] Watts JC, Prusiner S. Mouse models for studying the formation and propagation of prions. J Biol Chem 2014;289:19841–19,849.

[76] Anon. The mouse model: less than perfect, still invaluable. Johns Hopkins Medicine; 2010. Available from: http://www.hopkinsmedicine.org/institute_basic_biomedical_sciences/news_events/articles_and_stories/model_organisms/201010_mouse_model.html. [Accessed 15 March 2019].

[77] Dawson TM, Ko HS, Dawson VL. Genetic animal models of Parkinson's disease. Neuron 2010;66 (5):646–61.

[78] Choi DW, Armitage R, Brady LS, Coetzee T, Fisher W, Hyman S, et al. Medicines for the mind: policy-based "pull" incentives for creating breakthrough CNS drugs. Neuron 2014;84:554–63.

[79] Strange K. Drug discovery in fish, flies, and worms. ILAR J 2016;57:133–43.

[80] Pandey UB, Nichols CD. Human disease models in *Drosophila melanogaster* and the role of the fly in therapeutic drug discovery. Pharmacol Rev 2011;63:411–36.

[81] Washington NL, Haendel MA, Mungall CJ, Ashburner M, Westerfield M, Lewis SE. Linking human diseases to animal models using ontology-based phenotype annotation. PLoS Biol 2009;7, e1000247.

[82] Chow CY, Reiter LT. Etiology of human genetic disease on the fly. Trends Genet 2017;33:391–8.

[83] Novick P, Field C, Schekman R. Identification of 23 complementation groups required for post-translational events in the yeast secretory pathway. Cell 1980;21:205–15.

[84] McGary KL, Park TJ, Woods JO, Cha HJ, Wallingford JB, Marcotte EM. Systematic discovery of non-obvious human disease models through orthologous phenotypes. Proc Natl Acad Sci U S A 2010;107:6544–9.

[85] Gissen P, Maher ER. Cargos and genes: insights into vesicular transport from inherited human disease. J Med Genet 2007;44:545–55.

[86] Rubinsztein DC. Protein–protein interaction networks in the spinocerebellar ataxias. Genome Biol 2006;7:229.

[87] Palikaras K, Tavernarakis N. Caenorhabditis elegans (Nematode). In: Brenner's encyclopedia of genetics. 2nd ed. Philadelphia: Elsevier; 2013. p. 404–8.

[88] No attributed author. Tuberous sclerosis complex in flies too? a fly homolog to TSC2, called gigas, plays a role in cell cycle regulation. July 27. Available from: http://www.ncbi.nlm.nih.gov/books/bv.fcgi?rid=coffeebrk.chapter.25; 2000.

[89] Hariharan IK, Bilder D. Regulation of imaginal disc growth by tumor-suppressor genes in drosophila. Annu Rev Genet 2006;40:335–61.

[90] Howe K, Clark MD, Torroja CF, Torrance J, Berthelot C, Muffato M, et al. The zebrafish reference genome sequence and its relationship to the human genome. Nature 2013;496:498–503.

[91] Spitsbergen JM, Kent ML. The state of the art of the zebrafish model for toxicology and toxicologic pathology research – advantages and current limitations. Toxicol Pathol 2003;31(Suppl):62–87.

[92] Kelsh RN, Eisen JS. The zebrafish colorless gene regulates development of non-ectomesenchymal neural crest derivatives. Development 2000;127:515–25.

[93] Smolowitz R, Hanley J, Richmond H. A three-year retrospective study of abdominal tumors in zebrafish maintained in an aquatic laboratory animal facility. Biol Bull 2002;203:265–6.

[94] Wojciechowska S, van Rooijen E, Ceol C, Patton EE, White RM. Generation and analysis of zebrafish melanoma models. Methods Cell Biol 2016;134:531–49.

[95] Tobin DM, Vary Jr JC, Ray JP, Walsh GS, Dunstan SJ, Bang ND, et al. The lta4h locus modulates susceptibility to mycobacterial infection in zebrafish and humans. Cell 2010;140:717–30.

[96] Curtis J, Kopanitsa L, Stebbings E, Speirs A, Ignatyeva O, Balabanova Y, et al. Association analysis of the LTA4H gene polymorphisms and pulmonary tuberculosis in 9115 subjects. Tuberculosis (Edinb) 2011;91:22–5.

[97] Beckwith LG, Moore JL, Tsao-Wu GS, Harshbarger JC, Cheng KC. Ethylnitrosourea induces neoplasia in zebrafish (*Danio rerio*). Lab Investig 2000;80:379–85.

[98] Berman JJ. Neoplasms: principles of development and diversity. Sudbury: Jones & Bartlett; 2009.

[99] Christie AE, Kutz-Naber KK, Stemmler EA, Klein A, Messinger DI, Goiney CC, et al. Midgut epithelial endocrine cells are a rich source of the neuropeptides APSGFLGMRamide (*Cancer borealis* tachykinin-related peptide Ia) and GYRKPPFNGSIFamide (Gly1-SIFamide) in the crabs *C. borealis*, *Cancer magister* and *Cancer productus*. J Exp Biol 2007;210(Pt 4):699–714.

[100] Sorensen PH, Shimada H, Liu XF, Lim JF, Thomas G, Triche TJ. Biphenotypic sarcomas with myogenic and neural differentiation express the Ewing's sarcoma EWS/FLI1 fusion gene. Cancer Res 1995;55:1385–92.

[101] Harrison DF. Biomechanics of the giraffe larynx and trachea. Acta Otolaryngol 1980;89:258–64.

[102] Finnerty JR. The origins of axial patterning in the metazoa: how old is bilateral symmetry? Int J Dev Biol 2003;47:523–9.

[103] deLussaneta MH, Osseb JWM. An ancestral axial twist explains the contralateral forebrain and the optic chiasm in vertebrates. Anim Biol 2012;62:193–216.

[104] Abrams MJ, Basinger T, Yuan W, Guo C, Goentoro L. Self-repairing symmetry in jellyfish through mechanically driven reorganization. PNAS 2015;112:E3365–73.

[105] Dunitz JD. Symmetry arguments in chemistry. Proc Natl Acad Sci U S A 1996;93:14260–14,266.

[106] Garcia-Bellido A. Symmetries throughout organic evolution. Proc Natl Acad Sci U S A 1996;93:14229–32.

[107] Baldauf SL. An overview of the phylogeny and diversity of eukaryotes. J Syst Evol 2008;46:263–73.

[108] Frias-Lopez J, Shi Y, Tyson GW, Coleman ML, Schuster SC, Chisholm SW, et al. Microbial community gene expression in ocean surface waters. Proc Natl Acad Sci 2008;105:3805–10.

[109] Demain AL. Regulation of secondary metabolism in fungi. Pure Appl Chem 1986;58:219–26.

[110] Theis N, Lerdau M. The evolution of function in plant secondary metabolites. Int J Plant Sci 2003;164:S93–S102.

[111] Matsushima T, Matsumoto H, Shirai A, Sawamura M, Sugimura T. Mutagenicity of the naturally occurring carcinogen cycasin and synthetic methylazoxymethanol conjugates in *Salmonella typhimurium*. Cancer Res 1979;39:3780–2.

[112] Wales JH, Sinnhuber RO, Hendricks JD, Nixon JE, Eisele TA. Aflatoxin B1 induction of hepatocellular carcinoma in the embryos of rainbow trout (*Salmo gairdneri*). J Natl Cancer Inst 1978;60:1133–9.

[113] Pichersky E, Gang D. Genetics and biochemistry of secondary metabolites in plants: an evolutionary perspective. Trends Plant Sci 2000;5:439–45.

[114] Henry M. Super-saturated chemistry. Inference Int Rev Sci 2016;2(4).

[115] Perez-Iratxeta C, Palidwor G, Andrade-Navarro MA. Toward completion of the Earth's proteome. EMBO Rep 2007;8:1135–41.

[116] Frank DN, Pace NR. Gastrointestinal microbiology enters the metagenomics era. Curr Opin Gastroenterol 2008;24:4–10.

[117] Yang X, Xie L, Li Y, Wei C. More than 9,000,000 unique genes in human gut bacterial community: estimating gene numbers inside a human body. PLoS One 2009;4, e6074.

[118] Banuls A, Thomas F, Renaud F. Of parasites and men. Infect Genet Evol 2013;20:61–70.

[119] Yu J, Hu S, Wang J, Wong GK, Li S, Liu B, et al. A draft sequence of the rice genome (*Oryza sativa* L. ssp. indica). Science 2002;296:79–92.

[120] Madar S, Goldstein I, Rotter V. Did experimental biology die? Lessons from 30 years of p53 research. Cancer Res 2009;69:6378–80.

[121] Zilfou JT, Lowe SW. Tumor suppressive functions of p53. Cold Spring Harb Perspect Biol 2009; a001883.

[122] Vogelstein B, Lane D, Levine AJ. Surfing the p53 network. Nature 2000;408:307–10.

[123] Waterham HR, Koster J, Mooyer P, van Noort G, Kelley RI, Wilcox WR, et al. Autosomal recessive HEM/Greenberg skeletal dysplasia is caused by 3-beta-hydroxysterol delta(14)-reductase deficiency due to mutations in the lamin B receptor gene. Am J Hum Genet 2003;72:1013–7.

[124] Piatigorsky J. Gene sharing, lens crystallins and speculations on an eye/ear evolutionary relationship. Integr Comp Biol 2003;43:492–9.

[125] Piatigorsky J, Wistow GJ. Enzyme/crystallins: gene sharing as an evolutionary strategy. Cell 1989;57:197–9.

[126] Wistow G. Evolution of a protein superfamily: relationships between vertebrate lens crystallins and microorganism dormancy proteins. J Mol Evol 1990;30:140–5.

[127] Land MF, Fernald RD. The evolution of eyes. Annu Rev Neurosci 1992;15:1–29.

[128] Andreeva A, Murzin AG. Structural classification of proteins and structural genomics: new insights into protein folding and evolution. Acta Crystallogr 2010;F66:1190–7.

[129] Schnoes AM, Brown SD, Dodevski I, Babbitt PC. Annotation error in public databases: misannotation of molecular function in enzyme superfamilies. PLoS Comput Biol 2009;5, e1000605.

[130] Jones C, Brown A, Baumann U. Estimating the annotation error rate of curated GO database sequence annotations. BMC Bioinformatics 2007;8:170.

[131] Kohler J, Munn K, Ruegg A, Skusa A, Smith B. Quality control for terms and definitions in ontologies and taxonomies. BMC Bioinformatics 2006;7:212.

[132] Gersbach CA, Perez-Pinera P. Activating human genes with zinc finger proteins, transcription activator-like effectors and CRISPR/Cas9 for gene therapy and regenerative medicine. Expert Opin Ther Targets 2014;18:835–9.

[133] Lv Q, Yuan L, Deng J, Chen M, Wang Y, Zeng J, et al. Efficient generation of myostatin gene mutated rabbit by CRISPR/Cas9. Sci Rep 2016;6:25029.

[134] Shah RR, Cholewa-Waclaw J, Davies FCJ, Paton KM, Chaligne R, Heard E, et al. Efficient and versatile CRISPR engineering of human neurons in culture to model neurological disorders. Wellcome Open Res 2016;1:13.

[135] Zhang C, Liu J, Zhong JF, Zhang X. Engineering CAR-T cells. Biomark Res 2017;5:22.

[136] Anderson FJ. An illustrated history of the herbals. iUniverse; 1999.

[137] Berman JJ. Armchair science: no experiments, just deduction. Kindle ed. Amazon Digital Services, Inc.; 2014.

[138] Wegener A. Die Entstehung der Kontinente und Ozeane. 2nd ed. Braunschweig, Germany: F. Vieweg; 1920.

[139] Gandolfo MA, Hermsen EJ, Zamaloa MC, Nixon KC, Gonzalez CC, Wilf P, et al. Oldest known eucalyptus macrofossils are from South America. PLoS One 2011;6, e21084.

[140] Frederic MY, Lundin VF, Whiteside MD, Cueva JG, Tu DK, Kang SY, et al. Identification of 526 conserved metazoan genetic innovations exposes a new role for cofactor *E*-like in neuronal microtubule homeostasis. PLoS Genet 2013;9, e1003804.

[141] Wetterbom A, Sevov M, Cavelier L, Bergstrom TF. Comparative genomic analysis of human and chimpanzee indicates a key role for indels in primate evolution. J Mol Evol 2006;63:682–90.

[142] Neme R, Tautz D. Phylogenetic patterns of emergence of new genes support a model of frequent de novo evolution. BMC Genomics 2013;14:117.

[143] Erwin D, Valentine J, Jablonski D. The origin of animal body plans. Am Sci 1997;85:126–37.

[144] Graur D, Zheng Y, Azevedo RBR. An evolutionary classification of genomic function. Genome Biol Evol 2015;7:642–5.

[145] Graur D, Zheng Y, Price N, Azevedo RB, Zufall RA, Elhaik E. On the immortality of television sets: "function" in the human genome according to the evolution-free gospel of ENCODE. Genome Biol Evol 2013;5:578–90.

[146] Alfoldi J, Lindblad-Toh K. Comparative genomics as a tool to understand evolution and disease. Genome Res 2013;23:1063–8.

[147] Samollow PB. The opossum genome: insights and opportunities from an alternative mammal. Genome Res 2008;18:1199–215.

[148] Mikkelsen TS, Wakefield MJ, Aken B, Amemiya JL, Chang S, Duke M, et al. Genome of the marsupial *Monodelphis domestica* reveals innovation in non-coding sequences. Nature 2007;447:167–77.

[149] Zheng J, Xia X, Ding H, Yan A, Hu S, Gong X, et al. Erasure of the paternal transcription program during spermiogenesis: the first step in the reprogramming of sperm chromatin for zygotic development. Dev Dyn 2008;237:1463–76.

[150] Faustino NA, Cooper TA. Pre-mRNA splicing and human disease. Genes Dev 2003;17:419–37.

[151] Tanackovic G, Ransijn A, Thibault P, Abou Elela S, Klinck R, Berson EL, et al. PRPF mutations are associated with generalized defects in spliceosome formation and pre-mRNA splicing in patients with retinitis pigmentosa. Hum Mol Genet 2011;20:2116–30.

[152] Horike S, Cai S, Miyano M, Chen J, Kohwi-Shigematsu T. Loss of silent chromatin looping and impaired imprinting of DLX5 in Rett syndrome. Nat Genet 2005;32:31–40.

[153] Preuss P. Solving the mechanism of Rett syndrome: how the first identified epigenetic disease turns on the genes that produce its symptoms. Research News Berkeley Lab; 2004. 20 December.

[154] Soejima H, Higashimoto K. Epigenetic and genetic alterations of the imprinting disorder Beckwith-Wiedemann syndrome and related disorders. J Hum Genet 2013;58:402–9.

[155] Agrelo R, Setien F, Espada J, Artiga MJ, Rodriguez M, P rez-Rosado A, et al. Inactivation of the lamin A/C gene by CpG island promoter hypermethylation in hematologic malignancies, and its association with poor survival in nodal diffuse large B-cell lymphoma. J Clin Oncol 2005;23:3940–7.

[156] Bartholdi D, Krajewska-Walasek M, Ounap K, Gaspar H, Chrzanowska KH, Ilyana H, et al. Epigenetic mutations of the imprinted IGF2-H19 domain in Silver-Russell syndrome (SRS): results from a large cohort of patients with SRS and SRS-like phenotypes. J Med Genet 2009;46:192–7.

[157] Chen J, Odenike O, Rowley JD. Leukemogenesis: more than mutant genes. Nat Rev Cancer 2010; 10:23–36.

[158] Martin DIK, Cropley JE, Suter CM. Epigenetics in disease: leader or follower? Epigenetics 2011; 6:843–8.

[159] McKenna ES, Sansam CG, Cho YJ, Greulich H, Evans JA, Thom CS, et al. Loss of the epigenetic tumor suppressor SNF5 leads to cancer without genomic instability. Mol Cell Biol 2008;28:6223–33.

[160] Feinberg AP. The epigenetics of cancer etiology. Semin Cancer Biol 2004;14:427–32.

[161] Hardison RC. Evolution of hemoglobin and its genes. Cold Spring Harb Perspect Med 2012;2: a011627.

[162] Storz JF. Gene duplication and evolutionary innovations in hemoglobin-oxygen transport. Physiology (Bethesda) 2016;31:223–32.

[163] Sorek R, Dror G, Shamir R. Assessing the number of ancestral alternatively spliced exons in the human genome. BMC Genomics 2006;7:273.

[164] Pagani F, Baralle FE. Genomic variants in exons and introns: identifying the splicing spoilers. Nat Rev Genet 2004;5:389–96.

[165] Fraser HB, Xie X. Common polymorphic transcript variation in human disease. Genome Res 2009;19:567–75.

[166] Venables JP. Aberrant and alternative splicing in cancer. Cancer Res 2004;64:7647–54.

[167] Srebrow A, Kornblihtt AR. The connection between splicing and cancer. J Cell Sci 2006;119: 2635–41.

[168] USFDA. FDA approval brings first gene therapy to the United States: CAR T-cell therapy approved to treat certain children and young adults with B-cell acute lymphoblastic leukemia. U.S. Food and Drug Administration; 2017. 30 August.

[169] Ren J, Zhang X, Liu X, Fang C, Jiang S, June CH, et al. A versatile system for rapid multiplex genome-edited CAR T cell generation. Oncotarget 2017;8:17002–17,011.

[170] Chmielewski M, Abken H. TRUCKs: the fourth generation of CARs. Expert Opin Biol Ther 2015;15:1145–54.

[171] Morgan RA, Yang JC, Kitano M, Dudley ME, Laurencot CM, Rosenberg SA. Case report of a serious adverse event following the administration of T cells transduced with a chimeric antigen receptor recognizing ERBB2. Mol Ther 2010;18:843–51.

[172] Wang D, Gao G. State-of-the-art human gene therapy: part II. Gene therapy strategies and applications. Discov Med 2014;18:151–61.

[173] Collins F. Statement on NIH funding of research using gene-editing technologies in human embryos, https://www.nih.gov/about-nih/who-we-are/nih-director/statements/statement-nih-funding-research-using-gene-editing-technologies-human-embryos; 2015. 28 April.

[174] Erwin DH. The origin of bodyplans. Am Zool 1999;39:617–29.

[175] Valentine JW, Jablonski D, Erwin DH. Fossils, molecules and embryos: new perspectives on the Cambrian explosion. Development 1999;126:851–9.

[176] Bromham L. What can DNA tell us about the Cambrian explosion? Integr Comp Biol 2003;43:148–56.

[177] Budd GE, Jensen S. A critical reappraisal of the fossil record of the bilaterian phyla. Biol Rev Camb Philos Soc 2000;75:253–95.

[178] Love GD, Grosjean E, Stalvies C, Fike DA, Grotzinger JP, Bradley AS, et al. Fossil steroids record the appearance of Demospongiae during the Cryogenian period. Nature 2009;457:718–21.

[179] Benvenuti S, Arena S, Bardelli A. Identification of cancer genes by mutational profiling of tumor genomes. FEBS Lett 2005;579:1884–90.

[180] Weaver BAA, Cleveland DW. The role of aneuploidy in promoting and suppressing tumors. J Cell Biol 2009;185:935–7.

[181] Swanton C. Intratumor heterogeneity: evolution through space and time. Cancer Res 2012;72:4875–82.

[182] Wu X, Kumar V, Quinlan JR, Ghosh J, Yang Q, Motoda H, et al. Top 10 algorithms in data mining. Knowl Inf Syst 2008;14:1–37.

[183] Kothandapani A, Sawant A, Dangeti VS, Sobol RW, Patrick SM. Epistatic role of base excision repair and mismatch repair pathways in mediating cisplatin cytotoxicity. Nucleic Acids Res 2013;41: 7332–43.

[184] Combarros O, Cortina-Borja M, Smith AD, Lehmann DJ. Epistasis in sporadic Alzheimer's disease. Neurobiol Aging 2009;30:1333–49.

[185] Lobo I. Epistasis: gene interaction and the phenotypic expression of complex diseases like Alzheimer's. Nat Educ 2008;1:1.

[186] Chi YI. Homeodomain revisited: a lesson from disease-causing mutations. Hum Genet 2005;116: 433–44.

[187] Gerke J, Lorenz K, Ramnarine S, Cohen B. Gene environment interactions at nucleotide resolution. PLoS Genet 2010;6, e1001144.

[188] Estivill X, Bancells C, Ramos C. Geographic distribution and regional origin of 272 cystic fibrosis mutations in European populations. Hum Mutat 1997;10:135–54.

[189] Omim. Online Mendelian inheritance in man. Available from: http://omim.org/downloads; 2013. [Accessed 20 June 2013].

[190] Salmena L, Carracedo A, Pandolfi PP. Tenets of PTEN tumor suppression. Cell 2008;133:403–14.

[191] Wagner PJ, Ruta M, Coates MI. Evolutionary patterns in early tetrapods. II. Differing constraints on available character space among clades. Proc R Soc B Biol Sci 2006;273:2113–8.

[192] Glansdorff N, Xu Y, Labedan B. The last universal common ancestor: emergence, constitution and genetic legacy of an elusive forerunner. Biol Direct 2008;3:29.

[193] Bergsten J. A review of long-branch attraction. Cladistics 2005;21:163–93.

[194] Berman JJ. Data simplification: taming information with open source tools. Waltham, MA: Morgan Kaufmann; 2016.

[195] Weatherall DJ. Molecular pathology of single gene disorders. J Clin Pathol 1987;40:959–70.

[196] Nachman MW, Crowell SL. Estimate of the mutation rate per nucleotide in humans. Genetics 2000;156:297–304.

[197] Roach JC, Glusman G, Smit AF, Huff CD, Hubley R, Shannon PT, et al. Analysis of genetic inheritance in a family quartet by whole-genome sequencing. Science 2010;328:636–9.

[198] Oller AR, Rastogi P, Morgenthaler S, Thilly WG. A statistical model to estimate variance in long term low dose mutation assays: testing of the model in a human lymphoblastoid mutation assay. Mutat Res 1989;216:149–61.

[199] Bierig JR. Actions for damages against medical examiners and the defense of sovereign immunity. Clin Lab Med 1998;18:139–50.

[200] Nagel ZD, Chaim IA, Samson LD. Inter-individual variation in DNA repair capacity: a need for multi-pathway functional assays to promote translational DNA repair research. DNA Repair (Amst) 2014;19:199–213.

[201] Martincorena I, Roshan A, Gerstung M, et al. High burden and pervasive positive selection of somatic mutations in normal human skin. Science 2015;348:880–6.

[202] Lynch M. Rate, molecular spectrum, and consequences of human mutation. Proc Natl Acad Sci U S A 2010;107:961–8.

[203] Angert ER, Clements KD, Pace NR. The largest bacterium. Nature 1993;362:239–41.

[204] Xu EY, Lee DF, Klebes A, Turek PJ, Kornberg TB, Reijo Pera RA. Human BOULE gene rescues meiotic defects in infertile flies. Hum Mol Genet 2003;12:169–75.

[205] Padgett RW, Wozney JM, Gelbart WM. Human BMP sequences can confer normal dorsal-ventral patterning in the Drosophila embryo. Proc Natl Acad Sci U S A 1993;90:2905–9.

[206] Hamada N, Backesjo CM, Smith CI, Yamamoto D. Functional replacement of Drosophila Btk29A with human Btk in male genital development and survival. FEBS Lett 2005;579:4131–7.

[207] McGinnis N, Kuziora MA, McGinnis W. Human Hox-4.2 and Drosophila deformed encode similar regulatory specificities in Drosophila embryos and larvae. Cell 1990;63:969–76.

[208] Grifoni D, Garoia F, Schimanski CC, Schmitz G, Laurenti E, Galle PR, et al. The human protein Hugl-1 substitutes for Drosophila lethal giant larvae tumor suppressor function in vivo. Oncogene 2004; 23:8688–94.

[209] Koonin EV, Fedorova ND, Jackson JD, Jacobs AR, Krylov DM, Makarova KS, et al. A comprehensive evolutionary classification of proteins encoded in complete eukaryotic genomes. Genome Biol 2004;5:R7.

[210] Koonin EV, Galperin MY. Sequence, evolution, function: computational approaches in comparative genomics. Boston: Kluwer Academic; 2003.

[211] de Vooght KMK, van Wijk R, van Solingel WE. Management of gene promoter mutations in molecular diagnostics. Clin Chem 2009;55:698–708.

[212] Mencia A, Modamio-Hoybjor S, Redshaw N, Morín M, Mayo-Merino F, Olavarrieta L, et al. Mutations in the seed region of human miR-96 are responsible for nonsyndromic progressive hearing loss. Nat Genet 2009;41:609–13.

[213] Dunn CW, Giribet G, Edgecombe GD, Hejnol A. Animal phylogeny and its evolutionary implications. Annu Rev Ecol Evol Syst 2014;45:371–95.

[214] Vulliamy T, Beswick R, Kirwan M, Marrone A, Digweed M, Walne A, et al. Mutations in the telomerase component NHP2 cause the premature aging syndrome dyskeratosis congenita. Proc Natl Acad Sci U S A 2008;105:8073–8.

[215] Yamaguchi H. Mutations of telomerase complex genes linked to bone marrow failures. J Nippon Med Sch 2007;74:202–9.

[216] Sender R, Fuchs S, Milo R. Revised estimates for the number of human and bacteria cells in the body. PLoS Biol 2016;14, e1002533.

[217] Bodey B. Spontaneous regression of neoplasms: new possibilities for immunotherapy. Expert Opin Biol Ther 2002;2:459–76.

[218] National Academies of Sciences, Engineering, and Medicine. Examining the state of the science of mammalian embryo model systems: proceedings of a workshop. Washington, DC: The National Academies Press; 2020.

[219] Okita K, Ichisaka T, Yamanaka S. Generation of germline-competent induced pluripotent stem cells. Nature 2007;448:313–7.

[220] Takahashi K, Tanabe K, Ohnuki M, Narita M, Ichisaka T, Tomoda K, et al. Induction of pluripotent stem cells from adult human fibroblasts by defined factors. Cell 2007;131:861–72.

[221] Tanimoto Y, Iijima S, Hasegawa Y, Suzuki Y, Daitoku Y, Mizuno S, et al. Embryonic stem cells derived from C57BL/6J and C57BL/6N mice. Comp Med 2008;58:347–52.

[222] Takahashi K, Murakami M, Yamanaka S. Role of the phosphoinositide 3-kinase pathway in mouse embryonic stem (ES) cells. Biochem Soc Trans 2005;33:1522–5.

[223] Fulton DL, Sundararajan S, Badis G, Hughes TR, Wasserman WW, Roach JC, et al. TFCat: the curated catalog of mouse and human transcription factors. Genome Biol 2009;10:R29.

[224] Lee TI, Young RA. Transcriptional regulation and its misregulation in disease. Cell 2013;152:1237–51.

[225] Seidman JG, Seidman C. Transcription factor haploinsufficiency: when half a loaf is not enough. J Clin Invest 2002;109:451–5.

[226] Ng BG, Kranz C, Hagebeuk EE, Duran M, Abeling NG, Wuyts B, et al. Molecular and clinical characterization of a Moroccan Cog7 deficient patient. Mol Genet Metab 2007;91:201–4.

[227] Holmes I. Transcendent elements: whole-genome transposon screens and open evolutionary questions. Genome Res 2002;12:1152–5.

[228] Kapitonov VV, Jurka J. RAG1 core and V(D)J recombination signal sequences were derived from Transib transposons. PLoS Biol 2005;3, e181.

[229] Lerat E, Semon M. Influence of the transposable element neighborhood on human gene expression in normal and tumor tissues. Gene 2007;396:303–11.

[230] Kivela T. Trilateral retinoblastoma: a meta-analysis of hereditary retinoblastoma associated with primary ectopic intracranial retinoblastoma. J Clin Oncol 1999;17:1829–37.

7

The Periodic Table

Chapter outline

> *Corpora nonagunt nisi ligata (A substance is not effective unless it is linked to another).*
>
> **Paul Ehrlich**

Section 7.1. Setting the Periodic Table

At first blush, the Periodic Table does not seem to fit the criteria for a classification insofar as it appears to be nothing more than a multicolumned listing of the elements. The elements are not grouped into discernible classes and subclasses. There is no lineage or ancestry associated with the table, as we would hope to see in any self-respecting classification. This being the case, then why is the Periodic Table discussed in this book about classifications?

On closer inspection, we see that the cells of the periodic table are, in fact, classes. They happen to be a special type of class known as a singleton; classes having just one member. The Periodic Table is all about the relationships among the singleton classes, each of which is assigned a unique identifier based upon its atomic number (i.e., number of protons in the nucleus). The relationships among the singletons determine the configuration of the table.

All of the singleton classes have the same parent class, which happens to be the root class. So, the lineage for each class is one generation in length. We must remember that classifications must be mono-parental (i.e., each class must have one and only one parent class). There is no limit to the number of child classes coming from one parent class. In this case, the parent class of all the singletons is the root class. The root class of the

343

elements is an abstract class that exists by implication. It doesn't have a name, but we can reasonably assert that the root of the periodic table contains the protons, neutrons and electrons, and the forces that operate upon them. All of the child classes are composed of protons, neutrons, and electrons inherited from the root class.

Do the child classes (i.e., the elements) have subclasses? Maybe. Each element of the table is an amalgam of all the isotopes of the element. The isotopes of an element are the different atoms containing varying numbers of neutrons and accounting for the noninteger atomic weights of elements. Each of the isotopes of an element has a unique atomic weight, expressed as an integer value equal to the sum of the number of protons and neutrons in the nucleus. In addition, each isotope of an element has its specific properties (i.e., instability, half-life, radiation emissions). The Periodic Table does not list the isotopes of individual elements, but chemists know where to find them when needed.

The first versions of a periodic table of the elements, in formats that we might easily recognize as forerunners of the modern Periodic Table, appeared in the mid-19th century. The best version for its time is credited to Mendeleev and was published in 1869. At the time, there were just a few dozen known elements, and the nature of elemental atoms was largely conjectural. It would be another 40 years or so before electrons were proven to exist and the so-called atomic theory was experimentally validated. As its name would suggest, the novelty of the Periodic Table derived from its focus on the periodic behavior of elements of increasing atomic mass. Mendeleev made an intuitive leap of faith that was not wholly validated until after his death, in 1907. All told, it took a scant few years to create the first serviceable version of the Periodic Table of the Elements; we've spent the ensuing 160 years learning its secrets. Today, a quantum physicist can benefit from the Periodic Table as much as any chemist.

Before we begin to discuss how we might interpret the table, let's stop a moment and see what we can say about the Periodic Table taken as a whole, without regard to any particular element.

1. The classification of the elements needed to be discovered, not created

Some of Mendeleev's peers saw no advantage in creating a classification of the elements. It was suggested, back when Mendeleev was struggling with early versions of the table, that his efforts were all in vain. His colleagues suggested dropping the matter and simply publishing a simple alphabetic list. All they wanted were the names of the known items, and perhaps a bit of information about each one. The value of classification was completely beyond their grasp.

Let's imagine that the Periodic Table of the Elements did not exist and that Mendeleev's contemporaries got the list that they were hoping for. What would be the harm in that?

When you search through the available college textbooks on chemistry, you won't find any of them consisting of 94 chapters, with each chapter devoted to one of the 94 naturally occurring elements. Budding chemists do not learn their discipline by reading a chapter on Americium, then a chapter on Antimony, and so on up to chapter 94 on Zirconium. If such a book existed, our students would come away with a lot of detailed knowledge about each element, but without any conceptual depth. They would not understand valence, and they would not understand how elements bond to one another to form chemicals, and they would not understand the fundamentals of physical chemistry. For the elements, just like anything else in our universe, science is about discovering relationships. When we learn the relationships among the different elements, as captured in the Periodic Table, we begin our training as true chemists. This point was lost on many of Mendeleev's contemporaries, but Mendeleev understood what he was trying to accomplish.

2. One atom of an element is identical to any other atom of the same element, and is demonstrably different from all of the atoms of all other elements

Identicality is something that we can never achieve in the macro world. We talk about identical twins, but we know that identical twins are not identical. They may have started life with the same genetic sequence in their respective zygotes, but the genome does not account for everything in an organism, and identical twins are, at best, a close approximation of one another. When we consider anything made by humans, in the hope of achieving uniformity of form and substance, we know that we must settle for something less than identicality. Chemists in the 19th century may have supposed that elements, like everything else they observed, were composed of similar (not identical) units. In this case, the collection of elements could have been viewed as a kind of spectrum, where one element blends into the next element, with only arbitrary cut-points to distinguish their boundaries. If such were the case, it would be futile to build a classification of the elements, because there would be no sensible way of assigning atoms to individual classes.

Thanks to John Dalton, the theoretical justification for classification of the elements was made possible. Dalton, building on the works of Antoine Lavoisier and Joseph Proust, published his atomic theory of matter in the first decade of the 19th century. In it, he asserted that all atoms of an element are identical and that atoms of different elements can be distinguished by the size and mass of their atoms. The notion that each element, and the atoms it contains, is fundamentally different from every other element establishes that the elements can be classified. The identicality of the atoms of an element establishes that elements can sit in singleton classes. Assuming that Dalton's atomic theory was correct (a big assumption at the time), Mendeleev had only to discern the periodic relationships among elements to compose the Periodic Table.

Today, when we speak of the identicality of an element's atoms, we acknowledge the existence of indivisible subatomic particles, for which all particles of a particular kind are identical and, hence, interchangeable. We know today that all atoms are composed of the same particles and that the position of the element in the Periodic Table is determined by the number of protons in the element's nucleus. In "Section 8.2. Invariances are our laws," we will come to learn that the identicality of particles is a fundamental property of spacetime and forms the basis of invariances that determine the physical laws of our universe.

For the moment, let's just stipulate that all elements have the same components: electrons, protons, and neutrons. We can split an atom, but we cannot split any of the fundamental particles. An electron is either there or is gone. We cannot have half of an electron or a third of an electron. Such things do not exist. The unique identifier for an element is its atomic number (i.e., number of protons). Elements may have varying numbers of associated neutrons, accounting for the different isotopes of the element. However, all of the neutral (i.e., zero net charge) isotopic atoms of an element are identical to one another, in terms of component particles.

3. The physical form of an element was not considered when designing the Periodic Table

Depending on conditions (e.g., temperature, pressure), any given element can be in a gaseous, solid, or liquid state. Furthermore, one element, such as carbon, can appear as a black rock or as a diamond, depending on its past conditions, but not depending on current conditions. Therefore, the definition of the class properties of elements must be independent of form or function [1].

4. The atomic number of an atom must determine its precedence of position in the Periodic Table

The fundamental class property of each element was eventually determined by the relationship between atomic number (i.e., number of protons in the nucleus) and electron number. As it happens, the atomic number of an element exactly equals the number of electrons orbiting the nucleus of a neutral atom. The number of electrons, and their configuration in the outer shell, account for much of chemistry and quantum physics.

5. The behavior of elements is periodic (i.e., the properties of elements recur in periodic progressions based on their atomic weight)

As we move across the Periodic table, from left to right, the number of electrons in the outer, valence shell is represented. The elements in column 1 have one electron in the outer shell. The elements in column 18 have the outer shell completely filled. Each row of the table represents a period. When we end one row, we end a period and begin the next period at the beginning of the subsequent row.

We will see in "Section 7.3. All the matter that matters" how the periods of the table help us predict chemical bonds in polyatomic compounds.

6. The Periodic Table is gapless

There is a mathematical relationship among the elements that can be expressed as follows:

> The number of protons in an atom is always an integer, and for every element having n protons in each atom, there is another element having n-1 protons in each atom, for n greater than 1.

This simple expression tells us a great deal about the elements, first and foremost of which is that the Periodic Table is gapless (i.e., there are no empty cells in the table). It also tells us something about the indivisibility of protons, insofar as the number of protons in the nucleus of an atom is always an integer value and never a fractional number. Before all of the elements had been discovered, chemists of the late 19th century and early 20th century had inferred that the early gaps of the table would be filled, over time. This allowed them to confidently include elements that were unknown at the time, and to predict a great deal about the properties of those elements.

Because the Periodic Table is gapless, and we know something about all of the elements, we can infer that there are no elements whose nucleus consists entirely of neutrons, with no protons. We can also observe that every element has a set of electrons that accompanies the nucleus, and that the number of electrons in ground-state atoms exactly matches the number of protons. This equality would apply to a single atom of an element or a collection of atoms of the same kind (e.g., a gold ingot) or a mixture of atoms from different elements (e.g., a metal alloy). If we assumed that everything in the universe is a collection of elemental atoms (a false assumption, but let's not quibble), then we would infer that the total number of protons in the universe is equal to the total number of electrons in the universe. Because the Periodic Table is complete, and we need not consider that elements may exist that violate the equal number of protons and electrons in ground state elements, then we can reasonably guess that there is some universal physical law balancing positive and negative charges in elemental atoms.

We don't see all the electrons occupying the same ground state (i.e., the lowest orbital, lowest energy state). This tells us that there must be some laws that forbid an excess of electrons in any given orbital. It also tells us that as the nucleus increases in protons, we must see an increase in electrons and that these electrons must occupy higher and higher orbitals at higher and higher energies.

7. There is a practical limit to the number of elements in our universe

Completeness tells us a great deal about the natural limits of classified objects. For example, the fact that there are only 94 naturally occurring elements suggests that there is a limit to the atomic number of elements. Under extreme laboratory conditions, we can produce about two dozen additional elements that exist briefly, before decaying.

Why are there only 94 naturally occurring elements? Why can we not make heavier and heavier atoms, without restraint? We will answer this question in "Section 7.4. Great deductions from anomalies in the Periodic Table."

8. The Periodic Table is universal

Spectrographic analysis of light from distant stars indicates that the elements here on earth are the same elements found in our galaxy and every other galaxy; and no elements are occurring in other galaxies that are not also present here on earth. This should not surprise us. We know that the same physical laws that apply on earth must also apply everywhere else in the universe (see "Section 8.2. Invariances are our laws"). Hence, the physical laws that account for the synthesis of the elements must apply everywhere in the universe. Hence, the elements must be the same everywhere in the universe. This thinking is nothing new. Back in 1884, before anyone knew anything about atomic particles or the big bang, and before there was much data to validate his hypotheses, Robert Chambers inferred that the elements are the same everywhere, writing:

> *Analogy would lead us to conclude that the modifications of the primordial matter, forming our so-called elements, are as universal, or as liable to take place everywhere, as are the laws of gravitation and centrifugal force. It, therefore, appears likely that the gases, the metals, the earth, and other simple substances (besides whatever more of which we have no acquaintance), exist under proper conditions, as well as in the astral system, which is thirty-five thousand times more distant than Sirius, as within the bounds of our solar system or our globe.*
> Robert Chambers, in Vestiges of the Natural History of Creation, *published in 1884 [2].*

Note that Chambers refers to the stuff from which our elements are built as "primordial matter". He guessed correctly that the elements were not the original form of matter in the universe, but that there was some primordial type of matter that was acted upon by universal physical forces to produce all of the elements that we encounter today.

Section 7.2. Braving the elements

One of the great strengths of the Periodic Table is that it is informative, no matter how we choose to examine it.

1. The Periodic Table can be viewed by rows or by columns

As every high school student knows, the consecutive rows of the Periodic Table can represent consecutive shells that encircle the nucleus, that fill, electron-by-electron (i.e., column by column), as we move from left to right through the table.

Each row of the table is a period, representing the outer shells of the sequential elements lining the row. When the final element of a row is reached, the outer shell is full. An element with a full outer shell of electrons is chemically nonreactive. Hence, the last column of the table is filled with elements that exist as inert, monoatomic gases. These are often referred to as the Noble elements, presumably because they snobbishly refuse to have anything to do with atoms of other elements. They are so snobbish that they have nothing to do with atoms that are identical to themselves. Even at very low temperatures, when the nonnoble gases such as hydrogen, nitrogen, and oxygen have frozen as a solid matrix of closely packed atoms, the noble elements remain aloof and gaseous. Helium, the lightest of the noble elements, is the only element that cannot be solidified by cooling under standard pressure (i.e., 1-atm pressure), even when the temperature hovers near absolute zero.

2. The Periodic Table can be viewed by outer orbital configurations

The Periodic Table can be neatly carved into blocks of contiguous related elements, according to their outer electronic configurations. Elements whose outer shell electrons are generally confined to the s orbital (i.e., lowest energy orbital in the shell) fall into one block. Elements whose outer shell electrons are generally confined to the s or p orbitals, where the p orbitals are the next higher energy orbitals in the shell) form another block. As a general rule, elements belonging to the same block have similar reactivities (Fig. 7.1).

3. The Periodic Table can be viewed by levels of instability

As we go from top to bottom, the elements become less and less stable. Eighty of the first 82 elements in the periodic table have at least one stable isotope. By the time we reach radon, we've got elements that simply have no stable isotopes. These elements spontaneously vanish, leaving behind a chain of decay elements.

4. The Periodic Table exhibits decreasing atomic radii, from left to right

As we move from left to right, along each row of the table, the radii of atoms generally decrease. When we move from the end of one row to the beginning of the next row, the atomic radius suddenly increases, only to slowly decrease again, as we move along the row.

What is happening here? As we move from left to right along any row, the atomic number of the successive elements increases, by increments of 1. The increasing charge of the nucleus attracts the orbiting electrons, including the electrons orbiting in the outermost shell. This attraction tends to decrease the size of the outermost shell, thus decreasing the atomic radius. When we move from the last element in a row to the first element in the next row, we transition to a new outer shell, at a greater distance from the nucleus than the preceding atom's outer shell. Consequently, the atomic radius (which is determined by the distance from the nucleus to the outer shell) abruptly increases. Subsequent atoms (moving from left to right on the row), tend to reduce radial size due to their increasing mass and charge.

The abrupt increase of atomic radius as we go from the last element of one row to the first element of the next row provided support for some of the early theories of atomic structure (i.e., a heavy positively charged nucleus surrounded by shells of orbiting negatively charged electrons).

We should note that the decreasing radius of atoms, as we move from left to right along a period (row) does not always hold. As is so often the case, we can learn a great deal by examining exceptions to our rules. Let's look at the example of lead and gold, both of which lie along the same row in the Periodic Table. Gold has atomic number 79 and lead, three elements further along the row, has an atomic number of 82. By all rights, lead atoms, with their greater mass and positive charge, should have a smaller atomic radius than gold. But we can infer from a very simple observation that this is absolutely not the case.

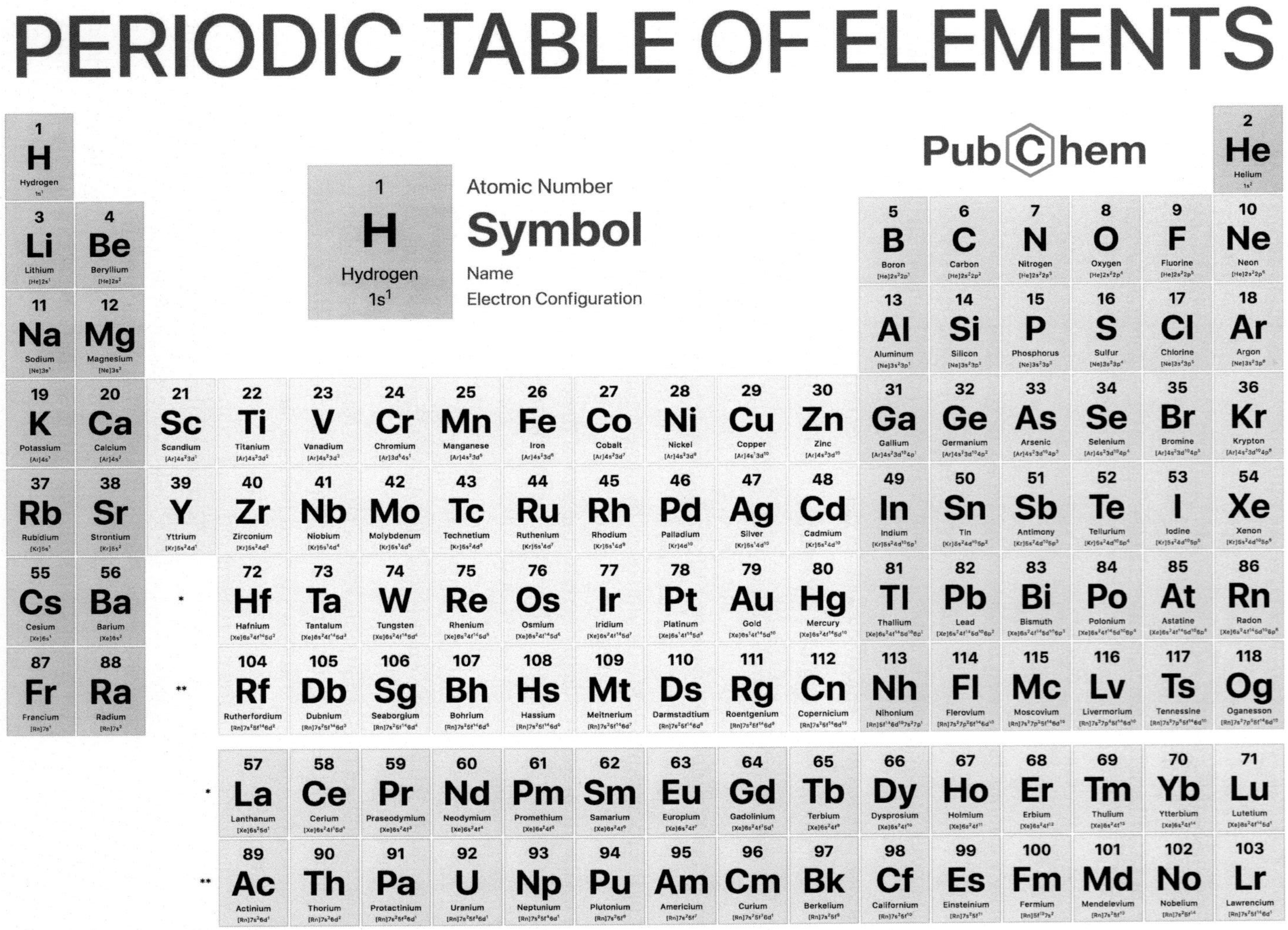

PERIODIC TABLE OF ELEMENTS

PubChem

FIG. 7.1 A simple Periodic Table, divided into blocks, according to the outer shell configuration of electrons. *Source: A government work produced for the National Library of Medicine, National Institutes of Health.*

It happens that a bar of gold weighs much more than a bar of lead, of equal volume. In fact, a cubic meter of gold weighs 22,588 kg, while a cubic meter of lead weighs only 11,340 kg. This tells us that gold is denser than lead, which would suggest that the atoms of gold (which are lighter than the atoms of lead) must be much more densely packed than the atoms of lead. This would also suggest that the atomic radius of a gold atom or the interatomic distances of gold atoms are much smaller than that of lead. In point of fact, both of these inferences are true. The atomic radius for gold is 135 picometer. The atomic radius for lead is 180 picometer. The gold-gold bond length is 288 picometers. The lead-lead bond length is 350 picometers. Hence, a given volume of space will accommodate more gold atoms than lead atoms. Hence, the smaller size of gold atoms, and the smaller distance between individual gold atoms account for the greater density of gold, compared with lead. But, at this point, we have not explained why gold atoms have a smaller atomic radius than lead atoms.

As we shall see in "Section 7.4. Great deductions from anomalies in the Periodic Table," heavy elements such as gold and lead contain electrons that are moving at relativistic speeds. For instance, the electrons of gold atoms, in the ground state (i.e., lowest energy), travel at about 58% of the speed of light. When we reach the bottom rows of the Periodic Table, complex relativistic effects account for deviations from the expected trends of decreasing atomic radii as we move from left to right along a row.

5. The Periodic Table can be viewed by elemental abundances in the universe

As we move diagonally, from top left to bottom right, the atoms get heavier and heavier, and their abundance in the universe drops precipitously. Hydrogen is the most abundant element in the universe (nearly 92% of atoms), Helium comes next (nearly 8% of atoms). Elements heavier than Helium altogether account for no more than 2% of observable matter. The least abundant elements are the man-made elements, at the very bottom of the table. Here are the 10 most common elements in the Milky Way Galaxy estimated spectroscopically: [3].

```
    Element            per million atoms

 1  Hydrogen              739,000
 2  Helium                240,000
 8  Oxygen                 10,400
 6  Carbon                  4,600
10  Neon                    1,340
26  Iron                    1,090
 7  Nitrogen                  960
14  Silicon                   650
12  Magnesium                 580
16  Sulfur                    440
```

Later in this chapter, we will learn why this is so.

6. The Periodic Table can be viewed by epoch in which the elements first came into existence

The Periodic table is something akin to an atomic clock, on a grand scale. As we move down the table, we move through time, beginning with the Big Bang, and ending with the present day. One second after the Big Bang, give or take, we start to find hydrogen atoms forming. By 3 min, some helium and lithium enter the mix. We need to wait another few dozen million years for the first stars to form before we begin to see some fusion of helium into carbon, and the consequent fusion products of nitrogen, oxygen, neon, and magnesium. The very last of the elements in the Periodic Table was created by humans, within the past century, 15 billion years after hydrogen appeared.

7. The Periodic Table can be viewed by almost any property of elements

We could also view the Periodic Table by electron affinities, and by ionization energies of elements. There is no limit to our options because the Periodic Table, like every good classification, is a way of organizing relationships among classes [1]. The table captures the essential nature of elemental atoms composed of a massive, positively charged nucleus orbited by negatively charged electrons, all of whose allowable states are strictly limited by quantum considerations (i.e., quantum numbers and the Schrodinger wave function). The Periodic Table is a conceptual representation of the chemical universe.

Section 7.3. All the matter that matters

Great classifications, like the Periodic Table of the elements, help us understand the universe through opposing viewpoints. We can use the relationships embedded in the table as a set of rules, upon which we can predict the rules of chemistry. Or, we can use our understanding of how the atoms and chemicals behave to explain the properties of the table. In the previous section, we saw that the Periodic Table tells us a great deal about the organization of the universe. In this and the next sections, we'll try to explain the scientific laws that account for some of the versatility of the table.

Law of Compositionality

The Law of Compositionality holds that things constructed from component objects are less numerous than their components. This is a fairly obvious law of nature, but we can use the Law of Compositionality to draw quite a few inferences about our universe. First, knowing that large things are composed of small things, we can infer that there are more large things than there are small things. For examples:

more stars than galaxies
more planets than stars [4]
more moons than planets
more meteors than asteroids

more pebbles than rocks
more grains of sand than pebbles
more smithereens than smithers

When we are certain of the compositional relationships among small and large objects, we can confidently predict the relative abundance of objects. For example, The Law of Compositionality also tells us that there are more small planets, like Earth, than there are giant gas planets, like Jupiter. If we are currently finding more large planets than small planets, it is only because large planets are easier to detect than small planets. Moving into the realm of biology, we can infer that there are more single-celled eukaryotic organisms than animals; because animals are composed of single-celled organisms. Likewise, we can also infer that there are more mitochondria than eukaryotic cells; because just about every eukaryotic cell contains more than one mitochondrion.

The Law of Compositionality tells us that if the universe is composed of the 94 naturally occurring elements, then we would expect the smaller elements to be most abundant, while the larger elements would be relatively scarce. As we noted in the prior section, hydrogen, the smallest and simplest of atoms, accounts for most of everything. Helium, the second smallest atom, accounts for nearly everything else. We can extend this generalization to include chemical compounds composed of elements. Among the polyatomic chemicals found in deep space, polycyclic aromatic hydrocarbons, consisting only of hydrogen and carbon, are the most abundant. It should come as no surprise that polycyclic aromatic hydrocarbons play a major role in the chemistry of life on earth [5].

As we proceed downwards from the top row of the Periodic Table (consisting of just Hydrogen and Helium), the abundance of the natural elements diminishes. When we get to the bottom row of the table, we come upon the elements that have only existed in laboratories, and only for small fractions of a second. Hence, the Periodic Table embodies the Law of Compositionality, and it does so on a universal scale. Can we extend the Law of Compositionality to make one additional inference? It seems straightforward to suggest that if there are many more light elements than there are heavy elements, then the heavy elements may somehow be composed of the lighter elements, just as large sedimentary rocks are composed of small particles of sand. As it happens, this inference is true. Fusion occurring in stars creates heavy atoms by fusing lighter atoms. In general, as the mass of stars increases so does the mass of the atoms they are capable of producing. Giant stars can fuse helium into carbon and can produce nitrogen, oxygen, neon, and magnesium. Supergiant stars can fuse lighter atoms to produce transition metals. When super-giants erupt as a supernova, they may produce uranium and even heavier elements. The most prolific creators of heavy elements are neutron stars [6]. Not surprisingly, rare collisions between two neutron stars appear to be an especially rich source of heavy elements [7]. Finally, in a shameless display of one-upsmanship the heaviest elements are formed in laboratories here on earth, by curious humans.

Predicting chemical bonds

Sometimes it appears to me that a bond between two atoms has become so real, so tangible, so familiar that I can almost see it. But then I awake with a little shock: for the chemical bond is not a real thing, it does not exist, and no one has ever seen or will ever see it. It is a figment of our imagination.

Charles A. Coulson [8].

We can be certain that when the original version of the Periodic Table was fashioned by Mendeleev, he was looking for something much more than a cheat sheet for associating the name of an element with its atomic weight. Mendeleev understood that the Periodic Table imposed a natural order that would serve as a tool for predicting the behavior of elements, including the behavior of elements that were not yet identified but which would logically fit in the tabular gaps between known elements. If a classification merely provided a place to assemble collections of objects according to one observable feature, then it has no value other than possibly serving as a student's study aid.

One of the most important uses of the Periodic Table has involved the prediction of chemical bonds between different elements. What can we infer about chemical bonds, from examining the Periodic Table? Firstly, bonds between elements seem to form without any obvious relationship to increasing atomic numbers. Most elements, regardless of their atomic weight, form chemical bonds with other elements. The exception is the elements belonging to column 18 of the table (i.e., the column on the far right), which never form bonds with other elements; not even with themselves. We see that the elements of column 18 vary from very small atomic numbers to very large atomic numbers, and they all exist as monatomic gases. The bonding activity among elements seems to be influenced by the electron configuration of the atom; not by anything observable in the nucleus.

Why is it that nearly all of the mass of the atom is in the nucleus, while nearly all of the reactivity of the atom is determined by the electrons? The simple answer is that chemical bonds are transactions carried out by outer shell electrons in a gambit that results in lower potential energy of the combined atoms compared with the total potential energy of the atom individually. In the process, energy is released. The nucleus plays almost no role in the formation of polyatomic bonds.

Why is the positive charge of the nucleus exactly balanced by the negative charges of the atom's electrons? Conservation of energy would dictate that the total of all the positive charges in the universe would equal the total of all the negative charges. The homogeneity of space would dictate that conservation laws operate locally (i.e., one piece of space is much like any other). Hence, conservation of the energy carried by charge should apply to atoms to which no external energy is applied.

The Schrodinger equation is a wave function that allows us to predict the probable location of electrons belonging to an atom. All of the electron configurations represented in the Periodic Table are observed solutions of the Schrodinger equation. Chemical bonding is just a description of the electron configurations of the outer shell electrons of one atom paired with the outer shell electrons of one or more other atoms. All such configurations are determined by the same Schrodinger equation [9]. Hence, solving the Schrodinger equation tells us everything we need to know about chemical bonding. As the number of atoms increases, finding the solutions to the Schrodinger equation becomes increasingly difficult. We are currently unable to compute exact solutions of Schrodinger's equations for multiparticle bonds, but we can come fairly close with some clever approximation algorithms [10] (Fig. 7.2).

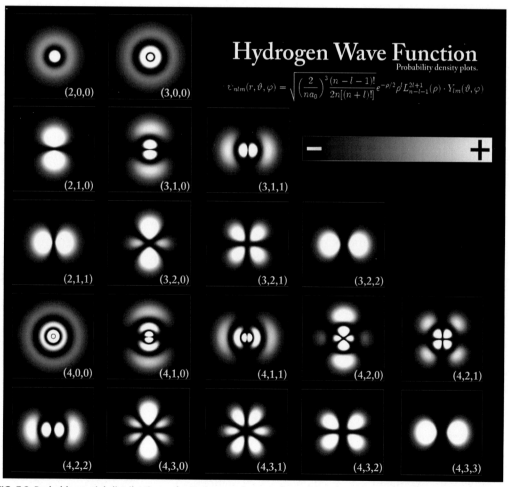

FIG. 7.2 Probable spatial distributions of a Hydrogen electron, for various quantum states, as predicted by the Schrodinger wave function. The oddly-shaped clouds in each of the 19 diagrams represent zones where an electron may be found, with equal probability. *Source: Wikipedia, and entered into the public domain by its author, PoorLeno.*

Schrodinger notwithstanding, the Periodic Table alone has done an adequate job of predicting chemical bonds for well over a century. As we move across the Periodic table, from left to right, the number of electrons in the outer, valence shell is represented. The elements in column 1 have one electron in the outer shell. Elements of column 1 may easily lose their single electron in the outer shell, rendering the atom's charge positive. Elements in column 17 are missing an electron in their outer shell, rendering them prone to collecting an additional electron, and rendering the atom's charge negative. Elements in between are in the best position to share outer shell electrons through chemical bonds. Elements in column 18 have a full outer shell that cannot accommodate any additional electrons, rendering these elements inert. The Periodic Table serves as a handy and quick, but not always perfect, indicator of how elements may combine to form any existing compound. [Glossary Valence]

Does matter really matter?

The visible world tends to reinforce the false impression that matter is the only thing that matters. What remains are mere abstractions we invent to help us describe the strange properties of matter. In our simple worldview, electricity is just the flow of electrons, a component of matter. Gravity is just the force that makes matter fall. Magnetism is something that is produced by magnets. Our language reinforces this thinking. When we say that something matters, it means that it is important. When we say that something is immaterial (literally, not made of matter), then we're saying that it is unimportant and irrelevant. When we say that something is abstract, then we are saying that it exists only in our imagination, and has no status in the real world.

As our thinking becomes more sophisticated, we may acquire a more nuanced appreciation of things. We come to think of matter and energy as being interchangeable. Electrons, having both wave and particle properties, can now be thought of as conveyers of charge. For the quantum physicist, electrons are mere points in space, having no size and barely qualifying as a component of matter. Some might say that the Periodic Table reduces chemistry to physics, insofar as it permits us to understand all of the elements in terms of the types of particles they contain (e.g., protons, neutrons, electrons) and a few fundamental laws of physics that control particle behavior.

Section 7.4. Great deductions from anomalies in the Periodic Table

Science commits suicide when it adopts a creed.

Thomas Huxley (1885)

Classifications are meant to be challenged. We benefit greatly whenever we uncover flaws in their design. When we look back at the history of the development of all the natural classifications, we find that many of the most important advances in our understanding of life, chemistry, and universal laws of physics have come from trying to explain anomalies in classifications. There is a simple reason why this is the case. **Natural Classifications encapsulate the operating system of our universe, and every item in the classification must conform to the general rules that account for class relationships. When we find an anomaly in our classification, we can assume that its explanation will involve some new insight into how our universe functions**. The process of explaining or correcting potential flaws in the classification is an essential part of the classification process.

How quantum theory spilled out from a hot cup of coffee

Along with the Periodic Table of the Elements came a physical model of atoms that fit its framework. Basically, each element was characterized by a nucleus accounting for most of the weight of the atom, encircled by small, orbiting electrons. The orbiting electrons provided a negative charge that exactly equaled the positive charge provided by the much larger nucleus. Each period (i.e., row) of the Periodic Table reflected the tendency of the outermost orbit of the atoms to attract additional electrons or to lose electrons. In the last column (the column furthest to the right) of every row were the elements that had the perfect complement of electrons, with no tendency to lose or gain electrons. All of the elements in the last column of the Periodic Table are gases, indicating that they have no tendency to bond with (by sharing electrons) other atoms.

The Periodic Table, at the end of the 19th century, seemed to make perfect sense, but one problem, from the field of thermodynamics, spoiled the harmony of the moment. We can summarize the problem by close observation of an everyday object. It has been experimentally determined that a hot cup of coffee emits infrared radiation, but does not emit X-rays. The same is true for an ingot of iron thrust into a forge. As objects get hotter and hotter, their molecules become increasingly energetic; moving at higher and higher speeds, and emitting light at higher and higher energies. Physicists knew that the velocities of molecules in a gas increased as a function of temperature. In the 19th century, it was known that heat, along with increasing the velocity of gas molecules, also increased the frequency of light emitted by objects. It was assumed that the same distribution that accounted for the increased velocity of heated molecules should also apply to the distribution of electromagnetic radiation emitted by heated objects. If this were the case, as objects are heated to higher temperatures, the distribution of electromagnetic waves emitted by the object should include radiation of higher and higher energy and frequency. This would mean that a hot cup of coffee, in addition to producing low-energy infrared waves, would produce some visible light waves, some ultraviolet waves, maybe some X-rays. Certainly, an extremely hot fire, such as used in iron forges, would be expected to produce huge amounts of X-rays. Fortunately for us, such is not the case. We cannot get a tan by sitting next to a hot cup of coffee. We cannot use an iron forge as a source of radiation for hospital X-ray machines. As it happens, the distribution of electromagnetic radiation emitted by heated objects does not follow the same statistical distribution as that observed for the velocities of heated molecules of gas. For a heated object to produce appreciable amounts of high-energy electromagnetic radiation, temperatures must be many times higher than the temperatures predicted with classical (i.e., 19th century) physics.

Early in the 20th century, Max Planck introduced the world to the notion of quantum mechanics. His theory held that energy shifts occur in integer steps (e.g., $n=1$, $n=2$, $n=3$), which he referred to as quantized partitions. The electromagnetic radiation emitted when such quantized energy shifts occur is restricted to a particular wavelength. Each quantum shift that releases electromagnetic energy requires an exponentially greater amount of energy than the prior shift. Hence, as the temperature of an object increases, the distribution of observed electromagnetic waves occurs as a set of wavelengths that are limited in range and cannot be represented as a wide statistical distribution of radiation emitted at all frequencies (Fig. 7.3).

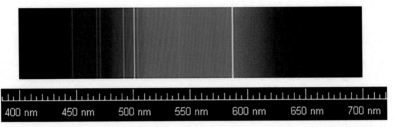

FIG. 7.3 Emission pattern of helium. Elements, when heated, radiate at characteristic wavelengths. *Source: U.S. National Aeronautics and Space Administration.*

Planck played a major role in establishing the general field of quantum physics. The new theory of quantum physics improved upon the conception of the atomic theory that was reflected in the Periodic Table of the Elements. The simple orbitals conceived in the 19th century were replaced by quantized orbitals that were predicted (in 1926) by Schrodinger's wave functions. It came to be that the Periodic Table could be conveniently divided into blocks, based on the quantum orbitals of electrons. Thus, an observation that threatened the atomic theory underlying the Periodic Table was instrumental in improving how the Periodic Table is currently used (Fig. 7.1).

Attack of the Anomalous Zeeman Effect

After the Periodic Table of the Elements was established as a reasonable way to classify atoms, Niels Bohr set about providing a physical justification for the periodicity of properties displayed by atoms. Bohr suggested that the electrons were arranged in shells that orbited the nucleus. Each shell had a certain number of allowed electrons, and when the allowance was met, the shell was complete. Any additional electrons would need to occupy a higher orbit. The reactive properties of atoms were determined largely by the total number of electrons of the atom, and these electrons were distributed into the different orbitals within shells. As more was learned about quantum theory, Bohr saw that electrons could transition between available spaces in shells by absorbing or releasing quanta of energy. The spectrum of light produced by a heated element consisted of a series of discrete lines corresponding to the characteristic quanta of energy absorbed when electrons shifted orbitals (Fig. 7.4).

FIG. 7.4 The emission spectrum of Iron. The spectrum consists of discrete lines corresponding to quanta of electromagnetic energy at specific frequencies that are emitted when electrons transition to lower orbitals. Each element has its characteristic emission spectrum consisting of discrete lines. This observation served as an important clue to the quantum nature of our physical reality. *Source: Wikipedia.*

The known observations of the elements in the periodic table, fit well with Bohr's atomic theory, except for two blips - one theoretical and the other experimental. The first blip was quite simple. If the nucleus of an atom is positively charged, and the electrons are negatively charged, then the large nucleus should attract the orbiting electrons. Why don't the orbits of electrons degenerate under the attractive force of the nucleus? In other words, what keeps electrons from falling into the nucleus?

The other objection to Bohr's theory was the mysterious Anomalous Zeeman Effect. In the 1890s, Pieter Zeeman had shown that when excited atoms were placed in a magnetic field, the spectral lines produced when electrons transitioned to lower orbitals were increased in number. Bohr and Summerfield launched a new theory to explain this phenomenon. In the new theory, each electron is provided with a set of 3 quantum numbers (n = orbital shell number, k = the shape of the orbital shell, and m = the direction in which the orbit is pointing). The quantum of electromagnetic energy released during an orbital shift is determined uniquely by the set of these three quantum numbers. In the presence of a magnetic field, the m value changes (i.e., the direction in which the orbit points change), with six allowable values for m. Thus, according to the Bohr-Sommerfeld theory, the spectral lines produced by transitions between orbitals can increase sixfold under the influence of a magnetic field.

Again, the Periodic Table and the emission spectra under a magnetic field seemed to be self-consistent. Soon, however, very fine analyses of emission spectral lines revealed even more spectral lines than were predicted by the Bohr-Sommerfeld theory. Quantum theory was in jeopardy. We can now introduce Wolfgang Pauli, who provided an explanation that, as far as anyone can determine, has withstood every experimental test. His solution, now known as the Pauli Exclusion Principle, established one of the most fundamental laws of the universe. Let's spend a little time explaining what Pauli suggested, and what it tells us about the behavior of matter.

Several physicists. Back in 1925, discovered a fourth quantum number (in addition to n, k, and m) which came to be known as spin and abbreviated as "s." The spin quanta are characterized by one of two numbers: spin plus one-half or spin minus one-half. History credits Ralph Kronig, George Uhlenbeck, Samuel Goudsmit, and Wolfgang Pauli for their nearly synchronous contributions to this important breakthrough in quantum physics. In the same year, Pauli asserted that every electron in an atom is characterized by all four quantum numbers and that no two electrons are characterized by the same four quantum numbers. In other words, it is impossible to push an electron into an orbital occupied by another electron having the same 4 quantum numbers. This assertion is now known as the Pauli Exclusion Principle, which applies to all particles with half-integer spin (i.e., fermions) and which excludes all particles with integer spin (i.e., bosons). Because Pauli's Exclusion Principle does not apply to bosons (which includes photons), it would be theoretically possible to superposition any number of boson particles at the same location.

At this point, Pauli's new quantum number, spin, seemed to explain the Anomalous Zeeman Effect. The extra spectrographic lines emitted by atoms in a magnetic field were the result of spin (one line for transitions of the spin 1/2 electron in an orbital, and another line for transitions by the spin −1/2 electron in the same orbital). How did the Exclusion Principle relate to our understanding of the Periodic Table? It turns out that when spin is taken into account, the allowable quanta exactly match the completed shells observed in the rows of the Periodic Table. Hence, spin theory reconciled the empiric closed-shell numbers used in Bohr's early atomic theory with the allowable numbers predicted by Pauli.

On a certain level, the Pauli Exclusion Principle is trivial. Of course, two identical particles cannot exist in the same place. But what does it mean for two particles to be identical, and what does it mean for two particles to exist at the same place? From the point of view of the quantum physicist, two particles of a kind are identical if they have the same set of quantum numbers (i.e., orbital shell number, the shape of the orbit, direction, and spin). In this case, identicality is perfect, in the sense that there is absolutely no way in which the two particles can be distinguished, and either particle could substitute for the other particle in all possible events, in all locations in space, and at all times. We will see in "Section 8.2. Invariances are our laws," that the identicality of particles is one of the fundamental symmetries of the universe.

When we speak of two particles occupying the same place, the Pauli exclusion principle moves us away from the traditional idea of a "place" being determined by an x, y, and z coordinate, and replaces it with the idea of a set of quantum numbers that refer to a probability or wave configuration. We no longer pretend to know the exact coordinates of a particle. Instead, we use a quantum configuration characterized by a wave function. Two particles of an atom are in the same place, in the quantum world, if they have the same quantum number. Before quantum theory and the Pauli Exclusion principle, physicists asked themselves why a table does not descend through the floor, as its atoms ooze through the spaces between atoms in the matter below. Today, we accept the idea that electrons cannot occupy the wave function of another electron (having the same quantum numbers), which defines a probabilistic space larger than a single point. Hence, we cannot walk through solid walls, and we do not sink to the center of the planet. Wolfgang Pauli, in one breath, solidified two tables: the table that sits in my dining room, and the Periodic Table of the elements.

Now we can return to one of the original questions that challenged the validity of the Periodic Table. If atoms are characterized by a positively charged nucleus and encircled by negatively charged electrons, then why don't the electrons, attracted by an opposite charge, fall into the nucleus? Again, the Pauli exclusion principle provides an answer. Each electron has its allowable quantum states, in which the unexcited electron is energetically stable. In the lowest state, also known as the ground state, the electron zooms around without losing energy. In this state, its only option is to move to a higher quantum level if energy is added to the system. Even if the temperature of the molecule is lowered to absolute zero, the ground state electron will continue to travel in its ground state indefinitely. Crashing into the nucleus is simply not a quantum option.

The quantum theory of the atom, strange as it may seem, is self-consistent (i.e., it makes internal sense). It is also consistent with observations of the Periodic Table, explaining electron shells, orbitals, and valence; and it is consistent with experimental observations. Until further notice, Pauli's exclusion principle meets the criteria of universal law. [Glossary Stern-Gerlach experiment, White dwarf gravitational degeneracy]

Special relativity is elemental

There are just 94 naturally occurring elements. Heavier elements have been formed in laboratories, but the man-made elements are unstable and pass out of existence after mere fractions of a second. Is there an upper limit to the number of elements, and can we assign a specific number to the highest allowable atomic number?

It turns out that as the mass of an element increases, the velocity of the electrons must increase to avoid being falling into the nucleus. The speed of innermost orbital electrons for any element is determined by the element's atomic number. The equation describing the relation between electron speed and an element's atomic number is:

    v(relative) = Z/137

v is the velocity of the inner orbital electron relative to the speed of light, Z is the atomic number of the element, and 137 is the constant of the universe known as the fine structure constant. We can see that when the atomic number of the element is 137, the electrons in the inner orbit would travel at the speed of light, a relativistic impossibility. Hence, there can never be an element of atomic number 137 or higher. Of course, arriving at the number 137, as the limit for the Periodic Table, is a theoretical exercise. Various scientists, using different models, have arrived at other upper limits for the Periodic Table [11]. Everyone in the field seems to agree that an upper limit must exist, as it becomes increasingly difficult to create new elements, even under extreme laboratory conditions.

A ground-state electron in gold ($Z = 79$) will travel at 58% of the speed of light. As an electron travels at relativistic speeds, its mass increases, according to the following formula (Fig. 7.5). The increased mass of the electrons in gold, traveling at relativistic speeds, contracts the electron radius of gold atoms, accounting for the high density of gold. Incidentally, the same contraction produces shifts in electron orbitals, producing light emissions of a characteristic wavelength, accounting for the stunning golden color of metallic gold.

$$m_{rel} = \frac{m}{\sqrt{1 - \frac{v^2}{c^2}}}$$

FIG. 7.5 The relativistic mass (left side of the equation) can be calculated from the mass measured in an invariant frame of reference (also known as the rest mass) and the velocity of the mass relative to the speed of light. Notice that as the velocity approaches the speed of light, the relativistic mass becomes infinitely large.

What have we learned from this discussion of special relativity as it relates to the heavy elements in the Periodic Table? Aside from the curious fact that the electrons in heavy atoms, such as gold, travel at relativistic velocities (58% of the speed of light), we have learned that the physical attributes of elements found under normal conditions (i.e., ambient temperature and pressure) are influenced by the laws of relativity. In our high school physics courses, we are taught Newtonian physics, and we are advised that Newtonian physics accounts for the observable physical phenomena encountered under normal conditions. Special relativity, we are often told, only applies to the extremely unrealistic conditions when objects travel near the speed of light. We now know that special relativity is quite ordinary. We see physical expressions of special relativity every day. It is Newtonian physics that is special, insofar as it applies only to the special case wherein objects are moving at very slow speeds, not routinely encountered in the atoms that constitute observable matter (e.g., gold, lead, mercury) [12–14]. So-called "special relativity" is not at all special; it is the physics that is observed in all possible frames of reference, and it leads us to the most general ways of understanding physics and chemistry.

Violations of intransitivity in the Periodic Table

One of the greatest classifications of the natural world violates a fundamental requirement of all proper classifications: the intransitivity rule. If we recall from "Section 2.1. Classifications defined", the instances belonging to a class cannot shift their class. A mouse cannot become a lion, and Gregor Samsa cannot awaken one morning to find that he has metamorphosed into some kind of bug. Yet, when we look at the elements of the Periodic Table, we find that one element may become a series of alternate elements. [Glossary Intransitive property]

Although every element is classified by the number of protons in its nucleus, we observe that the number of neutrons in the nucleus is somewhat variable. The various forms of an element, determined by the number of neutrons in its nucleus, are known as isotopes. Some isotopic forms of an element may be stable, while others are energetically unstable and undergo events in which some of their energy is dispersed, through radioactive decay. Unstable isotopes can disperse energy through the emission of particles (i.e., alpha particles, beta particles, protons, neutrons) or through the production of electromagnetic waves (i.e., gamma rays), or through nuclear fission. As a result, one element may transform into another element (Fig. 7.6).

We tend to think that most elements are completely stable and that the transmutation of elements through radiation decay is a rare event. This is not the case. As noted earlier, the occurrence of unstable isotopes increases as atomic number increases. Of the first 82 elements, 80 elements have one or more stable isotopes. The two exceptions are technetium (element 43) and promethium (element 61) which have no stable isotopes. As we move to to the larger naturally occurring elements (element 83 to element 94), unstable isotopes are extremely common. Elements containing more than 94 protons occur only in the laboratory. They are all highly unstable and short-lived.

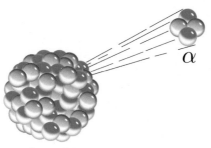

FIG. 7.6 Schematic of alpha decay, one of several decay processes whereby unstable elements transform into other elements. An atom's nucleus emits an alpha particle and is replaced by another atom with a mass number decreased by 4 and an atomic number decreased by 2. *Source: Wikipedia, and entered into the public domain by its author, Inductiveload.*

Let's take a moment to look at Radon (element 86). Radon has no stable isotopes, meaning that every isotope of radon will eventually enter a decay chain. The end-product of decay is a stable isotope of lead (element 82) (Fig. 7.7).

Because radon is a noble element, with a filled outer orbital, it is a nonreactive chemical and forms no bonds with other elements. Hence, radon, whose atoms are heavier than atoms of lead, exists in a purely gaseous state. When humans inhale radon, the decay chain may lead to the production of lead, which can precipitate in the human body. It seems remarkable that inhaled radon gas will produce a lead residue in our lungs, but such is the power of elemental transmutation.

The transmutation of elements through radioactive decay is a problem for the purists among us, insofar as it violates the intransitive rule for classifications. For the rest of us, who do not insist on having definitionally pure classifications, transmutation adds tremendously to our understanding of the world. As an example, let's consider, how zircon forms. Zircon is a mineral whose chemical name is Zirconium Silicate ($ZrSiO_4$). During the formation of zircon, two other elements may substitute for Zirconium; these two elements being Hafnium and Uranium. Strangely enough, when Zircon rocks are assayed for their constituent elements, lead is a common contaminant. How is it that lead, which cannot substitute for Zirconium and which plays no part in the formation of Zircon, is found at the precise crystal locations where Zirconium, or Uranium, or Hafnium are known to occupy?

The mystery is analogous to one of those whodunits wherein the murder victim was alone, in a room locked from the inside. How did the murderer commit the crime? In the case of zircon, the Lead molecules gained access to the crystal matrix via transmutation from Uranium. Radioactive isotopes of Uranium, entombed in zircon, slowly decay, eventually yielding Lead. In the process of decaying, ionization focally damages rock, internally, producing micro-fractures in the crystal; a phenomenon known as metamictization. Using a microscope or a hand lens, an astute mineralogist can detect the presence of radioactive decay in rocks, without resorting to sophisticated and technical

Radon-222 Decat Chain

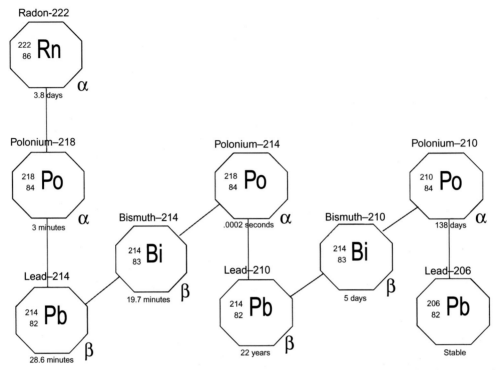

FIG. 7.7 Decay chain of Radon. Notice that Radon-222's decay chain leads to a stable isotope of lead. *Source: Public domain image provided by the U.S. Environmental Protection Agency. radon-222-decay-radon-222-decay-.*

measurements of radiation. If we know the concentration of the various Uranium isotopes that were incorporated into zircon, as it formed, and if we know the rate of radioactive decay of these isotopes, and if we know the concentration of Lead molecules in the present-day zircon, we can calculate the date that the zircon formed. Doing so has yielded a great deal of information about the process of crystal rock formation. Of the rocks that have been sampled for radioactive dating, the oldest seem to be somewhat greater than 4 billion years old; an indication that the earth was sufficiently cool to form solid rocks within about a half billion years of its birth. Moreover, these findings confirm that some present-day rocks are incredibly ancient, enduring for 4 billion years, or more (Fig. 7.8).

Our major allotment of radioactively decaying atoms was attained when planet earth formed, from space debris. Many of the atoms composing earth today are "spent" having formed from unstable elements that have completed their decay chain. There are more than a dozen elements that existed on the early earth, but which have become extinct, through radioactive decay and consequent transmutations [15].

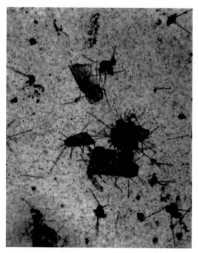

FIG. 7.8 Photograph of alpha tracks in rock, emitted by Uranium molecules, and traveling through a silver-based photo-emulsion, developed after a 5-day exposure. The black (i.e., developed silver grains) areas with radiating lines are sites of Uranium molecules or uranium daughter products. Each radiating line is an alpha particle track. If we were to prepare another photo-emulsion image of the same rock, after we wait a few hundred million years, the number of new alpha tracks on the image would be fewer, as a portion of the Uranium atoms will have decayed into nonradioactive Lead. *Source: U.S. Department of the Interior. Report of photographic methods of Uranium determination released; February 26, 1951.*

Let us look at a list of 16 extinct radioactive elements that formerly resided on our planet, arranged in order of decreasing half-life.

Samarium-146:	Isotope Half-life in Millions of years 103.5
Niobium-92:	Isotope Half-life in Millions of years 34.7
I-129:	Isotope Half-life in Millions of years 15.7
Curium-247:	Isotope Half-life in Millions of years 15.65
Lead-205:	Isotope Half-life in Millions of years 15.3
Hafnium-182:	Isotope Half-life in Millions of years 8.9
Palladium-107:	Isotope Half-life in Millions of years 6.5
Mn-53:	Isotope Half-life in Millions of years 3.7
Dysprosium-154:	Isotope Half-life in Millions of years 3.01
Cesium-135:	Isotope Half-life in Millions of years 2.33
Technetium-98:	Isotope Half-life in Millions of years 4.23
Iron-60:	Isotope Half-life in Millions of years 2.62
Technetium-97:	Isotope Half-life in Millions of years 2.6
Gadolinium-150:	Isotope Half-life in Millions of years 1.798
Zirconium-93:	Isotope Half-life in Millions of years 1.53
Al-26:	Isotope Half-life in Millions of years 0.7

The half-lives of extinct radioactive isotopes fall into a range from about zero up to a little over 103 million years. There are many radioactive elements with half-lives much longer than 103 million years; half-lives of billions and trillions of years are not particularly unusual. The revealing finding is that none of the naturally occurring isotopes with half-lives greater than 103 million years are extinct, while all of the isotopes with half-life less than 103 million years are extinct. What is the significance of the 103-million-year half-life cut-off that separates extinct elements from extant elements?

The mystery has a solution. The earth formed from space debris that contained various elements, including the unstable elements that became extinct, over time. The earth is not old enough to provide sufficient decay time for radioactive elements that have a half-life exceeding 103 million years. Unstable elements less than 103 million years have slowly diminished to the point where they can no longer be detected. If we could compute the length of time for an element with a half-life of 103 million years to decay to the point that it can no longer be detected, then we would know the age of the earth. As it happens, it takes about 40 half-lives for an element to decay to the point that it can no longer be detected by current monitors. With each half-life being 103 million years, the age of the earth can be no shorter than 40×103 or 4.12 billion years. At this point, the skeptical reader may ask, "If these elements, all having a half-life of fewer than 103 million years, cannot be found on earth, how could we possibly know that they existed at any time in earth's history?" The answer is simple. Extinct elements, as they decayed, produced characteristic daughter isotopes in the process, and these byproducts of decay are still present on earth. By observing the daughter isotopes, we safely infer the former presence of the extinct parent isotope [15].

In summary, transmutation detracts from our strict set of rules for classification by violating intransitivity. On the flip side, transmutation elucidates our understanding of radioactive decay and adds to our knowledge of the chronology of planet earth. The field of classification, like so much in life, generally benefits from compromise.

Could we have built a better Periodic Table?

As previously noted, the Periodic Table stands as an exception among classification for three reasons:

1. Each element in the Periodic Table forms its singleton class (e.g., the class of elements known as Helium contains Helium and nothing else).
2. Each class is determined by its unique class property (i.e., atomic number), and all other class properties derive from the atomic number.
3. Each class has no subclasses specified.

Whereas most classifications look like branching trees, the Periodic Table looks like a homemade brick barbecue pit, with a few excess bricks laid end to end off to the side. Although the Periodic Table has served as a handy utility, it hardly qualifies as a thing of beauty. Ingenious scientists have attempted, dating back to its inception in the 1860s, to improve upon its form. In 1863, Alexandre-Emile produced a cylindrical version of the Periodic Table, with elements spiraling up the sides [16]. Only the clunky, current version has held its popularity.

What is the secret to the durability of the Periodic Table? The Periodic Table, like all good classifications, is a multipurpose tool that can be used outside the narrow discipline of its creators. In "Chapter 6. The Classification of Life," we saw that paleontologists, geologists, embryologists, zoologists, geneticists, all look at the Classification of Life through the eyes of their particular profession, and each sees something else entirely, but they're all looking at the same thing. The Periodic Table has taught us much about chemistry, but we should not overlook its contributions to physics. Over the past 120 years, quantum physicists have learned a great deal from the table. This is an amazing turn of events insofar as the field of quantum physics did not come into existence until about 40 years had passed after the first version of the table was published. In the next chapter, we will see that the field of quantum physics advanced by explaining or preserving the physical relationships predicted by the rows, columns, and numeric order of the traditional Periodic Table.

Glossary

Intransitive property One of the criteria for classification is that every member belongs to exactly one class. From this criterion comes the intransitive property of classifications; namely, an object cannot change its class. Otherwise, over time, an object would belong to more than one class. It is easy to apply the intransitive rule under most circumstances. A cat cannot become a dog and a horse cannot become a sheep. What do we do when a caterpillar becomes a butterfly? In this case, we must recognize that caterpillar and butterfly represent phases in the development of one particular member of a species, and we do not create separate caterpillar classes or butterfly classes.

Stern-Gerlach experiment When Wolfgang Pauli provided a mathematical description of quantum spin, he thought he was creating particles that make no physical sense; and this troubled him deeply. Electrons are point particles (having no size). Their only function is to carry a charge. How can a particle with no size spin? Additionally, in the case of electrons, the mathematics would indicate that the two allowable quantum states for a spin could be either $1/2$ or $-1/2$. Pauli's own calculations indicated that an electron would need to spin around twice, just to get back to its starting point (a seeming impossibility). Pauli is quoted as saying, "I have done a terrible thing. I have postulated a particle that cannot be detected."

As it happens, electron spin is easily detectable. In fact, electron spin was detected in 1922, 3 years before Pauli's mathematical description of spin, and one century before this book was published. The corroborating experiment, known today as the Stern-Gerlach experiment, demonstrated that quantum spin was real and that fermions (e.g., electrons) and bosons (e.g., photons) behave much as their symmetry group (i.e., the irreducible Representations of the double cover of the Poincare group) would predict. Specifically, fermions have spin $1/2$ and photons have spin 1.

The experiment, conceived by Stern and conducted by Gerlach, has been described in great detail and involves passing a beam of electrons, through a magnetic field. Doing so splits the beam in two; one beam deflected upwards, and the other beam deflected downwards, and each beam is composed of the same number of electrons. The reason that the electron beam was split into two equal beams is that the original electron beam contained equal populations of electrons that were alike in every way, but with half the electrons having spin $1/2$ and the other half having and an equal and opposite spin of $-1/2$, the two allowable spin states described by Pauli. The spin $1/2$ electrons moved in one direction under a magnetic field, and the spin $-1/2$ electrons moved in the other direction. This phenomenon seemed to echo the Zeeman effect; wherein spectrographic emission lines split into two closely-spaced lines when atoms were subjected to a magnetic field.

By blocking the electrons of one or the other of the split beam, a beam of electrons having a "polarized" spin of exclusively one spin is produced, and the experimental system acts as a spin directional filter. If two such filters are placed in tandem and rotated with respect to one another, the doubly-filtered output beam is observed to vary in intensity from 100% (when the filters are aligned) to 0% when the filters are oriented at 180 degrees.

If we duplicate this experiment, using a beam of photons (i.e., a light beam) instead of an electron beam, and using a polarizing filter instead of magnets, we get similar results, with a filtered beam that can be doubly filtered by a second polarizing filter. As in the case of an electron beam, we find that we can vary the intensity of the doubly filtered light beam by changing the orientation of the polarizing filters with respect to each other. When the polarizing filters are aligned, the beam strength is at maximal intensity. When we rotate the filters, the beam strength drops to 0% when the filters are oriented at 90 degrees.

Wait a minute! In the electron beam experiment, the doubly-filtered beam strength drops to zero when the filters are 180 degrees out of alignment. In the light beam experiment, the doubly-filtered beam strength drops to zero when the filters are 90 degrees out of alignment. How is this possible? Electrons (a type of fermion) have spin 1/2, while photons (a type of boson) have spin 1. The electron must spin twice to come to its original configuration; while the photon needs to spin only once. This explains the two-fold difference in the effect of orientation angle on the intensity of the filtered electron and light beams.

Pauli thought that spin was an abstract property, that could not be interpreted in a classically physical manner. He was wrong. Stern and Gerlach's physical observations fit perfectly with the strange, abstract notion that an electron must spin around twice, to come back to its original configuration.

Valence The number of electrons that an atom uses when bonding with another atom. In general, the valence can be determined by examining the configuration of the outer shell of electrons. If the outer shell is full, then the atom will not bond with other atoms. Predictions of bonding are based upon the ability of two atoms to complete their respective outer shells by sharing electrons. In doing so, one electron may seem to occupy the outer shell of two atoms, at once. For example, an atom with one electron in its outer shell might form a bond with an atom that needs one electron to complete its outer shell. The shared electron completes the outer shell of the first atom by seemingly moving away from the atom, thus emptying its shell, and moving towards the second atom, where it seemingly completes the second atom's outer shell. Because the two atoms stay close to one another (i.e., in a chemical bond), sharing an electron that resides in a zone overlapped by both atoms is credible.

White dwarf gravitational degeneracy Almost immediately following Wolfgang Pauli's announcement of his exclusion principle, cosmologists applied it to astronomical phenomena, another example wherein fundamental advances in one field (quantum physics in this case) often lead to the solutions of seemingly intractable puzzles in other fields (cosmology).

When stars collapse, they reduce their size to something comparable to the diameter of the earth, achieving enormous densities of a plasma consisting of bare nuclei and electrons. Why does the collapse of neutrons and electrons stop when it does, instead of collapsing even further, to the extent that there is no space whatsoever between particles, or even to the point where particles superpose upon themselves (i.e., where two particles occupy the same space)? This problem had been vexing cosmologists, but Ralph Fowler, in 1926, applied Pauli's Exclusion Principle and showed that at a certain point, even at absolute zero, the Pauli Exclusion Principle determines that the collapse of a white dwarf cannot continue indefinitely [17,18].

References

[1] Jensen WB. Classification, symmetry, and the periodic table. Comput Math Appl 1986;12B:487–510.

[2] Chan EF, Gat U, McNiff JM, Fuchs E. A common human skin tumor is caused by activating mutations in beta-catenin. Nat Genet 1999;21:410–3.

[3] Croswell K. Alchemy of the heavens. New York, NY: Anchor; 1996.

[4] Cassan A, Kubas D, Beaulieu J, Dominik M, Horne J, Greenhill J, et al. One or more bound planets per Milky Way star from microlensing observations. Nature 2012;481:167–9.

[5] Hudgins DM, Bauschlicher CW, Allamandola LJ. Variations in the peak position of the 6.2 µm interstellar emission feature: a tracer of N in the interstellar polycyclic aromatic hydrocarbon population. Astrophys J 2005;632:316–32.

[6] Siegel E. Starts with a bang! Forbes June 12, 2017.

[7] Kasliwal MM, Nakar E, Singer LP, Kaplan DL, Cook DO, VanSistine A, et al. Illuminating gravitational waves: a concordant picture of photons from a neutron star merger. Science 2017;358:1559–65.

[8] Coulson CA. The contributions of wave mechanics to chemistry. J Chem Soc 1955;2:69–84.

[9] Bonolis L. From the rise of the group concept to the stormy onset of group theory in the new quantum mechanics: a saga of the invariant characterization of physical objects, events and theories. Riv Nuovo Cimento 2004;27:1–110.

[10] Neese F, Atanasov M, Bistoni G, Maganas D, Ye S. Chemistry and quantum mechanics in 2019: give us insight and numbers. J Am Chem Soc 2019;141:2814–24.

[11] Ball P. Would element 137 really spell the end of the periodic table? Philip Ball examines the evidence. Chem World 2010.

[12] Ahuja R, Blomqvist A, Larsson P, Pyykko P, Zaleski-Ejgierd P. Relativity and the lead-acid battery. Phys Rev Lett 2011;106, 018301.

[13] Pyykko P, Desclaux JP. Relativity and the periodic system of elements. Acc Chem Res 1979;12:276–81.

[14] Pitzer KS. Relativistic effects on chemical properties. Acc Chem Res 1979;12:271–6.

[15] Berman JJ. Logic and critical thinking in the biomedical sciences, volume I: deductions based upon simple observations. Cambridge, MA: Academic Press; 2020.

[16] Lemonick S. The periodic table is an icon. But chemists still can't agree on how to arrange it. C&EN; 2019.

[17] Fowler RH. On dense matter. Mon Not R Astron Soc 1926;87:114–22.

[18] Koester D, Chanmugam G. Physics of white dwarf stars. Rep Prog Phys 1990;53:837–915.

8

Classifying the universe

Chapter outline

> *God, Thou great symmetry,*
> *who put a biting lust in me*
> *From whence my sorrows spring,*
> *For all the frittered days*
> *That I have spent in shapeless ways*
> *Give me one perfect thing.*
> **Anna Wickham, from poem "Envoi", 1921 [1].**

Section 8.1. The role of mathematics in classification

> *The horizons of physics, philosophy, and art have of late been too widely separated,*
> *and, as a consequence, the language, the methods, and the aims of any one of these*
> *studies present a certain amount of difficulty for the student of any other of them.*
> *Hermann L. F. Helmholtz, 1885 [2].*

Practitioners of the "hard" sciences (e.g., mathematics, physics, and chemistry) occasionally remark that taxonomists (i.e., the toiling folk who build classifications) are little more than stamp collectors. Such casual scorn should be discouraged. Mathematics, physics, and chemistry are fundamentally all about classification; the principal difference between one field of science and another often comes down to a matter of vocabulary. All of the sciences are devoted to describing relationships among abstract or physical objects; and the relationships among like objects are classes.

In modern times, mathematicians and physicists have concentrated most of their best efforts into mastering class properties, understanding the relationships among

Classification Made Relevant. https://doi.org/10.1016/B978-0-323-91786-5.00003-3

different classes, and thereby drawing new inferences in the form of proofs, for mathematicians, and in the form of natural laws, for physicists. Back in "Section 1.3. Relationships, classes, and properties," we made the point that mathematical equations are formal statements of the relationships among mathematical objects (e.g., variables and constants, coordinates and vectors, integrals, and integrands), and we used Euler's identity as our example of a relational equation. Mathematicians know exactly what they are dealing with in their equations of abstract objects; because they are the ones who have defined the abstractions. Their limitation, from the viewpoint of nonmathematicians, is that the abstract objects they define may have no physical counterparts. Physicists, like mathematicians, use equations to express the relationship among measurable quantities of matter and energy (e.g., mass, electricity, heat, and magnetism, charge, photons), but the very real quantities that physicists measure may lack explanatory definition, other than their somewhat recursive or self-referential mathematical relationships to one another.

For example, consider Einstein's famous equation relating energy to mass (Fig. 8.1).

$$\mathbf{E} = mc^2$$

FIG. 8.1 Einstein's mass-energy equivalence formula relates energy to mass, but it does not tell us the meaning of mass or the meaning of energy.

Einstein's equation establishes a relationship between energy and mass, but when we try to understand the meaning of energy or mass, we are stymied. We know that energy is something that can perform work, such as heating an object or causing it to move. We also know that mass is something that can move if you push it with a force. Neither of these statements concerning mass and energy rises to the level of definitions; they merely frame additional relationships (i.e., the relationship between energy and heat and work; the relationship between mass and resistance to movement). In fact, if we were to collect all of the formulas of physics, we would find that they all establish relationships between one measurable quantity and some other measurable quantity, without actually helping us define those properties in any absolute sense. Nobody can satisfactorily define electricity or magnetism in absolute terms. Karl Pearson described the situation accurately and succinctly in his 1899 book, The Grammar of Science when he wrote "That all science is description and not an explanation."

After a physicist has established a formulaic relationship between measurable objects, she will naturally determine the groups of objects to which the relationship applies and the groups of objects to which the relationship does not apply. The process of doing so results in the discovery of classes and class relationships. Before very long, the physicist has created something akin to a classification. The story is much the same for mathematicians, who create, from their imaginations, classes of abstractions. Much of their careers are devoted to attaining a deep understanding of the class properties that apply to the classes of mathematical objects (e.g., groups, algebras, geometries, topologies) and to use such insights to determining the relationships among those classes.

As you recall, one of the key features of any classification is completeness; its ability to contain and describe every item in its claimed domain. Most physicists and mathematicians are reductionists, believing that the universe is a closed system of matter, energy, and space, all operating according to a few natural laws. For the reductionists, their job comes down to explaining everything we see based on what we can learn about the fundamental operating principles of the universe. Thus, the reductionist would welcome a classification of the universe that is complete, containing all of the relationships that account for everything we can observe today and for all of our tomorrows. The naturalists, who were influential in the first half of the 20th century, took reductionism one step further, asserting that man has no special place in the universe, and there can be no miracles or magical events that intervene in our lives.

Of course, good scientists are always eager to challenge their peers. One of the most forceful rebuttals to naturalism came from a somewhat modest essay written by Eugene Wigner, a quantum physicist, and Nobelist. In 1960, he published "The Unreasonable Effectiveness of Mathematics in the Natural Sciences," which focused on several physical properties of the universe that were perfectly described by mathematics [3]. The question raised by this essay is as follows: "If mathematics is a human construction, and if the operation of the universe is wholly indifferent to human activity, then why do the abstractions of mathematics fit so perfectly with the natural laws of the universe?" In fact, absent any satisfactory naturalistic explanation, mustn't we conclude that a physical universe operated under a mathematical equation is itself magical, and proof of man's special place in a mystical realm?

The notion of a universe described perfectly by mathematical formulas has stirred philosophers for centuries [4]. Is there something special about humans and our tiny planet earth that permit us to compose the mathematical rules that describe all of creation? Are the naturalists simply wrong? A point often raised by opponents of naturalism comes from the seemingly miraculous finding that the fundamental laws of the universe can be constructed from observations made on planet earth. Certainly, one might argue, the earth must have some special significance if the universe operates according to earth-bound principles. Of course, this is simply backward thinking. A less geo-centric way of approaching reality posits that everything on earth operates under universal laws, and therefore the universal laws can be studied without leaving earth.

We approach the question of reductionism through the process of classification. Does our struggle to create a classification of the universe lead us to a complete understanding of reality, or does it lead us into mystery? Are we stepping into light or into darkness? In either case, it will be through the process of classification that we answer the deep questions posed by physicists and mathematicians.

Has our study of the science of classification equipped us to conquer the universe? Not quite. As it happens, our universe is best understood by mathematical relationships among abstract classes, and all of these are expressed using mathematical notation. Accordingly, when we study the classes of objects in the universe (e.g., particles, forces, spacetime, and their symmetries), we are bound to find that they have been prepackaged into mathematical abstractions that we nonmathematicians cannot easily grasp. We will sidestep some of the higher mathematics, instead concentrating on a very general understanding of mathematical abstractions, and how physicists use abstraction to understand and predict the behavior of our universe. In particular, we will be studying the relationships found in symmetry groups, such as those included in the Classification Theorem of the Finite Simple Groups. Those of us whose attention is focused primarily on the theory and practice of classification may not be particularly interested in learning anything at all about group theory, and understandably so. To soften the intellectual blow, we are about to receive, here is a preview of this chapter, in one short paragraph:

> The universe operates under a set of conservation laws (conservation of momentum, conservation of energy, etc.), and these conservation laws are determined by natural symmetries (i.e., conditions that do not vary through space and time). When we observe the physical nature of the universe (e.g., the speed of light, the measurable effects of electricity and magnetism, and gravity), we find that our sets of observations are describable as properties of various symmetry groups. Physicists can take empiric observations concerning subatomic particles, atoms, gravity, light, multiverses, wormholes, or anything that suits their interest, and look to see if those observations fit classified groups, finite or continuous. If so, we can use the known properties of the group to predict the behavior of the universe.

Now that the secret is out, let's start by showing that the most profound laws of our universe result from invariances (i.e., things that do not change).

Section 8.2. Invariances are our laws

Que nous representent en effet les phenomenes naturels, si ce n'est une succession de transformations infinitesimales, dont les lois de l'univers sont les invariants? (What do natural phenomena represent other than a succession of infinitesimal transformations, whose invariants are the laws of the universe?)

Sophus Lie, 1895 [5].

All of the universal laws of science are simple relationships that apply to the fundamental building blocks of our universe: matter and its constituent particles, and energy and its various forces. We will see, as the chapter progresses, that all such laws are built on invariances, and that the invariances of the universe can be expressed by symmetry groups. For now, let's take a moment to review the general features of scientific laws so that we can best appreciate their nature.

General features of scientific laws:

1. Testable and validated. A law doesn't mean much if you cannot put it to the test. If a law passes every test that scientists can devise, we often say that it has been validated (i.e., shown to be true, as far as anyone can determine).

2. Universally applicable. One of the very nice things about our universe is that it provides us with laws that apply everywhere. We can determine that the light (electromagnetic waves) received from galaxies billions of miles away obeys the same scientific laws as light produced by our smartphone screens. We can observe that orbiting stars in distant galaxies obey the same laws of gravitation that cause hammers to fall here on earth. Furthermore, our laws seem to be stable over time. Nothing much seems to have changed since the Big Bang.

3. Simple. Most scientific laws are very short equations, and the brevity of these laws has been an enduring puzzle among scientists and nonscientists alike. In this chapter, we will see that scientific laws are almost always based on invariances (i.e., situations in which things do not vary under transformations). When we look at things that do not vary, we might expect that the equations that describe relationships would be simple; nothing changes. This happens to be the case, and every student of physics should be grateful that the most significant scientific laws can all fit comfortably on a single index card.

As mentioned in point 3, above, scientific laws are relationships among fundamental things (i.e., matter and energy) that depend on some universal invariance. An invariance is, as its name implies, anything that does not change when some specified conditions are altered. If an object has the same properties when moved through space, then we say that the properties are spatially invariant. If a circle looks that same, when flipped across any axis that passes through its center, then we say that the circle is invariant under that particular rotation (i.e., geometrical invariance).

Conserved quantities, such as the conservation of energy, or the conservation of charge are both invariances over time. If the quantity being measured does not change over time, then we say that the quantity has been conserved. Hence, conservation laws can be thought of as the subset of invariance laws in which the invariance is observed over time.

We tend to take invariances for granted, as though they are all so obvious that they could have no significance and could not possibly be worthy of our attention. In this section, we will look at some invariances that have a profound influence on our understanding of the universe, and how the laws derived from these invariances took humans thousands of years to fully grasp.

Let's start with a simple invariance that is taught to every middle school student: the law of inertia.

The law of inertia, also known as Newton's first law, states that if a body is at rest or moving at a constant speed in a straight line, it will remain at rest or keep moving in a straight line at constant speed unless it is acted upon by a force.

According to Newton, if a rocket ship is moving through empty space at 50,000 miles per hour, it will maintain that speed forever, without requiring any additional fuel, and will eventually traverse the entire universe, given sufficient time. This is quite an amazing property of the universe, providing us with the ability to travel for eternity, at a constant speed, without any investment of energy. It would seem that the law of inertia is one of the energy conservation laws because the total energy of the system does not change, and there is something conserved. Specifically, the momentum of the rocket ship, calculated as the mass of the ship times its velocity, remains constant and is thus conserved. More fundamentally, the law of inertia tells us something about the invariance of spacetime. Because the speed of the rocket ship stays the same, regardless of where it is translated (i.e., movement in a straight line) and when it is observed, we can conclude that space is homogeneous and that momentum is spacetime invariant.

What about that part of the law of inertia that deals with masses at rest staying at rest, unless acted upon by a force? The homogeneity of spacetime implies that one frame of reference is just as valid as any other because the universe doesn't change when positions are translated through space and time. We can see now that the mass moving at a constant velocity, when observed in a frame of reference moving at the same velocity, is equivalent to a mass at rest. So, of course, the mass at rest stays at rest unless acted upon by a force.

Time shift invariance

An object can be stationary in space, but it cannot be stationary in time. Time is always flowing in one direction, and it is for this reason that poets liken time to a river. Poets have a tougher time finding the words to describe the traditional three-dimensional coordinates, which are disdainfully described as whatever happens to lie between point A and point B.

Similarly, time seems to move forward endlessly, without any "push" to our clocks. Any actions occurring at any moment can be repeated at later moments, without variance. This signifies that no time is any different from any other time, and time moves forward without the expenditure of energy or mass. Then there's light. If you shine a flashlight into space, its beam moves forward forever, to the ends of space and time. We don't need to give the light an extra push every once in a while, just to keep it moving. When we determine the speed of light in a vacuum, it's always the same in space-time units (e.g., miles per second). Altogether, it seems that our universe provides us with a lot of conserved space-time happenings, with no energy being lost from objects and no energy being added to the system to keep things moving along. Because there is no "payment" exacted for movements of matter and energy through time, we conclude that time itself is an invariant. [Glossary Time symmetry]

Invariance of the speed of light

Einstein's special theory of relativity was developed from two fundamental assertions about the universe [5]:

1. Physics works the same way in all uniformly moving frames of reference (an extension of Galileo's principle of relativity).

2. The speed of light is the same in all frames of reference (as demonstrated by the Michelson-Morley experiment [6]).

When we think about it, Einstein only needed the first assertion to develop his remarkable theory. The second assertion follows as a consequence of the first. When we say that the observers in any frame of reference observe the same physical laws and the same outcomes of those laws, then we can infer that the observers must observe the same measurements of the speed of light in every frame of reference. Therefore, the speed of light must be the same in every frame of reference. Michaelson and Morley's experiment merely confirmed a foregone conclusion.

We can also interpret the constancy of the speed of light as a conservation law. Time invariance tells us that experiments performed at a certain time will produce the same results if they are performed under the same conditions at another time. Hence, whether we measure the speed of light today, or tomorrow, within our frame of reference, the speed of light remains the same, never slowing down or speeding up. We also know that the same constancy of light will be true in every frame of reference. Hence, the speed of light is constant in every frame of reference, at all times; and this is a conservation law.

Einstein went on to demonstrate that normal matter cannot travel at the speed of light, no matter how much energy is devoted to providing an accelerating force. At the same time, no energy is required for a beam of light to maintain its constant speed forever, as it travels endlessly through the universe. This profound difference between matter and light suggests that these two objects belong to two fundamentally different classes. As it happens, fermions are responsible for atoms, and light is mediated by bosons, each having its representations of a particular symmetry group. More about this later.

In 1904, Hendrik Antoon Lorentz introduced a set of mathematical variables that preserves the symmetry of transformations in space and time (Fig. 8.2).

$$c^2 t_1 t_2 - x_1 x_2 - y_1 y_2 - z_1 z_2 = c^2 t\prime_1 t\prime_2 - x\prime_1 x\prime_2 - y\prime_1 y\prime_2 - z\prime_1 z\prime_2$$

FIG. 8.2 Solutions to translations in time and space that are invariant with a frame of reference must satisfy the following equation. Time is denoted by "t," and the spatial coordinates are x, y, and z. The primed variables indicate coordinates in an alternate frame of reference. The unit of time is converted to distance by multiplying by the universal constant, c, measured by distance per second, times "t" measured in seconds.

At the time, Lorentz did not fully appreciate the physical significance of his work [5]. Soon afterward, Poincare demonstrated how the Lorentz transformations could be extended to represent all the invariances described in Maxwell's equations. Einstein's theory of relativity was soon re-interpreted as the physical expression of Poincare's extension of the Lorentz transformations. All of these great works stemmed from the simple observation that electromagnetic waves move at a constant speed in all frames of reference. At last, we saw the light!

Homogeneity of empty space and the inverse square law

Suppose there is a hammer on the left side of your desk, and you choose to move it over to the right side of your desk. This little maneuver, like the hammer itself, is totally within your grasp. When the hammer is horizontally translated across the desk, all of the molecules of the hammer move in perfect unison, maintaining their locations with respect to the other trillions of molecules of the hammer. The hammer is unchanged, whether it is on the left of your desk or the right. We owe this amazing outcome to the homogeneity of space and the molecular organization of the hammer. The individual molecules of the hammer can take up residence in some new location, without forfeiting their positions in the hammer, because the relationships among the molecules of the hammer are determined by atomic forces that act independently of the hammer's spacetime coordinates. One point in spacetime is much like another, and any point will do.

Using the homogeneity of empty space, we can derive the inverse square law, with a little help from the law of conservation of energy. When energy emanates through empty space from a point source it spreads through time in all spacetime coordinates equally. This tells us that a point source of light will spread out as a sphere that expands over time. At any moment, any point on the surface of the sphere will have the same light exposure as any other point on the surface of the sphere. Due to conservation of energy, the total energy moving through a spherical shell at radius "r" will equal the total energy moving through a spherical shell at radius "2r" and radius "4r" and so on.

The area of a 3-dimensional sphere is $4\pi r^2$. This means that the total energy moving through a sphere of radius r will be equally distributed over the area $4\pi r^2$. As the energy expands outward, the total energy (a constant) moving through a sphere of radius 2r will be distributed over an area of $4\pi(2r)^2$, or 4 times the total area of the smaller radius. This means that the passing energy measured per unit surface area is reduced by 1/4 when we double the distance from the original point source.

Generalizing, the expanding energy reduces as the inverse square of the distance from the emanating point source. This is known as the inverse square law. Physicists have shown this law to be true, by actual measurements. We can say that our conclusion was made independently of any experimental evidence, and solely based on the three conditions: the conservation of energy, the invariance of spacetime, and the Euclidean geometry of our universe.

Employing the same line of logic, the inverse square law for 3-dimensional space can be generalized to higher dimensions (Fig. 8.3).

$$I \propto \frac{1}{r^{n-1}}$$

FIG. 8.3 General formula for the inverse power law for n-dimensional Euclidean space. The intensity of the field (e.g., light), falls off as the inverse (*n*-1)th power as the radius (distance from the light source) grows.

As an aside, we can use the homogeneity of space to derive the conservation of momentum law. Because no location in space is any different from any other location in space, the momentum of moving objects stays the same over its spacetime locations (i.e., is conserved). Hence, the homogeneity of space accounts for the law of conservation of momentum.

Shift invariance of time and the conservation of energy

Since no moment is different from any other, the total energy of the universe shifted to any given time should be the same as the total energy at any other time. Hence, the shift symmetry of time accounts for the law of conservation of energy.

Keeping the relationship between time and energy in mind, let's briefly consider a moment 14 billion years ago, when the universe as we know it was born in a Big Bang. To the best knowledge of physicists, none of whom were witnesses to the event, the Big Bang produced everything in our universe, emanating from a small point of spacetime.

How much energy did the Big Bang produce? According to the conservation law, and the invariance of time, the Big Bang produced a net zero of energy. There was no energy at the moment preceding the Big Bang; therefore, there must have been no net energy at the moment after the Big Bang. Time symmetry tells us that net positive energy cannot come from a net-zero energy.

But the universe is full of energy! Where did it all come from? The easiest explanation is that the Big Bang produced equal amounts of positive energy and negative energy. We've become accustomed to observing positive energy, but the negative energy evades our attention.

It has been speculated that negative energy is what holds protons together, in a dense nucleus, against the repulsive forces that would otherwise tear apart particles having the same charge (i.e., positive-positive repulsions among protons). Likewise, we might expect that there is an equal number of antiparticles hiding somewhere in our universe, to balance the creation of the particles that serve as the familiar ingredients of ordinary matter. In summary, our universe should have begun with a net-zero energy, and we have been running on empty ever since.

Conservation of angular momentum and rotational symmetry

Imagine that you are in a rocket ship moving at a constant velocity through empty space. For the sake of discussion, imagine that you have run out of fuel, and the rocket is simply coasting. When might you expect the rocket to come to a complete halt? The answer is "never." With nothing to impede the rocket's flight, it will continue along its current path, at its current speed, until the end of time. Forward momentum is conserved because no energy is being expended to counter its movement. Suppose you were to suddenly bump into a large, stationary object, with twice the mass as your rocket ship. Your rocket would stop in its tracks, and the larger object would suddenly fly off, much like a billiard ball hitting another billiard ball. At what speed would the more massive rocket fly? We know that momentum is conserved, and that momentum is mass times velocity. If your ship comes to a full stop after colliding with an object having twice the mass, then the more massive object will move away at half your former velocity, thus conserving momentum.

Now, imagine that you are spinning in space, at a constant angular velocity. Just as forward momentum continues for eternity, in empty space, so does the angular momentum of a spinning object. A sphere that is set spinning in space will continue to spin at a constant angular speed, forever. Suppose that the sphere suddenly, and mysteriously shrinks, without changing its mass, and without the exchange of energy. The angular momentum that was present in the larger sphere will be conserved in the smaller sphere.

Angular momentum is proportional to the mass of the rotating object multiplied by its radius. If the radius shrinks by half, the velocity of the rotating sphere will increase by a factor of 2, to conserve the angular moment that was present in the larger sphere. Likewise, if the radius shrinks by a factor of 100,000, then the rotational speed will increase by a factor of 100,000 (Fig. 8.4).

v=L/mr L is constant
m = 1 and r = 1,000,000

v=L/mr
L is unchanged, m is
unchanged, r = 1,000

FIG. 8.4 When a large, spinning object is suddenly transformed into a small object having the same mass, its angular momentum, L, does not change (i.e., angular momentum is conserved). To preserve angular momentum, its angular velocity will increase by the same factor that the radius has decreased.

An increase in the speed of angular rotation will result when a spinning mass condenses in size. The appearance of a neutron star, that can rotate on its axis in under a second, suggests that it condensed from a very large size to a very small size. We can infer that a fast-spinning, a neutron star is formed by the collapse of a slowly spinning conventional (i.e., nonneutron) star. As it happens, the gravitational collapse of massive stars produces a concentrated ball of neutrons. In the process of neutron star formation, a star that has a radius of a million kilometers will shrink down to a star with a radius of about 10 km, a 100,000-fold difference. Angular momentum is conserved, and the neutron star spins with a velocity about 100,000 times the velocity of the parent star, sometimes revolving hundreds of times per second.

The identicality of the types of fundamental particles

We tend to assume that all fundamental particles are identical to their kind (e.g., all electrons are alike, all protons are alike). In point of fact, the identicality of particles, by type, happens to be true; but we did not know this to be true until it was proven so.

It turns out that in the late 19th century, before the advent of quantum mechanics, and even before atoms were proven to exist, physicists had a clever way of demonstrating the identicality of particles. The basic argument for the identicality of fundamental particles rested on the second law of thermodynamics, which holds that the entropy of isolated systems left to spontaneous evolution always achieves a state of thermodynamic equilibrium for which the entropy is maximal (i.e., maximal particle randomness). A strange phenomenon occurs, defying simple explanation, when we mix different types of gases; the so-called mixing paradox. If there are two different gases, held under the same conditions (volume, pressure, temperature, and a number of atoms), the total entropy of the system, when the two gases are mixed, will be greater than the total entropy if we had mixed two volumes of the same gas. The mixing paradox is an apparent violation of the second law of thermodynamics that occurs whenever one gas is mixed with another gas of a different type [7]. Its satisfactory explanation has been an ongoing labor involving contributions from the fields of quantum chemistry, quantum thermodynamics, and classical entropy physics. For whatever reason, the mixing paradox, also known as the Gibbs paradox, seems to be an empiric fact that applies when gases of different types are mixed. Because gases of the same type, when put together, do not display the mixing paradox, we infer that the individual atoms of the gas are identical to one another; otherwise, entropy would increase when the atoms are mixed. Because atoms are composed of fixed numbers of electrons, protons, and neutrons, we can infer that each of these fundamental particles is identical to the particles of the same type; (e.g., one electron is completely identical to, and interchangeable with, any other electron).

Using the mixing paradox (which we do not fully understand) to support an argument for the identicality of atoms and particles (which we do not fully understand) seems to lack some of the rigor that we have come to expect from physicists. Let's backtrack and consider just the issue of the identicality of electrons. An electron is considered to be a "point" particle (i.e., a particle without size). An electron is functionally defined as a particle that carries a negative charge and that can be described as a wave. From the geometric point of view, all points are identical to one another. Hence all electrons are identical to all other electrons.

While we're on the topic of identicality, we can take our discussion one step further; specifically, we can take the identicality of particles and extend it to the identicality of the charge carried with each particle. We all know that protons carry a positive charge, and electrons carry a negative charge. Can we prove that the opposite charges carried by protons and electrons are exactly equal in magnitude? Yes. Let's stipulate that matter is composed of an enormous number of atoms, with each atom composed of equal numbers of protons and electrons. If the charge on an electron and a proton were even the tiniest bit unequal, then matter would have an excess electric charge (i.e., the sum of the differences in charge between electrons and protons). Hence, every sample of matter would be mutually repulsive to every other sample of matter; because like charges repel. Once again, the universe as we know it could not exist.

Maxwell's equations are all about invariances

We've all heard of Maxwell's equations, and we've all enjoyed the T-shirts emblazoned with Maxwell's formulas expressing how changing electric and magnetic fields are related to charges and currents. The original set of equations were published in the 1860s and were in a much less elegant mathematical syntax, employing differential equations. Oliver Heaviside, using vector calculus, produced the short format that fits neatly on a shirt (Fig. 8.5).

$$\nabla \cdot \mathbf{D} = \rho$$

$$\nabla \times \mathbf{E} = -\frac{\partial \mathbf{B}}{\partial t}$$

$$\nabla \cdot \mathbf{B} = 0$$

$$\nabla \times \mathbf{H} = \mathbf{J} + \frac{\partial \mathbf{D}}{\partial t}$$

FIG. 8.5 Maxwell's equations, Heaviside form. From top to bottom: Gauss's law, Faraday's law of induction, Gauss's law for magnetism, and Ampere's circuital law. Nonmathematicians can appreciate the simplicity of the formulas, and, overlooking the difference between a curl and a divergence, the visual resemblances of one formula to another. [Glossary Curl and divergence]

Without going into mathematical detail, all of these equations express basic invariances that apply to energy fields. The underlying principle of Maxwell's equations is represented in the fundamental continuity equation for conserved quantities (Fig. 8.6).

$$\frac{\partial \rho}{\partial t} = -\nabla \cdot \mathbf{J}$$

FIG. 8.6 The general continuity equation for a conserved quantity. All conservation laws, including most of Maxwell's equations, can be written in a form that expresses relationships in much the same way as the general continuity equation.

Conservation laws, when expressed mathematically, have a form that closely resembles the continuity equation, allowing for a different set of variables depending on which quantity happens to be conserved. In fact, the continuity equation here is identical to Maxwell's equation for charge conservation. In the equation for charge conservation, J is the current density measured in amperes per square meter, and ρ is the charge density measured in coulombs per cubic meter.

Why do all these field laws look just about the same, when expressed as a mathematical formula, and why do the field laws look much like the continuity equation for conserved quantities? If we have any conserved quantity in space (e.g., a magnetic field), we know that the change in the density of the field in its region of space must be exactly equal to the flux of the field through a surrounding area, where the flux is the quantity of the field that has moved through the surrounding area). Put another way, if we have a conserved quantity that changes within a volume, then any change in the quantity must be exactly equaled by the quantity that leaves or enters the volume, and whatever leaves or enters the volume must pass through the area that surrounds the volume. The continuity equation provides a neat mathematical representation of this simple concept. Because all of Maxwell's laws express conserved quantities moving through space over time (i.e., invariances), they all look much like the continuity equation (Fig. 8.7).

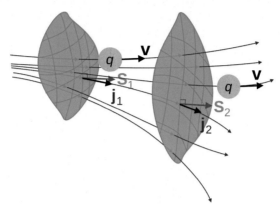

FIG. 8.7 Diagram illustrating the principle underlying the Continuity Equation; namely, that the changes in the density of a conserved quantity within a volume are balanced by the outflow of the quantity through the surrounding surface area. *Source: Wikipedia, and entered into the public domain by its author, Maschen.*

Incidentally, why do electricity and magnetism travel together, in phase, and perpendicular to one another? The changing magnetic field creates a changing electric field as described by Faraday's law. The resulting electric field creates a changing magnetic field through Maxwell's addition to Ampere's law.

Conservation of electric charge

As noted in the discussion of Maxwell's equations, the continuity equation is identical to Maxwell's equation for charge conservation, and all empiric evidence confirms that charge is neither created nor destroyed. On an atomic level, the exact balance of positive charge (i.e., protons) and negative charge (i.e., electrons) prevents atoms from having a net electric charge, which would render atoms mutually repulsive. On a cosmologic level, we note that atoms account for all observed matter in the universe and are the source of all electric charges, in the form of electrons. Because the charge of individual atoms is balanced between positive and negative, we can surmise that the total amount of positive charge held in all the atoms in the universe is exactly balanced by the total amount of negative charge held by atoms.

It's reasonable to think that all of the atoms in the universe contribute no net charge, on a grand scale, but does charge conservation hold on a small scale. In particular, would it be possible to suddenly create one unit charge somewhere in space, at the expense of a little energy? Charge conservation, on any scale, was formally proven as a consequence of a mathematically sophisticated theory, principally developed by Weyl, now known as gauge invariance [8,9,5]. The mathematics of this theory lies beyond the scope of this book and the expertise of this author, but it is possible to summarize the argument in words. Certain quantitative items in nature cannot be directly measured. These are only understood and described in relative terms. One such item is voltage. It is impossible to simply measure the voltage (electrical potential) of a point in space. We can only measure the difference in potential between points. Traditionally, the voltage at a point is measured by comparison to the reference potential of the earth. Restated, voltage is always a relative quantity and has no absolute meaning. These kinds of relative values serve to give forces and fields an analytical equivalence to geometric frames of reference. Just as we see invariances related to geometric frames of reference, we see invariances of fields, and the mathematical description of these types of field invariances are referred to as gauge theories. [Glossary Gauge theories]

Given that voltage is only measured in relative terms, then let us consider a gedanken experiment in which we imagine that charge is not locally conserved. In this alternate universe, we can create a new unit of charge or destroy a unit of charge, at will. A unit of charge would be the charge carried by a single electron. The energy carried by a unit charge is known to be equal to the charge times the voltage: [Glossary Gedanken]

```
The energy of charge creation = (charge produced) x (voltage at the
point in space where the charge is produced)
```

Hence, if we measure the energy that was spent producing a single quantum of charge, we could calculate an absolute value for the voltage. However, doing so would violate gauge invariance of voltage, which is known to be a quantity that cannot be measured absolutely. That is to say that voltage is always a relative measurement of the differences of electrical potential at two points. Thus, if the charge is not conserved, then gauge invariance is violated. Gauge invariance cannot be violated. Therefore, the charge is conserved, even for one lonely electron.

Invariance of inertial and gravitational mass and the theory of general relativity

Let's start with Galileo, and his assertion that all objects fall at the same speed, regardless of their respective weights. Every student learns that Galileo proved that objects of different weights fall at the same speed. Fewer people know that Galileo's famous experiment in Pisa merely confirmed what Galileo had already deduced, from a simple gedanken experiment. Imagine that you have a 2-pound ball and an 8-pound ball, connected by a string. Let's pretend that heavy objects fall faster than light objects. In this case, the 8-pound ball would drop faster than the 2-pound ball. If this were so, then when the connected balls were dropped, the 2-pound ball, traveling slower than the 8-pound ball, would put a drag on the descent on the 8-pound ball; slowing its fall. Hence, a 10-pound composite weight would travel slower than a single, 8-pound weight; a contradiction of the original premise, that heavier objects fall faster than lighter objects (Fig. 8.8).

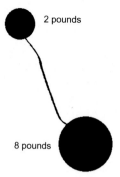

2 pounds

8 pounds

FIG. 8.8 Galileo deduced, before his experiment at the Tower of Pisa, that all objects fall at the same speed, regardless of weight. The premise of his argument is that any object is composed of objects having a lesser weight. In the case of the illustration, a 10-pound weight is equivalent to an 8-pound weight and a 2-pound weight, joined together.

Had we begun with the opposite assumption, that lighter objects fall faster than heavier objects, then the fast-traveling 2-pound weight would speed the descent of the attached 8-pound weight. Hence, the composite 10-pound weight would travel faster than the component 8-pound weight. Again, the original premise would be contradicted. Only if both connected weights, 2-pound, and 8-pound, fell at the same rate, could this contradiction be avoided.

If we were to substitute a feather for the 2-pound ball, the same argument would hold. If heavy objects fall faster than lighter objects, then the attached feather would slow the heavier ball, and the sum of the weights of the feather and the ball, which exceeds the weight of the ball, would fall more slowly than the ball without feather, contradicting our premise. If objects fell at different rates, based on weight, or molecular composition, we would have a universe in which the various types of particles composing atoms (e.g., protons, neutrons, electrons) would each be expected to have their own relationship to gravity.

Galileo understood that the experiment at the Tower of Pisa was basically all for show. His application of logic had settled the issue. Unfortunately for Galileo, experiments do not always work as they should. When the balls were dropped from the Tower, the larger ball beat the smaller ball to the ground, by a smidgen. We now know that the difference is accounted for by air resistance. When an equivalent experiment is conducted in a vacuum, the advantage of the heavier ball is lost, and the two balls of different weights drop at the same speed. At the time, Galileo's skeptical colleagues showed no tolerance for imprecision. The heavier ball beat the smaller ball to the ground; that fact was sufficient to conclude that heavy objects fall faster than light objects. His detractors were wrong, of course, but Galileo learned an important lesson in the sociology of science; that experimental results are easily misinterpreted. [Glossary Precision]

Galileo's analysis applied the Law of Compositionality. A large object is composed of smaller objects, and the properties of the large object cannot violate the properties of the objects it contains. Had Galileo been just a bit more insightful, he may have taken his conclusion one step further, preempting one of Einstein's most important theories. Galileo had correctly reasoned that all objects fall at the same rate under the influence of gravity, regardless of their weight. From this assertion, Galileo could have inferred that gravity is not a physical force. How so? Forces that act on objects must contend with the physical properties of the object, such as mass, molecular composition, and the properties of the individual molecules that compose the object. Much of physics can be reduced to the mathematical description of the interplay between forces and atoms. When we think about gravity, the physical properties of objects are removed from the equation. When we drop two objects, they fall at the same rate, without regard to their respective masses, and without regard to their chemical compositions. Moreover, gravity seems to be everywhere, at once. Whether you drop two objects from the Leaning Tower of Pisa, or the mountains of mars, the objects will fall as one, although the speed of the fall will be somewhat different on earth than on mars. We cannot shield an object from the effects of gravity; nor can we measure the speed at which gravity exerts its effect. It is as though gravity is not created through an application of measured energy. Hence, Galileo, back in the year 1590, could have inferred that gravity must be part of the fabric of space. About 315 years later, Albert Einstein concluded that gravity is not an interatomic force; it is a curvature in space-time, basically removing the distinction between geometry and physics. When objects fall, they are slipping along a curve in spacetime (Fig. 8.9).

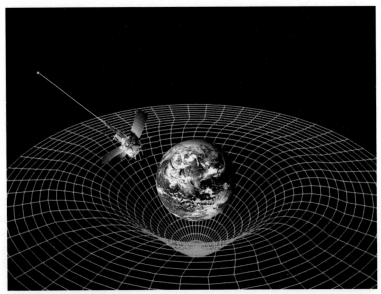

FIG. 8.9 Artist's conception of a satellite orbiting in the spatial distortion caused by the earth. *Source: U.S. National Aeronautics and Space Administration.*

Einstein approached the concept of gravity using a somewhat novel take on invariance. Specifically, Einstein focused his thoughts on the invariance of inertial and gravitational mass. Einstein asserted that there was no way to distinguish between a mass on earth falling due to the force of gravity and between a mass (such as a rocket ship in space) being accelerated at 1 g (i.e., the acceleration of a falling mass on earth, about 32 ft per second squared). If you were to step on a scale here on earth, and the scale measured 160 pounds, then if you were to step on a scale in a rocket ship accelerating through space at 32 ft per second squared, you would also weigh 160 pounds. Furthermore, if your spaceship suddenly stopped accelerating, your weight on the scale would drop to 0 pounds. Likewise, if you stepped off a cliff on earth, while still standing on a scale, your weight would drop to 0 pounds (until you collided with the ground). Basically, gravitational masses are weightless while falling, and inertial masses are weightless when not being accelerated. These same observations would apply to any mass, in any frame of reference, regardless of its chemical composition. Einstein concluded that there is no fundamental difference between gravitation and the acceleration of an inertial mass. When bodies fall, there is no force to overcome (i.e., falling bodies have zero weight). There is only an accelerating trajectory in spacetime. Einstein found a relationship that balanced gravity against the geometry of spacetime. The relationship between spacetime geometry and gravity is represented by the Einstein Field Equations.

The simple observation that gravitational mass and inertial mass are invariant eventually led to Einstein's general theory of relativity, a theory that has since been validated by all manner of scientific tests. Einstein's use of invariance principles to develop his theories of both special and general relativity was truly revolutionary. Until then, invariance has always been considered a phenomenon derived from the known laws of nature. Einstein turned this way of thinking around, showing the world that the laws of nature are derived consequences from the invariances of our universe [5].

One last thought. We now know how to relate mass and gravity, but the only way we understand the meaning of mass is through its relationship to other things that are themselves understood through other relationships (e.g., inertia, momentum, gravity, kinetic energy). It is one of the most powerful properties of classifications that we can relate to things that we cannot understand individually. We speak of "mass" only in terms of formulas that describe its relationship to other classified items, such as momentum, and kinetic energy. The relationships are provided by classifications, but the meaning of the related objects is left to our imaginations. We must remind ourselves that classifications are a device for organizing class relationships and are not designed to define the items contained in classes.

The universe is complete and classification-ready

The final invariance that we will be discussing is the invariance of the composition of the universe. From the moment of the Big Bang until the present moment, the universe, which consists of matter and energy, has been complete. The conservation of matter and energy tells us that nothing is being added to the universe, and nothing is being subtracted from the universe. There is nothing new under the sun. What we may think of as "new" things are just old things that has been transformed. For example, every human being is formed by chemicals in the environment, many of which are recycled molecules from the remains of previously living organisms. Ultimately, every atom in our bodies has been "used" previously.

Likewise, so-called "new" data is just old data updated to the current time. For example, when we collect new data on the most current weather in our region, we can be certain that the current weather is an incremental modification of the weather from the preceding moment; and therefore, not new.

The "completeness" of our universe provides another justification for a "classification of everything." At the moment we have laws that establish the relationships among classes of items in our prevailing concept of the universe, and those laws are predicated upon observable invariances.

Section 8.3. Fearful symmetry

The best that most of us can hope to achieve in physics is simply to misunderstand at a deeper level.

Wolfgang Pauli

Up until now, we have stressed invariance as a key condition accounting for much of what we know about the operational laws of the universe. Modern textbooks of physics have largely abandoned the term "invariance," and have emphasized a related term that closely aligns physics with mathematics. This new term is "symmetry." The term "symmetry" has been used in the field of geometry to indicate that a geometric object can be moved in space (i.e., rotated, flipped, reflected, or translated laterally) without changing the way it looks. For example, when a circle is bisected along its diameter, the left half of the circle is identical to the right half of the circle, and the bisection of the circle provides an axis of rotational symmetry. If we have an equilateral triangle, we can flip it any way we like, and it will fit perfectly into its original silhouette. Modern physicists have extended the notion of symmetry to operations upon anything (not just geometric objects) in which the result of the operation is invariant. Thus, we can start to think of the symmetries that might involve time, matter, energy, gravity, and all of the fundamental components of our universe. Furthermore, the invariances that we have described earlier in this chapter all qualify as symmetry operations since each of the invariances involves an operation in spacetime (movement at a constant velocity, angular rotation of an object, flipping one object and another of the same type). Let's return to our example of the speed of light, which is invariant (the speed does not slow down or speed up, and all beams of light travel at the same speed), and a conserved quantity (light does not involve the addition of energy to maintain its speed, and light is not lost as it travels in empty space). Does the speed of light have symmetry? Yes. Light exhibits translational symmetry in that it is constant in all frames of reference!

If we wished, we could describe all manner of equivalences between symmetries and invariances. For example, the homogeneity of space is a type of invariance (i.e., one point in space is just like another). It is also a geometric symmetry (i.e., symmetry under rotation and translation). The invariance of time (i.e., the property that an action will produce the same result, whenever it is repeated), can be thought of as a shift symmetry in time. Likewise, we can describe equivalences between symmetries and conservation laws.

The mathematically rigorous rule that describes the fundamental relationship between conservation laws and symmetry is known as Noether's theorem, published by Emmy Noether, in 1918 [10]. Emmy Noether's theorem has been interpreted many different ways, depending somewhat on the field in which it is being applied. Here are three interpretations of her highly influential theorem.

- Correct but inscrutable to nonphysicists version: Every differentiable symmetry of the action of a physical system has a corresponding conservation law.
- Simplified version: Every continuous symmetry of a physical system corresponds to conservation law of the system.
- Imprecise but memorable version: Every symmetry has a conservation law, and every conservation law has a symmetry.

In one sweeping contribution to physics, Noether connected the classical laws of conservation (e.g., conservation of energy, conservation of momentum, conservation of angular momentum, a uniform center of mass motion, time and space translations and rotations, and Galileo's and Lorentz's frame of reference transformations), with symmetry transformations. In fact, all of Maxwell's equations, which are conservation laws, can be imagined as expressions of Noether's theorem.

Let's just look at one example where we can apply Noether's theorem: the conservation of energy. It happens that the energy of a system in space is independent of the direction of our observation. Specifically, the energy levels of an isolated atom do not depend on the direction from which the atom is observed [5]. This tells us that atoms have rotational symmetry, and this, according to Noether's theorem, would suggest that the energy associated with rotation is conserved.

What is so special about the concept of "symmetry"? Why must we abandon the familiar term, "invariance" and replace it with "symmetry," a term from geometry that has no obvious association with anything we were taught when we studied physics in high school and college? The key difference among these alternate ways of looking at the same thing (i.e., a conserved quantity as an invariance, or a conserved quantity as a symmetry) is that invariant and conserved physical transformations happen to be symmetry operations that we can study as a mathematical group. As it happens, symmetry transformation groups have an abundance of interesting properties that permit us to reach scientific conclusions that would have been extremely difficult to attain by other analytic approaches. Simply put, symmetries have groups and invariances do not. Under Noether's theorem, physical laws are represented by geometric symmetry groups, and group theory is a subject that mathematicians have studied, for centuries.

At this point, we need to make a slight diversion to discuss the concepts of groups and, in particular, symmetry groups.

Let's begin by defining a group. A group is a set having the properties of closure and associativity under an operation; having an identity element; and having an inverse element for every member of the set.

Specifically, for some operation (which we'll call "x" in this example), closure tells us that for all a, b in group G, the result of the operation, a x b, is also in G.

Associativity tells us that for all a, b, and c in G, (a x b) x c = a x (b x c).

To have an identity element, there must exist an element e in G such that, for every element a in G, the equation e x a = a x e = a holds. The identity element is unique within a group, and we speak of "the" identity element.

To have an inverse element, there must exist for each a in G, an element b in G, such that a x b = b x a = e, where e is the identity element. No matter what a group's operator happens to be, we know that we can always apply operations on group elements to return the original element. Specifically, there will always be a b such that a x b x a = a. Hence, every group has an operational symmetry that is built into its definition.

A simple group is a group G that does not have any normal subgroups except for the trivial group and G itself. A finite simple group is a simple group having a finite number of group elements.

Before we continue, we need to discuss the term "symmetry group." A symmetry group, more accurately known as a symmetry transformation group, is a group consisting of transformations on objects that preserve certain defined properties of the objects. The elements of the group are the transformations. Not to put too fine a point on this concept, but when mathematicians refer to the symmetry of an object, they are most often referring to the group of symmetry transformations that preserve the object (i.e., the symmetry group of the preserved object). When physicists refer to "groups" or to "symmetries" they are most likely referring to symmetry transformation groups.

One of the greatest conceptual hurdles that nonmathematicians have, when approaching the topic of symmetry groups, involves understanding why group theory has been conflated with the study of symmetry. What does one thing have to do with the other? The reason for the confusion lies in the subtle way in which mathematicians use abstract transformations (not numbers or variables or the objects upon which the transformations act) as group elements.

For example, the very first group that is commonly described in introductory group theory textbooks is the group of transformations that can be performed on an equilateral triangle that produces a new triangle that is the same size and shape as the original triangle. The group consists of six transformations (three rotations including the identity rotation) and three reflections. This group (i.e., the symmetric transformations on an equilateral triangle) happens to be equivalent to S3, the group of all possible permutations of three objects. In either of these cases, the group consists of a set of transformations (i.e., transformations on a triangle or transformations on three objects). The triangle is not an element of the triangle symmetry group. The triangle is just something that the group of transformations acts upon. In the case of the permutation group, the set of three objects is not included in the group. The group is the set of permutations (another type of symmetry transformation) that act upon three objects. **Basically, what we call a symmetry group is just a group in which the group elements are symmetry transforms**.

Felix Klein summarized the situation in 1872 when he wrote (translated from German) that "what is important are not geometrical figures, but the groups of transformations under which they remain invariant" [5].

It just so happens that most of the interesting applications of group theory have involved symmetry transformation groups. Hence, physicists have little or no interest in groups other than symmetry transformation groups. In addition, Cayley's theorem (published 1854) established that every finite group (including nonsymmetric groups) is isomorphic to a subgroup of the symmetric group acting on it. Without belaboring the point, Cayley's theorem tells us that all groups are related to symmetry transformation groups. Whenever we read any scientific literature that deals with symmetry transformation groups, we might find that the authors truncate the term to just "groups" or even just "symmetries." In this matter, we must indulge the mathematicians and physicists.

Symmetry groups are commonly named for the types of structures that their transformation elements preserve. For example:

- a crystal group preserves a crystal lattice
- a fixed point group preserves one particular element
- a homeomorphism preserves a topology
- a linear group preserves a linear structure
- an isometry preserves a metric
- an isomorphism preserves an algebraic structure
- an orthogonal or unitary group preserves distance from a fixed point

Let's look at one example where physicists have used the concept of geometric symmetry groups to establish physical law. The group of all rotations about the origin of 3-D Euclidean space is known as SO(3), an abbreviation for Special Orthogonal Group for 3 dimensions. A rotation about the origin is a transformation that preserves the origin, Euclidean distance, and orientation. Every rotation is described by an orthogonal 3×3 matrix which, when multiplied by its transpose, results in the identity matrix. All of the laws of physics are SO(3) invariant because they apply equally when observed from any direction in space. Specifically, the rotational symmetry between time and space coordinate axes gives us the Lorentz transformations which account for the theory of special relativity. SO(3) can be represented by equivalent groups whose elements are matrices and whose group operations (i.e., the symmetry transformations) are matrix operators. The matrix representations of SO(3) led to the discovery of the Pauli Exclusion Principle (discussed in "Section 7.4. Great deductions from anomalies in the Periodic Table"). The atomic model represented in the Periodic Table of the Elements is, in turn, based on the principles of rotational symmetry and the Pauli Exclusion Principle. [Glossary Group nomenclature]

Now that we have discussed symmetry groups, we can return to Noether's theorem, which happens to involve the symmetries of something known as the Lagrangian. To understand how Noether's theorem is employed by physicists, we need to discuss the Lagrangian, and its action integral. The Lagrangian is a mathematical function that encapsulates all the forces operating within the coordinates of space. It is suited for solving sets of equations where the forces are conserved.

In mathematical terms, the Lagrangian is the difference between the kinetic energy of the system (i.e., the sum of the kinetic energy of all the parts of a system) and the potential energy of the system. In effect, the Lagrangian describes the physical system (Fig. 8.10).

$$L = T - V$$

FIG. 8.10 The nonrelativistic Lagrangian. L is the Lagrangian, T is the total kinetic energy, and V is the potential energy.

When we speak of symmetries under the Noether theorem, we are referring to symmetries of the Lagrangian. That is to say that we are dealing with those symmetries that leave the Lagrangian unchanged. The "action" of the Lagrangian is the Lagrangian's integral (Fig. 8.11).

$$S = \int_{t_1}^{t_2} L \, dt$$

FIG. 8.11 Formula for a Lagrangian's "action," denoted here as S.

The mathematical evidence of an unchanged transformation of the Lagrangian (e.g., unchanged over time, unchanged over translation by distance) is determined by the so-called "Least Action" of the Lagrangian (Fig. 8.12).

$$\delta S = \delta \int_{t_1}^{t_2} L(q, \dot{q}, t) dt = 0$$

FIG. 8.12 The equation for "Least Action." When the Action does not change, its derivative (the Least Action) is zero. All of Newton's laws can be derived from the Least Action, as applied to objects in motion.

The Principle of Least Action holds that physical systems do not change the value of the action. The Principle of Least Action is a mathematical representation of the conservation laws that account for most of the laws of physics. Furthermore, the symmetry transformation groups that obey the Principle of Least Action (i.e., whose transformations leave the Lagrangian stationary) are the symmetry groups that represent the physical laws of the universe.

If you have read through the preceding treatment of group theory and Lagrangians, you should be very proud of yourself. Einstein himself had difficulties applying group theory to physics, and he called upon the talents of a mathematician-friend to help with the tough parts [5]. Many of Einstein's colleagues resisted applying group theory to theoretical physics. These physicists had been raised on classical mathematical analysis, and they chafed at the thought of mastering another branch of mathematics. They showed their contempt by employing the term "Gruppenpest" (pesty groups) to describe the field [5].

For those readers who skipped over the descriptions of group theory, the chapter so far can be summarized as follows:

1. Conservation principles determine many of the fundamental laws of energy and matter, including all of Newtonian physics, Maxwell's equations, and special relativity.
2. Conservation laws tell us that there is symmetry in the universe, as described by Noether's theorem (vida infra). In fact, all of the aforementioned physical laws can be approached as special cases of Noether's theorem.
3. Symmetry in the universe tells us that matter and energy can be represented by mathematically defined groups, and analyzed with the methods of group theory.
4. Group theory, a field of mathematics, was well-established by the middle of the 19th century. There is now an established classification of all the finite simple groups, and the properties of the classes of all such groups are defined.
5. Much of modern physics involves relating an invariance or a conserved quantity as a symmetry group. How do we identify the symmetry group that represents a physical reality (e.g., motion, rotation, force carrier (i.e., particle), energy, field)? The symmetries we find are symmetries of the Lagrangian. That is to say that the laws of physics are based upon the various transformations that leave the Lagrangian unchanged; the symmetry of the Lagrangian being the mathematical expression of Noether's Law.
6. Once we have identified the various groups that represent the fundamental particles of matter and the carriers of energy, we can use the mathematical properties of the group to predict the properties of matter and energy.
7. The predictions based on group-theoretical analyses of matter and energy have been validated by experimental studies, and have attained the status of physical law.
8. Today, the field of modern theoretical physics is built upon mathematical group theory, a field whose foundations were developed two centuries ago.

To summarize bluntly, physical reality has symmetries, and symmetries have groups. Once you've found the group that corresponds to a physical symmetry, you can use the known features of the group, or, more often, of the matrix representation of the group, to determine physical law.

Section 8.4. The Classification Theorem

The complete classification (of the finite simple groups) is arguably the greatest achievement of 20th-century mathematics.

Kishore Marathe

Humanity's Greatest Intellectual Achievement: Classification Theorem of the Finite Simple Groups.

Title of a lecture delivered by Hugo De Garis

What does classification mean to a mathematician? Essentially, it's the same definition that a biologist uses, but with terminology rooted in set theory. Beginning with a set of objects, mathematicians find equivalence relationships between groups of elements to form classes of the set. The mathematician further stipulates that the classes are nonoverlapping and that every element belongs to a class. Each class is itself a set of objects that can be subclassified according to the same definition. This mathematical conceptualization encompasses completeness (every element belongs to a class), exclusivity (classes are nonoverlapping), lineage (classes can be subclassed), and inheritance (each subclass has the common equivalence that defines its parent class).

As they pertain to any branch of science, a classification embodies everything in its domain (i.e., relationships, classes, members, and properties). In the case of the Classification Theorem, Daniel Gorenstein, one of the key mathematicians involved in the effort to classify the finite simple groups, wrote "to me, classification refers to an attempt to understand the intrinsic structure of a given mathematical system [11]." Basically, a classification explains itself.

When creating a classification, mathematicians are held to a higher standard than the members of any other scientific discipline. Mathematicians cannot simply measure a few consistent instances and claim that an assertion is true, empirically. Mathematicians earn their living by proving their assertions, and classifications are one of the most important tools used to prove conjectures and theorems. There are two properties of mathematical classifications that have particular utility as components of proof:

1. Argument by completeness

If a mathematician needs to prove that a particular assertion applies to all the possible members of a particular class of abstractions, but she cannot build a generalized argument that covers all class members, she might attack the proof piecemeal by developing a proof tailored to each of the subclasses. A mathematical classification is always complete, so the mathematician can be certain that the classification will list every possible subclass. With the list of subclasses in hand, it becomes a straightforward process to build a compilation of little proofs that add up to a complete proof for the class.

2. Argument by isomorphism

If you visit some of the blogs where mathematicians discuss their work, you'll encounter steps in proofs that involve showing that a component of a conjecture or theorem is isomorphic to a particular class (i.e., the component has the same properties as the class). Mathematicians have many different classes whose properties are known (e.g., finite simple groups, Clifford algebras). When an isomorphism has been established, the properties of the isomorphic class can be applied to the component of the conjecture, and this often takes the mathematician one step further along in her proof.

Let's take a moment to discuss group isomorphisms, a topic having particular relevance in this chapter. A group isomorphism is a function between two groups that sets up a one-to-one correspondence between the elements of the groups in a way that preserves that mapping after group operations. A group and its isomorphisms compose a class of groups. [Glossary Bijection, Class of groups]

Knowing what it means for two groups to be isomorphic to one another, what inference can we draw regarding group isomorphisms? Because two isomorphic groups have a one-to-one correspondence between their elements, and because operations on one group are preserved in the second group, then the groups have the same properties and are equivalent to one another.

Let's look at an example. We can show that the group of real numbers are isomorphic to the group of logarithms of the real numbers. There is a one-to-one mapping among the group elements, and the operation of multiplication in the first group is equivalent to the operation of addition in the second group. We can find an isomorphism between the group of real numbers and the group of the logarithms of the real numbers (also real numbers). When we multiply any two real numbers in the first group, we get the isomorphic element obtained by adding the two logarithms of those two real numbers and then mapping back to the first group. Because logarithms make it easy to multiply and divide real numbers, we might choose to conduct all such activities in the equivalent isomorphic group of logarithms, and save ourselves a lot of time and effort.

One of the most useful isomorphism tricks used in group theory is to create an isomorphic image of an abstract group to a matrix group, especially matrix groups that are multiplicative. It is often easier to conduct group operations using matrix algebra than to create a set of operations tailored to an abstract group. For the most part, physicists and mathematicians rely upon three matrix operations (multiplication, transposition, determinants), and upon whether a group's operations are commutative. [Glossary Commutative, Matrix determinants, Matrix multiplication, Matrix transposition]

If mathematicians use classifications and class relationships to prove conjectures, then why is it so hard to be a great mathematician? It seems like a simple process to pick a ready-made group or class, with proven and defined class properties, and apply these to a conjecture. The simple truth is that it takes a great mathematical mind to attain a deep understanding of abstract classes and to perceive how relationships within classifications can be extended to solve mathematical problems.

History of the Classification Theorem

The current version of the Classification Theorem's proof has been published in eight ponderous volumes. Technically, the proof began back in 1832, when Galois introduced the notion of subgroups. Mathematicians have been classifying groups ever since. A concerted effort to produce an all-encompassing proof of the Classification Theorem dates back to 1972 when Daniel Gorenstein proposed a multi-step program for classifying finite simple groups. With the participation of hundreds of mathematicians, a first-version classification and proof closely adhered to Gorenstein's original outline. A forthcoming revisionist proof is expected to have a length of at least 5000 pages of dense text. It should be pointed out that mathematicians traditionally work in isolation. You can well imagine that a sustained worldwide effort of a large number of theorists to produce a unified product marks a unique event in the annals of mathematics.

Notably, the Classification Theorem is a purely mathematical construct. As stated several times previously, this book is devoted to classifications within the natural sciences; these sciences being physics, chemistry, and biology. The natural sciences involve the observation and the explanation of natural phenomena, neither of which are strong suits for mathematicians. This being the case, it is truly wondrous that group theory and the Classification Theorem have had an enormous influence in physics and chemistry, serving as a testament to the enduring unreasonable effectiveness of mathematics.

Statement of the Classification Theorem

The Theorem states that every finite simple group is either cyclic, or alternating, or it belongs to a broad infinite class called the groups of Lie type, or else it is one of 26 or 27 exceptions, called sporadic. Mathematicians may sometimes write the theorem to include the names of included classes:

- The cyclic groups of prime order, including all the abelian simple groups (of which there is one general class),
- The alternating groups of degree at least 5 (of which there is one general class).
- The groups of Lie type (of which there are 16 general classes).
- One of 26 groups is called the "sporadic groups." These being the five Mathieu groups; the seven groups related to the Leech lattice, including the three Conway groups; the "monster" group M, plus seven other related groups; and six pariah groups [12].
- The Tits group (which is sometimes considered a 27th sporadic group). [Glossary Cyclic groups]

Admittedly, the Classification Theorem seems to be a poor fit to our concept of a traditional classification. It consists of what, on the surface, seems to be nothing more than a list of mathematical abstractions. It is difficult to imagine what all the fuss is about or why The Classification Theorem would be featured as a prototypical classification in this book.

Let's try to understand why the Classification Theorem satisfies the fundamental definition of a true classification, and why it may represent the ideal classification.

1. The Classification Theorem is purely relational

We should remember that the purpose of classification, in contrast to an index or a dictionary, is to understand the relations among the classes within a domain. The Classification Theorem provides the relationships that define groups and does not characterize or list the objects that undergo group operations. This means that we can fill a group with electrons, or photons, or gravitons, or whatever we wish, so long as the items in the group conform to the defining group operations. We refer to the fundamental operation of a group as its "action." Because the Classification Theorem is based on group actions and does not specify the items acted upon, we can consider the Classification Theorem to be purely relational.

Although the concept of classification as an organizer of relationships holds true for the Classification of Life and the Periodic Table of the Elements, it is only in the case of the

Classification Theorem that we find a purely relational construct, with nothing physical to cloud our vision. All we see are relationships, and we will see that group relationships model the operating principles for everything in our physical universe.

2. The Classification Theorem is complete

Completeness is one of the basic properties common to all classifications. As discussed in "Section 2.3. The gift of completeness," when we are certain that every class in a domain has a place within the classification, then we can begin to infer what exists and what cannot exist. When we know that a group exists, and we know that it has properties such as those we might find in a finite simple group, then we know that we can assign it a place somewhere within the groups listed in the Classification Theorem. In particular, we can be certain that there is a symmetry group for every physical symmetry. The challenge for physicists involves finding the correct symmetry group for an observed physical symmetry.

3. The Classification Theorem is hierarchical

All of the groups contained in the Classification Theorem fall into 1 of 5 major classes, each having class properties that extend to all of its subclasses.

4. The Classification Theorem simplifies reality

There are an infinite number of possible finite simple groups. We can play endlessly with elements and actions that conform to the definition. The Classification Theorem tells us that any such group will be isomorphic to one of the classes listed in the theorem. [Glossary Isomorphism]

Groups preserve invariances

Felix Klein summarized the situation in 1872 when he wrote (translated from German) that: "any geometry consists of a space of points and a group of transformations that move the figures in the space around while preserving the properties appropriate to that geometry" [5]. What Klein wrote for geometry applies generally. As we have seen, invariances account for the fundamental laws of physics. Hence, symmetry transformations preserve the physical invariances described by metrics.

In addition, Cayley's theorem (published in 1854) established that every finite group is isomorphic to a subgroup of the symmetry group acting on it. Without belaboring the point, Cayley's theorem tells us that all groups are related to symmetry transformation groups. Consequently, group theory is generally defined as the branch of mathematics that deals with symmetries [13].

In summary, because most physical laws involve geometric operations (e.g., rotations, reflections, translations) or metrics (e.g., energy, mass) or structures (particles, molecular lattices), we can examine physical symmetries as symmetry groups. Because we know a great deal about the properties of symmetry groups, we can apply such knowledge to understand the nature of physical reality.

Physical reality and sporadic groups

One of the surprises of the Classification Theorem was the finding that there are highly complex finite simple groups that do not seem to fit into any of the classes that have interested physicists for the past century or more. These outlier groups are called "sporadic," conveying the idea that these groups are unexpected, somewhat inscrutable, and probably less useful than the better-known finite simple groups. It would be intellectually easy to assume that the sporadic groups have no connection to physical reality. Such does not seem to be the case, as mathematicians and physicists are finding the physical relevance of sporadic groups whose full range of properties lie outside human comprehension. Examples include [12]:

-   The Leech lattice leads to the optimal transmission of coded messages [12].
-   The Monster group leads us to a deeper understanding of string theory, vertex operators, and black holes [12].
-   Compactification in string theory reduces the operation space from 10 dimensions to 4 [12].

Section 8.5. Symmetry groups rule the universe

Numbers measure size, groups measure symmetry.

Mark A. Armstrong

Why physical laws are tethered to symmetry groups

As we have seen, Noether's theorem tells us that for every conservation law, there is symmetry. Group theory tells us that for every symmetry, there is a symmetry group. Because nearly every fundamental law of physics is a conservation law, we can infer that nearly all of physics can be modeled by symmetry groups. The logic seems straightforward, but we should stop a moment to think a bit more about what it means to assign a set of physical phenomena to a particular mathematical group. When a physical system is modeled by a group, then the system acquires all of the properties of that group. To oversimplify, modern physicists search for a symmetry group that satisfies the requirement for invariance (i.e., all those conservation laws that we have previously discussed) under the group of local transformations; and then apply what is known about the group properties to determine the physical laws of the system.

The full potential of classifications cannot be appreciated unless we take a look at how class properties can be applied to real-world problems in the natural sciences. Fortunately for us, it is possible to understand the power of group theory without becoming world-class mathematicians or physicists. All we need to have, is an understanding that reality can be modeled by classes of mathematical abstractions whose properties accurately predict the behavior of particles and fields.

Students will love this next list, but all self-respecting mathematicians will deplore it for its misleading assumptions and inaccurate comparisons. Nonetheless, the following line of reasoning has a semblance of truth and may serve as a convenient stepping stone leading to a rigorous appreciation of the subject:

1. If nothing varies, then there is conservation.
2. If there is conservation, then there is a symmetry.
3. If there is a symmetry, then there is a symmetry group.
4. If there is a symmetry group, then there is an isomorphism.
5. If there is an isomorphism, then there is an irreducible representation.
6. If there is an irreducible representation, then there is a matrix algebra.
7. If there is a matrix algebra, then there is a simple calculation
8. If there is a simple calculation, then there is a simple mathematical relationship
9. If there is a simple mathematical relationship, then there is a general physical reality expressed by the relationship. [Glossary Irreducible representations, Representation]

To simplify even further, much of physics involves converting your physics problem into a symmetry group problem, then determining the symmetry group that applies and using the properties of that group to determine the behavior of the system under study. Physicists find the appropriate symmetry group by studying the Lagrangian. The appropriate symmetries are the ones that leave the Lagrangian unchanged after transformation. When the appropriate symmetry group is found, physicists depend on mathematicians to prove the theorems that determine the useful properties of groups, that can be understood as physical laws. Einstein once lamented, in a letter written to Antoon Lorentz on August 14, 1913, that mathematicians had not yet developed group theory sufficiently for his needs [5].

Physics seems ridiculously simple when trivialized in this manner. Throughout this section, we will be reviewing several examples where physicists have used the properties of symmetry groups to discover the fundamental nature of our universe. Of course, we'll skip some of the essentials as we bypass much of the mathematics. No matter. Our discussions will always return to the central theme of this book; namely the relevance of the process of classification to the advancement of science.

What we have learned from symmetry groups

Groups in crystallography

If we wished, we could have added a fourth classification to our list of the great classifications of the natural sciences; this being the classification of naturally occurring crystals. As it happens, the crystals result from symmetry transforms of repeating geometric units, and are represented as cyclic finite simple groups contained within the Classification Theorem. Hence, the classification of crystals is discussed here as a subclassification within the Classification Theorem and is logically included within this chapter.

The scientific principles of crystallography draw from the fields of chemistry (e.g., silicon crystal semiconductors), quantum physics (e.g., atomic nature of matter, X-ray crystallography), electrical engineering (e.g., piezoelectric crystals ubiquitous within transducers), mathematics (e.g., symmetry point groups), and biology (e.g., the chirality of molecules involved in metabolism). Our current understanding of crystallography is based on the intellectual triumphs of the 19th century. The story of crystal geometry, and its legacy of fundamental advances in all of the natural sciences, demands our attention.

As discussed briefly in "Section 2.3. The gift of completeness," all crystals can be assigned to one of 32 classes, with each class consisting of a point symmetry group. To appreciate the meaning of a point symmetry group, we need to know a few things about crystals. Every crystal has an irreducible structure, the so-called unit cell of the crystal, that repeats itself to form the visible crystal. There are 7-unit cell structures, and these are known as Bravais lattices [14]. Hence a crystal that can be held in the hand has the same structure as a crystal that is viewed under the microscope. The unit cell lattices of different crystals can all be transformed by any combination of symmetry operations (i.e., transformation that leave the structure unaffected; and these operations for unit cells include reflection through particular planes, or inversion with respect to the center, or rotations around axes through the center). The angles of rotational symmetry transformations are limited to 2 pi/n, where n must be either 2,3,4, or 6. Point groups are the various combinations of symmetry transformations that can be performed around a fixed point on a unit cell. As mentioned, there are 32 crystal point groups. Using the point symmetry groups and the translational symmetries (all being groups included in the Classification Theorem), we find a total of 230 space groups for crystals. Furthermore, all of the crystal symmetry groups can be represented by matrix algebras, greatly facilitating their mathematical analysis. This information laid the groundwork for X-ray crystallographic analysis, a field that did not yet exist when the classification of crystals was being finalized [15]. [Glossary Bravais lattices]

Pierre Curie worked in the field of crystal symmetries in the 1880s [16]. His studies led to a new way of conceptualizing the physical implications of symmetries, remarking that "When certain causes produce certain effects, the elements of symmetry in the causes ought to reappear in the effects produced" (translated from the French [5]). The physical symmetry that Curie discovered was piezoelectricity. When certain classes of crystal are squeezed, an electrical current can be produced, resulting from the polarization of charge in crystal unit cells. The physical symmetry, in this case, involves the application of an electrical current to a crystal, producing a reciprocal deformation in the unit cells. The property by which a structure is reciprocally altered by two different forces (electric current and physical pressure in this case) is known as transduction. Microphones and speakers operate through piezoelectric transduction. When an electronic signal is sent to a transducing crystal, and physical changes in the crystal are converted to pressure waves (i.e., sound waves), then we have a speaker. When we do the reverse, then we have a microphone. Curie and his colleagues, back in the 1880s, were among the first scientists to use the symmetries of crystals to study symmetric physical effects. [Glossary Signal]

Pierre Curie had a deep understanding of the close relationship between physical phenomena and spatial geometry. Specifically, he was able to describe electricity and magnetism in terms of their respective geometric symmetry groups. Curie famously declared that electric fields have the symmetry of truncated cones while magnetic fields have the symmetry of rotating cylinders [5,17]. He also understood that physical systems operating with a combination of forces, each having their symmetries, must obey physical laws determined by the symmetries held in common by the unified system.

One of the examples of Curie's approach to symmetry physics is demonstrated by his explanation of the Hall effect. The Hall effect is the production of a voltage difference between the two sides of a plate carrying an electric current when a magnetic field is applied perpendicular to the direction of current flow (Fig. 8.13).

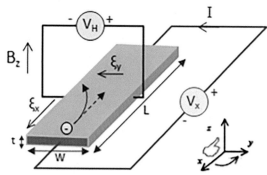

FIG. 8.13 The Hall effect. A directional magnetic field, B, is perpendicular to the conductive plate. A voltage difference is measured between the top and bottom of the plate. *Source: Wikipedia, from a public domain image.*

The Hall effect, discovered by Edwin Hall in 1879, was something that Pierre Curie understood in terms of the geometric symmetries of electricity and magnetism. Let's look at the geometric equivalent of the Hall effect, using a cylinder rotating clockwise as it stands in a moving current of water, between two shores (represented by the straight lines) (Fig. 8.14).

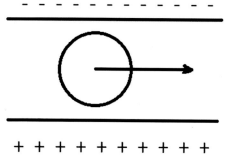

FIG. 8.14 The clockwise-rotating cylinder stands in water between two shores (top line and bottom line). The current of water flows in the direction of the arrow, as illustrated in a paper by Shubnikov [17].

As the cylinder spins, it accelerates the water moving over its top half because the water and cylinder's top is moving in the same direction. At the same time, the cylinder decelerates the water moving over its bottom half because the water and the cylinder bottom are moving in opposite directions. Consequently, the water level rises on the bottom shore and drops on the top shore.

As noted, Curie determined that a magnetic field has the symmetry of a rotating cylinder, while an electric field has the symmetry of a straight arrow (leading a cone). The cylinder standing in a current of water has the same symmetry as a magnetic field applied perpendicular to an electric conductor. Hence, in the electronic equivalent of the same symmetry operation, the electric field will rise on one side of the plate and drop on the opposite side, producing a voltage between the top and bottom of the conductor (i.e., the Hall Effect) [17].

Pierre Curie might well have understood the equivalence of spatial geometry and physics better than any other scientist of his time. His untimely death, in 1906, at the age of 47, deprived the world of one of the most productive and insightful minds of his era. It is ironic that at the moment when Pierre Currie died, the world was just beginning to digest three marvelous manuscripts published by Albert Einstein, in 1905. What Curie had done to equate the laws of space with the laws of physics, Einstein had taken another giant step further, equating the laws of spacetime with the laws of physics.

Beyond Pauli's exclusion principle

In the list of steps by which modern physics is modeled by symmetry groups, two of the steps required some additional explanation, namely:

If there is an isomorphism, then there is an irreducible representation.
If there is an irreducible representation, then there is a matrix algebra.

In these two steps, physicists transform their symmetry groups into representations that can be examined as matrices, using standard matrix algebra. It is in these two steps that a physical symmetry can yield a set of scientific laws determined by the specific irreducible representations that may apply.

So, without straining our patience, what are the irreducible representations of a symmetry group, and how do we determine which particles or forces match each of the possible irreducible representations (better known as "irreps")?

Atomic states have physical symmetries, and these physical symmetries have symmetry groups (i.e., the transformations that preserve the physical symmetries). These symmetry groups are characterized by irreducible representations. For example, the double cover of the Poincare group is the symmetry group of spacetime. Its three irreducible representations have been used to predict the existence and the properties of fundamental particles having different quantum spins. When we look at the quantum states of electrons and bosons, they each match a different irrep of the Poincare Group (technically, the double cover of the Poincare group, or the symmetry group of spacetime) [18,12]. Fundamental particles must preserve space–time symmetry and must match one of the three irreps of the Poincare group. The irreps correspond to a spin of 0, 1/2, or 1. Electrons a have spin of 1/2. The properties of the irrep of 1/2 exclude any two fermions in an atom (i.e., electrons) from having the same set of quantum numbers. The statement that no two electrons in an atom may have the same set of quantum numbers is equivalent to saying that no two electrons will occupy the same orbit, which is another way of saying that electrons cannot be super-positioned. All of these statements are known as the Pauli Exclusion Principle.

We discussed the Pauli Exclusion Principle back in "Section 7.4. Great deductions from anomalies in the Periodic Table." The Pauli exclusion principle explains why electrons don't all occupy the same orbital when they are cooled down to absolute zero, achieving their lowest energy. It also explains everything we know about chemical valences. More importantly, it means that there is an inviolate condition, that stops electrons from one atom from simply passing through the electron orbitals of any other atom. Without this condition, there simply would be no solid matter.

The irreps of the Poincare group, in addition to accounting for the Pauli Exclusion Principle (for fermionic particles of spin 1/2, such as electrons), must lead us to conclude that there exist particles having integer spins of 0 or of 1. The putative particles with integer spin were called bosons, and the particle with spin 0 was named the Higgs boson. The irrep of the Poincare group having integer spin does not exclude two particles having the same set quantum numbers. Therefore, bosons, can superposition upon one another (i.e., two bosons may occupy the same location).

Perhaps the most remarkable lesson learned from the laws of superposition (forbidden for fermions and allowed for bosons) is that the laws of physics have been transformed into the matrix representations of geometric symmetry groups. [Glossary Principle of superposition]

Special relativity as the invariant theory of a group

It is often said that when Einstein published his special theory of relativity, there were only a handful of physicists capable of understanding his contributions. There may be a bit of hyperbole at play here, but it is certainly true that most classical physicists living at that time were puzzled by Einstein's theory. The scientists who were most definitely not challenged by Einstein's special relativity were the group theorists. Felix Klein, in particular, simply accepted special relativity as the invariant theory of the Lorentz transformations [5]. Similarly, Hermann Minkowski equated all of the special relativity to the observation that Maxwell's equations happen to be invariant under the group of Lorentz transformations [5]. Poincare had observed that the Lorentz transformations form a group that could be characterized by those linear substitutions of the four variables x, y, z, t which leave the quadratic form $x^2 + y^2 + z^2 - c^2 t^2$ invariant. Hence, all of Einstein's spacetime relativity is represented by the Poincare group.

To trivialize the situation still further, the mathematicians who studied group theory saw special relativity as a direct application of their abstract work, to the physical realm. As pure mathematicians, they were not particularly interested in applications. [Glossary Lorentz group, Poincare group]

Particle identicality as a geometric principle

In the prior section, in our discussion of physical invariances, we discussed the identicality of like particles. That is to say, there is a physical invariance of like particles. It turns out that the identicality of the fundamental particles is one of the most important features of existence. If fundamental particles were not identical, then there would be no Pauli's exclusion principle (i.e., every particle would occupy its specific quantum state).

What links particle identicality to Pauli's exclusion principle? The identicality of particles led to the inference that systems of identical particles are unchanged by permutation of the coordinates of their particles [5]. A system of identical particles and their symmetry transformations are a group that can be represented through irreducible representations (irreps). The irreps happen to account for the quantum spin values that account for all fermions (e.g., electrons) and all bosons [12]. The identicality of like particles was the first of the nonspacetime symmetries to enter the realm of quantum physics [5].

Gauge symmetries and the Standard Model

There are many things in our observable universe that we cannot measure directly. For the most part, these things produce some measurable effect that we can easily measure, and we tend to substitute such ersatz measurements for the real thing. For example, we really cannot measure gravity, but we can easily measure how much we weigh or how fast a ball accelerates when it is dropped off a cliff. Examples of things that we do not directly measure are electromagnetic fields, gravitational fields, and fields that characterize the forces carried by elementary particles. We glibly speak of electrons having a charge of −1, when we really would like to speak in terms of the charge field carried by a point particle (i.e., a particle having no size) that we refer to as an electron. A gauge theory relates unobservable things (usually fields) to their observable effects. Gauge invariance occurs when measurements of observable field effects do not change under transformations acting upon their unobservable fields. Such invariances are symmetries and are known as gauge symmetries.

The Standard Model of particle physics describes three of the four known fundamental forces (the electromagnetic, weak, and strong forces, and not including the gravitational force) in the universe. The known elementary particles are the carriers of these forces. Because the three forces are only observable through their indirect measurable effects on particles, the Standard Model involves gauge symmetries. The general method by which the theory was developed involved choosing a set of symmetries (i.e., invariant transformations) for the system, and then constructing a Lagrangian that observes these symmetries (by leaving the Lagrangian unchanged). Bypassing all of the mathematics, these gauge symmetries correspond to the symmetry groups U(1) for the electromagnetic force, SU(2) for the weak force, and SU(3) for the strong force [13]. [Glossary SU(2), SU(3), U(1)].

Asymmetries

Lest we believe that everything in the universe is the product of symmetrical transformations, we must point out that asymmetry applies to many physical phenomena.

Furthermore, our prior observations of symmetries have very much to tell us about asymmetries. Let's discuss a few examples.

Earlier in this section, we touched upon the perfect identicality of particles and atoms. This being the case, we can infer that when we are preparing the steel infrastructure for a 100-story skyscraper, we must use the same sized iron atoms that we would use to create a small model of the skyscraper suitable for display in a showroom. Consequently, we cannot take a structural design that is suitable for a 2-ft model and directly scale it (atoms included) for the skyscraper. The symmetry that we observe with individual atoms prohibits us from achieving symmetry of scale.

A considerable amount of science fiction is devoted to shrinking ("The Incredible Shrinking Man") or enlarging ("Attack of the 50 Foot Woman") hapless humans. We should remember that an enlarging ray cannot change the size of individual atoms without violating one of the most fundamental symmetry laws of the universe. This being so, a 50 Foot Woman would certainly collapse under her weight. Her bones, designed with a more petite woman in mind, would snap under the load. Likewise, the cells of a whale are no different in size than the cells of a mouse, both being composed of the same-sized atoms and similarly-sized cells. Hence the proportions for bone and muscle that work well for a tiny mouse will not scale up for a whale.

Less fancifully, consider the asymmetry of the wavelength of light and the speed of light. The speed of a star does not affect the speed of the received light, but it has a profound effect on the wavelength of the received light, as observed in the redshift. As the star moves away from us, the wavelength of the light received lengthens, shifting toward the red. The faster the star recedes, the greater the redshift. Thanks to the asymmetry of wavelength (and the symmetry of the speed of light), we can routinely use red-shift measurements to calculate the distance of the star from the earth. [Glossary Redshift]

Section 8.6. Life, the universe, and everything

If you want to make an apple pie from scratch, you must first create the universe.
Carl Sagan

To repeat an often-repeated theme, classifications are how we organize relationships. In this chapter, we have seen that the fields of physics and mathematics are all about relationships. All of the physical laws that we learn in school are simple relationships between measurable quantities, and all of the seemingly abstract mathematical equations we memorize are fundamentally formal statements of relationships. The higher we advance in the fields of physics and mathematics, the more we learn to rely on the principle of classification to determine the "relationships among the relationships" of physics and mathematics.

The classes of relationships that govern geometry, forces, and the carriers of forces (i.e., particles) lead to our understanding of chemistry and biology. The progression is as follows:

1. Universal laws obey symmetries.
2. The known properties of classified symmetry groups predict the existence and physical properties of matter, charge, and spacetime geometry.
3. The classification of chemistry (i.e., The Periodic Table of the Elements, and the properties of molecules built from combinations of the elements) is determined by natural laws of physics.
4. Replicating forms of life are composed of chemicals and the chemicals in living organisms obey the same natural laws as chemicals located anywhere in the universe.
5. Hence, everything we observe in our universe is interrelated, and these relationships are discovered through the process of building and exploring a simple lineage of classifications (Fig. 8.15).

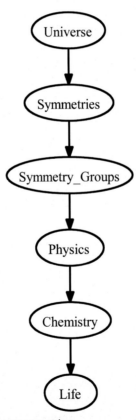

FIG. 8.15 The natural sciences are built one upon another.

The relationships of mathematics, physics, and chemistry are, at some level, the same relationships that govern chemical reactions and living organisms. There are no differences between one discipline of science and another. The perceived differences are imposed by us as a matter of convenience insofar as it's hard for any individual to master all the different tools used in the pursuit of science. So we say anatomists should use this and that tool and physicists should use some other set of devices and techniques. All scientists shop in the same hardware store; just in different aisles.

Of course, applying this same line of reasoning, we can be lulled into a weird sense of "oneness" in which all of the nuance and complexity of our universe is swallowed into a single thought. Consider the following line of reasoning:

1. The operating system of the universe is encapsulated in a few simple rules, which are best expressed as mathematical relationships.
2. These rules account for all of the elementary particles that compose matter, and all of the forces that compose energy.
3. There are no classes of things in the universe that are not fully determined by these basic relationships.
4. Because the components of our universe inherit the same fundamental laws, we can infer that they must all fit into a unifying classification [19].
5. This being the case, the goal of every classification builder is not to create an isolated classification with its own set of laws and relationships. The goal of the classification builder is to find the higher classification under which her classification may fit.
6. A "root" class provides the fundamental laws that apply to all subclasses.
7. What is the "root" class of the universe? Nobody knows, but as far as we can tell, the relationships we observe today seem to have begun with the Big Bang (Fig. 8.16).

The hierarchical nature of the natural sciences would suggest that a living organism cannot defy the natural laws of chemistry and that a molecule cannot defy the natural laws of physics. Hence, we can count on the fact that classifications of organisms, molecules, and particles, and the laws that govern their actions, must all come together, at some point. Specifically, any hypothesis we might apply to the Classification of Life must fit with what we know about the elements that constitute the molecules that compose living organisms and must also make sense from what we know about the symmetries of physics. Conversely, anything we know about symmetry physics must also fit our observations and inferences drawn from chemistry and living organisms. As we are constantly checking our hypotheses, we draw closer and closer to classifications that are consistent with one another. Hence, all classifications of the natural world will make sense, eventually.

At the beginning, when all the natural classifications met, for the very first time

In just a smidge more than a quarter-century, from 1846 to 1872, the theory and structure of the three great classifications of nature were laid out. It is likely that nobody, at the time, fully comprehended that their works contributed to the unification of all naturally occurring things and greatly facilitated the most profound intellectual advances in human history that would soon follow.

At this point we can look at the chronology of advances in the science of classification, occurring between 1846 and 1872, and we can appreciate the enormous impact of this short period on our current understanding of the field.

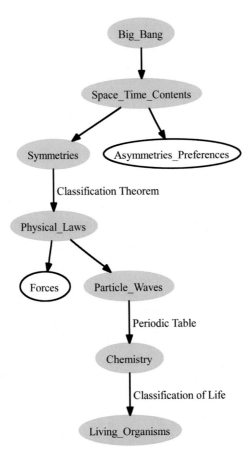

FIG. 8.16 Graphic indicating how the great classifications of the natural world, may have developed from some "root" class (represented here as the Big Bang).

The foundational years for the natural classifications and the consequent unification of the sciences

1846 → Works by Evariste Galois and Augustin Louis Cauchy (French), building upon earlier works, firmly establish Group Theory.

1850 → Auguste Bravais (French) publishes symmetry groups (known today as Bravais lattices or Bravais classes) for crystal classification [14].

1854 → Arthur Cayley (English) proves theorem (known now as Cayley's theorem) stating that every finite group is isomorphic to a subgroup of the symmetric group acting on it, providing a reason to pursue a Classification of the finite groups. [Glossary Cayley's theorem]

1858 → Rudolph Virchow (German) publishes *Die Cellularpathologie (Cellular Pathology)*

1859 → Charles Robert Darwin (English) publishes *The Origin of Species*

1859 → Gustov Robert Kirchoff (German) announces that every element produces characteristic spectral lines.

1865 → Gregor Mendel (Austrian) publishes the four laws of genetics, a work that is ignored for the next 33 years.

1865 → James Clerk Maxwell's (Scottish) equations unify electricity and magnetism and light. First unification in physics

1866 → Ernst Haeckel (German) publishes a classification of living organisms in *Generelle Morphologie der Organismen (General Morphology of Organisms)*

1869 → Dmitri Mendeleev (Russian) prepares Periodic Table of the Elements.

1872 → Ferdinand Julius Cohn (German) publishes a 3-volume classification of bacteria into genera and species.

1872 → Felix Klein (German) publishes his *Erlangen Program,* classifying geometries by their symmetry groups. [Glossary Geometry]

In the 26 years between 1846 and 1872, the scientific world had prepared the basis for a complete classification of the natural universe. Early forms of the Classification of Life and the Periodic Table of the Elements were available for study. The important concepts of group theory were known, and an understanding of groups as symmetry transformations, within the realm of geometry, was appreciated. The conservation/invariance laws of physics were known and were formalized as equations. The equivalence between conservation laws and symmetries would later be elucidated by Emmy Noether (1916).

American readers may notice that all of the important seminal advances in the realm of classification, as applied to the natural sciences, were performed by European scientists. Although American scientists play a dominant role in the sciences today, their total absence at the most crucial time in the development of the field of classification is astonishing. What happened?

In the period 1846–1872, America was preparing for, fighting in, or recovering from a terrible civil war. It seems that half of America was fighting for the freedom to deny other people their freedom (i.e., the right to own slaves). It is difficult to imagine a more absurd excuse for revolution, but there it is. Perhaps war activities were enough of a distraction to remove Americans from their usual scientific pursuits. On the plus side, war spurs engineers to meet wartime production goals, and the U.S. emerged, in the remaining decades of the 19th century, as an economic and industrial powerhouse.

It must not be lost on us that the time when scientists achieved the greatest advances in the field of classification corresponded to the time in earth's history when scientists achieved the greatest advances in all of the natural sciences. Many of these scientific advances were made possible by the Classification of Life, the Periodic Table of the Elements, and by symmetry groups that would eventually be included in the Classification Theorem. We like to think that we are living in a moment when science is advancing at a pace unequaled by prior generations. Historians of the natural sciences will be quick to tell us that scientific discovery slowed down in the latter half of the 20th century, despite a huge influx in research spending and a large increase in the number of professional scientists [20]. It is reasonable to wonder whether science might advance faster if more scientists were trained in the theory and practice of classification. [Glossary Science in the latter 20th century]

The title of this final section of this final chapter is also the title of a brilliant and funny novel by the late Douglas Adams. *Life, the Universe, and Everything* is one of the five Hitchhiker's Guide books. The title suggests that all the mysteries of the universe are fully explained within the pages of the Hitchhiker's Guide. In a sense, *Classification Made Relevant* seeks to contain all of the natural sciences (biology, chemistry, physics, and mathematics) under one classification. The moment we can see the relationships among all the classes that encapsulate our universe is the moment that we understand everything.

Glossary

Bijection Refers to functions that map each element of one set to exactly one element of a second set, and in which each element of the second set is mapped to exactly one element of the first set. Group isomorphisms are always bijective.

Bravais lattices Crystals are highly ordered physical structures, consisting of repeated units of a single geometric shape (the so-called unit cell). Various investigators in the 19th century observed that there were a limited number of geometric structures that could serve as unit cells for space-filling repeated arrays. For any crystal, we can determine all of its symmetry operations (i.e., reflections through planes, inversions with respect to the center, and rotations through the axes through the center) [5].

In 1850, Bravais found 7-unit cell structures, now known as Bravais lattices [14]. Each type of lattice has the property that from any point in the repeating unit of the crystal, the array leading off from that point appears to be identical. To illustrate, let's consider the honeycomb structure, which has most of the features of a Bravais lattice (Fig. 8.17).

A honeycomb is an endlessly repeating array wherein the unit cell of the array is a hexagon. However, a honeycomb does not qualify as a Bravais lattice insofar as the array is not identical from the viewpoint of every point in the array. Consider points A, B, and C. If you stood at point A and looked to the right, you would see the same endless array as you would see if you stood at point C and looked to your right. However, if you stood at point B and looked to your right, you would see a slightly different array. Only by flipping the image 180 degrees about point B would you see the same array of points as is seen from points A or C.

Bravais lattices are isomorphic to symmetry groups included in the Classification Theorem. Symmetry groups that are isomorphic to one another are equivalent to one another. Hence, when we describe physical phenomena in terms of a symmetry group, and the symmetry group is isomorphic to a crystal group (i.e., a Bravais lattice), then the properties of the Bravais lattice will apply to the physical phenomenon.

Cayley's theorem States that every finite group G is isomorphic to a subgroup of the symmetric group acting on G. Stated differently, if we have a finite group G, we can find a symmetry transformation that will take the elements of G and produce another group. This other group will contain subgroups that are isomorphic to the original group G (i.e., equivalent to G). This being the case, Cayley's theorem tells us that finite groups are embedded in symmetry groups.

Class of groups A class of groups satisfies the property that if G is a group in the class, then every group isomorphic to G is also in the class.

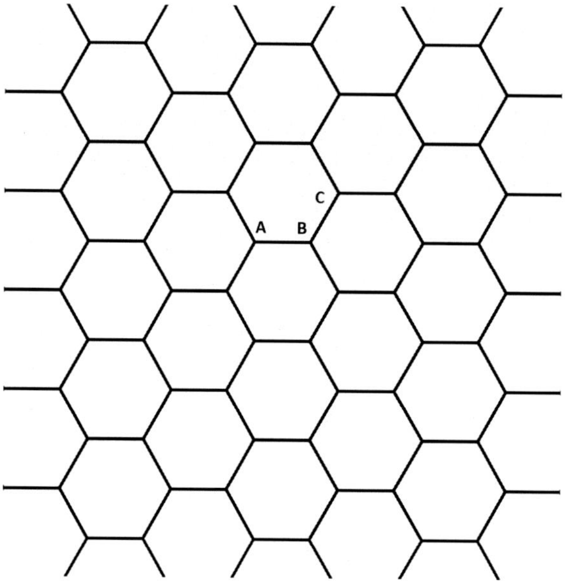

FIG. 8.17 A honeycomb is an endlessly repeating array wherein the unit cell of the array is a hexagon. However, a honeycomb does not qualify as a Bravais lattice.

Examples of classes of groups:

empty class of groups.
class of abelian groups.
class of all groups.
class of cyclic groups.
class of finite groups.
class of finite simple groups.
class of finite solvable groups.
class of finite super-solvable groups.
class of nilpotent groups.

Commutative A binary operation is commutative when changing the order of the operation does not change its result. For example, using the additive operator on "a" and "b":

a + b = b + a

In an abelian group, all operations on all elements are commutative.

Because we are all raised to learn arithmetic, in which numeric operations are strictly commutative (i.e., addition, multiplication), we might tend to think that the mathematics of physical and geometric systems must also be commutative. This is not the case, and the noncommutative symmetry groups have proven themselves extremely useful. Groups representing geometric invariants may have irreducible representations as matrix algebras, and matrix operations are generally noncommutative. We can thank noncommutative symmetry groups for the Pauli Exclusion Principle.

Curl and divergence The curl represents the rotation of a vector field in space. The magnitude of the curl is the magnitude of rotation. The divergence represents the rate of change of a vector as it rotates. In the case of Maxwell's equations described in the text, two of Maxwell's laws involve a curl (Faraday's law and Ampere's law), and two involve divergences (Gauss's law and Gauss's law for magnetism).

Cyclic groups A cyclic group is generated by a single element (the generator of the group, usually referred to as "g"). Every infinite cyclic group is isomorphic to the integers (which have a generator element, "1" and an additive operation).

Gauge theories Gauge theories account for forces that cannot be directly measured, but whose effects are observable, and determined by scientific laws. Examples of things that we do not directly measure are electromagnetic fields, gravitational fields, and fields that characterize the forces carried by elementary particles. A gauge theory relates unobservable things (usually fields) to their observable effects. Gauge invariance occurs when measurements of observable field effects do not change under transformations acting upon their unobservable fields. Such invariances are symmetries and are categorized as gauge symmetries. Gauge symmetries account for the fundamental forces described in the Standard Model: The electromagnetic, the weak, and the strong force. These gauge symmetries correspond to the U(1), SU(2), and SU(3) symmetry groups [13].

Gedanken Gedanken is the German word for "thought." A gedanken experiment is one in which the scientist imagines a situation and its outcome, without resorting to any physical construction of a scientific trial. Albert Einstein, a consummate theoretician, was fond of inventing imaginary scenarios, and his use of the term "gedanken trials" has done much to popularize the concept. The scientific literature contains many descriptions of gedanken trials that have led to fundamental breakthroughs in our understanding of the natural world and the universe [21].

Geometry For high school students, geometry deals primarily with Euclid's theorems, and proofs of congruencies. For modern mathematicians, geometry deals with symmetry transformations (e.g., rotations, reflections, translations) in space. Felix Klein (1849–1925), a German mathematician and an early proponent of group theory, asserted that "any geometry consists of a space of points and a group of transformations that move the figures in the space around while preserving the properties appropriate to that geometry." [5]. Hence, all the geometry can be approached using symmetry groups.

Group nomenclature Mathematicians have a shorthand name for many of the common symmetry groups. Let's look at a few examples:

- Sn is the symmetric group Sn is the group of bijections from any set of n objects. An element of this group is called a permutation of the n elements. The group operates in Sn is the composition of mappings. The order of Sn is n!.
- SO(3) is the group of all rotations about an origin, in 3-D Euclidean space. A rotation about the origin is a transformation that preserves the origin, Euclidean distance, and orientation. Every rotation is described by an orthogonal 3×3 matrix which, when multiplied by its transpose, results in the identify matrix.
- SU(2) is the special unitary group of 2×2 matrices. The S stands for special and tells us that the determinate of the representative group matrices is 1. The U stands for unitary, which tells us that the transpose of a group matrix multiplied by the matrix is 1. The number in parenthesis tells us the size of the square matrices.

Irreducible representations Also known as irreps. Very loosely, representations are isomorphisms to groups wherein the group elements are matrices and the group operations (i.e., the symmetry transformations) are matrix operators. Irreducible representations are representations that cannot be decomposed into nontrivial subrepresentations. The collection of a group's irreducible representations can serve as nonequivalent components of a group.

Irreducible representations play a major role in quantum physics because they can be used to determine the existence and the behavior of different types of particles that are modeled by a symmetry group. For example, atomic states (i.e., quantum numbers) are determined by irreducible representations of fundamental symmetry groups [5]. The different irreducible representations of the group tells us much about the properties of a different type of particle.

Quantized atomic states have physical symmetries, and these physical symmetries have symmetry groups (i.e., the transformations that preserve the physical symmetries). The symmetry groups are characterized by irreducible representations. For example, the double cover of the Poincare group is the symmetry group of spacetime. Its three irreducible representations have been used to predict the existence and the properties of fundamental particles having different quantum spins.

Isomorphism An isomorphism is an element-to-element mapping between two structures (groups in this case) that can be reversed by an inverse mapping. For example, the logarithm operation is a mapping function that creates an isomorphism from the positive real numbers to their logarithms. The antilog operation is an inverse mapping that reverts the logarithm of a real number to the original real number from which it was mapped. When an isomorphism exists between two groups, we say that the groups are isomorphic.

All isomorphisms are symmetric. If we apply the original operation taking a group to its isomorphism, and then apply the inverse operation taking the isomorphism back to the original group, the full process is invariant (i.e., you end up with what you started with), and hence, symmetric.

One of the values of isomorphic groups is that a group's isomorphism may be more amenable to calculations than the other. We can take elements of one group, then determine their isomorphisms, conduct our calculations on the isomorphic elements, and use the inverse operation to map back to the original group.

In terms of mathematical proofs, we can draw logical inferences related to a group, from the known and proven properties of its isomorphism.

Lorentz group The Lorentz transformations are the substitutions of the variables x, y, z, t that leave the quadratic form of the equation in Fig. 8.18 invariant. The transformations form a symmetry group, known as the Lorentz group. The Lorentz group accounts for special relativity insofar as special relativity represents spacetime invariance and can be considered equivalent to the group of rotations in spacetime (i.e., the 4 coordinates x, y, z, and t) (Fig. 8.18).

$$c^2 t_1 t_2 - x_1 x_2 - y_1 y_2 - z_1 z_2 = c^2 t\prime_1 t\prime_2 - x\prime_1 x\prime_2 - y\prime_1 y\prime_2 - z\prime_1 z\prime_2$$

FIG. 8.18 Invariance under Lorentz transformation.

Group theorists recognize the Lorentz group as O(1,3), the indefinite orthogonal group of linear transformations of n-dimensional space, where n=p+q (i.e., 1+3=4, in this case, being the 3 real coordinates x, y, z plus the 1 imaginary coordinate, t). Expressing the Lorentz Group in this form permits mathematicians to treat the group as matrices having a particular set of properties.

Matrix determinants A determinant is a number derived from a square matrix. In a simple 2×2 matrix, the determinant is computed by multiplying the top left and bottom right elements and subtracting the multiplication of the top right and bottom left elements. Determinants of greater size can be computed by laboriously breaking them down to combinations of 2×2 matrices, a task best left to computers.

Here is a short Python script, matrix_determiant.py that computes the determinant for a 3×3 matrix.

```
import numpy as np
from numpy import linalg
A = np.array([[3,4,7],[2,5,2],[1,0,4]])
print(A)
print("determinant is:")
print(np.linalg.det(A))
```

Output of script:

```
c:\>matrix_determinant.py
[[3 4 7]
 [2 5 2]
 [1 0 4]]
determinant is:
1.0
```

Determinants have a variety of very useful properties, including reflection (the determinant is unchanged when rows are changed into columns and the columns into rows and invariance) and invariance (the determinant is unchanged under particular types of transformational operations). For example, matrices with a determinant of 1 preserve volume. When a matrix of determinant 1 transforms the points inside a shape, the proportional change in the volume of the resulting shape is the determinant of the matrix.

Matrix multiplication Matrix multiplication can be difficult to perform manually, particularly when the size of the matrix exceeds two or three rows. Luckily, computers have no problem performing matrix algebra. When we can represent a group as a linear system, we can convert our group to matrices and use computers for all of our calculations.

In matrix multiplication for two matrices, the number of columns in the first matrix must be equal to the number of rows in the second matrix. The resulting matrix has the number of rows in the first matrix and the number of columns in the second matrix.

Here is a short example of matrix multiplication using the Python programming language.

```
import numpy as np
from numpy import linalg
A = np.array([[3,4,7],[2,5,2],[1,0,4]])
B = np.array([[1,0,1],[2,1,1],[1,4,1]])
C= A.dot(B)
D= B.dot(A)
print(A,B,C,D, sep='\n\n')
exit
```

Let's look at the script's output:

```
Matrix A
[[3 4 7]
 [2 5 2]
 [1 0 4]]
```

```
Matrix B
 [[1 0 1]
  [2 1 1]
  [1 4 1]]

A x B
 [[18 32 14]
  [14 13  9]
  [ 5 16  5]]

B x A
 [[ 4  4 11]
  [ 9 13 20]
  [12 24 19]]
```

Notice that the product of Matrix A with Matrix B is not commutative (i.e., A x B does not equal B X A).

Matrix transposition A matrix is transposed by exchanging rows and columns so that row i of A becomes column i of the transposed matrix.

Python example: script of matrix_transpose.py.

```
import numpy as np
from numpy import linalg
A = np.array([[3,4,7],[2,5,2],[1,0,4]])
print(A, end="\n\n")
print(A.transpose()) #transposes matrix A


c:\ftp\py>matrix_transposeMatrix.py
 [[3 4 7]
  [2 5 2]
  [1 0 4]]

 [[3 2 1]
  [4 5 0]
  [7 2 4]]
```

Poincare group The Poincare group, which is short for the double cover of the Poincare group is a symmetry group containing all of the transformations that leave invariant the Minkowski metric (i.e., the computation of distances in Minkowski space). This statement implies that the double cover of the Poincare group is the fundamental symmetry group of spacetime.

Precision Precision is the degree of exactitude of measurement and is verified by its reproducibility (i.e., whether repeated measurements of the same quantity produce the same result). Accuracy measures how close your data comes to being correct. Data can be accurate but imprecise or precise but inaccurate. If you have a 10-pound object, and you report its weight as 7.2376 pounds, every time you weigh the object, then your precision is remarkable, but your accuracy is dismal.

What are the practical limits of precision measurements? Let us stretch our imaginations, for a moment, and pretend that we have just found an artifact left by an alien race known throughout the galaxy for its prowess in the science of measurement. As a sort of time capsule for the universe, their top scientists decide to collect the history of their civilization, encoded in binary. Their story looked something like "001011011101000..." extended to about 5 million places. Rather than print the sequence out on a piece of paper or a computer disc, these aliens simply converted the sequence to a decimal length (i.e., 0.001011011101000...") and marked the length on a bar composed of a substance that would never change its size. To decode the bar, and recover the history of the alien race, one would simply need to have a highly precise measuring instrument, that would yield the original binary sequence. Computational linguists could translate the sequence to text, and the recorded history of the alien race would be revealed! Of course, the whole concept is built on an impossible premise. Nothing can be measured accurately to 5 million places.

We live in a universe with practical limits (e.g., the speed of light, the Heisenberg uncertainty principle, the maximum mass of a star, the unpredictability of highly complex systems, division by zero). There are many things that we simply cannot do, no matter how hard we try. The most precise measurement achieved by modern science has been in the realm of atomic clocks, where the accuracy of 18 decimal places has been claimed [22]. Nonetheless, many scientific disasters are caused by the ignorance of our limitations, and our persistent gullibility, leading us to believe that precision claimed is precision obtained [23].

Principle of superposition In its most general form, the principle of superposition holds that for all linear systems, the response produced by multiple stimuli is the sum of the responses that would have resulted from each stimulus acting alone. A function that satisfies the superposition principle is a linear function, and an example of which is the Schrodinger equation.

When applied to quantum systems, the principle of superposition would indicate that a superposition of physically possible states is also a physically possible state. This, in turn, implies that many different physically possible states can coexist at the same moment. This condition (i.e., multiple states coexisting) is somewhat at odds with our empiric understanding that we can only observe one state at any one time, a problem sometimes referred to as Schrodinger's cat paradox. The principle of superposition permits Schrodinger's cat to be alive and dead at the same time.

Redshift The speed of a star does not affect the speed of the received light, but it has a profound effect on the wavelength of the received light, as observed in the redshift.

```
z = wavelength observed - wavelength at rest/wavelength at rest
```

If a galaxy emits a spectral line of 91 nm that is observed as 640 nm (shifted toward red) on earth, then the redshift is 640–91/91 or 6.03.

For galaxies moving at far less than the speed of light, the relationship between z (red-shift) and v, the velocity of the galaxy is:

```
z = v/c
```

Measurements of the redshift indicated that nearly all galaxies are moving away from us. From this, Edwin Hubble reasoned that the universe must be expanding in all directions.

Hubble found a linear relationship between a star's distance from earth and its speed.

```
(Distance of galaxy from the earth) = (velocity of a galaxy moving away from
earth)/Hubble's constant
```

Hubble's constant happens to be approximately 2.3×10^{-18}/per second. He used the relationship between a star's distance from earth and its speed as a handy way of calculating the distance of any galaxy from the earth.

Representation In group theory, a representation is a mapping from a group element to a vector space in such a way that the group properties are preserved. Representations are typically used to map a group to a matrix (that represents vectors) while preserving group properties, and allowing calculations to be performed on matrices. The goal is often to find all of the inequivalent, irreducible representations of a given abstract group [5]. Because the group and its representations are homomorphic (i.e., being of the same algebraic type and preserving operations) we can directly apply the properties of the group to its matrix representations. This is a desirable situation because, in most instances, it is easier to work with matrices than to work with abstract groups.

SU(2) Abbreviation for Special Unitary Group of degree 2 (i.e., the special unitary group of 2 × 2 matrices). The S stands for special and tells us that the determinant of the representative group matrices is 1. The U stands for unitary, which tells us that the transpose of group matrices multiplied by the matrix is 1. The number in parenthesis tells us the size of the square matrices. Generalizing, the special unitary group of degree n, denoted SU(n), is the Lie group of n x n unitary matrices with determinant 1.

SU(3) Abbreviation for Special Unitary Group of degree 3. In mathematics, SU(3) is the Lie group consisting of all 3 × 3 unitary matrices with determinant 1. In physics, this group is used to model objects with internal rotation (i.e., objects composed of components that rotate). Murray Gell-Mann, in 1964, used the SU(3) representation to show that there are only three baryonic elementary particles (i.e., 3 quarks) [24].

Science in the latter 20th century Most of the scientific advances that shaped the world today were discovered before 1960. In 1960, we had home television (1947), transistors (1948), commercial jets (1949), computers (Univac, 1951), nuclear bombs (fission in 1945, fusion in 1952), solar cells (1954), fission reactors (1954), satellites orbiting the earth (Sputnik I, 1957), integrated circuits (1958), photocopying (1958), probes on the moon (Lunik II, 1959), practical business computers (1959), lasers (1960). When you watch an old movie circa 1960, and you look at streets and houses, and furniture, and clothing, do you see any great differences between then and now? Not much [20].

Medical advances in the past 60 years pale in comparison to the achievements made in the prior 60 years, bringing us to 1960. We had the basic principles of metabolism, including the chemistry and functions of vitamins; the activity of the hormone system (including the use of insulin to treat diabetes and dietary methods to prevent goiter), the methodology to develop antibiotics and to use them effectively to treat syphilis, gonorrhea, and the most common bacterial diseases. We had effective vaccines that protected us from deadly viruses, such as smallpox. Sterile surgical technique was practiced, bringing a precipitous drop in maternal postpartum deaths. We could provide safe blood transfusions, using A, B, O compatibility testing (1900). X-ray imaging had improved medical diagnosis. Civil engineers prevented a wide range of common diseases using a clean water supply and improved waste management. Safe methods to preserve food, such as canning, refrigeration, and freezing saved countless lives. In 1941, Papanicolaou introduced the smear technique to screen for precancerous cervical lesions, resulting in a 70% drop in the death rate from uterine cervical cancer in populations that implemented screening. By 1947, we had overwhelming epidemiologic evidence that cigarettes caused lung cancer [20].

When we entered 1950, Linus Pauling had largely invented the field of molecular genetics when he demonstrated that a single amino acid mutation accounted for the defective gene responsible for sickle cell anemia. In 1950 Chargoff discovered base complementarity in DNA. Also, in 1950, Arthur Vineburg routed an internal mammary artery, in place, to vascularize the heart. In 1951, fluoridation was introduced, greatly reducing dental disease. Then came isoniazid, the drug that virtually erased tuberculosis (1952). Also, in 1952, Harold Hopkins designed the fiberscope, heralding fiberoptic endoscopy. In 1953, Watson and Crick showed that DNA was composed of a double helix chain of complementary nucleotides encoding human genes. John Gibbon performed the first open-heart surgery using a cardiopulmonary bypass machine (1953), and D.W. Gordon Murray used arterial grafts to replace the left anterior descending coronary artery (the coronary artery bypass graft). Oral contraceptives (birth control pills) were invented in 1954. That same year, Salk developed an effective killed vaccine for polio, followed just 3 years later with Sabin's live polio vaccine. Thus, in the 1950s, the two most dreadful scourges of developed countries, tuberculosis, and polio, were virtually eradicated [20].

The U.S. Department of Health and Human Services has published a sobering document, entitled, "Innovation or Stagnation: Challenge and Opportunity on the Critical Path to New Medical Products" [25]. The authors note that fewer and fewer new medicines and medical devices are reaching the Food and Drug Administration [26]. The last quarter of the 20th century has been described as the "era of Brownian motion in health care" [27,28].

If the rate of scientific accomplishment is dependent upon the number of scientists on the job, you would expect that progress would be accelerating, not decelerating. According to the National Science Foundation, 18,052 science and engineering doctoral degrees were awarded in the U.S., in 1970. By 1997, that number had risen to 26,847, nearly a 50% increase in the annual production of the highest-level scientists [29]. The growing workforce of scientists failed to advance science very much, but it was not for lack of funds. In 1953, according to the National Science Foundation, the total U.S. expenditures on research and development was $5.16 billion, expressed in current dollar values. In 1998, that number has risen to $227.173 billion, greater than a 40-fold increase in research spending [29].

Signal In a very loose sense, a signal is a way of gauging how measured quantities (e.g., force, voltage, pressure) change in response to, or along with, other measured quantities (e.g., time). A sound signal is caused by the changes in pressure, exerted on our eardrums, over time. A visual signal is a change in the photons impinging on our retinas, over time. An image is a change in pixel values over a two-dimensional grid. Because much of the data stored in computers consists of discrete quantities of describable objects, and because these discrete quantities change their values, with respect to one another, we can appreciate that a great deal of modern data analysis is reducible to digital signal processing.

Time symmetry In our spacetime universe, time is a dimension through which we move, much the same way as we move through the familiar x, y, and z dimensions of Euclidean space. Euclidean space permits us to move reversibly through any dimension. We can move forward or backward in the x, y, and z dimensions. A forward motion is equivalent to a backward motion, played in reverse.

When we think about the forward and backward motions in time, we encounter some practical limits to time reversibility. For example, as we watch a movie depicting a high-octane car chase culminating in a fiery crash, we know that the movie is progressing forwards in time. If the movie were played in reverse, with a car suddenly being assembled from the shattered remnants of an explosion, then instantly speeding backward down the street, we would all agree that what we were seeing was physically impossible. We would conclude that time, unlike the Euclidean x, y, and z coordinates, cannot be reversed. Hence, time is asymmetric, meaning that it proceeds in one direction but not the other.

Let's imagine another movie, in which there are only a few particles moving in space, occasionally bumping into one another. In this case, if we watched a movie of those particles, and played the movie backward, we would have no way of distinguishing whether the movie was playing forwards or backward (i.e., in reverse). For a small number of particles, assigning forward time and backward time is arbitrary and, hence, reversible, and symmetric.

When physicists think about time symmetry, they tend to confine their thoughts to shifts in time, wherein repeated experiments will have the same observed outcome, regardless of the time at which the observations are made.

U(1) Geometrically, U(1) is the rotational symmetry of a circle. It is represented by 1×1 matrices.

U(1) is the symmetry group that characterizes quantum electrodynamics. Its representations account for the existence of electrons and photons and determines the properties of electrons and photons that preserve symmetry.

References

[1] Wickham A. Envoi. In: The contemplative quarry. New York, NY: Harcourt, Brace and Company; 1921.

[2] Helmholtz HLF. On the sensations of tone as a physiological basis for the theory of music. 2nd English ed. London: Longmans, Green, and Co.; 1885.

[3] Wigner E. The unreasonable effectiveness of mathematics in the natural sciences. Commun Pure Appl Math 1960;13:1–14.

[4] Dembski WA. Review of the applicability of mathematics as a philosophical problem by Mark Steiner. Books Cult 1999;5.

[5] Bonolis L. From the rise of the group concept to the stormy onset of group theory in the new quantum mechanics: a saga of the invariant characterization of physical objects, events and theories. Riv Nuovo Cimento 2004;27:1–110.

[6] Michelson AA, Morley EW. Influences of motion of the medium on the velocity of light. Am J Sci 1886;31:377–86.

[7] Gibbs JW. On the equilibrium of heterogeneous substances (originally published in Connecticut Acad Sci, 1875–1878). Selected papers on thermodynamics and statistical physics. London: Cambridge University Press; 1951.

[8] Weyl H. Raum, Zeit, Materie. Berlin: Springer-Verlag; 1918.

[9] O'Raifeartaigh L. The dawning of gauge theory. Princeton: Princeton University Press; 1997.

[10] Noether E. Invariante variations probleme. Nachr Ges Wiss Gottingen Math Phys Kl 1918;1918: 235–57.

[11] Gorenstein D. Classifying the finite simple groups. Bull Am Math Soc 1986;14:1–98.

[12] Boya LJ. Introduction to Sporadic Groups. In: Proceedings of the workshop, supersymmetric quantum mechanics and spectral design. Benasque, Spain; 2010.

[13] Schwichtenberg J. Physics from symmetry. 2nd ed. Springer International Publishing Switzerland; 2018.

[14] Bravais A. Memoire sur les systemes formes par les points distribues regulierement sur un plan ou dans l'espace. J Ecole Polytech 1850;19:1–128.

[15] Dunitz JD. Symmetry arguments in chemistry. Proc Natl Acad Sci U S A 1996;93:14260–6.

[16] Curie P. Sur la symetrie dans les phenomenes physiques: Symetrie d'un champ electrique et d'un champ magnetique. J Phys 1894;3:393.

[17] Shubnikov AV. On the works of Pierre Curie on symmetry. Comput Math Appl 1988;16:357–64.

[18] Mandel-Tsveig VB. Irreducible representations of the SU3 group. Sov Phys—JETP 1965;20:1237–43.

[19] Anderson PW. More is different. Science 1972;177:393–6.

[20] Berman JJ. Machiavelli's Laboratory. Kindle ed. Amazon Digital Services, Inc.; 2010.

[21] Berman JJ. Armchair science: no experiments, just deduction. Kindle ed. Amazon Digital Services, Inc.; 2014.

[22] Bloom BJ, Nicholson TL, Williams JR, Campbell SL, Bishof M, Zhang X, et al. An optical lattice clock with accuracy and stability at the 10–18 level. Nature 2014;506:71–5.

[23] Berman JJ. Data simplification: taming information with open source tools. Waltham, MA: Morgan Kaufmann; 2016.

[24] Koerber C. Lie algebra representation theory: SU(3)-representations in physics. North Carolina State University, Department of Mathematics, Publication MA725; December 3, 2013.

[25] Anon. Innovation or stagnation: challenge and opportunity on the critical path to new medical products. U.S. Department of Health and Human Services, Food and Drug Administration; 2004.

[26] Angell M. The truth about the drug companies. N Y Rev Books 2004;51 [book review].

[27] Quality of Health Care in America Committee, editor. Crossing the quality chasm: a new health system for the 21st century. Washington, DC: Institute of Medicine; 2001.

[28] Wurtman RJ, Bettiker RL. The slowing of treatment discovery, 1965–1995. Nat Med 1996;2:5–6.

[29] National Science Foundation. National Science Board, Science & Engineering Indicators—2000. Arlington, VA: National Science Foundation; 2000 [NSB-00-1].

Index

Note: Page numbers followed by *f* indicate figures and *ge* indicate glossary terms.

Printed in the United States
by Baker & Taylor Publisher Services